THE PUZZLE OF LATIN AMERICAN ECONOMIC DEVELOPMENT

THE PUZZLE OF LATIN AMERICAN ECONOMIC DEVELOPMENT

THIRD EDITION

Patrice Franko

ROWMAN & LITTLEFIELD PUBLISHERS, INC.
Lanham • Boulder • New York • Toronto • Plymouth, UK

ROWMAN & LITTLEFIELD PUBLISHERS, INC.

Published in the United States of America
by Rowman & Littlefield Publishers, Inc.
A wholly owned subsidary of The Rowman & Littlefield Publishing Group, Inc.
4501 Forbes Boulevard, Suite 200, Lanham, Maryland 20706
www.rowmanlittlefield.com

Estover Road, Plymouth PL6 7PY, United Kingdom

British Library Cataloguing in Publication Information Available

Library of Congress Cataloging-in-Publication Data

Franko, Patrice M., 1958–
   The puzzle of Latin American economic development / Patrice Franko.
     p. cm.
   Rev. and updated ed. of: The puzzle of Latin American economic development.
   Includes bibliographical references and index.
   ISBN-13: 978-0-7425-5353-8 (pbk. : alk. paper)
   ISBN-10: 0-7425-5353-1 (pbk. : alk. paper)
   1. Latin America—Economic conditions—1982–. 2. Latin America—Economic policy.
I. Franko, Patrice M., 1958–. Puzzle of Latin American economic development. II. Title.
   HC125.F682 2006
   338.98—dc22   2006025479

Printed in the United States of America

♾™The paper used in this publication meets the minimum requirements of American
National Standard for Information Sciences—Permanence of Paper for Printed Library
Materials, ANSI/NISO Z39.48–1992.

CONTENTS

Tables, Figures, and Boxes

Tables

vii

FIGURES

Boxes

PREFACE

This book explores the puzzle of economic development in Latin America. Despite a similar starting point in the late 1800s, why didn't Latin America continue to grow at the pace of North America? How can we understand the economic path it took? What are the contemporary opportunities and constraints? This is not a general textbook on development, but it tries to provide tools from development, trade, and finance for students to evaluate policy outcomes in Latin America. Without ignoring the historical antecedents, the central task of the text is an analysis of contemporary problems in Latin America. It is essentially the story of the character and contradictions of the new economic model in Latin America.

The text begins with the conceptual and historical foundations of development in Latin America. After briefly raising questions about the meaning of development and issues on the Latin America economic agenda in chapter 1, chapter 2 sets a broad historical context with a focus on inputs and outputs to characterize the period leading up to World War II. The question of primary product exports as an engine for growth is a central theme. Chapter 3 takes up import substitution industrialization, providing a theoretical and applied context for state-led development policy in the region. The debt crisis and macroeconomic stabilization attempts are treated in chapters 4 and 5. Questions of credibility and confidence return as constraints on flexible adjustment in the 1990s.

The challenge of the first part of the text was compressing into five chapters readings that at one time constituted the bulk of a course on Latin American development. Beloved material is missing. But if a course on Latin America is to be one semester, we no longer have the luxury of spending two weeks on dependency theory and then another two unraveling structuralism and import substitution industrialization. Whereas I used to spend nearly a month debating the debt problem and hyperinflation, if we do so now there is less room for capital markets, trade integration, social policy, and the environment. Yet students need to understand the historical antecedents to appreciate the difficulties of contemporary policy. This book provides the background in a condensed approach, then moves on to the neoliberal model and contemporary challenges.

The second part of *The Puzzle of Latin American Economic Development* begins with an exploration of the role of the state in chapter 6. After discussing the downsizing of the state and efforts to enhance revenues, the chapter takes up the question of the appropriate role of the state in Latin America, setting up a debate among the neoliberal view of a reduced state, the neoinstitutionalist prescription for institutional deepening, and a neostructuralist perspective of selective state action. This question of how much state intervention is appropriate in the economic arena arises in subsequent chapters. After discussing new capital flows to the region in chapter 7, we debate interventions by states to reduce vulnerability. In chapter 8, after a review of trends in trade liberalization, cooperative state action in integration efforts is discussed and the potential for a free trade area of the Americas is evaluated. Chapter 9 looks at the way in which globalization and marketization have affected competitiveness of industry and associated input markets for labor and technology, while chapter 10 takes up the contemporary challenges of agriculture. The unifying theme of these chapters is the optimal degree of policy intervention in the face of opportunities and constraints presented by globalization of finance and production.

The final group of chapters addresses the social and environmental challenges that the region faces. After analysis of the problem of persistent poverty and inequality in the region in chapter 11, chapters 12 and 13 grapple with the problem and promise of health reform and education. The chapter on the environment in Latin America reinforces the environmental dimension that has run through the text. Social, gender, and environmental issues pervade the text because they are intimately connected with problems of stabilization, liberalization, and competitiveness in the global arena. The chapters on poverty, education, health, and the environment focus the student on these issues not as the effects of other policies but as profound challenges that must be addressed for Latin America to meet the goals of sustainable, equitable development. This third edition attempts to capture the dynamic changes and challenges in a region confronting deep internal divides and stiff global competition. As social and environmental deficits have dominated the political agenda, heterogeneous patterns of economic policy responses have emerged. The students are asked to evaluate these changes in light of the historical pendulum swing of policies in the region.

This book is written for students with varying economics competencies. My students often ask whether they should take this course before or after taking trade, finance, and development. My experience is that the benefits accrue either way. If the student has strong theoretical tools, the depth of understanding of the problem of development in Latin America is more nuanced. However, engaging the difficult choices facing Latin American economic policymakers provides an applied context to acquire conceptual tools to solve the puzzle of strong, sustainable, and equitable growth in the region. For many students, the luxury of how to sequence economics courses is a moot point. They come to a course on the economics of Latin America after realizing through a study-abroad program or through interdisciplinary course work that an understanding of economic trends in the region is critical to a comprehension of contemporary politics and society. This may be their only course in Latin American economic development. This book therefore has no prerequisites other than an introductory sequence of economic principles. Throughout the text terms are explained, and box presentations provide illustrations and real-world examples. Words in bold type are defined in the glossary at the end of the book. This is designed to minimize the distraction to the better-equipped student eager to cut to the heart of the development issue.

Unlike many of the fine edited collections that provide a rich array of reading material, this text presents the fundamentals alongside the issues. An instructor may want to use a supplementary edition, create a personalized reader from some of the terrific pieces cited in the endnotes of each chapter, or supplement readings with case studies. Writing this book has been a gratifying and humbling experience. There was so much engaging work on the problem of economic development in Latin

America from which to draw. The explosion of papers on the Internet has made the third edition particularly challenging. It was of course always daunting to condense a thoughtful, provocative, and well-researched article or book into a two- or three-line summary. Notes have been left in throughout the text to indicate to even the beginning student that the theory of economic development in Latin America is the product of a mosaic of ideas and policies. The more advanced student should aggressively track down these readings, which provide the nuanced texture of the debate in the field that a single text could never hope to convey. My thanks to all upon whose work I liberally drew, and my apologies for any errors or omissions. I look forward to hearing from readers of this book to clarify pieces that I may have misrepresented or point out works that I neglected to consult.

This book is the legacy of years of teaching bright and engaged students in my course on contemporary economic policy in Latin America at Colby College in Waterville, Maine. My students pushed me with their insightful questions (some of which I hope are answered herein) and motivated me with their enthusiasm for understanding Latin American economic development. My research assistants over the past few years have been active collaborators in this book effort. Justin Ackerman, Jeana Flahive, Katie Gagne, Erwin Godoy, Luisa Godoy, Justin Harvey, Meg Knight, Louise Langhoff-Roos Bigger, Jill Macaferri, Joanna Meronk, Gillian Morejon, Josh Schneider, Jacqueline Smith, and Mary Beth Thomson became data sleuths and Internet wizards; each has left an indelible imprint on the text. Former students now with professional lives of their own in the field—M. Holly Peirce, Marina Netto Grande Campos, Kristin Saucier, and David Edelstein—were valuable sources of information. Courtney Fry made substantial contributions to the revisions of the chapters on health, education, and poverty. Work on the third edition was managed by Mariah Hudnut, Leonardo Aguilar da Costa, and Melanie Scott. I also have a debt to the students and faculty in the Georgia Tech Executive Masters Program in Logistics (EMIL) for providing the incentive (and inputs) to think more clearly about microeconomic foundations in Latin America. I am very grateful for all of my students' hard work and dedication. Much appreciated administrative assistance was provided by Colby's economics secretary Dianne Labreck. Of course, any mistakes are mine alone. The enthusiastic and patient guidance of my editor, Susan McEachern, transformed what could have been an unpleasant struggle into a productive and energizing process. Yvonne Ramsey and Carol Bifulco skillfully handled the copyediting and production processes. My family, especially my mother and late father, unconditionally supported my efforts not only on this text but throughout my academic endeavors. My stepchildren and their spouses, Dana and Erik Anderson and Josh and Eden Maisel, inspire me by their own commitments to teaching and policy work. But my greatest debt of gratitude is to my husband, Sandy Maisel, who believed in my ability to see this project through even when I wasn't sure myself; he provided the pragmatic advice, personal inspiration, untiring encouragement, and steaming coffee every morning to take this project from conception to reality. When the explosion of material for the third edition overwhelmed me, he graciously picked up the slack in so many areas of our lives. I dedicate this book to him with all my love.

ABBREVIATIONS

AFL-CIO	American Federation of Labor-Congress of Industrial Organizations
APDH	Permanent Assembly of Human Rights
ASEAN	Association of South East Asian Nations
A2R	Axial RR
BECC	Border Environment Cooperation Commission
BEFIEX	Special Fiscal Benefits for Exports
BIS	Bank for International Settlements
BNDE	Brazilian State National Development Bank
BSCH	Banco Santander Central Hispano
CAC	command and control
CACM	Central American Common Market
CAFTA	Central American Free Trade Agreement
CAN	Community of Andean Nations
CAP	Compaña de Acero
CBA	cost-benefit analysis
CCAD	Central American Commission on Environment and Development
CCT	conditional cash transfer
CD	certificate of deposit
CDM	Clean Development Mechanism
CEA	cost-effectiveness analysis
CEC	Commission for Environmental Cooperation
CEPAL	United Nations Economic Commission for Latin America and the Caribbean
CERs	Certified Emissions Reductions
CET	common external tariff
CLUSA	Cooperative League of the United States of America
CNS	Consejo Nacional de Salud (National Health Council)
CORFO	Corporación de Fomento de la Producción
CSIS	Center for Strategic and International Studies
CSUTCB	Sole Union Confederation of Rural Workers of Bolivia
CVRD	Companhia Vale do Rio Doce
DRIFs	demand-driven rural investment funds
EAP	economically active population
ECLA	UN Economic Commission for Latin America
ECLAC	UN Economic Commission for Latin America and the Caribbean
EFA	Education for All
ESF	emergency social fund
EU	European Union

FDI	foreign direct investment
FIESP	Federation of Industries of São Paulo
FORMABIAP	Formación de Maestros Bilingües de la Amazonía Peruana
FOSIS	Chilean Solidarity and Social Investment Funds
FTA	free trade area
FTAA	Free Trade Area of the Americas
GATT	General Agreement on Tariffs and Trade
GDP	gross domestic product
GEF	Global Environment Facility
GEM	Gender Empowerment Index
GM	General Motors
GNI	gross national income
GNP	gross national product
HDI	human development index
HFA	Health for All
HPI	Human Poverty Index
IADB	Inter-American Development Bank
IAF	Inter-American Foundation
ICT	information and communications technology
IDB	Inter-American Development Bank
ILO	International Labor Organization
IMF	International Monetary Fund
IMIP	Institute Materno-Infantil de Pernambuco
IPO	initial public offering
ISI	import substitution industrialization
ITIN	Individual Taxpayer Identification Number
LAWG	Latin American Working Group
LIBOR	London Interbank Offer Rate
MBIs	market-based instruments
MDGs	millennium development goals
MDI	Mesoamerican Development Institute
Mercosur	South American Common Market
MEXFAM	Fundacion Mexicana para la Planeacion Familiar
MNCs	multinational corporations
MOH	Ministry of Health
MST	Movimento Sem Terra
NAFTA	North American Free Trade Agreement
NAFTA-TAA	NAFTA Transitional Adjustment Assistance
NGO	nongovernmental organization
NIE	new institutional economics
NPE	new political economy
NPV	net present value
NTAEs	nontraditional agricultural exports
OAS	Organization of American States
ODA	official development assistance
OECD	Organization for Economic Cooperation and Development

OPEC	Organization of Petroleum Exporting Countries
ORIT	Inter-American Regional Workers Organization
PAHO	Pan American Health Organization
PAREIB	Basic Education Development Project
PAS	Programa de Agentes de Saúde
PES	payment for environmental services
P&G	Proctor and Gamble
PHC	Pew Hispanic Center
PPP	purchasing power parity
PPPs	public private partnerships
PREAL	Partnership for Educational Revitalization in the Americas
PREDEG	Program for Farm Conversion and Development
PRGF	Poverty Reduction and Growth Facility
PRI	Mexican Revolutionary Party
PROCYMAF	Proyecto de Conservación y Manejo Sostenible y Recursos Forestales (Community Forest Project)
Proexsal	Producers and Exporters of El Salvador
PRSPs	poverty-reduction strategy papers
PTAs	preferential trade agreements
R&D	research and development
S&D	special and differential
SIFs	social investment funds
SMEs	small- and medium-sized enterprises
SOEs	state-owned enterprises
SSI	social security institutes
TNCs	transnational corporations
UNCTAD	UN Conference on Trade and Development
UNDP	United Nations Development Programme
UNEP	United Nations Environment Programme
URV	real unit of value
USAID	United States Agency for International Development
USDA	U.S. Department of Agriculture
VAT	value added tax
WHO	World Health Organization
WOLA	Washington Office on Latin America
WTO	World Trade Organization
YPFB	Yacimientos Petrolíferos Fiscales Bolivianos

North and South America

Scale 1:67,000,000

Azimuthal Equal-Area Projection

0   500   1000   1500   2000 Kilometers
0   500   1000   1500   2000 Miles

Boundary representation is not necessarily authoritative.

802532 (R02283) 11-96

South America

Central America and the Caribbean

CHAPTER ONE

DEVELOPMENT IN LATIN AMERICA

Conceptualizing Economic Change in the Region

Latin America contains cities of splendor . . . *(Photo by Patrice Franko)*

I

. . . and pockets of poverty. *(Courtesy of David Mangurian and the Inter-American Development Bank)*

Latin Americans live in a complex economic system, ~~simultaneously inhabiting the frontiers of finance and technology while also appearing hopelessly mired in a vicious circle of poverty.~~ Consider the following stories.

Carlos Slim Helu is the richest man in Latin America and one of the wealthiest men in the world. Primarily invested in telephone industry, Carlos Slim runs Mexico's and the region's largest cellular phone company (América Movil), as well as the virtual Mexican monopoly on landlines (Telmex). Said to have a Midas touch for selecting business acquisitions, he moved beyond the Mexican fixed line and mobile market to consolidate his telecom empire by snapping up companies throughout the region.[1] But Slim's greatest asset is diversification. His investment group Grupo Carso is a Mexican conglomerate that today ranges from North America to Tierra del Fuego; he owns an ISP (Prodigy), an online bank, department stores, a cigarette company (Cigatam), and a restaurant chain with hundreds of locations.[2]

Although he has made his money in markets, Carlos Slim has become a vocal critic of free trade as a development strategy for the region, arguing that the Mexicans have nothing to show for it and that the state must be a major investor in education and infrastructure.[3] Said to have one of Latin America's largest collections of Rodin sculptures, he is also the founder of Foundation of the Historic Center of Mexico City, dedicated to restoring colonial buildings in Mexico City's historic city center.[4] Additionally, as part of his philanthropic work, he heads the Latin America Development Fund project. Telmex and Grupo Carso each have foundations, with a combined fund of $850 million, which will reach $1 billion this year. In 2005 the organizations gave out 17,000 scholarships to college students, paid bail for 5,000 first-time arrestees accused of minor crimes (so that they wouldn't sit for years in jail waiting for the slow justice system to move), funded infant nutrition programs, and helped cover the expenses of 11,000 surgical operations in rural areas.[5]

Brazilian soccer superstar Ronaldo has reached the apex of soccer fame, becoming one of the highest-paid players in soccer history. After battling knee injuries for two and a half years, his remarkable comeback led Brazil to win its fifth World Cup title. A striker for the Spanish team Real Madrid, he has signed deals with Nike and the Italian milk company Parmalat, as well as Brazil's number-one beer maker, Brahma. Born in a poor *favela,* or slum, in Rio de Janeiro, Ronaldo had to quit soccer as a young boy because he didn't have the bus fare. Sixteen of Ronaldo's relatives live at the home where he grew up sleeping on the sofa with his older brother. The home is simply furnished—no telephone but a freezer and a television. Ronaldo is currently involved with a program in Brazil that takes poor kids out of the *favelas* and puts them in soccer camps to ensure that others have a chance for a future.[6]

Jessy Contreras, a cosmetology student, has long dreamed of logging onto the Internet to study the latest Parisian trends. But saving enough money for a computer and access in a poor country like Peru, where average income is less than $300 per month and few have private phones lines, seemed too far a stretch. Fortunately, Peruvians are signing on in droves through the Peruvian Scientific Fund, a network begun with $7,000 in seed money from the UN Development Fund and other cooperative arrangements with universities, hospitals, and nongovernmental organizations. Manuel Molla Madueno, a psychologist making somewhere in the range of

Peruvians sign on to the Internet. *(Courtesy of David Mangurian and the Inter-American Development Bank)*

$400–$500 a month, is able to access international journals and participate in bulletin boards. Local teachers are able to monitor Spanish culture from around the world. Unfortunately, expansion is limited by the slowness of Telefonica, the telephone company, in installing telephone circuits.[7]

Judith Yanira Viera, from El Salvador, is eighteen years old. For over a year she worked in the Taiwanese-owned Mandarin International *maquiladora* factory in the San Marcos Free Trade Zone where she made shirts for the Gap, Eddie Bauer, and JCPenney. From Monday to Thursday her shift went from seven in the morning until nine at night. On Fridays she would work straight through the night, starting at 7 A.M. and working until 4 A.M. She and her coworkers would sleep overnight on the factory floor. The following day, they would work from 7 A.M. until 5 P.M. Despite these very long hours, the most she ever earned was 750 *colones,* about $43 per month.[8]

Blasio and Claire Lehman struggle with the help of their two teenage sons to make approximately $900 a year as tobacco farmers in Brazil. With a simple home on a small piece of land, their dream when they married twenty-two years ago was a future in tobacco. But competition in the global tobacco market has soured their dream. Small farmers are forced, in a feudal-like arrangement, to take bank loans to buy kits comprised of seeds, pesticides, herbicides, fertilizers, a plastic sheet to cover the soil, and protective gear for applying chemicals. When purchasing the kits they must pledge to sell their harvest to the companies that sold them. Fifteen percent of the payment for the first harvest is withheld to ensure complete delivery. If growers try to hold back crops because they disagree with the companies' valuation of the product, police assist the companies in seizing the crops. Illiteracy prevents farmers from mobilizing. Some farmers work in the tobacco processing plants to supplement crop income. The Lehmans' son Ismail has offered to quit school to make his family's ends meet—to save the $35 a month in bus fare. His future would brighten if the family could switch to another crop—but that would take money for start-up costs. Too bad that the fiscal incentives provided to the big tobacco companies—including Philip Morris—couldn't find their way into more affordable transportation.[9]

Economically, Latin Americans range from the very wealthy Carlos Slim to the desperately poor Judith Yanira Viera. Resources available to create working lives may be the tobacco plant or the complex strands of the Internet. International markets—for clothing, fruit, or sports—may propel some to relative affluence, but there are always the masses left behind in Ronaldo's *favela.* Economic life in Latin America is multilayered, from traditional rural life to dirty assembly factories to ultramodern skyscrapers in cosmopolitan cities. Latin American economic **development** is a puzzle. This text invites you to make some sense of this complex problem. Questions that we will explore in trying to unravel this puzzle include the following:

- How do so many fragments of different levels of economic life join to form a coherent whole?
- With a far wider income range than industrial countries, with available technologies running from a simple shovel to a sophisticated financial machine,

what kind of macroeconomic policies can address the complex microeconomic structure of Latin America?

- How does this multilayered economy interface with the world market?
- How have the pressures of globalization and the international market transformed the varied lives of Latin Americans?

As an introduction to the puzzle of Latin American economic development, this book attempts to clarify the complexity of economic life in Latin America. We will try to understand the potential that Carlos Slim has been able to tap, as well as the constraints keeping many farmers and factory workers in poverty.

A CONCEPTUAL MAP: WHAT IS ECONOMIC DEVELOPMENT?

To understand the multilayered economic home of Jessy Contreras and Carlos Slim, we first need to contextualize it within a theory of economic development. The objectives of this chapter are to explore briefly the meaning of development and to highlight selected characteristics of economic policy and performance in Latin America. In an ideal world, readers of this text would have taken courses in economic development, international trade, and international finance before embarking on a study of Latin American economics. However, many students come to understand the economic importance of Latin America late in their academic careers and simply don't have the time (or may even lack the interest) to backtrack through this important theoretical framework. The economic component may be only a small part of your broader interest in the region. For you, this section raises some of the questions that would be grappled with over a longer period of time in a course on development theory. Students with a background in development theory are invited to draw on that broader conceptual framework and apply it to the case of Latin America to answer a fundamental question of this book: How can we understand the process of economic development in the Latin American region? How can we reconcile the different lives of Ronaldo and the Lehmans within a single economic system?

Characteristics of Development

What characteristics do we normally associate with developed and less-developed countries? Try ranking the United States, Mexico, Brazil, Ecuador, Canada, and France on the following measures:

- Which countries have the highest rates of urbanization?
- Which countries have the highest per capita rates of **growth**?
- Which countries have the highest weight of international trade in the economy as measured by net exports and gross domestic product (GDP)?
- Which countries have the highest per capita carbon dioxide emissions?

The answers might surprise you. In Brazil, 84.2 percent of the population lives in urban areas; this is followed by 81.1 percent in Canada and 80.8 in the United States, 76.7 percent in France, 76 percent in Mexico, and 62.8 percent in Ecuador. Average growth of per capita GDP in 2004 ranged from 1.7 percent in France and 1.8 percent in Canada, to 2.9 percent in Mexico, 3.2 percent in the United States, 3.5 percent in Brazil, and 5.4 percent in Ecuador. Trade plays the greatest role in Canada, where exports represented 38.3% of GDP in 2003, followed by Mexico at 27.8%, France at 25.7%, Ecuador at 23.8%, Brazil at 16.4%, and the U.S. at just 9.6%. The United States has the dubious honor of leading the list of per capita carbon dioxide emissions at 19.92 metric tons in 2002, followed by Canada at 16.54, France at 6.34, Mexico at 3.84, Ecuador at 1.99, and Brazil at 1.92.

This short exercise raises a few questions. What do we mean by a developed (versus an underdeveloped) country? Are countries neatly classifiable? What is the diversity of economic experience within Latin America itself? How can we begin to think about a development strategy with relatively divergent conditions? You might want to open the most recent *World Development Report* or log onto the World Bank homepage at www.worldbank.org to look at some of the other data within the Latin America region and comparisons between Latin America and the rest of the world. Tables 1.1 and 1.2 summarize some of these statistics. You may be surprised at the diversity you find.

In table 1.1, we can see that although some countries in Latin America exhibit poor performance on indicators of child malnutrition and child mortality, others perform extremely well. Honduras and Guatemala, for example, are the worst performers, with nearly one in five children underweight, but in Chile only 1 percent of children suffer from hunger. Similarly, Bolivia, Guatemala, Honduras, and Nicaragua demonstrate tragic rates of infant mortality, whereas Chile, Costa Rica, and Uruguay demonstrate strong records. In Ecuador and Venezuela, only 80 and 71 percent of the population have access to improved sanitation facilities. Colombia, Panama, Mexico, Paraguay, Uruguay, Costa Rica, and Chile all have rates higher than 90 percent. Access to improved sanitation and safe water increases the chances that a child will make it to her fifth birthday or that he won't be plagued by diarrhea and other intestinal problems associated with underweight children. Throughout the region the growth of private consumption has been uneven, with slow rates in many countries reflecting small changes in the material well-being of the population. As we will see in this text, the long, hard road of economic adjustment to the debt shocks and the tough macroeconomic stabilization packages of the 1980s and the currency shocks of the 1990s left many Latin Americans with little more in their homes than they had when they started the decade.

Table 1.2 gives a few measures of what you might expect in terms of material life in the Americas. Residential energy use is a measure of electric gadgets and appliances in the home. Brazil uses 13 percent of the U.S. value, Mexico 19.4 percent. As a measure of technology penetration, the number of personal computers is far more limited in the region as compared to the United States or Canada, restricting access to the wealth of information on the web via the Internet. The number of cell phone users has boomed, connecting people as well as opening possibilities for employment. (Try getting or holding a job when you can't contact your

Clean, potable water is a step forward for the community, but its collection is part of the double duty of work that women perform in the developing world. *(Courtesy of the Inter-American Development Bank)*

Table 1.1.   Quality of Life Indicators

	Final Consumption Expenditure, etc. (annual % growth)	Improved Sanitation Facilities, Urban (% of urban population with access)	Life Expectancy at Birth, Total (years)	Mortality Rate, Under 5 (per 1,000)	Prevalence of Underweight Children <5 (MDG 4) (%)
	2003 or 2004	2002	2004	2004	2004
Argentina	8	..	75	18	5
Bolivia	2	58	65	69	8
Brazil	1	83	71	34	6
Canada	4	100	80	6	..
Chile	−1	96	78	8	1
Colombia	4	96	73	21	7
Costa Rica	3	89	79	13	5
Ecuador	5	80	75	26	12
El Salvador	2	78	71	28	10
Guatemala	4	72	68	45	23
Honduras	3	89	68	41	17
Mexico	5	90	75	28	8
Nicaragua	3	78	70	38	10
Panama	5	89	75	24	7
Paraguay	4	94	71	24	5
Peru	3	72	70	29	7
United States	3	100	77	8	..
Uruguay	14	95	75	17	..
Venezuela, RB	16	71	74	19	4

Source: World Bank World Development Indicators 2006, www.worldbank.org, and The State of Food Insecurity in the World, 2005, for data on malnutrition.

employer.) Access to health care exhibits a wide range, with poorer countries registering a scarcity of physicians, nurses, and doctors. Of course, we want to be careful with these data; cross-country data are always difficult to collect, especially when you are estimating houses with access to sanitation or computers. Furthermore, we don't want to suggest that computers or mobile phones are the bellwethers of what it means to be developed. We need to be aware of data difficulties even as we develop more sophisticated measures to evaluate progress and poverty in the region in later chapters.

What do we mean by development? When we think about the challenges of development and underdevelopment in Latin America, what do we really mean? Are mobiles and toilets the goal of development? How does "promoting development" translate into something concrete for the policymaker to target? U.S. president Harry S. Truman, in his inauguration speech in January 1949, envisioned a bold new program, based on "the concepts of democratic fair-dealing," to make the "benefits of our scientific and industrial progress available for the improvement and

Table 1.2. Indicators of Standards of Living

| | Residential Energy Use per Capita | | Human Resources per 10,000 Pop | | | | | |
| | Kg Oil Equivalent per Person 2001 | % of 2001 US Value | Physicians c2001 | Nurses c2001 | Dentists c2001 | Personal Computers | Internet Users | Mobile Phones |
						(per 1,000 people) 2003		
Argentina	239.7	27.01	32.1	3.8	9.3	82.0	112	178
Bolivia	75.9	8.55	10.2	12.3	1.3	22.8	32	152
Brazil	116.4	13.12	7.6	3.2	1.2	74.8	82	264
Canada	963	108.51	20.6	5.2	9.5	487.0	513	417
Chile	314.9	35.48	11.5	6.6	4.4	119.3	272	511
Colombia	113.8	12.82	12.7	6.1	7.8	49.3	53	141
Costa Rica	118.9	13.40	11.5	7.1	3.3	197.2	193	111
Cuba	78	8.79	60.4	71.4	4.9	31.8	11	2
Ecuador	105.7	11.91	16.4	5.3	1.7	31.1	46	189
El Salvador	209.3	23.58	12.6	8.1	5.5	25.2	84	176
Guatemala	300.1	33.81	9.5	3.6	1.6	14.4	33	131
Honduras	192	21.63	8.7	3.2	2.2	13.6	25	49
Mexico	172.5	19.44	15.6	10.8	1	82.0	118	291
Nicaragua	232.3	26.17	16.4	1.4	2.9	27.9	17	85
Panama	184.6	20.80	13.8	11.2	2.8	38.3	62	268
Paraguay	239.1	26.94	5.6	2.2	0.8	34.6	20	299
Peru	138	15.55	11.7	8	1.1	43.0	104	106
United States	887.5	100.00				658.9	551	543
Uruguay	211.5	23.83	39	8.7	12.4	110.1	119	193
Venezuela	147.3	16.60	20	7.9	5.7	60.9	60	273

Source: World Resources Institute, Earthtrends online database, www.earthtrends.wri.org, derived from International Energy Agency data, 2004; Population Division of the Department of Economic and Social Affairs of the United Nations Secretariat, 2004; and World Bank, World Development Indicators 2005 (Washington, D.C.: World Bank, 2005).

Lack of access to adequate housing leaves millions in misery. *(Courtesy of David Mangurian and the Inter-American Development Bank)*

growth of underdeveloped areas."[10] Although the word "underdeveloped" had been introduced in 1942 by Wilfred Benson, a member of the secretariat of the International Labor Organization, development economists such as Paul Rosenstein-Rodan spoke of "economically backward areas," and Arthur Lewis characterized the emerging challenge as the gap between rich and poor countries throughout the 1940s. Truman popularized the term "underdevelopment" but did not clearly define it. Since Truman, the goal of development has been to undo the hardships of underdevelopment—without a clear statement of the positive objective. What does it mean to be developed? With the advent of the Cold War, the world was divided into industrial market economies, the communist or "second" world, and finally the rest of the globe or the "third" world. These nations were once again the residual—what was left over when the rest of the counting was done. Since the collapse of the Berlin Wall, the second world has euphemistically been referred to as "transitional economies." What exactly are they transitioning toward? What is a usable definition of the goal of "development"?

In common language, development describes a process in which the potential of an organism is released to achieve its mature form. Dictionary definitions point to growth or expansion to bring about a more advanced state. When we think of the development of a tree or an animal, we have a clear idea of the appearance of the mature, advanced form. In economics we find ourselves in a bit of trouble. We can measure degrees of industrialization or access to a wider array of consumer products, but things become murky when we try to associate the terms "modern," "mature," and "developed" with societies having well-articulated economic infrastructures. Given the long list of ills associated with modern society, we should be clear in our understanding that more sophisticated production techniques and a wider range of electronic toys do not necessarily imply a better or happier society. In addition, we don't know which members of society have access to the gains of economic growth. More industrialization—particularly with the associated environmental costs—does not necessarily mean an increase in the well-being of citizens.

How then should we think about development? Is a developed country simply the opposite of a poor country? Is a developing country a rich country in the making? Box 1.1 presents the thoughts of development economists and practitioners on defining the term. Generally, they find it easier to agree on what constitutes the alleviation of poverty and meeting the basic needs of a population than on what represents the achievement of wealth or the satisfaction of material wants. This text looks at development as a process of meeting the basic human needs of the population and enhancing options for the allocation of economic resources both today and in the future to increase the choices citizens have in their daily lives. It pays particular attention to how much is produced and for whom, and it addresses the environmental sustainability of production for future generations. One measure to promote progress on development was the adoption of the millennium development goals or MDGs. These goals, depicted in box 1.2, were adopted at the United Nations Millennium Summit in 2000 and broadly seek to reduce global poverty by 2015 as well as to improve health and educational outcomes among the world's least advantaged people.

Box 1.1.   Development, Underdevelopment, and Growth: An Evolution of Defnitions

WEBSTER'S DICTIONARY

"The act, process, or result of developing; the state of being developed; a gradual unfolding by which something is developed, a gradual advance or growth through progressive changes."

W. ARTHUR LEWIS (1954)

"The central fact of economic development is rapid capital accumulation, including knowledge and skills with capital."[11]

CELSO FURTADO (1964)

"Economic development, being fundamentally a process of incorporating and diffusing new techniques, implies changes of a structural nature in both the systems of production and distribution of income. The way in which these changes take place depends, to a large extent, on the degree of flexibility of the institutional framework within which the economy operates."[12]

P. BAUER AND B. YAMEY (1967)

"The widening of the range of alternatives open to people as consumers and producers."[13]

B. HIGGINS (1968)

"A discernible rise in total and in per capita income, widely diffused throughout occupational and income groups, continuing for at least two generations and becoming cumulative."[14]

THEOTONIO DOS SANTOS (1968)

"Development means advancement towards a certain well-defined general objective which corresponds to the specific condition of man and society or can be found in the most advanced societies of the modern world. The model is variously known as modern society, mass society and so on."[15]

DENIS GOULET (1971)

"Underdevelopment is shocking: the squalor, disease, unnecessary deaths, and hopelessness of it all! No man understands if underdevelopment remains for him a mere statistic reflecting low income, poor housing, premature mortality, or underdevelopment. The most empathetic observer can speak objectively about underdevelopment only after undergoing, personally or vicariously, the 'shock of underdevelopment.'"[16]

CHARLES K. WILBER (1973)

"Development itself is simply a means to the human ascent."[17]

DUDLEY SEERS (1972)

"The questions to ask about a country's development are therefore: what has been happening to poverty? What has been happening to unemployment? What has been happening to inequality? If all three of these have declined from high levels, then beyond doubt this has been a period of development for the country concerned."[18]

SIMON KUZNETS (1973)

"A country's economic growth may be defined as a long-term rise in capacity to supply increasingly diverse economic goods to its population, this growing capacity based on advancing technology and the institutional and ideological adjustments that it demands."[19]

JAMES J. LAMB (1973)

"If there is to be a possibility of choosing a human path so that all human beings may become the active subjects of their own history, it must begin at the level of new analysis. Development should be a struggle to create criteria, goals, and means for self-liberation from misery, inequity, and dependency in all forms. Crucially, it should be the process a people choose which heals them from historical trauma, and enables them to achieve a newness on their own terms."[20]

PAUL STREETEN (1979)

"A basic-needs approach to development starts with the objective of providing the opportunities for the full physical, mental, and social development of the human personality and then derives ways of achieving this objective."[21]

PETER J. A. HENRIOT (1981)

"'Underdevelopment' is seen as the flip side of the coin of 'development.' It refers to the process whereby a country, characterized by subsistence agriculture and domestic production, progressively becomes integrated as a dependency into the world market through patterns of trade and/or investment."[22]

ORTHODOX PARADIGM (1980s)

"The view of the historical process contained in the orthodox paradigm is clear from this characterization: it is one in which developing societies move toward ever greater availability of goods and services for their citizens."[23]

WORLD COMMISSION ON ENVIRONMENT AND DEVELOPMENT (1987)

"Humanity has the ability to make development sustainable—to ensure that it meets the needs of the present without compromising the ability of future generations to meet their own needs. . . . [S]ustainable development is not a fixed state of harmony, but rather a process of change in which the exploitation of resources, the directions of investment, the orientation of technological development, and institutional change are made consistent with future as well as present needs."[24]

GERALD M. MEIER (1995)

"Although requiring careful interpretation, perhaps the definition that would now gain widest approval is one that defines economic development as the process whereby the real per capita income of a country increases over a long period of time—subject to the

continued

continued

stipulations that the number of people below an 'absolute poverty line' does not increase, and that the distribution of income does not become more equal."[25]

AMARTYA SEN (1998)

"It is not hard to see why the concept of development is so essential in general. Economic problems do, of course, involve logistics issues, and a lot of it is undoubtedly 'engineering' of one kind or another. On the other hand, the success of all this has to be judged ultimately in terms of what it does to lives of human beings. The enhancement of living conditions must clearly be an essential—if not the essential—object of the entire economic exercise and that enhancement is an integral part of the concept of development."[26]

JOSEPH E. STIGLITZ (1998)

"It used to be that development was seen as simply increasing GDP. Today we have a broader set of objectives, including democratic development, egalitarian development, sustainable development, and higher living standards."[27]

NANCY BIRDSALL (2005)

"Global inequality poses enormous challenges for managing and civilizing globalization so that it works for the developing world. Monetary inequality matters to people. Moreover, in developing countries, where markets and politics are by definition far-from-perfect, inequality is likely to be destructive, reducing prospects for growth, poverty reduction, and good government. Globalization is too often asymmetric, i.e. benefiting the rich more than the poor, both within and across countries. The world is not 'flat,' as *New York Times* columnist Thomas Friedman has suggested. Rather, what appears to be a level playing field to people on the surface is actually a field of craters in which other people are stuck—and hard to see."[28]

Box 1.2.   Millennium Development Goals

Goals	Targets
Eradicate extreme poverty and hunger	Halve, between 1990 and 2015, the proportion of people whose income is less than $1 a day
	Halve, between 1990 and 2015, the proportion of people who suffer from hunger
Achieve universal primary education	Ensure that, by 2015, children everywhere, boys and girls alike, will be able to complete a full course of primary schooling

Goals	Targets
Promote gender equality and empower women	Eliminate gender disparity in primary and secondary education preferably by 2005 and in all levels of education no later than 2015
Reduce child mortality	Reduce by two-thirds, between 1990 and 2015, the under-five mortality rate
Improve maternal health	Reduce by three-quarters, between 1990 and 2015, the maternal mortality ratio
Combat HIV/AIDS, malaria, and other diseases	Have halted by 2015 and begun to reverse the spread of HIV/AIDS Have halted by 2015 and begun to reverse the incidence of malaria and other major diseases
Ensure environmental sustainability	Integrate the principles of sustainable development into country policies and program and reverse the loss of environmental resources Halve, by 2015, the proportion of people without sustainable access to safe drinking water Have achieved, by 2020, a significant improvement in the lives of at least 100 million slum dwellers
Develop a global partnership for development	Develop further an open, rule-based, predictable, nondiscriminatory trading and financial system (includes a commitment to good governance, development, and poverty reduction—both nationally and internationally) Address the special needs of the least developed countries (includes tariff- and quota-free access for exports enhanced program of debt relief for HIPC and cancellation of official bilateral debt, and more generous ODA for countries committed to poverty reduction) Deal comprehensively with the debt problems of developing countries through national and international measures in order to make debt sustainable in the long term

Source: United Nations, www.un.org.

Growth versus Development

From the definitions in box 1.1, we can see that most economists agree: development is far more than economic growth. It is useful, however, to clarify the difference between the two terms. Joseph Schumpeter distinguishes growth as a process of gradual change, with all quantities, such as wealth, savings, and population, increasing slowly and continuously; development is characterized as rapidly propelled by innovations.[29] Robert Lucas defines growth as the increase of income proportional to the increase of population and development as the process whereby income increases more rapidly than population. In other words, growth does not presuppose technical change; development does.[30] For both Schumpeter and Lucas—economists of very different dispositions—development centrally engages the question of how **technological change** takes place in an economy. A key element in development is the management of technological change or how technology is used to transform the economic structure. This of course presupposes that technology is in scarce supply and that its use has a price. In this sense, policy matters very much. Economic development is not simply driven by factor endowments or the quantity of resources but by how land, labor, and capital are combined in new ways to increase productivity and the choices available to a population.

New technologies require new ways of doing things. The leap from feudalism to early capitalism was propelled by technological changes—the introduction of the horse and plow as well as the three-field crop rotation system—that made an agricultural surplus possible. But like the transition into early capitalism, the contemporary process can be politically and socially tumultuous. Development policy can be viewed as the implementation of economic tools when political and social structures as well as economic institutions are rapidly changing. In contrast to the thrust of standard economic theory, where in principle we begin with the *ceteris paribus* condition, or "all else held constant," development policy is harder to carry out consistently due to simultaneous changes in a number of arenas. An economic policymaker in an industrialized country may be able to rely on a bit of automatic pilot under stable conditions; in the developing world, navigation is far more demanding with a variety of new challenges at each turn.

This text chronicles the development journey of Latin America. We begin by trying to understand the attempts of Latin American policymakers to promote growth and development in the region. Chapter 2 focuses on the engine of trade and Latin America's export performance in the late colonial and early independence periods. Chapter 3 looks at a growth strategy widely adopted in the region from roughly the 1950s through the 1980s: import substitution industrialization. We can see, in both cases, that the strategy centered largely on the problem of growth and made less progress in the arena of social and environmental change. In chapters 4 and 5 we discuss two unintended results of the development strategies adopted: high rates of inflation and increased vulnerability to macroeconomic shocks. The policy response to economic disequilibrium was to step back and rely more on markets and less on state intervention in the economy. Chapter 6 takes up this changed role of the state under the neoliberal model; chapters 7 and 8 look at its implications for international capital flows and trade. How industry and agriculture have fared under a more open, internationalized economic model is taken up in chapters 9 and 10. Although policies that transformed the structure of Latin American economies from closed to open markets have been largely successful in macroeconomic terms, the rest of our book explores some of the deficits in human and social development hindering sustainable growth.

Basic Human Needs versus Growth as Measures of Development

In addition to thinking about how economies change, we must raise the question of growth: Who benefits from new economic opportunities? Technological change— new combinations of capital and labor to produce a surplus—does not address the general well-being of society. Does the process of economic development help the rich or the poor? A modest goal of development might be for a developed nation to meet the basic human needs of its population. Paul Streeten defines enhancing basic human needs as improving income-earning opportunities for the poor, reforming public services that reach the poor, augmenting the flow of goods and services to meet the needs of all members of the household, and increasing the participation of the poor in the policy-making arena.[31] Streeten goes on to suggest why growth itself is not a good measure of economic development. Rather than generating the predicted theoretical results that growth would trickle down to the poor or that governments would extend benefits through progressive taxation or social services, Streeten argues that growth has been accompanied by increasing **dualism.** That is, when countries grow as measured by annual GDP growth rates, the rich often become richer and the poor more destitute in the process of change. We see the expansion of the modern, capitalist sector alongside a traditional, backward sector—two distinctly different worlds growing side by side. Dualism—the simultaneous existence of modern and traditional economies—complicates the policymaker's task. More important, if an economy magnetized by growth neglects the plight of the poor, people without assets are marginalized by the growth process and made even worse off. Those without land, capital, or education, such as the poor peasant in feudal times who lost access to the agricultural commons, can be pushed into the margins of society. Without access to resources, the poor can become poorer. Their attempts to scrape together a subsistence existence often pressure the environment as desperation drives people to use up land or forests or dump open sewage or waste today without thought of tomorrow—for tomorrow holds little promise when they struggle with hunger or sickness.

For development economists such as Michael Todaro, growth must be accompanied by a change in the economic and social rules of the game. Todaro defines development, in addition to raising people's living levels, as "creating conditions conducive to the growth of people's self-esteem through the establishment of social, political, and economic systems and institutions that promote human dignity and respect and increasing people's freedom by enlarging the range of their choice variables."[32] But this is a difficult task. As we will see in chapters 11 through 13, the social deficit in Latin America must be addressed to promote an equitable and sustainable development policy. As we investigate poverty in chapter 11, we will analyze ways of measuring human development including the human development index (HDI), which is a composite index comprising three indicators: life expectancy (representing a long and healthy life), educational attainment (representing knowledge), and real inflation-adjusted GDP (representing a decent standard of living). Poverty and the associated social challenges of promoting education and health are discussed in chapters 12 and 13.

The United Nations, in its *Human Development Report,* suggests that a human development paradigm incorporates four elements: productivity, **equity,** sustainability, and **empowerment.** People must be enabled to increase their own productivity and participate as fully in the economy as their own talents allow. Gender barriers to achievement must be confronted. Economic growth is therefore a subset of human development models. To encourage fair outcomes, people must have access to equal opportunities. Economic and environmental sustainability is enhanced when all forms of capital—physical, human, and environmental—are replenished to promote access to opportunity, which must be for future generations as well as the present. Finally, development must be by people, not for them. People must participate fully in the decisions and processes that shape their lives for the benefits of genuine development.

Is There a Development Theory?

If the goal is to imitate industrial countries, is the road to a modern economy well marked by stages? Or are there different pathways to modernization? If countries are to progress economically and improve the quality of life for their inhabitants, what is the best way to do it? Is there a theory of economic development that is distinct from the economic theory we apply to our understanding of industrially advanced countries?

These are questions that economists have been grappling with for centuries. Adam Smith in *The Wealth of Nations* puzzled over how nations can best mobilize resources to produce the greatest wealth for their citizens. Box 1.3 highlights some of the conceptual guides that pioneers of development theory have offered in response to these questions. In contemporary times economists have struggled with the problem of understanding why some countries grow and others do not. This text does not assume that countries undergoing rapid economic change will necessarily follow the same pathway to achieve improvements in the quality of life. There may be different strategies to achieve the goal of raising the well-being of their citizens. The new global context for growth that Latin American economies face as we begin the twenty-first century requires a different set of policies from the ones used by the United States and Europe during the Industrial Revolution. A country's place in the region, its size, and its natural endowments may also condition its development strategy. Development theory and practice are dynamic, evolving over time.

Box 1.3.   Pioneers in Economic Development

WALT W. ROSTOW (NEW YORK CITY, 1916–2003)

Walt W. Rostow, an American economic historian, is known for his theory of the stages of economic growth. For Rostow, development was a linear process that began with traditional society, which then moved into the stage of "preconditions for takeoff into self sustaining growth." The economy would then "take off," follow "the road to maturity," and finally hit "the age of high mass consumption." Rostow believed that the "takeoff" would be caused by an increase in investment, leading manufacturing sectors, and the existence of an institutional framework consistent with expansion.

PAUL ROSENSTEIN-RODAN (AUSTRIA-HUNGARY, 1902–1985)

Development economist Paul Rosenstein-Rodan advanced the concept of balanced growth. He believed that in order to achieve sustained growth, an economy must develop various industries simultaneously, requiring a coordination of investment or a "big push." He was one of the first economists to emphasize market failure and the need for state intervention.

RAGNAR NURSKE (ESTONIA, 1907–1959)

Ragnar Nurske, like Rosenstein-Rodan, advocated balanced growth and further elaborated upon his colleague's work. For Nurske, small market economies were victims of a vicious cycle hindering growth. The small size of the market was responsible for the limited amount of production and income and for the perpetual poverty and stagnation. To break the cycle, an economy needed a "big push" coordinated by a government properly allocating domestic and foreign resources.

ALBERT OTTO HIRSCHMAN (GERMANY, 1915–)

Economist Albert O. Hirschman provided a contrary thesis: the idea of unbalanced growth as the principal strategy for development. Building on the concept of development as a state of disequilibrium, Hirschman identified and attacked bottlenecks to growth. Like Nurske and Rosenstein-Rodan, he called for government intervention to achieve sustained growth. Yet Hirschman believed that decision-making and entrepreneurial skills were scarce in underdeveloped economies. Governments should therefore concentrate this scarce resource in a few sectors rather than on the entire economy. Planners and policymakers would need to use "forward and backward linkages" between industries to attack the bottlenecks within an economy.

W. ARTHUR LEWIS (WEST INDIES, 1915–1991)

W. Arthur Lewis, a Nobel Prize winner in economics in 1979, formulated a model in the 1950s known as "economic development with unlimited supplies of labor." Lewis's structure of the economy has a dualistic nature, with divisions into the subsistence sector and the capitalist sector. According to Lewis, underdeveloped economies are characterized by a large subsistence sector with surplus labor and a small capitalist sector, which contributes directly to a low savings rate. Economic growth occurs when there is an increase in the savings rate, which is made possible only when the capitalist sector expands and absorbs the surplus labor from the agricultural sector.

continued

continued

RAÚL PREBISCH (ARGENTINA, 1901–1986)

Raúl Prebisch was an Argentine economist and former chairman of the UN Economic Commission for Latin America (ECLA). Prebisch is well known for the "Prebisch-Singer thesis," which claims that the export of primary products prevalent in developing countries results in a decline of terms of trade—the price of exports compared to the price of imports. There are two important implications of the thesis: first, that a decline in terms of trade results in the transfer of income from the periphery (the developing countries) to the center (the developed countries), and second, the periphery then needs to export more and more to be able to import the same quantities as before. Prebisch's pessimism on terms of trade was used to support import substitution industrialization policies in Latin America.

PAUL ALEXANDER BARAN (UKRAINE, 1910–1964)

Paul Baran is known for his neo-Marxist view of development and for his contributions to the dependency school of thought. Although not completely agreeing with Marx, Baran used Marxist principles to locate the causes of underdevelopment. Countries suffer from low per capita income because the ruling classes fail to productively use the surplus extracted from peasants and wage laborers. Instead, they hold monopoly power over production and the political system. To break this monopoly power and achieve growth, a revolution must take place to replace the dominant classes with one committed to social and economic development.

GUSTAV RANIS (GERMANY, 1929–) AND JOHN FEI (GERMANY, 1923–1996)

Gustav Ranis's early work focused on the economic development of Japan in the post-Meiji period and used it as a successful case of transition to modern growth. From there he began to focus on balanced growth and teamed up with another economist, John Fei, to further develop concepts used by Rostow and Lewis. For both Ranis and Fei, the process of "takeoff," as introduced by Rostow, would occur when the industrial sector absorbed both redundant labor and the disguised unemployed, using Lewis's process of absorption of surplus labor.

IRMA ADELMAN (ROMANIA, 1930–)

Irma Adelman is well known for a forty-three-nation cross-country study done with Cynthia T. Morris. The results of the study show an increase in income inequality as poorer nations grow. Both women also provided a quantitative analysis of the effects of social and political factors on economic conditions. Prior to their work, social and political factors had been ignored. Adelman also worked with Sherman Robinson in the areas of policy analysis and economic planning for developing countries and the application of computable general equilibrium models. Her current interests include land reform, trends in income distribution and poverty, agriculture development-led industrialization, and the modeling of institutional change.

ANNE KRUEGER (NEW YORK, 1934–)

Anne Krueger's work on foreign trade controls creating windfall gains, known as rent-seeking behavior, and its relationship to corruption in developing countries influenced a new theory in development: the new political economy. Her early work concentrated on international trade and payments theory. She is currently researching policy reform in developing countries, the political economy of policy formation, and U.S. economic policy toward developing countries.

REFERENCES

Blaug, Mark. *Great Economists since Keynes: An Introduction to the Lives of One Hundred Modern Economists.* Totowa, N.J.: Barnes and Noble, 1985.
———. *Who's Who in Economics.* Cambridge, Mass.: MIT Press, 1986.
Blomstrom, Magnus, and Bjorn Hettne. *Development Theory in Transition: The Dependency Debate and Beyond, Third World Responses.* London: Zed, 1984.
Hunt, Diana. *Economic Theories of Development: An Analysis of Competing Paradigms.* Savage, Md.: Barnes and Noble Books, 1989.
Lewis, John P., and Valeriana Kallab, eds. *Development Strategies Reconsidered.* U.S.-Third World Policy Perspective, No. 5. Washington, D.C.: Overseas Development Council, 1986.
Meier, Gerald M. "From Colonial Economics to Development Economics." In *From Classical Economics to Development Economics.* New York: St. Martin's, 1994.
Meier, Gerald M., and Dudley Seers. *Pioneers in Development.* Oxford: Oxford University Press, 1984.
Toye, John. *Dilemmas of Development.* 2nd ed. Oxford: Blackwell, 1987.

Challenges for Development Policy in Latin America

Developing countries must contend with a set of economic issues that make economic policy more difficult—and for a student perhaps more interesting—than traditional theory. Throughout this text we will analyze how these issues have been addressed in Latin America from its earliest economic history through contemporary times. It is useful to raise some of these challenges here to help you begin to think about the dilemmas of economic policy making in the region. It is important to remember, however, that each of these challenges plays out differently in each country in Latin America; the diversity of experience is probably as great as the set of common problems.

INTERNAL VERSUS EXTERNAL MACROECONOMIC BALANCE

Developing countries, in large part because by definition they are capital poor, find themselves reliant on international capital to fuel the growth process. Unlike the United States (which until recently focused little on domestic economic policy effects of the international sector because they were relatively small), Latin American countries have had to weigh carefully the effects of changes in domestic macropolicy—traditional money supply and fiscal tools—against their effects on the external sector. There is a constant tension between internal and external balance. Lessons from economic history in Latin America will show that a one-sided focus on either the internal or the external sector results in imbalances and the deterioration of the economic plan. Integrating a nation into international capital markets raises important complexities. This may be done in the form of debt (as in the 1890s and 1970s) or through foreign direct investment in the economy, raising questions of multinational presence (such as in the control of the United Fruit Company in Guatemala in the 1950s) or contemporary questions of international labor standards. Countries that orient themselves toward the international export economy—as in Chile through copper or in Ecuador through oil—may have to sacrifice domestic goals to maintain an exchange rate that is compatible with international market conditions. One response to the trade conundrum has been to pursue alternate trade regimes in the form of integration efforts such as the Central American Common Market (CACM) or the South American Common Market (Mercosur). We will be grappling with the need to achieve internal and external balance throughout this text.

Internationalization creates a wide range of opportunities, but it also introduces constraints in domestic policy making. For new entrepreneurs such as Carlos Slim it creates profit, but it may limit the relative well-being of the Lehman family. For now, remember that developing economies are especially sensitive to the internal versus external balance.

STABILITY VERSUS CHANGE: THE QUESTION OF TIMING

The process of development involves rapid structural change, yet economic agents like certainty. In traditional economic models we assume perfect information held by all agents. We know that divergence from the assumption of perfect information leads to inefficiencies in the market. How to handle economic agents' need for greater certainty and good information in an environment that is almost by definition (when it is working best) characterized by change is a challenge for policymakers in the developing world. Officials in Latin America must at once be agents of change, flexibly adapting to the dynamic needs of the economic transformation while also acting as strict guardians of confidence and stability. The ability to walk this policy tightrope as both motivators and moderators of change often defines policy success. When governments fail to navigate and anchor the economy, they suffer a loss of confidence. Given rapid rates of change, past policy responses have often been volatile and unpredictable, creating uncertainty. Latin American governments have a smaller store of institutional credibility than, for example, the Bank of England or the U.S. Fed—where the big news might be a 0.25 percent increase in the interest rate and not the freezing of all bank accounts, the 30 percent devaluation of a currency, or the implementation of a currency peg. During Ismail Lehman's young life, for example, the Brazilian currency changed names five times. Confidence building in economic policy making is a long and slow process—one not easily achieved when the economic waters are rough and choppy. Students of Latin American economic policy always need to ask how the proposed policy is going to affect the confidence and long-run credibility of economic agents.

POLICY FOR WHOM?

Economic policy affects various groups within an economy differently. One of the fundamental challenges facing policymakers in Latin America is the deep divisions that exist in its socioeconomic structure. Latin America is characterized by high degrees of income inequality. There is a huge gap between the lives of Carlos Slim and Judith Yanira Viera. The goal becomes promoting not only growth but some form of equitable growth—quite a tall order. Income inequality introduces complications in the measurement of growth. If equality is important, the change in a poor person's income should carry roughly the same weight as that of a rich person. But given inequality, if a rich person earns twenty times more than a poor person, changes in the income of the wealthy receive twenty times the weight of changes in income of the poor in the national growth calculation.[33] If growth is supposed to measure economic performance, even the measures are far from the mark.

In many cases inequality is exacerbated by an ethnic and cultural mosaic of approaches to economic life. Traditional forms of social organization in indigenous communities may clash with the marketization of economic life. Gender also plays a key role in the assessment of policy outcomes. In a society often conditioned by traditional gender roles, policymakers sensitive to the gender divide must ask, how accessible terms of credit or access to technology are to the widest range of citizens. Although these problems are not unimportant in policy making in more industrialized countries, the range of difference confronts the policymaker with hard choices. Women in Santiago, for example, may be well-educated, active economic contributors, whereas their sisters in the Altiplano live a far more traditional life. In assessing policy in Latin America, do not neglect to ask: Policy for whom? Whose needs should policy be designed to meet? Judith Yanira Viera's? Or Carlos Slim's?

PRESENT VERSUS FUTURE VALUE: THE ENVIRONMENTAL DIMENSION

Promoting not only development but also sustainable development—or a strategy that leaves future generations as well-off as the present—may seem unrealistic when more than half of a population lives on the verge of starvation or when inflation eats away at the meager earnings of the working poor. Policymakers in the developing world—like those anywhere—are constrained by political and financial capital. There are only so many things that can be done with limited energy and finances. Daily crises take precedence over long-term planning. This becomes quite evident in the environmental arena. The challenge becomes how not to forfeit future growth while confronting present dilemmas. Even in industrial market economies, characterized by less sensational economic twists and turns, it is hard enough to promote incentives for sustainable use of resources. Imagine the difficulties in a developing country. Enforcement of environmental laws in industrial economies, with stronger institutional and financial resources, is often lax or ineffective. Yet without an environmental sensitivity to the future, policy will not be sustainable over time. Bad choices today have costs tomorrow. Policy to promote rational environmental decision making in Latin America must be carefully crafted—and perhaps supplemented with external capital—for long-term investment in the future. Macro- and microeconomic policies must be assessed through environmental lenses to protect resources for future generations.

THE STATE AND THE MARKET: PROMOTING PARTNERSHIP

Who should be the primary development actor in the region? What should be the relative balance between the state and the market in promoting development in Latin America? These questions have framed much of the twentieth-century policy debate in the region. We will see that the pendulum has swung from a market-led to a state-dominated economy. Social protest in the first years of the twenty-first century by those who have been marginalized by growth has forced a reevaluation of the belief in the return to the market. Whether or not you support a stronger role for the state in economic decision making may be conditioned by your view of the relative sophistication of economic institutions in the region. Irma Adelman and Cynthia Taft Morris, two highly respected development economists, suggest that the crucial factor affecting development is the effectiveness of economic institutions and how economic institutions mediate the way in which gains from growth are distributed.[34] Are the economic institutions—central banks, capital, land and labor markets, redistributive agents, and laws governing property rights—sufficiently strong to promote equitable and sustainable growth without much day-to-day state interference? If independent market institutions or the property code is weak, is policy intervention warranted? Defining where the state can and should supplement the activity of the market is an important element in crafting effective policy for development in Latin America.

Three broad schools of thought can be identified with respect to the role of the state in development policy.[35] During the 1950s and 1960s, the success of the socialist model in jump-starting industrialization in the Soviet Union led to a **planning model** that accorded a strong role to the state in promoting development. The economists within Latin America who broadly believed that state intervention was critical to promoting development were called **dependency theorists**. Since markets were viewed as incomplete and unable to send strong and accurate price signals to economic agents, the state was viewed as an essential vehicle to orchestrate the growth process. Without an interventionist state, markets alone would not spontaneously generate growth. State-run activity was seen as necessary in providing infrastructure, such as roads and railways, and public services in education and health. In addition, state activity was encouraged in the direct production of goods and services in which private initiative had failed. The state was also supposed to help to counterbalance the power of domestic and international elites. We will consider the extension of this model to Latin America in chapter 3 on import substitution industrialization. Today, the potential gains from globalization and international trade, the benefits of entrepreneurship and the profit motive, and the difficulties introduced by problems of accountability and enforcement have created a shift away from the planning model.

The second broad approach falls within the **institutionalist tradition.** Institutionalists accord a strong role to nonmarket institutions. In particular, institutionalists suggest that rather than relying solely on price signals, other forms of organization—judges, chieftains, priests, or community councils—may intervene to settle disputes arising from the conflict over scarce economic resources.[36] Economic problems must therefore be treated within the context of legal, social, and political systems. Economic outcomes were often determined as much by power as by price signals. As the wealthy would be better able to command resources, high degrees of inequality would bias development against the poor. For institutionalists, with a variety of factors influencing outcomes, development does not tend toward equilibrium but may be a bumpy and discontinuous process. As we will see in chapter 3, the planning model and dependency theorists as well as institutionalist thought informed the position of some of the structuralist thinkers and policymakers in Latin America. **Structuralists**—economists who believed that the particular structure of developing economies warranted a different policy approach—dominated regional policy from the 1940s through the 1970s. Neostructuralists suggest that the modern demands of global red markets require a balancing hand of the state.

A third school of thought in development economics is the **neoclassical tradition.** Linked in part to the **Chicago School** of **orthodox** economic policies, it places the market at the center of the development equation. The orthodox key to development policy is in ensuring that economic agents face accurate price incentives without interference to make the best of all possible economic decisions. State-led activity in infrastructure and public services is seen to have a poor performance record. Well-intended short-term market interventions are argued to perpetuate unintended long-run misallocations of resources.[37] Strict neoclassical theorists therefore see a minimalist role for the state as a guarantor of rules and property rights and a provider of a limited array of public goods such as defense. The private sector, through the profit motive and Adam Smith's invisible hand, will generate the greatest good for all. Foreign trade and international prices should become the engine for growth. Under the leadership of the late Milton Friedman, the Chicago School was the principal articulator of the Pinochet model in Chile, and it broadly informs the neoliberal policies that have dominated development strategies in Latin America in the 1990s.

All development approaches do not necessarily fall into one of these three policy boxes. However, the three tend to define answers to the critical question: Is the market the best of all possible mechanisms to organize economic activity and promote growth, or is state intervention a necessary ingredient to development policy in Latin America? The planner would argue for the hand of the state to guide development policy, the institutionalist would suggest that mechanisms beyond the market are critical in determining economic outcomes, and the subscriber to the Chicago School would staunchly support market-based policies. As we proceed through the puzzle of development in Latin America, you will need to resolve for yourself the most beneficial mix of market, state, and complementary institutions to promote development in the region. We will address this question in chapter 6 as we take an in-depth look at the contemporary role of the state in development.

These five issues—external balance, credibility, distribution, environmental sustainability, and the role of the state—pervade our examination of the backdrop to development policy in the region and our treatment of contemporary issues. In chapters 2 and 3 we will see how they played out in early development theories in the region. Chapters 4 and 5 address two of the dramatic legacies of imbalances of past mistakes—hyperinflation and debt. Chapter 6 introduces the new economic model in the region and chapter 7 chronicles the return of Latin America to international capital markets. In chapter 8 we consider contemporary trade performance, and then we go on to analyze sources of industrial competitiveness as well as the potential of the agricultural sector in chapters 9 and 10, respectively. We will see the radical economic changes adopted by the region in the 1990s and evaluate their significant gains. But challenges remain. In chapter 11 we take up the problem of poverty, and in chapters 12 and 13 we assess educational and health systems in the region. Finally, although we pay attention to the environment throughout this text, in chapter 14 we look at environmental priorities in Latin America and suggest an agenda for action. We conclude in chapter 15 with an evaluation of the relative weight of the state and the market in addressing the challenges to a sustainable and equitable development strategy in Latin America.

Key Concepts

Chicago School
dependency
development
dualism

empowerment
equity
growth
institutionalist tradition

planning model
sustainable development
technological change

Chapter Summary

Development: Definitions and Theory

- Development is a word not easily defined in the context of economic advancement. Questions arise as to what kinds of characteristics "developed" countries have or should have.
- A distinction exists between development and economic growth. Development is multidimensional, involving political and social institutional change. Growth focuses on increased output.
- The goals of development extend beyond economic growth. These goals may include meeting basic human needs, increasing economic opportunities for the poor, empowering marginalized groups, and ensuring economic benefits for future generations.
- Economists have not been able to agree on a well-defined theory of development. The development processes for less-developed nations are likely to differ from those followed by industrialized nations. Approaches to develop-

ment will depend upon the location, size, and natural endowments of each country.

- Three schools of thought for development policy provide policy guides to development strategy: the planning model, the institutionalist tradition, and the neoclassical tradition. Each of these defines a degree to which the state should intervene in the development process and the extent to which the process should be left in the hands of the market.

Challenges in Development Policy in Latin America

Policymakers face five major challenges when designing development policy in Latin America. First, they must establish a delicate balance between the external sector and domestic macropolicy. Second, they must be attentive to the changing nature of the global economic environment as well as preserve confidence and stability within their own economies. Third, to attain equitable growth, they must fashion policies to target different economic, ethnic, and gender groups. Fourth, their policies must balance the allocation of resources between meeting the needs of present as well as future generations. Finally, policymakers are faced with the challenge of deciding the extent to which each state should supplement the activities of its own market to facilitate equitable, sustainable development.

Notes

1. Dionne Searcey and David Luhnow, "Verizon Pulls Out of Latin America," *Wall Street Journal,* April 4, 2006; wsj.com, A18.

2. Profile on *Forbes Magazine* retrieved on March 9, 2006.

3. Geri Smith, International—Latin American Cover Story, *Business Week,* February 21, 2000, Business Week.com.

4. "Billionaires by Rank," *Forbes,* www.forbes.com.

5. Smith, International—Latin American Cover Story, *Business Week.*

6. Excerpted from Monica Larner and Ian Katz, "It's Ronaldo's World," *Business-Week,* June 22, 1998, 204; and Alex Bellos, "Ronaldo's Fame Hasn't Hit Home," *Minneapolis Star Tribune,* 10 July 1998, 6c.

7. Calvin Sims, "A Web Entree for Peruvians without PCs," *New York Times,* 27 May 1996, sec. 1, p. 29 (accessed via LEXIS-NEXIS database).

8. "In the Gap and Sweatshop Labor in El Salvador," *NACLA Report on the Americas* 29(4) (January–February 1996): 37.

9. Diana Jean Schemo, "Brazil Farmers Feel Squeezed by Tobacco Companies," *New York Times,* April 6, 1998, online edition.

10. Harry S. Truman, inaugural address, January 20, 1949, in *Documents on American Foreign Relations* (Connecticut University Press, 1967), as quoted in Wolfgang Sachs, ed., *The Development Dictionary: A Guide to Knowledge as Power* (London: Zed, 1992), 2.

11. W. Arthur Lewis, "Economic Development with Unlimited Supplies of Labour," *Manchester School* 22(2) (1954). Reprinted in A. N. Agarwala and S. P. Singh, eds., *The Economics of Underdevelopment* (New York: Oxford University Press, 1963).

12. Celso Furtado, *Development and Underdevelopment,* trans. Ricardo W. de Agruar and Eric Charles Drysdale (Berkeley: University of California Press, 1965), 47. Originally published as *Dialectica do desenvolvimento, Rio de Janeiro* (Berkeley: University of California Press, 1964).

13. Peter Bauer and Basil Yamey, *The Economics of Underdeveloped Countries* (New York: Cambridge University Press, 1967), 151.

14. Benjamin Higgins, *Economic Development: Problems, Principles, and Policies* (New York: Norton, 1968), 148.

15. Theotônio Dos Santos, "La crisis de la teoría del desarollo y las relaciones de dependencia en América Latina," *Boletin de CESO* 3 (1968). This article appeared in English as "The Crisis of Development Theory and the Problem of Dependence in Latin America" in *Underdevelopment and Development,* ed. H. Bernstein (Harmondsworth, UK: Penguin, 1973).

16. Denis Goulet, *The Cruel Choice: A New Concept in the Theory of Development* (New York: Atheneum, 1971), 23.

17. Charles K. Wilber, *The Political Economy of Development and Underdevelopment* (New York: Random House, 1973), 355.

18. Dudley Seers, "What Are We Trying to Measure?" *Journal of Development Studies* (April 1972).

19. Simon Kuznets, "Modern Economic Growth: Findings and Reflections," *American Economic Review* 63(3) (June 1973): 247.

20. Kenneth P. Jameson and Charles K. Wilber, *Directions in Economic Development* (Notre Dame, Ind.: University of Notre Dame Press, 1979), 38. Originally in James J. Lamb, "The Third World and the Development Debate," *IDOC-North America* (January–February 1973): 20.

21. Paul Streeten, "A Basic Needs Approach to Economic Development," in Jameson and Wilber, *Directions,* 73.

22. Peter J. Henriot, "Development Alternatives: Problems, Strategies, Values," in *The Political Economy of Development and Underdevelopment,* 2nd ed., ed. Charles K. Wilber (New York: Random House, 1979), 11.

23. Jameson and Wilber, *Directions,* 7.

24. World Commission on Environment and Development, *Our Common Future* (Oxford: Oxford University Press, 1987), 8–9.

25. Gerald M. Meier, *Leading Issues in Economic Development,* 6th ed. (Oxford: Oxford University Press, 1995), 7.

26. Amartya Sen, "The Concept of Development," in *Handbook of Development Economics,* Vol. 1 (Netherlands: North-Holland, 1988).

27. Boris Pleskovic and Joseph E. Stiglitz, eds., *Annual World Bank Conference on Development Economics, 1997* (Washington, D.C.: World Bank, 1998), 19.

28. Nancy Birdsall, President, Center for Global Development, email correspondence, November 2005, based on concepts in her 2005 Annual WIDER Lecture *Rising Inequality in the New Global Economy* at the United Nations University's World Institute for Development Economics Helsinki, October 2005.

29. Schumpeter (1939), as presented in Paolo Sylos Labini, "The Classical Roots of Development Theory," in *Economic Development: Handbook of Comparative Economic Policies,* ed. Enzo Grilli and Dominick Salvatore (Westport, Conn.: Greenwood, 1994), 3–26.

30. Lucas (1988), as presented in Sylos Labini, "The Classical Roots of Development Theory," 3.

31. Paul Streeten, "From Growth to Basic Needs," in *Latin America's Economic Development: Institutionalist and Structuralist Perspectives,* ed. James L. Dietz and James H.

Street (Boulder, Colo.: Lynne Rienner, 1987). Originally appeared in *Finance and Development* 16 (September 1979).

32. Michael P. Todaro, *Economic Development,* 5th ed. (White Plains, N.Y.: Longman, 1994), 670.

33. Gerald K. Helleiner, "Toward a New Development Strategy," in *The Legacy of Raúl Prebisch,* ed. Enrique V. Iglesias (Washington, D.C.: Inter-American Development Bank, 1994), 178.

34. Irma Adelman and Cynthia Taft Morris, "Development History and Its Implications for Development Theory," *World Development* 25(6) (1997): 831–840.

35. Karla Hoff, Avishay Braverman, and Joseph Stiglitz, "Introduction," in *The Economics of Rural Organization,* ed. Karla Hoff, Avishay Braverman, and Joseph Stiglitz (New York: Oxford University Press/World Bank, 1993).

36. Ibid.

37. John Martinussen, *Society, State, and Market: A Guide to Competing Theories of Development* (London: Zed, 1997), 260.

CHAPTER TWO

HISTORICAL LEGACIES

Patterns of Unequal and Unstable Growth

Historical patterns of land distribution have left a legacy of high inequality in the region. *(Courtesy of the Inter-American Development Bank)*

In *One Hundred Years of Solitude,* Colombian novelist Gabriel García Márquez warns us that Latin America recycles its past. To evaluate contemporary policy we must understand the historical legacies of the region. The economic history of Latin America, a continent with diverse national stories and richly textured social histories, is far more complicated and nuanced than this short chapter on historical legacies can ever hope to convey. Here we can only abstract some of the patterns shaping development in the region. Perhaps some of the questions raised in our study of contemporary policy in the region will motivate the serious student of Latin America to revisit the historical pattern of growth at another time.[1] Some questions we will consider include the following:

- What factors shape the growth patterns of countries?
- Why, despite relatively similar starting points, did Latin America fall behind the United States and Canada in terms of growth?
- What are the characteristics of primary product-led growth?
- What were the social forms of economic organization conditioning development patterns?
- What were the environmental implications of the early pattern of development in Latin America?

This chapter assumes the overwhelming challenge of putting contemporary development into a simplified historical framework. It explains how the colonial and early independence periods shaped later development problems by focusing on the inputs and outputs of production. This brief foray is designed to provide a context for policy making today. Like the Buendía family in the García Márquez novel, this chapter highlights the opportunities and the cyclical constraints in the development experience in Latin America.

THE PUZZLE OF COMPARATIVE GROWTH PATTERNS

What early patterns of economic organization in Latin America shaped later growth? Rather than a conventional time line, our discussion is organized around the inputs to development: availability of labor, capital, and technology to promote agricultural and industrial growth at home and abroad. How did available resources constrain and shape development? In table 2.1 we can see that in 1700, per capita gross domestic products (GDPs) in Mexico and the United States were roughly equal. As late as 1850, Argentina and Brazil enjoyed per capita GDPs higher than Canada's. Table 2.2 presents similar results based on a different study; by 2001 GDP per capita in the United States had risen to roughly five times that of Latin nations. In terms of overall GDP, the U.S. economy is more than twice the size of all Latin American economies combined. Why did Latin America stagnate in the twentieth century while the United States and Canada surged ahead?[2]

Table 2.1.   Historical Per Capita Growth of GDP (in 1985 US$)

	1700	1800	1850	1913	1989
Argentina	NA	NA	874	2,377	3,880
Brazil	NA	738	901	700	4,241
Chile	NA	NA	484	1,685	5,355
Mexico	450	450	317	1,104	3,521
Peru	NA	NA	526	985	3,142
Canada	NA	NA	850	3,560	17,576
United States	490	807	1,394	4,854	18,317
% of U.S. per Capita GDP					
Argentina	NA	NA	62.70	48.97	21.18
Brazil	NA	91.45	64.63	14.42	23.15
Chile	NA	NA	34.72	34.71	29.24
Mexico	91.84	55.76	22.74	22.74	19.22
Peru	NA	NA	37.73	20.29	17.15
Canada	NA	NA	60.98	73.34	95.95
United States	100.00	100.00	100.00	100.00	100.00

Source: Stanley Engerman and Kenneth Sokoloff, *Factor Endowments, Institutions and Differential Paths of Growth among New World Economies: A View from Economic Historians of the United States,* National Bureau of Economic Research Historical Paper No. 66 (Cambridge, Mass.: National Bureau of Economic Research, 1994).

THINKING ABOUT INPUTS, OUTPUTS, AND ECONOMIC CHANGE

Economic development may be thought of as a process whereby the structure of the economy evolves to adapt to the changing needs of a growing population. Growth of output must outstrip population growth to improve the resources available to people. Population, or labor, constitutes one of the inputs of production. How is it organized and combined with other inputs to produce output? It is useful to think about the fundamentals shaping the structure of an economy. These in turn condition the economy's performance in meeting the requirements of society. Why do economies begin to produce certain goods? How do specializations evolve and change over time? One way to answer this is to consider the inputs available for production and the characteristics of the output market that define product demand. What inputs are available to be made into desired output? What technology is available—and who controls it—to facilitate the process? Whose tastes and desires—local, international, rich, poor—are the target market? Looking at the factors affecting supply and demand will allow us to say something about the structure of an economy and to evaluate how policy was used historically to improve the responsiveness of an economy to the needs of its citizens. Table 2.3 summarizes some of these factors shaping patterns of growth.

What factors condition the menu of goods and services that a country produces? Resources, raw materials, and the physical characteristics of land affect production

Table 2.2.   Historical Population and GDP Data

	1820	1870	1913	1950	2001
Population (million people)					
Total Western Europe	133.0	187.5	261.0	304.9	392.1
Japan	31.0	34.4	51.7	83.8	126.9
Total Asia (excluding Japan)	679.4	730.8	925.7	1,298.6	3,526.6
Africa	74.2	90.5	124.7	227.3	821.1
United States	10.0	40.2	97.6	152.3	285.0
Mexico	6.6	9.2	15.0	28.5	101.9
Argentina	0.5	1.8	7.7	17.2	37.9
Brazil	4.5	9.8	23.7	53.4	177.8
Chile	0.9	1.9	3.5	6.1	15.3
Peru	1.3	2.6	4.3	7.6	27.5
Uruguay	0.1	0.3	1.2	2.2	3.4
Total Latin America	21.7	40.4	80.9	165.9	531.2
World	1,041.8	1,271.9	1,791.1	2,524.3	6,149.0
Per Capita GDP (1990 international Geary Khamis dollars)					
West European Average	1,204	1,960	3,458	4,579	19,256
Japan	669	737	1,387	1,921	20,683
Asian Average (excl. Japan)	577	550	658	634	3,256
Africa	420	500	637	894	1,489
United States	1,257	2,445	5,301	9,561	27,948
Mexico	759	674	1,732	2,365	7,089
Argentina	..	1,311	3,797	4,987	8,137
Brazil	646	713	811	1,672	5,570
Chile	..	..	2,653	3,821	10,001
Peru	..	..	1,037	2,263	2,263
Uruguay	..	2,181	3,310	4,659	4,659
Latin American Average	692	681	1,481	2,506	5,811
World	667	875	1,525	2,111	6,049
GDP (million dollars)					
Total Western Europe	160.1	367.6	902.3	1,396.2	7,550.3
Japan	20.7	25.4	71.7	161.0	2,624.5
Total Asia (excluding Japan)	392.2	401.6	608.7	822.8	11,481.2
Africa	31.2	45.2	79.5	203.1	1,222.6
United States	12.5	98.4	517.4	1,455.9	7,965.8
Mexico	5.0	6.2	25.9	67.4	722.2
Argentina	..	2.4	29.1	85.5	308.5
Brazil	2.9	7.0	19.2	89.3	990.1
Chile	..	..	9.3	23.3	153.3
Peru	..	..	4.5	17.3	99.8
Uruguay	..	0.7	3.9	10.2	25.4
Total Latin America	15.0	27.5	119.9	415.9	3,087.0
World	695.3	1,112.7	2,732.1	5,329.7	37,193.9

Source: The World Economy: Historical Statistics.

Table 2.3. Factors Shaping Patterns of Growth

Natural resources	Is the country resource abundant? Who owns resources?
Land	How is land distributed? Who decides who owns land? Are landholdings concentrated or spread out among small stakeholders? Are the claims or titles to landholdings clear? What is the quality of available land?
Labor resources	How abundant is labor? What is the skill level of workers?
Financial capital	Is there a domestic surplus available for reinvestment? Do domestic investors find better returns at home or abroad? Is growth dependent on an external infusion of funds?
Technology	What is the technological base of the nation? Who controls the access to technology? Do international patents restrict the free flow of technology?
Policy environment	Is the driving force behind growth the market or the state? Is the policy inwardly oriented or open to the international economy?

Source: Patrice Franko.

possibilities. Does a country's geographic location matter? Is a country rich in natural resources? Is there a diversity of available resources? Or does the country rely on a limited number of natural commodities? Who owns resources and how they are distributed throughout the population both matter enormously. Asset ownership confers the ability to make a profit on the sale or use of that factor of production. Is the ownership of key resources concentrated in a small, powerful group, or it is evenly spread around the population? Do these assets—land or mines or timber or fish—generate a profit for the owners above and beyond subsistence needs? The development of a group of people with a profit or surplus above and beyond personal subsistence requirements creates an elite class of potential capitalists or investors. These capitalists can then reinvest the surplus to create new growth opportunities—or they can send it out of the country to earn money elsewhere. If this pool of national capital falls short of domestic investment demand, the country finds itself dependent on international sources of funds for growth. The choices that domestic elites make about where to invest their money also shape the available stock of technology employed in the production process. Investments in technological inputs may enhance the productivity of the labor force, or resources may be directed toward producing sophisticated products outside the reach of the common consumer. As we can see, land, capital, and labor—the primary inputs to production—help define the productive structure.

But this structure does not operate in a vacuum. Public policies fashion the productive environment. The legal structure defines property rights and social responsibilities. The policy environment may be shaped by a market philosophy limiting the sphere of government activity, or there may be a demand for the government to address collective needs or redress some of the imbalances created by economic growth. A nation's institutions may continue to be influenced by its colonial past. Furthermore, what a country produces, as well as how and by whom, is conditioned by what the rest of the world is doing. Borders are generally permeable to ideas, goods, services, and prices; countries view productive capabilities relative to the endowments and technological achievements of other nations. Relative advantage matters. A country's position in the international economic order also defines possible pathways to growth. A late-developing country may find that others have already cornered the market in a particular product or process. These supply characteristics of inputs, and production rules interact with demand. The most efficient producer of an undesired good goes broke. The characteristics of a product—how responsive people are to price changes, the number of substitutes, the frequency and size of purchase—as well as the internal and external market size for a country's tradable goods create the opportunity for profit.

Fundamental supply and demand conditions affect and are affected by macroeconomic variables. Supply constraints or excess demand may give rise to inflation; failure to capture a surplus for reinvestment may result in anemic or slow growth. Attempts to jump-start an economy may simply fuel inflation; policies to manipulate the exchange rate to gain competitive advantage may have unintended domestic effects. The macroeconomic environment therefore shapes the activity of producer and consumer in the market.

How have the supply conditions—land, labor, capital, and technological availability—interacted with the demand factors and the macroeconomic environment to condition historical growth in Latin America? What were the available resources? Who controlled them? What technology was available to the owners of resources? What were the rules of the market? How did demand for products from Latin America affect growth patterns? How and where were profits reinvested? Finding answers to these questions gives us a sense of the historical factors shaping growth in the region.

Natural Abundance: Geography and the Rewards of the Extractive Economy

Geography was an important determinant in shaping the economic fortune of Latin America. Geography affects long-term growth through health conditions, productivity of land, availability of natural resources, transportation costs, and economies of scale in market size.[3] The diverse physical and human geographies of Latin America—from the peaks of the Andean range to the low, moist floors of the rainforests—create physical barriers to overcome. The geographic diversity of the region has shaped growth patterns. Before the completion of the Panama Canal in 1914, Andean economies were seriously disadvantaged in distance from trade markets; moving a ton of goods from Lima to Bogota cost 52.9 pounds as compared to 2 pounds to Buenos Aires or Montevideo.[4] Trade with port cities promoted an outward focus in a region where overland shipping could be as expensive as sending goods halfway around the world. In Bolivia and Ecuador, for example, costs from the port city to the capital were between four and five times the cost of shipping from England.[5]

Isolation from contact with European settlers may have preserved indigenous cultures but also created obstacles to integration in the global market. Colonizers rejected harsh conditions of the tropical Central American countries and instead invested in institutional development in the more hospitable southern latitudes. Hard-to-control disease vectors, rusting machines, and perennially soggy clothing were not for the weak. Health conditions such as malaria reduced growth by as much as 1 percent.[6] European immigrants flocked to temperate lands, bringing education and market customs.[7] To promote the extraction of rich natural resources, Europeans imposed institutions—sets of rules governing human behavior—that protected their rights to New World wealth.[8] Where resources were abundant, colonial powers placed extractive institutions in elite hands; geographies less generously endowed led to establishing institutions of private property that allows access to broader stakeholders in society to receive returns on investment. Even within countries, geography conditioned the development of settlements and future wealth.[9] Although inhospitable geography should not be seen as fatally consigning countries to poverty, the effects of poor land and frail institutions persist today.

The exploitation of natural resources was at the heart of the colonial period of Latin American development. Latin America was resource rich. Exploration of the region was driven by the Spanish mercantilist search for silver and gold. The New World provided new opportunities for wealth in Europe. Monopoly control over mines and land in the New World was accorded through the **encomienda** system, with a share of the output, or **repartida,** owed in return. Under the encomienda system, rights to land were parceled out by the monarchy, with an associated portion of the profits to be shipped back to Europe. Labor, however, was scarce. In 1503 Queen Isabella of Spain "entrusted" the Indians to the landlords, requiring the heads of the estates, or **caciques,** to provide payment, protection, and instruction in the Christian faith in exchange for their services. Indian laborers were also entrapped through debt into purchasing goods from the owner at inflated prices. Extractive activities also laid a toll on the local labor force to bring the silver and gold to Spain. Indigenous peoples were obliged to provide the labor for mining, and Indian populations were decimated by European diseases—smallpox, yellow fever, malaria, and bubonic plague. As indigenous communities were broken up in support of an emerging agricultural sector, the "biological holocaust," as some have called it,[10] claimed the lives of the large majority of the continent's indigenous population.

The Portuguese, given claim to Brazil by the Treaty of Tordesillas in 1494, were initially less driven by the search for precious metals. When the Portuguese arrived, they did not find and conquer the highly organized indigenous civilization of the Incas or the Mayans to lead them to a fabulous pot of silver or gold. Furthermore, with the indigenous population scattered throughout the vast Amazon, labor was a problem. Agriculture took hold before mining. The early importation of African slaves solved labor shortages in the emerging sugar industry. The gold rush began in Minas Gerais, Brazil, in the late 1600s and continued through the middle 1700s, increasing Portuguese interest in the colony. But the relatively early development of Brazilian agriculture exerted a stabilizing influence on the early development pattern. As in the United States, importing slaves relieved the labor constraint in production.

LABOR AND SOCIAL RELATIONS

The exploitation of indigenous labor supplies, the importation of Africans, and European immigration radically changed the racial composition in the region. Around 1900, there were approximately twenty million Latin Americans, a regional population about equal to that of Great Britain and double that of the United States. The small national populations were seen as a constraint on development. Argentina and Brazil were the second and third most popular intercontinental destinations for European immigrants in the late 1800s and early 1900s, but they attracted only 20 percent of the immigration flow, compared to 60 percent for the United States.[11] Four million African slaves were introduced to Brazil from 1531 to 1855.[12] As we can see in table 2.4, limited immigration flows set up different racial patterns in the region. In Spanish America, by 1935 blacks accounted for 13.3 percent of the population and Indians 50.4 percent; in Brazil, African Brazilians made up 35.5 percent of the population, surpassing the Indian population. Interestingly, slavery in Latin America was abolished soon after independence in most Latin American nations, with little of the turmoil that accompanied the transition in the United States. Even in Brazil, where slavery lasted until 1888, racial integration has been far more harmonious than in North America.

Differing racial patterns in Spanish America and Brazil as compared to the United States and Canada had a clear economic dimension. The production of export crops such as sugar and mining activities relied on imported slave labor and

Table 2.4.   Racial Composition in New World Economies (percentages)

		White	Black	Indian
Spanish America	1570	1.3	2.5	96.3
	1650	6.3	9.3	84.4
	1825	18.0	22.5	59.5
	1935	35.5	13.3	50.4
Brazil	1570	2.4	3.5	94.1
	1650	7.4	13.7	78.9
	1825	23.4	55.6	21.0
	1935	41.0	35.5	23.0
United States and Canada	1570	0.2	0.2	99.6
	1650	12.0	2.2	85.8
	1825	79.6	16.7	3.7
	1935	89.4	8.9	1.4

Source: Stanley Engerman and Kenneth Sokoloff, *Factor Endowments, Institutions and Differential Paths of Growth among New World Economies: A View from Economic Historians of the United States,* National Bureau of Economic Research Historical Paper No. 66 (Cambridge, Mass.: National Bureau of Economic Research, 1994), table 3.

forced Indian labor. Although the southern United States also solved its labor constraint through slavery, 80 percent of the population in the United States and Canada was white in 1825, whereas whites composed only between 20 and 25 percent of the population in Spanish America and Brazil. But this small white minority held extraordinary economic power. The white Europeans in Latin America, small in number, were granted property from the monarchies, whereas slaves or manual laborers without assets were the bulk of the population.[13] Income—derived from the ownership of assets—was highly unequal and tied to race from the start in Latin America. Mentally combine the data on per capita GDP in table 2.1 with our information about the small share of the white population. Since the per capita estimates are an average of the population, imagine how well the white European elite must have lived compared with the rest of the population. Income inequality shaped institutional development in the region. Wealthy elites preferred low tax rates on income and property—resulting in the limited capacity of governments to provide public goods of education and infrastructure. The status quo served vested interests. The Portuguese even prohibited the operation of printing presses in colonial Brazil and stifled the development of a university system.[14]

Despite differences in the emphasis on mining and agricultural activity between Brazil and the rest of the region, early social relations in both the Spanish and the Portuguese colonies tended to be feudal. The traditional authority of the Catholic Church reinforced these social patterns. The *encomienda* system accorded property rights to a small number of landholders, concentrating ownership and crowding the indigenous and mestizo, or those of mixed heritage, onto less-productive land. This system of the *latifundia,* the feudal **hacienda** estates in Spanish Latin America, and the *fazenda* system in Brazil set up a highly unequal socioeconomic system. Furthermore, since internal markets were relatively small, the *latifundia* largely fostered an agricultural sector directed toward Europe. Profits were repatriated, leaving little at home for reinvestment. By 1800 residents in Bourbon, Mexico, paid more taxes than Spaniards in the Metropolis.[15] Powerful elites blocked taxation at the local levels, precluding investment in public schooling at the heart of the North American model. Political opposition to such privilege was weak; by the mid-nineteenth century all Latin American countries retained wealth and literacy requirements to vote.[16] Those eking out a subsistence existence on the *minifundia,* the small parcels of land the peasants farmed, could do little more than feed themselves with their meager earnings. Compared to the United States, greater inequality in wealth, human capital, and political power likely promoted the evolution of weaker internal markets in Latin America.[17] The poor didn't have much money to buy goods. Elites retained positions of political power, blocking forces of economic change.

INDEPENDENCE: POLITICAL CHANGE WITHOUT ECONOMIC TRANSFORMATION

National independence, achieved regionally by 1822 (with the exception of Cuba and Puerto Rico), allowed for a change in rules regarding property rights and trade. However, the violence, lawlessness, and political turmoil of the period of independence reinforced the legitimacy of the *latifundia* as a form of political and economic organization. Lawlessness and revolt were common. People wanted security. The growing pains of nations—the difficulty in raising taxes and providing public services—highlighted the stability of the semifeudal system of social, political, and economic protection that the *coronel,* or the head of the *latifundia,* provided. Accompanied by wars and uncertainty, independence did not deliver conditions for sustained economic growth.[18] The preservation of elite political interests, rather than institutional modernization favoring equal legal rights for citizens, may have had the effect of slowing growth in Latin America as compared to the North.[19] Elites in extractive societies had much to lose from institutional reform and instead preserved their power to extract resource rents.[20] Weak central governments were subordinated to local military and political caudillos. Fiscal deficits emerged, creating a vicious cycle whereby vulnerable governments succumbed to challenges by political elites and civil strife ensued.[21]

The pattern of land tenure was perhaps unnecessarily concentrated. Although we can trace the roots of unequal landholdings to the colonial land tenure system, it is important to point out that after independence, new national governments missed opportunities to redistribute land from conquest, held by the former crowns, or further appropriated from indigenous communities. The lack of change is not surprising. Literacy and wealth requirements limited the vote to the powerful oligarchies.[22] If political elites tied to this system had not been so powerful, fundamental land reforms would have created greater competition in the agricultural sector. With a larger number of small holdings, competitive pressure may have fostered activity in other sectors. Infrastructure, including transportation and energy, was also weak, making it difficult to set up local manufacturing. Thin domestic capital markets made it tough to raise money. In addition, local market demand was too small and product quality was too low for manufacturing to exploit the international sector. Political and economic structures did not help create a climate conducive to institutional change.

Contributing to the desire to maintain a political oligarchy was the fact that people were relatively well-off. By the end of the 1800s, the per capita income in Latin America was $245, at a time when it only reached $239 in North America.[23] Unfortunately for national growth, income was concentrated, and reinvestment of profits in entrepreneurial activity was limited. The lack of political change hindered economic transformation. Given the control of the political system by elites, it made little sense to venture into risky investments. The security of the *latifundia* system mitigated against economic risk taking. With political and economic gains consolidated, why embark on an investment likely to fail?

THE GIANT SUCKING SOUND OF SINGLE-COMMODITY EXPORTS

As shown in table 2.5, nations tended to hitch their economic star to a dominant commodity. Coffee, sugar, bananas, and their associated feudal structures of production dominated the export profile. Exports were seen as the engine of economic

Table 2.5.   Single-Commodity Exports As a Percentage of Total Exports

Country	Commodity	% Total Exports, 1938
El Salvador	Coffee	92
Venezuela	Petroleum	92
Cuba	Sugar	78
Panama	Bananas	77
Bolivia	Tin	68
Guatemala	Coffee	66
Honduras	Bananas	64
Colombia	Coffee	61
Dominican	Sugar	60
Chile	Copper	52
Haiti	Coffee	51
Costa Rica	Coffee	49
Nicaragua	Coffee	47
Brazil	Coffee	45

Source: Simon Hanson, *Economic Development in Latin America* (Washington, D.C.: Inter-American Affairs Press, 1951), 107.

growth. There are winners and losers in the global export game. Despite the similarities in socioeconomic systems, there was a great deal of diversity in economic performance throughout the region, largely connected to the so-called **commodity lottery.**[24] The luck of natural endowment and agricultural advantage—copper and silver in Chile; sugar in Cuba; coffee in Brazil, Colombia, and Costa Rica; cattle in Argentina; bananas from Central America; guano in Peru—defined the winnings in the international export market. International demand had expanded with the opening of the British agricultural market and industrialization in Europe and the United States. In the late 1800s through the early 1900s, a broad consensus for agriculture-led export growth prevailed. This **golden age of primary product exports in Latin America** was facilitated by political stability, expansion of transportation systems encouraging geographic integration, improvements in capital markets promoting capital investment, and secondary industrialization taking place in textiles, food packing, and transportation in support of the agricultural sector. Indeed the period from 1870–1913 has been argued to parallel the current era of globalization.[25] Latin America responded to new demands from the industrializing international system by providing raw materials, including key minerals and food.[26] The Latin American economies sampled in figure 2.1 were more strongly export-oriented than those in Europe in 1929. During this period, Central America began the export of bananas, and Brazil entered the rubber boom.

Single-commodity exports, however, were an unstable basis for balanced, sustainable economic growth. Development policy was preoccupied with the needs of the export sector, with little attention to the links with domestic production and demand. In bananas, much of the production was dominated by U.S. multinationals functioning as an export **enclave** contributing little to the social development of the country. The powerful United Fruit Company, for example, did not pay a cent of tax

Figure 2.1.   Merchandise Exports to GDP, 1929

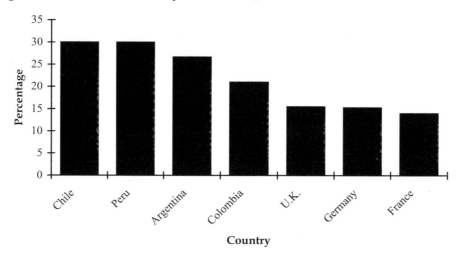

Source: Angus Maddison, "Economic and Social Conditions in Latin America, 1913–1950," in *Long-Term Trends in Latin American Economic Development,* ed. Miguel Urrutia (Washington, D.C.: IADB and Johns Hopkins University Press, 1991), table 1.13.

to the Costa Rican government, and its workers bought goods imported duty-free in the company store.[27] Central American economies became inextricably linked to an international political economy beyond domestic control. As table 2.6 shows, the problems of single-commodity exports were exacerbated by a high concentration in market destination. Demand for the product was essentially determined abroad. The old saying that when the United States sneezes Latin America gets pneumonia begins to apply in this period.

**Table 2.6.   Geographic Distribution of Latin American Exports, 1929
(% of total exports)**

Country	United States	United Kingdom	France	Germany	Four Country Export Concentration
Cuba	76.6	12.6	2.1	0.8	92.1
Colombia	75.2	4.7	0.5	2.1	82.5
Mexico	60.7	10.3	3.9	7.6	82.5
Brazil	42.2	6.5	11.1	8.8	68.6
Peru	33.3	18.3	1.3	6.1	59.0
Venezuela	28.2	1.9	2.9	4.7	37.7
Chile	25.4	13.3	6.1	8.6	53.4
Uruguay	11.9	23.0	11.9	14.5	61.3
Argentina	9.8	32.3	7.1	10.0	59.2
Average	40.4	13.6	4.2	7.0	65.2

Source: Angus Maddison, "Economic and Social Conditions in Latin America, 1913–1950," in *Long-Term Trends in Latin American Economic Development,* ed. Miguel Urrutia (Washington, D.C.: IADB and Johns Hopkins University Press, 1991).

Placing bets in the commodity casino leaves a country vulnerable to the vagaries of the international market. Commodity wealth—gold, silver, tin, coffee, rubber, sugar, oil—can exert negative effects on the process of development. With strong international demand for a particular product, national resources are sucked into the production or extraction of a single commodity. As international prices boom, so do profits at home. Given comparative advantage, it makes great sense to concentrate production on addressing international demand. Resources move to the hot sector, pressuring input prices throughout the economy. Dubbed the **Dutch disease** because of Holland's experience with natural gas, this produces a distorted pattern of development precariously predicated on the hot commodity. International resources are drawn in, overvaluing the exchange rate. When a commodity is booming, why should investors place their money in a less-lucrative outlet? If tin mining is returning high rates of profit, why invest in a dress factory? Furthermore, if profits from the boom are unequally distributed, a broader multiplier effect of the windfall income in industrial development is even less likely. Investors have monopoly or oligopoly control on the industry, and their continued access to profits or monopoly rents appears assured.

But booms have their busts. When commodity prices in the international market fall, they drag the whole economy down with them—because the commodity has essentially become the economy. For example, in 1920, sugar, a key crop for several Latin American nations, sold at 22.5 cents in May but tumbled to 3.625 cents by the end of that same year.[28] By the end of the decade it reached an all-time low of 1.471 cents—a devastating fall for an economy revolving around "king sugar." Coffee prices dropped 40 percent from 1929 to 1930—a tough shock to national coffers.[29] Another dramatic example was the guano economy in Peru. Between 1840 and 1880, Peru's economy revolved around guano deposits left by birds on the island coasts off Peru, where it barely rains. When substitutes were found for this valued fertilizer, Peru's economy crashed. Because most governmental receipts came from taxes on foreign trade, the effect of a commodity bust was magnified by contractionary fiscal policy.

ENGEL'S LAW AND DECLINING TERMS OF TRADE

In addition to price volatility, concentration in primary product exports is also complicated by the nature of primary product demand. Primary products, particularly agricultural goods, are relatively price and income inelastic. If prices go up for coffee or sugar, as in a boom period, people cut back only slightly on their consumption of these perceived necessities. But on the downslope, with prices falling, people don't buy much more at a lower price. There is a limit to how much coffee or sugar people want. Furthermore, we observe a statistical relationship called **Engel's law,** that as income increases there is a weak increase in the demand for primary products. As world income grows and people become wealthier, the demand for agricultural products does not keep pace, unlike that for most manufactured products. If your country is an agricultural producer, compared to the rest of the world getting richer through manufactured goods, you stagnate. The net result

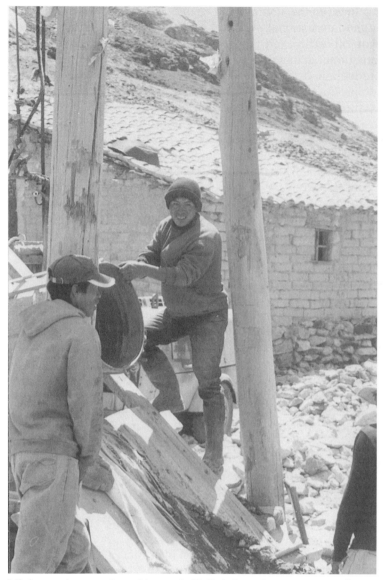

Mining projects such as this one in Bolivia have been a source of
export revenues but also introduce questions of export price
instability and declining terms of trade. *(Courtesy of Amanda McKown)*

of the **declining terms of trade** is that high rates of growth in the primary product
sector may not be enough to act as a catalyst for development. Latin America's
terms of trade declined by about 105 from 1880 to 1900 and fell approximately
20 percent more by 1930.[30] **Export pessimism**—the belief that exports would not
be the engine of growth—began to characterize the policymaker's mind-set by the

early 1920s. In addition to declining terms of trade, the export engine was not strong enough to pull large, low-productivity nontradable sectors.[31] Although the golden age of exports may have acted as a handmaiden to growth, the cycle had turned against Latin America.

THE EFFECTS OF WEAK INDUSTRIAL LINKAGES AND HIGH TARIFF TAXATION

Despite declining terms of trade and export pessimism, primary product export growth is not necessarily a bad thing. Indeed, export growth can provide the opportunity for a country to capture a surplus, reinvest this profit, and reduce dependency on the agricultural product. In Latin America, however, weak links between export industries and the rest of the economy, labor shortages in the manufacturing sector, and foreign competition in industry depressed relative returns. Much export production exhibited characteristics of enclaves isolated from the rest of the economy. Linkages between commodity production and other products were relatively low. For example, coffee did not send signals back down the production chain for much in the way of capital necessary for production (a **backward linkage**), nor did it generate the demand for new industries or products (a **forward linkage**). (The Starbucks coffee bar had yet to be developed!) Cattle ranching is an example of an industry that did contribute to forward linkages in leather processing and the shoe industry, but for the most part, commodity-led industrialization did not stimulate production in other sectors of the economy. In addition, with the notable exception of Argentina, immigration policies limited the labor market, creating shortages in the industrial sector. Ironically, compared to today, high-priced labor in Latin America made manufacturing costly. Domestic markets for financial capital were relatively weak, and foreign investment flowed to areas in which technological or capital constraints restricted entry of local firms. Military conflicts in the newly emerging states drained finances—money most easily acquired by levying import duties. Throughout the region, ad valorem rates reached as high as 40 percent in the late nineteenth century, dampening the positive effect that imported inputs may have had on the economy. By 1865 tariff rates in Latin America were, with the exception of the United States, the highest in the world. Export-led growth was oddly accompanied by import protection used to finance wars.[32]

DOMINANCE OF FOREIGN CAPITAL DURING THE FIRST WAGE OF GLOBALIZATION

Investment flows to Latin America postindependence were large and volatile.[33] New government bond issues garnered the attention of London financiers in the 1820s, but most ended in default. By the late 1860s capital flows resumed and dominated large sectors of some economies. Primarily public, loans were used to roll over old debts and finance military spending and railway construction. Brazil was favored for its relative stability, while other nations, still rocked by wars, were riskier bets. By the end of 1880, 58 percent of British bonds in the region were in default, cementing in investors' minds the untrustworthiness of sovereign borrowers in Latin America. In the private sector, the British had lucrative interests in railways, sanitation, telegraph companies, banking, shipping, and mining. Private sector lending grew for the next several decades, largely tied to the trade boom. Inflows were concentrated in Argentina, Mexico, Brazil, Chile, and Uruguay, emerging stars outstripping slow-growing republics in the region. Capital flowed to support infrastructure and industry—widening the gap between rich and poor in the region. Nonetheless, even dynamically growing countries' investors paid dearly for capital flows—returning high profits for risk.

In the first decade of the twentieth century lenders diversified to include North American, French, and German holdings; in this period the ratio of foreign capital to GDP was 2.7, dwarfing Asia at .4 and Africa at 1.1. Based on these flows, roughly one-third of the capital stock in the region was supplied by external sources—a significant benefit but one that required market discipline and engendered dependency on constant inflows. Crisis and volatility marked the period as hot money over-inflated economies, foreshadowing the stop-and-go nature of debt crises in the 1980s. This epoch of globalization from 1870 to 1914 of open trade and finance, like its parallel a century later, created winners and losers in the region. When foreign capital withdrew in the war years, poorly articulated domestic financial markets were not up to the task of raising and allocating scarce capital. The combination of high levels of foreign investment with commodity export economies tended to generate low returned value to the host economy, depressing possibilities for future growth.[34]

One notable exception to the weakness of domestic capital markets was the case of Brazil. It has been suggested that Brazilian coffee barons were able to underwrite the industrial base of São Paulo while continuing to expand coffee production. It is theorized that this took place because the coffee land was not suitable for agricultural diversification, and *fazendeiros* found themselves in the manufacturing sector in search of new profits.[35] Furthermore, coffee production itself needed so little in the way of reinvestment of surplus that profits were best placed outside the sector.[36] Nonetheless, even under these relatively favorable conditions, development stalled when British financiers fancied more lucrative alternatives.[37]

Table 2.7 illustrates the high rate of foreign investment as a percentage of GDP in the beginning of the century. When foreign capital was withdrawn during World War I, local financial systems were not sufficiently developed to intermediate capital needs. Reflecting the importance of external finance and trade, Argentina, for example, did not have a central bank until 1935. Instead, its monetary authority, the Caja de Conversión, was responsible for guaranteeing the external value of the currency, with no domestic lender of last resort in the system.[38] The role of foreign and domestic commercial lenders was also differentiated. Because international bankers dominated short-term, less risky portfolios, domestic institutions were left with longer-term loans to firms and real estate. When foreign banks pulled out, domestic institutions were not able to liquidate their assets quickly enough to respond to the capital shortage, and they could not respond to the needs of the local economy to finance the accumulation of physical capital.[39] International crises created local reverberations as money was withdrawn from Latin

Table 2.7.   Foreign Investment in Latin America, circa 1913

Creditor	Capital (in millions U.S.$)	Percentage
Great Britain	3,700	43.5
France	1,200	14.1
Germany	900	10.6
United States	1,700	20.0
Others	1,000	11.8

Source: Werner Baer, "Leteinamerica und Westeuropa. Die Wirtschaftsbeziehungen bis zum Ende des Zweiten Weltriegs," in *Lateinamerica-Westeuropa-Vereinigte Staaten Ein atlantisches Dreieck,* ed. W. Grabendorff and R. Roett (Baden-Baden, 1985); cited in Walther L. Bernecker and Hans Werner Tobler, eds., *Development and Underdevelopment in America: Contrasts of Economic Growth in North and Latin America in Historical Perspective* (Berlin: Walter de Gruyter, 1993).

America to supplement European war chests.[40] Dependence on foreign capital has decreased over the course of the century, but vulnerability to the whims of the international capital market has remained a constant challenge for policymakers in the region.

THE ENVIRONMENTAL DIMENSION

The environmental costs of an agricultural and extractive economy geared to export markets were substantial. Ecologically sustainable systems of communal agriculture had been practiced in Mesoamerica since at least 1500 B.C.E. The Spanish Conquest succeeded in its goal of extracting natural riches and also destroyed ancient communal villages and practices.[41] After the mines were stripped, colonists cleared the land for agricultural crops. The introduction of sugar and coffee prompted vast ecological change, transforming the Central American region from subtropical forest to an agricultural export economy by clearing and planting, pushing the frontier, and exhausting the soil. Cattle were introduced, making further claims on land. Land held by the Catholic Church or publicly held Indian lands called **ejidos** came to be seen by liberal free market reformers as constraints on further development of the export economy. By 1880, every Central American country had titling laws granting coffee growers rights to land formerly held by Indian communities. Exports surged, but so did the devastation of indigenous groups. The confiscation of traditional lands led Indians to the ecologically more fragile mountains or lowlands, compounding environmental problems. When coffee estate owners faced labor shortages, the government forced communities to provide workers for the labor-intensive harvest through the **mandamiento** program, often under brutal working conditions. The expansion of banana production in the 1920s and 1930s increased pressure on the land and local food crops as firms dominated by multinationals competed with less powerful *campesinos* for the best high-nutrient soils.

Devastation was not limited to Central America. Brazilian B. F. Brandão provided one of the earliest accounts of environmental destruction in 1865 in this description of his youth on a Brazilian *fazenda:*

> At six o'clock in the morning the overseer forces the poor slave, still exhausted from the evening's labor, to rise from his rude bed and proceed to his work. The first assignment of the season is the chopping down of the forests for the next year's planting. . . . The next step is destruction of the large trees. . . . They set fire to the devastated jungle, and then they cut and stack the branches and smaller tree trunks which have escaped the fire . . . and could hinder development of the crop. . . . Centuries-old tree trunks which two months before had produced a cool, crisp atmosphere over a broad stretch of land, lie on the surface of a field ravaged by fire and covered with ashes, where the slaves are compelled to spend twelve hours under the hot sun of the equator, without a single tree to give them shelter.[42]

Initially trees were burned in a short-term effort to increase soil fertility; they were also felled because they were thought to compete with coffee for limited moisture.[43] Over time, the result was economic devastation.

In mining, industry, and some agricultural activities, local governments allowed control by foreign multinational firms. As characterized by Eduardo Galeano, Latin America's open veins of tin and copper poured into multinational coffers with little commitment to sustainable environmental policy. For example, a New York firm was granted a concession to mine in the Cerro de Pasco region of Peru's Central Andes. It constructed a network of roads, railroads, smelters, mining camps, hydro-electric plants, and haciendas to serve the mines; in 1922 it opened a smelter refinery using timber, promoting deforestation, and polluting air and rivers with sulfuric acid and iron-zinc residues. Products were sold globally, but the devastation was local.

But foreign capital was not entirely to blame. In the 1940s Brazil's president expressed the following philosophy: "To conquer the land, tame the waters and subjugate the jungle, these have been our tasks. And in this centuries-old battle, we have won victory upon victory."[44] Resource-based growth was premised on taking advantage of the riches the land had to offer—at a clear cost to the environment. Even where an early consciousness of environmental protection existed, institutional resources for implementation were weak. The Brazilian government implemented a forest code in the 1930s, prohibiting deforestation along watercourses, limiting cutting on property, and protecting rare species. With limited financing, however, it was unenforceable.[45] Moreover, the demand for economic growth far outpaced environmental concerns.

THE ISOLATION OF THE WAR YEARS: A BLESSING IN DISGUISE?

World War I had a profoundly dislocating effect on Latin America. The fall of the gold standard fomented financial instability. Oil-producing countries such as Venezuela benefited, but the confusion surrounding world war masked fundamental structural changes taking place in the global economy. As advanced industrial products were developed, the value of agricultural trade declined. New products such as synthetics displaced traditional raw materials. The Great Depression exacerbated global commodity market instability, leaving the externally oriented development strategy without robust markets for products. Growing protectionism abroad further limited export potential. The terms of trade—what a country receives for its exports relative to what it pays for its imports—fell between 21 and 45 percent when international markets collapsed. International capital inflows to fuel industrial development virtually dried up by 1929.[46]

But there was a silver lining to this cloud. As a result of these external shocks to the trade-driven model, Latin America was forced to adjust. It turned inward, adopting a set of economic policies called import substitution industrialization, the subject of chapter 3, to address the cycle of instability and vulnerability it faced under the externally oriented commodity export model. Although import substitution industrialization was not the solution to the puzzle of Latin American development, new strategies to meet growing internal and external economic challenges were introduced. Unfortunately, as we will see in the following chapters, a changed focus toward internal growth did little to change the fundamental pattern of asset ownership, reinforcing the highly unequal pattern of growth in the region.[47]

HISTORICAL LESSONS

To conclude our rapid tour of Latin American history, we have summarized some of the factors influencing growth in the region in table 2.8. Natural resource dependence, geography, unequal distribution of land, and labor, capital, and technological constraints shaped early development outcomes. What kind of lessons can we draw about these historical factors affecting Latin American development? We need to be very careful about concluding too much about historical causality, especially given the diverse set of circumstances in the region, but we can point to several legacies.

First, the colonial pattern of asset distribution in the region was unequal and tied to privilege. The political and economic power of the elites was replicated in the postindependence period and set the stage for contemporary policy. Persistent and rising inequality is the defining characteristic of the region's growth. Because international capital was relatively abundant, it did not have to turn to enhancing labor productivity as a source of growth. The poor in Latin America were rarely invested in.

Second, as a region rich in resources and blessed with agricultural abundance, Latin America first pursued a strategy of export promotion. Geography mattered enormously. Finanical resources were drawn to the dynamic export sectors, to the neglect of balanced development strategies. Colonial inequality was reinforced by the region's successful integration into the global economy and its access to relatively cheap external capital and technology. Government efforts were focused not on improving the local human capital of the peasants but on attracting external capital as the source of growth.[48] The *encomienda* system established the pattern of depleting and not replenishing the region's human capital.[49]

Third, given the openness to world trade, Latin America was unable to protect itself from external shocks in the global economy. When the booms turned to busts and prices fell, entire economies suffered. The Great Depression and the war years

Table 2.8.   Stylized Characteristics of Early Growth Patterns in Latin America

Natural resources	Resource abundant although often dependent on a single commodity Ownership was concentrated Geographic terrain and distance to markets Conditioned settlement patterns and institutions
Land	Land was initially distributed by the crown Landholdings were concentrated in large *latifundia* or *fazendas* Peasants did not hold clear title to the land they worked Land quality varied; lack of title for peasants decreased incentive for investment
Labor resources	Labor in agriculture and mining was scarce; slavery and Indian labor in addition to immigration relieve the labor constraint Low skill level; little investment in education Investment flows to Latin America were large and volatile
Financial capital	Part of the surplus was returned to Europe; concentrated ownership protected high returns in agriculture and resources creating little incentive for domestic investment in industry During periods of commodity booms, high returns in agriculture make investment in industry risky A domestic savings gap creates international financial dependency
Technology	Weak science and technology infrastructure Domestic technological gaps begin to emerge between industrial North and Latin America Technological control by the North begins High asset inequality allowed elites to build institutions to protect privilege
Policy environment	The golden age of exports gives way to import substitution in the post–World War II period International protection through trading companies limited export options

Source: Patrice Franko.

produced dramatic structural changes in Latin America that forced a reconsideration of the externally oriented primary product model.

Finally, the commodity export model exacted a high environmental and social price. The dislocation of indigenous communities and devastation of the land had enduring consequences. Pristine forest lands and diverse wildlife fell under the reign of sugar-, coffee-, and banana-exporting economies. Contemporary patterns of social conflict in the region—for example, the thirty-six-year civil war in Guatemala or the movements of the landless people in Brazil—certainly find their roots in the historical pattern of unequal land distribution.

The dissatisfaction arising from the externally oriented commodity export model gave rise to a new model of development in Latin America: import substitution industrialization. Import substitution industrialization located the answer to the question of why Latin America stagnated after the war period while Europe and the United States took off in the vulnerability of external orientation and dependency on international primary product markets. As we will see in the next chapter, the focus on substituting imports with a wider array of domestically produced goods was envisioned as a means of diversifying the source of growth and harnessing the emerging locomotive for growth: technological change.

Key Concepts

backward linkage
caciques
commodity lottery
Dutch disease
ejidos
enclave
encomienda

Engel's law
export pessimism
fazenda
forward linkage
golden age of primary
    product exports

hacienda
latifundia
mandamiento
minifundia
repartida

Chapter Summary

Growth Patterns

- Growth patterns demonstrate that disparities between industrialized nations and Latin America did not develop until the twentieth century.
- Historical factors including geography, natural endowments, the allocation of factors of production, policy frameworks, and macroeconomic environments have determined patterns of growth in Latin America.
- Geography conditions settlement patterns and trade profiles; it also shapes institutions associated with extractive industry.

An Extractive Economy

- Throughout the colonial period, Spanish and Portuguese conquistadors extracted abundant natural resources from Latin America. Their exploitative techniques utilized indigenous populations and imported slaves under the *encomienda* decree as well as marginalized peasants and concentrated land-holdings under the *latifundia* system. These methods resulted in elite control of capital and political power, a weak internal market, and severe income disparities.
- Despite the opportunity to alter rules of property rights during the period of Latin American independence, the political elite maintained concentrated

landholdings. During the late 1800s and early 1900s, Latin America benefited from agricultural exports. The boom, however, was short-lived. Development policy was driven by the export sector, ignoring domestic production, and demand for exports was determined abroad.

- Single-commodity exports faced various problems. First, Dutch disease promoted unbalanced development. The dependence on any one export proved problematic when prices declined and revenues diminished.
- Second, single-commodity exports of primary products faced inelastic demand —that is, despite significant increases in consumer income, the consumption of a particular product may only rise slightly. Growth potential is therefore limited.
- Third, Latin American countries largely failed to reinvest profits from single-commodity exports. Furthermore, the characteristics of export commodities did not stimulate production in other sectors of the economy through forward or backward linkages. The influx of foreign capital, moreover, failed to foster the development of domestic financial institutions.
- Finally, the environmental costs of single-commodity exports in extractive economies were high. Conquistadors interrupted traditional agricultural practices and substituted environmentally unsustainable methods. World War I and the Great Depression forced Latin America to address the cycle of instability and vulnerability it faced under the externally oriented export model and to decrease its dependence on single-commodity exports.

Notes

1. Suggested starting points are Bradford E. Burns, ed., *Latin America: Conflict and Creation: A Historical Reader* (Englewood Cliffs, N.J.: Prentice Hall, 1992); and Benjamin Keen, *Latin American Civilization,* 3rd ed. (Boston: Houghton Mifflin, 1974). Even a few hours dabbling in these readers will help capture the rich and complex regional history. New work in the economic history of Latin America has been spurred by the confluence of research by the New Institutional Economics (led by Douglas North) and the work on the New Economic History, which analyzes technological and institutional sources of growth. For an overview see Stephen Haber, *How Latin America Fell Behind* (Stanford, Calif.: Stanford University Press, 1997), chap. 1.

2. Leandro Prados de la Escosura, "Colonial Independence and Economic Backwardness in Latin America," GEHN Working Paper Series, Working Paper No. 10/05, www.lse .ac.uk, February 2005, favorably compares Latin American growth to other African and Asian cases, indicating that the decline in Latin America was relative to the United States—and not to more geographically comparable cases.

3. Inter-American Development Bank, "Why Geography Matters," box 1.2 in *Latin America at the Turn of the New Century, Economic and Social Progress in Latin America 2000 Report,* 21.

4. Luis Bertola and Jeffrey Williamson, "Globalization in Latin America before 1940," *NBER Working Paper* No. W9687, May 2003, 4.

5. Prados, "Colonial Independence and Economic Backwardness in Latin America," 18.

6. John Luke Gallup, Alejandro Gaviria, and Eduardo Lora, *Is Geography Destiny?* (Washington, D.C.: The Inter-American Development Bank, 2003).

7. Bertola and Williamson, "Globalization in Latin America before 1940," 15.

8. Daron Acemoglu, "Root Causes: A Historical Approach to Assessing the Role of Institutions in Economic Development," *Finance & Development,* June 2003, 27–30.

9. Gallup, Gaviria, and Lora, *Is Geography Destiny?*

10. See, for example, Bill Weinberg, *War on the Land: Ecology and Politics in Central America* (Atlantic Highlands, N.J.: Zed, 1991).

11. Colin M. Lewis, "Industry in Latin America," in *Dependency and Development in Latin America,* ed. Fernando Henrique Cardoso and Enzo Faletto (Berkeley: University of California Press, 1979).

12. Bertola and Williamson, "Globalization in Latin America before 1940," 15.

13. Stanley Engerman and Kenneth Sokoloff, *Factor Endowments, Institutions, and Differential Paths of Growth among New World Economies: A View from Economic Historians of the United States,* National Bureau of Economic Research Historical Paper No. 66 (Cambridge, Mass.: NBER, 1994).

14. Thomas E. Skidmore, "Brazil's Persistent Income Inequality," *Latin American Politics and Society* 46(2) (2004): 138.

15. Prados "Colonial Independence and Economic Backwardness in Latin America," 4.

16. Kenneth Sokoloff, "Inequality and the Evolution of Institutions of Taxation: Evidence from the Economic History of the Americas," in *Growth Institutions and Crises: Latin America from a Historical Perspective,* ed. Sebastian Edwards (Cambridge, Mass.: NBER, 2005).

17. Engerman and Sokoloff, *Factor Endowments,* 30.

18. Prados, "Colonial Independence and Economic Backwardness in Latin America," 7.

19. John Coatsworth, "Notes on the Comparative Economic History of Latin America and the United States," in *Development and Underdevelopment in America,* ed. Walther Bernecker and Hans Werner Tobler (New York: Walter de Gruyter, 1993).

20. Acemoglu, "Root Causes," 29.

21. Prados, "Colonial Independence and Economic Backwardness in Latin America," 9.

22. John H. Coatsworth and Jeffrey G. Williamson, "Always Protetctionist? Latin American Tariffs: Independence to the Great Depression," *Journal of Latin American Studies* 36(2) (May 2004): 205–232.

23. There is some inconsistency in the historical data. Although estimates of Latin American income at the time were almost certainly biased upward, Bulmer-Thomas, *The Economic History of Latin America since Independence,* 27, notes that "Latin America's relatively privileged status within what is now the third world at the end of the 18th century is difficult to dispute."

24. Bulmer-Thomas, *The Economic History of Latin America since Independence,* uses the term "commodity lottery" to describe the effects of export orientation in the 1800s. Much of the discussion of economic history in this chapter relies on Bulmer-Thomas's illuminating text.

25. Michael Bordo and Christopher Meisner, "Financial Crisis 1880–1913: The Role of Foreign Currency Debt," in Edwards, *Growth Institutions and Crises.*

26. Rosemary Thorp, *Progress, Poverty, and Exclusion: An Economic History of Latin America in the 20th Century* (Baltimore: Johns Hopkins University Press/Inter-American Development Bank, 1998), 49.

27. Daniel Farber, *Environment under Fire* (New York: Monthly Review Press, 1993), 34.

28. Simon Hanson, *Economic Development in Latin America* (Washington, D.C.: Inter-American Affairs Press, 1951), 107.

29. Ibid., 106.

30. Bertola and Williamson, "Globalization in Latin America before 1940," fig. 2.

31. Prados, "Colonial Independence and Economic Backwardness in Latin America," 9, citing Bulmer-Thomas.

32. Bertola and Williamson, "Globalization in Latin America before 1940," 18–23.

33. This section draws heavily from Alan Taylor, "Foreign Capital in Latin America in the Nineteenth and Twentieth Centuries," March 2003 *NBER Working Paper* No. W9580, which later appears as a chapter in the *Cambridge Economic History of Latin America,* edited by Victor Bulmer-Thomas, John Coatsworth, and Roberto Cortés. This short section hardly does justice to the rich detail in the article.

34. Thorp, *Progress, Poverty, and Exclusion,* 69.

35. Lewis, "Industry in Latin America," 295.

36. Thorp, *Progress, Poverty, and Exclusion,* 56.

37. Nathaniel H. Leff, "Economic Development in Brazil, 1822–1913," in *How Latin America Fell Behind: Essays on the Economic History of Brazil and Mexico, 1800–1914,* ed. Stephen Haber (Stanford: Stanford University Press, 1997).

38. Gerardo Della Paolera and Alan M. Taylor, "Finance and Development in an Emerging Market: Argentina in the Interwar Period," in *Latin America and the World Economy in the Nineteenth and Twentieth Centuries: Explorations in Quantitative Economic History,* ed. John Coatsworth and Alan Taylor (Boston: Harvard University Press, 1998), 12.

39. Ibid., 18.

40. Thorp, *Progress, Poverty, and Exclusion,* 64.

41. Farber, *Environment under Fire,* 15.

42. Burns, *Latin America,* 40.

43. Thorp, *Progress, Poverty, and Exclusion,* 57.

44. John Ryan, "The Shrinking Forest," *NACLA Report on the Americas* 25(2) (September 1991): 19.

45. Thorp, *Progress, Poverty, and Exclusion,* 21.

46. Vittorio Corbo, "Economic Policies and Performance in Latin America," in *Economic Development: Handbook of Comparative Economic Policies,* ed. Enzo Grilli and Dominick Salvatore (Westport, Conn.: Greenwood, 1994), 299.

47. Thorp, *Progress, Poverty, and Exclusion,* 6.

48. Coatsworth, "Notes on the Comparative Economic History of Latin America and the United States," 24.

49. Timothy Yeager, "Encomienda or Slavery? The Spanish Crown's Choice of Labor Organization in Sixteenth-Century Spanish America," *Journal of Economic History* 55(4) (December 1995).

CHAPTER THREE

IMPORT SUBSTITUTION INDUSTRIALIZATION

Looking Inward for the Source of Economic Growth

Many of the state-led investments under import substitution industrialization were in large-scale industries such as petrochemicals. *(Courtesy of the Inter-American Development Bank)*

At the beginning of the twentieth century Argentina was one of the world's wealthiest nations. Why did the elegant and luxurious buildings in Buenos Aires begin to seem locked in time as other nations modernized? Why did much of Latin America, despite its rich natural resources, experience slow growth? The export-led model discussed in chapter 2 did not deliver the anticipated growth. Distribution also had not improved. Why were the peasant *campesinos* stuck in a cycle of poverty? Emerging from the Great Depression and the world wars, Latin America lagged behind its neighbors in the Northern Hemisphere. Once behind international competitors, how could Latin American nations ever hope to catch up?

Hoping to answer these questions, Latin American policymakers compared the performance of the region with that of North America and Europe; they also looked with interest at the takeoff of the Soviet Union. Two answers to the puzzle of slow growth emerged: first, an explanation for Latin America's falling behind and, second, a prescription for what to do about it. Political economists such as Paul Baran and Andre Gundar Frank suggested that Latin America was not falling behind but was being *pushed* back by the exploitative development process in the powerful industrial countries. Raúl Prebisch and those at the Economic Commission for Latin America and the Caribbean (ECLAC) defined the development problem as the need to promote growth in the face of an international system controlled by the center countries. This chapter explores these tools of inward-looking development in the policy of **import substitution industrialization (ISI)**. It treats the role of the state as a developmental actor and introduces the exchange rate and trade tools used to promote industrialization. It concludes by evaluating the performance of ISI as an answer to the puzzle of how to promote development in Latin America. The following questions form the core of our investigation:

- How did theorists make sense of Latin America's declining position in the world economy?
- How did the theory of ISI propose to overcome the constraints on Latin American economic development?
- What were the key elements in the ISI toolbox?
- Was the approach successful in practice?

Understanding ISI is an important step in unraveling the puzzle of Latin American development. This gives us a sense of the historical backdrop to contemporary policy and also locates one end of the policy spectrum with respect to the role of the state in development against which we can evaluate current practices. Box 3.1 provides a glimpse of the evolution of thought on development in the region by looking at the life of one significant contributor, Raúl Prebisch.

DEPENDENCY THEORY: AN EXPLANATION FOR BACKWARDNESS

For some analysts, answering the question of why some nations were growing and others were stagnating required looking not at countries in isolation, as individual

Box 3.1.   Raúl Prebisch (1901–1986)

The Argentine economist Raúl Prebisch was born in 1901 in the town of Tucuman.[1] He was strongly influential in the development of Latin American economic policy, and his contributions to development economics broke with the neoclassical. Although later criticized, his views and ideas questioned the extent to which the free market and free trade could solve the problem of underdevelopment.

Prebisch was educated at the University of Buenos Aires,[2] and during the 1920s he worked as a statistician for the Sociedad Rural, a stockbreeder's association.[3] Toward the beginning of his career, Prebisch believed in neoclassical economics, but the Great Depression and the writings of economist John Maynard Keynes shattered his faith in the free trade model.[4] Prebisch began to formulate different theoretical views in the early 1940s. This shift was first manifested in *The Economic Development of Latin America and Its Principal Problem,* written in 1949.[5] By this time Prebisch had served as director general of the Argentine Central Bank (1935–1943) and had witnessed the devastating effects of the Depression on Argentina, which suffered from falling prices and debt payment difficulties. His 1949 manifesto reflected the effect of these external influences on economic development.

Prebisch divided the world in two, labeling one part the center and the other the periphery. The center referred to advanced economies, producing primarily industrial goods; the periphery included developing countries, producers of primary products. Prebisch defined a skewed relationship between the two, with the center gaining at the expense of the periphery. For Prebisch, productivity gains in the North (the center) were translated into rising wages, not falling prices, due to the market power of business and unions. In the South (the periphery), surplus labor kept wages low, and slow productivity growth in agriculture and mining acted as a drag on the economy.[6] The unequal distribution of economic gains was due primarily to **declining terms of trade,** as developing countries would have to export more and more to be able to import the same quantities as before. It is clear that by this point Prebisch rejected the idea that comparative advantage was the answer to growth for developing countries and opted for other policy prescriptions.

In 1948, the UN Economic Commission for Latin America was created; Prebisch became its influential chairman in 1949.[7] Prebisch's diagnosis for the causes of underdevelopment led him to advocate ISI. From 1964 to 1969, Prebisch was the secretary-general of the UN Conference on Trade and Development (UNCTAD).[8] During this time period, Prebisch put aside his theoretical thinking and formulated policies that were later ignored by both the developed and the developing worlds. When Prebisch returned to his theoretical endeavors after the UNCTAD years, he suggested that a post-ISI policy was required, including removing protection from certain industries and encouraging non-traditional exports. He pointed to the need to develop internal savings to decrease reliance on external debt, suggested institutional changes in the labor market and financial sector, and advised budgetary reforms to consolidate change in Latin America.[9]

plants in a garden, but rather at how countries interacted with each other in the international system. Proponents of **dependency theory** postulated that a country did not thrive or falter simply because of its own national endowments. Rather, progress could be attributed to the power it had to set the rules of the international economic game. **Center** countries, or the industrialized countries, defined the rules; the **periphery,** or developing countries, were pawns in the international pursuit of profit. As dependency theorist Andre Gundar Frank postulated, underdeveloped countries were not developed countries in the making; rather, industrial countries had caused underdevelopment in other nations in the process of economic expansion. For Frank, underdevelopment was generated by the same historical process that produced economic development: the march of capitalism.[10] Industrialized countries had access to cheap inputs for growth through the extraction of resources, the export of minerals, and the exploitation of cheap labor in the underdeveloped world. Rich countries became rich by making other countries poor.

The owners of the resources—the wealthy in the underdeveloped region—benefited from the international market. According to dependency theorist Paul Baran, local elites formed alliances with international capitalists, hindering long-term, dynamic growth in favor of short-term profits. Baran pointed to the feudal coherence of the *latifundia* system and the monopolistic market structure as impediments to vigorous long-run growth.[11] A social glue bonding local and international elites cemented economic privilege for the upper class. Those with power had no interest in sharing it. Relatively concentrated markets weakened competitive pressures. For Baran and for Frank, while the periphery was tied to the center, there was no possibility of sustainable growth. As long as traditional elites remained in power, periphery countries would be shackled to center country interests. Revolution, therefore, was in order.

Other theorists, such as Fernando Henrique Cardoso and Enzo Faletto, disagreed with the revolutionary prescription. Although concurring with the assessment that the center countries controlled the dynamic of growth, Cardoso and Faletto argued that autonomous development was indeed possible within the periphery. It would, however, involve an active state policy to counterbalance the greedy hand of the international market. A powerful state acting in the national interest could counteract the strength of local and international economic elites to promote genuine development in the periphery.

From Dependency Theory to Development Policy: ECLA and the Structuralist School

The dependency theorists' critique of the international economic system informed but did not completely define the position of the **structuralists** at the United Nations Economic Commission for Latin America (ECLA).[12] Under the leadership of Raúl Prebisch (see box 3.1), ECLA analysts looked at the disappointing economic performance of Latin America in the first half of the century, focusing on the volatility of primary product exports and the progressive difficulty of paying for more technologically sophisticated (and expensive) products with the limited agricultural returns.[13] Technological progress was controlled by the powerful center-industrialized countries and spread slowly into the periphery. ECLA researchers in the 1950s were also fascinated by a seeming correlation between the interruption of normal trade patterns with the industrialized countries during the war periods and accompanying robust internal growth in the Latin America region. Isolation from the international system apparently helped growth at home.

In part the disadvantaged position of periphery countries in the international system derived from the kind of goods they offered. Developing countries principally traded primary products, such as raw materials and agricultural goods, for more technologically advanced products in the international arena. Within this unequal framework, they faced what was seen as declining terms of trade for their products. There are only so many bananas that people want to eat or so much coffee that they can drink. Given the low income elasticity for agricultural products, as the global economy grows, the relative demand for primary products declines. Instead, rewards tend to accrue to those engaged in technological entrepreneurship. Technological sophistication adds value to a good, increasing its market price well beyond the cost of basic inputs. Declining terms of trade for primary products reflected the argument that as the prices of sophisticated goods rose, developing countries would need to export more and more oranges or wheat to pay for the more expensive technological machinery. Without mastering technology, countries had little hope of advancement.

In addition to the position that all goods do not generate equal rewards, structuralists also offered a view contrary to that of traditional economists on how economies functioned. Challenging the tenets of neoclassical economic theory, which assumes that rational, self-interested profit maximizers operating in open and competitive international markets will produce the greatest good for all, structuralists argued that the economy was shaped by power and politics. For the structuralists, economic activity is conditioned by interest-group politics. Markets in Latin America are controlled by concentrated oligopolies in which firms are price makers and elites establish patterns of consumption. Powerful advertising conglomerates shape global tastes; elites tend to demand sophisticated goods produced by industrial economies. Importing these items would do little to spur local growth. The promises of trickle-down economics hold no magic for the masses of the poor in the developing world. In the structuralist's eyes, the development process is not a movement toward equilibrium but rather is driven by imbalances and tension. Although the neoclassical model predicts benefits for poor countries from international trade, structuralists contend that international trade exacerbates inequality between and within nations because those countries and companies with control set the rules of the game in their favor. For the structuralist, the neoclassical model does not conform to the hard, cold facts of the international economy. Of course, neoclassical economists hold a different view, one suggesting that the dependency approach repackaged reality to fit its worldview. Some economic historians suggest that the unexpected growth under postwar isolation that prompted the strategy was neither as dynamic nor as isolated as the stylized facts of the dependency theorists suggest.[14]

FROM STRUCTURALISM TO ISI

The arguments of the dependency theorists and the structuralists shaped the ISI policy package widely adopted in Latin America. Perceiving the international game as stacked against them and with multiple external shocks repeatedly destabilizing the economy, Latin American policymakers turned inward to promote internal sources of economic growth. Instead of relying on the international economy as the engine of growth, ISI policies sought to develop industries in a protected environment. The goal was to create industries capable of producing substitutes for expensive imports while simultaneously promoting industrial growth and the expansion of internal economies. The notion was that ISI would induce a process of learning driven by exposure to new ideas and processes that would dynamically spill over into the whole economy.[15] Raúl Prebisch and ECLA structuralists placed the role of technological change at the center of the development process and identified a strong role for the state in promoting national technological capabilities.[16] Without mastering technological processes, developing countries had no chance to catch up. The only economic actor strong enough to counterbalance the weight of multinational corporations was the state.

The strategy of ISI was informed by Albert Hirschman's concepts of bottlenecks and linkages. For Hirschman, imbalances in the system, such as supply shocks and bottlenecks, were central to development as signals for investment.[17] Hirschman characterized the development process as a bottle with a thin neck. Inputs—land, labor, capital—were constrained from freely flowing from the bottle by the constricting neck of scarce complementary factors such as technology, infrastructure, or entrepreneurial capital. If the state could break the bottlenecks in crucial industries, resources would flow back up the production chain, stimulating the demand for intermediate inputs, or they would flow forward in the consumption pattern to create the demand for new products. Therefore, by promoting a steel sector, for example, **backward linkages** such as those to the iron ore and smelters would stimulate the growth of these supplier industries, while **forward linkages** would stimulate the auto or machine industries. If the state could target those industries with the largest backward and forward linkages, it could act as an engine of development.

A strong state was critical to the structuralist program. ISI theorists pointed to a simple fact: if the market could work on its own, why had it not been successful in promoting growth in Latin America? **Market failure** to produce sustainable growth provided the rationale for state intervention. Given the weak private sector and the large economies of scale attached to industrial endeavors, an active state was viewed as a necessary complement to the market economy.[18] The ability of the state to deliver on public project investments contributed to the perceived need of governments to also meet the demand for social projects. This emanated from the highly unequal income distribution in Latin America.

The political demands of populism, of attending to the broad needs of the domestic population in the name of social peace, were consistent with the ISI economic theory. Populism drew on the charismatic power of leaders such as Juan Perón of Argentina or Getulio Vargas of Brazil to mobilize support within labor and industrial elites in the service of a nationalist development strategy. Traditional populist strategies encouraged support for a developmentalist model to meet the changing needs of society without explosive class conflict. By co-opting key labor and industrial groups into the quest for change, support for interventionist policies could be maintained. **Economic populism,** a term applied to the developmental strategies of the 1950s, 1960s, and 1970s, emphasized growth and redistribution of income to the neglect of internal and external constraints. That is, as long as financing was available, the state kept attempting to buy off each group in the conflictual process of development. Labor, politically powerful, was given strong protection under the law. Industrialists were favored with development schemes. State-led strategies to reduce poverty and promote infrastructure were pursued to keep local political leaders happy. But constraints on development—inflation, fiscal deficits, external imbalances—were often ignored until it was too late and crisis erupted.[19] Political demands to moderate the distributional tensions of development were consistent with the state-led ISI model.

THE ISI TOOLBOX

ISI relied on a variety of economic tools to achieve its aim. The toolbox can be broken down into three categories: active industrial policy, protective international instruments, and accommodationist fiscal and monetary policy complemented by a careful program of transnational participation. It is important to note that although these tools were at the disposal of all policymakers in the region, they were applied in varying degrees in each country. We will discuss these three broad tools in turn.

Active Industrial Policy: The Role of SOEs

Industrial policy was anchored in the formation of state-owned enterprises (SOEs) throughout the region. Under the assumption that the state was the only able domestic actor with the resources to produce in relatively underdeveloped markets, state firms were formed in a wide range of heavy industries, including oil, petrochemicals, telecommunications, steel, and aircraft. In some cases these enterprises were wholly owned by the state, and in others they operated as mixed enterprises, incorporating state and private capital. State firms had access to public funds for investment, research, and development. Backed by sovereign guarantees, they also had easier access to international financial markets to borrow for large development projects. State ministries could assist in the negotiation of international technology transfer packages to jump-start production. Such firms had the resources to hire some of the brightest national scientists, engineers, and managers to run operations. Additionally, the pressures of producing initial annual profits were relieved as state firms were able to extend their time horizon for investment returns.

Although the public enterprise status held many advantages, there were also restrictions. Hiring and pay scales were subject to national standards, sometimes placing a ceiling on the pay for skilled labor. State firms were subject to the whims of politicians and often became agencies for employing large numbers of constituents. Furthermore, the services of industries in basic infrastructure, such as the electrical or telecommunications sectors, were often underpriced to provide cheap inputs to stimulate the growth of the private sector. Cheap inputs allowed for a local manufacturing boom; however, underpricing electricity or phone service led to losses that were absorbed by the SOEs. As resources became increasingly constrained, underpricing also resulted in underinvestment over time. Because firms were carrying losses, they couldn't afford to expand to meet the demand.

Despite the difficulties that SOEs confronted, they proliferated rapidly from the

Table 3.1.   State Enterprise Share in the Brazilian Economy, 1973

	Proportion of Assets in State-Owned Firms
High Degree of State Participation (≥50%)	
Railways	100
Port services	100
Water, gas, and sewers	99
Telegraph and telephone	97
Electricity	79
Mining	63
Developmental services	51
Chemicals	50
Medium Degree of State Participation (20–49%)	
Water transport	45
Banking and Finance	38
Metal fabrication	37
Services	36
Air transport	22
Low Degree of State Participation (<20%)	
Construction and engineering	8
Rubber	6
Road transport and passengers	6
Agriculture and forestry	4
Nonmetallic mineral	2
Transport equipment	2
Food and beverages	1
Machinery	0
Wood products and furniture	0
Textiles and leather products	0
Tobacco	0
Printing and publishing	0
Radio and television	0
Commerce	0

Source: Adapted from Peter Evans, *Dependent Development* (Princeton, N.J.: Princeton University Press, 1979), 221, table 5.1.

1950s to the 1970s in Latin America. In table 3.1 we see what types of industries were most subject to state ownership and ISI policies in the case of Brazil. High rates of state ownership existed particularly in industries that required significant investment, such as public goods enjoyed by all citizens and critical industries, including national security enterprises.

In an analysis of the cause for state intervention, Tom Trebat identifies six reasons for state enterprises: a weak private sector, economies of scale, public externalities, dynamic public managers, natural resource rents, and public historical factors. In steel, electrical energy, and telecommunications, state-owned firms were formed after private-sector failures. Particularly in Brazil, developmental nationalists believed that state intervention was the pragmatic response to the failure of the free market. Economies of scale and the need for large investments to lower costs provided further grounds for state activity. In industries with clear public value, such as railroads, energy, and ports, it was argued that there were benefits to state provision of these services, especially when private providers had not emerged in the market. Because of public visibility and prestige, some state enterprises were able to attract the most dynamic managers. Finally, where industrialization was resource based, such as in oil and mining, it was argued that these resources belonged to the nation and should therefore be managed on the public's behalf.[20] Thus, there was an economic rationale (although perhaps not always a compelling one) for state activity in the industrial sector.

The High Tariff Walls of ISI: Protectionism as a Tool of ISI

International economic tools facilitated the industrialization process. If your grasp of international economics is rusty, box 3.2 provides a quick review of terms. The growth of state and private enterprises was encouraged under the protection of high tariff and trade restrictions. These protective walls were designed to give less-competitive national industries, conceived of as infant industries, the chance to develop without the competition of large multinational firms. There was a perceived need for protection while an economy developed the necessary conditions to promote learning and innovation within the firm.[21] The policy objective wasn't to ignore exports; rather, the hope was that temporary protection would lead to the development of new products.[22]

We can measure the degree of protectionism by looking at tariff rates. Average nominal protection over consumer and manufactured goods was 131 percent in Argentina, 168 percent in Brazil, 138 percent in Chile, 112 percent in Colombia, 61 percent in Mexico, and 21 percent in Uruguay in 1960.[23] In the case of Mexico in 1970, the effective rate of protection—the nominal tariff rate adjusted for the protection also present in the purchase of intermediate goods used to produce the final good—was as high as 671 percent for fertilizer and insecticides, 226 percent for synthetic fertilizers, 206 percent for pharmaceuticals, 102 percent for automobiles, and 67 percent for electrical equipment. Across the board, for durable consumption and capital goods in Mexico in 1970, effective protection rates averaged 35 percent.[24] Import licenses were used in intermediate and consumer durable goods to encourage growth.[25] High import tariffs often induced multinational firms to set up factories within the country. In 1970 in Mexico, 62 percent of the machinery sector, 49.1 percent of transport vehicles, and 79.3 percent of electric equipment were dominated by foreign enterprises.[26] Although ownership was not national, labor learned new production techniques, and the technological level of production was raised.

Somewhat ironically, in the first stages of ISI, national imports usually rose. Steel, for example, could be produced only with huge furnaces, and they had to be bought somewhere. To promote the import of these critical inputs, states tended to maintain **overvalued exchange rates,** making imports relatively cheaper to purchase. Imports and access to this underpriced foreign exchange were often licensed

Box 3.2.   A Review of the Tools of Protectionism

export subsidy   A fiscal incentive, sometimes in the form of a tax break, for reaching export targets. Export subsidies promote the development of export industries at home, arguably to unfair advantage compared to the international firms.

foreign exchange controls   To restrict the quantity of imports or to direct imports to certain sectors, the government may ration foreign exchange. This generally involves compelling exporters to sell foreign exchange to the government at a fixed price. Selective importers of key goods are offered preferential prices for foreign exchange, whereas importers of luxury items or those wanting to travel pay more local currency for their dollars, yen, or pounds. Foreign exchange controls are therefore linked to a system of multiple exchange rates. Not surprisingly, as there are therefore different prices for the same commodity—money—a black or a parallel market often develops. The black market price can sometimes be used as an indicator of how far the exchange rate has been taken off course by policy distortions.

import licensing   The legal requirement to obtain a license to import a certain kind of good. Import licensing boards evaluate national availability of goods to assess whether the import is critical or whether the need can be met by national production.

industrial incentives   Direct payments or tax breaks to a firm engaging in a particular line of production. These credits act as a protectionist device if an international competitor cannot meet the lower, subsidized price in the local market.

quota   A quota is a quantitative limit on imports. A quota presents a fixed limit on the quantity of goods that may be imported. Quotas may be assigned to suppliers or they may be auctioned, creating revenue for the central government.

tariff   A tariff, the most common type of protectionism, is a tax on imports. A tariff works best when the demand for the good in question is elastic or price sensitive. If buyers do not respond to the higher price, a tariff will not limit imports. With a tariff, the central government collects revenues. Nominal tariff protection is measured by looking at the tariff rate on the final manufactured good. Effective rates of protection adjust this rate for tariffs on intermediate inputs.

to limit imported goods to those critical to the industrialization process. As reviewed in box 3.2, import licensing boards evaluated the quality and availability of national substitutes, their prices, and their importance in the production process before allocating cheap foreign exchange.[27] International trade and foreign exchange tools insulated the economy from rival foreign firms dominating the market. Box 3.3 contrasts the effects of various exchange rate regimes in development strategies.

Additional Tools of Industrial Policy: Targeted Lending, Multinational Activity, and Passive Monetary Policy

Ownership was not the only tool of industrial policy in Latin America. Industrial policy was accommodated by monetary and fiscal measures. The state provided subsidies to domestic firms, and it granted tax credits and soft credit to jump-start the national industrial motor. National development banks were formed, such as

Box 3.3.   Exchange Rate Policy and Development

An exchange rate is simply the price of one currency in terms of another. Ideally, exchange rates should equate the value of one nation's goods with those of another.[28] There are three broad types of exchange rate regimes: fixed, flexible, and crawling pegs. Under the gold standard (1870–1914) and the Bretton Woods systems (1945–1973), countries fixed their currencies to an anchor—gold or the U.S. dollar. A fixed exchange rate has the advantage of promoting stability. A critical economic price—the price of domestic goods in terms of international goods—is fixed. The rules of a fixed regime require that a country running a balance of payments deficit must clear its accounts by exporting gold or defend its rate by selling dollars or reserves. Because money supplies are anchored to dollars or gold, the decrease in money contracts the economy and few goods are imported. The economy should therefore expand only at the rate of its accumulation of real reserves—that is, gold or dollars in circulation. The best way to understand this concept is to visualize the old trade rules: if France imported more from Great Britain, it had to send or "export" gold to pay for it, thus lowering the national money supply. In the next period France could buy less—and Britain more—balancing imports and exports.

Today many countries pursue a floating exchange regime. Under a floating system, if a country is running a balance of payments deficit, the price of foreign exchange adjusts or depreciates. Rather than a country exporting gold, the market changes the value of national money. The price of the currency is determined by the demand for a country's goods. As imports surge, residents sell their own currency to buy the foreign currency needed to purchase the imported goods. As a result, imports become more expensive and exports appear cheaper in international markets. If consumers are responsive to price change, flows should begin to balance. A large stock of reserves is not needed to defend the rate. Nevertheless, whereas the fixed exchange rate promotes price stability, a floating exchange rate may exacerbate inflation. Depreciation makes crucial imports more expensive, exerting an upward pressure on domestic prices.

Finally, some countries attempt to have both the stability of a fixed anchor and the flexibility of floating rates with the use of a crawling peg. Under this exchange rate system the currency is set to a central value but is allowed to fluctuate around that target in the short run.

What is the "right" exchange rate in the long run? Essentially, the same good should sell for the same price in two different markets. If it does not, and transportation costs are minimal and trade is free, some enterprising person will buy goods in the cheaper market and sell them where they are dear. Not surprisingly, using the exchange rate as a tool of industrial promotion interferes with arriving at the "right rate." Imbalances emerge that become difficult to sustain over time.

Chile's Corporación de Fomento de la Producción (CORFO) and Brazil's State National Development Bank (BNDE), to target investments in the economy. A national development bank has an advantage over commercial lenders in planning strategic investment projects. As a state bank, it has a longer return horizon and is able to be active in more risky sectors because bottom-line profits are not the objective. Key industries such as machinery, automobiles, shipbuilding, and telephones were targeted as central to industrial growth. In Mexico, the Law of New and Necessary Industries provided select tax exemptions to promote growth in a limited number of unrepresented but critical sectors in the economy. Economic policy flexibility adjusted to changes in product and monetary markets. Governments saw

ISI contributed to the development of manufacturing such as this Brazilian auto parts manufacturer. *(Photo by Patrice Franko)*

budget deficits as reasonable investments in the future, financing them either through borrowing or running the printing presses. Quite simply, economic policy supported a countercyclical dimension—an approach untenable in later years of macroeconomic crises.[29]

In "strategic" sectors such as autos or steel, **transnational corporations** were welcomed as providers of needed technology and capital within the ISI model. In table 3.2 we can see the significant role played by multinational corporations in manufacturing. In or about 1970, 24 percent of manufacturing in Argentina, 50 percent in Brazil, 30 percent in Chile, 43 percent in Colombia, 35 percent in Mexico, 44 percent in Peru, and 14 percent in Venezuela was under foreign control. Some of this participation predates the ISI period, but the strong involvement of transnationals, particularly in industrial production, was seen throughout the postwar ISI period.[30]

The entry of transnational corporations was somewhat paradoxical. ISI, after all, was attempting to reduce dependency on the international structure of production. However, there was also a degree of pragmatism at work. Transnationals provided critical financial capital and technology. The goal became to utilize these assets selectively, employing state bargaining power to transform the rules of the game. ISI policies set new rules: to produce and sell in the domestic market, trans-

Table 3.2.   Foreign Share of Selected Industries, circa 1970 (percentages)

	Argentina	Brazil	Chile	Colombia	Mexico	Peru	Venezuela
Food	15.3	42.1	23.2	22.0	21.5	33.1	10.0
Textiles	14.2	34.2	22.9	61.9	15.3	39.7	12.9
Chemicals	34.9	49.0	61.9	66.9	50.7	66.7	16.5
Transport equipment	44.4	88.2	64.5	79.7	64.0	72.9	31.1
Electrical machinery	27.6	83.7	48.6	67.2	50.1	60.7	23.2
Paper	25.7	22.3	7.9	79.3	32.9	64.8	20.1
All manufacturing	23.8	50.1	29.9	43.4	34.9	44.0	13.8

Source: Excerpted from Rhys Jenkins, *Transnational Corporations and Industrial Transformation in Latin America* (New York: St. Martin's, 1984), table 2.4.

national companies had to commit to technology transfer and the training of labor. Under the threat of market closure to the sale of their products, transnational firms agreed to joint ownership arrangements and the use of local inputs. In the automobile industry in Brazil, for example, GM do Brasil was a joint venture between Brazilian capital and General Motors (GM). Along with Ford, Volkswagen, and Fiat, it sparked the development of an industrial park. With high tariff rates, local production was the only viable way to sell cars nationally. Multinational firms defended market shares against the possibility of being shut out through local manufacture. If a multinational corporation did not participate according to local rules, its international competitors would. Development of local parts suppliers was promoted by requiring 99 percent local content by weight for passenger cars produced locally.[31] Mexico was able to prod concessions in creating national joint ventures in the electrical industry by playing one multinational against another.[32] In addition to local content laws, contracts often stipulated the training of local managers to improve national managerial capacity, an assurance of transfer of technological processes (not simply sending the more sophisticated parts preassembled in the United States or Europe), and limits on the repatriation of profits to promote local reinvestment of revenues.

A large domestic market enhanced national bargaining power in establishing contract terms with the multinationals. Clearly, Brazil and Mexico had greater bargaining power than Ecuador or Paraguay, as there were many more likely Brazilian or Mexican buyers of locally produced cars. Yet even in the Mexican and Brazilian cases, exports of locally manufactured multinational products were necessary to take advantage of economies of scale. Despite technology and export earnings, multinationals were not welcomed in all sectors. Even where bargaining power was strong, nationalist sentiments reserved strategic industries, such as oil in Mexico, to wholly local ownership.

For the most part, a loose monetary policy greased the fiscal wheels of development. From the mid-1960s to the 1980s, the dominant political system in Latin America was an authoritarian government. Developmental nationalists saw it as their mission to promote development as a critical element of security. Rules were changed to decrease the autonomy of central banks, forcing them to accommodate fiscal spending programs. Nonetheless, in areas of monetary, fiscal, or international affairs, reliable data about developing nations were sorely lacking, and many macro-economic decisions were made by guesswork and intuition.[33]

THE PERFORMANCE OF ISI

How well did ISI work? Box 3.4 summarizes the tools at work. By the barometer of average annual growth rates of 5.5 percent over the period 1950–1980, one could call import substitution a successful strategy. Throughout the 1950s, Latin American economies were growing comparatively faster than the Western economies, and between 1950 and 1970 Latin American gross domestic product (GDP) tripled.

As illustrated in table 3.3, performance varied by country, with Brazil, Ecuador, and Mexico exhibiting the strongest growth rates over the ISI years of roughly 1950–1980. The production of basic consumption goods was widespread throughout the region, and some countries successfully initiated heavy-machine goods industries as well.[34] Production outstripped population growth, making progress on this problem (identified in chapter 2). While the population of the region roughly doubled over the period 1945–1980, GDP in real terms quintupled.[35]

Import performance was uneven. Most countries did not see a decline in imports

---

BOX 3.4.   ISI TOOLBOX: A SUMMARY

INDUSTRIAL POLICY

Form state-owned firms
Form mixed economic enterprises—part state, part private
Require government purchases from national firms
Require foreign firms to establish joint ventures
Pressure foreign firms to increase local content

INTERNATIONAL INSTRUMENTS

Tariffs on final goods
Quotas on imports
Exchange rate overvaluation
Exchange rationing
Import licenses

FISCAL AND MONETARY POLICY

Subsidies for cheap inputs such as electricity
Subsidies for public transportation
Tax breaks in production
Preferential interest rates
Accommodating monetary policy

Table 3.3. Percentage Growth in GDP per Capita

Country	1941–1949	1950–1959	1960–1969	1970–1979	1980–1989
Brazil	1.6	3.6	2.8	6.1	0.8
Ecuador	4.1	2.4	1.8	7.0	−0.1
Mexico	3.7	3.1	3.5	3.2	−0.3
Dominican Republic	3.0	3.4	1.4	4.6	0.7
Panama	−2.2	1.8	4.8	1.9	−0.6
Costa Rica	4.7	2.8	2.2	3.3	−0.8
Colombia	1.6	1.8	2.1	3.2	1.6
Peru	2.5	3.0	2.5	1.2	−2.1
El Salvador	9.3	1.8	2.2	1.8	−2.6
Guatemala	0.3	0.5	1.9	3.1	−2.1
Paraguay	0.6	−0.7	1.1	5.0	0.9
Argentina	2.3	0.8	2.8	1.3	−2.3
Honduras	1.5	−0.1	1.8	2.4	−1.0
Chile	1.5	1.3	1.9	0.6	1.9
Uruguay	2.5	1.0	0.3	2.5	0.1
Nicaragua	4.2	2.4	3.6	−2.5	−3.8
Bolivia	0.6	−1.7	3.2	1.9	−3.0
Venezuela	6.7	2.9	0.0	−0.1	−3.4

Source: ECLA data as found in Vittorio Corbo, "Economic Policies and Performance in Latin America," in *Economic Development: Handbook of Comparative Economic Policies,* ed. Enzo Grilli and Dominick Salvatore (Westport, Conn.: Greenwood, 1994), 308.

as a ratio of GDP. Brazil was more successful, as indicated in a comparison of 1964 with 1949. Imports in the Brazilian economy decreased substantially as a percentage of total national supply, ranging from 19.0 percent in 1949 to 4.2 percent in 1964. Predictably, during the first stages of ISI in Brazil, the import of capital producer goods doubled from 1949 (15.8 b Cr) to 1959 (29.2 b Cr) as machines were needed to produce other goods. However, by 1964, imports of capital producer goods had fallen to nearly half the rate of the 1949 levels. Over the same period, domestic production of consumer and producer goods rose substantially, with national production of all manufactured products increasing 266 percent from 1949 through 1964.[36]

Less-tangible gains also accrued.[37] Import substitution created forces for the development of an urban middle class, which demanded infrastructure entitlements in public utilities such as water and sewage systems. A national business class and a parallel labor union movement emerged, changing the agrarian balance of power. This coalition supporting the model, however, often intervened in policy making to thwart changes such as exchange rate valuations that might have prevented the accumulation of large fiscal imbalances.

THE CRISIS OF ISI

Despite the apparent gains, ISI was both unsustainable over time and produced high economic and social costs. In theory, ISI should have developed an internal momentum, expanding industrialization through interindustry linkages. Employing his concept of linkages, Hirschman predicted that industrial growth should have occurred based on targeted investments. However, some contend that given the limited size of the internal market in Latin America, ISI became "exhausted." It was postulated that as one moves to ever more sophisticated production, especially heavy machinery, the minimum plant size increases. Successful substitution would therefore be limited to sectors in which the internal demand for the good exceeded plant size—or where exports could make up the difference. The export vent, however, was largely closed due to the unfavorable exchange rates and less competitive industries. One study suggested that with such a high degree of income inequality, a massive devaluation to make Latin American exports globally competitive would have been politically and socially explosive.[38] Some programs were successful, such as the Brazilian BEFIEX (Special Fiscal Benefits for Exports) scheme, which provided incentives for exports. In many cases nationally manufactured goods did not meet international quality standards after growing up under protective tariffs, and firms were not forced by competition to become efficient. ECLA economists advocated economic integration within the region to expand the economies of scale, but the integration process was stalled. Economic performance was too varied across the region, the base of consumers with an ability to pay was too small, and political differences made subregional integration difficult at times.

Others explained the crisis of ISI in political and sociological terms. Because the industrial process was largely in the hands of elites, it failed to create a new entrepreneurial class that would have given the process greater dynamism. Given elite power, ISI may have provided more support to industrialists than to industry.[39] Many of the tools used to manage ISI—import licenses, investment permits, and government contracts—created the possibility of profitable personal rents for those able to control them.[40] Corruption became economically expedient under the ISI model. This led to the views of the new political economists (which will be discussed in chapter 5), suggesting a minimalist role for government.

ISI exacerbated inequality in the region. With more than a third of the region's population living in poverty, internal demand was severely limited. Consumption patterns imitated those of the center elite instead of attending to the needs of the masses. ISI may also have been a more reactive and a less-coherently implemented strategy than is often supposed. That is, the policy-making process frequently may have been responding to balance of payments crises in erecting tariffs rather than proactive protection.[41] Finally, instead of promoting risk-taking behavior, the comfort of state ownership and international protection coddled the business culture. ISI fostered the creation of inefficient economic institutions that have persisted into the contemporary period.[42]

With resources focused on industrialization, agriculture was neglected. Necessary investments in agricultural infrastructure were not made as capital was directed to the industrial sector. Labor also gravitated toward urban industrial regions, pressuring cities. In some cases the decline in agricultural production meant an increase in the quantity of food imports, further pressuring the balance of payments. The neglect of agriculture weakened not only a source of profits but also the food security of nations. The urban, industrial bias was unsustainable. ISI was an imbalanced strategy.

Inefficiencies and inconsistencies abound under ISI. Even Raúl Prebisch, founder of the ECLAC school, was not blind to the emerging challenges in the region in the late 1960s and early 1970s.[43] Prebisch noted that overvalued exchange rates biased growth against the export sector. Where exports are a source of international or hard currency, this introduces a foreign exchange gap to finance development. Differences in domestic expenditures and revenue in state-owned firms lead either to persistent deficits or to monetary expansion that results in inflation. We will consider these inflationary biases in chapter 5. Internal and external resource gaps were met through external borrowing, adding annually to debt obligations (see chapter 4). As long as international financial markets were willing to extend financing, the model could be sustained; however, once the spigots of international finance were turned off, internally driven industrialization ground to a halt.

LESSONS FOR DEVELOPMENT: WAS ISI INHERENTLY FLAWED?

Does the failure of ISI in the 1980s mean that it was a misguided policy from the start? Some contend that the triumphant adoption in the 1990s of the neoliberal model throughout the region testifies to the inherent flaws of ISI. Others such as economist Werner Baer suggest that ISI was the appropriate policy for the period but that times changed.[44] Indeed, it could be argued that the development of the industrial sector under ISI made the dynamic private sector model possible in the 1990s. The international environment also changed substantially, with expanding globalization. After we look more closely at the neoliberal model in chapters 6–9, consider the counterfactual question: Would industrial development have been so successful without ISI? Although we will come to no definitive conclusion, entertaining this question may foreshadow some of the future needs in Latin America with respect to the role of the state. Remember Gabriel García Márquez's warning (see chapter 2) about the repetitious cycles in Latin American history. Before we discard the goals and tools of ISI forever, we might do well to consider that in the future the past may reappear, with a stronger need for the state to address some of the problems of market failure.

But this is getting well ahead of our story. In the next chapter we will look more carefully at some of the problems associated with the later ISI period: macroeconomic instability and the debt crisis. This will then position us for a careful look at the neoliberal model, with a strong role for the private as opposed to the public sector.

Key Concepts

backward linkages	forward linkages	overvalued exchange
declining terms of trade	import substitution	rates
dependency theory	industrialization (ISI)	structuralists
economic populism	market failure	transnational corporations

Chapter Summary

The Dependency and Structuralist School

- The dependency theory states that the center (industrialized nations) expanded at the expense of the periphery (developing nations). Capitalism therefore created underdevelopment. Local elites forged alliances with international capital, blocking development.
- The structuralist school, as defined by the UN Commission for Latin America, had two main characteristics. First, declining terms of trade hindered economic development for Latin America. Second, concentrated oligopolies and elites determined prices and consumption patterns that proved incompatible with growth for the region.

Import Substitution Industrialization (ISI)

- In response to dependency theory and the structuralist school, Latin America pursued ISI. This inward-oriented approach sought to promote and protect domestic industries through an interventionist state that would attack bottlenecks and market failure.
- ISI relied on various tools to promote industrialization:
  - active industrial policy through the use of SOEs;
  - protective international instruments such as tariffs, quotas, import licenses, foreign exchange controls, industrial incentives, and export subsidies to protect infant industries;
  - targeted lending to industries such as machinery and automobiles;
  - subsidies and tax exemptions for particular industries, including transnational corporations that provided critical financial capital and technology;
  - strict investment rules such as local content laws and minority foreign ownership;
  - and passive monetary policy to finance projects under ISI.
- Although data show that ISI had a positive effect on growth until the 1980s, there were also negative consequences. Nationally manufactured goods often failed to meet international quality standards, making them uncompetitive in the global market. ISI exacerbated inequality by preserving the power of the elite and failing to create an entrepreneurial class. In addition, the agricultural sector was neglected, which weakened a source of profit and food security. There was also a bias against export growth through overvalued exchange rates, leading to differences in domestic expenditures and revenue that contributed to persistent deficits and inflation.

Notes

1. Gerald M. Meier and Dudley Seers, *Pioneers in Development* (Oxford: Oxford University Press, 1984), 173.

2. Meier and Seers, *Pioneers in Development,* 173.

3. Ronald V. A. Sprout, "The Ideas of Prebisch," *CEPAL Review* 46 (April 1992): 178.

4. James L. Dietz and James H. Street, eds., *Latin America's Economic Development: Institutionalist and Structuralist Perspectives* (Boulder, Colo.: Rienner, 1987), 81.

5. Meier and Seers, *Pioneers in Development,* 176.

6. Henry Bruton, "A Reconsideration of Import Substitution," *Journal of Economic Literature* 36 (June 1998): 905.

7. Meier and Seers, *Pioneers in Development,* 176.

8. Sprout, "Ideas of Prebisch," 179.

9. Ibid., 182; and Nancy Birdsall and Carlos Lozada, "Recurring Themes in Latin American Economic Thought: From Prebisch to the Market and Back," in *Securing Stability and Growth in Latin America,* ed. Ricardo Hausmann and Helmut Reisen (Paris: OECD Publications, 1996).

10. Andre Gundar Frank, *Capitalism and Underdevelopment in Latin America* (New York: Monthly Review Press, 1967).

11. Paul A. Baran, "On the Political Economy of Backwardness," *Manchester School* 20(1) (1952); reprinted in *The Economics of Underdevelopment,* ed. A. N. Agarwala and S. P. Singh (New York: Oxford University Press, 1963), and in *Political Economy of Development,* ed. Charles K. Wilber (New York: Random House, 1973). See also the classic piece written by Gabriel Palma, "Dependency: A Formal Theory of Underdevelopment or a Methodology for the Analysis of Concrete Situations of Underdevelopment?" *World Development* 6(7–8) (July–August 1979): 881–924.

12. The Spanish acronym for ECLA is CEPAL, the Comisión Económica Para América Latina. ECLA later became ECLAC, with the "C" reflecting the incorporation of the Caribbean.

13. Enrique V. Iglesias, ed., *The Legacy of Raúl Prebisch* (Washington, D.C.: Inter-American Development Bank, 1994).

14. Stephen Haber, *How Latin America Fell Behind* (Stanford, Calif.: Stanford University Press, 1997), chap. 1.

15. Henry Bruton, "Import Substitution," in *Handbook of Development Economics,* vol. 2, 3rd ed., ed. Hollis Chenery and T. N. Srivivasan (New York: Elsevier, 1996), 1609.

16. Vittorio Corbo, "Economic Policies and Performance in Latin America," in *Economic Development: Handbook of Comparative Economic Policies,* ed. Enzo Grilli and Dominick Salvatore (Westport, Conn.: Greenwood, 1994).

17. Charles K. Wilber and Steven Francis, "The Methodological Basis of Hirschman's Development Economics: Pattern Modeling vs. General Laws," *World Development,* Special issue 14(2) (February 1986): 181–191.

18. For a discussion of the role of the state in economic development, see Thomas Trebat, *Brazil's State-Owned Enterprises: A Case Study of the State as Entrepreneur* (New York: Cambridge University Press, 1983).

19. Rudiger Dornbusch and Sebastian Edwards, "The Political Economy of Latin America," in *The Macroeconomics of Populism in Latin America,* National Bureau of Economic Research Conference Report, ed. Rudiger Dornbusch and Sebastian Edwards (Chicago: University of Chicago Press, 1991), 9. See also Alan Knight, "Populism and Neo-Populism in Latin America, Especially Mexico," *Journal of Latin American Studies* 30 (1998): 223–248.

20. Trebat, *Brazil's State-Owned Enterprises.*

21. Bruton, "Import Substitution," 1607.

22. Rosemary Thorp, "Import Substitution: A Good Idea in Principle," in *Latin America and the World Economy: Dependency and Beyond,* ed. Richard J. Salvucci (Lexington, Mass.: Heath, 1996), 140–146. The Salvucci book is a good reader to accompany chapters 2–3 of this text.

23. Victor Bulmer-Thomas, *The Economic History of Latin America since Independence* (New York: Cambridge University Press, 1994), 280. "Nominal" refers to the tariff rate on the final good without adjusting for tariffs on intermediate inputs.

24. Adriaan ten Kate and Robert Bruce Wallace, "Nominal and Effective Protection by Sector," in *Protection and Economic Development in Mexico,* ed. Adriaan ten Kate and Robert Bruce Wallace (Hampshire, UK: Gower, 1980), 122, 151.

25. Gerardo Esquivel and Graciela Marquez, "Some Economic Effects of Closing the Economy: The Mexican Experience in the Mid-Twentieth Century," in *Capital Controls and Capital Flows in Emerging Economies: Policies, Practices and Consequences,* ed. Sebastian Edwards, *NBER,* June 2005.

26. Tom Warts, "Protection and Private Foreign Investment," in *Protection and Economic Development in Mexico,* 198.

27. Robert Bruce Wallace, "Policies of Protection in Mexico," in *Protection and Economic Development in Mexico.*

28. This is based on the theory of purchasing power parity and the law of one price. Two sweaters should sell for the same price in two markets (adjusted for transportation costs). If they didn't, some enterprising person would buy sweaters where they are cheap and sell them where they are dear.

29. Petro Lains illustrates this idea in "Before the Golden Age: Economic Growth in Mexico and Portugal, 1910–1950," p. 7 in Edwards, "Growth Institutions and Crises: Latin America from a Historical Perspective." Table 4 shows total public debt rising from 2.48 percent a year to 12.97 percent from 29–39 to 39–50 and M1 growth from 4.14 to 19.18 over the same period (p. 23).

30. Rhys Jenkins, *Transnational Corporations and Industrial Transformation in Latin America* (New York: St. Martin's, 1984), 40.

31. Gary Gereffi and Peter Evans, "Transnational Corporations, Dependent Development, and State Policy in the Semiperiphery," *Latin American Research Review* 16(3) (1981): 31–64.

32. Richard S. Newfarmer, "International Oligopoly in the Electrical Industry," in *Profits, Progress, and Poverty* (Notre Dame, Ind.: University of Notre Dame Press, 1984), 147.

33. Henry Bruton, "A Reconsideration of Import Substitution," *Journal of Economic Literature* 36 (June 1998): 910.

34. Robert J. Alexander, "Import Substitution in Latin America in Retrospect," in *Progress toward Development in Latin America: From Prebisch to Technological Autonomy,* ed. James L. Dietz and Dilmus James (Boulder, Colo.: Lynne Rienner, 1990).

35. Albert O. Hirschman, *A Propensity to Self Subversion* (Cambridge, Mass.: Harvard University Press, 1995), 156.

36. Bela Belassa, "Brazil," in *The Structure of Protection in Developing Countries* (Baltimore: Johns Hopkins University Press, 1971), table 6.2, p. 107.

37. This paragraph draws from Rosemary Thorp, *Progress, Poverty and Exclusion: An Economic History of Latin America in the 20th Century* (Baltimore: Johns Hopkins University Press for the IADB, 1998), 197.

38. James E. Mahon Jr., "Was Latin America Too Rich to Prosper? Structural and Polit-

ical Obstacles to Export-Led Industrial Growth," *Journal of Development Studies* 28(2) (1992): 242.

39. Alan M. Taylor, "On the Costs of Inward-Looking Development: Price Distortions, Growth, and Divergence in Latin America," *Journal of Economic History* 58(1) (March 1998): 20.

40. Bruton, "A Reconsideration," 923.

41. Bruton, "Import Substitution," 1616.

42. Taylor, "On the Costs of Inward-Looking Development," 21.

43. Enrique V. Iglesias, "The Search for a New Economic Consensus in Latin America," in *The Legacy of Raúl Prebisch,* ed. Enrique V. Iglesias (Washington, D.C.: IADB, 1994).

44. Werner Baer, "Changing Paradigms: Changing Interpretations of the Public Sector in Latin America's Economies," *Public Choice* 88 (1996): 365–379.

CHAPTER FOUR

LATIN AMERICA'S DEBT CRISIS

The Limits of External Financing

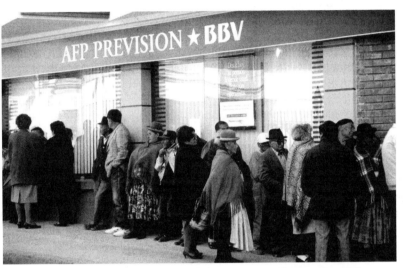

The macroeconomic crisis threatened the meager savings and social security of Latin America's poor. *(Courtesy of David Mangurian and the Inter-American Development Bank)*

The debt crisis in Latin America was a development crisis. It called into question the viability of the import substitution industrialization model of development and shaped the economic future of the region.

How did the crisis come about? Borrowing to finance development is not in itself a bad thing. Developing countries are by definition capital poor. Funding is needed for investment and growth. If a country, like a person, wants to grow or expand, borrowing provides necessary capital for change. As a student, you might be borrowing money to finance educational expenses in anticipation of a better future. This is rational behavior. Borrowing becomes a crisis when an individual or a country fails to make payments on the outstanding value of the loan. If the investment you make in your education doesn't generate a decent salary by the time your first loan payment is due, you will have a personal financial crisis. For a nation, if the returns on the investments don't match the debt obligations when they come due, a crisis also ensues. Unfortunately, the development model in Latin America was dependent on a continuous infusion of capital, with new lending required to finance the development of long-term projects. When conditions in the international market changed dramatically in the early 1980s, Latin American economies, one after another, collapsed under the mountain of external debt. The debt crisis transformed economic policy in the region—at a very high price.

In this chapter we begin by analyzing how borrowing to support import substitution industrialization became an unstable foundation for growth. We then consider the problem of debt-led growth and why a change in external conditions brought inward-looking development to a halt. Finally, we turn to the changes in development policy that enabled economies to survive the crisis, and we analyze the economic and social costs to the region. Questions that will shape our analysis include the following:

- What fueled the accumulation of external debt?
- What role did internal and external factors play in precipitating a crisis?
- How did countries and the international financial community respond to the crisis?
- What are the legacies of the debt crisis?
- Is the Latin American debt crisis over?

THE MOUNTAIN OF DEBT: AN UNSTABLE FOUNDATION FOR DEVELOPMENT

Economic growth under the import substitution model of development was fueled by external savings. With thin domestic financial markets, by 1982 Latin America had borrowed more than $300 billion from the rest of the world. Figure 4.1 shows this accumulation of Latin American total disbursed external debt during 1980–2004. Under the import substitution model, the first stage of industrialization was driven by the import of capital goods—particularly machinery—to be used to produce goods domestically. In many cases, the capital was also used to finance large infrastructure projects such as roads, electricity, telecommunications, or water supply,

Figure 4.1.   Total External Debt of Latin America

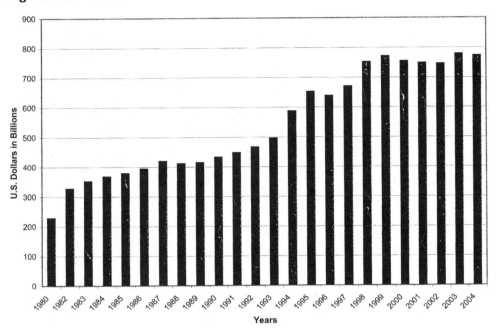

Source: World Bank, *World Debt Tables* (various years) and *Global Development Finance 2005.*

all of which are vital to a nation's advancing growth. Borrowing in itself is not a bad strategy. Problems arise, however, when the borrowing requirements for long-term projects outpace the ability to repay past loans. Crises may erupt due to the mechanics of borrowing or the **debt trap** (unproductive investments or investments with very long time horizons that do not generate returns in time to help service loans), internally inconsistent economic policies that impede the success of projects, or external shocks that derail the domestic economy. Let's consider these causes in turn.

It is easy to fall into a debt trap when lending is for long-term projects but obligations to repay begin in the short term. This problem is made clear with a simple mathematical example. Assume the following (rather lenient) borrowing conditions. You contract to borrow $1,000 dollars a year for a project that is going to take ten years. You agree to pay $50 a year back in principal for each $1,000 borrowed over twenty years at an interest rate of 10 percent per year on the outstanding balance of the debt. As can be seen in table 4.1, in the first year you receive $1,000 and repay $50, leaving a balance of $950. At 10 percent interest your net outflow, the interest plus the principal, is $95 plus $50 or $145. In the second year you again receive $1,000 of new money to continue your project, pay $100 in principal (the first and second $50 principal payments), leaving $185 of interest to be paid on the balance of $1,850. Your principal plus interest therefore totaled $285. Your annual net transfer, the $1,000 coming in minus the $285 going out, is $715.

This formula of new money minus principal and interest payments goes on for

Table 4.1.   The Debt Trap: Long-Term Project Lending

Year	New Lending	Total Debt Incurred	Principal ($50/year for twenty years)	Out-standing Debt	Interest Payment (10%)	Total Outflow = Interest + Principle	Net Transfer = Disbursement Outflow
1	1,000	1,000	50	950	95	145	855
2	1,000	2,000	100	1,850	185	285	715
3	1,000	3,000	150	2,700	270	420	580
4	1,000	4,000	200	3,500	350	550	450
5	1,000	5,000	250	4,250	425	675	325
6	1,000	6,000	300	4,950	495	795	205
7	1,000	7,000	350	5,600	560	910	90
8	1,000	8,000	400	6,200	620	1,020	−20
9	1,000	9,000	450	6,750	675	1,125	−125
10	1,000	10,000	500	7,250	725	1,225	−225
11	1,000	11,000	550	7,700	770	1,320	−320

Source: John Charles Pool, Stephen C. Stamos, and Patrice Franko, *The ABCs of International Finance,* 2nd ed. (Lexington, Mass.: Lexington Books, 1991).

several years. Notice that each year, because of the obligation to pay the principal on past loans and the increasing interest burden, the net transfer—the amount of money coming in after payments have been made—substantially dwindles. Indeed, by the eighth year the $1,000 of new money doesn't even cover your payments on past obligations, much less fund new investment. If your multiyear project is incomplete or if it is not yet generating significant returns, you would need to borrow even more just to make payments. You have landed flat in the debt trap.

Mismatched Projects and Returns

Import substitution was fueled by regular infusions of capital not unlike our example above. In part, the import substitution industrialization model was driven by the failure of the private sector to provide critical goods and services in the economy. We remember that this took place most frequently in industries with large economies of scale and in sectors in which the complementary infrastructure was not available. This led to state investment in sectors with high capital requirements for entry as well as in large-scale projects to develop needed infrastructure in energy, telecommunications, and transportation. Unfortunately, the payback period for these multiyear investments was not always consistent with the terms of commercial lending. Furthermore, the returns to social investments by the state are not easily captured in state tax coffers for repayment of debt obligations.

Even when lending for large-scale infrastructure projects was efficient and well managed, multiyear development projects were not easily financed. If a road, for example, is constructed over a ten-year period and then it takes another ten years for businesses to move into the area and pay taxes, the project itself may not generate returns—and repayment of debt—until well into the future. Debt-generated investment should create the ability to service that debt in the future. Investments must have a sufficient rate of return within a compatible term structure. When this is not possible in huge undertakings, the government often steps in with public lending. Although it is a function of government to sequence projects and manage these flows, the magnitude of large-scale investments under import substitution industrialization left Latin American governments vulnerable to the willingness of capital markets to finance the gap between the period of investment and the long-term returns on the project. Given sovereign guarantees and the low likelihood of countries defaulting (as opposed to companies), markets were willing to lend. Debt was accumulated to service past debt.

Unsustainable Domestic Policies

In addition to the simple mathematical lesson of the debt trap, the intersection of politics and economics promoted debt-led development. Latin America has a long history of populism, or the use of political rhetoric to mobilize the masses. Old-style populists, such as Juan and Eva Perón of Argentina, charismatically co-opted labor and middle-class groups as well as domestic industrial elites to maintain power. But buying off the masses costs money. As we saw in chapter 3, **economic populism** in the 1970s emphasized growth and income redistribution and de-emphasized the risks of inflation and deficit finance, external constraints, and the reaction of economic agents to aggressive nonmarket policies.[1] The populist political culture encouraged spending, which was made possible by favorable conditions in the international financial markets.

Unfortunately, the large state-run development model also lent itself well to inefficiency and corruption in lending. In some instances, lending was for pharaonic megaprojects with limited utility for social development. The history of Latin America contains numerous stories of a state firm's payrolls padded with dead people, construction taking place only on paper, and misguided attempts at development such as the Transamazonian Highway. Debt was incurred for projects that would never generate the ability to repay.

External Shocks

Of course, at some level, politicians understood that one day the piper would have to be paid. However, extraordinarily attractive international prices for capital played into the short-term political incentive to borrow. Real international interest rates—that is, interest rates adjusted for global inflation—were negative from 1974 until 1977. As shown in table 4.2, the U.S. prime rate adjusted for inflation (the real prime rate) ranged between −2.9 and −1.4 percent. If someone asked you whether you would like to borrow money today, have the use of that money for some period of time, and repay less than what was borrowed, how would you respond? Although much of the lending was on a floating rate basis—that is, each year your interest

Table 4.2.   Real International Interest Rates, 1974–1984

Year	U.S. Nominal Prime Rate (%)	U.S. Inflation Rate (%)	U.S. Real Prime Rate (%)
1974	10.81	13.1	−2.2
1975	7.86	11.1	−2.9
1976	6.84	8.3	−1.3
1977	6.83	8.5	−1.4
1978	9.06	7.2	1.7
1979	12.67	9.2	3.2
1980	15.27	11.9	3.0
1981	18.85	10.1	8.1
1982	14.77	7.5	6.8
1983	10.81	5.1	5.5
1984	12.04	4.8	6.9

Source: ECLAC, *Economic Survey of Latin America and the Caribbean* (Santiago, Chile: ECLAC, various years); IMF, International Financial Statistics, 1987 (Washington, D.C.: IMF, 1987), 113.

rate would change to reflect market conditions—after several years of negative real rates and the possibility that you wouldn't even be in office when repayment time came around, the decision to borrow could be seen as a rational response to price. It would be as if the interest rates in the debt trap example presented earlier were −2 percent rather than +10 percent. At that rate it would take twenty-one years, perhaps five different government administrations, for net flows to become negative. Within that time, the project may be bearing returns. Given those conditions, it would be hard for a politician to do anything but incur the loan!

Although the demand for finance was driven by developmental needs as defined by the import substitution model and the populist politics of its implementation, lending would never have taken place on such a broad scale without an ample supply of global cash. During the 1970s banks needed to recycle the proceeds from the quadrupling of oil prices, called petrodollars. Unless banks lent these petrodollar deposits, they would be unable to pay interest to the OPEC creditor nations. Many lenders simply saw it as easier and more lucrative to advance megaloans to state-owned enterprises (SOEs), backed by sovereign governments, than to package small business or agricultural loans in the United States. The competition to lend was ferocious.

Distinct Patterns, Same Result: Crisis

It is important to note that Latin American countries pursued a variety of economic strategies during this time period—yet all were strongly hit by crisis. Table 4.3 compares three cases: Mexico, Brazil, and Argentina. The Mexican debt crisis was driven by an attempt to expand the oil sector while maintaining social peace at home through domestic spending programs. International bankers were only too happy to lend to Mexico because the loans were collateralized by the black gold of

Table 4.3.   Debt and Distinct Patterns of Development

Policy Instruments	Mexico	Brazil	Argentina
Long- and short-term external debt (billions of 1985 U.S.$)	96.8	106.1	50.9
Fiscal policy	Overexpansion of fiscal policy driven by investments in the oil sector; new oil discoveries led to expanded investments by Pemex; fiscal deficit exploded to 17% of GDP	Respond to global recession with growth of domestic demand; maintain high protective tariffs; wages increased	Inconsistent fiscal policy; 1976 military regime adopted orthodox model
Monetary policy	Loose monetary policy with low interest rates led to massive capital flight; outflows reached $8.4 billion in 1981 and $6.6 billion in 1982; inflation soars	Economy indexed to respond to inflation; money supply passively accommodates expansionary fiscal policy	High *peso* interest rates initially generated strong capital inflow; when confidence was lost, capital flight ensued
Exchange rate policy	Maintains fixed exchange rate policy despite inflation; overvaluation results	Limited devaluation of *cruzeiro* to 50% despite inflation rates twice as high; overvaluation results	Overvalued exchange rate depressed exports and accelerated imports; acute reserve loss led to borrowing just to maintain the exchange rate
Exogenous shocks	Tightening U.S. monetary policy raised real interest rates; oil prices plunged	Oil crisis pressures balance of payments; high interest rates; commodity price shock; contagion effects from Mexico	Tight U.S. policy raised cost of capital
Comments	As an oil exporter, Mexico had access to capital; its problem derived from its attempts to limit social conflict through state spending while simultaneously expanding the oil sector	Brazil attempts to maintain state-led development model despite changes in the international economy; its large size allows it to pursue this strategy too long	Argentina pursued an aggressive liberalization policy with exchange rate priced to restrain inflation—not promote exports; the model was therefore internally inconsistent

Source: Derived from information presented in SBC Warburg Dillon Read, *The Latin American Adviser* (February 1998).

new oil discoveries. Domestic expansion exploded into inflation, which the government attempted to restrain through a fixed exchange rate. This exchange rate became overvalued, compromising the ability of the non-oil export sector to perform. As described below, Mexico sounded the first alert to the international community of the debt crisis in August 1982 when it announced its inability to meet its financial obligations.

Brazil also enjoyed easy access to international finance. Because it was one of the ten largest economies in the world, lenders believed that investments in this emerging powerhouse were well placed. Loans to state enterprises were seen as backed by the **sovereign guarantee** of the government of Brazil—investors thought that the government would not default on obligations. As international financial conditions changed in the 1980s, Brazil's size also slowed the incentive for its adjustment. It was able to maintain its inward-looking model of development and turn to domestic money creation to service external debt. Inflation soared, but a sophisticated system of indexing interest rates, wages, and prices minimized the pain for economic agents. We will consider these macroeconomic responses in chapter 5. A rate of devaluation of the exchange rate slower than the rate of inflation was designed as a brake on rising prices but had the unfortunate effect of reducing export performance.

Whereas debt accumulation in Brazil and Mexico was driven by investments through state firms, Argentina's inward-looking development model ran out of steam under the populist Peronist regime. The military took over in 1976 and radically opened the economy. Unfortunately for Argentina, borrowing was used for financial purposes and did not result in an increase in the productive capabilities of the nation. Instead, a misguided attempt to maintain an overvalued exchange rate led to borrowing to defend the fixed currency price. Money flowed into the country in the form of short-term loans used to support the exchange rate, but those same dollars quickly exited in private portfolios betting against the ability of the Argentine government to restrain inflation and jump-start growth. At the crux of the Argentine problem was the fact that the overvalued exchange rate, used as an anchor for inflation, could not simultaneously promote exports. Box 4.1 provides a review of overvalued exchange rates.

Despite these differences in internal development models, Mexico (an oil exporter), Brazil (a nation inwardly focused on its large domestic market), and Argentina (an economy open to the international economy) were all rocked by changes in the international economy that transformed a heavy debt profile into an insupportable burden. Unsustainable domestic policies left each nation vulnerable; external pressure exposed the fragility of the debt-led development model.

The Crisis Builds: External Shocks and Capital Flight

The accumulation of external liabilities to finance development is not a crisis. However, external conditions changed radically, and evidence began to mount that called into question the ability of governments to service their debt. In 1979 U.S. president Jimmy Carter appointed Paul Volcker as chairman of the Federal Reserve

Box 4.1.   Overvaluation of Exchange Rates and the Debt Crisis

An overvalued exchange rate can be seen as both a cause of the accumulation of debt and an effect of the macroeconomic instability perpetuated by the debt crisis.

Before explaining the economic cause and effect of an overvalued rate, we should clarify what is meant by an overvalued exchange rate. An overvalued exchange rate exists when the currency is artificially too strong, allowing the purchase of more foreign currency than trade patterns might indicate. With a strong currency, people buy more from abroad. An undervalued rate is "too weak," favoring exports. Imports become prohibitively expensive, and exports are cheap. Most overvaluation exists when the price of a currency is established under a fixed exchange rate system.

The Goldilocks question of figuring out which rate is "just right" goes back to a theory of exchange rate determination called purchasing power parity, or PPP. In its simplest form, PPP argues that a good should sell for the same price in two countries when prices are adjusted for the exchange rate. Holding transportation costs constant, if Costa Rican coffee does not sell for the same price in San Jose, Costa Rica, and San Jose, California, people will buy it where it is cheap (Costa Rica) and sell it where it was dear (California), driving the price up in Costa Rica and down in California. Because one would need *colones* to purchase the coffee in Costa Rica, this would drive up the value of the *colon* until the value of the two goods was identical in the two markets. If the exchange rate were set by the government (rather than being a floating market rate), the "right" price for the currency should generate one price for coffee. However, if tastes changed and people drank less coffee and demanded fewer *colones* to buy it, an unadjusted exchange rate would become overvalued.

Alternatively, if the Costa Rican government increased the money supply, the *colon* should be worth less than the dollar. For example, if prices in Costa Rica were rising at 20 percent per year but in the United States they were only rising by 5 percent a year, this means that Costa Ricans could purchase 15 percent $(20 - 5)$ less a year with the same income as those in the United States. Under a floating system, this should be reflected in a 15 percent fall in the value of the currency, or the exchange rate. Once again, if the exchange market isn't functioning smoothly or if the government intervenes to fix a currency price and does not allow the devaluation to take place, we would say that this currency is overvalued.

A look at table 4.4 shows that from 1979 through 1981, currencies became significantly overvalued in Latin America. The numbers presented are indexes that set 1980–1982 as a base year. By 1981, for example, Argentina's currency was 7 percent too strong,

continued

Table 4.4.   Real Exchange Rate Indexes (1980–1982 = 100)

	Argentina	Brazil	Chile	Mexico	Venezuela
1976–1978	73	116	75	98	95
1979	101	96	79	98	94
1980	116	85	95	104	93
1981	107	103	108	114	100
1982	76	112	97	82	110
1983–1985	74	85	86	86	98

Source: Selected from Rudiger Dornbusch, *Stabilization, Debt, and Reform: Policy Analysis for Developing Countries* (Englewood Cliffs, N.J.: Prentice-Hall, 1993); original source Morgan Guarantee, World Financial Markets.

continued

Brazil's 3 percent, Chile's 8 percent, and Mexico's 14 percent; only Venezuela's was "just right." (We see, however, not for long.)

Why would a country allow overvaluation to take place? First, if the country is pursuing import substitution, the strong currency value allows companies to purchase intermediate inputs at a lower cost. Because the policy was often to discourage the importation of final consumer goods, import licenses at these preferential rates were sometimes required. Second, countries may choose to link their currency to a vehicle currency such as the dollar as an inflation-fighting anchor. Just as global currencies were set to the dollar under the Bretton Woods system following World War II or under the gold standard, developing countries have at times viewed the link as a stabilizing force. Currency boards have also been used to establish a one-to-one link, constraining the growth of the domestic money supply to the number of dollars held in reserve. Whether the link is firm or whether the government uses the dollar value as a guide to monetary policy, under a fixed exchange rate regime this should be anti-inflationary. Nonetheless, if all inflation is not immediately squeezed out of the economy and a rate is fixed, when the local currency should be losing value to reflect inflation but it isn't, overvaluation is taking place.

Finally, even when a country knows that a devaluation is indicated, at times it is reluctant to do so. In addition to incurring a political cost (citizens concluding that the government was unable to control inflation), the devaluation can serve as an additional inflationary shock because imports now become more costly. The vicious circle between inflation causing the need for devaluation and then a devaluation increasing prices in the economy pressuring for a further devaluation is the economic minister's nightmare.

Capital flight makes the pressure toward devaluation worse. If indications point to the possibility of a devaluation, investors will move their assets out of the country. The rationale is clear. Say you have 1,000 pesos in the bank and that initially they can buy you 1,000 dollars worth of goods at a 1:1 exchange rate. Now assume that you have a 20 percent devaluation of the peso. This means that to buy the same US$1,000 worth of goods, you will have to come up with 1,200 pesos. Therefore, if you think there will be a devaluation, you will sell pesos and hold dollars (perhaps in a Miami bank account or perhaps under your bed). Selling pesos, not surprisingly, weakens the peso. Under a fixed exchange rate, the government must intervene in the market, selling dollars and buying pesos to maintain the value. It is forced to sell the dollars that it holds in reserves for such foreign exchange transactions. However, a fall in reserves in the balance of payments numbers erodes confidence. Everyone knows that reserves are dwindling and that a devaluation is inevitable because the central bank does not have infinite resources to defend the currency. Capital flight accelerates in the face of a possible devaluation, making that change in the currency value inevitable. Pressures on overvalued exchange rates resulted in many countries moving from a fixed to a floating rate.

Board. Volcker's inflation-taming efforts drove the U.S. prime rate to 18.8 percent in 1981. Floating rate obligations skyrocketed to a real, or inflation-adjusted, positive 12 percent. In addition to facing escalating interest payments, countries found it difficult to generate the hard currency—usually dollars—to pay the debt. Debt in Latin America was generally dollar-denominated, since no international bank would issue a loan in pesos when the peso was likely to be devalued. To repay the loan, the country therefore had to earn or buy dollars. The most direct means of augmenting dollar holdings was to sell Latin American goods in the United States. Unfortunately, Volcker's inflation-fighting tools also generated recession, shrinking the United States as a market for Latin American goods. The slowdown became

Table 4.5.   Capital Flight from Selected Latin American Countries (billions of U.S.$)

	1979	1980	1981	1982	1983	1984
Argentina	2.2	3.5	4.5	7.6	1.3	−3.4
Brazil	1.3	2.0	−1.4	1.8	0.5	4.0
Mexico	−1.1	2.2	2.6	4.7	9.3	2.6
Venezuela	3.0	4.8	5.4	3.2	3.1	4.0

Source: Robert Cumby and Richard Levich, "On the Definition and Magnitude of Recent Capital Flight," Working Paper 2275 (Cambridge, Mass.: National Bureau of Economic Research, 1987); cited in Sebastian Edwards, *Crisis and Reform in Latin America: From Despair to Hope* (New York: Oxford University Press and World Bank, 1995), 23.

global, and the region found itself with increasingly burdensome obligations and a limited ability to earn the money owed.

Evidence of the unsustainability of the debt began to mount. Table 4.5 shows the capital flight from unsustainable policies in Argentina, Mexico, and Venezuela from 1979 through 1984. Capital flight as a percentage of total external debt reached 76.9 percent in Argentina, 73.3 percent in Mexico, and 131.5 percent in Venezuela. Capital flight takes place when a national makes a deposit or investment outside the home country. On one hand, capital flight is simply good international investing. A Brazilian economist once commented, "Why is it that when an American puts money abroad it is called 'foreign investment' and when an Argentinean does the same it is called 'capital flight'? Why is it that when an American company puts 30 percent of its equity abroad it is called 'strategic diversification' and when a Bolivian businessman puts only 4 percent abroad it is called 'lack of confidence'?"[2] On the other hand, if one's portfolio preference is decidedly against domestic investment or if investors or savers actively circumvent laws to prevent scarce capital from leaving the country, capital flight has taken place. Capital votes with its feet. Many Latin American families, for example, have savings accounts in Miami to guard against the possibility that the value of all of their savings would be decimated by poor economic management, followed by a devaluation. As shown in box 4.1, overvaluation of a currency contributes to capital flight because agents do not want to be caught holding assets denominated in a currency that is likely to be devalued. In some cases corruption exacerbated capital flight. Dollars coming in as loans to SOEs found their way out of the countries in the coffers of corrupt public agents.

Capital flight further destabilizes macroeconomic management. In an attempt to bribe capital to stay at home, interest rates may be set too high and retard investment. When capital leaves the tax base, the government's ability to raise revenues is weakened. There is stronger incentive for **seignorage, the process of printing money to cover the deficit**. Because people want to sell the local currency and trade it in for dollars, the excess supply of the local currency is inflationary. We will come back to this problem in chapter 5.

Other measures of indebtedness fueled uncertainty, aggravating capital flight and the loss of confidence in economic management in the region. Since export earnings finance debt payments, it is important to look at the weight of debt to exports as well as debt service—the interest and principal that must be paid for by

Table 4.6.   Debt Indicators for Latin America and the Caribbean, 1980–1990

Year	Total Debt/Exports of Goods and Services	Total Debt/GNP	Total Debt Service/Exports of Goods and Services	Interest/Export of Goods and Services	Interest/GNP
1980	206.0	36.2	36.9	19.6	3.4
1981	210.9	37.8	21.6	11.1	2.0
1982	269.1	46.9	47.6	30.3	5.3
1983	309.1	58.6	43.0	29.8	5.6
1984	291.4	59.3	39.9	27.2	5.5
1985	312.9	61.3	38.2	27.9	5.5
1986	376.6	63.2	43.6	27.5	4.6
1987	377.6	66.1	37.4	23.0	4.0
1988	332.6	56.7	39.6	24.1	4.1
1989	293.3	50.1	32.1	16.6	2.8
1990	277.4	45.0	26.3	13.0	2.1

Source: World Bank, *World Debt Tables* (Washington, D.C.: World Bank, various years).

exports. A measure greater than 200 percent in the level of total external debt to exports or a debt service to export ratio over 40 percent is unhealthy, pointing to great pressure on exports for debt payments and leaving little capital for other investment. We can see in table 4.6 that by 1982 total debt over exports had reached 269 percent and that total debt service over the exports of goods and services was edging toward 50 percent. Interest payments alone ballooned to 30 percent of exports, without reducing future liabilities. Latin America was in trouble.

CAN'T PAY, WON'T PAY

In August 1982, Mexico announced to the international financial community that it could no longer service its debt. When the financial community saw that the sovereign government of Mexico would not or could not make good on its obligations, confidence in all developing countries eroded. It was a crisis for Mexico that quickly spread through the region and all developing countries and threatened the international finance system. At the time that Mexico signaled the international financial community of the severity of the crisis, exposure to debt was a problem not only for the countries but also for the banks. As can be seen in table 4.7, the exposure of the nine major banks to six highly indebted countries exceeded an average of 174 percent of shareholders' equity in the banks. Exposure to either Mexico or Brazil alone would have been approximately half of shareholders' capital.

The International Monetary Fund (IMF) Approach

When Mexico rang the alarm bell on the mountain of external debt accumulated by developing countries, the depth of the problem was poorly understood. The inter-

Table 4.7.   Exposure of Nine Major U.S. Banks to Six Highly Indebted Countries, 1984

	% of Shareholders' Equity (common and preferred)
Manufacturers Hanover	268.5
Chase Manhattan	212.7
Citicorp	206.7
Chemical	196.7
Bankers Trust	177.6
Bank of America	150.9
Morgan Guarantee	143.5
Continental Illinois	129.9
Wells Fargo	129.8
First Chicago	126.9
Average	174.3

Source: John Charles Pool, Stephen C. Stamos, and Patrice Franko, *The ABCs of International Finance,* 2nd ed. (Lexington, Mass.: Lexington Books, 1991), 113.

national financial community diagnosed the difficulty primarily as a liquidity crisis. The *World Development Report* of 1983 noted, "Debt problems of most major developing countries are caused by illiquidity, not by insolvency."[3] Returning to the analogy of personal finances, **illiquidity** might mean that because you were laid off from your job or because you went wild with your credit cards, you cannot make your payments when due. However, with time and budgeting, you could honor your commitments and not be forced into bankruptcy or insolvency. In the banking world, the assumption was that debtors would regain creditworthiness through a combination of internal adjustments and more favorable global economic conditions. Box 4.2 reviews other debt-related terms.

The internal adjustments were, for most countries, tough medicine to swallow. The presumption was that countries were living beyond their means and therefore had to reduce domestic **absorption** of resources. If fewer goods were consumed at home, more could be exported to service the debt. If we allow Y to represent national income and A to stand for the domestic consumption of goods and services (including imports), we can see in the simple formula $Y - A = B$ that B (the balance) is the residual. A trade surplus, then, would help restore financial health by decreasing the need to finance imports, leaving the balance to pay off the debt. Absorbing less at home left more for hard currency-earning exports.

The Absorption Approach: $Y - A = B$

How should domestic absorption be decreased? The IMF prescription for achieving balance revolved around decreasing government and personal absorption of resources and increasing the attention to the international sector. In contrast to the state-centered import substitution strategy, the IMF recommended that states decrease

Box 4.2.   Key Debt Terms

arrears   The amount of past-due payments (interest and principal) on outstanding debt owed by any given debtor.

bilateral loans   Loans from governments and their agencies, from autonomous bodies, and from official export credit agencies. These differ from private creditors (commercial banks and bonds) who did the bulk of the lending leading to the debt crisis.

concerted lending   **Involuntary lending** by a bank. When the Mexican crisis began in 1982, large banks formed bank advisory committees to represent all banks and to keep them informed of debt negotiations. These committees, along with industrialized countries and the IMF, pressured smaller banks to continue lending to prevent defaults.

debt service   The sum of principal repayments and interest payments actually made.

disbursements   Earnings on loan commitments during the year specified.

LIBOR (London Interbank Offer Rate)   Traditional benchmark interest rate for international lending by private European banks.

loan default   A bank declaration that a borrower is not expected ever to repay its debt, usually following an extended cessation of principal and payments by the debtor.

long-term external debt   Debts with a maturity of more than one year owed to nonresidents, payable in foreign currency, goods, or services.

moratorium   A declaration by a debtor country of its intent to stop principal and interest payments to its creditors.

net flows   Disbursements minus principal repayments.

net transfers   Net flows minus interest payments during the year.

sovereign default   A government's decision to default on its external debt obligations.

REFERENCES

Biersteker, Thomas J. *Dealing with Debt.* Boulder, Colo.: Westview, 1993.

Krugman, Paul R., and Maurice Obstfeld. *International Economics: Theory and Policy.* 3rd ed. New York: HarperCollins, 1994.

World Bank. *World Debt Tables, 1995–1996.* Washington, D.C.: World Bank, 1996.

spending on public works, privatize SOEs, and eliminate subsidies on goods and services. To combat inflation, monetary policy should be contractionary. If wages were indexed to a public minimum wage, it was generally suggested that wage increases be minimal. Devaluation was indicated to adjust overvalued exchange rates, and liberalization of markets through the reduction of tariffs and quotas was favored. The devaluation was designed to change the relative price of goods, making imports more expensive and exports cheaper. This creates incentives for expenditure switching by raising the opportunity cost of tradable goods. Fewer tradables will be consumed at home, and more will be released for sale abroad. Rather than borrowing, foreign investment was seen as the vehicle for the capital necessary for growth. The overriding principle was to get prices right. Resources should be directed to their most productive use through accurate price signals.

The IMF package was inherently contractionary, premised on decreasing fiscal spending and monetary emission. The hope was that the infusion of capital from abroad and initiative from the local private sector would fuel growth. The program generated a good deal of economic dislocation. Workers in bloated SOEs were laid off. Recipients of state-subsidized milk or tortillas faced dramatic price increases. The price of public transportation rose, and spending on infrastructure fell. Companies that had grown up behind the protection of high tariff walls found it difficult to compete with international firms. Tight money meant high interest rates, which retarded investment. Devalued exchange rates sent price shocks through imported consumer goods. Agricultural exports were rapidly promoted, often at high environmental cost.

But the bitter IMF pill was seen as necessary if countries were to maintain access to finance. When a country found itself unable to make payments on its external obligations, banks would lend no more until the country had signed a letter of intent with the IMF to implement the tough economic policies. Targets for macroeconomic performance would be set, and if countries adopted the conditions specified to achieve these goals, IMF funding would be released. **Conditionality**—the adoption of strict fiscal, monetary, and trade policies in exchange for the release of funds—was designed to alert the private sector that substantial change in the spending habits of the country was under way. This signaled a green light for further lending.

The lending, however, was not fresh money for new projects. Instead, given the severity of the financial crisis, the loans were intended to provide the capital to make payments on past liabilities coming due. For a price—and at a higher interest rate—old loans were rolled over into new loans with maturity dates further in the future. The presumption was that when these repackaged loans came due again, the benefits of the tough economic medicine would be available to service the obligations. Called **involuntary lending,** this rolling over of obligations was designed to provide financial breathing room until payments could be made from more productive economies.

Unfortunately, international macroeconomic conditions did not cooperate. Real interest rates did not decline rapidly, and the prices that countries received for their exports—primarily agricultural commodities—were depressed. By 1985 Latin American countries had not returned to good standing in the international market. The problem was clearly more than a short-term liquidity issue. But was the IMF approach wrong?

Criticism of IMF conditionality packages centered on the IMF's diagnosis of the problem as well as the policy measures to bring about change. In Latin America, the theoretical debate was led by the structuralist school. It faulted the IMF approach as too standardized. The same IMF recipe, based upon the assessment of the need to reduce excess demand, was applied in all cases. The structuralists focused instead on the particular economic characteristics of each country. They puzzled at how a country with an unemployment rate of 15 percent and a capacity utilization rate of 75 percent could have excess demand. Furthermore, they challenged the IMF proponents to explain how a crisis triggered by the external shock of high global interest rates and expensive oil imports could be solved by domestically reducing aggregate demand. The structuralists argued that IMF programs were unnecessarily recessionary and increased inequality. They contended that the restrictive short-run targets set by the IMF exacerbated the negative impacts. Finally, the structuralists argued that the international financial community played a significant role in the accumulation of debt and should therefore bear some of the adjustment burden.[4]

Despite the standardized prescriptions, this first stage of the debt crisis was defined by a case-by-case approach to the resolution of the problem. That is, a region-wide approach was rejected by creditors. The politics of the case-by-case strategy on the part of the IMF, the World Bank, and the creditor countries may explain in part why Latin America did not default on the debt. Despite the fact that at the outset the debtor countries had some bargaining power given the exposure of money center banks, collective action was not effective. In the Declaration of Quito (1984), Latin American countries called for an immediate response from the creditor countries to ameliorate the dramatic fall in living standards. In June 1984 the Cartagena Consensus Group of debtors argued that the burden of Latin American foreign debt threatened both the very stability of the international monetary system and the emergence of democracy in the region. But the Declaration of Quito was all talk and no action. Although some countries such as Peru declared a partial moratorium, stating that it would devote no more than 10 percent of exports to debt, and Brazil announced in 1987 a unilateral moratorium on the payment of interest of $68 billion of medium- and long-term money, the carrots for good behavior—the flow of new money into countries—were sufficiently enticing to keep countries largely in line.[5]

The Market Reacts to the Continuing Crisis

While countries were engaged in difficult adjustment measures, the financial sector quietly found ways to reduce its exposure to debt. Through the process of **provisioning,** or setting aside profits before dividend payments against risky loans, banks set aside the capital to guarantee their positions in the event of a default. Banks also found means to reduce their exposure to unwanted debt through innovative new market instruments. A **secondary market** for debt developed. Because loans were assets, they could be resold to other, more risk-inclined, buyers for a discount. The new holder of a million-dollar loan to Mexico might have paid only $510,000 for this asset if it were purchased in August of 1987. The value of the discount would be steeper the lower the likelihood the country would ever repay the full amount. As we can see in table 4.8, by 1987 expectations were so low that Peru would ever make good on its external obligations that its debt could be purchased for between two and seven cents on the dollar.

Beyond allowing those who were more risk-averse—particularly the medium-sized regional banks—to exit, the secondary market produced another innovation, **debt-for-equity swaps.** For example, a firm wishing to build a factory in a Latin American country could use the secondary market to purchase the debt note. In August 1987 a firm wanting to invest in Chile could purchase $100,000 worth of debt for about $64,000. The country then owed the firm instead of the bank. However, the firm could turn to the government and say, "I don't need to be paid in dollars (hard earned through exports). In fact, in setting up this factory, I need pesos to buy supplies and pay my workers locally." In this way the debt purchased at a discount could be presented at the central bank for payment in local currencies. If the country had a strong bargaining position, such as good firm location, it too could

Table 4.8.   Secondary Market Prices of Latin American Debt (% of face value)

Country	July 1985	January 1986	January 1987	August 1987	October 1987
Argentina	60–65	62–66	62–65	45–47	34–38
Brazil	75–81	75–81	74–77	52–54	35–40
Chile	56–69	65–69	65–68	64–66	52–56
Colombia	81–83	82–84	86–89	80–82	75–80
Ecuador	65–70	68–71	63–66	41–43	31–34
Mexico	80–82	69–73	64–57	51–53	46–49
Peru	45–50	25–30	16–19	7–10	2–7
Venezuela	81–83	80–82	72–74	72–74	50–54

Source: George Anayiotos and Jaime de Piniés, "The Secondary Market and the International Debt Problem," *World Development* 18(2) (1990): 1655–1660.

negotiate a deal and agree to pay only $90,000 worth of pesos to the firm. Firms were satisfied because the secondary market gave them access to discounted funds, and governments could pay in local currency, not scarce foreign exchange.

On the surface, debt-for-equity swaps are a win-win proposal. The banks sell their poorly performing loans; the company makes a profit on the difference between the discount and the local payment; and the country, in addition to reducing its debt in hard currency, gains in jobs through the foreign direct investment. Indeed, Chile reduced 10 percent of its external obligations this way. However, it was not the perfect scheme. It is important to identify how the local currency was raised. If the central printing presses were simply run a little longer, there could be inflationary impacts. If the government borrowed internally to finance the pesos, indebtedness hadn't really changed—the holders just switched from international to domestic lenders. It was also questionable whether the investments by firms would have taken place anyhow—perhaps bringing hard currency into the country. Some critics raised concerns over sovereignty, charging that foreign firms were using cheap money to compete against local entrepreneurs. (Domestic firms were prevented by international banking conventions from buying back their own debt.) Finally, use of debt-for-equity swaps was a strategy suited for only the best performers. Logically, it would work only if multinational corporations wanted to operate in the host country. If economic adjustment had not been substantial, it was unlikely that foreign capital was going to be banging down the doors.

Despite these drawbacks, the appeal was strong. The secondary market was also used to facilitate **debt-for-nature swaps.** In this instance, rather than purchase materials, international organizations purchased the discounted notes and offered cancellation or partial payment in exchange for the country's promise to establish a nature preserve. As discussed in box 4.3, Costa Rica, in particular, pursued this alternative.

Beyond Muddling Through: The Baker Plan

"Muddling through" (as some called the first period of adjustment to the debt crisis) did not work to restore creditworthiness and growth to the region. Adjustment

Box 4.3.   Debt-for-Nature Swaps

Although the debt crisis was catastrophic for Latin America, it had a silver lining for international environmental nongovernmental organizations (NGOs) trying to persuade Latin American governments to adopt sustainable development policies. Third world debt, in the form of debt-for-nature swaps, gave NGOs a bargaining tool to influence the creation of environmental measures. Some countries were persuaded to implement environmentally sound projects and policies in exchange for a reduction in their outstanding debt.

Debt-for-nature swaps were first proposed in 1984 by the then vice president of the World Wildlife Fund, Thomas Lovejoy. Yet it was not until 1987 that Bolivia, Costa Rica, and Ecuador engaged in this form of debt reduction. Pointing to the negative environmental effects of debt service through natural resource exploitation to earn dollars, Lovejoy and others argued for a proenvironmental policy. Debt-for-nature swaps could reduce hard currency indebtedness while making investments critical to the environment.

To carry out a debt-for-nature swap, three requirements must be met. There must be a donor, usually an NGO, who funds the initiative by purchasing a portion of a developing country's debt from the secondary market. In addition, the country's central bank must be willing to accept the debt note and able to finance the negotiated environmental programs. Finally, a private or governmental agency must carry out the environmental programs. Two types of debt-for-nature swaps have taken place: bond-based programs, where the interest on government bonds is used to pay for environmental and conservation activities, and policy programs, where the government commits to implementing a series of environmental policies. The process for both types is similar. The donor negotiates with the debtor government on the terms and then purchases debt from the secondary market at a price lower than the face value of the outstanding debt. The debtor country now owes the donor instead of the creditor. If a bond-based program was negotiated, the purchased debt is converted to government bonds issued in the name of a local NGO that receives the interest over the life span of the bond. On the other hand, if a policy program is negotiated, in exchange for the debt note, the government agrees to implement environmental policies such as creating environmental reserves or ensuring that forests are managed sustainably. Finally, the funds are transferred to a local private or government agency for the implementation of negotiated projects.

Although debt-for-nature swaps sound like fabulous deals that benefit every party involved, they have limitations. They reduce little debt. In fact, the maximum debt reduction took place in Costa Rica, where less than 5 percent of external debt was reduced. There is a fear that the central bank will engage in money creation, triggering inflation. Further, conservation projects may take precedence where other, more critical sustainable development projects are needed. This also raises the question of sovereignty among nationalists who see foreign NGOs dictating the national environmental agenda.

Despite these restrictions, Costa Rica made good use of debt-for-nature swaps. The major reason for Costa Rica's success is the high level of government participation. To safeguard against inflationary tendencies, officials set a ceiling on the number of swaps allowed yearly. Costa Rica demonstrated that used properly, debt-for-nature swaps can help reduce some of its external debt. More important, debt became an instrument to achieve another policy goal: promoting environmental sustainability.

REFERENCES

Caldwell, Laura. "Swapping Debt to Preserve Nature." *Christian Science Monitor,* 11 September 1990.

Patterson, Allen. "Debt for Nature Swaps and the Need for Alternatives." *Environment* 21 (December 1990): 5–32.

World Bank. "Other Financial Mechanisms: Debt-for-Nature Swaps and Social Funds." www.esd.worldbank.

under IMF programs was largely unsuccessful. The burden of debt service had become painfully obvious. As seen in figure 4.2, high debt service costs resulted in a persistent outflow of resources from Latin America from 1982 through 1990. This loss of capital resulted in the flat growth in gross national product (GNP) seen over the same period in figure 4.3. As growth slowed, unemployment rose in the 1980s, and real wages did not increase to improve the standard of living for the masses.

The costs of adjustment were enormously painful. As will be discussed in later chapters, poverty increased and environmental damage was exacerbated. Political and social dislocation led to labor strikes, supermarket looting, and bus burnings in response to depressed wages and higher prices. Fragile democratic regimes were threatened as people began to idealize the stability and prosperity of military rule. To promote prosperity and stability, in 1985 U.S. Treasury secretary James Baker announced a plan designed to jump-start growth. The premise of the Baker plan was that countries could not continue to service their debt through contractionary policies. Growth and adjustment became linked. The Baker plan targeted fifteen less-developed countries for $29 billion of new money, $20 billion from commercial banks and $9 billion from the IMF and the World Bank.

The Baker plan was important in shifting policy from austerity to growth. It also identified a new role for the World Bank in promoting institutional change. The failure of traditional IMF measures to resolve the debt crisis changed the understanding of the debt crisis from a short-term liquidity problem (with primary responsibility lodged in the IMF) to a long-term problem of **structural adjustment.** Debt came to be understood as a development problem, and the World Bank was charged with assisting in the management of the adjustment process. As a result, the World Bank began to engage in macroeconomic policy, formerly the

Figure 4.2.   Net Flows and Resource Transfers

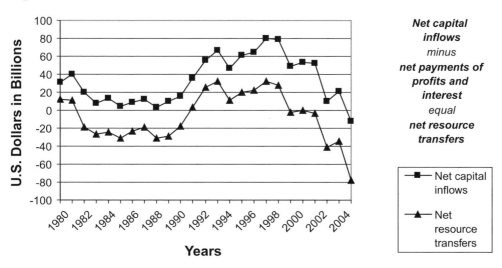

Source: ECLAC on the basis of figures from the IMF and national sources.

Figure 4.3.   Gross National Product of Latin America and the Caribbean, 1980–2000

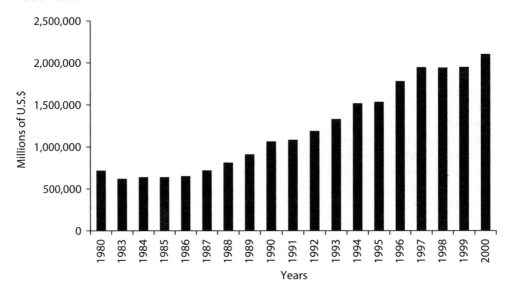

Source: World Bank, *Global Development Finance* (Washington, D.C.: World Bank, various years).

purview of the IMF, and the IMF was forced to design lending facilities to support long-term structural change. There was general agreement that adjustment with growth would be led by the export engine, but there was a greater appreciation for the fact that severely contractionary monetary policy would not favor investment, the deepening of markets, or democracy.

This conceptual shift was important, but the Baker plan itself was too little, too late. Twenty-nine billion dollars may have made a difference if it were targeted toward one or two countries, but given the almost trillion dollars in external obligations on the part of developing countries at the time, it was inconsequential. Furthermore, commercial banks were unconvinced that new lending to debtor countries made any sense. In their view, why throw good money after bad?

Registering its "no confidence" vote for the success of the Baker plan, in 1987 Citicorp announced that it would allocate $3 billion from the loan loss reserves it had been setting aside against its developing country debt portfolio. Some had feared that such a move would lower Citicorp's stock value (since its assets are its loans, which were now worth less); instead, the stock market greeted the news with applause. The consensus was that the banks were prepared to take a realistic position on developing country debt: it would never be repaid in full. Accompanied by a $200 million write-off in the same year by the Bank of Boston, this was seen as the death of the Baker plan. Jump-starting growth would not work until the debt burden was reduced two years later under the Brady plan.

The Social and Environmental Costs of Debt Adjustment

The burden of adjustment to the debt crisis may have fallen disproportionately on women. Several studies showed that in poor households, women were responsible for changes in work, child care, and consumption patterns. Household incomes were maintained by increasing the number of workers per home. Unlike the effects of the Great Depression in the United States, where women tended to withdraw from the workforce in favor of men, in Latin America women entered the workforce during austerity to help meet family needs; their entrance appears permanent.[6] Skilled men were eligible for unemployment compensation; their wives sometimes went into the informal sector to compensate for income loss. The entrance of men into the informal sector of unregulated, poorly compensated jobs tended to be inversely related to skill level.[7] Girls often assumed more domestic tasks, including child care of younger siblings, sometimes leaving school to do so. People cut back on food expenditure, eating fewer meals and consuming less protein and fresh vegetables. Health care was also postponed, often until a medical condition became severe. Households were forced to dig into savings, pawn their possessions, and borrow from relatives or loan sharks. Pressures to make ends meet took an emotional toll on families as they struggled to survive the adjustment to the debt crisis.[8]

From Adjustment through Growth to Debt Reduction: The 1989 Brady Plan

The 1989 Brady plan addressed the need for debt reduction as a necessary step toward stable growth in developing countries. The Brady plan offered three options: decreasing the face value of debt, extending the time period of obligations, or infusion of new money. Countries were officially able to decrease the face value through buybacks in the secondary market. Whereas earlier buybacks were considered cheating and not sanctioned as indicating good performance in servicing loans, countries such as Costa Rica were able to reduce official debt by $1.1 billion.[9] Alternatively, countries were able to swap old loans for thirty-year bonds with a 30–35 percent discount on the face value at a variable interest rate or swap loans without the discount but at a fixed interest rate of 6.25 percent. The longer time period of the Brady bonds made them consistent with the long-term strategies needed for growth. A novel feature of Brady deals were the guarantees to the lender. The United States, Japan (a primary financier), and the developing country put up guarantees (usually in the form of U.S. Treasury bonds) to safeguard payment in the event of default, encouraging investor confidence. Finally, new money could be extended to cover interest in the early years and smooth the transition to the market economy. To be eligible for any of the three options, countries had to show political will and a strong track record in economic reform.

The Mexican Brady deal in 1989 restructured $48 billion of its liabilities by floating $20.8 billion in bonds that had been discounted from the face value at 35

BOX 4.4.   MILEPOSTS IN MEXICAN DEBT

Date	Event
1978–1981	Three-month London Interbank Offer Rate (LIBOR) jumps from 8.8 percent to 16.8 percent
February 1982	President Lopez Portillo vows to "defend the currency like a dog" but is forced to devalue
August 12, 1982	Moratorium placed on dollar-denominated deposits held in Mexican banks
August 15, 1982	Mexico announces it can no longer meet interest payments on foreign debt
Fall 1982	Mexico signs standby agreement with the IMF
1986	Peso devalued
October 1987	Mexican stock market collapses, losing 74 percent of its value in less than forty days; inflation at annual rate of 159 percent
December 1987	Unsuccessful Baker plan provides only $1.1 billion in debt relief for Mexico
April 1989	Mexico signs three-year, $3.64 billion loan agreement with the IMF
July 1989	U.S. Treasury secretary Brady introduces collateralized Brady bonds, reducing Mexican debt to foreign banks by US$48.5 billion and cutting annual debt payments by US$3 billion for next four years

Source: Helen Shapiro, *Mexico: Escaping the Debt Crisis,* Harvard Business School Case (Boston: Harvard Business School, 1991).

percent and $22.4 billion in par value bonds at 6.25 fixed interest. In addition, Mexico received $4.4 billion in new money at the rate of LIBOR plus 13–16 percent.[10] The World Bank estimated that this debt relief reduced net transfers by $4 billion per year, nearly 2 percent of the gross domestic product (GDP), from 1989 through 1994.[11] Box 4.4 recalls the tough economic road Mexico faced up to the debt relief of the Brady plan, underscoring how crisis drove policy throughout the decade.

The commercial sector responded more enthusiastically to the Brady options than it did to the Baker plan. The former's realistic appraisal of the need to reduce the debt overhang, as well as its insurance guarantees, made it appealing. Investors found the plan pragmatic and less risky than the traditional short-term financial commitments. It is also important to note that by 1989, Latin America had already undertaken substantial reforms and was emerging as an intriguing investment arena. Brady bonds arrived as a vehicle for investment in a region that, after much painful adjustment, was beginning to be viewed as ripe for growth.

Is the Debt Crisis Over in Latin America?

Tough adjustments in Latin America appear to have paid off in the region. Data for the 1990s in figure 4.2 mark the return of positive net transfers in the region. Table 4.9 shows the decline in the ratio of external debt to exports of goods and services, as well as interest as a percentage of exports of goods and services. By 2000 total external debt had reached the manageable level of 38.5 percent of GNP, and exports, or the ability to earn hard currency, had expanded while interest rates had fallen, bringing the drain of interest payments on the export bill down to 11.8 percent. This is not to say that Latin America is no longer vulnerable to its external obligations. When international financial crises in Asia, Russia, and Brazil hit the region in the late 1990s, the burden of debt servicing increased as well. Nonetheless, crisis was averted. As we will see in chapter 7, international capital has returned to the region, but it has been unpredictable in both magnitude and type of capital flow.

Latin America's recovery from the debt crisis has been a long and painful process. The turnaround in the region is quite dramatic. Many nations are emerging as major players in the world's debt and equity markets. Some countries have initiated their own stabilization and emergency funds to circumvent the need for a future return to the IMF. As we will see in chapter 7, financial flows have moved away from loans to bonds, portfolio stock flows, and foreign direct investment.

A second important sign of the maturity of Latin American markets is the shift in focus of Latin American firms to domestic markets to raise capital. Many Latin American firms are turning to the region's private pension and mutual funds for financing. Care must be taken, however, not to simply replace international liabilities with domestic debt. Internal debt can also be a cause for serious concern. In the Brazilian case, for example, the total net public debt exploded from 30 percent of

Table 4.9.   Debt Indicators for Latin America and the Caribbean, 1980–2003

Year	Total Debt Stocks/Export of Goods and Services	Total Debt Stocks/GNP	Total Debt Service/Export of Goods and Services	Interest/Export of Goods and Services	Reserves/ Months
1980	201.0	34.4	36.2	19.2	4.3
1990	254.5	44.6	24.4	12.2	3.6
1995	212.9	40.0	26.4	12.2	4.8
1996	201.0	38.0	31.3	11.7	5.2
1997	190.8	36.6	35.6	11.2	4.7
1998	212.7	41.1	34	11.9	4.2
1999	208.4	41.8	41.6	13.0	4.0
2000	172.6	38.5	39	11.8	3.5
2001–2003 averages	205.8	?	23.6	7.7	5.3

Source: World Bank, *World Debt Tables & Global Development Finance* (Washington, D.C.: World Bank, various years).

GDP in 1984 to more than 60 percent in 2002. Only about 30 percent of this debt is in dollars, but the internal obligation ties the hands of the government. The Brazilian government must maintain a fiscal surplus to keep interest rates down or risk a debt-led collapse of the Brazilian economy. The key to predicting the stability of Brazilian debt is estimating the tolerance of domestic institutional investors. The debt to GDP ratio in Italy and Belgium has exceeded 100 percent. Do Brazilians have this kind of confidence that their government will honor its obligations?[12]

These changes in the Latin American markets point to an overall increase in confidence for developing nations. Although there is still much progress to be made, recent trends suggest that Latin America may be ready to take on a more influential position in the world market. However, underneath the shiny new exterior, the mountain of external debt still remains to be paid in full.

Debt Relief for the Region's Poorest Countries

The postcrisis return to the financial market has not reached the poorest countries in Latin America. Table 4.10 shows debt burdens by income classifications. As a result of pressure from the international community, the World Bank and the IMF launched the **HIPC** (or highly indebted poor country) initiative in 1998. Unlike earlier refinancing that actually increased the debt stock of poor countries, the objective of HIPC is to reduce the stock of debt to sustainable levels. A 1999 reform accelerated the relief given to countries with track records of credible reform. Countries receiving HIPC assistance must directly link debt relief to assistance to the poor with poverty-reduction strategy papers (PRSPs) developed in consultation with civil society. Comprehensive, well-targeted, and credible PRSPs include measures to achieve job-creating growth, especially in agriculture; realignment of public expenditure toward poverty reduction; improvements in access to basic health and education; action to improve governance; transparency and accountability; and processes to maintain the engagement of civil society.[13] The strategies are intended to be country-owned, developed as a result of national consultation, and implemented collaboratively with other development agencies, especially the UN system.

HIPC lending proceeds in two phases. At the end of the first period of adoption of IMF–World Bank Reforms, a decision point is reached based on an analysis of **debt sustainability;** if a country's debt obligations as a percentage of exports exceed 150 percent, it qualifies for assistance. Once eligible, the country must establish a further track record of adjustment and adopt a national PRSP; further assistance will be provided at this time. The national process of consultation embodied in the PRSP is designed to promote accountability and to decrease the chances that debt relief will only benefit corrupt politicians or become fungible money for military spending. Funding is then allocated through the Poverty Reduction and Growth Facility (PRGF), the IMF's low-interest lending facility for low-income countries.

Evidence suggests that the poorest HIPC-eligible countries are, for the first time in decades, spending more on social services than on debt service. Critics argued that the reduction of approximately two-thirds of outstanding debt didn't go far enough—there should instead be 100 percent cancellation. Others suggested that

Table 4.10. Latin American Economies by Income Group and Indebtedness, 2003

Income and Debt Classification	Severely Indebted PV of Debt/XGS >220% or PV Debt/GNP >80%	Moderately Indebted PV of Debt/XGS >132% and <220% or PV Debt/GNP >132% and <80%	Less Indebted PV of Debt/XGS <132% or PV Debt/GNP <48%
Low income: pc GNP <$765			Haiti, Nicaragua
Lower middle income: pc GNP $766–$3,035	Brazil, Ecuador, Peru	Bolivia, Colombia, El Salvador, Honduras, Paraguay	Dominican Republic, Guatemala
Upper middle income: pc GNP $3,036–$9,385	Argentina, Belize, Panama, Uruguay	Chile, Venezuela	Costa Rica, Mexico

Source: Extracted from The World Bank, *Global Development Finance 2005,* statistical appendix, table A50.
Note: PV is the present value of debt which is the sum of all future debt service obligations (interest and principal) on existing debt discovered by the market interest rate.

the definition of sustainable debt levels is sensitive to the volatile external market shocks that poor countries face. For example, sustainable debt to export ratios can quickly become burdensome if foreign markets dry up. The calculation is also cumbersome; the World Bank's online handbook to advise countries on document presentation runs more than one thousand pages. The fear that relief was too slow and not substantial enough to alleviate the current misery of the poor also motivates opposition to HIPC.[14] Critics also pointed to inadequacies in the consultative process with civil society. Authentic participation takes time to develop—time that may not be consistent with the timetables of the IMF.[15] Some believe that HIPC is a good step, but only a baby step given the desperate lives of those living on less than $1 a day.

In Latin America four countries qualified for HIPC: Bolivia, Guyana, Nicaragua, and Honduras. Bolivia, in 1998 the first country in the world to reach the so-called completion point—the successful completion of negotiations over progress indicators—received nearly $2 billion in debt relief, reducing its external debt by half. Debt service as a percent of exports fell from 23 to 16 percent, releasing funds for poverty programs.[16] Guyana, Nicaragua, and Honduras qualified in 1998, 2004, and 2005, respectively. Table 4.11 provides a summary of the measures Nicaragua implemented to achieve the completion point debt relief. In 1999, Nicaragua's debt-to-exports ratio was 540 percent; debt relief of $3.267 billion was achieved by 2004, despite adverse economic circumstances in the country. Additional support in the amount of $129 million from 2002–2005 under the PRGF was allocated by the IMF to promote poverty-reducing growth. Budgetary savings from debt relief led to a $165 million increase (approximately 4 percent of GDP) in spending on poverty programs in 2002–2003, with a focus on education, health, water, housing, and protection for vulnerable groups. Debt to exports fell to 161 percent—a significant decline, but still about the 150 percent benchmark commonly accepted as manageable.[17]

But debt relief was not enough to alleviate the burden that remaining debt

Table 4.11.   Nicaragua's Measures to Reach the Completion Point under the HIPC

Poverty reduction	Prepare a fully participatory poverty reducation strategy paper and implement it for one year Use interim savings from HIPC to implement the PRSP
Macroeconomic stability	Maintain stable macro frameworks and performance under PRGF
Human capital & social protection	Approve school autonomy law encouraging parental participation Approve health regulatory changes to grant autonomy to hospitals and local health systems Adopt action plan to introduce social protection
Strengthen governance	Implement a civil service law to reduce political interference in hiring/firing Introduce sound management of public sector procurement Strengthen the comptroller's office Legal reform and training programs for penal procedures
Pension reform	Create supervisory authority for pension funds with adequate staff; restructure social security administration
Privatization	Divest ENITEL Electricity generating units of ENEL

Source: IMF.org.

repayment placed on social spending and poverty reduction. As a result of a social movement begun in 1995, and propelled by the Jubilee coalition, in 2005 the G-8 nations—the world's industrialized nation group—agreed to 100 percent cancellation of the debt of HIPC countries that is owed to the IMF, the World Bank, and the African Development Fund under the Multilateral Debt Relief Initiative. The four HIPC Latin American countries qualify (Bolivia, Honduras, Nicaragua, and Guyana), taking part in the overall $55 billion debt relief. HIPC has established a track record for the reallocation of resources from debt service to investments in social capital. Relief for countries where per capita income is less than $380 will come from gold sales by the IMF; financing for countries where average income is over the $380 threshold will come from bilateral contributions to the PRGF. This has been questioned by some proponents of full reduction who worry that debt relief should provide additional resources for development. Under this program—which at present includes adhering to the conditionality of the HIPC process—Nicaragua, for example, expects to receive $1.01 billion in additional debt relief. It is not clear, however, that the job of debt relief is complete. Countries that did not qualify for HIPC such as Peru or Brazil but still fight persistent extreme poverty under the burden of debt payments remain pressured by their financial liabilities.

LESSONS OF THE DEBT CRISIS

What are the lessons of the debt crisis? The most salient and the most painful lesson is that strong fundamentals matter. Unlike the populist policies of the past, countries must attend to price stability and budget constraints. Responsible fiscal policy—keeping the domestic house in order—has clear effects on a country's external balance. This is perhaps more important today in highly integrated capital markets. Information travels quickly, and negative performance on critical indicators carries a high price. Maintaining the confidence of the market is a vital ingredient for success. Without credible and predictable policies, capital will quickly respond to uncertainty by fleeing to less risky instruments. Politics and market psychology are intertwined with sound economic policy.

But generating the necessary macroeconomic stability in the region was no easy task. In the 1980s and early 1990s, several countries in the region had annual inflation rates exceeding 1,000 percent. In the next chapter we will consider how governments in Latin America took on the inflation problem. Tied to the ability to restrain inflation has been a reengineering of the role of government. In contrast to the central role of the state under ISI, Latin American governments had to redefine the boundaries between the public and the private sectors. We will consider this revolution in political and economic space in chapter 6. The transformation of the inward-oriented model to an export-driven growth strategy has engendered strategic changes in the behavior of firms and states in the region. This will be discussed in chapter 8. These radical changes in the rules and goals of the economy in Latin America have not been without cost. Poverty rose throughout the region, and the environment suffered from the natural resource export drives—the subject of chapters 10 and 14. As we explore these issues, we will see that the resolution of the debt crisis fundamentally transformed the development model in the region.

Key Concepts

absorption	debt trap	provisioning
capital flight	economic populism	secondary market
conditionality	HIPC	seignorage
debt-for-equity swaps	illiquidity	sovereign guarantee
debt-for-nature swaps	involuntary lending	structural adjustment
debt sustainability		

Chapter   Summary

The Accumulation of Debt

- The debt crisis was a natural consequence of spending practices in the 1950s, 1960s, and 1970s. Careless borrowing for large-scale projects with high capital requirements was partly responsible for the accumulation of debt in Latin America. Many of these multiyear investments, with unpredictable returns, led to a debt trap. Economic populism, inefficiency, and corruption contributed to further unnecessary and extravagant fiscal spending financed through more loans.
- Negative real interest rates and the influx of petrodollars into the banking system made borrowing attractive and easy during the 1970s. In real terms, countries had to pay back less than what they borrowed and had seemingly unlimited funds.
- As evidenced by the cases of Mexico, Brazil, and Argentina, not every Latin American country pursued the same policies. The end result of accumulated debts, however, was the same.

On the Road to Crisis

- In 1979 the Federal Reserve Bank of the United States raised interest rates. The effects were detrimental for Latin America. While countries' interest payments for past loans increased, the U.S. market for Latin American exports fell, effectively limiting the foreign exchange needed to repay loans.
- The excess supply of local currency fueled inflation. Locals deposited their money abroad in hopes of higher returns, and capital flight ensued. Governments' ability to raise revenues was therefore greatly weakened.
- Mexico's inability and unwillingness to pay its debt signaled to the international community that the economies of Latin America were on the verge of crisis.

Responses to the Debt Crisis

- Under the assumption that Latin American countries needed to reduce domestic absorption, the IMF prescribed a decrease in fiscal spending, tight monetary policy, and strict trade policies. What has become known as IMF conditionality spurred criticism from various circles, including the structuralist school, for unnecessarily contracting the economy without addressing its structural problems.
- In response to the crisis, a secondary market for debt developed. The secondary market was used to facilitate debt-for-equity and debt-for-nature swaps.
- The Baker plan was "too little, too late," representing a shift away from IMF

conditionality. A new role was given to the World Bank, focusing on structural adjustment.
- The Brady plan decreased the face value of debt, extended the time period of obligations, or infused new money.

After the Crisis

- The return of international capital to Latin America, the shift toward domestic markets for financing, and an increase in the degree of trust in domestic currencies are signs of an increase in the maturity of Latin American markets.
- The HIPC initiative links debt reduction for the poorest countries with poverty alleviation measures.
- Debt sustainability: Under the enhanced HIPC initiative debt burden thresholds were adjusted downward, enabling a broader group of countries to qualify for debt relief.

Notes

1. Federico A. Sturzenegger, "Description of a Populist Experience: Argentina, 1973–1976," in *The Macroeconomics of Populism in Latin America,* ed. Rudiger Dornbusch and Sebastian Edwards (Chicago: University of Chicago Press, 1991), 79.

2. John T. Cuddington, *Capital Flight: Estimates, Issues, and Explanations,* Princeton Studies in International Finance, No. 58 (Princeton, N.J.: Princeton University Press, 1986), 10.

3. Sebastian Edwards, *Crisis and Reform in Latin America: From Despair to Hope* (New York: Oxford University Press, 1995), 17.

4. Patricio Meller, "IMF and World Bank Roles in the Latin American Foreign Debt Problem," in *The Latin American Development Debate: Neostructuralism, Neomonetarism, and Adjustment Processes,* ed. Patricio Meller (Boulder, Colo.: Westview, 1991).

5. "'Til Debt Do Us Part," *The Economist,* 28 February 1987, 85.

6. Irma Arriagada, "Unequal Participation by Women in the Working World," *CEPAL Review* 40 (April 1990): 83–98.

7. Helena Hirata and John Humphrey, "Workers' Response to Job Loss: Female and Male Industrial Workers in Brazil," *World Development* 19(6) (1991): 671–682.

8. Frances Stewart, *Adjustment and Poverty: Options and Choices* (London: Routledge, 1995), 189. Stewart summarizes results of studies published in the late 1980s.

9. U.S. Department of State, *1996 Country Reports on Economic Policy and Trade Practices,* a report submitted to the Senate Committee on Foreign Relations, the Senate Committee on Finance, the House Committee on Foreign Affairs, and the House Committee on Ways and Means, January 1997 (available at www.state.gov/www/issues/tradereports/latinamerica99/costarica96.html).

10. Edwards, *Crisis and Reform,* table 4.3.

11. Ibid., 81.

12. "Brazil: Domestic Debt Dynamics and Implications," *ING Barings Emerging Markets Weekly Report,* March 5, 1999, 1–3.

13. Statement of U.S. Treasury secretary Lawrence H. Summers at the Joint Session of the International Monetary and Finance Committee and the Development Committee, Prague, Czech Republic, September 24, 2000, www.imf.org.

14. Drop the Debt, "HIPC Initiative Offers No Guarantee against Future Debt Problems," www.dropthedebt.org.

15. Dijkstra presents a comprehensive and thoughtful analysis of the weakness in the process. Geske Dijkstra, "The PRSP Approach and the Illusion of Improved Aid Effectiveness: Lessons from Bolivia, Honduras and Nicaragua," *Development Policy Review* 23(4) (2005): 443–464.

16. World Bank News Release 2001/369/S, "Bolivia: World Bank and IMF Support US$1.2 Billion in Additional Debt Service Relief for Bolivia under Enhanced HIPC Initiative," www.worldbank.org. See also "Debt—Undermining Development," www.globalissues.org and www.oxfam.org.

17. "Completion Point under the Heavily Indebted Poor Countries Initiative," *Inter-American Development Bank* 8 (March 2004).

CHAPTER FIVE

MACROECONOMIC STABILIZATION

A Critical Ingredient for Sustained Growth

The debt crisis contributed to the lost decade of development in Latin America. *(Courtesy of Amanda McKown)*

Inflation plagued Latin American economies from the 1980s through the first part of the 1990s. Imagine the difficulty—as was experienced in Argentina, Brazil, Nicaragua, and Peru—of living with inflation rates exceeding 2,000 percent per year! These were not isolated exceptions; as we can see in table 5.1, only Costa Rica, Panama, and Bolivia had rates under 20 percent in 1990, and as we will see, Bolivia paid a huge social price to achieve this ratio and tame inflation in the mid-1980s.

Inflation exacts a high cost. Real wages—earnings after the inflationary bite—fall, reducing purchasing power. Inflation hits the poor particularly hard; the wealthy can insulate themselves through financial mechanisms indexed to the inflation rate. Macroeconomic instability creates uncertainty and undermines the investment climate. Inflation compromises the business environment, complicating long-run decision making. It erodes tax earnings and reduces the ability of the government to provide public services. It promotes consumption today, reduces savings, and creates environmental pressure. Inflation hurts nearly all economic actors.

Despite these costs, excessive inflation persisted in Latin America for nearly fifteen years. Our discussion in this chapter revolves around several questions:

- Why was Latin America so inflation prone?
- What caused inflationary pressures in the region?
- Why was inflation so intractable?

Table 5.1.   Inflation of Latin American Countries, 1990

Country	Hyper (>2000%)	High (>30%)	Medium (>20%)	Low (<20%)
Nicaragua	7,485.0			
Peru	7,481.5			
Brazil	2,937.0			
Argentina	2,313.7			
Uruguay		112.5		
Guyana		63.6		
Ecuador		48.5		
Guatemala		41.2		
Venezuela		40.6		
Paraguay		38.2		
Colombia			29.1	
Mexico			26.6	
Chile			26.0	
El Salvador			24.0	
Honduras			23.3	
Suriname			21.7	
Costa Rica				19.0
Bolivia				17.1
Panama				0.8

Source: IADB, *Economic and Social Progress in Latin America* (Washington, D.C.: Johns Hopkins University Press, various years); and IMF, *World Economic Outlook 1997* (Washington, D.C.: IMF, 1997), 148.

- What mechanisms were used to bring inflation under control in the region?
- What worked?
- Is inflation in Latin America now gone for good?

Latin America has been a virtual laboratory for macroeconomic experiments. This chapter will address these issues of macroeconomic stabilization, underscoring the causes and costs of inflation and highlighting the measures used to address it. It will look at the range of policies introduced to provide some insight on the difficult problem of maintaining stable prices while an economy is going through the complex and sometimes tumultuous process of economic growth.

Theories of Inflation: Monetarists versus Structuralists

Policies to attack inflation rest on an understanding of inflation's causes. Two broad schools of thought address the problem: the monetarists and the structuralists. For monetarists, or orthodox theorists, the cause of inflation is rather simple: too much money chasing too few goods. Monetarists such as Milton Friedman and the Chicago School look to the equation of exchange as a key to the cause of inflation. With M representing the quantity of money, V equal to the velocity or the number of times per year a unit of currency is used to purchase final goods and services, P as the price level, and Q standing for national output or gross domestic product (GDP) in real terms, monetarists argue that

$$M \times V = P \times Q$$

If the rate of growth of output and velocity are assumed to be constant in the short run, prices are determined by the quantity of money in circulation. A rising level of money in circulation causes price acceleration. Although in the short run resource price shocks or shortages may accelerate prices temporarily, monetarists perceive that inflation over time is caused by excess liquidity in the system. Understanding persistent inflation for the monetarist involves highlighting why monetary authorities would continue to make policy errors by increasing the money supply in the face of rising prices. Monetarist explanations for such excess in Latin America include irresponsible deficit financing, erosion of the tax base, and mismanagement of the debt crisis. Let's consider these in turn.

Deficit Financing

If a government is spending more than it is taking in, the deficit must be financed. This can be done in three ways: print money, issue domestic debt, or borrow from foreign sources. As John Maynard Keynes pointed out in 1923, a government can live for a long time by printing money.[1] A government's ability to buy goods and services by printing money is called **seignorage.** Indeed, if the economy is growing at a strong pace, the quantity of goods and services available increases and the price effect may be moderate. However, once growth slows down, there is too much money chasing too few goods. Deficits in Latin America imply different dynamics than in the United States. The U.S. dollar is the world's most important reserve currency. If the Federal Reserve issues more dollars—and if the world continues its appetite for dollars as a safe investment—investors throughout the world absorb the dollars and reinvest in America's sophisticated capital markets. If the Bank of Mexico emits pesos, a strong international demand is far less likely. The value of the peso erodes, confidence vanishes, and a crisis erupts. There may come a time when the demand for dollars weakens sufficiently to present binding constraints. For now it is enough to appreciate that tough budget problems in Latin America resolved by printing money are more likely to result in inflation and balance of payments crises.

The alternative to printing money is issuing debt to finance government spending. Governments are often precluded from issuing domestic debt—the equivalent of a U.S. Treasury bond—by underdeveloped local capital markets. If the public cannot be induced to hold bonds, a government must borrow externally or print money. When the debt crisis hit Latin America in the early 1980s, the external borrowing option dried up, and the simplest response to deficits was to monetize them.

We can observe the pattern of macroeconomic instability in Latin America up to the 1990s in tables 5.2, 5.3, and 5.4. In table 5.2, we note the trend of strong

Table 5.2.   Overall Fiscal Surplus or Deficit in Latin American Countries, 1982–1990 (percentage of GDP)

Country	1982	1983	1984	1985	1986	1987	1988	1989	1990
Argentina	−3.7	−10.1	−5.7	−2.9	−3.2	−4.4	−3.8	−2.6	−1.7
Bolivia	−13.7	−17	−18.3	−9.3	−1.7	−3.7	−5	−2	−1.3
Brazil	−3.1	−4.3	−5	−11.1	−14	−12.6	−16.3	−17.5	−6.2
Chile	−2.6	−3.7	−3	−1.9	−0.5	2.3	3.6	5.0	1.4
Colombia	−2	−1	−4.3	−2.7	−1.3	−0.5	−1.4	−1.7	−0.1
Costa Rica	−3.2	−3.4	−3.1	−2	−3.3	−2	−2.5	−4.1	−4.4
Ecuador	−4.4	−3	−0.6	1.9	−2.2	−6.2	−2	0.4	3.5
El Salvador	−5.9	−4.1	−3.2	−2	−3.6	−0.9	−3	−3.7	−1.5
Guatemala	−4.7	−3.6	−3.7	−1.8	−1.5	−1.3	−1.7	−2.9	−1.8
Guyana	−34.3	−40.1	−44.5	−56.1	−58.8	−42.4	−31.6	−6.6	−22.9
Honduras	−9.7	−9	−9.8	−7.2	−6	−5.8	−4.1	−6	−4.1
Mexico	−11.9	−8.2	−7.2	−7.6	−13.1	−14.2	−9.7	−5	−2.8
Nicaragua	−13.3	−30	−22.5	−21.3	−14.5	−16	−25.1	−3.5	−18.7
Panama	−11.4	−6.2	−7.4	−3.4	−4.5	−4.2	−5.2	−6.9	6.8
Paraguay	−1.5	−4.7	−3.5	−2.3	0.0	0.4	0.6	2.4	3.2
Peru	−3.1	−7.3	−4.4	−3	−4.3	−6.9	−3.9	−6.3	−3.5
Suriname	−1.7	−17.6	−18.4	−21.4	−26	−24.8	−21.3	−14	−6.3
Uruguay	—	−4.2	−5.8	−3.1	−1.3	−1.3	−2	−3.4	−0.1
Venezuela	−2.1	−0.6	2.8	2.0	−0.4	−1.6	−7.4	−1	−2.1

Source: IADB, *Economic and Social Progress in Latin America* (Washington, D.C.: Johns Hopkins University Press, various years).

Table 5.3.   Average Annual Rates of Growth of Money Supply in Latin America, 1982–1990

Country	1982	1983	1984	1985	1986	1987	1988	1989	1990
Argentina	154.2	362.0	582.3	584.3	89.7	113.5	351.4	4,168.2	1,023.2
Bolivia	228.8	207.0	1,798.3	5,784.6	86.1	36.6	35.3	2.4	39.5
Brazil	68.5	102.7	204.1	334.3	330.1	215.4	426.9	1,337.0	2,333.6
Chile	2.8	15.6	22.8	24.2	43.3	21.0	46.5	17.2	23.3
Colombia	25.4	23.4	24.1	10.7	—	—	25.7	—	—
Costa Rica	70.3	38.9	17.6	7.7	31.0	0.3	53.2	–2	3.9
Ecuador	14.0	31.9	39.6	25.6	20.1	34.7	52.7	43.8	59.0
El Salvador	3.7	–1.3	13.8	27.0	19.1	–0.4	8.1	13.5	22.3
Guatemala	1.4	6.0	4.3	54.9	19.5	9.8	14.4	20.7	33.0
Guyana	25.3	17.4	20.2	20.3	19.4	51.4	54.8	34.0	54.5
Honduras	13.5	13.6	2.5	–3.2	8.2	26.6	11.9	20.0	23.6
Mexico	62.6	40.3	60.0	49.5	67.2	118.1	67.8	37.3	63.1
Nicaragua	25.7	67.1	83.5	162.8	252.2	637.0	11,673.4	2,368.3	6,286.7
Panama	5.4	–1.8	2.2	7.5	9.8	–1.6	–31.3	1.0	41.0
Paraguay	–3.6	25.6	29.4	28.0	26.7	53.6	34.8	31.7	28.3
Peru	40.4	96.5	104.4	281.2	88.0	122.0	515.0	1,654.9	6,710.0
Suriname	17.7	8.0	26.9	52.5	39.6	27.1	24.5	11.3	4.0
Uruguay	19.8	9.0	48.4	107.6	86.1	58.1	63.7	72.9	101.0
Venezuela	4.5	25.0	27.0	8.9	5.3	40.8	22.7	22.2	54.6

Source: IMF, *International Financial Statistics 1996* (Washington, D.C.: IMF, 1996), 81.

and persistent fiscal deficits throughout the region from 1982 to 1990. Only two countries—Chile and Paraguay—had surpluses nearly as often as deficits. Brazil's consistent deficit averaged 10 percent of GDP over the period. Although we should be careful not to overinfer about the cause of the growth of the money supply, indeed we can see that in the countries with strong and persistent deficits, the average annual

Table 5.4.   National Interest Rates in Latin America (central bank discount rates, end of period in percent per annum)

Country	1982	1983	1984	1985	1986	1987	1988	1989	1990
Brazil	174.0	194.0	272.0	380.0	89.0	401.0	2,282.0	38,341.0	1,083.0
Colombia	27.0	27.0	27.0	27.0	33.8	34.8	34.3	36.9	46.5
Costa Rica	30.0	30.0	28.0	28.0	27.5	31.4	31.5	31.6	37.8
Ecuador	15.0	19.0	23.0	23.0	23.0	23.0	23.0	32.0	35.0
Guatemala	9.0	9.0	9.0	9.0	9.0	9.0	9.0	13.0	18.5
Guyana	14.0	14.0	14.0	14.0	14.0	14.0	14.0	35.0	30.0
Honduras	24.0	24.0	24.0	24.0	24.0	24.0	24.0	24.0	28.2
Nicaragua	—	—	—	—	—	—	12,874.6	311.0	10.0
Paraguay	—	—	—	—	—	—	10.0	21.0	30.0
Peru	44.5	60.0	60.0	42.6	36.1	29.8	748.0	865.6	289.6
Uruguay	83.7	112.7	133.2	145.1	138.4	143.4	154.5	219.6	251.6
Venezuela	13.0	11.0	11.0	8.0	8.0	8.0	8.0	45.0	43.0

Source: IMF, *International Financial Statistics 1996* (Washington, D.C.: IMF, 1996), 96.

rates of growth of the money supply are startling. In Brazil, Argentina, Nicaragua, and Peru, the rate of growth of the money supply exceeded 1,000 percent in 1990. In an attempt to raise money internally to finance deficits as well as to stem capital flight, national interest rates in 1990 exceeded 1,000 percent in Brazil and were above 30 percent in eight countries. But this was something of a losing battle. Although these interest rates were necessary to attract money for debt servicing, they also made borrowing for business investment problematic. The result was simultaneous inflation and recession.

Inflammatory financing of the fiscal deficit creates a vicious circle. Persistent inflation lowers the cash balances that people want to hold, because the value of the currency is declining quickly. People prefer to purchase goods to retain the value of their earnings, driving up prices in the market. Inflation therefore begets inflation. A second perverse effect has also been identified. Whereas deficit spending in most industrial countries is countercyclical, in Latin America it has largely been procyclical. That is, instead of spending to stimulate the economy during a recession, Latin American governments tend to contract during recession. This is tied to access to funds. As recession erodes the government's ability to raise money in international markets, it must reign in spending. Unfortunately, such procyclical policies, by their very nature, exacerbate macroeconomic volatility.[2]

The Tax Connection

If a government has lost credibility or if its population is very poor, tax collection as a percentage of government expenses is very low. Furthermore, as inflation rises, the real value of tax collection falls. Taxes for 1986 are due in 1987; because they are paid in 1987 dollars, they are worth less after inflation. The phenomenon by which inflation eats away at the value of tax receipts is called the **Olivera-Tanzi effect.** An extreme case was Bolivia, where by 1984 only 2 percent of government expenditure was covered by taxes.[3] More printed money was therefore needed to cover the deficits. Inflation, as a result, exceeded 8,000 percent. We will return to the problem of taxation in the region in chapter 6.

Effects of the Debt Crisis

As access to foreign loans dried up, there was more pressure to raise money domestically to service existing debt. This left printing money as the most popular action to purchase the foreign exchange to make the interest payments on debt. This was the case in Argentina after 1982.[4] Furthermore, the devaluation often required in International Monetary Fund (IMF) stabilization packages increased the value of the external debt in domestic terms. That is, as the currency became worth less, it took more of it to buy the dollars to service the external debt. This increased the temptation to print money to service the debt. Running up a down escalator may be a good metaphor for this type of policy.

Is Inflation Too Much Money?

At the center of the monetarist explanations for inflationary financing were profligate governments running budget deficits. The monetarist solution to restrain inflation in the region was therefore quite straightforward: decrease government spending. If the monetarists are right and inflation is tied to excessive government spending, the solution is clear: eliminate deficit-driven policies. Yet this was easier said than done. Deficit reduction proved politically tough.

Why do governments run large fiscal deficits despite the inflationary risks associated with them? The research in this area indicates that countries with less stable political systems are more likely to engage in deficit financing. As political instability increases, politicians see it in their own interest to buy political favor and to avoid making hard choices.[5] Politically threatened governments find it difficult to carry through on promises of fiscal responsibility. Political change can therefore make economic stabilization more problematic. Clearly this plays out in cases such as Peru or Nicaragua. Political change from an authoritarian government to a democracy was taking place over this period for countries such as Brazil and Argentina. Instability likely played a role in the capacity of states to follow sound economic programs.

In contrast to these monetarist explanations, for the **structuralists** the explanation of deficit-led instability was too simple. Structuralists do not deny that excess liquidity or budget deficits can cause inflation, but they do not believe that these are the sole or even central causes of inflation in Latin America. Attention to monetary variables is complemented by the study of a host of other factors. Because structuralists add other factors to the orthodox focus on the money supply, their policy is sometimes called **heterodox.** Structuralist or heterodox explanations focus on the structure of the underdeveloped economy as the propagating mechanism for inflation. Instead of making the equilibrium assumptions of the classical model upon which the monetarist theory is based, structuralists contend that economies in Latin America can best be understood as incomplete markets that do not automatically tend toward full employment equilibrium. For the structuralists, bottlenecks in both the agricultural and the industrial sectors create price pressures. If input markets cannot quickly adjust to price signals to meet supply requirements, inflation will result. External price shocks from the international economy can also introduce or exacerbate instability in the domestic market.

Cost-Push Elements

Cost-push elements were therefore central to the structuralist explanation. Internal shortages and external price shocks such as the oil crisis interact with the structure of industry and labor organization to fuel an inflationary struggle. In contrast to the perfect competition assumption in neoclassical models, both output and labor markets in Latin America are highly concentrated. Under oligopolistic conditions, prices are sticky downward. Shortages ratchet up prices, but during periods of slack demand or recession, prices rarely fall. Furthermore, firms may engage in markup pricing to maintain profit margins. Large firms often have internal sources of capital as well, circumventing the need to pay high interest rates for money. When prices increase, powerful labor unions demand wage increases—which firms are able to cover because they pass the cost on to the consumer. Inflation then reflects the distributive conflict between capital and labor. If all agents assume inflation, each side wants to build predicted price increases into its share of the pie.

Monetary authorities may passively accommodate the demand for money. Central banks in the region were often not independent of the executive branch and were therefore subject to political pressure. In Brazil the central bank was ordered by the military government to finance the public deficit automatically from 1971 to 1974; from 1974 until 1994, the politically dependent minister of finance had overwhelming control of the central bank. In 1994 Brazil finally formed a National Monetary Council as a supervisory and coordination organ for money policy, accountable not only to the presidency but also to Congress.[6] For the structuralists, underdeveloped political systems, the lack of accountability of military governments, and later nascent democracies unable to handle competing demands contributed to inflationary tendencies.

In the structuralist model, inflation becomes embedded in the economy. People begin to anticipate inflation. Such **inertial inflation** results when economic agents come to expect inflation and automatically adjust for it in their wage demands and pricing patterns. Not surprisingly, expected inflation is a self-fulfilling prophecy as people adjust behaviors accordingly. However, for the structuralist, inflation was an unwelcome but not unexpected result of the conflicts inherent in the process of economic development. Since markets in developing countries had unique characteristics that did not favor equilibrium, the recessionary costs of forcing austerity under these circumstances were just too high. Structuralists were willing to live with inflation as a price associated with growth in the developing world. The policy challenge became reducing the costs of living in an inflationary society.

PERPETUATING INFLATION: INDEXATION, INFLATIONARY EXPECTATIONS, AND VELOCITY

In the 1980s structuralist thought dominated much policy making in the Latin American region. Given that inflation was seen as a function of the structure of the economy, measures were introduced to minimize the costs of inflation. Most wages were indexed to a public minimum salary that was adjusted monthly to accommodate inflation. A teacher's contract might, for example, be written for seven times the national minimum wage. As the minimum wage rose each month, salaries tracked inflation. Some prices were also indexed to inflation. If you got into a taxi in Rio de Janeiro, you would not pay the price on the meter. Rather, the meter reflected a price on a *tabela,* or list of prices, that could be adjusted by decree. In stores, clothing was tagged with letters of the alphabet. Although K might mean a Cr$50 dress one day, a week later a buyer might have to come up with Cr$65. Interest on bank accounts was also indexed. Checking accounts were interest bearing (similar to U.S. NOW accounts), and borrowers had to pay the real rate of interest plus inflation. Rents were likewise increased alongside interest and bond rates through this inflation adjustment, sometimes euphemistically called the "monetary correction."

In some periods the official rate of **indexation** was set at less than the rate of inflation to act as a brake against future inflation. But people quickly figured this out, and they took it into account in setting wage demands and prices. Ironically, although indexation was introduced as a defense against inflation, it made the transfer of inflation from the present to the future automatic, even when the government tried to manipulate expectations by lowering the percentage adjustment for inflation. Because it was built into the system, people came to expect it. Indexing made inflation easier to live with while inadvertently reinforcing its place in the economy.

Vicious Circles

Although indexation was designed to mitigate the costs of inflation, it created unintended inflationary side effects. **Inflationary expectations** became ingrained in the culture. People expected inflation, the government accommodated inflation, and the public got inflation. Inflation today was equal to inflation in the past period plus additional demand pressures and the effects of any supply shocks. As inflation accelerated, it made tax collection less efficient, pressuring fiscal balances and often leading to a further increase in the money supply. Inflation complicated exchange rate management. If the exchange rate was fixed, the erosion of the value of domestic money made it worth less relative to international or hard currencies. If the fixed rate was not adjusted, the currency was posted at an overvalued rate, creating a bias against exports. If the rate was devalued or if the currency was allowed to float freely, the higher prices of imported goods introduced additional inflationary pressures in the economy. To account for inflation and risk, nominal interest rates were high, often retarding investment.

The **velocity of money** changed in response to economic agents learning to live with inflation. A review of velocity will help illuminate this problem. Velocity is the number of times money turns over in a system each year. If the payment for a dinner to a restaurant owner is quickly used to purchase linens for a beach house, and those receipts are rapidly used (in concert with other receipts) by the curtain maker to buy a new sewing machine, and that revenue in turn is immediately used to pay workers, a given physical quantity of money is supporting the purchase of many goods. Velocity is a measure of how much output is supported by the stock of money, or GDP divided by the money supply (M). If velocity is increasing—that is, if a decreasing stock of money supports a given amount of output—increasing that stock of money without changing the productive capability of the economy will result in inflationary pressures.

In an inflationary economy, people have the incentive to transform their rapidly worthless currency into goods. If a worker in Brazil waited until the end of the month to buy groceries or other goods from a monthly paycheck, in 1990 prices would have risen by approximately 70 percent by the month's end, leaving 70 percent less in the grocery basket. It made good sense to buy quickly. Of course, the shortages that the "buy now" behavior created further increased prices.

The banking system may respond to the pressure to turn money over quickly, further increasing velocity. If you deposit a check and it takes three days to clear, you may not use that money for three days without bouncing another check. However, if your checks clear instantaneously, it is time to go shopping again! A higher velocity will support the purchase of more goods and services per dollar. Once a system has adapted to a higher velocity rate, modest increases in the money supply will have a stronger expansionary effect. If supply constraints prevent the rapid provision of goods and services in response to the increase in the money base, inflation will be ignited.

The velocity numbers are dramatic in the Brazilian case. During an inflationary period the velocity of money in Brazil was an astounding 125, compared to 16 in the United States. The highly efficient system of interest-bearing transactions balances allowed money holders to escape from the direct use of currency through something similar to checkable money market funds. The Brazilian money supply therefore supported a higher volume of goods and services per dollar than that in the United States. Changes in the money supply would be magnified in inflation rates.

How Much Inflation Is Too Much?
Timing and Adjustment Problems

The monetarist versus structuralist policy debate in part boils down to a decision as to how much macroeconomic imbalance is tolerable in the medium term. Monetarists argue that imbalances should be swiftly redressed. Excesses in external accounts or in fiscal deficits should not be tolerated because they will quickly aggravate inflation. Structuralists contend that it is not that simple. Given the underdeveloped nature of markets in the developing world, they expect imbalances in domestic accounts or in external spending. Harsh and rapid adjustment, for the structuralist, is too high a price. Rapid reductions in the money supply to reduce domestic absorption might also have the effect of strangling long-term growth.

Monetarists and structuralists also had different views of the degrees of freedom of countries in their abilities to isolate themselves from the effects of the "inconsistent trinity" or the "trilemma." Recall that most Latin American countries in this period adhered to a fixed exchange rate system. Policymakers face inevitable tensions in balancing goals of domestic monetary policy, fixed exchange rates, and capital mobility.[7] A country cannot have all three. Under a fixed exchange rate regime, if international capital is mobile and governments accept the rules of the game—that is, that a current account deficit will result in a decrease in money supply—autonomy in domestic monetary policy is forfeited. If a fixed exchange rate is maintained to preserve an international price anchor, capital controls and sterilization may give temporary relief, but exchange rate crises will certainly erupt if adjustment is incomplete. Governments might be tempted to pump up the money supply, but this will result in ballooning trade deficits. If nations want to pursue monetary autonomy they can certainly abandon the fixed rate and let the exchange

---

BOX 5.1.   MACROECONOMIC POLICY TRILEMMA

Tool	Objective	Conflict
Domestic monetary autonomy	Activist monetary policy to shorten recessions and restrain inflation	Under fixed exchange rate "rules of the game" (deficit requires decrease in the money supply) weaken independent monetary policy; if domestic capital is not also mobile, central bank can perform offsetting domestic interventions (sterilization)
Fixed exchange rate	Price anchor—tie exchange rate to a firm anchor and force real adjustment	Lose monetary independence; could float exchange rate but lose price anchor; if capital is immobile, can create different domestic prices for money
Capital mobility	Encourage international investment; buoy confidence	Interest rates must be equal to international rates plus inflation; lose interest rate wedge in monetary policy; could float, but lose inflation anchor

---

price float, but without high credibility in international markets this is likely to introduce an inflationary bias into the economy. Unless markets believe that the government is pursuing a stable monetary policy, the expected depreciation of the currency will raise import prices and foment inflation. Facing this trilemma, monetarists largely counseled abandoning domestic monetary policy and linking to a hard international currency; structuralists suggested exchange controls to preserve domestic autonomy. Rather than forfeit autonomous monetary policy or the exchange anchor, structuralists preferred to restrain capital mobility. Box 5.1 summarizes this trilemma of open economies. It is worth recalling that such capital controls were before the days when globalization and liberalized markets were the trademarks of sound policy.

How did stablization policies play out in practice in Latin America? Drawing on elements of both schools, Latin American nations adopted a variety of approaches to macroeconomic stabilization. The fixed versus floating rate constraint was softened somewhat in practice by using intermediate exchange rate solutions such as crawling pegs or exchange rate target zones and other forms of managed exchange rate regimes. In these cases a target is set—either pegged to a hard currency such as the dollar or set within a range, with a ceiling and a floor between which it can fluctuate. Depending on pressures on the currency, the monetary authority intervened by buying or selling to stabilize the currency but was not bound to defend a fixed price. This kind of flexibility accounted for the fact that inflation in developing countries is generally higher than in the industrial world.

Flexibility in exchange rate policy promotes competitiveness in international markets. However, if the central bank lacks credibility, inflation will resurge. The tradeoff between credibility and competitiveness has shaped exchange rate policy in Latin America as countries struggle to produce stable growth fueled by export engines.[8] Table 5.5 illustrates the pros and cons of a fixed versus a flexible rate. In the late 1980s and early 1990s, raging, uncontrollable inflation led many countries to pursue **exchange rate-based stabilization programs.** By tying a country's currency to another, stable international currency, countries tied their own hands and their own ability to pursue independent monetary policies. Some suggest that these programs were a necessary medicine to create the conditions for price stability.[9] However, once stabilization of the exchange rate and prices was achieved, new problems emerged. Linking a currency to another—either through a hard link such as dollarization or a softer approach in a firm fix—means that real prices must adjust. That is, if a country is less productive than its anchor partner, real prices must actually fall to make that country's goods competitive on international markets. If prices don't adjust, the fixed exchange rate becomes overvalued and a target for financial runs. Exchange rate crises in the late 1990s led to an increasing preference for floating systems in the first decade of the twenty-first century.

Table 5.6 shows the choices of monetary frameworks and exchange rate regimes in 2005. Some countries retain an exchange rate anchor to monetary policy. Whether they have dollarized such as El Salvador and Ecuador or require central bank intervention to maintain a fixed or crawling peg as in Venezuela or Costa Rica, the anchor provides a foundation for price stability. Domestic monetary autonomy is sacrificed, and competitiveness must be achieved through real changes in the economy. You will notice, however, that the countries pursuing an exchange rate anchor tend to be smaller countries with strong bilateral trade with the United States. Venezuela is an exception in this respect, but recall that internationally, petroleum sales are largely priced in dollars, hence the need for a strong dollar link. Under the pressure of currency crises in the late 1990s, several countries have abandoned exchange rate stabilization for firm and transparent monetary policy rules to promote credibility in central bank operations. Called inflation targeting, this has been defined as a framework for policy decisions in which the central bank makes an explicit commitment to conduct policy to meet a publicly announced numerical inflation target within a particular time frame.[10] Allowing the exchange rate to float to reflect market value, the central banks of Brazil or Peru, for example, set a preannounced target for inflation and adjust money supplies to meet that target. Transparency in inflation targeting regimes circumvents any market suspicion that politics, not sound economics, is driving national money machines. Other countries such as Paraguay do not follow strict targets; Argentina is a case where relatively flexible targets remain. A full-fledged targeting system with tight, preannounced bands requires a leveling out of macroeconomic variables, greater credibility by markets, and enhanced autonomy of the central bank.

A crawling peg or target zone can allow for small, regular devaluations to take inflation differentials into account and prevent an overvaluation of a currency.

Table 5.5. Advantages and Disadvantages of Fixed versus Floating Rates

	Fixed Rate	*Floating Rate*
Advantages	Limits exchange rate risk for international transactions	Neutralizes the impact of external shocks
	Lowers risk premium and therefore cost of access to international financial markets	Neutralizes the impact of real shocks
	Decreases domestic interest rates as domestic rates need not include exchange rate premiums	Neutralizes the effect of inflation on export competitiveness
	Facilitates disinflation with an exchange rate anchor	Cheaper export prices promote competitiveness
	Impedes monetary financing of the fiscal deficit because monetary policy is impotent	Price mechanism (e.g., an exchange rate depreciation) reallocates resources from the nontradable to the tradables sector
Disadvantages	Credibility is fragile; subject to speculative attacks in currency markets	Source of imported inflation through increasing import prices
	In case of crisis, adjustment may be costly	Negative effect of strong volatility on trade and financial transactions; agents like predictable prices
	Dependence on the monetary policy of the peg country; may not meet national needs	Countries can engage in competitive devaluations, creating regional instability
	Strong sensitivity to external and real domestic shocks; a fall in global demand, for example, must be matched by a fall in the money supply to maintain the promised peg rate	Can lead to postponement of required structural adjustments; the change in prices may mask underlying rigidities
	Risk of real exchange rate appreciation; if national inflation exceeds the peg's inflation rate, the local currency becomes overvalued	In case of crisis, can make the servicing of external and internal debt unpredictable; more local currency units are needed to repay obligations
	An overvalued currency creates a current account imbalance; countries would have to lower costs to maintain competitiveness	Hyperinflationary past may impede necessary central bank credibility
	Current account imbalances will require financing; if confidence dries up, a crisis ensues	Stability is only as strong as underlying central bank institutions

Source: Adapted from Helene Poirson, "How Do Countries Choose Their Exchange Rate Regime?" IMF Working Paper WP/01/46, April 2001, www.imf.org, 26, table A3.

Table 5.6.   Monetary Policy Framework and Exchange Rate Regime

	Exchange Rate Anchor	*Monetary Aggregate Target*	*Inflation Targeting Framework*	*IMF supported or other monetary program*	*Other (monitor various indicators)*
Dollarized	Ecuador Panama El Salvador				
Conventional Fixed Peg	Belize Venezuela				
Crawling Peg	Bolivia Costa Rica Honduras Nicaragua				
Managed Float with no pre-determined path		Guyana Jamaica	Colombia Guatemala Peru	Argentina Haiti	Paraguay
Independently Floating		Uruguay	Brazil Canada Chile Mexico		United States Dominican Republic

Source: IMF Annual Report 2005, Appendix, table II.13.

There is some suggestion that the exchange rate regime conditions inflation. In a fixed regime, inertial factors weigh more heavily. Countries under a fixed regime should pay close attention to labor market rigidities and corporate structure. Under a floating regime, deficit financing predominates. This may lead to a resurgence of inflation in the region as more countries have abandoned fixed anchors.[11] A radical alternative to either fixed or floating is no exchange rate at all—that is, simply dollarize and give up your currency. This option is discussed in box 5.2. There are rich lessons in the experience of macroeconomic stability in Latin America. Here we consider three cases: structuralist policies in Brazil, a monetarist approach in Bolivia, and a change from a structuralist to a monetarist stance in Argentina.

HETERODOX APPROACHES TO INFLATION STABILIZATION IN THE 1980S: BRAZIL

Brazilian policymakers diagnosed inflation in the 1980s as structural. The external oil price shocks of 1973 and 1978–1979 in conjunction with the interest rate shocks of the early 1980s intersected with a highly concentrated industrial sector able to pass on cost increases to the public. Maxidevaluations of the currency in 1979 and 1983 took place because of current account pressures, fueling price increases. Ortho-

BOX 5.2.   DOLLARIZATION

In the midst of the debate on fixed versus flexible exchange rates, one option that has gar-nered attention is abandoning national currencies—and the question of the appropriate exchange rate—and adopting the dollar.[12] Exchange rate pegs can be seen as invitations to speculative attacks, pushing countries to abandon the exchange rate anchor or float. The dollar, an international currency, is not subject to the same kind of speculative attacks and currency runs. By taking away exchange rate uncertainty—and not leaving domestic monetary policy subject to political manipulation—nations could decrease the cost of borrowing in capital markets. Proponents point to the falling cost of capital for European nations such as Italy with the adoption of the euro and suggest that, as it did in Europe, a single currency would hasten regional integration. Dollarization enhances credibility, making tough changes irreversible.

Dollarization is not without its drawbacks. It implies a loss of seignorage, the money that a government makes by issuing money. Printing money that can be used for schools, roads, and hospitals is equivalent to a no-interest loan to the government. The central bank can also use currency, which does not bear interest, to purchase interest-bearing assets, such as foreign reserves. These show up as central bank profits and are transferred to the government. Clearly, dollarization implies a loss of monetary autonomy, including the ability of the central bank credit to provide liquidity to the banking system. Dollar-ization can also threaten competitiveness. The dollarized real exchange rate can become overvalued for the country in question. Real devaluation must be achieved through a fall in wages and prices. If labor markets are not flexible, such price reduction is problematic. Finally, dollarization may be a high-risk strategy for rebellion. Trashing the local currency challenges nationalist pride.

Approaches to the process of dollarization differ. Some recommend slow, evolu-tionary dollarization. With a starting point of complementary banking, fiscal, and trade reforms, dollarization would be the coronation after a long period of preparation. But those driven to dollarization by crisis may benefit from shock treatment. Rapid dollariza-tion will force labor market adjustments—there is no choice but for unions to recognize that there are few alternatives. It hardens the government's fiscal constraint. The hope is that the term structure of debt will lengthen with less risk and the country will have enhanced access to commercial credit lines. Dollarization should create synchronization of business cycles through the interest rate.

Rapid dollarization is called the Nike approach—just do it. Countries most likely to benefit from dollarization are those most highly integrated with the United States, including a wide degree of informal dollarization through dollar-based savings and trans-actions. The optimal currency literature suggests that the best candidates include those with small size, a high degree of openness, a high degree of cross-border trade, similar shocks, and dollar-based debt structures. Williamson suggests that by these criteria the small Central American countries are strong candidates for dollarization; the Andean countries are an intermediate case. Mexico, an oil-based economy, is subject to different shocks, and **Mercosur** countries in search of a monetary anchor might better think of cre-ating their own monetary union than tie their fates to the distant dollar of the north.[13]

Panama adopted the dollar as legal tender in 1904, leaving the balboa as a symbolic relic. It has a low rate of inflation and low cost of capital and has eliminated exchange rate risk. But dollarization isn't a magic wand. Due to its inability to control public finances and a high rate of external borrowing, Panama unpleasantly claims the second-largest number of IMF programs in the world. No exchange rate regime—not even a nonregime—can avoid the tough problems of reconciling the demand for government services with weak revenues.

continued

continued

> After proclaiming a few days before that dollarizing was "a jump into the abyss," Ecuador's President Jamil Mahuad switched to the greenback in January 2000. It cost him his job two weeks later, but the results have been more successful than most analysts expected. Ecuador had run out of options. It faced erratic oil prices, debilitating capital flight, bank failures, international loan defaults, and devastating floods. Nearly half its twelve million people are considered impoverished by World Bank standards. The sucre had plunged from 7,000 to 25,000 per US$1, igniting price explosions. Without consulting the IMF, Ecuador moved to a dollar standard. Ecuador dollarized at a discount, opening the door to international competitiveness. An IMF program in 2000 consolidated the gains of dollarization and further pushed structural reform, including the fiscal accounts and banking reform. By 2001, growth hit 5 percent, inflation was under 25 percent, and the people felt the benefit in the positive growth in the real minimum salary. Nonetheless, a delicate banking and financial system and vulnerability to oil prices, the weight of external debt, and falling global demand leave Ecuador's recovery fragile to external shocks. The boost from the initial devaluation has weakened; competitiveness will be contingent on improvements in productivity, labor reforms, and privatization in telecommunications and electricity, very tough microeconomic changes to engineer.[14]

dox policies to reduce inflation had been tried under the military governments with painful social results. Sectoral conflicts between industry and agriculture as well as social conflicts between powerful labor and industrial organizations were thereafter resolved through spending. The state itself played an active role in the economy through state-owned enterprises (SOEs), especially in the provision of infrastructure such as electricity and key inputs such as steel. In these sectors prices were held down to spur development of industry, but the difference was made up in deficit spending. As inflation accelerated, bonds, credit, and wages were indexed with increasingly frequent intervals. The lack of independence of the Bank of Brazil from the Treasury left it in a passive role to accommodate expansion.

When monthly inflation hit 459.1 percent in January 1986,[15] a radically different stabilization plan was called for. The **Cruzado Plan** included a general price freeze and a partial freeze on wages following an 8 percent readjustment. If the consumer price index increased more than 20 percent, wage increases would be permitted. Indexation of contracts with less than one year's duration was prohibited. A new currency was created called the cruzado, set equal to 1,000 cruzeiros. After a devaluation, the cruzado was fixed at 13.84 cruzados to the dollar. Popular favor was cultivated as Brazilian president José Sarney deputized all Brazilians as *fiscais,* or price inspectors, to police the price freeze in supermarkets and shopping malls. Citizens could arrest store managers for raising prices. People felt empowered by the fight against inflation. The goal was to eliminate the inertial aspect of inflation, creating expectations for price stability rather than inflation.

The preliminary results were dramatic. By April prices actually fell 4.5 percent, and in May they rose only 1 percent. Because inflation was not eating away at paychecks, Brazilians enjoyed a real wage increase for the first time in years, and economic growth was led by the strong demand for consumer durables. However, Brazilian industry was not able to meet the surge in consumer demand, and the economy began to overheat. Shortages emerged. The sustainability of the plan was

The price of a currency is a key macroeconomic variable.
(Photo by Patrice Franko)

called into question. As businesses lost faith in the plan, they withheld goods from the market, anticipating that the price freeze could not last indefinitely. Fiscal reform was limited, and monetary policy accommodated the deficit pressures. With state and gubernatorial elections in the fall of 1986, politics would not permit austerity. By December 1986 monthly inflation was back in triple digits. Following the elections, adjustments were made to the price framework, and a crawling peg for the exchange rate temporarily relieved the pressure for devaluation. Contracts were once again indexed to ease the costs of inflation. But credibility was destroyed, and a year and a half after the introduction of the plan, inflation topped 1,000 percent. Although the plan worked initially to reduce inflation dramatically, when the economy was unable to respond to the increased demand, credibility eroded in the government's ability to manage the economy.

Brazil continued its heterodox experiment with the **Bresser Plan** in mid-1987. The Bresser Plan also froze wages, although the caps were designed to be readjusted every ninety days to minimize misallocation and shortages. The exchange rate was managed through a series of mini devaluations. Interest rates were targeted above inflation to keep the lid on the consumer boom that overheated the economy under the Cruzado Plan. Finance Minister Luiz Carlos Bresser Periera placed heavy emphasis on controlling the public deficit in theory but was unable to realign the political priorities of the Sarney administration. A follow-up "summer plan" included another revaluation of the currency, lopping off three zeros once again and calling it the novo cruzado. However, it did little to change the underlying politics of the Brazilian situation. Fiscal pressures continued, inflation accelerated, and confidence was low.

In 1990 a new president—the first directly elected by the people in nearly thirty years—came into office with a strong mandate to "kill inflation with a single bullet." President Fernando Collor de Mello engineered the most dramatic of stabilization plans, with both heterodox and orthodox elements. With annual inflation nearing 3,000 percent, and consistent with prior stabilization plans, Collor froze wages and prices, and once again readjusted the monetary unit, renaming it the cruzeiro. Agreeing with the monetarists that inflation indeed had a strong monetary component, Collor implemented a radical liquidity freeze, immediately reducing the money stock by 80 percent. All bank accounts in excess of $1,000 were frozen. Brazilians were shocked. People who had, for example, sold one house but were in the process of buying another could not go ahead with their purchases. By law, they were not allowed access to their own money. The economy—including prices—was essentially at a standstill. These drastic measures were accompanied by planned reductions in the shape of government, including privatizations and layoffs of government employees.

The plan backfired. Rather than change expectations toward a low-inflation economy, it eroded confidence in the government as a guarantor of the rules governing the economic game. If the government could step in and freeze a family's life savings, what would it not do? The powerful business lobby, represented by the Federation of Industries of São Paulo (FIESP), was not consulted in the plan, leaving an angry and alienated industrial sector. The plan collapsed with a loss of legitimacy; Collor himself later fell to charges of corruption and was impeached. Changing the shape of government had not addressed some of the personalistic privileges that government officials had usurped. Nonetheless, this early test of Brazilian democracy led, after the interim presidency of Itamar Franco, to the election of Fernando Henrique Cardoso on the platform of price stabilization.

As Franco's economics minister, Cardoso introduced the **Real Plan.** The Real Plan was a pragmatic mix of orthodox and heterodox elements. Its premise was heterodox in spirit: eliminate the inertial elements of inflation to break out of a cycle of indexed price increases that adjusted for past inflation. The preliminary stage of the plan lasted three months. It began in December 1993 by identifying disequilibria, eliminating price distortions, and introducing emergency fiscal adjustments. In March monetary reform was introduced. All wages, prices, and taxes, and the exchange rate, were redenominated in a new accounting unit, the real unit of value (URV), roughly set at par to the U.S. dollar. The URV was a kind of superindex as an intermediate step on the path back to using money as the measure of value. Indexation to other rates was prohibited, and the money supply was tightened, indicating a monetarist bent. By July a new currency, the real, was introduced; it was tied initially one to one to the URV accounting unit. Once again this new currency was designed to erase the inflationary memory associated with the old unit. What was different in the case of the real was that the policy changes implemented in association with the Real Plan were credible to the public. The gradual, preannounced

Table 5.7.   Macroeconomic Indicators for Brazil, 1982–2004

Year	Consumer Prices	Growth	Urban Unemployment
1982	100.3	0.6	6.3
1983	178	−3.4	6.7
1984	209.1	5.1	7.1
1985	239	8	5.3
1986	58.6	7.5	3.6
1987	394.6	3.4	3.7
1988	993.3	0.3	3.8
1989	1,863.6	3.2	3.4
1990	1,584.6	−4.2	4.3
1991	475.8	0.3	4.8
1992	1,149.1	−0.3	5.8
1993	2,489.1	4.5	5.4
1994	929.3	6.2	5.1
1995	22	4.2	4.6
1996	9.1	2.5	5.7
1997	4.3	3.1	5.7
1998	2.5	0.1	7.6
1999	8.4	0.7	7.6
2000	6	3.9	7.1
2001	7.7	1.3	6.2
2002	12.5	1.5	11.7
2003	9.3	0.6	12.3
2004	7.6	4.9	11.5
2005	5.7	2.3	9.8
2006*	4	2.8	10

Source: ECLAC, *Economic Survey of Latin America and the Caribbean* (Santiago, Chile: ECLAC, various years). Data for 2005 from David Fleischer, Brazil Focus e-newsletter, email fleischer@uol.com.br. *Forecasts.

nature of each step served to calm expectations. Furthermore, after more than two decades of unsuccessfully battling inflation, the public was simply ready to bite the bullet. Expectations of inflation were changed. As President Cardoso said on the second anniversary of the Real Plan, "Brazil used to be like a casino. Everyone, not only banks, speculated here. This is coming to an end."[16] By 1996 the inflation rate was the lowest in Brazil in thirty-nine years. As we can see from the data in table 5.7, growth resumed, buoyed by consumer confidence, and unemployment did not rise.

The real was a stable anchor against inflation through mid-1998, but imbalances began to emerge in the Brazilian economy. Government deficits, fueled by a lack of fundamental restructuring in fiscal outlays, became alarming. Strong spending—led by workers finally able to save enough to buy consumer durables—created trade balance problems. The real was becoming overvalued relative to economic fundamentals. As we will discuss in chapter 7, when currency crises shook Asia and Russia, the unstable Brazilian economy was unable to withstand the capital outflows. The government abandoned the fixed exchange rate, allowing the

currency to float on international markets. The associated 30–40 percent depreciation raised fears of igniting another inflationary round in Brazil.[17]

Restraining the resurgence of inflation was a top priority. Under pressure of
financial turmoil and the loss of an IMF rescue package, President Cardoso was able
to extract important fiscal reforms from Congress and restrain inflation to about 10
percent, a significant achievement given the country's hyperinflationary past. This
was no small task in Brazil, where the 1988 constitution hampers the president's
ability to change a complex system of taxes and entitlements controlled by a powerful Congress. A tightening of monetary policy by the central bank sent interest rates
soaring to 43 percent by March 1999—a strong signal that the government was
serious about fighting inflation without an exchange rate anchor.[18]

Without the fixed exchange rate anchor (or its second cousin the crawling peg),
Brazilian monetary authorities had to generate market confidence in their ability to
manage the independent monetary policy associated with a float. The third central
bank president in as many weeks, Arminio Fraga, brought his Wall Street experience to Brasilia. The central bank announced a transparent commitment to inflation
targets. Concerned about the inflation pass-through from the devaluation (estimated
to be approximately 30–40 percent), interest rates were raised to 45 percent to
restrain the impact of import price escalation. Fraga hit the international financial
markets with forceful international economic diplomacy, successfully garnering
external financial support. Inflationary expectations fell, and interest rate pressures
were relieved. Panic behind it, the Brazilian central bank was able to lengthen the
term structure of the government's domestic debt and regularize publication of
inflation targets and performance on its website (www.bcb.gov.br).[19] By mid-1999,
Brazil adopted an inflation-targeting scheme with strict targets that enhanced the
credibility of the new regime. Despite pressure from the East Asian crises (discussed in chapter 7), the devaluation of the Brazilian real and the dismantling of
the exchange rate–based stabilization scheme did not lead to a full-blown currency
crisis in 1999, in large part because the monetary move was accompanied by substantial reform.[20]

To reign in public finances, Brazil passed a fiscal responsibility law in 2000 that
sets limits on borrowing by states and municipalities, forbidding the expenditure
of more than 60 percent of revenues on wages. Aimed at budgetary balance, unintended effects included hiring fewer doctors, teachers, and security guards. Offend-
ing mayors can be banned from office. The federal government is also forbidden to
bail out states and cities in trouble. By limiting fiscal excess and promoting more
efficient tax collection, Brazil promoted international credibility and improved its
bond ratings in international markets, lowering the cost of capital critical for growth.

The 2002 elections of Luiz Inácio "Lula" da Silva, the left-leaning Workers
Party candidate, rocked Brazilian markets, resulting in a 40 percent depreciation of
the real and a $30 billion IMF lifeline in the face of an uncertain economic direc-
tion for Brazil. To the surprise of many, however, Lula has turned to pursue conservative fiscal and monetary policies, bowing to the pressure of international markets
to maintain budget and trade surpluses. From a nominal fiscal deficit in 1999 of
14 percent of GDP, Brazil has reduced this measure of the burden of government in
the economy to 10 percent in 2000 and 2–2.5 percent in 2005.[21] If interest payments

owed by the government are held aside, Brazil posts a 2005 primary surplus of 5.1 percent. Brazil's ability to promote growth remains constrained by its need to maintain financial market credibility. With government debt at a weighty 51.7 percent of GDP, Brazilian growth is highly sensitive to bringing down interest rates. A 2005 move by the Brazilian central bank to lower the interest rate to 19 percent was greeted with praise for those looking to pump up the economy—but caution emerged as well to not move in the opposite direction of U.S. interest rates. If the extravagant spread between riskier Brazilian investment and safer U.S. options shrinks too much, foreign investment in Brazil may suffer. If falling investment increases the risk factor of investing in Brazil, this premium will be reflected in rising rates—just what the government is trying to avoid.[22]

What lessons for inflation stabilization can we take from the Brazilian case? Clearly, heterodox policy alone is not enough. Simply focusing on expectations and taming the inertial component does not eliminate the imbalances creating the expectations. Fiscal and monetary fundamentals also need to be adjusted. Without reshaping the fundamentals, it is not possible to generate confidence that the imbalance in the domestic economy has been corrected. A pure orthodox approach was simply not dramatic enough to generate confidence and support. In the Brazilian case, merely restraining the money supply had perverse effects. When the money supply was cut and interest rates rose as a result, economic agents perceived this as a rise in the nominal interest rate—or a signal that inflation was heating up again. They therefore increased their demands for higher wages or prices to adjust for expected future inflation. Without a change in expectations of inflation, without a clear sense of a change in the rules of the game, inertial aspects of inflation will plague the orthodox strategy.

The fight for shares, the struggle to adjust to inflation by stepping on the back of other economic agents, was indeed prevalent in the Brazilian case. In an economy characterized by a high degree of inequality and structural constraints on the road to equilibrium, this battle between capital and labor cannot be ignored. With Brazil's relatively closed economy, agents did not have to look to the external sector for competitive price setting. By the same token, resolving the problem of conflict over social shares cannot be passed around like a hot potato by ineffective government. Confidence in the ability of government to mediate this conflict, to stabilize the playing field, is crucial to a compact on the part of all agents in restraining inflation. Not surprisingly, this confidence begins at home, with a transparent and credible plan for managing fiscal accounts.

Solving chronic budgetary problems is the key to sustainable prices over time. By accompanying monetary with fiscal change, Brazil was able to move from an exchange rate–based stabilization program to an inflation target. Although the exchange rate–based stabilization program was likely necessary to overcome inflationary expectations and launch a credible currency, the real, an increasingly overvalued exchange rate constrained Brazil's international competitiveness. With a worsening current account, the Brazilian government had to raise interest rates to attract capital to finance the international imbalance—choking off domestic growth in the process.[23] Although Brazil must continue to pay attention to an international balancing act between the need to attract capital and a progrowth interest rate, an inflation target combined with a floating exchange rate has given the country a bit of breathing space to promote growth through exports. Brazil's success in the short term of restraining speculative attacks on the real under the float will be cemented only by a long-term commitment to resolving the tough distributional issues that drive Brazil's deficits.[24]

EARLY MONETARIST APPLICATIONS: BOLIVIA

The Bolivian stabilization experience provides an interesting orthodox contrast to the Brazilian case. Bolivia had also embarked on a period of hyperinflation by 1985. External factors such as the crash of international tin prices from $6 to $3.5 between 1982 and 1985 severely contracted tax revenues. Tin export earnings fell from $234.8 million to $75.1 million. At the same time, foreign debt service requirements increased from 0.4 percent of GDP in 1979 to 10.8 percent in 1983. As in other developing countries, due to the debt crisis, there was virtually no access to new funding in international markets. In addition to the fall in revenues, inflation was eating away at the value of tax receipts. Because the government was pursuing an expansionary policy, financing the internal and external deficits required monetary emissions, or increases in the money supply. By 1984 the government deficit had risen to nearly one-fifth of gross national product (GNP). The jump in the money supply, or seignorage to finance government spending, mirrored the decline in resource flows from abroad. In interesting contrast to the Brazilian case, wage and price indexation was not widespread. In a futile attempt to provide a monetary anchor, the exchange rate was fixed. Rather than price stability, the result was an overvalued exchange rate. When an exchange rate is fixed and exchange controls are imposed to restrict the amount of hard currency in the system, international currencies are strongly demanded in black—or, as they sometimes were called to reflect the openness of the transactions, parallel—markets. In Bolivia by 1985 the controlled rate was at 67,000 bolivianos per dollar while the free black market rate was running at 1,143,548. This 1,600 percent overvaluation made legal exports unprofitable. Underground transactions therefore emerged as evidenced by oddities in international data. Peru, for example, despite its lack of tin mines, became a tin exporter (of illegal Bolivian exports) during this period. Of course, illegal exports were not taxed, further eroding the ability of the Bolivian state to finance its affairs. Speculation in foreign exchange became quite profitable. If a person could buy the overvalued official boliviano (sometimes illegally), money could be made in selling cheaply acquired dollars on the black market. Politically, Bolivia had a weak government trying to adjudicate increasing claims on the state to address problems of poverty and inequality. A powerful military and labor movement pressured the spending arm of the state. Falling external prices made these constraints that much more acute.

In 1985, Victor Paz Estenssoro came to power and announced the New Economic Policy to address the extreme macroeconomic deterioration (shown in table 5.8). A devaluation of the exchange rate followed by managed floating addressed the priority of getting international prices right.[25] The state-led development strategy

Table 5.8. Macroeconomic Indicators for Bolivia, 1982–2004

Year	Consumer Prices (annual % change)	Growth Rate of GDP (annual % change constant 2000$)	GDP/Capita (US$)	Public Deficit as % of GDP
1982	296.5	NA	1,069	−13.7
1983	328.5	−5.3	986	−15.7
1984	2,176.8	1.2	972	−17.6
1985	8,170.5	−0.1	945	−9.0
1986	65.9	−1.9	902	−1.6
1987	10.6	2.6	901	−3.6
1988	21.5	−1.3	809	−4.5
1989	16.6	3.8	822	−1.8
1990	18.0	4.6	840	−1.0
1991	14.5	5.3	864	−1.4
1992	10.5	1.7	857	0.8
1993	9.3	4.3	872	−1.0
1994	8.5	4.8	891	−4.2
1995	10.6	4.7	911	−3.8
1996	9.9	4.5	926	−1.9
1997	6.7	4.9	942	−3.3
1998	4.4	5	966	−4.0
1999	3.1	0.3	947	−3.8
2000	3.4	2.3	1,019	−3.7
2001	0.9	1.6	952	−6.9
2002	2.5	2.7	905	−9.0
2003	3.9	2.4	872	−7.0
2004	4.3	3.9	1.6	−5.4
2005	4.9	4.1	1.8	−3.5

Source: ECLAC, *Economic Survey of Latin America and the Caribbean* (Santiago, Chile: ECLAC, various years); and IADB, *Economic and Social Progress in Latin America* (Washington, D.C.: Johns Hopkins University Press, various years).

was abandoned. Enterprises were privatized or scaled down, resulting in a reduction of the public-sector wage bill. In particular, COMIBOL, the powerful state tin producer, reduced its employment from thirty thousand in 1985 to seven thousand in 1987. Public-sector revenues were increased through tax reform. Greater confidence in the government also resulted in higher compliance with tax obligations. Debt was rescheduled, and funding from multilateral institutions and foreign governments was secured in exchange for the adoption of these orthodox economic policies. Widespread liberalization of trade and capital accounts was implemented to attract private capital inflows. An amnesty was declared for the return of dollars that had fled abroad. Dollar deposits were also legalized without proof of origin, permitting the entry of coca dollars into the economy.[26]

The immediate result of this austere package was a call for a general strike. However, after three years of hyperinflation, the public chose to support the government rather than the workers, and the tough package was upheld. To minimize the social costs of adjustment, an emergency social fund (ESF), financed by the Inter-

American Development Bank (IADB) and the World Bank, was implemented. It provided funds for small-scale, labor-intensive projects proposed and implemented by local nongovernmental organizations. The projects financed were mostly in infrastructure; they are estimated to have created nearly forty-one thousand jobs and added 2 percent to the GNP over the period.[27] We will return to the use of social funds in chapter 11, which discusses poverty.

Despite the innovations of the ESF, the costs of inflation stabilization in Bolivia were enormous. While inflation was dramatically controlled, the price was a long period of recession. Over the period 1985–1996, the rate of growth of GDP per capita ranged from −10.21 percent in 1988 to +2.86 percent in 1991. If the goal of development is to improve the well-being of its population, falling or stagnant rates of growth of GDP do not present opportunities for economic advancement. By 1994 GDP finally climbed back to the 1982 level—a lost decade of development for Bolivians. GDP per capita in 1996 did not reach 1982 levels. The Bolivian orthodox strategy eradicated inflation, but at a high price for growth.

The Case of Argentina: From the Austral Plan to the Convertibility Plan

Stabilization in Argentina was conceptually path-breaking with its heterodox attempt in the 1980s and its orthodox plan in the 1990s. The Argentine **Austral Plan** of 1985 provided many of the elements followed by Brazil. Inflation was diagnosed as having a strong inertial component. A decade of failed stabilization attempts taught economic agents to expect inflation and adjust for it in wage and price setting. The Austral Plan therefore froze wages and prices (including the exchange rate) and introduced a new currency with a promise not to print money. Fiscal adjustment was the third element of the plan. There was a close relationship between fiscal deficits and money creation in Argentina. Eliminating deficits would stem the need for seignorage, or money printing, as the last resort for financing. Initially the plan succeeded as inflation decreased from 350 percent in the first half of 1985 to 20 percent in the second.

Nonetheless, the Austral Plan collapsed as signs of disequilibrium emerged. The exchange rate became overvalued, and external accounts deteriorated. The government made adjustments for price flexibility, but the credibility of the plan was undermined. Argentines needed to have their expectations grounded in a firm and credible long-run strategy. They found this in the 1991 **Convertibility Plan** introduced by Minister Domingo Cavallo in the Menem administration. President Carlos Menem succeeded President Raúl Alfonsín as the second democratically elected president after years of military rule. International markets held their breath because Menem was a renowned populist of the Peronist Party. However, the old style of populist spending to appease conflicts between industry, labor, and the military was surprisingly transformed into a personal populism that allowed Menem to introduce one of the toughest austerity programs in the region. The Convertibility Plan locked the Argentine peso to the U.S. dollar. Through a currency board independent of the Treasury, by law the money supply could be increased only if the

U.S. dollars held in reserve were to rise. This took the central bank out of the position of being the lender of last resort and removed the temptation to finance domestic deficits with new money creation. Monetary policy was nondiscretionary, fixed to the long-run performance of the external sector. Liberalization of the economy promoted exports and the inflow of foreign investment to increase the stock of dollars in Argentina. The peso, which formerly lost value daily, became indistinguishable from the U.S. dollar. Indeed, in bank machines in Buenos Aires one could select whether to receive cash in dollars or pesos. Fiscal adjustment was dramatic but incomplete. The government embarked on a large-scale privatization program, putting fifty-one firms on the auction block between 1989 and 1992 and generating approximately US$18 billion.[28] Tax reform increased revenues to balance government books. Smaller government demanded less inflationary financing.

As we can see in table 5.9, inflation tumbled in Argentina from the peak of more than 3,000 percent to an astoundingly low rate of 0.1 percent in 1996. Domestic and international capital believed in the long-run commitment of the plan. International capital flowed to Argentina, convinced of the sustainability of the program and lured by the values of the privatized firms on the stock exchange. The plan was remarkable. Despite high social costs of 17 percent unemployment, Cavallo was tough and held firm on the Convertibility Plan. When the Mexican peso crisis of 1994–1995 rocked the international financial community's faith in Latin America, Argentina stuck to the plan even as capital temporarily fled the region. Cavallo left the administration in July 1996 with the economy contracting at a rate of 4.6 percent in 1995; nonetheless, the new economics minister, Roque Fernandez, continued to ground the Argentine peso firmly in the value of the dollar. Despite the recession, Fernandez attacked the budget deficit, increasing taxes and cutting spending. The costs of not erasing the inflationary memory in Argentina were simply much greater than the pain of recession.

When its trading partner, Brazil, let the real float in 1999, fragilities in the Argentine model were exacerbated. The accompanying devaluation of the Brazilian real improved competitiveness and the Brazilian trade balance; at the same time, the strengthening dollar compounded the overvaluation of the peso. External accounts deteriorated, unemployment remained stuck at socially unacceptable levels in the range of 18 percent, and fiscal deficits were not brought under control. As we will see in chapter 7, challenges from Brazil, the inability to restrain fiscal spending by the provinces, and rising external debt burst the viability of the peso-dollar lock, and Argentina tumbled into economic chaos.

A perfect storm hit Argentina in 2001. Still weak from financial contagion of the Asian currency crisis and the Brazilian real crisis, Argentina began running into balance of payments difficulty. Tied to the U.S. dollar, the exchange rate anchor became a dead weight on the Argentina economy without significant internal improvements in productivity and competitiveness. As credibility eroded, capital rapidly flowed out of Argentina. Debt obligations became unsustainable as interest rates soared and growth slowed. Despite radical changes in the shape of the state under President Menem, tough adjustments in fiscal accounts lagged behind. Given that its monetary hand was tied by the convertibility law, the government should have adopted greater fiscal conservatism during periods of growth to cushion the

Table 5.9. Macroeconomic Indicators for Argentina, 1970–2004

Year	Inflation (average annual growth of consumer prices)	Annual Growth Rate of GDP	Urban Unemployment
1970	13.6	—	—
1971	34.7	—	—
1972	58.4	3.1	6.6
1973	61.2	6.1	5.4
1974	23.5	6.5	3.4
1975	182.9	−1.3	3.7
1976	444.0	−3	4.5
1977	176.1	6.4	2.8
1978	175.5	−3.4	2.8
1979	159.5	7.1	2.0
1980	100.8	1.4	2.3
1981	104.5	−6.2	4.5
1982	164.8	−5.2	4.8
1983	345.0	2.6	4.2
1984	627.5	2.4	3.9
1985	672.5	−4.4	5.3
1986	85.7	6.0	4.6
1987	123.1	2.1	5.3
1988	348.3	−1	6.0
1989	3,080.5	−1.9	7.6
1990	2,314.7	−6.1	7.4
1991	171.7	0.0	6.5
1992	24.9	8.8	7.0
1993	10.6	5.9	9.6
1994	4.2	5.8	11.5
1995	3.4	−2.9	17.5
1996	0.1	5.5	17.2
1997	0.3	8.0	14.9
1998	0.7	3.8	12.9
1999	−1.8	−3.4	14.3
2000	−0.7	−0.6	15.1
2001	−1.5	4.4	17.4
2002	41.0	−10.8	19.7
2003	3.7	8.7	17.3
2004	6.1	9	13.6
2005	12.3	9.2	11.6
2006*	11	8.5	—

Source: ECLAC, *Preliminary Overview of the Economy of Latin America and the Caribbean,* various years (Santiago, Chile: ECLAC, various years); Economic Commission for Latin America and the Caribbean, *Statistical Yearbook of Latin America and the Caribbean,* various years (Santiago, Chile: ECLAC, various years); and IADB, *Economic and Social Progress in Latin America* (Washington, D.C.: Johns Hopkins University Press, various years).
*Forecast.

fall during a downturn—but it wasn't so prudent. The IMF, perhaps a bit too tied to Argentina as its Washington Consensus poster child, extended additional loans without requiring stronger fiscal adjustment. An emergency loan called the "blindaje" or armor was arranged to protect the Argentine economy against external shocks.[29] Money market managers were drawn to the high returns that risky Argentine assets offered. So long as they could convince markets of the viability of future gains in Argentina, money poured in to make more money. Of course the $14 billion loan was not a grant—increasing Argentina's indebtedness in a desperate attempt to save the Convertibility Plan and promote growth.

Yet investors began to suspect that the one-to-one link of dollars to pesos couldn't hold. There was significantly stronger demand for dollars—a demand that the central bank could not meet with its meager reserves. Argentines began to withdraw pesos from the system, running on banks to the tune of $15 billion in the second half of 2001. As GDP growth ground to a halt, the debt to GDP ratio, an indicator of the ability to pay, rose, indicating an impending crisis. The only way to generate more growth was to issue more debt—creating a debt time bomb with exploding debt dynamics.[30] The unsustainability of the program became apparent—but as confidence waned, an exit strategy from the Convertibility Plan became more problematic. Convertibility was legally binding—if this promise was broken, what could markets trust?[31]

To stem the tide, the Argentine government imposed a little fence or "corralito" on funds, placing a $1,000 a month ceiling on bank withdrawals. The public became furious and took to the streets to protest. Political uncertainty spiked investor anxiety, and funds continued to flee Argentina. Governments tumbled, leaving four presidents in as many weeks. By February of 2002 Argentina was forced to default on $155 billion of public debt, the largest default of any country in history. Desperate attempts to impose credibility on the system backfired. The announced zero deficit policy to restrain fiscal spending came at just the wrong time to wring a 13 percent cut in expenditure, as the economy was already in a painful contraction. Average income fell to almost a quarter of its level reached in the late 1990s, and more than half of the Argentine population sank under the poverty line.

By 2003, the IMF attempted to stave off default of an additional $6.6 billion coming due to the fund from Argentina. Rewarding it for tough measures to reduce the deficit following default, the IMF was helping the government of President Eduardo Duhalde to stay in good stead at the IMF until a new government was elected that spring. Incoming President Néstor Kirchner and his economy minister Roberto Lavagna then played hardball with markets. Using funds that would have gone to meet interest and principal payments to invest in the Argentine economy, growth recovered to 8 percent in 2004. Arguing that creditors who piled money into Argentina should bear some of the risk, in June 2005 the government forced hundreds of thousands of bondholders of the defaulted debt to take a huge "haircut"— a shaving of 66 percent on the $103 billion outstanding liabilities, exchanging the defaulted paper for new discounted offerings. Given the megadevaluation of the dollar, this is the amount that Argentina felt it could reasonably repay. Argentines, tired of tough adjustment policies, rallied to the defiance of markets, reducing social tensions at home.

Despite the dire warnings that a default would preclude new capital flows to Argentine, by July 2005 a new bond issue of $500 million was oversubscribed. Argentina's unprecedented primary budget surplus of 4 percent of GDP, its current account surplus, and low global interest rates left markets enamored, once again, with the Argentine financial tango.[32] Nonetheless, with a less than independent central bank, monetary emissions and a weak exchange rate were fueling the inflation engines to approximately 12 percent for the year.[33]

Argentina provides us a case study of an effective instrument of stabilization—the one-to-one convertibility of the dollar to the peso—that later became a debilitating liability. Once inflation was tamed, the value of the peso reflected underlying conditions in the dollar-based economy—not those in Argentina. Because real productivity was dramatically different, Argentina became overwhelmingly constrained in its efforts to grow.

LESSONS FOR STABILIZATION

Box 5.3 summarizes the variation of the stabilization experiences we have just studied. What lessons can we draw from these cases of stabilization in Latin America? As Jeffrey Sachs notes, there are three components to inflation reduction: (1) finding a solution to chronic budgetary problems at the core of high inflation; (2) identifying a means of eliminating inertial inflation, principally wage and price indexation; and (3) introducing one or more nominal anchors to the price level at the start of stabilization to ground expectations and the behavior of central bank authorities.[34] In all the cases, without clear and credible attention to the fiscal crisis, inflation will resurge in the economy. Fiscal imbalances will prevent stabilization, and the government will likely respond by monetizing the difference.

Restructuring the role of government in the economy has an additional benefit: creating the perception that business as usual has changed. Generating the confidence that the government is serious about reform and will—and can—remain committed to a stable policy is critical to success. This involves erasing the inflationary memory, the backward-looking behavior of agents that reflexively drives price increases. Tying the currency to an anchor—either firmly as in the case of Argentina or loosely in terms of a crawling peg to the dollar—provides monetary restraint. But with this stability comes a loss of flexible exchange rate changes to reflect different macroeconomic conditions. Beyond these tools, the population needs to believe in the benefits of inflation fighting. In Argentina the public was so tired of struggling to live with inflation that it was willing to quit cold turkey. Much like an alcoholic, the public understood that one little ounce of price inflation would tip the economy into an inflationary binge. Over time, however, the objective of a credible anchor gave way to the need for job creation and competitiveness. Bolivians, also subject to ravaging hyperinflation, were willing to swallow the tough contractionary pill. In Mexico the support was negotiated through El Pacto, providing a framework for sharing the burden of stabilization. Brazilians have been able to stave off some of the more dramatic social conflicts, perhaps in part due to the size of their economy and the ability to insulate it to some degree from the shock

Box 5.3. Variations on the Stabilization Experience

	Brazil's Cruzado Plan 1986	Brazil's Real Plan 1994	Argentina's Convertibility Plan 1991	Bolivia's New Economic Policy 1985
Diagnosis of inflation	Structural; inflation is a fight over social shares; address inertial inflation	Provide nominal anchor tied to exchange rate, de-index economy, and correct fiscal imbalances	Erase inflationary memory and control expectations; provide firm price anchor	Monetary emissions to accommodate government spending; fall in tax revenue forces seignorage; exchange rate overvalued
Fiscal policy	Reform unsuccessful	Short-run emergency adjustment; long-run change stalled in Congress	Restrictive; cut expenditures; strong privatization; tax increase	Tax reform; increase public sector prices; cut SOEs
Monetary policy	Increases due to fear of raising nominal interest rate giving inflation signal	Contractionary	Nondiscretionary; tied to U.S. dollar reserves	Tight
Exchange rate policy	Fixed at 13.84Cr = US$1	Crawling peg set to dollar	Fixed on par with U.S. dollar; money supply tied to reserves	Establish stable, unified rate; devalue then dirty float
Wage and prices	Freeze	Flexible	Flexible	No controls
Currency	1Cz = 1,000Cr	New currency real tied to URV loosely set to dollar	Peso interchangeable with dollar	
Political	Price inspectors			Restrain influence of labor unions
Trade	Continued internal orientation	Temporary erection of tariffs	Aggressive liberalization	Liberalization

continued

continued

	Brazil's Cruzado Plan 1986	Brazil's Real Plan 1994	Argentina's Convertibility Plan 1991	Bolivia's New Economic Policy 1985
Indexation	Prohibit contracts of less than one year with indexation clauses	All indexation except to new URV prohibited	None	
Initial results	Inflation falls from 22 percent monthly in February to .3 in May; growth surges led by strong consumer durables	Inflation lowest in nearly forty years; consumption exploded with increase in real income; some tightening	Dramatically low inflation	Drove hyperinflation out
Persistent imbalances	Shortages, withholding of goods; plan collapses as expectations escalate	Fiscal imbalance; real structural change awaits congressional approval	Unemployment at 17 percent	High social costs; anemic growth rates
Balance of payments	Trade surplus shrinks; reserves fall; exchange rate held fixed too long to maintain internal-external balance	Loss of export dynamic due to overvalued currency		

of international competitiveness. Whether this will prove to be a good thing in the long run remains to be seen.

Resolving deficit financing involves putting an end to persistent deficits. Expenditures have outpaced volatile revenues in Latin America. An Organization for Economic Cooperation and Development (OECD) study shows that industrialized countries collect an equivalent of 23 percent of GDP, while Latin American governments take in less than 15 percent—of generally smaller GDPs.[35] The ability to raise tax collection is crucial to enhancing education, health, and technology systems. Fiscal policy in Latin America also tends to be procyclical, fueling booms and protracting recession. In addition to tough questions of taxing politically powerful elites versus the penniless poor, questions of corruption and legitimacy plague reform efforts. Tax reform is a difficult balancing act, invariably asking some group to give more for the sake of the public good.

Sustained stabilization may also involve the development of new financial markets. One of the defining features of underdeveloped economies is the lack of a long-term capital market. In part this is a self-fulfilling prophecy—instability decreases the incentive for long-term investments. But this makes macroeconomic stabilization in the short term problematic. Without long-term confidence, bond markets cannot be used as an effective instrument of open market operations to smooth cyclical variations in the economy. This lack of monetary instruments places increasing pressure on governments to use the blunt tools of decreasing fiscal expenditures to stabilize growth.[36] Banking systems are also in need of reform. Banks in Latin America are more vulnerable during crises because most deposits are short-term (due to lack of confidence in the government's policies), banking institutions tend to put a great share of assets in land, and the value of their holdings of government securities is more volatile. During crises, banks find it hard to raise external financing; this is exacerbated by the fact that domestic capital markets are thin.[37] As banks struggle with bad loans and missed payments during a downturn, confidence in the banking system's financial health is called into question. Macrocrises are exacerbated by these fragilities of banking systems. Many countries have therefore adopted reforms in the banking sector. They have tightened prudential guidelines for lending, established minimum capital requirements that banks must hold relative to their loan base, and adopted monitoring systems to assess loan quality and risk. Banks are subject to wider supervisory review and are required to provide more comprehensive financial information consistent with international standards. There is, however, a wide degree of variance in regional banking reform. Brazil's banking sector was able to withstand the pressure of the depreciation of the real in part due to reforms of the mid-1990s; Argentina and Chile are also leaders in reform efforts. Other nations need to improve supervisory capabilities, including the ability to monitor cross-border operations for those with significant offshore financial sectors.

FROM STABILIZATION TO GROWTH

The dramatic achievements in price stabilization are evidenced in table 5.10 with a fall in the increase in consumer prices from an annual rate of 440.8 percent in 1990 to approximately 8.1 percent in 2000. Imagine the benefits of this price stability to agents trying to plan for the future. Real GDP growth accelerated to a high of 5.3 percent before falling to .2 as a result of the global slowdown in 1999; regional output grew at a slow 1.7 percent in 2001, again reflecting a sharp slowdown in global conditions. Growth in per capita GDP is lower, however, reflecting the mismatch between the rate of growth of the economy and the needs of growing populations in the region.

The process of economic stabilization has not been smooth. The IADB's 1996 report characterizes the pattern of reform in five phases: stabilization and implementation of reforms, economic recovery or boom, stress, correction or crisis, and

Table 5.10. Selected Latin American Macroeconomic Indicators

Year	Increase in Consumer Prices (%)	New Data	Increase in Real GDP per Capita (%)	New Data	Increase in Real GDP (%)	New Data
1990	440.8	87–96 avg. 181.9	–1.6	87–96 avg. 0.9	0.6	87–96 avg. 2.7
1995	36.0	97–06 avg. 8.0	–0.6	97–06 avg. 1.3	1.7	97–06 avg. 2.8
1996	21.2		2.0		3.6	
1997	12.9	11.9	3.5	3.6	5.3	5.2
1998	9.9	9.0	0.6	0.7	2.3	2.3
1999	8.8	8.2	–1.1	–1.1	0.2	0.4
2000	8.1	7.6	2.5	2.4	4.2	3.9
2001	6.2	6.1	–1.1	–1.0	1.7	0.5
2002	4.9	8.9	1.5	–1.5		x
2003		10.6		0.7		2.2
2004		6.5		4.2		5.6
2005*		6.3		2.7		4.1
2006*		5.4		2.4	3.6	3.8

Source: ECLAC, *Preliminary Overview of the Economies of Latin America and the Caribbean* (Santiago, Chile: ECLAC, various years).
*Forecast.

postreform growth.[38] As in Brazil's or Argentina's first packages, successful stabilization measures discussed above created consumer and investor confidence that leads to economic recovery or boom. Growth increases at a rate 4 percent higher than normal, and the resulting increase in income tax revenues improves fiscal balances. The boom, usually lasting about three years, creates imbalances. Credit tightens and interest rates rise. Higher domestic spending leads to an appreciation of the currency, squeezing exports. The economy slows, and fiscal deficits emerge. Investors, including foreign capital, become wary. Confidence erodes, and the economy enters into a period of stress. Pressures are often exacerbated by political factors. The reform process can be temporarily derailed by the crisis. However, if corrections are swift and credible, while slower growth can be expected, the downturn need not be traumatic. Chile provides an example of a country that, after more than twenty years of reform, has entered into the final stage of postreform. This is not to say that the economy is perfectly functioning. Challenges, particularly the social challenges of poverty and inequality, require response. But policy making has achieved a level of continuity and normalcy that encourages measured, long-run responses.

THE PRICE OF PRICE STABILITY: THE CHALLENGE OF RESOLVING THE SOCIAL DEFICIT

Despite stabilization, the magic of the market has not completely fulfilled the promise of development in Latin America. It is important to recall the huge human cost of austerity measures designed to stabilize inflationary economies. Like adjustment to the debt crisis, policies to reduce inflation come at the expense of current consumption—and for the poor, reducing a thin margin means human suffering. The fragility of this model was clearly demonstrated as strikes and demonstrations have evidenced frustrated expectations of growth. Domestic difficulties call into question the ability of governments to continue to apply tough austerity measures at home in hope of maintaining investor confidence abroad.[39] Large portions of the populations are left out of the process of growth. The social deficit—the enormous unmet need in the region for education, housing, medical services, transportation, and other public services—may not be resolved by the market. Contemporary social and political tension in Bolivia today can be traced to two decades of struggle. Women have borne the brunt of macroeconomic stabilization. As the guardians of the family, they are left with the task of designing strategies of survival. They must do more with less. Because they are forced outside the home for long hours to make up lost income, their daughters must fill motherly roles with younger siblings. Macrocrises can be considered a social "tax" on women's time.[40]

The road to economic reform in Latin America has been rocky. In all cases the social costs of stabilization have been the daily reality of Latin Americans. Poverty and inequality in the region rose, and human capital investments have suffered from the cuts in government programs in education, health, and social services. Macroeconomic equilibrium is seen as a necessary but not sufficient condition for development. Development, as we remember from chapter 1, revolves around the question of structural change. Several problems must be addressed to move from stability to growth. Sufficient savings must be generated and channeled into productive investment, resources must be allocated efficiently, and a setting must be developed that is conducive to generating the incentives to find new, potentially better ways of doing things.[41] The broad framework should move beyond macroeconomic policy reform to address trade liberalization, private-sector development, innovative policies for technological change, and reform of the state, focused on greater equity, efficiency, participation, and environmental sustainability.[42] We will take up these issues in the following chapters.

Key Concepts

Austral Plan	heterodox	Olivera-Tanzi effect
Bresser Plan	indexation	Real Plan
Convertibility Plan	inertial inflation	seignorage
cost-push elements	inflationary	structuralists
Cruzado Plan	expectations	velocity of money
exchange rate-based	Mercosur	
stabilization programs		

Chapter Summary

Monetarist Theory of Inflation

- Monetarists believe that persistent inflation in Latin America was caused by irresponsible deficit financing, the erosion of the tax base, and the debt crisis. With weak capital markets, and with foreign sources of capital drying up after the debt crisis, Latin American governments financed their deficit through seignorage, or the printing of money, inducing inflation. Unable to generate revenue with a deteriorating tax base, governments again looked at seignorage as a form of financing deficits. The debt crisis exacerbated conditions, making it difficult to finance the deficit through other means. The monetarist solution was to decrease government spending—although this was politically difficult.

The Structuralist Theory of Inflation

- The structuralists focused on cost-push elements as the main factors inducing inflation. Bottlenecks causing shortages, oligopolies, external shocks, and labor interacted to push prices up and prevented them from falling under normal market conditions. The political power of business and labor made it difficult to resist accommodating money demands. Inflation then became imbedded in the system and, for the structuralists, a necessary price for growth in the developing world.

- With ingrained expectations of inflation, some countries adopted indexation to adjust to the increase in prices. At the same time, indexation propelled inflation as price increases were automatically passed around the economy. Inflationary expectations also increased the velocity of money. With higher velocity, an increase in the money supply has a stronger expansionary and inflationary effect.

- Latin America is a laboratory of inflation-fighting policies. Brazil, characterized by a culture of inflation, began its fight against inflation with the Cruzado Plan, which initially was successful. It failed due to a loss of credibility and political pressures. The next attempt was the Bresser Plan in 1987, which fell to shortages and balance of payments pressure. President Collor tried to bring the economy to a standstill by eliminating inflationary expectations but succeeded only in eroding credibility. Using a mix of heterodox and orthodox measures, Finance Minister (later President) Cardoso introduced the Real Plan, which managed to bring down inflation. The fixed exchange rate aspect of the plan was abandoned, however, as international capital was wary of the lack of fundamental reform in the wake of the Asian crisis. Inflation appears to have stabilized.

- The decrease in foreign capital in the mid-1980s induced Bolivia to finance government spending through seignorage. To reduce the inflationary effects of its policies, Bolivia adopted a monetarist approach by devaluing the currency, privatizing, instituting tax reform, liberalizing trade and capital accounts, and rescheduling the debt. The austerity package brought about a general strike, but the government was able to uphold its package. Tough contractionary measures resulted in low growth throughout the 1980s and into the 1990s.

- The 1985 Austral Plan to bring down inflation in Argentina initially succeeded but, like the Cruzado Plan in Brazil, ultimately collapsed as inflationary expectations resurged. Populist president Carlos Menem surprised the country by introducing an austerity program to fight inflation in 1991. Menem tied the Argentine peso to the dollar to limit any increases in money supply and liberalized the economy. Though inflation came down from 3,000 percent to 0.1 percent, Argentina continues to suffer social costs of high unemployment. The Convertibility Plan collapsed in 2001 under the weight of fiscal deficits, weak competitiveness, and extreme debt.

- Lessons for stabilization include the need for fiscal sustainability, confidence in the ability to tackle tough choices, and the development of new sources of finance. The human and environmental costs of stabilization have been high, resulting in a huge social deficit and environmental degradation.

Notes

1. Rudiger Dornbusch, *Stabilization, Debt, and Reform: Policy Analysis for Developing Countries* (Englewood Cliffs, N.J.: Prentice Hall, 1993), 19.

2. Michael Gavin, Ricardo Hausmann, Roberto Perotti, and Ernesto Talvi, *Managing Fiscal Policy in Latin America and the Caribbean: Volatility, Procyclicality, and Limited Creditworthiness,* IADB, Office of the Chief Economist Working Paper No. 326 (Washington, D.C.: IADB, 1996), 4.

3. Victor Bulmer-Thomas, *The Economic History of Latin America since Independence* (New York: Cambridge University Press, 1994), 393.

4. Dornbusch, *Stabilization, Debt, and Reform,* 20.

5. Sebastian Edwards, "The Political Economy of Inflation and Stabilization in Developing Countries," *Economic Development and Cultural Change* 42(2) (January 1994): 235–266.

6. G. Tullio and M. Ronci, "Brazilian Inflation from 1980 to 1993: Causes, Consequences and Dynamics," *Journal of Latin American Studies* 28 (October 1996): 635–666.

7. Obstfeld and Taylor refer to these as the macroeconomic policy trilemma for open economies. As cited in Alan M. Taylor, "On the Costs of Inward-Looking Development: Price Distortions, Growth, and Divergence in Latin America," *Journal of Economic History* 58(1) (March 1998): 22.

8. Jeffrey Frieden and Ernesto Stein, *The Currency Game: Exchange Rate Politics in Latin America* (Washington, D.C.: Johns Hopkins University Press for the IADB, 2001), 9.

9. Anoop Singh, Agnés Belaisch, Charles Collyns, Paula De Masi, Reva Krieger, Guy Meredith, and Robert Rennhack, "Stabilization and Reform in Latin America: A Macroeconomic Perspective on the Experience since the Early 1990s," Occasional Paper 238, International Monetary Fund, February 2005.

10. Federal Reserve Bank of San Francisco, "U.S. Inflation Targeting: Pro and Con," FRBSF Economic Letter 98–18, May 29, 1998.

11. Prakash Loungani and Phillip Swagel, "Source of Inflation in Developing Countries," IMF Working Paper 01/198 (Washington, D.C.: The International Monetary Fund, December 2001).

12. Andrew Berg and Eduardo Borensztein, "The Dollarization Debate," *Finance & Development,* March 2000.

13. John Williamson, "Dollarization Does Not Make Sense Everywhere," Institute for International Economics, Speeches 2000, available at www.iie.com.

14. ECLAC, "Balance preliminar de las economías de América Latina y el Caribe, 2001," available at www.eclac.cl/publicaciones/DesarrolloEconomico/3/LCG2153PE/lcg2153sur.pdf and www.imf.org/external/np/sec/nb/2001/nb01129.htm.

15. Inflation series from Donald V. Coes, *Macroeconomic Crises, Policies, and Growth in Brazil, 1964–90* (Washington, D.C.: World Bank, 1995), table A.10.

16. Interview with President Fernando Henrique Cardoso on the occasion of the second anniversary of the Real Plan, as reported by the Foreign Broadcast Information Services, Latin America (FBIS-LAT-96-129, July 3, 1996), first appearing on Rede Globo (the Brazilian television station) at 10:30 Greenwich Mean Time, July 1, 1996.

17. The range for the depreciation depends on the day it is measured. On January 30, 1998, for example, it had depreciated 37 percent from its initial value.

18. Edmund Amann and Werner Baer, "Anchors Away: The Costs and Benefits of Brazil's Devaluation," *World Development* 31(6) (2003): 1040.

19. Arminio Fraga, "Monetary Policy during the Transition to a Floating Exchange Rate: Brazil's Recent Experience," *Finance & Development* 37(1) (March 2000), www.imf.org,

and Victor Bulmer-Thomas, "The Brazilian Devaluation: National Responses and International Consequences," *International Affairs* 7(4) (1999): 729–741.

20. Amann and Baer, "Anchors Away," 1042.

21. Viviane Monteiro, "Fiscal Resolve Is Crucial to the Economy, Says Finance Minister Palocci," *NoticiasFinancieras,* Groupo de Diarios America InvestNews (Brazil), September 13, 2005.

22. "Coming Up Roses," *Latin American Economy & Business,* Intelligence Research Ltd, October 25, 2005.

23. Amann and Baer, "Anchors Away," 1044.

24. Eliana Cardoso, "Brazil's Currency Crisis," in *Exchange Rate Politics in Latin America,* ed. Carol Wise and Riordan Roett (Washington, D.C.: Brookings Institution Press, 2000), 70–92.

25. "Managed floating" refers to an exchange rate policy in which the price is largely market determined; the government may intervene in the market by buying and selling currency to stabilize the value.

26. Adapted from Juan Antonio Morales and Jeffrey Sachs, "Bolivia's Economic Crisis," in *Developing Country Debt and the World Economy,* ed. Jeffrey Sachs (Chicago: University of Chicago Press, 1989).

27. Diana Tussie, *The Inter-American Development Bank,* vol. 4 of *The Multilateral Development Banks* (Ottawa: North-South Institute, 1995), 112.

28. Sebastian Edwards, *Crisis and Reform in Latin America: From Despair to Hope* (New York: Oxford University Press, 1995), 196.

29. For a gripping insider account of the bankrupting of Argentina, see Paul Blustein, *And the Money Kept Rolling In (and Out)* (New York: Public Affairs, a member of the Perseus Group, 2005). The blindaje is discussed on p. 106.

30. Blustein, *And the Money Kept Rolling In (and Out),* 80, quoting IMF official El-Erian.

31. Blustein, *And the Money Kept Rolling In (and Out),* 96.

32. Peter Hudson, "Issue by Argentina Is Greeted Warmly," *Financial Times* news alerts, July 20, 2005.

33. Mary Anastasia O'Grady, "Argentina Land of the Incredible Shrinking Peso," *Wall Street Journal,* October 21, 2005.

34. Jeffrey Sachs and Alvaro Zini, "Brazilian Inflation and the Plano Real," *World Economy* 19(1) (January 1996).

35. Federal Reserve Bank of Atlanta, "Imbalances in Latin American Fiscal Accounts: Why the United States Should Care," *Econ South* 2(1), www.frbatlanta.org.

36. José María Fanelli and Roberto Frenkel, "Macropolicies for the Transition from Stabilization to Growth," in *New Directions in Development Economics: Growth, Environmental Concerns and Government in the 1990s,* ed. Mats Lundahl and Benno J. Ndulu (London: Routledge, 1996), 46.

37. Robert Rennhack, "Banking Supervision," *Finance & Development* (March 2000): 27.

38. As characterized by Michael Gavin, "Surviving Economic Surgery," *The IDB* (December 1996): 4–5.

39. "A New Risk of Default," *Euromoney,* September 1996, 283.

40. Lance Taylor and Ute Piper, *Reconciling Economic Reform and Sustainable Human Development: Social Consequences of Neo-Liberalism,* United Nations Development Programme Discussion Paper Series (New York: UNDP, 1996).

41. Fanelli and Frenkel, "Macropolicies," 41.

42. Colin Bradford Jr., "Future Policy Directions and Relevance," in *The Legacy of Raúl Prebisch,* ed. Enrique V. Iglesias (Washington, D.C.: IADB, 1994), 164.

CHAPTER SIX

THE ROLE OF THE STATE

From a Smaller to a Smarter State

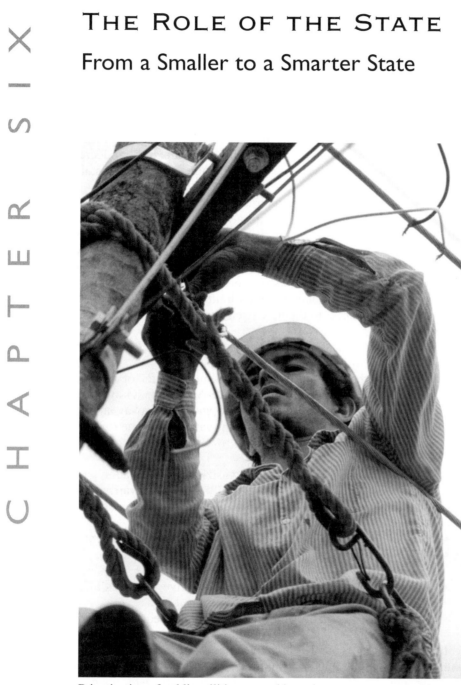

Privatization of public utilities created huge investment opportunities.
(Courtesy of the Inter-American Development Bank)

145

The shape and the function of the state in Latin America changed dramatically in the 1990s. We saw the state sputter as the engine of growth under import substitution industrialization (ISI). Coincident with a political transformation to democracy throughout the region, an economic transformation producing a smaller state sector also took place. We recall that debt crises and macroeconomic instability forced a reconsideration of the capabilities of the state. From chapter 5, we remember the pattern of deficit financing that emerged in Latin America in the 1980s. These deficits were compounded by interest rate and commodity price shocks. Capital flight contributed to the erosion of the tax base. Government spending was a source of macroeconomic instability. Fiscal reform, in terms of both decreasing expenditures and increasing revenues, was essential to macroeconomic stabilization in the region.

With greater vulnerability to international capital markets, Latin American policymakers must exercise fiscal discipline more rapidly and strictly than counterparts in industrial countries.[1] Given the fiscal crisis of the state, one aspect of reform has been the downsizing of the public sector. Another element of this reform is the privatization of state enterprises, changing the shape of state activity in the region. Decreasing the financial liabilities of the state included decreasing state provision of public services. As we analyze these dramatic changes in the region, key questions emerge with respect to the new streamlined Latin American state:

- How have decreases in the quantity of resources controlled by the state changed the role of government in the region?
- What were the mechanics of the massive transfer of resources from state-owned enterprises (SOEs) to the private sector? Just how are enterprises privatized without creating a garage sale, give-it-all-away atmosphere?
- What has been the record to date on privatization in the region? What remains to be done?

Driven by crisis, the first stage of downsizing—cutting aggregate public expenditure and privatizing firms—was relatively straightforward. Deficits had to be reduced to sustainable levels. The next stage is more problematic.

- What size and roles should the new streamlined government assume?
- What should be the balance between the state and the market in Latin America?
- How have corruption and poor administrative practices affected the legitimacy of the state in Latin America?
- What kind of instructions promote sustainable, equitable growth?

In a sense, the first stages of stabilization were easier—by decree governments lowered tariffs, reducing gross inefficiencies and improving macrodisequilibria. What lies ahead includes the tougher steps for Latin American states: an era of institution building.[2] Institutional arrangements, particularly how policymakers are elected to office and the rules of the game in allocating budgets among competing priorities, affect levels and efficiency of spending.[3]

THE NEW ROLE FOR THE STATE IN LATIN AMERICA

Privatization and fiscal stabilization revolutionized the traditional role of the strong state in Latin America. Altering levels of expenditures and mechanisms for raising revenue should be undertaken in the light of a clear vision of the appropriate role of the state in Latin America. The traditional state in Latin America was subject to a paradox; it was both omnipresent and extremely weak. Large and unwieldy, it was unable to accomplish its functions efficiently. A source of political favors and populist responses, it was also captured by numerous interest groups that competed to extract rents from the state.[4] Macroeconomic crisis brought with it unintended benefits. Internal and external shocks shook up interest group politics. Ruling coalitions broke down in many countries as exogenous shocks led to the fiscal crises of the state. What should be the new shape of the state in the region?

According to Dani Rodrik, the huge capacity gap between what the state promised and what it was actually able to deliver prompted an era of excessive pessimism with respect to state intervention in the economy. State effectiveness in delivering public goods changed the shape of the Latin American state. Rodrik suggests further that having overcome "excessive pessimism," we are on the threshold of a serious reconsideration of the role of the state in development.[5] The question remains, however, of the character and scope of efficient and effective government intervention in Latin American economies. How should the state behave to promote economic development?

Two broad forces indicate a possible increase in state intervention: globalization and the social challenges in the region. According to Peter Evans, international trade is increasingly organized as a flow of goods within productive networks that are structured globally rather than nationally.[6] Goods are produced transnationally, not within a single country's borders. Decisions taken in multinational headquarters are as important to workers as policy choices of the national central bank. Globalization has also increased the power of global capital markets in relation to governments. Globalization produces winners and losers. Should governments intervene to ameliorate the effects of globalization?

Rodrik finds a correlation between exposure to such global trade networks and government expenditures. More open states appear to employ greater intervention. He concludes that globalization may require larger states to insulate their citizens from the uncertainty of globalized markets.[7] In addition to the external forces of globalization, the legacy of the debt crisis and macroeconomic instability has been a huge social deficit. As we will see in later chapters, while the market may contribute to solutions, effective state leadership is critical in investing in health and education systems.

But developing countries find it difficult to decrease vulnerability to external shocks and promote human capital development at home. First of all, unless they solve the puzzle of how to raise tax revenues, they do not have the fiscal capacity to protect citizens from the costs of globalization or prepare them as healthy, educated, global citizens. Second, international lending practices constrain activity by developing states. Although they are beginning to change their position on this, multilateral development institutions frown upon intervention favoring free market outcomes. Intervention in the domestic interest may have an international financial cost. Given conditionalities by multilateral institutions, a question arises as to where the main accountability of the state lies—with the voters in a fragile democratic system or with the external aid organizations that hold significant purse strings? As the state in Latin America shapes new roles, questions of internal and external accountability will have to be resolved.

The Market for Government Services

Within a restricted market for state activity, how should governments respond to different demands for services? One can think of the state as the arbiter of demands by competing interest groups. As Barry Weingast notes, "A well functioning and stable state in which all interest groups are represented and can interact freely must exist before efficiency-enhancing policies can emerge."[8] Consolidation of democratic procedures and deepening of institutional reform is critical. Without a state apparatus that can fairly mediate competing concerns, policy will be driven by the interests of the powerful—clearly the historical legacy in Latin America. As Evans argues, "Civic engagement flourishes more easily among private citizens and organized groups when they have a competent public sector as an interlocutor."[9] If development policy is to respond to the needs of the people, there must be some sort of political "market" where these demands can be expressed. Moves toward decentralization of power are designed to allow for bottom-up, demand-driven policies.

Decentralization has encouraged local participation. *(Courtesy of the Inter-American Development Bank)*

A system of fiscal federalism can limit arbitrary behavior of the central government by introducing accountable institutions at lower levels and restricting the ability of central governments to overtax.[10] However, if local institutions are dominated by local elites, this effect can be overrun. Accountability and transparency are critical ingredients of good governance. Given the history we considered in chapter 2, this, of course, is a tall order for Latin America.

World Bank economists indicate that states should do less in areas where markets can be relied upon, working with market forces and not against them.[11] Two criteria should be met: government actions should address serious marketplace imperfections, and they should be designed such that their benefits outweigh their costs.[12] In other words, governments should intervene when markets break down, but only if government action in this arena is preferable to other uses of scarce government funds. Intervention should be selectively targeted in areas of greatest possible returns.

A successful market-based strategy relies on complementary institutions. Particularly in developing countries, where markets may not function perfectly, state-sponsored institutions can promote better flows of information, encourage standards for production, and facilitate communications and the diffusion of knowledge among firms. As illustrated in the case of Chilean foreign trade, this growth-enhancing collaboration between state agencies and private groups is especially important in promoting exports and diversifying production.[13] CORFO, the Chilean state-owned production development corporation, searched out the best foreign practices and fostered networks of small producers to supply large, modern processing firms in promoting agroexports. Chile's market-based "miracle" was in part based on the knowledge sharing, quality control, and improved technical capabilities encouraged by the state that made Chilean exports competitive in international markets. PROCHILE, a state agency created in 1975, assisted firms in breaking into unknown foreign markets and cofinanced export projects with coalitions of firms. Most recently, state promotion has been targeted at modernization with social equity. The Chilean example underscores the fact that achieving sustainable growth involves building economic institutions to address informational and organizational constraints in the developing world.

Theoretical Approaches to State Activity in Development

Despite the significant statement on the part of the World Bank that the state and the market are complementary institutions, a formulaic mix of just how much state versus how much market is not provided. This echoes Adam Smith's seminal question: Just how much should states do to promote the wealth of nations? In part, the answer to this policy question has to do with the assumptions about states and markets that you bring in approaching the problem of economic development in Latin America. Box 6.1 outlines some of the conditions under which market solutions are optimal. As we consider the specific circumstances of state participation in the areas of international trade, finance, social policy, and the environment in the following chapters, we can look to three broad theoretical perspectives to pattern policy

BOX 6.1.   WHEN DO MARKETS WORK BEST?

- Markets are most effective for goods that can be consumed by one person at a time, or when the characteristic of subtractability is present. For example, with a finite supply, one person's use of scarce water subtracts from that available to a community, but one person's use of a road does not significantly diminish its future availability for others.
- Individuals must face the threat of being easily prevented from consuming the good, or excludability, to be willing to pay. For example, people cannot be easily excluded from breathing air.
- Common pool goods such as common pastures and irrigation water are difficult because there is high subtractability but low excludability. The use of water that threads through many farms takes away from that available downstream, but it is hard to prevent one farmer from taking more than a fair share. Incentives for cooperation and persuasion through local participatory institutions work best with common pool problems. Community involvement can promote local resource management.
- When subtractability is missing, or when the use by one person does not reduce the availability to others while excludability is also low, as in the case of public goods, powerful incentives exist to free ride and not pay for resources. It is hard to get individuals to pay to clean the air, because if some individuals choose not to pay, you can't say "don't breathe." A mix of hierarchy to enforce payment and local community involvement can help solve the public-good problem.
- Toll goods with characteristics of low subtractability and high excludability such as piped water not in scarce supply can be managed through a combination of market and hierarchy. Regulated private water companies, private concessions, or autonomous public corporations may be used depending on local conditions. Fair and transparent administration of private contracts to manage public resources is a key ingredient to success.
- Private markets work best when both excludability and subtractability are present. For smooth functioning of markets, a strong institutional framework ensuring private property rights is key.
- To decrease some of the conflicts generated by unfettered free markets such as pollution externalities or overuse of natural resources, the private voluntary sector or nongovernmental organizations can be effective in mobilizing grassroots energies to counter negative market effects. Lester Salamon notes that "we are in the midst of a global associational revolution that may prove to be as significant to the latter twentieth century as the rise of the nation-state was to the latter nineteenth." New institutional capital created by the voluntary sector may be a critical ingredient in holding market-based strategies together.

Source: Adapted from Robert Picciotto, *Putting Institutional Economics to Work: From Participation to Governance,* World Bank Discussion Papers, No. 304 (Washington, D.C.: World Bank, 1995).

responses: the **new political economy (NPE)**, the **new institutional economics (NIE)**, and the **neostructuralists.** These broad schools are really archetypes, modeling general schools of thought. In the economics and the political economy literature you will find different, more nuanced variants of these three broad categories of thought.[14]

The first model is loosely based on NPE, which grounds its assumptions in the material self-interest and rational calculus of economic actors. A position long espoused by economist Milton Friedman and the Chicago School, NPE suggests that people make their own best individual economic choices. Intervention by the state distorts the necessary market signals for accurate decision making. Interfering with market signals by providing a soft social cushion, for example, will only prolong the long-run process of adjustment.[15] New political economists assume that self-promoting politicians and bureaucratic elites will form coalitions to control resource allocation in accord with their own narrow interests. Corruption on the part of public officials is seen as systemic because it is in their self-interest.[16] For new political economists, sometimes broadly called **neoliberals,** markets save on scarce administrative capacities. These decentralized institutions oriented by profit signals avoid the pitfalls of big bureaucracies and are more responsive to consumer needs.

New political economists do agree that outcomes in developing countries may have an internal logic inconsistent with long-run efficiency. For example, a peasant farmer may continually divide the family fields into small plots that make cultivation difficult. Although there is an associated loss of efficiency and output, the peasant rationale is simple: diversification of risks among the local community.[17] Nonetheless, the presumption of the model is that the same assumptions about individual maximization of utility adhere in the developing world as in industrial market economies. Rolling back the size of the state will facilitate the reach of the market and the ability of economies to get price signals right. Foreign trade will introduce competitive price pressure and create incentives for external orientation and transparency in public policy. For neoliberals, the free market is the best of all possible worlds.

NPE is transformed by NIE—associated with economists Ronald Coase, Douglass North, and Oliver Williamson—to include the importance of institutions. They support the tenets of individual choice within neoclassical economics but conclude that mainstream economics has ignored transaction costs, particularly those associated with market failure. Institutions have developed to minimize transaction costs, although they may not always be efficient organizations. Institutions are defined as the rules of the game of the society and are composed of formal rules such as statute laws, common laws, and regulations as well as informal constraints including conventions, norms of behavior, and self-imposed codes of conduct. Organizational players include political bodies such as parties, city councils, or regulatory agencies; economic bodies including firms, unions, and cooperatives; and social bodies such as churches or clubs and educational bodies.[18] An institutional structure evolves historically, determining who the strategic actors are and the constraints on their choices. Economic change is a complex interplay between the stock of knowledge, institutions, and demographic factors.[19]

New institutionalists suggest that neither the state nor the market may be the best way to organize the provision of goods and services.[20] This belief is driven in part by a different view of the market. For the new institutionalists the market is not the "impersonal economic exchange of homogeneous goods by means of voluntary transactions on an equal basis between large numbers of autonomous, fully informed entities with profit-maximizing behavioral motivations able to enter and leave freely" on which neoclassical theorists build their models.[21] Instead, NIE assumes that information is rarely complete and that there are transaction costs in finding out relevant prices, negotiating contracts, and monitoring and enforcing them.[22] Economic performance depends crucially on the setting in which market transactions occur. NIE emphasizes the economic benefits of institutional arrangements that help bring down transaction costs, including transparent, effective, and accessible legal and judicial arrangements. It allows that cultural norms and values may create institutional outcomes distinctly different from those in industrial market economies, where traditional norms might mediate questions of allocation and income.

Economic modernization for the new institutionalist depends on a favorable institutional environment. A core concept is that strong market institutions make for market friendliness. North lays out four essential conditions for successful industrial development: secure property rights, effective and impartial judicial systems, transparent regulatory frameworks, and healthy institutional arrangements to promote complex interpersonal exchange, including enforcement of contracts, establishment of limited liability corporations, and easy entry and exit of firms.[23]

Rodrik presents four functions for economic institutions: market creating, market regulating, market stabilizing, and market legitimizing.[24] To create markets, property rights must be protected and contracts enforced. Regulation is necessary to deal with externalities, economies of scale, and imperfect information. For example, regulatory agencies will enhance efficiency in telecommunications, transportation, and financial services. Market stabilizing institutions are primarily macroeconomic, ensuring low inflation, minimizing macroeconomic volatility, and averting financial crises. Examples include central banks, exchange rate regimes, and budgetary and fiscal rules. Finally, market legitimizing institutions provide social protection and insurance, involve redistribution, and manage conflict. Examples include pension systems, unemployment insurance schemes, and other social funds. For the new institutionalists, capacity building in state institutions will facilitate market outcomes. Markets left alone will be inefficient; developing states need to foster the development of strong market institutions. New institutionalists do not believe that markets develop spontaneously; they must be nurtured by careful state policy.

In contrast, neostructuralists see a broader scope for state activity. Building upon the assumptions of the structuralists studied in chapter 3 that the facts describing developing economies do not conform to those of industrial market economies, they suggest a case for effective selectivity in state intervention in the economy. Calling for a modernization strategy that would respond to socioeconomic backwardness and excessive vulnerability, neostructuralists recognize a vital role for the state in making up for market failures. They specifically suggest intervention to promote or simulate missing markets (such as long-term capital markets), strengthen incomplete markets (including technology), eliminate or correct structural distortions (heterogeneous production structures, concentration of property), and eradicate or compensate for the most significant market imperfections arising from economies of scale, externalities, and learning.[25] They part with their intellectual fathers in the dependency school in placing greater emphasis on outward-looking export development as opposed to inward-directed import substitution and place less faith than the new institutionalists (and certainly the new political economists) in the ability of markets to meet the difficult challenges of development without significant state activity. The neostructuralists believe that markets alone—even relatively efficient ones—will not solve intractable problems such as poverty or the environment or meet the challenge of promoting dynamic technological change in a globally integrated world, for the markets are a necessary but not sufficient condition for economic development. Instead, an effective state is key to sustainable development.

This is not to say that neostructuralists naively believe that all state intervention is positive. In a typology of states, one can distinguish between states that are captured by elite constituencies and those able to maintain policy independence. The first type has been called a factional state; it may be either democratic or authoritarian. The second has been characterized as autonomous. The autonomous state may be seen as either guardian or predatory. A guardian state may attempt to maximize the welfare of its subjects or despotically create its own rules under the assumption that it is more enlightened than its constituency. The predatory state focuses on the extraction of resources from the population for its own benefit. Gains may accrue to a single ruler or to enhance the power of state bureaucracy.[26] Clearly, the goal is to establish parameters for public policy that would encourage the development of an autonomous guardian state responding to the will of the people.

Some neostructuralists have suggested a non–Washington Consensus in counterpoint to the policies of recent years.[27] Such a package would include an appreciation for fiscal equilibrium but add an additional focus on the links between the fiscal, foreign, and savings gaps with a particular eye to the distributional and political aspects of fiscal equilibrium. The non–Washington Consensus advances the position that getting prices right is neither easy nor without cost and that wage reductions resulting from economic reforms adversely affect human capital development. The orthodox interpretation of sound macroeconomic policy backfires into an anemic state and economic stagnation, and privatization in itself is not desirable. Investment in a better-educated, better-paid, and healthier labor force is a long-term process with limited payoffs in short-run economic expansion. Finally, preset blueprints for macroeconomic policy do not apply to all cases. Each country has its own set of historical circumstances and institutional norms that need to be taken into consideration when designing policy. State economic policy must be carefully crafted to local conditions.

Not surprisingly, new political economists disagree with many of the neostructuralist prescriptions. New political economists might agree that markets will not generate perfect outcomes, but in their eyes government, even when acting in a benevolent fashion, does not know more than markets in terms of the "right" intervention schemes. Government does not have enough information or sharp-enough tools to minimize the costs of intervention and maximize the benefits. Market prices—the quintessential magnification of disaggregated decision making—are a better guide to resource allocation.[28] New political economists contend that markets will move the economy toward the best of all possible levels of economic growth. New political economists, consistent with their orthodox roots, suggest that intervention in the market will only divert the economy from its long-run efficient equilibrium. Under the guise of making things better in the short run, intervention will only leave the economy worse off over time. Furthermore, when policy interventions are possible, agents are encouraged to engage in rent-seeking behavior to influence outcomes. Nonmarket activities such as lobbying or offering bribes become a mechanism for securing preferences by the state.[29]

As we continue in our text to investigate development challenges in Latin America, the broad framework of the new political economists, the new institutionalists, or the neostructuralists may guide your policy perspective. Do you believe that the market alone will generate the best of all possible outcomes? Do you support the proposition that transaction costs might interfere with the efficient workings of the market, warranting different institutional arrangements? Or do you subscribe to the view that the state has a legitimate role as an actor in economic development in the region? Clarifying your position on the appropriate mix of market and government activity will facilitate your ability to formulate coherent policy positions.

THE POLICY PENDULUM IN LATIN AMERICA

The decade of debt and macroeconomic instability of the 1980s in Latin America left states with few options in economic policy. An active state role costs money; most Latin American states were broke. If state promotion of economic development was to be financed through noninflationary means, Latin governments would have to attract international capital. Financial markets, wary of investing again in the same state-led structure that had led them to write down significant outstanding debt, were looking for fresh approaches to investment. Market-led as opposed to state-directed development gained ascendancy. A pragmatic marriage of cash-strapped governments and return-seeking capital markets took place.

A smaller minimal state with a focus on macroeconomic stabilization and market fundamentals emerged. Fiscal and monetary discipline were seen as prerequisites to growth. The state exited most of its activities as a producer of goods and services in the commercial sector, with the exception of some public goods such as electricity and natural resource–based activities. Broad social subsidies for food inputs, education, and health were redirected to means-tested programs. Lower marginal tax rates combined with broadening the tax base was intended to encourage local entrepreneurship while balancing the fiscal books. The focus moved from inward development to the export engine for growth—with widespread trade liberalization leading the way. Regulations governing capital flows were also loosened to encourage both portfolio and direct investment inflows. Market magic—and the promise of healthy returns—captured investors' imaginations. SOEs put on the auction block offered exciting investment opportunities. The International Monetary Fund (IMF) encouraged many of these measures through its rigid stabilization programs, and the World Bank participated in helping to facilitate structural adjustment from relatively closed to open, globalized economies.

In 1990 John Williamson named this constellation of market-based policies operative in Latin America the "Washington Consensus"—a term he later regretted.[30]

Column 1 of table 6.1 summarizes the key elements of the consensus. Williamson later noted that the term came to describe "an extreme and dogmatic commitment to the belief that markets can handle everything."[31] The extreme version is perhaps better captured by the term "neoliberalism" or George Sorros's "market fundamentalism."[32] It most clearly maps into the NPE view of the world. In the following chapters we will carefully analyze the market-based elements in trade, finance, agriculture, and industry—and the effects that these policies have had for poverty, inequality, gender, and the environment. In retrospect, what is most surprising about these packages was their boldness: governments, in their attempts to cultivate political favor among elites at home and international investment abroad, went beyond the recommendations of the international financial institutions to implement bold, radical market-based approaches to stabilization and growth. Kurt Weyland suggests that the drastic Fuji shock in Peru, President Carlos Menem's convertibility program in Argentina, and Fernando Collor de Mello's single bullet to kill liquidity in Brazil all went beyond multilateral bank recommendations in the wholesale adoption of market-based mechanisms.[33] Weyland argues that prospect theory—a psychological concept that suggests that when people are faced with large losses they are willing to take high risks to avoid collapse—explains how crises triggered bold actions that engendered systematic overshooting of international financial institutions' recommendations. A big bang approach could serve to jolt market participants to attention.

The consensus originally described by Williamson was more nuanced in terms of its understanding of what markets can and cannot accomplish than the programs put in place to curry votes and dollars. As market fundamentalism marched forward, attention to the social sector and infrastructure investment languished. The need to complement the market with strong institutions for growth in a globalized world was downplayed. Strong industrial market economies around the world are supported by strong governments to regulate fair play and intermediate social investments. Where the need for building educational and health institutions or strong regulatory regimes to promote fair competition was recognized in Latin America, the financing for such difficult institutional development was most often lacking. Without the critical contributions of institutional development, market growth has been unruly and volatile. Figure 6.1 shows the disappointingly slow growth in Latin America as compared to Asian counterparts. Much of the so-called second generation reforms during the 1990s in Latin America—the tough, slow, plodding work of changing law and building institutions—has been directed at these deficiencies. However, while it is relatively straightforward to implement bold macroeconomic policies by decree, changing the delicate social balance of entitlements through legislatures and courts is a more difficult political challenge.

In 2001 Nancy Birdsall and Augusto de la Torre highlighted the need to counterweight market fundamentalism with economic policies explicitly targeting social equity in their report "Washington Contentious."[34] The last column of table 6.1 summarizes their recommendations. Although the market remains the central tool for growth, social policies intermediated by a selective state are seen as necessary for equitable, sustainable growth. A broader recognition that reforms had bogged down throughout the region and the need to round out a myopic emphasis on growth with

Table 6.1. The Washington Consensus versus Washington Contentious

The Washington Consensus (Williamson 1990)	Prescription of Market Fundamentalism?	Too Weak or Too Much: Insufficient Progress or Going beyond IFI Recommendations?	Washington Contentious (Birdsall and de la Torre)
Fiscal discipline	Yes; prerequisite to growth	Some plans such as Peru and Venezuela seen as too radical by IFIs to contain domestic opposition—but were pursued at breakneck speed; other plans did not insert significant budgetary discipline	Rule based fiscal discipline remains a necessary ingredient
Redirect spending priorities from things like indiscriminate subsidies to basic health and education	Not necessarily market; role for a smarter state	Financing for social development scant	Bring the state back in to create automatic social safety nets; education policy to target the poor; redistributive policies for growth
Lower marginal tax rates and broaden the tax base	Yes, in increasing incentive for private investment	Tax reform a political nightmare of contending interest groups	Focus on taxing the rich
Interest rate liberalization & monetary stabilization	Yes; get market money prices right —free markets and sound money	Systematic overshooting of IFI targets in radical stabilization plans	Reduce volatility; focus on smoothing booms and busts
A competitive exchange rate	Yes; get relative international prices right	Disputes within the IFIs on exchange rate regimes; fear of Argentine convertibility plan	Floating exchange rate is most dominant with some exceptions

Trade liberalization	Yes; open to Smith and Ricardo's gains from trade	Unilateral trade liberalization preceded the time frame mandated under WTO or PTA agreements	Genuine liberalization to include reducing rich country protectionism
Liberalization of FDI inflows	Yes; open to international capital flows	Controversy around the use of capital controls to manage problems of exchange rate overvaluation	Capital flowing to more dynamic economies leaves slow growth economies behind
Privatization	Yes; increase the role for the private sector	Star element of package, although momentum of capital inflows falls off as best investment opportunities are completed	Consumer driven public services
Deregulation, in the sense of abolishing barriers to entry and exit	Yes, in increasing private scope but also need complementary institutions to promote competition	Progress on competition policy too slow to regulate private sector activity	Promote competition policy to give small businesses a chance
Secure property rights	Yes, in guaranteeing property rights but need laws and practices to guarantee rights at all levels	Legal system of contracts too weak to guarantee investment	Deal openly with discrimination, repairing land markets and protecting workers rights

Source: Patrice Franko.

Figure 6.1.   Slow Latin Growth 1990–2003

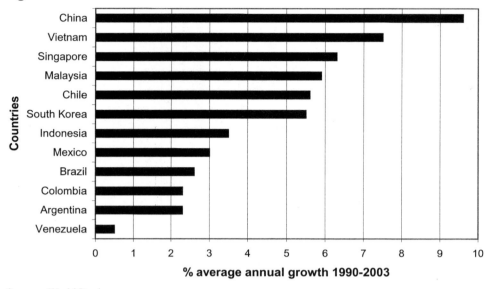

Source: World Bank.

investment in poverty reduction and social investment has begun to take hold among policymakers.[35] As Dani Rodrik noted, jump-starting and sustaining growth are two different processes—the first can be initiated by market magic, but the latter must be aligned with incentives balancing social costs and benefits.[36] The market has lost its luster for the Latin American public. The percentage of Latin Americans who believe that the market economy is good for their country plummeted from a high of 77 percent in 1998 to 18 percent in 2003.[37] This is not altogether surprising. As shown in figure 6.2, per capita growth rates have been either negative or anemic since the onset of the debt crisis in 1981. Social disillusionment has sprouted into protest and violence throughout the region. Bolivia, Ecuador, and Nicaragua are under the pressure of weak institutions, fractious politics, and gaping social divisions that threaten democracy.[38] In April 2005, Lucio Gutierrez became Ecuador's third consecutive president to be driven from office by social unrest polarized by a deep ethnic divide. Youth gangs in Central America—disillusioned by the lack of upward mobility in these societies—threaten the fabric of traditional societies.

Pressures to bring the state back in to address redistributive crises are strong. As Bernardo Kliksberg notes, this is not a step back to the 1960s' state-led development strategy but rather "a step forward to construct an efficient, participatory and equitable state: an intelligent state."[39] A smarter state might intervene selectively to address the gaps left by market magic. Williamson himself, in assessing the post–Washington Consensus, specifies that "in addition to pursuing economic growth, the objectives should include 'sustainable development, egalitarian development, and democratic development.'"[40] Table 6.2 summarizes the productive role of the state in open economies advocated by the Economic Commission for Latin

Figure 6.2.   Growth and Productivity Changes

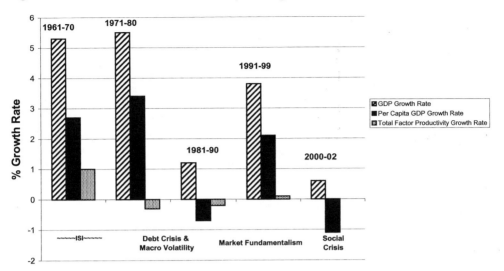

Source: Loayza et al (2002) and World Bank 2001 as reported in Lora et al 2003.

America and the Caribbean (ECLAC). Nobel laureate Joseph Stiglitz contends that "what is at issue is not just the size of government, but its role—what activities should it undertake—and the balance between government and the market. The post–Washington Consensus recognizes that there is a role for a market; the question is, to what extent do the neo-liberals recognize that there is a role for the state, beyond the minimal role of enforcing contracts and property rights."[41]

What roles should the state undertake in promoting Latin American growth in

Table 6.2.   ECLAC's Road Map for Productive Development in Open Economies

- Consolidate macroeconomic management, expand ability to apply counter-cyclical policies, promote higher and less volatile growth; manage diverse risks
- Encourage public and private investment, improve infrastructure, promote competition, improve regulations, increase public sector flexibility in spending; better environmental management
- Improve the quality of external participation through stable and secure access to world markets and diversification of products
- Deal with shortfalls in information that the market cannot resolve—"exchanging more market, less government" for a model based on "smoothly functioning markets and quality government"
- Recognize the diversity of the economic and social structure; place income distribution at center; identify policies for a complex three-tiered economy, including multinationals, medium and small informal firms

Source: Jose Luis Machinea, ECLAC Executive Secretary.

the new millennium? Your views may be shaped by the views you might hold as a new political economist, an institutionalist, or a neostructuralist. Although you may agree that the market has failed to deliver on its promised growth, do you believe that a smarter, more selective state can do better? If you believe there is greater scope for state activity in modern Latin America, how much activity would you recommend? Do you believe that institutions ingrained over time can indeed be changed enough to promote stable, equitable growth—or that more aggressive, albeit smarter state action is warranted to generate sustainable outcomes? If a stronger state hand is necessary, how can it be financed? The rest of our text will grapple with these dilemmas across a variety of issue areas. As we test your predisposition to a market, an institutional, or a structuralist position across concrete policy problems, you may begin to unravel the puzzle of Latin American economic development. Or perhaps your answer may depend on where the pendulum has just been— each model creates its own weaknesses that need to be addressed by the strength of the other.

Before concluding this chapter, we will treat three issues central to the discussion of the state in Latin America: the contemporary size of the Latin American state as limited by the need to reduce corruption and enhance transparency, fiscal constraints, and the privatization record in the region.

Good Governance: Fighting Corruption and Enhancing Transparency

To be effective, government activity must be credible and legitimate. State activity in Latin America is plagued by lack of transparency, kickbacks in contracting to civil servants and politicians, and bribes to judges and the police. Rule of law is critical to well-functioning markets. Corruption—fueled by inadequate laws, weak public administration, and weak capacity for law enforcement—contributes to the low credibility of institutions. Table 6.3 illustrates the pervasiveness of corruption in the region. Only Chile ranks among Transparency International's top twenty-five cleanest countries as measured by the corruption perceptions index; most nations in the region find themselves in the bottom half of the global scale. In the Global Corruption Barometer, also by Transparency International, we can see that corruption is perceived as pervasive across a range of institutions—from political parties and legislatures to the police, the judiciary, and the private sector. Religious bodies and nongovernmental organizations (NGOs) score best but still worse than the average world score for the same institutions.

Corruption has an economic cost. One estimate for Colombia suggests that 1 percent of gross domestic product (GDP) is lost to corruption; in Brazil it is suggested that each Brazilian pays $6,000 annually due to corruption. The average Mexican household reportedly spends 14 percent of its income bribing civil servants to get a drivers license or permission to build a new house.[42] Unofficial estimates in Ecuador place the corruption burden at 11.2 percent of GDP. Estimates indicate that governments in Latin America pay corruption surcharges of 15–20 percent of their purchases, totaling $40–50 billion each year.[43]

Corruption adds to the cost of development projects. The comptroller general of Ecuador shows irregularities in handling funds in 95 percent of projects evaluated. In Paraguay the cost of roads in rural areas increased from $13 million to $24 million due to kickbacks. In Venezuela, seven hundred ghost employees were found on the rolls of public enterprises.[44] These high costs of corruption act as a deterrent to international investors.

The perception is that bribery smooths the work of public administration, but as César Gaviria of the Organization of American States (OAS) notes, it hinders trade, growth, and development, creating disincentives to investment. An underdeveloped civil society, where a large amount of power remains in the hands of an elite, creates incentives for corruption. Combined with an inefficient bureaucracy, corruption has become accepted by society as a mechanism to expedite business. Government officials rely on bribes to supplement low state wages, and the weakness of the rule of law means that corruption generally goes unpunished. Research by the World Bank shows that countries that tackle corruption and improve rule of law can increase national incomes by as much as four times in the long run. This 400 percent dividend would mean that a country with an income per capita of $2,000 could see its income rise to $8,000 in the long run.

In many countries the costs of corruption are becoming better understood. In response to public demand, governments have tried to promote clean government. Mexico's Vicente Fox set up the National Pact on Transparency and Fighting Corruption in February 2001, with special outreach to civil society. With the support of the United States Agency for International Development (USAID), El Salvador has implemented an ethics code for civil servants. In Peru, efforts to cut down on traffic ticket scams that increased costs particularly to taxi drivers included the hiring of female traffic officers—70 percent surveyed now say that traffic control has improved, in part because the women are perceived as less corruptible. In Colombia and Venezuela networks of citizen watchdog groups, including local chapters of NGOs such as Transparency International Latin America and Carribean have proliferated. Engaging the public is crucial to promoting accountability. Transparency measures supported by e-governance have helped to build credibility in public institutions. Regionwide the OAS has adopted the Inter-American Convention against Corruption; anticorruption measures have also been prominent in the Summit of the Americas meetings.[45]

Despite progress, much remains to be done. Star performer Chile finds that although its government auditing office, the Contraloria, has reigned in spending and corruption, it is important to complement clean government with measures of performance and efficiency to encourage good governance. Incentives to promote public servants' productivity are being tried to invigorate slow-moving bureaucracies. Uruguay is trying to change the tradition of patronage that handed out jobs to the one in four Uruguayans who work for the government. Government agencies were rewarded through access to special funds for labor cost savings, and employees who were released were given access to money to start small businesses, resulting in a savings of $56 million to the Uruguayan treasury.[46] Efforts to improve the quality of public administration could be translated into a doubling of spending on health and education if squandered resources are recovered.

Table 6.3.   Corruption Indexes

Transparency International 2005 Corruption Perceptions Index (CPI)

Global Country rank	Country	2005 CPI score*	Confidence range**	Surveys used***	
14	Canada	8.4	7.9–8.8	11	
17	United States	7.6	7.0–8.0	12	
21	Chile	7.3	6.8–7.7	10	
32	Uruguay	5.9	5.6–6.4	6	
	Costa Rica	4.2	3.7–4.7	7	
51	El Salvador	4.2	3.5–4.8	6	
	Colombia	4	3.6–4.4	9	=====>
	Brazil	3.7	3.5–3.9	10	For corruption barometer,
	Mexico	3.5	3.3–3.7	10	higher score is worse; for
	Panama	3.5	3.1–4.1	7	corruption perceptions
65	Peru	3.5	3.1–3.8	7	index, high score is better
97	Argentina	2.8	2.5–3.1	10	<=====
	Honduras	2.6	2.2–3.0	7	
107	Nicaragua	2.6	2.4–2.8	7	
	Bolivia	2.5	2.3–2.9	6	
	Ecuador	2.5	2.2–2.9	6	
	Guatemala	2.5	2.1–2.8	7	
117	Guyana	2.5	2.0–2.7	3	
130	Venezuela	2.3	2.2–2.4	10	
144	Paraguay	2.1	1.9–2.3	7	

LA Average ==>
World Average ==>

Explanatory notes: The Corruption Perceptions Index surveys businesses and elites.
* The CPI Score relates to perceptions of the degree of corruption as seen by business people and country analysts and ranges between 10 (highly clean) and 0 (highly corrupt).
** The Confidence range provides a range of possible values of the CPI score. This reflects how a country's score may vary, depending on measurement precision. Nominally, with 5 percent probability the score is above this range and with another 5 percent it is below. However, particularly when only few sources (n) are available an unbiased estimate of the mean coverage probability is lower than the nominal value of 90%.

Enhancing the effectiveness of markets often involves strengthening the role of nonmarket, nonstate actors: NGOs. This broader definition of the market actors includes local economic and social organizations and institutions. A concept of civil society–state synergy in which civic engagement may strengthen state institutions and effective state institutions may foster civic engagement has been proposed to strengthen market outcomes.[47] Examples of such organizations include community health cooperatives, soup kitchens, and farmers' extension groups. A key aspect of the synergy includes complementary or mutually supportive relations with a clear

Political parties	*Parliament / Legislature*	*Police*	*Legal system / Judiciary*	*Tax revenue*	*Business / private sector*	*Customs*	*Medical services*	*Media*	*Education system*	*Utilities*	*Registry and permit services*	*The military*	*NGOs*	*Religious bodies*

Global Corruption Barometer

Political parties	Parliament / Legislature	Police	Legal system / Judiciary	Tax revenue	Business / private sector	Customs	Medical services	Media	Education system	Utilities	Registry and permit services	The military	NGOs	Religious bodies
3.9	3.6	3	3.2	2.9	3	2.5	2.5	3.1	2.3	2.7	2.2	2.5	2.4	2.6
3.9	3.5	3	3.5	3.4	3.2	3	3.1	3.5	3	3	2.5	2.9	3	2.8
4.2	3.8	4	4.1	3.2	3.5	3.3	2.6	3	2.4	3	2.8	3	2.6	2.2
4	3.4	4	3.5	3	3.2	4	3.2	2.8	2.6	2.9	2.3	2.9	2.2	2.9
4.6	4.2	4	3.6	4.1	3.5	4	3.5	3.1	3.1	3.6	3.2	.	3	3.2
na	na	na	na	na	na	na	na	na	na	na	na	na	na	na
4.4	4.2	4	3.8	3.6	3.1	3.6	3.2	3	3	3.5	3.1	3.2	3	2.7
na	na	na	na	na	na	na	na	na	na	na	na	na	na	na
4.7	4.4	5	4.5	3.9	3.5	4.2	3.2	3.3	3.1	3.6	4	3.1	3.3	2.9
4.7	4.7	4	4.5	3.9	3.5	4	3.2	3.2	3.3	3.5	3.4	3.9	3	2.4
4.5	4.5	4	4.5	3.9	3.4	3.4	3.6	3.7	3.8	3.6	4.1	4.1	3.3	2.6
4.6	4.5	4	4.3	3.4	3.6	4.2	3	3.4	3	3.3	3.6	3.2	2.8	3
na	na	na	na	na	na	na	na	na	na	na	na	na	na	na
4.6	4.4	4	4.4	4.4	3.9	4.1	4	3.7	4.1	4.2	4.1	3.4	3.3	3
4.8	4.6	5	4.3	3.5	3.4	4.4	3.2	3	3.3	3.2	3.1	3.8	3.2	2.3
4.9	4.9	4	4.6	3.7	3.4	4.5	3.5	3.3	3.6	4.1	4.4	3.6	2.9	2.8
4.2	4	4	3.9	4	3.7	3.8	3.6	3.5	3.4	3.7	3.6	3.9	3.4	3.2
na	na	na	na	na	na	na	na	na	na	na	na	na	na	na
3.7	3.7	4	3.4	3.2	3.3	3.4	3.3	3.2	3.1	3.2	3.4	3.2	3.2	3.2
4.8	4.7	5	4.6	4.1	3.5	4.6	3.9	3.1	3.6	4	3.8	4.2	3	2.8
4.5	4.4	4	4.3	3.7	3.5	4	3.2	3.3	3.2	3.5	3.7	3.3	3.1	2.8
4	3.7	4	3.5	3.4	3.4	3.3	3.2	3.2	3	3	2.9	2.9	2.8	2.6

*** Surveys used refers to the number of surveys that assessed a country's performance. 18 surveys and expert assessments were used and at least 3 were required for a country to be included in the CPI.
Global Corruption Barometer: To what extent do you perceive the following sectors in this country/territory to be affected by corruption? (1: not at all corrupt, . . . 5: extremely corrupt) (Gallup surveyed 55,00 people in 69 counries).
Source: Transparency International.

division of labor between public and private actors. States can provide private citizens with inputs such as health care or agricultural extension that they could not have access to on their own. However, states should allow private actors to work with these inputs and not interfere where the private sector, including nonprofit community action groups, works best. A second ingredient of the synergy thrives on bridging the state-private divide to build relationships of trust and collaboration at the community level. Embedded relations between state and society build on reciprocal trust between, for example, health extension agents and their clients, making the state agencies a part of the communities where they work.[48]

The Size and Structure of the Latin American State

As you consider the conceptual framework for the role of the state, it is important to understand the realities and contemporary trends of state activity in Latin America. You may be surprised to know that the public sector in Latin America is roughly half the size of the typical industrial country government. Accounting for approximately 20 percent of GDP, the Latin American state spends less on social security, defense, health, and education than European counterparts, which spent approximately 40 percent. Interest payments on debt constitute 3.5 percent of GDP for both Latin American and industrial countries, but because the size of government is smaller, Latin American nations spend nearly twice the industrial average of 8 percent of central government expenditure on interest payments.[49] It is also important to note that less spending is not necessarily better for the market. As Carol Wise points out, Chile's successful performance has been correlated with one of the largest investments on the part of a state. The Chilean experience points to the need to invest in institutions and links to civil society to support broad market-based reforms.[50]

Why are Latin American states relatively small? The small size of the Latin American state is in part driven by its more limited capacity to raise revenues as compared to an industrial country government. This limited capacity stems from the region's large informal markets, which largely escape taxation, and from a weak bureaucratic structure for tax collection. Tax evasion is high, imposing higher costs on those complying with tax obligations. The administration of tax collection is weak, on average relying on 1 tax official per 6,649 inhabitants versus an average for industrial countries of 1 per 1,835.[51] Without an increased capacity to raise revenue and lacking the financial capacity to run persistent deficits, Latin American governments must limit the functions of the state. The tough lessons of overblown state sectors without the financial capacity to sustain them were made clear to Latin American governments in the high costs of debt service and macroeconomic instability.

Progress on reducing the fiscal deficit in Latin America has been far more dramatic than changes in the fiscal stance of industrial countries. Both began the 1970–1995 period with deficits of nearly 4 percent of GDP; isolating 1990–1995, Latin America had slashed its deficits to 2 percent with little change in industrial country deficits. Debt, the accumulated deficits of past years, was lower than the Organization for Economic Cooperation and Development (OECD) average for six Latin American countries and higher for eleven. Nonetheless, because domestic credit markets are more shallow in Latin America, governments are more vulnerable and exposed than in industrial countries. Relative to the size of the domestic financial system, Latin American deficits were three times the OECD average for the 1970–1994 period.[52] Debt can only be issued to the degree that markets think it profitable to hold it. Furthermore, the public is less interested in holding government debt when more secure international investment vehicles are available. The difficulty in raising money domestically pressures local interest rates and introduces macroeconomic disequilibrium. The downsizing of the Latin American state has left little room for further decreases in expenditures. Sustained macroeconomic stabilization is contingent on the ability of the state to increase revenues.[53]

Increasing Revenues: The Tax Problem

The challenge in Latin America is generating a sustainable increase in fiscal resources to permit the provision of needed services. Increasing spending on social services such as health, education, or environmental protection without provoking macro-economic instability is contingent upon increasing government revenue. How might this be done? Tax revenue derives from a number of different sources. Liberaliza-tion has made reliance on international trade taxes problematic and forced a shift toward domestic taxes. Tax reform in Latin America has been oriented toward the reduction of rates and the simplification of the individual income tax system as well as the widespread use of withholding.[54] With respect to direct income and property taxes, the threshold limit for income taxes has been raised and the maximum low-ered for individuals (from 47 to 28 percent) as well as for corporations (from 43.3 to 35.5 percent).[55]

The dismantling of ISI prompted a dramatic revision of the source of tax rev-enue. International trade taxes—tariffs on imports or taxes on exports—constituted 27.7 percent of total tax revenue in 1980; this ratio fell to 20.5 percent for the 1991–1995 period.[56] Most dramatic was the case of Argentina, where in 1980 inter-national trade taxes accounted for 45.8 percent of total tax revenue; by the first half of the 1990s this had fallen to 5.6 percent. Region-wide taxes on international trade only accounted for 5 percent of revenue in 2004.[57]

There is an apparent preference in the region for indirect taxation **value added tax (VAT)**. Advantages of VAT include its domestic, international, and intertem-poral neutrality and its self-monitoring nature.[58] VAT is seen as improving the like-lihood of tax compliance. By 1995, twenty-one countries in Latin America used VAT, which is a consumption tax. It is assessed at various levels of the production process, with each buyer of an input paying a percentage. It is therefore self-policing in that it is in the interest of the buyer to ensure that the tax at the previous level has been fairly paid to receive credit on the already taxed input. A large number of goods, including foodstuffs and most services, are excluded from VAT. Goods with negative externalities—such as alcoholic beverages, tobacco, and fuels—are generally taxed at a higher rate. VAT rates can also be used as an instrument to pro-mote gender equality because men and women tend to purchase different items. Those services that might decrease the burden of the double day that women face in the home and the marketplace might, for example, be taxed at a lower rate.[59]

In contrast, an income tax is difficult to administer because it is spread among a variety of activities, the number of potential taxpayers is large (but compliance low), and the administrative tax collection process does not generate a self-policing paper trail. Income tax collection relies on a process of withholding—a procedure that is thwarted by a large number of unregistered small firms or individuals in the informal sector. Low literacy rates complicate filing individual tax returns, and weak administrative capacity makes evasion widespread. The average income tax revenue for Latin America and the Caribbean is 4.3 percent of GDP, compared to 7 percent in Asia. Given difficulties in income tax collection, the VAT, which encourages the next agent in the chain to certify that the tax was paid at the stage before, is often seen as preferable.

Throughout Latin America the concept of decentralization—of redirecting state functions from centralized bureaucracies in state capitals to the local level—has taken hold. However, this is problematic in that decentralization has weakened the capacity to promote fiscal balance. The absence of accountability on borrowing at lower levels of government and the incentives for subregions to generate their own funds suggest that a decentralization of administration of tax services must accompany the political process of devolution of authority to the local level. Local politicians may be more prone to corruption. In Colombia, for example, many local governments are controlled by guerrilla groups or drug cartels.[60] Decentralization can also exacerbate inequalities by enhancing regional disparities in income. Wealthier regions can raise revenues while poor areas fall further behind in the provision of health care and education to a needy population. Increasing regional inequality may be a long-run constraint on sustained national development.

Despite advances in deficit reduction, fiscal reform in the region is incomplete. Policy alternatives include combating tax evasion, increasing direct taxation (especially the income tax), introducing green taxes to promote environmental compliance, and readjusting central versus local revenue-raising capabilities.[61] Mexico provides an example of decreasing the rate of evasion. In 1989 it introduced a tax on assets. Many firms did not pay income taxes, declaring a loss or no profits for the taxable period. In this case, if the firm had not paid taxes equal to 2 percent of its assets, it would be liable to that limit; credit would be given against the asset taxes for tax paid on profit.[62] Only by generating a stable and predictable level of revenue will the state be able to execute an active, developmental role.

THE PROMISE OF PRIVATIZATION

Beyond fiscal balance, privatization in Latin America became a dramatic and visible symbol to the international community of the depth of the commitment to a market model. But simply selling SOEs might not resolve some of the market inefficiencies that gave rise to the perceived need for state ownership in the first place. As Douglas North noted in his Nobel Prize acceptance speech, "Transferring the formal political and economic rules of successful Western market economies to third world economies is not a sufficient condition for good economic performance. Privatization is not a panacea for solving poor economic performance."[63] Changes in rules must accompany changes in ownership. Key questions must be resolved. Is a private monopoly any better than a state monopoly? Can the provision of important public services be guaranteed by market magic? What are the distributional implications of privatization? Will workers or consumers be hurt? Some of the concerns surrounding privatization can be addressed if the privatization process is carefully planned. How should that be done? This section will discuss the privatization record in Latin America with an eye to key complementary policies—particularly competition—that will reduce the costs and enhance the gains of privatization.

The Mechanics of Privatization

Privatization can be achieved in a variety of ways. An enterprise might be sold to the private sector by issuing stock in the corporation, a concession for the provision of public services can be auctioned off, or the regulations grounding market entry might be changed. These three types of privatization—sale of assets, contracting for services, and deregulation—are very much conditioned by the type of good or service produced and the existing market structure. If the market is relatively competitive, the outright sale of assets is most likely. Sometimes deregulating the market can enhance competitiveness. If the newly private firm will enjoy considerable market power, the state might choose to retain ownership and contract private services or introduce public regulations to make the private monopoly accountable to the public good. This may be appropriate in the case of natural monopolies. It is important to note, however, that privatization does not take place in a vacuum but rather is integrated as part of a comprehensive package of reforms. The success or failure of the privatization is intertwined with the overall progress of reforms.

The first wave of privatizations in Latin America in the 1980s generated significant resistance. At the time, state firms accounted for approximately 12 percent of GDP in Latin America.[64] Not surprisingly, managers and workers in state firms were threatened by the potential loss of jobs. Nationalist sentiments ran strong, contending that foreign capital would purchase the country's patrimony at bargain-basement prices. The military was concerned about the vulnerability of strategic industries, and the state itself did not want to lose the political power that control of jobs and production conferred.

Nonetheless, the potential gains from privatization were compelling. Many SOEs were inefficient and operating at a loss. Privatization, it was argued, would increase efficiency and decrease the pressure on state coffers. Whether the productivity gains and the desired fiscal effects were achieved was very much influenced by institutional capacity. Privatization involves a range of complementary measures; simply selling shares in a corporation does not guarantee competitiveness. Furthermore, particularly if a state-owned company was already relatively efficient, the revenue gains from the sale have only a one-time fiscal effect. That is, it is much like selling grandmother's silver to finance a vacation. The deficit may be helped temporarily, but once the heirloom is gone it carries no asset value.

To prevent shares from being sold at below their worth, valuations of the firm (usually using a net present value calculation) provide a minimum reference price below which shares are not sold. How shares are offered on the market can have distributional and efficiency consequences. If the firm had been owned by the public, should the citizenry continue to have an interest in the corporation through widely distributed shares, or does a tightly held corporation make more sense? Several methods can be employed: sale of stock to workers, private individuals, and corporate entities; sales of stock on an exchange; and competitive bidding through public auctions.[65] The selection of which method to use depends in part on the sophistication of markets and their ability to distribute shares in a fair, efficient, and transparent manner.

The speed and sequencing of privatization and regulatory reform matters. Rapid, comprehensive privatization signals strong political will to adhere to the market. However, if complementary measures to promote competition or regulate powerful private entities cannot be implemented at the same pace, privatization efforts are likely to falter. Market structure may indeed be more important than ownership in explaining the comparative performance of companies. Where privatized firms become natural monopolies without regulatory reforms, consumers may be no better off. Large private powerhouses can extract monopoly rents and provide low-quality services to consumers. Encouraging international competition may help mitigate monopolistic abuses, but questions of nationalism and ownership may then arise.

To promote successful, sustainable service to the population, privatization may need to be accompanied by measures to promote competition. In the privatization of utilities, telecommunications, water, and sewage, for example, state monopolies may become private monopolies without appropriate rules to govern behavior. In Chile, it was found that although privatization of these sectors led to improvements in the quality and quantity of services, without an enforceable regulatory structure prices did not fall with the privatization of services.[66] In the energy sector, energy losses were cut from 23 percent to 7 percent, and the number of clients per worker doubled. The number of phone lines increased sixfold from 1987 to 2001, and the average length of the waiting period for a new phone line fell from forty-one days in 1993 to only six days in 2001.[67] As monopolists, firms were able to charge the highest price the market would bear. The areas experiencing falling prices were those where competition emerged. Long-distance telephone rates, for example, fell 50 percent as new competitors entered the market; monopolized local rates rose by 35 percent. Regulation of utilities tends to be problematic given the classic problem of public regulation: asymmetry of information and regulatory capture. Only the firm knows the true cost of services; there is an incentive to inflate costs if the regulator's price formula is based on costs. Cozy relationships between firms and their overseers encourage corrupt and rent-seeking behavior. Strong and transparent regulation may challenge vested interests.

The rules for both national and international actors must be perceived as fair and transparent to build public support. The transition from SOEs to a competitive private market may be facilitated by multilateral support in preparing bids for sale, developing new management plans, or downsizing the workforce. International participation—either through a public agency such as the World Bank or a private concern such as an international consulting firm—has been important in safeguarding transparency and generating credibility in the fairness of the process. In the absence of transparency, the perception that private firms are "stealing" from what had been the national patrimony is fostered. Domestic political commitment at the highest level is critical to sustain privatization;[68] otherwise, the losers from the process will stonewall progress. Since losers are usually concentrated (people losing jobs) and gains dispersed (increased access), losers are likely to be more vocal and organized in opposing privatization. Public opinion, shaped by the pressure of opponents, has decidedly turned against privatization, with the majority of people in the region disagreeing with the statement that "the state should leave economic activity to the private sector."[69]

Privatization may include measures to reduce short-term labor costs. Measures may be introduced as part of the package to delay employment reduction or spread it over a longer period of time. Often the deal includes temporary protection of the labor force for a specified period after privatization. Fair severance packages and early warnings for mass layoffs can help cushion the blow to workers when jobs are not protected. Bonuses can induce voluntary layoffs to secure political support and the cooperation of unions in the privatization process. The state may also facilitate the movement of laid-off workers into other forms of employment through job search and mobility assistance, retraining, or vocational education programs. Political support for privatization can be expanded if it is construed as part of a wider process of increasing democratic participation in public decision making on issues such as whether to spend more on loss-making public enterprises or instead increase spending on health and public education. Consultation by government and the incoming private management with workers is critical in minimizing the social costs of adjustment in privatization efforts.[70]

Who Has Participated?

Generating sufficient investor interest in a wide array of newly private activities may be problematic when capital markets are thin. Foreign capital was a significant source of privatization revenues, accounting for 39.7 percent regionwide for the 1990–1995 period. In 1994 and 1995 foreign revenue jumped to 71.4 and 76.7 percent respectively. In Bolivia, Peru, and Uruguay, more than 80 percent of the privatization revenues flowed from abroad. A new trend has been intraregional **foreign direct investment** (**FDI**) through privatization. Latin Americans are now investing in other countries in the region. The Argentine steel producer SOMISA, for example, was acquired by a consortium composed of the Argentine group Technit, Chilean CAP (Compaña de Acero), Brazilian USIMAS and CVRD. Investment is coming not only from industrial countries but also from within the region.

For most countries, privatization revenues come in the form of FDI. Notable exceptions are Mexico, Argentina, Brazil, and Colombia, where more sophisticated capital markets allow for portfolio investors. Although portfolio investors such as mutual funds and insurance companies have invested in these markets heavily, they have no significant day-to-day control. In contrast, foreign direct investors acquire sufficient shares to control the strategic direction of the firm. Additionally, FDI generates additional flows to modernize plant and equipment. There may also be spillover effects beyond the particular company as the privatized firm improves the provision of key services and raises the profitability of investments in other sectors. One study found that worldwide, each dollar of FDI privatization revenue generates an additional eighty-eight cents of FDI transactions outside the privatization.[71]

Privatization therefore has the potential to generate future capital flows as the business climate improves in a country. We will return to the role of foreign investment in chapter 7, where we evaluate its effects on economic performance.

The Privatization Record

Privatization generated much excitement in Latin America in the 1990s. Seventy-seven percent of all privatizations in developing countries in 1998 took place in Latin America; in 1999 the region accounted for more than half of such privatizations.[72] Ambitious programs of privatization in Latin America were undertaken in Chile, Argentina, and Mexico. Chile has the longest regional track record in privatizations. In 1973 SOEs accounted for nearly 40 percent of Chilean GDP.[73] From 1974 to 1992, more than five hundred firms were privatized, primarily under the supervision of the state holding company CORFO. The first stage of the privatization, from 1974 to 1982, was largely debt-led, with workers and other buyers taking advantage of relatively cheap credit to finance purchases. The Chilean crisis in 1982 resulted in the failure of many of these vulnerable firms, and the second stage involved more equity than debt and was accompanied by sweeping regulatory reform. Public enterprises not privatized in the first wave were given a mandate to behave "as if" private and were forced to face competition in liberalized markets. Many of these firms were privatized in a later stage, reducing state ownership to 16 percent of GDP by 1989, or 6.6 percent if Codelco, the copper giant, is excluded from the count. In the case of the Chilean electric firms CHILGENER and ENERSIS, privatization contributed to higher profitability, improved productivity, and increased investment. The loser was the Chilean government, which was no longer able to appropriate the quasirents from electrical sales. The sale of CTC, the Chilean telecommunications monopoly, resulted in increased foreign investment, expansion of services, and improved labor productivity with a net gain to state coffers. A comparison of the two sectors underscores that the positive fiscal effect is a function of whether the firms were profitable or not in the first place. Furthermore, Chile was able to enhance the gains from privatization by requiring that foreign investors commit to investments to improve services. Workers gained in both sectors through participation in the ownership and appreciation of the shares they acquired. On balance, privatization improved the well-being of society.[74]

Privatization in Argentina has been extensive, including television, petroleum, trucking, gas and electric, water and sewage, railroads, ports, the postal service, manufacturing enterprises, telecommunications, and the airlines. International participants in Argentine privatizations included Chile (6 percent), Spain (15 percent), the United States (12 percent), Italy (9 percent), and France (7 percent).[75] One of the largest privatizations to take place in emerging markets was of the Argentine oil company YPF. Prior to privatization YPF was a huge conglomerate that included hospitals and schools in addition to an array of energy-related businesses. Not only was it poorly run, but it was also bled by other state agencies benefiting from underpriced energy and unpaid bills. Before the initial public offering (IPO), YPF was downsized, trimming the firm to its core activities where it had competitive advantage. It was then restructured, with a focus on upstream exploration and production, downstream refining and marketing, and well-defined business units for information processing and personnel. The capital was distributed such that the federal government retained 20 percent of the shares, provincial governments were accorded 11 percent, workers were given 10 percent, and the balance was offered in national, U.S., and international tranches. Despite a relatively weak oil market, the launching of the stock exceeded expectations, in large part due to enhanced efficiency prior to the sale. YPF has gone on not only to become a regional player, building upon a strong understanding of the South American business environment and the growth of trade in **Mercosur,** but also to acquire a U.S.-based subsidiary, Maxus Energy Corporation. Despite adverse economic conditions in Argentina from the 1995 Mexican peso crisis, YPF was able to turn itself and Maxus around to post historically high profits in 1997. In 1999 YPF was sold to Repsol of Spain for $13 billion and is now known as YPF Repsol.

Nonetheless, beyond the YPF success story, nationwide measures to promote competition were sacrificed in the name of speed. This was perceived as necessary because President Menem used the privatizations as a bold signal to the global market of the transformation of the Argentine economy. Deregulation of markets followed at a slower pace. Free competition opened in the Argentine telecom market in November 2000. The opening up of Argentina's phone monopoly was slated for 1999. Although the privatization of the national phone company created two geographically divided companies that have increased the number of lines from three to seven million, calling rates in this duopolistic market structure remain high by international standards due to the lack of competitiveness. The introduction of up to eight competing international companies was designed to increase service and lower prices in the local, long-distance, and cellular markets.[76] However, Argentina's macroeconomic collapse in 2002 derailed progress. Telecommunications operators suspended payments in debt incurred for expansion; some international participants withdrew from participation.[77] Privatization has largely ground to a halt.

Mexico has privatized between 2.1 and 3.2 percent of GDP, reserving strategic industries such as petroleum for national control. The state sector had grown to 1,155 enterprises accounting for 12.6 percent of GDP and receiving subsidies equal to almost 13 percent of GDP.[78] By 2003 the number of state firms in Mexico was reduced to 210.[79] Despite widespread restrictions, public utilities and energy firms remain in state hands. Privatization enjoyed more political support in Mexico than in other Latin American countries, in large part because it was tied to a tripartite agreement between labor, business, and the government. Labor ownership came to play a large role in the privatization effort. Foreign participation played only a minor role in the Mexican case. The success of the Mexican privatization effort can be attributed to strong commitment at the highest levels of Mexican government and transparency in the rules governing the process such that all parties could fairly evaluate conditions of sale. A big success story was the privatization of Teléfonos de México, the monopolistic provider of local and long-distance service, whose stock value soared from twenty-five cents (U.S.) a share to seven dollars a share after privatization. The negotiations governing the sale included commitments to expand the number of lines in service, increase coverage of small towns, add significantly to the number of public telephones, and improve the speed of repairs. Service and access dramatically improved along with profitability. Aeroméxico, a big money loser, was made profitable through privatization, in contrast to the privatization of another state airline, Mexicana, where productivity gains were not realized in the divestiture. One study of 218 privatized Mexican SOEs showed that the output of privatized firms increased by 54.3 percent, largely through incentive-related productivity gains. Although employment in privatized firms was cut in half, wages rose for remaining workers, and the need for subsidies, equal to 12.7 percent of GDP, was virtually eliminated.[80] Overall, divestiture in the Mexican case met its most important goal: cutting the budget deficit to facilitate macroeconomic stabilization.

Brazil came late to the privatization game with legal changes in 1990. Before the process began, the state held 100 percent of sales in public utilities, 67 percent of steel, 67 percent of chemicals and petrochemicals, 60 percent of mining, 35 percent of transportation services, 32 percent of gasoline distribution, 26 percent of fertilizers, and 21 percent of transportation equipment.[81] Raising $71 billion from 1990 to 1999, progress was substantial.[82] Privatization in Brazil was very much tied to the increase in capital inflows that we will study in the next chapter. Initial efforts were in the steel, petrochemical, and fertilizer industries. Privatization was extended to transportation, including railways and the energy sector.

Companhia Vale do Rio Doce (CVRD)—the world's largest iron ore exporter, Latin America's biggest producer of gold, Brazil's largest exporter, and the biggest foreign exchange earner in Brazil—was placed on the auction block in 1997. The privatization took place in three stages. In the first, the government released 45 percent of voting shares, out of its holdings of 51 percent, to enable a small group of strategic investors to gain control. Employees were allowed to buy 10 percent of the firm, facilitated by BNDES loans to acquire stock, with the rest sold through a global stock offering.[83]

Merrill Lynch did the valuation, with a minimum price set at $9.8 billion. The government held a golden share for the first five years, to be able to veto decisions. No single investor could hold more than 45 percent of equity, with no one firm holding more than 10 percent to prevent monopoly control. The CVRD privatization was the biggest privatization deal since the $3 billion offering of Argentine oil conglomerate YPF. Following the sale, costs were reduced by 30 percent, forty-five hundred people were let go, and new management systems contributed to profitable performance.[84] During 2001, the CVRD experienced a nearly 51 percent increase in profits over the same period in 2000, with $2.1 billion in gross revenue.[85] By 2006, CVRD had transformed itself from an iron-ore producer concentrated in Brazil to a global multiproduct mining giant. Predicated upon robust cash flow, prudent debt management, and a well-planned acquisition strategy, CVRD's market capitalization surged from $8.7 billion in 2000 to $41.2 billion at the end of 2005. CVRD is the world's third-largest mining company, behind Australian BHP and Billiton British Rio Tinto, and became the first Brazilian company to win an investment grade rating from Moody's and Standard & Poor's (both in 2005).[86]

Telebrás, Brazil's national telecommunications network, was auctioned off in twelve restructured pieces for $19.1 billion, topping London's privatization of British Telecom in the early 1990s. Despite protests from labor unions, the historically poor service of the company created public support for the sale. With just eleven phones and three mobiles per one hundred inhabitants and a two-year waiting list for phones in some areas, the telecom sale in the world's eighth-largest economy was characterized as a sale of "repressed demand" of the huge unanswered market of Brazilian talkers. The Spanish firm Telefónica won the crown jewel, São Paulo's Telesp, and MCI picked up another key piece, Embratel, Brazil's long-distance and international carrier.[87] We will return to the implications of improvements in the efficiency of the privatized Telebrás when we consider infrastructure deficits in chapter 9.

The sale of power sector and telecommunications companies has led privatization activity in Central America. Interestingly, despite an early start, Costa Rica is the least-privatized economy in the region; El Salvador has gone furthest in privatization efforts.[88] Nicaragua has had the furthest to go in restructuring after the central planning system of the Sandinista government. In Central America, the small size of capital markets has not allowed for widespread public offerings of privatized stock, resulting in less transparency and competition, two keys to privatization success. El Salvador's complementary policies to deregulate markets to promote additional competition compensated for few bidders in the sale itself. In Guatemala the lack of credible efforts to promote competition and irregularities in the bidding process compromised the privatization program.[89]

Despite difficulties throughout the Central American region, privatization has at least improved the climate for FDI, leading to greater investor interest. Privatization has also relieved pressures on cash-strapped governments. Nonetheless, the level of state ownership of enterprises is still high—8, 4, and 3.5 percent of GDP, respectively, for Costa Rica, Nicaragua, and Honduras—leaving room for gains in efficiency and profitability in moving firms into a well-regulated, competitive private sector.

Despite the strong success in transforming public enterprises into private-sector ventures, it is important to note the limitations of privatization. As shown in table 6.4, there has been a great deal of variation in privatization across the region—between countries and from year to year within countries. Privatization revenues tend to be lumpy. That is, the sale of a single large state firm such as a telecommunications entity has a big impact on the numbers. The other interesting number to analyze in table 6.4 is the ratio of privatization to FDI. The steady attraction of foreign direction investment is an important source of growth over time. If, however, FDI is driven primarily by privatization, there are diminishing returns to how many state enterprises are left on the auction block. Furthermore, although there may be important productivity gains in key sectors with private ownership, privatization does not reflect "greenfield" investment—that is, investment in new economic activity. Ownership patterns have changed and productivity may rise, but there is not a net addition to production.

The Special Case of the Banking Sector

Privatization has also extended to the banking sector. Under ISI, state banks were used to finance activities that were not attractive to the private sector but had

Table 6.4. Privatization Revenues in Latin America and the Caribbean, 1990–1999 (millions of U.S.$)

	1990	1991	1992	1993	1994	1995	1996	1997	1998	1999	Total	Privatization/ FDI (% 1999)	% Regional Total Revenue from Privatization, 1990–1999
Argentina	7,532	2,841	5,741	4,670	894	1,208	642	4,366	510	16,157	44,561	67.5	25.06
Bolivia	NA	NA	9	13	NA	789	34	40	10	151	1,046	14.9	0.59
Brazil	44	1,633	2,401	2,621	2,104	992	5,770	18,737	32,427	4,400	71,129	13.5	40.00
Chile	98	364	8	106	128	13	187	NA	181	1,053	2,138	11.4	1.20
Colombia	NA	168	5	391	170	NA	2,075	2,876	518	NA	6,203	NA	3.49
Mexico	3,160	11,289	6,924	2,131	766	167	1,526	4,496	999	291	31,749	2.5	17.85
Peru	NA	3	212	127	2,840	1,276	1,751	1,268	480	286	8,243	14.5	4.64
Venezuela	10	2,278	140	36	8	39	2,017	1,387	112	46	6,073	1.4	3.41
Other	71	147	120	393	1,289	132	140	726	2,447	1,231	6,696		3.77
Total	10,915	18,723	15,560	10,488	8,199	4,616	14,142	33,897	37,685	23,614	177,839		100.00

Source: World Bank, *Global Development Finance 2001*, 186.

developmental promise.[90] The Brazilian BNDES, for example, was instrumental in financing both state enterprises and private activity. Bank privatization presents a special case because of links with the international financial sector and domestic financial intermediation. States still have a strong incentive to maintain control. The experience of bank privatization in the region is mixed. Privatization has led to systemic financial instability in cases where new forms of regulation did not accompany the privatization. The nature of banking also results in a relatively concentrated market structure after privatization.[91] Early privatizations in Chile and Argentina suffered from coincident macroeconomic crises, leading to liquidity problems and bank rescues.

In part this has to do with the problems of **adverse selection** and **moral hazard** in lending that are exacerbated in a newly liberalized environment. Adverse selection is an asymmetric information problem—that is, a situation where one side of a deal has more information than another and leads to the selection of an undesirable outcome. For example, people who are conservative and risk averse are less likely to gamble on a chancy venture. Therefore, loan applicants are, as a group, likely to be risk takers. This results, over time, in banks lending less money because there is a smaller chance of getting a good loan candidate in the borrowers' pool. Moral hazards also stem from asymmetric information. Borrowers have more information than lenders about their own likely behavior after the sale. If sufficient collateral is not secured prior to the loan, the borrower has an incentive to pursue high-risk behavior because the gains will be high if the project succeeds but will be shared by the lender if it fails.[92]

Good information gathering on the part of the bank or predictable borrowing on the part of state-run firms can mitigate banking risks. With deregulation and privatization, however, the informational advantage further shifts from the bank to the private sector. Mexican banks that were nationalized in 1982 had directed roughly 50 percent of their lending to the government. Privatization in the early 1990s left the banks without formal credit bureaus to monitor and assess risk on household and small business loans. As the demands of the newly burgeoning private sector intensified, bank lending escalated from 10 percent of GDP in 1988 to more than 40 percent in 1994, quickly exceeding monitoring capabilities. An interest rate spike in January 1995 exacerbated the adverse selection problem, leaving only the most venturesome in the market for loans. With the peso crisis, increased uncertainty in stock markets and in firm balance sheets skewed the fundamental values upon which the loans were originally based. With the peso halved in value from December 1994 to March 1995, inflationary pressures escalated. Interest rates were ratcheted up to 100 percent to stem the bleeding, and the Mexican stock market fell 60 percent in dollar terms. International investors fled—particularly those with limited knowledge of the Mexican market—exacerbating the financial crisis. Many firms and households could not meet bank debt obligations, and a banking crisis ensued as their balance sheets deteriorated.

The collapse of the banking system was forestalled by government intervention to provide funds to protect depositors. (Remember that it was the depositors' money lent out to the now failed firms.) However, unlike an industrial country government, which can reflate the economy in a crisis, developing economies must guard against the perception of resumed inflation eroding confidence. Reflating the economy may also precipitate depreciation of the currency, and with many loans denominated in dollars, the debt burden on the firm in the developing country is extended. When the U.S. government injected liquidity into the economy following the 1987 stock market crash, there was little fear of inflation. However, recovery in a fragile and internationally dependent developing country is more complicated and fraught with pitfalls. Although bank privatization was not the root cause of financial instability in Mexico, the lack of a strong bank supervisory system coupled with rapid changes throughout the economy left the economy more vulnerable to a free fall. Independent, transparent, well-funded agencies need to be able to enforce adequate accounting and disclosure practices on the part of borrowers and the banking community to safeguard against banking crises. If an appropriate regulatory institution is not in place prior to privatization and deregulation, failure is likely.[93]

Identifying the need for prudent supervision does not mean that national banks bring efficiency gains to economies. One study shows, for example, that extensive state ownership can retard the development of the financial system and slow economic growth rates due to low productivity.[94] There is a delicate balance between the reach of a state bank and the efficiency of private financial services.

The Winners and Losers with Privatization

What have been the welfare consequences of privatization? A fair evaluation of the consequences of privatization for society involves an analysis of the particular market structure, the variables used to measure performance, and a control group of contrasting cases. It is difficult to know the counterfactual—what would have happened without privatization. Tracing the effects of privatization throughout the economy is problematic as relative price changes of key infrastructure inputs spill over into other sectors. Performance may have also changed due to other variables in the neoliberal, market-based package.[95] Finally, because a controlled experiment with both public and private enterprises operating in the same market under the same macroeconomic conditions cannot be run, it is difficult to attribute gains to privatization as opposed to liberalization or lower inflation.[96] The degree of competitiveness in input and output markets will determine whether gains accrue to society or are appropriated as monopoly rents to large, now private, firms.

The employment effects of privatization are ambiguous. It is difficult to separate the effects of privatization from other changes in the economy. Some argue that privatization will increase the capacity of the economy to create jobs through a more efficient use of capital and labor.[97] Others, however, suggest that privatizing existing industries will reduce the number employed in state agencies, which, as a political goal, had inflated employment. Recent studies show devastating short-run effects, decreasing employment by 40 percent in Argentina, 36 percent in Mexico, and 55 percent in Peru. Eventually, however, employment returned to long-run levels through rehiring and indirect job generation.[98] Profitability as a measure of performance may not always be consistent with long-run productivity gains or the social and environmental externalities generated through production. Some critics of privatization suggest that increased profitability derives from the ability to charge higher prices in an unregulated environment, although this may only be a partial explanation. Although efficiency based on sales per worker rose between 88 percent in Chile and 112 percent in Peru, state firms may have served other social objectives such as employment generation.[99] An evaluation of the divestiture process must take into account the trade-off that private firms might perform more efficiently but that the private means and ends might not be in the social good.

Special care should be taken in infrastructure privatization to evaluate the potential welfare effects on the poor. Questions of access and pricing are important equity considerations. The poor have largely benefited from privatization in expanding access to telephone, electricity, and water to the poorest segments of society. The urban poor are generally better served by firms looking to expand market share.[100] Access to telephone services in Bolivia doubled from 1988 to 1995. As evidenced by statistics in the Chilean case prior to privatization, only 2 percent of the poorest fifth of households had access to electricity, and only 3 percent had access to telephones. A decade later only 5.5 percent lacked electricity, and 60 percent lacked telephones.[101] However, increased access is usually accompanied by higher prices. In Cochabamba, Bolivia, the 43 percent price increase precipitated violent protests that led to the abandonment of water privatization. The social mobilization against privatization gave voice to broader discontent with the costs of neoliberal reform.[102] Nonetheless, privatization if properly regulated or accompanied by competition has the potential to lower prices. With competition, the price of services also dropped in Chile and Argentina by more than 50 percent—a benefit to the poor.

Natural Resource-Based Nationalization

The social backlash against the perceived welfare effects of privatization has swung the Latin American pendulum back toward a stronger role for the state. Booming commodity prices in the mid-2000s have led governments in resource-rich nations to respond to popular demand by appropriating rents for national gain. Populist leaders such as Evo Morales of Bolivia and Hugo Chavez of Venezuela have reasserted the state hand in the economy. In May 2006, President Morales ordered that all natural gas mined in Bolivia—a process principally performed by foreign firms such as Brazil's Petrobras—must now be sold through the state energy company Yacimientos Petrolíferos Fiscales Bolivianos (YPFB). "We're the absolute owners, this is what the nationalization has given us and as owners we have to receive all the financial resources from the gas that is being produced and sold," said Jorge Alvarado, president of YPFB.[103] In Venezuela, Chavez seized oil fields from France's Total and abrogated a contract with Italy's ENI SpA when they refused, unlike seventeen other oil companies, to hand over 60 percent of their Venezuelan interests to the state-run oil company PDVSA.[104]

Such moves to roll back the welcome for foreign capital have created a great deal of uncertainty in terms of guaranteeing the rights of capital in resource boom environments. It is worth observing that this is made possible by the strong revenues from the commodity price boom. If commodity prices fall—following a fairly predictable long run path—states may once again be constrained by fiscal realities.

CONCLUSION

Redefining the role of the state in Latin America has included elements of fiscal austerity, tax reform, and privatization to reduce the drag of deficits and the restructuring of the ownership role of the state. Reform of the state sector is a balancing act between a desirable and a sustainable level of state activity. We began our chapter with a discussion of the three schools of thought: the new political economists, the new institutionalists, and the neostructuralists. Because the new political economists believe that a small state is the most efficient outcome, reducing deficits and eliminating state responsibilities for production and provision of services should free the public sector from the need to raise additional money through taxes. Trimming the size of the state and improving its efficient delivery of a limited array of services is the focus of reform. Financing expenditures is more problematic for the new institutionalist and the neostructuralist. At least until market institutions mature and transactions costs are lowered, new institutionalists would call for a stronger mediating role for government in the marketization of the economy. They are concerned about the regulatory capabilities of states to oversee privatized monopolies. Regulation and supervision are not free, necessitating some new finance for public activity. Neostructuralists must match an active role for government as it supplements the activity in the market with an enhanced capacity to pay and to deliver needed services more efficiently. Committed to the notion that the state is an important actor in promoting equitable development, especially where markets are imperfect, neostructuralists face the challenge of convincing constituencies of the necessity to pay for public goods. For the neostructuralists, however, the long-run payoffs of decreased poverty and improved education and health are worth the long-run investment.

Key Concepts

adverse selection
foreign direct
    investment (FDI)
Mercosur
moral hazard

neoliberals
neostructuralists
new institutional
    economics (NIE)

new political economy
    (NPE)
value added tax (VAT)

Chapter Summary

The New Role of the Latin American State

- What should be the new role of the Latin American state? The state must balance accountability to multilateral organizations and voters. ECLAC argues a social covenant in which the state establishes a socioeconomic agreement with civil society. The World Bank in 1997 suggested that states should only engage in those activities in which they have the capacity to be effective, such as investing in basic social services.

The Theoretical Framework for State Intervention

- The theoretical framework for state intervention is divided into three main schools of thought: NPE, NIE, and neostructuralism. New political economists believe that state intervention will interfere with market signals; therefore, the role of the state should be minimal. New institutionalists claim that neoclassical economics ignores transaction costs. The principal tenet behind NIE is that market actors rarely receive perfect information. There is a need for institutional norms such as transparent, effective, and accessible legal and judicial arrangements to reduce transaction costs. Unlike the new institutionalists and new political economists, neostructuralists are not optimistic about the market's ability to enhance development. Neostructuralists call for effective state intervention when the market fails.

A Weak Public Sector

- The Latin American public sector is on average half the size of that of industrialized countries. Its small size stems primarily from a weak tax bureaucracy and a large informal sector that is difficult to tax.
- There has been a shift in the source of tax revenue from custom duties to domestic taxes. The most popular tax instrument has been the VAT because of its self-regulating mechanism. The next steps for Latin America are to combat tax evasion and increase revenue from direct taxes and green taxes.

Privatization

- Privatization of generally inefficient SOEs requires a complementary set of policies and their swift implementation. During privatization governments should promote competition to maximize the value of the sale by improving the efficiency of the firms prior to the sale. Foreign financing has played a major role in privatization in Latin America.
- Privatization of the banking sector presented a different kind of problem, one of asymmetric information where the borrower has the advantage. Successful banking sector privatization must be accompanied by an appropriate regulatory institution.

The Pendulum Swings Back

- A new wave of natural resource-based nationalism is reasserting the power of state firms in the economy.

• Dissatisfaction with the neoliberal model and the gaping social deficits have created demands in states benefiting from the natural resource boom to extract resource rents to finance the social sector.

Notes

1. Ricardo Hausmann and Ernesto Stein, "Searching for the Right Budgetary Institutions for a Volatile Region," in *Securing Stability and Growth in Latin America,* ed. Ricardo Hausmann and Helmut Reisen (Paris: OECD Publications, 1996), 247.

2. Shahid Javed Burki and Sebastian Edwards, *Latin America after Mexico: Quickening the Pace* (Washington, D.C.: World Bank, 1996).

3. Ernesto Stein, Ernesto Talvi, and Alejandro Grisanti, *Institutional Arrangements and Fiscal Performance: The Latin American Experience,* National Bureau of Economic Research Working Paper No. 6358 (Cambridge, Mass.: National Bureau of Economic Research, 1998).

4. Shahid Javed Burki and Sebastian Edwards, *Dismantling the Populist State* (Washington, D.C.: World Bank, 1996), 23.

5. Dani Rodrik, in Peter Evans, "The Eclipse of the State? Reflections on Stateness in an Era of Globalization," *World Politics* 50 (October 1997): 83.

6. Evans, "Eclipse," 66.

7. Dani Rodrik, "Why Do More Open Economies Have Bigger Governments?" *Journal of Political Economy* 16(5) (1998).

8. Barry Weingast, in Hans P. Binswanger and Klaus Deininger, "Explaining Agricultural and Agrarian Policies in Developing Countries," *Journal of Economic Literature* 35 (December 1997): 1978.

9. Evans, "Eclipse," 80.

10. Binswanger and Deininger, "Explaining Agricultural and Agrarian Policies," 1987.

11. John Martinussen, *Society, State, and Market: A Guide to Competing Theories of Development* (London: Zed, 1997), 266.

12. Joseph E. Stiglitz, "The Role of Government in Economic Development," in *Annual World Bank Conference on Development Economics 1996* (Washington, D.C.: World Bank, 1997), 12.

13. Paola Perez-Aleman, "Learning, Adjustment and Economic Development: Transforming Firms, the State and Associations in Chile," *World Development* 28(1) (2000): 41–55.

14. For example, see Kenneth P. Jameson, "Dollarization in Ecuador: A Post Keynesian Institutionalist Analysis," Department of Economics Working Paper 2004–2005, University of Utah, for an incisive explanation and application of post-Keynesian institutionalism.

15. Mick Moore, "Toward a Useful Consensus," in "The Bank, the State, and Development: Dissecting the World Development Report, 1997," *IDS Bulletin* 29(2), special edition (1998): 41.

16. Martinussen, *Society, State, and Market,* 262.

17. Popkin, as cited by Martinussen, *Society, State, and Market,* 244.

18. Douglas C. North, "The New Institutional Economics and Third World Development," in *The New Institutional Economics and Third World Development,* ed. John Harriss, Janet Hunter, and Colin M. Lewis (London: Routledge, 1995), 23.

19. Douglass C. North, *Understanding the Process of Economic Change* (Princeton, N.J.: Princeton University Press 2005), 48–49.

20. John Harriss, Janet Hunter, and Colin M. Lewis, "Introduction: Development and

Significance of the NIE," in *The New Institutional Economics and Third World Development,* ed. John Harriss, Janet Hunter, and Colin M. Lewis (London: Routledge, 1995), 1.

21. Barbara Harriss-White, "Maps and Landscapes of Grain Markets in South Asia," in *The New Institutional Economics and Third World Development,* ed. John Harriss, Janet Hunter, and Colin M. Lewis (London: Routledge, 1995), 87.

22. Harriss, Hunter, and Lewis, "Introduction," 3.

23. North, as cited by Martinussen, *Society, State, and Market,* 254.

24. Dani Rodrik and Arvind Subramanian, "The Primacy of Institutions (and What This Does and Does Not Mean)," *Finance & Development* (June 2003): 32.

25. Osvaldo Sunkel, *Development from Within: Toward a Neostructuralist Approach for Latin America* (Boulder, Colo.: Rienner, 1993), 7.

26. C. Gunnarsson and M. Lundahl, "The Good, the Bad, and the Wobbly," in *New Directions in Development Economics: Growth, Environmental Concerns, and Government in the 1990s,* ed. Mats Lundahl and Benno J. Ndulu (London: Routledge, 1996), 256–257.

27. As synthesized by Nader Nazmi, *Economic Policy and Stabilization in Latin America* (New York: Sharpe, 1996), 7–8.

28. Anne Krueger uses the term "benevolent social guardian" to characterize a well-intended but inefficient state. As described in Gunnarsson and Lundahl, "Good, Bad, and Wobbly," 256.

29. Gunnarsson and Lundahl, "Good, Bad, and Wobbly," 260.

30. John Williamson, "What Washington Means by Policy Reform," in *Latin American Adjustment: How Much Has Happened?* ed. J. Williamson (Washington, D.C.: Institute for International Economics, 1990).

31. John Williamson. "What Should the Bank Think about the Washington Consensus?" Institute for International Economics paper prepared as a background to the World Bank's 2000 World Development Report, July 1999, http://www.iie.com/publications/papers/paper .cfm?ResearchID=351.

32. Williamson, "What Should the Bank Think about the Washington Consensus?"

33. Kurt Weyland, *The Politics of Market Reform in Fragile Democracies* (Princeton, N.J.: Princeton University Press, 2002), 49.

34. Nancy Birdsall and Augusto de la Torre, "Washington Contentious," *Commission on Economic Reform in Unequal Latin American Societies,* sponsored by the Carnegie Endowment for International Peace and the Inter-American Dialogue, 2001.

35. Eduardo Lora, Carmen Pagés, Ugo Panizza, and Ernesto Stein, "A Decade of Development Thinking," Research Department, Inter-American Development Bank, Washington, D.C., 2004, 26.

36. IDEAS, "Reform Fatigue," Inter-American Development Bank Research Department, January–April 2004, 2, http://www.iadb.org/res/publications/pubfiles/pubI-Vol3e.pdf.

37. Latinobarómetro annual surveys of seventeen Latin American countries since 1996. Eduardo Lora, Ugo Panizza, and Myriam Quispe-Agnoli, "Reform Fatigue: Symptoms, Reasons, Implications," Paper presented at Rethinking Structural Reform in Latin America, Federal Reserve Bank of Atlanta, October 23, 2003.

38. "Latin America Sees Progress," *Washington Times,* August 9, 2005, reporting on the Inter-American Dialogue Policy Report by Sol M. Linowitz Forum, "A Break in the Clouds: Latin America and the Caribbean in 2005," http://www.washingtontimes.com/world/ 20050808-092143-3290r.htm.

39. Bernardo Kliksberg, "Public Administration in Latin America," *International Review of Administrative Sciences* 17(2) (2005): 325.

40. John Williamson, "What Should the Bank Think about the Washington Consensus?" Institute for International Economics Paper prepared as a background to the World Bank's

World Development Report 2000, July 1999, http://www.iie.com/publications/papers/paper .cfm?ResearchID=351.

41. Joseph E. Stiglitz, "Post Washington Consensus Consensus," Initiative for Policy Dialogue Working Paper Series, Columbia University, November 2004.

42. Robin Emmott, "Bribery Costs Mexicans Up to 14% of Income," *Financial Times,* October 31, 2001, www.ft.com.

43. "Lousy Deal," *IDB America* (May–June 2000): 2.

44. Transparency International, *Global Corruption Reports 2001,* www.transparency .org.

45. See www.oas.org for information on the convention and summit measures.

46. "Just Don't Call It Downsizing," *IDB America* (September–October 2000): 10–11.

47. Peter Evans, ed., "State-Society Synergy: Government and Social Capital in Development," *World Development* 24(6), special edition (June 1996).

48. Evans, "State-Society Synergy," 185.

49. Gunnarsson and Lundahl, "Good, Bad, and Wobbly," 109.

50. Carol Wise, "Latin America and the State-Market Debate: Beyond Stylized Facts," Paper presented at the Latin American Studies Association, Miami, March 16–18, 2000, 22.

51. Wise, "Latin America and the State-Market Debate," 84.

52. Michael Gavin, Ricardo Hausmann, Roberto Perotti, and Ernesto Talvi, *Managing Fiscal Policy in Latin America and the Caribbean: Volatility, Procyclicality, and Limited Creditworthiness,* IADB, Office of the Chief Economist Working Paper, No. 326 (Washington, D.C.: IADB, 1996), 4.

53. José María Fanelli and Roberto Frenkel, "Macropolicies for the Transition from Stabilization to Growth," in *New Directions in Development Economics: Growth, Environmental Concerns, and Government in the 1990s,* ed. Mats Lundahl and Benno J. Ndulu (London: Routledge, 1996), 41.

54. Guillermo Perry and Ana Maria Herrera, *Public Finances, Stabilization, and Structural Reform in Latin America* (Washington, D.C.: Johns Hopkins University Press/IADB, 1994).

55. ECLAC, *The Fiscal Covenant: Basis for Economic and Social Action by the State,* May 13, 1998, eclac.org.

56. IADB, *Economic and Social Progress in Latin America, 1995 Report: Overcoming Volatility* (Washington, D.C.: Johns Hopkins University Press, 1995), table 3.1, p. 126.

57. The World Bank, "World Development Indicators," *WDI Online,* www.worldbank .org.

58. IADB, *Latin America after a Decade of Reforms: Economic and Social Progress 1997 Report* (Washington, D.C.: Johns Hopkins University Press/IADB, 1997), 72.

59. Ingrid Palmer, "Public Finance from a Gender Perspective," *World Development* 23(11) (1995): 1984.

60. Vito Tanzi, *Fiscal Federalism and Decentralization: A Review of Some Efficiency and Macroeconomic Aspects,* Presented at the World Bank Conference on Development Economics, World Bank, May 1995 (as summarized by *The Economist,* 3 June 1995, 74).

61. ECLAC, *Fiscal Covenant,* 14.

62. Carlos Elizondo Mayer-Serra, "Tax Reform under the Salinas Administration," in *The Changing Structure of Mexico,* ed. Laura Randall (Armonk, N.Y.: Sharpe, 1996).

63. Douglas C. North, "Economic Performance through Time," Acceptance Lecture, 1993 Alfred Nobel Memorial Prize in Economic Sciences, published in *American Economic Review* 84(3) (1994).

64. Alberto Chong and Florencio López-de-Sibanes, "Privatization in Mexico," Inter-American Development Bank Working Paper No. 513, August 2004.

65. M. Sánchez, R. Corona, L. F. Herrera, and O. Ochoa, "A Comparison of Privatization Experiences: Chile, Mexico, Colombia, and Argentina," in *Privatization in Latin America,*
ed. M. Sánchez and R. Corona (Baltimore: Johns Hopkins University Press, 1994).

66. Eduardo Bitran and Pablo Serra, "Regulation of Privatized Utilities: The Chilean
Experience," *World Development* 26(6) (1998): 945–962.

67. Chong and López-de-Sibanes, "Privatization in Mexico," 25.

68. Emanuel Delovitch and Klas Ringskog, *Private Sector Participation in Water Supply
and Sanitation in Latin America* (Washington, D.C.: World Bank, 1995), 3.

69. John Nellis, Rachel Menzes, and Sarah Lucas, "Latino Barómetro Poll 2001 and
2002," as cited in, "Privatization in Latin America," Center for Global Development Policy
Brief, January 2004, Vol. 3, Issue 1.

70. Van der Hoeven and Sziraczi, *Lessons from Privatization,* 12–17.

71. Sader (1993) as cited in chapter 5, "Privatization," in *Economic and Social Progress
in Latin America 1996 Report* (Washington, D.C.: IADB), 179.

72. The World Bank, *Global Development Finance 2001,* appendix 4.

73. Ahmed Galal, Leroy Jones, Pankaj Tandon, and Ingo Vogelsang, "Divestiture:
Questions and Answers," in *Welfare Consequences of Selling Public Enterprises* (Washington, D.C.: World Bank, 1994), 184.

74. Galal et al., "Divestiture," 288.

75. This is in 1992. *World Investment Report 1994* (New York: United Nations, 1994), 93.

76. Clifford Krauss, "Argentina to Hasten End of Phone Monopoly," *New York Times,*
March 11, 1998, D4.

77. Elizabeth Mooney, "South American Economic Crisis Hits Telecom Operators,"
RCR Wireless News, April 2002, 25.

78. Galal et al., "Divestiture," 407.

79. Sebastian Edwards, ed., *Crisis and Reform in Latin America: From Despair to Hope*
(New York: Oxford University Press, 1995).

80. La Porta, Lopez-de-Silanes, and Shleifer, 1999, as summarized in William Megginson and Jeffry M. Netter, "From State to Market: A Survey of Empirical Studies of Privatization," *Journal of Economic Literature* 39 (June 2001): 349.

81. Werner Baer and Annibal V. Villela, "Privatization and the Changing Role of the
State in Brazil," in *Privatization in Latin America,* ed. Werner Baer and Melissa Birch (Westport, Conn.: Praeger, 1994).

82. World Bank, *Global Development Finance 2001,* 186, table A42.

83. "Privatization," *Euromoney,* September 1996, 294.

84. "Brazil's Iron King," *Financial Times,* June 29, 1998, 13.

85. Michael Kepp, "Refining Mining," *Latin Trade,* April 2002, 30.

86. "Deal of the Year 2005: Core Transformation," *LatinFinance,* February 2006, 24.

87. "Telebras Sold for US$19.1b," *Latin American Weekly Report,* August 4, 1998, 352;
and Seth Schiesel, "Brazil Sells Most of State Phone Utility," *New York Times,* July 30, 1998,
D1.

88. Felipe B. Larraín and Luis F. López-Calva, "Privatization: Fostering Economic
Growth through Private Sector Development," chap. 13 in Felipe B. Larraín, *Economic Devel-
opment in Central America,* Vol. 2, *Structural Reform* (Cambridge, Mass.: Harvard University
Press, 2001), 68.

89. Larraín and López-Calva, "Privatization," 96.

90. Baer and Villela, "Privatization," 2.

91. Kenneth P. Jameson, "The Financial Sector in Latin American Restructuring," in
Privatization in Latin America, ed. Werner Baer and Melissa Birch (Westport, Conn.: Praeger,
1994), 120.

92. This section draws extensively on Frederick Mishkin, "Understanding Financial Crises: A Developing Country Perspective," in *Annual World Bank Conference on Development Economics 1996* (Washington, D.C.: World Bank, 1997), 28–30.

93. Mishkin, "Understanding Financial Crises," 28.

94. La Porta, Lopez-de-Silanes and Shleifer, 2000, as summarized in William Megginson and Jeffry M. Netter, "From State to Market: A Survey of Empirical Studies of Privatization," *Journal of Economic Literature* 39 (June 2001): 333.

95. David Parker and Colin Kirkpatrick, "Privatization in Developing Countries: A Review of the Evidence and the Policy Lessons," *Journal of Development Studies* 41(4) (May 2005): 514.

96. Galal et al., "Divestiture," 13–14.

97. Van der Hoeven and Sziraczi, *Lessons from Privatization,* 11.

98. "The Privatization Paradox," *Latin American Economic Policies,* Inter-American Development Bank, Vol. 18, 2002, 3.

99. IADB, "The Privatization Paradox," 3.

100. Nancy Birdsall and John Nellis, "Winners and Losers: Assessing the Distributional Impact of Privatization," *World Development* 31 (10) (2003): 1626.

101. Antonio Estache and Danny Leipziger, "Utilities Privatization and the Poor: Lessons and Evidence from Latin America," *World Development* 29(7) (2001): 1181.

102. Nellis, Menezes, and Lucas, "Latino Barómetro Poll 2001 and 2002."

103. "Firms Now Pay Higher Gas Taxes to Bolivia," Associated Press/La Paz, Bolivia, June 8, 2006, www.businessweek.com.

104. "Venezuela on Wrong Path: Seizing Assets of Resource Firms Will Scare Off Foreign Investment," *Calgary Herald* (Alberta), April 10, 2006, A14.

CHAPTER SEVEN

FINANCING FOR DEVELOPMENT

Public and Private Capital Flows to Latin America

Foreign capital has flooded regional stock markets. *(Courtesy of David Mangurian and the Inter-American Development Bank)*

After the long period of painful structural adjustment to the debt crisis, Latin America became a magnet for international finance in the mid-1990s. Macroeconomic stability, opening of closed economies to international markets, lucrative privatizations, and subregional integration enticed private foreign capital to Latin America. By 1997, net resource transfers, which measure net capital flows minus payments of capital and interest, topped $32.6 billion. After a decade of isolation, Latin America was again a darling of international investors. Yet five short years later, capital was again flowing out of the region, as Latin America became a net capital exporter. What have been the causes and the consequences of cyclical capital flows to the region?

Answering this question involves distinguishing the types of capital in question. This chapter will begin with a discussion of the different kinds of private capital flows—debt flows through bank loans or bond, direct or equity investment. How do the different kinds of capital—**short- and long-term portfolio investments** as well as long-term **foreign direct investment (FDI)** through multinational corporations (MNCs)—affect development prospects in the region? Although new capital is of course a welcome way to spur growth, rapid inflows raise questions about sustainability and volatility. Are funds being channeled to improve the productive capacity of the region, or are they fueling asset bubbles or consumption booms? Are there ways of minimizing vulnerability while maintaining the confidence of international capital?

In addition to private capital flows, **official flows** in the service of development are also important to consider, particularly for the case of the poorest countries in the region. Who are the top international donors and recipients in the region? What kind of development programs are financed with international assistance? How can international dollars be leveraged for a stronger developmental impact?

Finally, you may be surprised to note that the largest source of capital flows into Latin American comes from Latin Americans themselves. In 2004 worker **remittances**—money sent home to families and communities in Latin America—accounted for 2.1 percent of regional gross domestic product (GDP). The importance of remittances has more than doubled over the past ten years. What explains these flows—and are they an important source of development financing in Latin America?

Understanding the changing nature of capital flows to the region will enhance our understanding of the promise and the limitations of liberalization as a strategy for Latin American economic development. Like trade, which we will study in the next chapter, the free flow of capital brings opportunities for growth but may be accompanied by an increase in uncertainty and volatility. Unlike the inward-looking model of import substitution industrialization, financial and trade liberalization make a nation more sensitive to changes in the global economy—the good *and* the bad.

AN INTRODUCTION TO THE BEHAVIOR OF CAPITAL FLOWS

The neoliberal market model places private capital flows at the center of development finance. Capital, it is argued, will flow to its most productive uses, where rates

Figure 7.1.   Net Resource Transfers

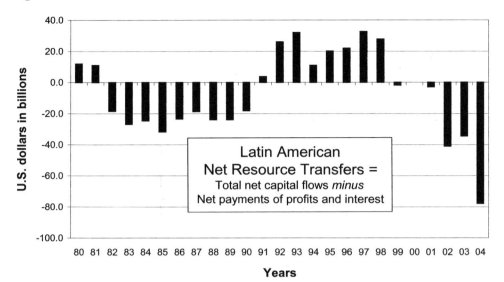

Source: Economic Commission for Latin America and the Caribbean (ECLAC), on the basis of figures from the International Monetary Fund (IMF) and national sources.

of return are highest. Tough austerity measures that transform the productivity of an economy should therefore be rewarded by improved access to international capital markets. This has, to some extent, taken place in the Latin American region. Figure 7.1 illustrates the cyclical nature of capital flows to Latin America. Here we measure net resource transfers, which include inflows on the capital and financial accounts, plus errors and omissions, International Monetary Fund (IMF) credit and exceptional financing minus the net payments of profit and interest. This gives us an overall estimate of the amount of capital available for investment in the region. We can see in figure 7.1 that capital flows in the 1990s were roughly 200 percent larger than those in the 1980s. This was an extraordinary vote of confidence on the part of international markets in Latin American economic reform.

By 2001, however, Latin America had become a net capital exporter to the rest of the world. Inflows stalled as Argentina entered crisis. Additionally, like other developing countries, Latin American nations began using current account surpluses to build up reserves against possible future currency crises and to pay down on past debt accrued.[1] New investments into the region were not sufficient to compensate for past debts accrued. Money was being drawn elsewhere.

To understand the nature of rapid capital reversals it is useful to analyze what drives the demand for foreign assets. As we have noted, the restructuring of Latin American economies created new growth potential. Remember that investors buy today in anticipation of returns in the future. Unlike buying a car or a computer, where you can pretty well predict what the asset will be worth next year, financial investments carry an uncertain future value. Purchases are made based on *expected* value. Do you think the value of the asset will rise or fall over the term of the invest-ment? This applies to investments in stocks, bonds, or commodities such as copper or tin. If there is a high degree of uncertainty as to the future performance of an asset, investors must be compensated for additional risk. If the asset is denominated in a foreign currency, the possibility that the currency may lose value over the term of the investment must also be taken into account. Stability, confidence, and pre-dictability are key to promoting sound financial investments.

Because international investment decisions are made one versus another—that is, investors evaluate *relative* returns—the policy or performance in Latin America may not be the sole factor. Relative returns on other assets—perhaps the dollar or maybe investments in Europe or Asia—could become more lucrative. Investors con-sider Latin America versus other investment options. The rise of China as an arena for FDI and former East European countries in the bond market have drawn capital flows to other regions. In part (depending on the type of capital), these trade-offs are accentuated by investor decisions to retain a certain portion of portfolios in riskier emerging market assets. Balancing risk against more stable industrial market returns may mean moving out of one emerging market as a portfolio becomes weighted in another. With expectations at play, emerging markets are especially vulnerable to shifts in investor sentiment. Alternatively, Latin America may be inter-esting because returns in other regions (or in industrial economies) are low—not because Latin economies are performing particularly well. But a country can't con-trol what is happening in the rest of the world. Periods of plenty and times of scarcity are subject not only to country performance but also to relative preferences of investors.

Figure 7.2 shows net private capital flows by region. Unlike the net resource

Figure 7.2.   Net Private Capital Flows

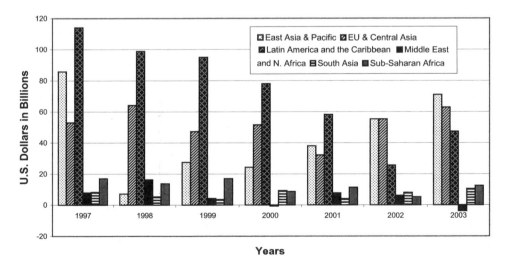

Source: Global Development Finance 2004, p. 8.

transfers in figure 7.1, which subtracted payments of profits and interest, net private capital flows measure private debt and investment finance. We can see that flows to Latin America have largely fallen as attention to East Asia and the Pacific as well as emerging European and Central Asian countries has grown. But regional totals may obscure trends at the country level. In 2003, globally ten countries accounted for 69 percent of FDI; five of these top ten recipients of FDI are Latin American countries. Some Latin American countries command significant market interest, but others are left out. As we will see later in this chapter, smaller, poorer countries require official assistance to supplement private flows.[2] But even for the larger Latin markets, FDI fell after 1999, driven primarily by the winding down of large-scale privatizations.

Even for the winners in attracting investment, capital inflows may have unintended costs. If capital—say, dollars—flows in, the supply of this foreign currency increases, and its price falls relative to the national currency. If the national currency as a result becomes stronger, this may compromise the ability of the country to pursue an aggressive export drive. Capital's helping hand may choke off the growth of exports. The gains to financing in the internal market may not be consistent with the external requirements of the economy. We will explore whether policy instruments are needed to balance capital flows in emerging markets, but first we need a better understanding of the types of capital.

The Short and Long of Capital Flows—Debt, Equity, and Private Transfers

The fact that capital is flowing to Latin America doesn't mean that investments there are always productive. Can Latin America productively absorb the capital flowing into the region? Can capital have negative repercussions—particularly if it is volatile? Understanding the benefits and costs of capital flows involves an appreciation of the types of capital coming into the region. The flow of capital into the region takes six forms: loans, bond purchases, FDI, portfolio equity flows, remittances, and lending directly to support trade.[3] Figure 7.3 shows the changing composition of capital flows (minus trade financing, which is limited in normal times) to the region from 1990 to 2004 as a percentage of GDP. In this section we will focus our attention on short-term capital flows—bank lending, bonds, and equity investments.

Bank lending has gone from the predominant source of capital in the 1960s and 1970s to a drain on regional resources as countries service total accumulated debt through interest and principal payments. Beyond debt drag, other forms of capital flows also have downsides. **Portfolio bonds** and **equity investments** can be transitory. Portfolio bond flows are bond issues purchased by foreign investors. These might be government bonds similar to U.S. Treasury bonds to finance public investments, or they might be corporate offerings. Remember that bonds are essentially a promise to pay in the future—an obligation incurred irrespective of whether the investment has generated returns. Moreover, developing country bonds have a second built-in risk, so-called original sin. Original sin is the inability of emerging markets to borrow abroad in their own currencies.[4] Investors have been leery of purchasing bonds issued in local currencies. Due to the state of being born or issued in

Figure 7.3.   Sources of External Financing

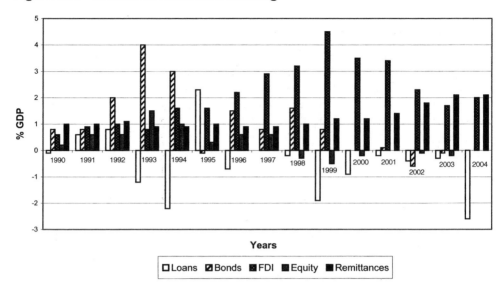

Source: ECLAC, Preliminary Overview 2004, table 2.1.

a developing country, the bond must be launched in an international currency such as the dollar, euro, or yen. If the local currency weakens (ostensibly by bad policy decisions as in the past), the bondholder doesn't pay for this. Instead, the developing country or local company must come up with more units of national currency to meet the obligations on the bond. The risk in bonds, then, is piled on the issuer. They are more attractive, however, than bank loans in that they are more liquid and hence tradable. Some developing countries, nonetheless, are moving beyond original sin to issue bonds in local currency units. In 2004 Colombia was the first issuer of a global bond denominated in Colombian pesos; in 2005 Brazil launched a $1.5 billion offering priced in the real, transferring currency risk to investors.[5] The benefit of greater macrostability is incurring less risk in raising capital.

Equity investments are the sum of country funds, depository receipts,[6] and direct purchases of shares by foreign investors. Equity investments, or the purchase of stocks, are also considered liquid, short-term capital, particularly if the holder maintains less than a 10 percent share. Equity or stock investments allow a company to share risk with investors. Short-term capital can leave as quickly as it arrives. If an economy or a firm experiences a downturn and the stock value plummets, stockholders lose. When hard times hit a company that has financed expansion through bonds (or through commercial bank loans), the firm or nation must still make good on that obligation or face the ramifications of default. Stocks, therefore, spread risk from firms to investors.

In addition to spreading the risk from borrowers to creditors, stock markets help to diversify risks among investments. Most people wealthy enough to hold a financial portfolio keep an array of assets—a bank account, bonds, stocks, and real estate.

From the borrower's perspective, corporate bonds or stock provide an important, cost-effective alternative to bank borrowing or internal profits to raise capital for investment. But stock and bond markets are weak in Latin America (and the rest of the developing world). Size is a key constraint. Market capitalization, the total value (price times current price), as a proportion of GDP in middle-income countries is about one-third of that in industrial countries. Stock exchanges in developing countries tend to lag technologically, making trading, clearance, and settlement problematic. Stock institutions are built on clear, credible rules; developing country institutions are more prone than industrial country institutions to corruption and weak regulation.[7]

Despite the potential for risk sharing, the outlook for capital markets in Latin America remains weak.[8] Latin American capital markets, characterized by dollarization, short-termism, and illiquidity, have lagged behind those in East Asia and Eastern Europe. The bond markets that have developed in Latin America tend to be dominated by public sector debt, much of it with short maturities. Firms have delisted and large companies have migrated to international exchanges. Although economic reforms have precipitated capital market deepening in other regions, in Latin America domestic trading has languished. Instead, the process of internationalization —where Latin companies are listed on foreign exchanges—seems to have replaced heartier domestic development of exchanges. In 1990 only 11 Latin firms engaged in international activity; by 2000, 249 firms participated in international equity markets such as the New York Stock Exchange. Equity capital raised abroad reached 91.9 percent of domestic capital in Latin America as compared to 17.1 for East Asia. Latin American participation in international bond markets rose from less than 9 billion in 1990 to almost 252 billion in 2001.[9] In addition to private firms, Latin governments also borrowed in international markets—9.8 percent of GDP as opposed to 3.8 percent international state borrowing in East Asia. In one sense this is logical—capital costs are cheaper in international markets where capital is more plentiful. However, borrowing in foreign currencies also opens governments up to exchange rate risks and weakens the number of players and liquidity at home.

We can measure market capitalization or market value by taking the share price times the number of shares outstanding on an exchange. Market size is an important predictor of a country's ability to mobilize capital and diversify risk. The level of stock market development closely tracks a country's overall development level. The growth of stock markets may increase liquidity and diversify risk.[10] At the end of 2002, stock market capitalization relative to GDP remained at only 28 percent in Latin America, as opposed to 72 percent in G-7 countries and 95 percent in East Asia.[11] Only a few Latin American firms are capable of issuing securities in amounts that will support ample liquidity; on the buy side there are only a few institutional buyers, driven in large part by domestic pension funds, further limiting liquidity in the market. Investors tend to buy and hold. The highly concentrated nature— in Chile and Argentina three companies account for almost 50 percent of market capitalization—makes for an illiquid market. Regionally, the top ten companies in Latin America account for more than 60 percent of the value traded; in the United States the comparable number is 15 percent.[12]

Should Latin American policymakers promote stock market development? Small markets are certainly constrained; diversification of stocks and improved liquidity is limited by asset scarcity. Institutions—including the legal framework, the regulatory system, supervisory capacity, accounting and disclosure standards—may need to be strengthened before capital market expansion.[13] Rules and incentives in pension fund investment systems may warrant revision. Well-functioning money markets, which link capital markets to the banking systems, must be strengthened. Expectations regarding local market potential may need to be revised, as internationalization appears to have squeezed out local development. Indeed, when the smallness of markets presents a binding constraint on liquidity, internationalization may be a pragmatic response. Nonetheless, smaller economies promoting pension investment funds may find it awkward to suggest using international investment vehicles— appearing as an official blessing to capital flight.[14]

Drivers behind Short Capital Flows to Latin America

Short-term (less than one year) capital with the exception of loans to finance trade is broadly characterized as speculative or "hot" money. It is this stateless, agile capital that concerns policymakers. As we learned in the chapter on the debt crisis in the 1980s, financing long-term development on short-term capital is a risky venture. Portfolio flows create problems for long-term sustainability. But access to this hot capital can also generate important growth in the region. Think for a moment about the landscape of U.S. growth minus our stock and bond markets—quite a bleak picture. Bonds and equity investments provide funding for projects. With interest rates still low in the United States, fund managers are desperate to obtain additional returns where they can chase capital investments around the globe. Not surprisingly, questions of volatility and sustainability arise.

A variety of factors explain the increase in both bond and equity capital flows and the interest in Latin America relative to other regions. Beginning with the supply side, international flows have responded to changes in international markets, following global integration. Technological changes facilitating the transfer of money and ideas have made the world a smaller place, reducing transaction costs for international investment. With better information and changes in the U.S. legal code, new groups of institutional investors such as pension and insurance funds have internationalized investment opportunities.[15] The aging of the baby boomers created a pool of capital in search of high returns. Low interest rates in the United States make domestic investments less attractive; fund managers are desperate to scavenge additional returns where they can. Excess global savings have continued to keep interest rates low despite the strong demand for money in the United States since 2001. These external supply factors, including developments in international financial markets, have been shown to be the primary determinant of capital flows to the region.[16] More investors are looking for productive opportunities around the globe. As discussed above, they prefer, however, to make these purchases on the New York Stock Exchange rather than directly in regional markets.

Why invest in Latin America instead of other regions? In addition to the factors that have increased the global supply of capital, structural changes in Latin America pulled financing into the region. Tough austerity measures improved financial solvency in the 1990s. In most countries in the region, changes in investment codes and macroeconomic policy are perceived to be permanent. National exchange rate regimes are less susceptible to megadevaluations. Investors have greater confidence in their ability to predict the long-term macroeconomic environment for business. Legislation has favored international investment, and privatization created new investment opportunities. Simultaneous political reform and the deepening of democracy reduced the political risk associated with investment. We can summarize these factors by saying that the relative yield of countries' assets as well as financial solvency improved, while political instability and potential losses due to devaluation or nationalization declined. In short, Latin America became a good investment risk in the 1990s.[17] Nonetheless, it is important to remember that no matter how well structured Latin America's reforms are, international capital chooses a home based on *relative* appeal: opportunities for profit not only have to be good, but they must be better than expected returns and adjusted for uncertainty and risk everywhere else. Latin America may be better placed to absorb capital than it was in the 1980s —but investors may find returns even more attractive in Eastern Europe.

REWARDS AND RISKS OF NEW CAPITAL FLOWS TO LATIN AMERICA

Hot money flows, or short-term capital investments, which, while used to finance investments and spur growth, introduce questions of volatility. What are the implications of short-term capital flows to Latin America? New capital flows to the region are the financial rewards for the painful process of structural adjustment. Greater global integration can be seen as a movement toward the more efficient worldwide utilization of capital. For advocates of new capital flows, maintaining access to international financial markets is simply the result of sound domestic economic management. They see international inflows as complementary to national capital. The infusion of funds will spur growth, which will then encourage savings.

Is money moving to the region because it is most efficiently employed in Latin America as compared to other investment alternatives? To evaluate the arguments of proponents of capital inflows, it is important to situate the theoretical argument in the context of the reality of Latin American markets. Latin American markets are not exactly like the Wall Street variety. If markets are relatively thin and uncompetitive, efficiency gains will be limited. Furthermore, the price signals driving capital to certain markets may be flawed. Given that finance deals with future information, expectations and opinions dominate over facts in decision making—and information about developing country markets may be less available than developments in more mature economies. Herding behavior and contagion may result as buyers jump on bandwagons with weak fundamentals. Informational bottlenecks and the institutional peculiarities of investors may interfere with market efficiency. Many new investment instruments are complex and not completely understood by participants, increasing the underlying risk. Transactions in many markets are unregulated, accounting standards are lax, balance sheets are inscrutable, and financial disclosure is not as strictly enforced as in the United States. With incomplete information, the globalization of capital may not generate as much efficiency as claimed.[18] Capital may be more fickle and less efficient than is sometimes assumed.

Some policymakers in Latin America are wary of long-run dependency on the new capital flows, particularly **short-term money,** because of its volatility and how it affects other variables. Because the decision to invest is made on relative rates of return, a country continuing to pursue a sound policy course might find itself out of favor in the international market as another nation or region becomes the Wall Street flavor of the month. A long history of negative effects of external price changes—such as the oil price and interest rate shocks precipitating the debt crisis of the 1980s—makes policymakers nervous concerning external vulnerability. Uncertainty is built into the structure of current financing. For example, bonds with an average maturity of four years are a major source of capital supporting infra-structure expansion. What if they are not renewed at expiration?[19] Can development planning be creatively financed with short-term inflows?

Given bandwagon effects and herding, capital flows tend to be procyclical. Money pours in during boom periods—and quickly exits with the bust. The lack of access to capital during periods of crisis further limits the government's ability to use countercyclical policies to manage a crisis. Evidence suggests that procyclical financial markets compounded by procyclical macroeconomic policies have exac-erbated the costs of volatility on growth. Major reversals of capital flows may have resulted in a decrease of 25 percent in the income of developing countries for a total of between $100 billion and $150 billion in lost GDP.[20]

In addition to volatility and a procyclical bias, capital inflows may adversely affect other economic variables. In particular, some economists are concerned about the degree to which capital inflows are consistent with sustainable levels of the exchange rate and the interest rate. Because capital inflows change the supply of money available for investment, they also change the price of money—both nation-ally, as measured by the domestic interest rate, and relatively, as measured by the exchange rate. If inflows are strong, finance becomes cheaper, and the interest rate falls. International money is more abundant, and therefore the local currency, rela-tively scarcer than it was before, appreciates. Low interest rates could have a nega-tive effect on national savings rates, discouraging local sources of financing. An appreciated exchange rate may stand in the way of pursuing an export orientation. In particular, if financial markets are shallow and uncompetitive, they may not be able to intermediate the capital surges effectively, exacerbating instability. If capital surges accelerate demand beyond the capacity of the economy, they may also create inflationary pressures. For some countries, the boom in capital flows is a high-risk venture that threatens national control over key monetary variables.

Financial innovation and international capital flows have decreased the degrees of freedom available to Latin American policymakers.[21] The speed of international capital markets requires greater flexibility in economic instruments; paradoxically, it also demands stability. Instantaneous movement of capital implies that markets are overly responsive to small policy mistakes, increasing the tendency toward in-stability.[22] The policymakers' tightrope is more threatening in international markets. Capital inflows, while acting as a spur to development, can also have a high cost.

International Capital Flows and Domestic Banking

A strong banking system can serve to dampen domestic macroeconomic instability and the challenges of short-term capital flows. Bank lending is the more traditional alternative to bond and stock markets in the region. Under a sound banking system, if domestic investors decide to sell long-term financial assets, they can move into domestic bank deposits. That is, if in the United States you are uncertain about the performance of the stock market or long-term mutual funds, you might opt for the safety of a certificate of deposit (CD). As people move into CDs, the greater availability of funds makes it easier to lend to companies, and expansion is encouraged, counteracting the downward trend in the market. However, if there is a lack of confidence in the banking sector, the substitute is international instruments, or **capital flight.**[23] When banks fail to provide domestic intermediation, the effects of crises are magnified. Furthermore, as has been demonstrated in the Asian financial crisis of 1997–1998, if domestic loans to large conglomerates—or, in the Latin case, *grupos*—sidestepped sound accounting procedures, a downturn may result in a resounding crash. The Chilean crisis in 1982–1993 and the Mexican crisis were exacerbated by loans made to huge conglomerates riding high on overinflated asset prices without corresponding real collateral to secure the megaloans. When the crisis hit in each country—and later in Asia—the high percentage of nonperforming loans magnified the contractionary effects on the economic system. Weak banks exacerbated rather than minimized the crisis.

The banking sector in Latin America was relatively fragile in the beginning of the 1990s. Years of high inflation and fiscal mismanagement had weakened the sector. **Capital controls** during the 1980s restricted competition, technological advances lagged, and most banking relationships were driven by personal or political ties.[24] The 1990s heralded a new era of openness, but institutional development is often slow. Privatization in Mexico, for example, led to a high degree of concentration, with fifty-eight institutions consolidated into eighteen commercial banks, of which six were considered national, with the balance regional. The presence of foreign banks is also increasing. Spain's Banco Santander Central Hispano (BSCH) is the dominant transnational bank in the region, along with Citibank (United States), Banco Bilbao (Spain), and Credit Suisse (Switzerland).[25] The low level of competitiveness in the sector has allowed banks to charge high fees and maintain large spreads between lending and deposit rates; it has also been more difficult for small- and medium-sized enterprises (SMEs) and the rural sector to access credit.[26] As noted in chapter 6, the speed of privatization—a bank was sold every three weeks—led to improper asset valuation, sloppy accounting, and a tendency toward political expediency in sales.[27] Few developing countries can muster the institutional resources necessary for a strong, functioning, independent regulatory authority.[28] Paradoxically, liberalization of capital markets decreases the ability and increases the need for sound government oversight at the national and international levels of lending practices of banks.[29] Opening up too fast may overwhelm institutional capacities to behave as financial watchdogs.

To deepen capital markets, necessary ingredients include macroeconomic stability, a sound legal framework, an efficient and reliable clearing and settlement system, an adequate accounting system, an efficient microstructure for trading securities, and a proper regulatory and supervisory framework.[30] However, this kind of institution building may take time. Some have suggested that financial liberalization may have taken place too quickly, not giving markets enough time to develop appropriate institutions.[31] In the Mexican case, for example, reprivatization of banks was simultaneously accompanied by lifting constraints on credit expansion. Overzealous lending without adequate supervision may have contributed to the depth of the ensuing financial crisis. Time and timing of changes matter. In the interim, the policy question becomes how to decrease the vulnerability of domestic financial systems to crisis and instability while strengthening financial institutions.

A Case in Point on Capital Flows: The Mexican Peso Crisis

The Mexican peso crisis of 1994–1995 highlights the problematic effects of international capital flows for internal macroeconomic stability. It underscores the conflict between domestic stabilization and attending to the international concerns of international capital in policy making. How should authorities balance national domestic concerns such as inflation and unemployment against external constraints of exchange rate stability and current accounts when there are two different judges of success: voters and international capital?

Mexico had become a darling of the international community. A poster child for liberalization, the country had, since the 1982 debt crisis, undertaken tough reform measures including fiscal stabilization, privatization, and the opening of internal markets to international trade. Markets were eager to lend to this nation that had battled budget deficits and revamped the rules of doing business. Unlike conditions during the debt crisis of the 1980s, much of the lending was in the private sector. Between 1987 and 1994 commercial credit expanded by more than 100 percent, with credits for housing ballooning 100 percent and consumption credit growing by 450 percent. GDP growth was strong, and prices were steady. Two-thirds of the $91 billion inflows were portfolio investments, quickly attracted to high returns in the new Mexico. Implementation of the North American Free Trade Agreement (NAFTA) promised new gains in markets and productivity. Relatively low interest rates in the United States made the returns in Mexico particularly lucrative. Mexican markets were hot.

This optimism created an asset price boom in Mexico. As investors were attracted to high returns, others, afraid to miss out on the rising market, jumped on the bandwagon. Incentives in the investment industry tend to draw clients in on an upward trend. Brokers are more frequently fired for missing a great opportunity than for crashing when everyone else around them is also falling.[32] Upward trends tend to reinforce themselves, overshooting real values and creating a divergence between the true investment potential and the asset bubble. Of course, the further the investment gets from its fundamental value, the harder is the landing when the market corrects itself. Small events can lead to major speculative attacks as investors who jumped on the bandwagon knowing little about the investment overreact without taking the time to obtain better information. Unfortunately, those who pay the highest price for the crash—the poor Mexicans who must bear the brunt of adjustment—are not necessarily those involved in creating the speculative bubble.

Oddly, in the midst of the Mexico market euphoria, the true performance of the Mexican economy was below the glowing predictions. Although both multilateral agencies such as the IMF and private-sector firms such as Bear Sterns painted a rosy picture, actual performance fell short of potential. While Mexico was being certified as low-risk investment-grade potential by J. P. Morgan and being heralded as a success story by the World Bank, real exchange rate appreciation caused by capital inflows was sending the wrong signal to the productive sector, eroding competitiveness.[33] The same price for the exchange rate was not clearing both financial and tradable goods markets.

Warning signs of unsustainability of the Mexican situation and an impending crisis appeared on the horizon. The Mexican peso began to appreciate substantially as a result of capital inflows. Adjusted for inflation differences with the United States, some estimated that it was overvalued by 30 percent. Others, including those within the Mexican government, contended that the appreciation was warranted by the improved productive potential of the Mexican economy. They argued that the currency was not overvalued but reflected stronger GDP growth. Why, they reasoned, would private capital continue to flow in if the underlying fundamentals weren't sound?

Nonetheless, there was a clear cost to the external account imbalance. Figure 7.4 shows that by 1994 Mexico's ballooning current account deficit had nearly reached 8 percent of GDP. Was this sustainable? Deficits on the current account, composed primarily of an excess of imports over exports, must be financed by surpluses on the capital account. Indeed, if imports are used to enhance productive potential (as opposed to luxury consumption), and if international capital is willing to finance

Figure 7.4.   Mexico's Current Account Deficit

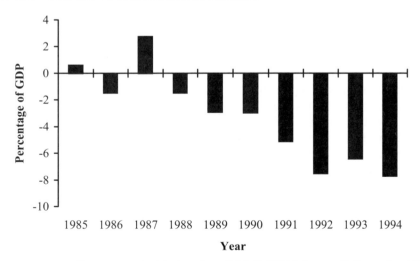

Source: Stephany Griffith-Jones, "The Mexican Peso Crisis," *CEPAL Review* 60 (December 1996).

these investments, trade deficits are not necessarily a bad thing. The question of sustainability revolves around the willingness of international markets to continue to supply funds to cover the deficits. If investors continued to believe that Mexico's future performance outpaced other alternatives, deficits could be sustained. Because inflows were largely private—albeit short-term—capital, Mexican authorities contended that they were a simple market reflection of Mexico's new growth potential.

Whether or not this argument was accurate, it was certainly politically expedient. The ruling party of Mexico, the PRI, was facing its first real electoral challenge from both the Right and the Left since the Mexican Revolution. Selling economic stability and the success of the Mexican liberalization plan were central to reelection efforts.

In hindsight we can see the folly of this argument. We can analyze current account sustainability through a simple formula:

$$C/y = gk*$$

C, or the current account, as a percentage of y, GDP, should be equal to the real growth rate of the economy, called g, times $k*$, or international investors' willingness to expose themselves to that nation's financial instruments, also as a percentage of GDP. The logic of this formula comes from the balance of payments rule that to be sustainable, a current account deficit must be financed by capital inflows. The allowable size of the deficit will vary with the growth rate of the country and foreigners' interest in holding that nation's liabilities. This willingness, as expressed here by $k*$, is largely determined by investors' assessment of the risk involved in holding the securities as well as the difference in expected returns between investments at home and abroad. A Mexican treasury bond is seen to be riskier than one issued by Uncle Sam; therefore, the Mexican government will have to offer higher interest rates to compensate investors for risk.

If we assume that initially a country is in a steady state, and we observe in this case that foreigners are interested in holding liabilities equal to 50 percent of GDP, and if the growth rate of GDP is 4 percent, a current account deficit of 2 percent of GDP is sustainable. (Fifty percent or one-half of 4 percent is 2 percent.) If, however, investors believe that risk has decreased or that expected returns have risen, say to 75 percent, the same rate of growth will sustain a 3 percent deficit. (Three-quarters or 75 percent of 4 percent is 3 percent.) Indeed, at their peak, foreign holdings of Mexican securities were in the 50 percent range, and growth was under 4 percent. By this formula, Mexico should have had a current account deficit of between 2 and 3 percent, not the nearly $50 billion, or 8 percent, shown in figure 7.4. Moreover, not only were deficits too high, but exchange rates overvalued by capital inflows indicated that they would continue to rise. Again in figure 7.5, we see a fall in the real exchange rate, indicating an overvaluation on the order of 30 percent.

Authorities ignored these signs and struggled to maintain market confidence, continually pointing to the soundness of the Mexican economy. Because disequilibrium in accounts was lodged in the private sector, they contended that private-market price signals should eventually correct this distortion. We don't know whether

Figure 7.5.   Mexico's Current Account Deficit and Real Exchange Rate

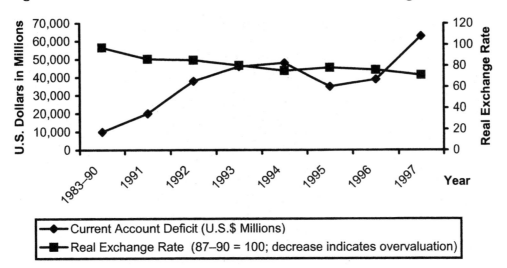

Source: Ricardo French-Davis, "Policy Implications of the Tequila Effect," *Challenge* (March–April 1998): 36.

this self-correction would have taken place in the long run. In the interim, political crises spooked markets. In January 1994, an armed uprising by insurgent rebels in the poor southern region of Chiapas panicked investors. Presidential candidate Luis Donaldo Colosio was then assassinated in March before the August elections. The selection of lesser-known Ernesto Zedillo Ponce de Leon as candidate did little to quell suspicions of Mexico's instability. Pressing social and political problems threatened economic gains. Investors began to wonder if Mexico was a political backwater or a strong emerging nation.

International capital began to vote with its feet. Because capital moves faster than trade patterns can adjust, Mexico's balance of payments deficits were being financed by dwindling international reserves. As importers went to the central bank to get dollars to pay suppliers, fewer dollars were available. To maintain the exchange rate, the central bank was forced to supply dollars from reserves. Mexico reportedly spent US$10 billion from March through May attempting to defend the peso in the wake of the Colosio assassination, although lags in the release of data decreased the transparency of events to the international community. The exchange rate, set using a crawling band, was under severe pressure, yet the government did not want to fuel inflationary expectations with a devaluation.

Nonetheless, knowing that the Bank of Mexico did not have the capacity to stem the outflow, both domestic and international investors came to expect a large devaluation to correct the trade imbalance. At the same time, the government didn't want to raise interest rates to keep capital at home, because this would have a recessionary effect on the domestic economy. Because the risk premium for holding foreign securities includes foreign exchange rate risk, investors needed to be compensated for the fact that if the devaluation took place, their assets would be worth less. If you are holding a financial instrument denominated in pesos and the peso is worth less, your asset value falls by the same proportion. To entice capital to stay, the government began to offer dollar-denominated treasury bonds, called ***tesobonos,*** to replace the peso-denominated *cetes.* In creating this option, the Mexican government essentially internalized the currency devaluation risk, simultaneously trying to send a signal that it perceived that the crisis was caused by short-term political factors. These would soon blow over, it argued, rendering a megadevaluation unnecessary.

Ruling-party PRI candidate Zedillo was elected president in August, and to the surprise of many in the international financial community, the government did not alter the exchange rate or the monetary or fiscal stance. With the support of business and labor under Mexico's El Pacto, President Carlos Salinas and President-Elect Zedillo forged ahead. The hope was that business as usual would reassure markets that the turbulence was temporary and that Mexico was ready to resume course. Mexican officials declared that a devaluation was out of the question.

But markets were unconvinced. By the end of November, reserves of $12.5 billion were insufficient to cover even half of the $27 billion short-term public debt, 70 percent of it in dollar-denominated *tesobonos.* When reserves reached critically low levels of around $6 billion in December, the government had little choice but to devalue. It adjusted the band on the peso by 15 percent. However, this attempt to release a little steam exploded. Investors felt that they had been deceived by Mexican authorities. Although instruments were dollar denominated, there was a lack of confidence that the government would be able to honor its obligations. The devaluation was not accompanied by any policy changes to assure markets that the disequilibrium would be addressed, and capital took a fast flight out of Mexico. After the Mexican government lost $4 billion in one day trying to defend the peso, it had no choice but to let it float—or, more appropriately, let it sink like lead—in international markets.

Emergency measures were taken to rescue the Mexican economy. An agreement with U.S., Canadian, and European banks allowed for $7 billion of financial guarantees to back the maturing short-term *tesobonos* coming due. Belated measures were taken to restructure the economy. The pace of privatization was quickened in railroads, satellites, and ports. The banking system was opened to foreign investment, labor unions agreed to hold down wages, and the government cut spending. Interest rates rose to 55 percent to hold investors at home, but this created a recessionary drag on the economy. Investor confidence further deteriorated, and uncertainty was extended to other Latin American economies. This so-called tequila effect created regional pressure, especially for Argentina with its currency board, to readjust internal accounts. Other Latin American countries were guilty by association.

Mexican adjustments were too little, too late. The initial devaluation had been announced in a policy vacuum, creating a panic disproportionate to the underlying fundamentals in the economy. As a result of consulting domestic business and labor prior to the devaluation, capital anticipated the devaluation, further depleting reserves. Timing was bad. The announcement of the devaluation took place on a

Tuesday, prior to Christmas. Fridays are better bad news days, giving investors the weekend to calm down before markets reopen for the week. Furthermore, holiday markets were thin, so there were fewer engaged in fishing the bottom for great deals to counter the downward market trend. Finally, the new administration's finance minister had yet to solidify ties with the international financial community. When panic erupted, there were few calming voices of reason because hardly anyone had the inside scoop as to the government's intentions. Credibility and confidence were shaken.

After conditions deteriorated further, the United States proposed a rescue package in January to assist its southern neighbor. Isolationist forces in the U.S. Congress resisted, and President Bill Clinton, not willing to see the positive gains that Mexico had achieved through liberalization evaporate, used his own emergency authorities to provide loan relief. The IMF and the Bank for International Settlements (BIS), the banker's bank, came up with $17.8 billion and $10 billion in loans, respectively, all of which was collateralized by Mexico's oil reserves. With a concerted international rescue, markets settled, and Mexico began another long and painful climb to economic recovery.

Several lessons emerged from the crisis. First is the importance of maintaining sustainable current account performance. Given confidence and economic growth, a sustainable deficit should not exceed 3 percent of GDP.[34] The composition of capital inflows to sustain the deficit is critical. Short-term capital inflows are extremely sensitive to political events. Changes to rely less on short-term international capital and more on internal sources of savings will encourage longer-term stable growth. Finally, the inflexibility of the exchange rate as an inflation anchor can be dangerous as economic fundamentals move out of line. The anchor becomes something of an albatross weighing down the process of flexible adjustment. Box 7.1 provides an epilogue to this story, evidencing that despite the severe economic pain of the crisis, good macromanagement has brought Mexico to a relatively strong position in capital markets.

The Chilean Case: Regulating Global Inflows

The rise and fall of the Mexican economy in the mid-1990s prompted a search for alternatives to the volatility of hot capital flows. Portfolio investments are tied to stock prices, reflecting increases in the real value of firms, and short-term capital flows or hot money respond to interest rate differentials or the expected appreciation of the currency—in Chile's case, the peso.[35] Speculative portfolio inflows rose in the early 1990s, concerning policymakers. Much attention was paid to the Chilean case. In Chile, net capital inflows ranged from 11 percent to 18 percent of GDP from 1979 to 1981. Over the period 1990–1993, the low was 1.9 percent and the high was 7.6 percent.[36] The composition of flows changed markedly as well, moving from medium- and long-term loans in the earlier period to FDI and Chilean investment abroad as well as portfolio investments and hot money in the 1990s. Laws governing FDI in Chile are highly favorable to foreign capital. The bulk of FDI in Chile has been in the export sectors, with more than half in mining alone.

BOX 7.1.   IS MEXICO STILL AN EMERGING MARKET?

Emerging markets are defined as developing economies with high risk coupled with attractive potential investment returns. From a borrowing perspective, emerging markets pay a penalty, called country risk, in credit markets.[37] Economists Jorge Blázquez and Javier Santiso suggest that Mexico has graduated from emerging market status. Mexico has received an investment grade rating, indicating lower risk, and has decoupled its economy from contagion in other emerging markets, and its sovereign spreads over international rates have fallen over the past half decade. Investor confidence is up, bolstered by a positive performance on its economic ability and its political willingness to service its debt. Its economy has become squarely internationalized over the past fifteen years and has diversified from an oil platform to become an exporter of industrial products. NAFTA has propelled a rise in the degree of openness, measured by the sum of imports and exports over GDP, from 27 percent in 1994 to 50 percent in 2001. The treaty has also acted as a credibility anchor, locking in promarket reforms by law and inspiring greater market confidence. Mexico has also significantly lowered its ratio of external debt to exports to 18 (as compared to Brazil's ratio of 71) and has promoted fiscal responsibility. Despite meager tax revenues relative to both the Organization for Cooperation and Economic Development (OECD) and other Latin American countries, the public debt has remained manageable since 1998. Inflation appears in check, and the political cycle is not controlling monetary policy. With these achievements, it can be argued that Mexico, following a development path of a country such as Spain, is moving beyond the category of an emerging market. However, this investment category does not focus on key deficits in the social sector that continue to plague Mexico and its drive to enhance productivity in the global economy.

Legal restrictions on the outflow of capital were liberalized in 1991, leading to significant investment abroad. In a new twist, Chilean companies poured billions into the rest of Latin America, the bulk of which flowed into just three countries: Argentina, Bolivia, and Peru. In Argentina, Chileans command a large share of the privatized electricity business as well as own assets in ceramics, disposable diapers, bottled gas, welded products, caddies, cables, and industrial oils. They operate the railways in Bolivia. In Peru, Chileans direct the fast-expanding pension fund industry and make everything from copper wire to spaghetti.[38]

Although new capital flows may appear to be beneficial, the effects on the exchange rate are the dark side of the inflow of speculative money. The Chilean development model is driven by the export sector. Throughout Latin America, structural adjustment was led by the export sector, yet paradoxically, good performance was rewarded by capital inflows that appreciated the currency and retarded export performance. Accounting for more than one-third of GDP, the diversified export sector has been a source of dynamism in Chilean growth. To the degree that capital inflows appreciate the peso, these financial flows undermine efforts in the real economy.[39] Ironically, countries can be hurt by their own successful adjustment. As the international market sees the assets of a country as a good investment, inflows appreciate the exchange rate, choking off the export drive that made for the success in the first place. The real exchange rate appreciation caused by capital inflows works against international competitiveness.[40]

Skyrocketing prices for copper in 2004 through 2006 have increased financial flows to pay for this hot commodity. As foreign money pours in, the increased supply means that the Chilean peso is relatively more expensive. Rising copper income has caused the peso to strengthen from 700 to the dollar to 510, past the 550 mark that most economists think is its long-term "normal" exchange rate.[41] The strengthening of the peso is threatening the diversification of the Chilean economy into fruit, wine, and wood products. Moreover, windfall gains from copper are being invested in spending in the social sector. This increased spending at home can overheat an already strong economy. To temper this, the new administration under Michelle Bachelet is using this opportunity to build up reserves. It is also investing in foreign assets to sop up the excess currency in the copper sector.

The policy dilemma becomes balancing external sector growth and internal stability. What should be done to offset these negative effects of financial flows? The Chilean central bank and Ministry of Finance utilized a combination of pragmatic measures designed to reduce short-term inflows. These included regulating short-term movements through reserve requirements, quotas, and fees; foreign exchange market intervention; and sterilizing the monetary effect of foreign exchange.[42] The goal of this policy has been to expand the leeway for domestic monetary policy by increasing domestic savings and decreasing the flow of international hot money.[43] Pragmatic management of the exchange rate has reduced Chile's vulnerability to capital swings, allowing it to pursue a more stable path in a highly liberalized market regime. The Chilean government has employed a crawling band system pegged to three international currencies; the peso has performed at the bottom of the band, indicating that appreciation would have been larger without intervention.[44] This is a case of government policy augmenting the stability of markets— and not the kind of zealous free market wizardry often associated with the Chilean model. The Chilean government also promoted FDI, in both traditional and nontraditional exports. Four out of the five largest fruit companies (which together account for half of fruit exports) are transnational corporations (TNCs). Several new mining projects involve TNCs. Capital continues to enter Chile, but it is on Chilean terms.

The downside to capital controls includes the fact that they are difficult to enforce, may signal risk and therefore drive up capital prices, and, if effective in the short term, may delay needed economic reforms. Furthermore, few countries have the long track record of adjustment demonstrated by Chile. Whereas the Chilean government has the accumulated credibility to apply brakes without coming to a screeching stop, other economies could be devastated by a chilly signal to international markets. No clear consensus has emerged on the overall effectiveness of capital controls, especially in affecting long-run levels of investment.[45]

The Asian and Russian Economic Crises and the Contagion Effect

The vulnerability of Latin American economies to global events is illustrated in the case of the Asian crisis. In the summer of 1997, the currencies of Thailand, Malaysia, and Korea came under attack. The loss of confidence in the once heralded

"Asian Tigers" quickly spread not only throughout Southeast Asia but to all emerging economies. Beset by the contagion effect, Latin America was confronted with a crisis not of its own making. Despite nearly two decades of adjustment since the eruption of the debt crisis in 1982, regional economies were challenged by a global loss of investor confidence in developing economies. The nosedive in stock and bond markets throughout the region had little to do with underlying economic fundamentals. Capital frightened of any emerging market risk indiscriminately pulled out of the region, leaving governments to sustain policies structured around open markets and the infusion of capital from abroad. Governments were forced to raise domestic interest rates as a means of bribing capital to stay at home. High domestic interest rates had contractionary effects on growth and increased unemployment. International commodity prices also fell as a result of global recessions. Sugar prices fell 21.14 percent, copper was down 22.7 percent, coffee declined 29.35 percent, and oil lost 32.6 percent with weakened Asian markets.[46] For commodity exporters such as Chile, this translated into balance of payments problems on the current account. The 30 percent devaluations of East Asian currencies also made manufactured goods from Korea, Malaysia, Thailand, Indonesia, and the Philippines more competitive in world markets, where they compete against goods from the larger Latin American industrial producers in Brazil and Mexico. Adjusting for the overvaluations throughout Latin America, the real cross-rate devaluations for South Korea, for example, range from 78.8 percent for Venezuela to 45.8 percent for Brazil. This is a hefty price difference for Brazilian or Venezuelan firms competing in international markets![47] Unfortunately, competitive devaluations by Latin American governments may lead to a feared resurgence in inflation.

When the Russian ruble collapsed in 1998, eyes turned to the last bulwark against total collapse in emerging markets: Brazil. In Brazil, the black market rate for dollars rose from the normal range of two cents over the official exchange rate to thirty cents, evidencing the stronger demand to convert into dollars, perhaps to send to bank accounts in Miami. Reserves fell by between $500 million and $1 billion a day in the wake of the uncertainty created by the Russian ruble.[48] The timing of the crisis was particularly unfortunate. President Fernando Henrique Cardoso, the architect of the Brazilian Real Plan, was engaged in a contest for reelection with Left-leaning "Lula," the nickname for contender Luis Inácio da Silva. Having already raised domestic interest rates, Cardoso was reluctant to further clamp down on the economy and irritate the vote of labor. Although he won the election, the margin was thin, reflecting national frustration with stabilization-induced high unemployment. After the election, Cardoso announced a fiscal austerity plan, including $20 billion in budget cuts. Devaluation, a key to increasing exports and jobs, was feared because of the possibility of reigniting inflation. The international community, perhaps belatedly, recognized the importance of Brazil, with an economy larger than those of South Korea, Thailand, and Malaysia combined.[49] It made ready a $41.5 billion IMF standby package to avoid seeing Brazil and the $800 billion Brazilian economy join Indonesia and other Southeast Asian nations in the international intensive care ward.[50]

The Asian crisis highlighted the fickle nature of international capital flows. Apart from the problem with commodity prices, the difficulties facing Latin America in large measure stemmed from a change in global risk aversion. Based on the fall of Asian markets, investors became wary of emerging market investments, without making distinctions for country performance. Said Chilean Finance Minister Eduardo Aninat, "It's the packaging effect. Analysts don't differentiate between regions, countries, or sectors anymore."[51] The difficulties facing Asian economies —especially the closed nature of business dealings dominated by cronyism—had already been in large part addressed through the painful adjustment of the 1980s and 1990s. Yet the rewards for good market behavior were not forthcoming.

International investor uncertainty was intensified by the reluctance of Brazilian politicians to pass Cardoso's budget. The ballooning government deficit had reached 8 percent of GDP and pushed domestic short-term interest rates above 40 percent in October 1998. A preliminary rejection of a key component of the plan, an increase in private contributions to the generous state-supported pension fund, frightened already jittery investors in early December. Local political feuds exacerbated uncertainty as the governor of a powerful state (and former president of the country) Itamar Franco declared a unilateral moratorium on obligations owed to the federal treasury. Fearing that Brazil would not be able to meet its financial obligations, investors began pulling out. Capital outflows accelerated. As international reserves plummeted, the government found it impossible to defend the Brazilian real and engineered an 8 percent devaluation on January 13 to relieve the pressure. Investors, having been burned by Asian devaluations, interpreted this as a sign of weakness and fled even faster. As we studied in chapter 5, the Brazilian government was forced to abandon the Real Plan, which had anchored the economy from inflation since 1994, and simply floated the currency on world markets. The currency fell another 20 percent, although stock markets in Brazil rallied on the news that the government would not continue to be bled of reserves in an uphill battle to defend the currency.

The price shock to Brazilians was dramatic. Imagine a Brazilian family with a child in an American university. Within days, the cost of tuition increased 30–40 percent. Many Brazilians who traveled during the holidays returned home to credit card bills now inflated by one-third or more. Import prices for medicines and supplies rose.[52] As the new higher costs worked their way through the supply chain, the specter of inflation rose on the Brazilian horizon. Tough contractionary measures, however, resulted in recession. Congress passed painful tax increases and cut government workers, although much tough work remained on the fiscal front. Auto workers in Brazil's multinational factories were laid off. The Brazilian government was able to weather this economic storm, but at considerable social cost. Capital flows, while they had brought strong investment and jobs, also carried costs associated with international volatility and vulnerability to external events.

The Argentine crisis of 2001–2002 presents a slightly different lesson. Argentines relied heavily on international capital flows to finance the gap between national spending and domestically available capital under the convertibility law of 1991. Powerful provincial governors thwarted the weak federal administration of President Fernando de la Rua from reducing fiscal deficits. The Brazilian devaluation of the real in 1998 had pressured external accounts as Argentina's export competitiveness eroded in the face of the cheaper Brazilian currency. When Argentina's international exposure became alarmingly high, international capital pulled out, leaving the nation to face default. The surprise in the Argentine crisis is the degree to which international markets appear to differentiate the problems of Argentina from the region's stronger performers. Contagion to other Latin American financial markets was limited, although Argentina's trading partners did suffer from real declines in exports.

DEBT RESTRUCTURING AND STABILIZATION AFTER PAST CAPITAL MARKET CAUSES

The Asian economic crisis of 1997–1998 forced a rethinking of conditionality. The cookie-cutter approach of reducing excess demand accompanied by changes in the size of the state simply didn't apply—and raised questions about the applicability of conditionality throughout Latin America and Africa as well. Although under IMF bylaws additional financing can only be provided if necessary changes in an economy are made, the expanded scope of conditionality of the 1980s and 1990s that extended beyond macroeconomic measures to microfoundations has been reversed in the new millennium. The first principle guiding reform is ownership of policies. Success of IMF policies has been shown to be tied to domestic political support for economic reform. Although reform may still be unpleasant economic medicine, if a package is arrived at in consultation with civil society, repeated failure of packages may be avoided. Secondly, conditionality is increasingly restricted to the IMF's core areas of competence in macroeconomic reform. Privatization and social conditionality is being left to coordination with other institutions such as the World Bank. Letters of intent are more clearly drawn to reflect those necessary macroeconomic changes for release of IMF funds as opposed to recommended structural changes in a country's reform program. Overall, the average number of conditions imposed has decreased by one-third. Changing conditionality will require greater flexibility and judgment on a case-by-case basis. Whether greater country specificity will encourage more sustainable reform will require the test of time. It is interesting to at least observe, however, that after twenty years of criticism—particularly by the neostructuralists that packages didn't address underlying national conditions—the IMF is finally beginning to listen.[53]

Changes in capital markets in the 1990s prompted the need to rethink how to handle sovereign crises. Unlike the debt crisis of 1982, when Argentina collapsed in 2002 there was no orderly mechanism to begin creditor negotiations. Twenty years ago major creditors—primarily large banks—would negotiate collectively through a steering committee that resolved intercreditor problems, assessed debtor offers, and preserved confidentiality. Today's claimants, largely diverse bondholders rather than syndicated banks, have little incentive and ability to solve crises collectively. Bondholders hold out, free riding in hopes of receiving payments in line with original contracts. Complex financial instruments such as derivatives make the problem worse as the underlying equity value is not always transparent. Yet the failure to act promptly to resolve a debtor's problems results in a deterioration of the nation's assets—a huge economic and social loss in no one's interest.

Lessons for Capital Mobility: Questions of Financial Sector Reform

The vulnerability of Latin America to the Asian and Russian crises renewed questions with respect to the sustainability of the externally driven model versus the need to promote stable domestic growth. Maintaining strong capital inflows over time will require either higher interest rates for bonds or loans or improved profitability of equity investments. Higher interest rates have a clear domestic cost. If higher rates are offered to attract capital, the domestic cost to borrowers—the firms that want to use this capital to expand—is necessarily higher. This also increases the cost to the government of servicing publicly held domestic debt.[54] Higher interest rates therefore act as a drag on productive domestic investment. They may also create pressures to appreciate the currency, making it more difficult for exporting firms and pressuring the balance of payments. Once again the exchange rate paradox emerges, because one indicator of country risk is a trade deficit.

Playing with the price of money is therefore unlikely to work in the long run. For capital inflows to remain stable, financial investments must be translated into real gains in productivity. If a disproportionate share of investments is directed toward the stock market or consumption, asset bubbles and imbalances will emerge.[55] Firms can be made more profitable through productivity improvements, but this is tough work. The "easy" stage of reorganization driven by privatization efforts is over. Firms must focus on long-run efforts to improve productivity, including human capital investments in health and education. Unfortunately, these take time and are not costless.

To escape the vicious circle of external vulnerability and internal recession, two other domestic policy possibilities emerge. Decreasing consumption in favor of domestic savings may lower the reliance on capital inflows for growth. Savings rates in the region have remained flat, at rates incompatible with sustainable growth. One of the reasons Latin American countries have been so vulnerable to international capital flows is the underdeveloped nature of long-term capital markets. Domestic savings in the region was 20 percent of GDP in 2000; savings rates in Asia range around 30 percent.[56] Increased reliance on domestic savings would reduce volatility, making them less vulnerable to the sudden withdrawal of foreign money. Changing savings rates, however, is a difficult long-term process. Rather than save, many Latin Americans have chosen to consume—much like U.S. counterparts. Weaning a country off capital flows requires substituting domestic for foreign savings to maintain growth. Encouraging savings may be accomplished by changing the relative opportunity cost of consuming today as compared to saving for tomorrow. Nevertheless, it is rarely popular with voters.

The second alternative is to promote tradable goods (exports) over nontradables, to strengthen the balance of payments. However, where the exchange rate is fixed in terms of the dollar, and thus represents a real and psychological anchor against inflation, changing relative prices between imports and exports becomes problematic.[57] Furthermore, primary product exports have their own source of instability. We will turn to the possibilities and limitations offered by the tradable goods sector in the next chapter.

In addition to changes that developing countries themselves might implement, others have suggested that the architecture of the global economy needs revision. Some contend that the IMF is too weak to grapple with the force and the ramifications of international capital flows and that the lending authority of the IMF may be too limited to deal with the needs of large countries such as Brazil or Mexico. They argue for an effective lender of last resort, much like the U.S. Federal Reserve system for domestic banks. International financier George Soros, believing that "international capital movements need to be supervised and the allocation of credit regulated," has called for the establishment of an international credit insurance corporation.[58] Diagnosing financial instability as in part caused by a "great asymmetry between an increasingly sophisticated and dynamic international financial market and the existing institutional arrangements, which are inadequate to regulate it," the Economic Commission for Latin America and the Caribbean (ECLAC) has called for a new institutional framework.[59] Arguing that the international community helps to create speculative crises, with risk-rating agencies drawing attention to "hot" countries and creating bubbles bound to burst, ECLAC urges negotiations to establish an institutional framework capable of providing accurate information in increasingly sophisticated and dynamic global markets.[60]

Others suggest, however, that an expansion of lending capabilities of the IMF or a new financial institution would create a moral hazard. That is, countries might act irresponsibly knowing that the IMF would be there to bail them out. This contention, however, is countered by those who say that governments would not risk paying the political price of austerity measures for some short-term emergency capital. The costs of adjustment are simply too high. At issue in policy circles is whether a new framework to provide enhanced international stewardship through improved early warning and data collection, as well as greater accountability to strengthened international regulations and accounting practices, might smooth the volatility—and its associated costs—in the international financial system.[61] The IMF itself is working to promote better transparency and dissemination of data, especially on short-term debt, but change can be accomplished only with the full support of the IMF's 184 member countries.[62] The IMF has encouraged members to release public information notices, letters of interest, and policy framework papers that accompany IMF consultations; indeed, with member consent, some of these documents can be found posted on the IMF web page at www.imf.org.[63] The IMF is also encouraging better dissemination of private banking data through expanded coverage of the BIS data and addressing gaps in banking supervision and adoption of standards. These efforts can be seen on the BIS home page at www.bis.org. As noted by then managing director of the IMF Michel Camdessus, in an era of intense integration of global capital markets, the most challenging aspect of reform has been the question of involving private-sector actors in forestalling and resolving crises.[64]

Solutions to the problems of instability and crises associated with international capital flows may be thought of using our three policy perspectives. A pure neoliberal or new political economy approach would suggest that interfering with the market allocation of private capital would promote inefficiency. Although the neoliberal might acknowledge the costs of volatility, intervention would only slow the path of adjustment. The best policy response would be to leave the market alone. The only warranted intervention might be to strengthen and clarify regulations and standards of reporting in domestic and international financial markets such that participants could make decisions on the best available data. A neoinstitutionalist would perhaps look to see if any of the transactions costs in global capital markets might be reduced. In particular, the neoinstitutionalist might suggest that while institutional deepening is pursued, countries should pursue countervailing measures to lessen the domestic costs of short-term capital. This may, for example, include a tax on short-term international capital flows along the lines of a Tobin tax of 0.1 percent of the value of a transaction to slow the wheels of international finance until markets could be made more efficient. The neostructuralist would be more concerned with the distributional implications of the international financial casino. The state might be called upon as a financial intermediary to generate domestic sources of savings, leaving countries less exposed to international capital flows. For example, special investment funds could be set up by the government and incentives created to promote opportunities to invest in small- and medium-sized firms, increasing both savings and income flowing to smaller businesses.[65] Your vision of the appropriate role of the state may guide you in outlining preferred policy options. The roles you assign to the state and the market may have something to do with the relative weight you place on each of three objectives of financial system reform: fostering efficiency and growth by allocating capital to areas of highest returns, reducing the risks of financial crises, and softening the impact and equitably sharing the burden of adjustment when crises hit.[66]

REMITTANCES: PEOPLE MOVING NORTH, MONEY MOVING SOUTH

In Latin America the largest source of international capital flowing into the region comes not from multinationals, investors, or development agencies but from Latinos themselves. How is Latin capital international? The largest source of foreign funds in Latin America is the money that emigrant workers send home.[67] In 2004, remittances—the economic resources sent by emigrants who live abroad to their families or communities in Latin America—overtook the total amount of FDI and overseas development assistance combined.[68] Why have remittances seen explosive growth? What is the impact of this capital flowing south? Can this money be better channeled for developmental purposes? This section takes up some of these questions.

Global money remittances from the twenty-five million adults born in Latin America living outside their country of origin to Latin America and the Caribbean soared from $11.7 billion in 1995 to $45 billion in 2004.[69] Thirty-three billion of this originated in the United States, nearly double the U.S. to Latin America flow rate of 18.6 in 2001.[70] For those adult Latinos living in the United States, 42 percent send money home regularly, usually between $100 and $300 a month, resulting in 187 million financial transactions a year.[71]

Remittances are becoming an important source of local income. Eighteen percent of all adults in Mexico, 23 percent in Central America, and 14 percent in

Ecuador are remittance receivers. Most are women. These links between husbands, fathers, and sons in the United States and communities at home give rise to a new phenomenon, transnational families.[72] Immigrants send home about 10 percent of their income—but for poor families in Latin America this can constitute 50–80 percent of household income. Unlike traditional migrations from Europe to the United States, people are not leaving Latin America primarily in search of a better life in a new country; instead, they are leaving to support their families back home. Countries now depend on these flows. Remittances account for more than 10 percent of GDP in El Salvador, Honduras, and Nicaragua; in Mexico only petroleum exports provide more foreign exchange. It has been suggested that migration is now not just an escape valve; it is also a fuel pump.[73] Nonetheless, it is a pump primed by the fact that there are not enough high-income jobs in the region. People are indeed moving north, draining towns of human capital but sending more money south.

Out-migration in search of better earnings is a key factor behind the surge in remittance dollars. The late 1990s saw record flows of immigrants from Latin America to the United States. The number of Latinos residing in the United States rose from 11.8 million in 1995 to approximately 17 million in 2002. Strong ties to families remaining in the United States are in part behind the 150 percent increase in remittance money since 2000. But the U.S. migrant population has only grown by 16 percent during this period.[74] Other factors including technology, competition, and legal changes have propelled the rapid rise in fund transfers.

Traditionally, migrants sent money back either through informal networks of contacts returning home or through companies such as Western Union and Money Gram. As banking services—such as the ubiquitous ATM machine—have become more prevalent even in the poor and rural sectors of Latin America, technological solutions have driven the market shares of wire transfer companies down. Banks have gotten into the business of offering binational banking services, increasing competition in the money transfer market and lowering the costs of sending money to family at home. As a result, the cost of transferring money has fallen from approximately 15 percent of the value of the transfer to 7 percent.

Legal changes have also facilitated banking the unbanked immigrants in the United States—making it possible for them to send money through formal channels. The U.S. Patriot Act allows financial institutions to accept both the Individual Taxpayer Identification Number (ITIN) and consular cards issued by the national consulate office in the United States as valid identification for opening a bank account.[75] This legal change has created inroads to economic citizenship in the United States—the ability to bank earnings and send them to loved ones at home. For example, with this card, Wells Fargo opened more than four hundred thousand new accounts between 2001 and 2004.[76] Moving the money through formal sectors also helps officials maintain better records of remittance flows—inserting a note of caution in the seeming explosion in remittance data. The dramatic rates of growth may also reflect money missed in balance of payments data as it passed through informal hands.

Whether the rate of growth of remittances is as robust as the data indicate is probably less important, however, than understanding and exploiting the impact of remittance dollars. Overall, the IMF in its *World Economic Outlook* found that remittances can play an important role in boosting growth, contributing to macro-stability, easing the impact of adverse shocks, and ameliorating poverty in developing countries. Remittances allow households to smooth consumption in hard times, augment it during better periods, and finance education or set up small businesses.[77] In association with microcredit organizations, there is some evidence that remittances are being channeled into business start-ups. But some research suggests the impact is overstated, demonstrating that remittances dollars do little to promote growth.[78] Furthermore, it should be recalled that the call of U.S. dollars leaves towns empty and depletes human capital pools. It is often the most motivated and energetic who emigrate, leaving those with fewer human capital assets at home. There is also an increasing concern that remittances dollars are creating inequality between families who receive support from absent relatives and those who do not.

Despite these problems, the benefits of remittance dollars are substantial as a source of foreign exchange and income support. Policymakers are investigating ways not only to improve the efficiency of the transfer but also to enhance the ways that remittance flows can truly make a contribution to development. The unofficial status of many immigrants leaves four out of five not using bank services to send money home—and forcing them into more expensive wire transfers or less reliable informal means.[79] Recipients are also without strong banking infrastructure; 35 percent of Ecuadorians, 64 percent of Salvadorans, and 75 percent of Mexicans are unbanked.[80] There is a need to strengthen the banking infrastructure in rural and periurban areas in Latin America and through education to build a financial culture among both senders and recipients. Democratization of the financial systems of countries of origin will not only strengthen the security of flows and lower costs but may also create other positive externalities such as prompting an increase in the rate of savings.[81]

An example of technologies reaching the marginalized includes a new binational credit card via Citicorp's acquisition of Banamex. Both the U.S. cardholder and the designated Mexican beneficiary are issued a Banamex credit card that can be used throughout Mexico; the sender can adjust the credit limit, and the beneficiary can also use it at an ATM. With this product, the number of Banamex bank transfer accounts soared 1,500 percent in first half of 2004.[82]

Beyond ease and cost of transfer, remittances can be leveraged to stronger developmental gains. A gaping social deficit in Latin America is the insufficient and unsafe, substandard, housing stock. In contrast to the building blocks of middle-class America, in Latin America owning a home tends to be the purview of the rich. With a history of inflation and weak banking services, manageable, long-term mortgages are difficult to obtain. Programs such as Mi Viviendo's (my home's) Quinto Suyo efforts are changing this by tapping the $1.7 billion sent home by Peruvians to build homes.[83] After saving 5 percent of a home's value in an overseas account, a government-backed mortgage can be obtained by Peruvians. The default rate is a low .3 percent, encouraged by a 20 percent government discount on monthly payments if the first six installments are made on time. Carlos Bruce, Peru's minister of housing, estimates that the strong initial interest in this program could translate into ten thousand housing units annually. Mexico and Ecuador offer similar programs. A family member may make money mortgage payments in pesos at a New Jersey bank branch through the Su Pedacito de Mexico.[84] Rather than being tempted to spend remittance dollars on consumption, families are encouraged to build capital for when the immigrant returns home.

In addition to mortgage schemes, some Mexican states offer two- or three-to-one matches for money sent back to the municipality by one of the 623 Mexican clubs or hometown associations registered in the United States.[85] These collective remittances totaled $300 million in 2004. They are used for paving roads or providing clean drinking water—with hopes of decreasing the amount of out-migration in the region. New programs such as Microfinance International Corporation's Mi Pueblo offer integrated banking facilities including account, money transfer, credit, loan, and money management services to Latin immigrants. Microfinance International has begun by focusing on the Salvadoran community in the greater Washington, D.C., area to make money themselves (the company projects revenues of $10 million in 2006) by focusing on the immigrant market. The Inter-American Development Bank (IADB) is partnering with similar microfinance organizations to begin to tap the 15–20 percent of remittance dollars channeled toward savings—with hopes of marshaling this money as a fund for entrepreneurs and new small business start-ups to leverage the developmental impact of remittances.

OFFICIAL DEVELOPMENT ASSISTANCE

Given the cold fact that capital will simply not flow to economies where abject poverty and low levels of human capital will retard returns, financing for development must also include official concessional flows. Official development assistance (ODA) plays an important role in bridging the gap between local resources and developmental needs in Latin America. ODA includes grants or loans by the official sector with the goal of promoting economic development and welfare; this excludes military assistance. Approximately 80 percent of the ODA to Latin America is in the form of grants (as opposed to loans); external debt reduction initiatives have accounted for a rising proportion of flows, up from 3 percent in 1990 to 10 percent in 2002. Whereas aid in the 1990s was directed at economic infrastructure, the focus has now shifted to support for social services and social infrastructure, which in 2002 accounted for 50 percent of aid dollars to the region.[86] In the 1990s total assistance for environmental protection in Latin America rose from $54 million in 1991 to more than $235 million in 2002, although funding has been characterized as irregular, complicating planning.[87]

Net aid per capita to the region is low, ten dollars per person as opposed to a global average of thirteen dollars. Overall Latin America attracted 8.3 percent of global aid dollars in 2002. Aid to Latin America represents approximately 25 percent of FDI; this may be seen in contrast to Africa, where net African ODA is seven times FDI. Nonetheless, for poorer countries in the region such as Nicaragua, Honduras, and Bolivia, aid dollars are important in financing development, reaching 13.58, 6.78, and 8.97 percent of gross national income (GNI) in 2002.[88] Regionally, ODA accounts for less than 1 percent (.35 in 2002) of GNI. Of aid coming into Latin America, just under a quarter is channeled through multilateral organizations such as the IADB or the World Bank; the balance of the aid is bilateral, delivered on a country-to-country basis.[89]

The downward trend in official development aid was reversed in 2003 following the signing of the Monterrey Consensus. This conference reaffirmed the need for assistance by wealthier countries to jump-start investments in support of reaching the Millennium Development Goals (MDGs) of reducing extreme poverty by half in 2015. Nonetheless, the increase to .25 of rich country GDI is a stretch from the .7 target—or even the more modest .44–.54 percent that some suggest is necessary to achieve the MDGs.[90] As shown in table 7.1, top donors to Latin America include the United States, Japan, and Spain. The United States gave 23 percent of all aid flowing to the region; this accounted for 10 percent of overall U.S. aid to all countries. Table 7.1 also shows the top ten recipients of aid, with Bolivia, Nicaragua, and Peru heading the list. It is perhaps interesting to note that aid is not perfectly correlated with need, as defined by GNI per capita. Other factors, including strategic concerns, enter into the aid allocation equation. Assistance to the region is primarily used for investment in social infrastructure and services. Education, health, population, water, civil society, employment, and housing programs receive 46 percent of the aid dollars, with another 11 percent going to infrastructure and 10 percent to agriculture, industry, and trade and tourism promotion. Other categories

Table 7.1.   Top Ten Aid Donors and Recipients in the Latin America Region

Top 10 Donors to LAC, 2002				Top 10 Recipients in LAC, 2002			
Donor	To LAC (USD Million)	% All Aid to LAC	% Each Donor's Aid World Total	Recipient	(USD Million)	% of Total LAC Aid	PC GNI, 2002 USD
United States	1,225	23	10	Bolivia	681	13	910
Japan	592	11	9	Nicaragua	517	10	720
Spain	414	8	41	Peru	491	9	2,020
Germany	355	7	10	Colombia	441	8	1,810
EC	315	6	3	Honduras	435	8	910
Netherlands	313	6	12	Brazil	376	7	2,860
United Kingdom	283	5	8	Guatemala	249	5	1,750
IDA*	248	5	5	El Salvador	233	4	2,080
France	175	3	4	Ecuador	216	4	1,490
IDB Sp. Fund	167	3	100	Dominican Republic	157	3	2,310
Other	1,131	22	6	Other	1,421	27	
Total	5,218		7	Total LAC	5,217	100	3,310 (average all LAC)

Source: www.oecd.org/dac, table 2.3, Aid by Region: Latin America.
*(International Development Association)

for assistance include multisector projects, program assistance, emergency assistance, and actions related to debt relief.

In the United States, official aid to Latin America is administered through the U.S. Agency for International Development (USAID), which focuses on policy in six areas: biodiversity, democracy, economic growth, education, health, and eradication of illegal narcotics. Assistance ranges from emergency response to natural disasters such as Hurricane Stan in Guatemala in 2005 that killed more than fifteen hundred people and wreaked havoc in an already fragile economy, to investments in a $50 million five-year biodiversity conservation program in the Amazon Basin, to facilitating the spread of microfinance in the region. Descriptions of policy objectives and case stories can be found at usaid.gov. USAID is promoting partnerships, such as that with Microsoft to bring computer training to disadvantaged Brazilian youth to expand the skill base in the region. USAID also partners with nongovernment organizations (NGOs) such as Mercycorps, Accion, and Project Concern in delivering emergency relief, sustainable development, and civil society programs in the region. Either in partnership with bilateral or multilateral organizations or through their own fund-raising, NGOs play a large role in building human and social capacity in the region. Private funding nearly doubles the U.S. foreign assistance budget—including the $1.5 billion in international giving by U.S. foundations, the $2.8 billion by U.S. businesses, the $6.6 billion from American NGOs, the $3.4 billion from overseas religious ministries, and the $1.3 billion in U.S. college scholarships to foreign students.[91]

The debate on development aid is fraught with controversy. Should aid be given to the most needy countries or to those that might assist in the donor's strategic interest? What conditions should be imposed on countries in return for the receipt of development assistance? Some overarching principles of economic justice might suggest allocating aid to the neediest—but if those in most need are governed by corrupt rules, will the aid simply be flushed through private coffers? Finally, how can aid be administered to strengthen institutions and not promote dependency on continual flows from donors? These are but some of the many questions swirling in the aid debate that also apply to the Latin American context.

LONG-TERM INVESTMENT: FDI AND THE ROLE OF MNCS

In contrast to short-term bond and equity flows, FDI largely represents a long-term capital flow with a commitment to local manufacturing. FDI is generally measured by acquiring a lasting management interest or 10 percent of the voting stock or by establishing a subsidiary or production branch. On average, FDI in Latin America accounts for approximately 2.2 percent of a country's GDP.[92] FDI is less risky than borrowing because if a project fails, it is the shareholders and not the local citizens bearing the cost. We can see in figure 7.6 that FDI grew enormously throughout the 1990s, with an increasing diversity of recipients. Flows for 2000 were 536 percent greater than for 1991, even adjusting for a downturn due to the Asian crisis. Multinationals from Spain, the Netherlands, Switzerland, and the United States snatched

Figure 7.6.   Net FDI Flows into Latin America

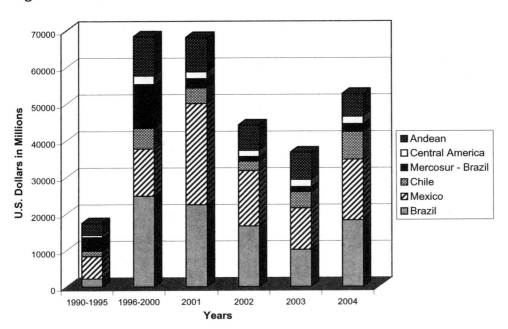

Source: ECLAC *Foreign Direct Investment in Latin America 2004.*

up cheaply priced Latin American firms in the telecommunications, banking, electric utility, and consumer finance sectors to strengthen their stakes in key markets in Brazil, Argentina, and Chile.[93] Inflows to Mexico and Argentina in the beginning of the decade have been supplemented by investment in Brazil, Venezuela, and other Latin American countries.

Nevertheless, the investment in the smaller countries of the region is about half that of Mexico or a quarter that of Brazil. In Ecuador, for example, foreign investors have shunned the unstable political and economic environment, with ventures largely limited to the oil sector.[94] FDI moves in response to dramatic swings in global markets. After a decade of extremely strong performance, FDI into Latin America and the Caribbean fell in 2002–2003, with recovery in 2004 driven by increased investment in Brazil. FDI in Latin America and the Caribbean increased 44 percent in 2004, to reach $56.4 billion, the first year that foreign capital has risen in the region since 1999, according to ECLAC. Whereas investment in the 1990s was driven primarily by privatization of state firms, recent activity has been motivated by the purchase of private firms. FDI rose 5 percent a year to reach $72 billion in 2005. The leading destination was Mexico, followed by Brazil, although flows to these countries were down 4 percent and 15 percent, respectively. Inflows rose to Colombia by 48 percent—not a trend but rather a single large purchase of the brewer Bavaria by South African Sab Miller.

Determinants of FDI

The decision by a multinational firm on where to build factories or buy businesses —FDI—is affected by many different factors as compared to short-term portfolio debt or equity flows. Foreign investment itself serves different purposes. Does the country want access to a market, raw materials, improved efficiency, or technological assets? Is the company in the goods or services sector? Table 7.2 details these strategies of TNCs by sector. Some multinationals search raw materials, often only available in a given location. Petroleum and gas producers in Andean countries are a good example. Quite often the capital costs of exploration and development of the resource are beyond local private capital. Multinationals might also profit from natural resources through tourism.

Beyond resources, the transnational might be looking to enhance efficiency in manufacturing by drawing upon lower-priced labor as in the clothing, electronics, or automotive sectors. Generally, this investment becomes part of a globally integrated production chain for export and depends upon the quality and cost of human

Table 7.2. Latin American and Caribbean Strategies of Transnational Corporations

| | Corporate Strategy | | |
Sector	*Efficiency Gains (labor costs) with export objectives*	*Natural Resource Seeking*	*Local Market Access*
Goods	Automotive: Mexico Electronics: Caribbean Basin, Mexico Clothing: Caribbean Basin, Mexico	Oil/gas: Argentina, Bolivia, Brazil, Colombia, Venezuela Minerals: Argentina, Chile, Andean	Automotive: Mercosur Agribusiness: Argentina, Brazil, Mexico Chemicals: Brazil Cement: Colombia, Dominican Republic, Venezuela
Services	Back office services, Costa Rica	Tourism: Mexico	Finance: Argentina, Brazil, Chile, Colombia, Mexico, Peru, Venezuela Telecommunications: Argentina, Brazil, Chile, Peru Electric power: Argentina, Brazil, Central America, Chile, Colombia Natural gas distribution: Argentina, Brazil, Chile, Colombia Retail trade: Argentina, Brazil, Chile, Mexico

Source: ECLAC, *Foreign Investment 2004,* table I.6.

resources, physical infrastructure, and international trade agreements. It is important to note that low wages are not in themselves a draw; the key is total compensation (which includes indirect costs from labor legislation) per unit of output. Low wages for low productivity are not a bargain. It has become clear that Latin America cannot compete on the basis of wages—it will be continuously trumped by China. Instead, the focus in the region must be on efficiently raising the output of workers per wage through investments in human capital.

Alternatively, a transnational might want access to a market closed either by policy such as a tariff or geographical constraints such as distance. Country size as expressed by GDP adjusted for the "effective market"—those consumers who can be reached with strong infrastructure such as good roads or ports—and distance from investors are two key factors that influence FDI decisions.[95] Automobiles were produced in Brazil for both reasons—to escape tariffs and to cut down on transportation costs of shipping heavy vehicles overseas. Infrastructure—particularly electric power, telecommunications, and electricity and gas distribution—are important service areas for transnational firms. Infrastructure investment depends on the regulatory environment in providing for after-contract services in areas such as telecommunications or water management.[96] Global retailers such as Wal-Mart have made strong inroads in the service sector in the region. Finally, multinationals might seek out technological advantages by locating in a country or region with a strong science and technology base. Latin America experiences little FDI of this type.

Across the four different types of FDI—natural resources, efficiency, market access, and technology seeking—several additional factors are at play. Distance works as a pro and con, depending on whether the company wants to sell either goods or infrastructure services in the foreign market (local production cuts down on transport costs) or desires to reexport to the home or other markets (where proximity to the target market is key). Legal codes that guarantee intellectual property right protection and investment dispute settlement mechanisms are important in decreasing a country's risk profile. The degree of transparency in a country's institutions is an important factor. One study suggested that on average a country could expect a 40 percent increase in FDI with a one-point increase in its transparency rankings.[97] Rather than grease the wheels, corruption adds to the burden of taxes and capital controls.

Who invests in Latin America? Figure 7.7 shows that the United States is the principal investor in the region, concentrating on manufacturers in Mexico and services such as electricity and gas distribution and telecoms in Mercosur. European firms are a growing presence, located in Mercosur and Chile in telecoms, energy financial services, automotive, agroindustry, and retail trade. The new kid on the block, Spain, is a significant investor in telecoms, financial services, electricity generation and distribution, and petroleum. Japan has limited investment in the region.[98] Firms seeking efficiency gains and lower wages tend toward the automotive and electronics sectors in Mexico and the Caribbean Basin. Natural resource-seeking investors are attracted to Venezuela, Colombia, Argentina, Chile, and Peru. Those seeking market access in manufacturing are interested in Argentina, Brazil, and Mexico, and firms taking advantage of liberalization and privatization of services have moved in throughout the region.[99]

Figure 7.7.   FDI in Latin America, Countries of Origin, 2004

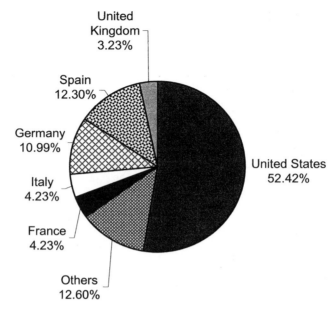

Source: ECLAC, *Foreign Investment in Latin America 2004.*

An increasingly important phenomenon in the region are the multi-Latinas or the trans-Latins—emerging Latin American transnationals that have made direct investments outside their home countries.[100] From a meager annual average of approximately US$52 million between 1970 and 1974, thirty years later outward investment from Latin America is approximately US$24.5 billion per year. Although outward investment by developing countries is dominated by Asian multinationals, Mexican and Brazil firms such as Cemex (cement), América Móvil (telecommunications), Petrobras (petroleum), CVRD (mining), Gerdau (metals), Grupo Bimbo (food), and Gruma (food) make it to the top fifty of nonfinancial transnationals from developing countries. Other important trans-Latins are from Argentina and Chile. In most cases, internationalization of firms has been market-seeking and has involved purchases of existing assets. Nonetheless, the existence of these firms demonstrates that multi-Latinas can indeed be competitive on a global scale.[101]

Worldwide, U.S. multinationals sell about two-thirds of their output in the host country, suggesting that the motivation for exports driven by cheap labor only adheres in a smaller percent of cases. In the Andean region, host-market serving and infrastructure arguments are even more compelling. U.S. manufacturing affiliates reach a striking 90 percent in Peru and Venezuela and average 75 percent for other nations, indicating that export orientation as a rationale for investment is limited.[102] This constrains foreign investment, because the number of consumers is relatively small. Despite a good deal of activity in natural resource-related activities, Andean countries will be limited by market size in attracting technology-based investment in manufacturing.

Multinational presence is strong in the automobile sector. *(Photo by Patrice Franko)*

Although the importance of single firms such as Chiquita Brands or General Motors in the economies of the subregion is not inconsequential, FDI is not the solution for all countries that want to spur development. That is, multinationals do not necessarily want to produce where conditions are unstable or the infrastructure is incomplete. They are also attracted to large markets such as Brazil or Mexico to sell the cars or machines produced there and avoid transport costs. FDI can be seen as preferable to short-term capital flows in that it reflects a long-term commitment to the nation. It should in fact translate into an increase in a country's productive potential—but it may work best where the country's industrial base is already relatively developed. On the negative side, however, multinational investment raises other questions with respect to balanced development, dependency, and domestic entrepreneurship.

MNCs are extraordinarily powerful, accounting for one-third of world production, with total sales exceeding the value of world trade. Table 7.3 shows the activity of the top twenty-five MNCs in the region. Compared to 1997, when auto and oil concerns dominated, in 2003 we see greater participation of telecoms and retailers. This penetration of firms into developing country markets raises the question of power and balance. Worldwide, ranked by output, fifty-one of the top one hundred "countries" are MNCs. That is, Wal-Mart is larger than the GDP of Argentina,

Table 7.3. Top Multinationals in Latin America

Rank 2003	Rank 1997	Corporation	Country	Sector	2003 Sales (millions of US $)	% of Global Sales	Principal Subsidiaries
1	1	General Motors Corp.	United States	Automotive	14,317	7.3	Mexico, Brazil, Colombia, Argentina
2	10	Telefónica	Spain	Telecommunications	14,112	44.7	Brazil, Chile, Peru, Mexico, Argentina
3	17	Wal-Mart Stores	United States	Commerce	12,031	4.6	Mexico, Brazil, Argentina
4	2	Volkswagen AG	Germany	Automotive	10,457	10.6	Mexico, Brazil, Argentina
5	4	DaimlerChrysler AG	Germany	Automotive	10,123	6.5	Mexico, Brazil, Argentina
6	—	Delphi Automotive Systems Corp.	United States	Motor Vehicle Parts	10,040	35.7	Mexico, Brazil
7	55	Repsol YPF	Spain	Petroleum/Gas	7,345	17.5	Argentina, Chile, Peru, Ecuador, Bolivia, Colombia, Venezuela
8	16	Endesa	Spain	Electricity	7,257	38.7	Chile, Brazil, Argentina
9	3	Ford Motor Co.	United States	Automotive	7,168	4.4	Mexico, Brazil, Argentina, Venezuela, Colombia
10	38	Telecom Italia SpA	Italy	Telecommunications	6,765	19.2	Brazil, Argentina, Chile
11	13	International Business Machines	United States	Computers	6,680	7.5	Mexico, Brazil, Argentina

12	—	Portugal Telecom	Portugal	Telecommunications	6,502	na	Brazil
13	7	ExxonMobil Corp.	United States	Petroleum/Gas	6,127	2.7	Brazil, Colombia, Argentina, Chile
14	36	AES Corp.	United States	Electricity	6,083	63	Brazil, Venezuela, Chile, Argentina
15	—	Bunge	United States	Agro-Industry	5,910	26.4	Brazil, Argentina
16	8	Carrefour Group	France	Commerce	5,633	7.1	Brazil, Argentina, Mexico, Colombia
17	4	Royal Dutch/Shell Group	Netherlands/ United Kingdom	Petroleum/Gas	5,514	2.7	Brazil, Chile, Argentina
18	20	Cargill, Inc.	United States	Agro-Industry	5,102	8.5	Argentina, Brazil
19	30	Hewlett-Packard (HP)	United States	Computers	4,771	6.5	Mexico, Brazil
20	14	Unilever	United Kingdom	Hygiene/Food	4,545	9.4	Brazil, Mexico, Argentina, Chile
21	12	Nestlé	Switzerland	Food	4,420	6.8	Mexico, Brazil, Colombia, Chile
22	22	Chevron Texaco	United States	Petroleum/Gas	4,192	3.7	Brazil, Colombia, Argentina
23	24	General Electric	United States	Various	4,157	3.1	Mexico, Argentina
24	—	Visteon Corporation	United States	Motor Vehicle Parts	3,581	20.3	Mexico, Brazil
25	28	Nissan	Japan	Automotive	3,574	5.4	Mexico

Source: ECLAC, *Foreign Investment 2004.*

or Nestle's sales exceeds the GDP of Peru. In addition, more than half of world trade consists of transnational firm trading activity, largely of an intrafirm nature.[103] This means that half of world trade is associated with firms such as Coca-Cola or Nike sending subassembly materials and final products among their own subsidiaries. Some worry about the cultural content contained in globalized products; others herald the arrival of cheaper, higher-quality products through retailers such as Wal-Mart. One study credits Wal-Mart's everyday low prices with ending a long history of hefty margins by national retailers and helping to reduce Mexico's inflation rate.[104] Others are less sanguine; Multinational Monitor calls Wal-Mart one of the ten worst corporations of 2004 for its labor practices in the United States.[105]

Box 7.2 summarizes the debate on the pros and cons of multinational production. Multinationals may provide technology, improve efficiency, and create jobs.

BOX 7.2.   IS MULTINATIONAL PRODUCTION GOOD FOR DEVELOPING COUNTRIES?

Pros	Cons
• With a technology gap, the farther behind you are the faster you can pick up the leader's innovations to catch up. MNCs provide a positive contagion effect.[106] • Spillover efficiency—even if the MNC does not directly share technology with local firms, it may have positive productivity effects through competition, as domestic firms are given an incentive to catch up; through training of labor and management; and through effects on local suppliers including higher standards of quality and delivery.[107] • Source of capital for investment (if not squeezing local capital out of domestic markets). • Employment source of jobs that generally pay higher wages than local firms.[108] • Provides needed management skills to the economy. • Improves export competitiveness. • Total factor productivity is higher in firms with foreign partnerships. • Higher levels of FDI are associated with higher wages.[109]	• Traditional dependency arguments— powerful international capital exploits workers, maintains control of technology, and preempts local development of production. • MNC production is culturally inappropriate, introducing products unsuited for local conditions. • MNCs engage in human rights abuse, unfairly taking advantage of female and child labor. • MNCs circumvent international law in the environmental arena. • Global production causes job loss in home economy—although one study shows that U.S. multinationals compete only at margins with affiliates.[110] • MNCs are production enclaves—there is a low level of linkages with local suppliers; evidence on this is mixed, depending on the type of MNC.[111] • Net capital outflow—after initial injection of capital, MNC may remit more in profits than it put in. • Use of technology inappropriate for local conditions—more capital intensive than appropriate. Big gap between local and MNC forestalls spillovers. • Reliance on foreign technology retards local development, causing negative effects on productivity.[112]

They can encourage the adoption of best production practices across borders. Some multinationals invest abroad to take advantage of cheaper labor or less stringent environmental standards. Producers of textiles, for example, have long moved to where unskilled workers, often women, can be paid a tenth of the going wage in the United States. Profits—made in part through the exploitation of cheap labor—are remitted to the home country rather than supporting growth in the local economy. Environmentalists worry that companies set up shop in countries with lax pollution laws, a phenomenon called environmental dumping. Governments, afraid of losing jobs and investment, may retreat from stricter environmental codes, promoting a race to the bottom of the environmental ladder. Evidence on this theory is incomplete; there is some suggestion that pollution costs are not a critical factor in location decisions and that at the national level governments tighten regulations as income rises.[113]

The degree to which MNCs contribute to local environments may be a function of the ability of the government to promote key backward linkages in the economy.[114] Overall, MNCs will employ technologies that best suit their own business needs. However, if an MNC is given incentives to source inputs locally, transfer of process and product information may take place. Government may play a key role in reducing the information gap between players by providing information about local producers, supporting the establishment of standards, testing and patent registration, and upgrading local human resource and technological capabilities.

The good news in enhancing the positive effects over the costs of multinationals is that globalization of information systems has decreased the ability of multinationals to get away with social and environmental abuse. As the Internet and CNN bring corporate activities into stockholders' living rooms, firms have been forced to comply with new standards. For example, after celebrity Kathie Lee Gifford was charged with exploitation of female workers in Central America in the production of her clothing line for Kmart, the negative publicity generated a fall in the stock price. The firm was forced to adopt codes of corporate conduct that improve the lives of workers. As dismal conditions and low wages have become well documented, college students across America have pressured for changes in sweatshop practices and adoption of a fair labor code by boycotting bookstore apparel.[115] Globalization of production has increased the multinational's reach but has made its activities more transparent.

Does the surge in multinational investment improve the productive capabilities of Latin American economies? As Latin America has moved away from protected state-run industries to allow greater multinational participation, how has productivity changed? One study of foreign production in Mexico shows that a high multinational presence is correlated with an increase in productivity in locally owned firms and that the rate of catch-up with international productivity standards is positively associated with the degree of foreign concentration in the industry. This suggests spillovers from multinational production to less-efficient local firms. Multinational firms may act as a catalyst to productivity growth, speeding up the convergence in productivity levels between developing and industrialized countries.[116] The authors warn, nonetheless, of extrapolating too much from the Mexican case because there is extensive movement of labor and capital between Mexico and the United States, especially in border production. Other studies of the Mexican case point out that the technology transferred may be too capital intensive and that subsidies provided by the Mexican government to attract firms may divert scarce resources from social investments.[117] Box 7.3 summarizes Mexico's long love-hate affair with foreign capital, illustrating the complex nature of FDI.

The gains and the costs of multinational production should be evaluated on a case-by-case basis; the costs and benefits vary by the reason for the multinational's presence and the strength of the state in providing a positive regulatory environment. One study showed that the positive effects of multinational transfer of technology were strong only when there was already a well-developed human capital base.[118] Some of the issues we consider in later chapters on social development and

---

BOX 7.3.   MEXICO'S LOVE-HATE AFFAIR WITH FDI

Mexico has progressed through a variety of positions in terms of the role of FDI in its economy, reflecting different views—sometimes simultaneously—of foreign investment in Mexico. Opposition to foreign intervention was a hallmark of early Mexican history since the days of the Spanish Conquest. Nonetheless Porfirio Díaz and his científico advisors espoused liberalization policies and encouraged foreign investment during the Porfiriato (1876–1911).

The Revolution to 1944 was marked by the establishment of state ownership, particularly in the mining sector and the 1938 nationalization of petroleum companies. The formation of the Banco de Mexico took the role of financing from foreign commercial banks. Ownership rules were defined by sector in the 1930s: strategic industries, including primary product exports and utilities, were dominated by state ownership. Manufacturing, under import substitution industrialization, drew on FDI, and the early maquilas used cheap labor to reexport goods to international markets.

Fears of foreign takeover of the Mexican economy led to the 1944 law requiring majority Mexican ownership except with permission of the secretariat of foreign relations. "Mexicanization" extended to radio, cinema, domestic airlines, buses, soft drink bottlers, publishing, and tires. Paradoxically, at the same time efforts were made to recruit foreign investment to fill the capital needs of industrialization. National ownership in banking, finance, and extractive industries was secured, while foreign investment boomed in areas of manufacturing.

The maquila program was introduced in 1965, allowing firms to import inputs tax free if they were to be transformed into exports. Mexico benefited through employment and foreign exchange, while the transnationals found high profit margins with cheap labor. In contrast, the 1973 Law to Promote Mexican Investment and Regulate Foreign Investment diverted policy inward, regulating foreign entry and enforcing Mexicanization and local majority ownership.

Capital constraints with the debt crisis again prompted a change of policy, including a 1989 liberalization law to encourage investment. Mexico acceded to the General Agreement on Tariffs and Trade (GATT) in 1985, lowering tariffs and reducing import controls. Signature of the North American Free Trade Agreement (NAFTA) formalizes this open investment regime and symbolizes Mexico's firm commitment through an international treaty to encourage international investment.

Source: Michael J. Twomey, *Multinational Corporations and the North American Free Trade Agreement* (Westport, Conn.: Praeger, 1993), 27–34.

education may therefore play a key role in shaping costs and benefits. Government policy in establishing the rules of the game for multinationals is important in evaluating outcomes. The size and number of other firms in a market also condition multinational behavior. If a multinational company is the only employer in a small town, it is less likely to treat workers well. If, however, if it is in competition with a large number of firms, it is more likely to provide good working conditions.

An ethical dilemma arises in considering labor standards for multinational production. Should home country or host country labor codes be employed? Labor standards in poor countries may approximate conditions in industrial countries fifty years ago. Should U.S. multinationals meet U.S. safety and health standards in a Guatemalan plant? Some contend that best practices should apply worldwide; others suggest local standards as a baseline while developing countries catch up. Proponents of FDI contend that although standards and wages may not match industrial country standards, they most often exceed the conditions and the pay in local factories. Sorting out the effects of multinational production poses tough ethical and policy dilemmas. Are workers worse off than they were without the new paychecks? How far can governments go in insisting on higher standards without driving investment and jobs away?

FDI, particularly in services, has been an important part of the privatization boom that we studied in chapter 6. Liberalization of global trade rules also encouraged FDI in telecommunications and financial services. We noted that the gains from the privatization of state monopolies were greatest when competition could be introduced or an effective regulatory structure implemented to limit private monopoly pricing. Yet the challenges for effective regulation and competition policy in markets dominated by large transnationals are especially difficult for developing-country officials. Regulators in developing countries must deal with multiple social objectives. They are still struggling with issues such as improving access to phones in rural and poor areas and guaranteeing basic levels of quality. The international dynamism in mobile cellular communications and Internet services introduces a whole set of complicated regulations. With generally weaker institutions, less experience, and fewer resources, regulatory agencies in developing markets must carry out traditional and new tasks. In doing so, regulators come up against some of the titans of the global marketplace—large and powerful megacorporations. In many cases—particularly those of the early privatizers—the rush to privatization granted long periods of exclusive operation to foreign investors in exchange for commitments to expand basic services. As these frameworks expire, the regulatory challenge will be to develop coherent sectoral strategies to achieve national policy goals as well as corporate objectives through an upgrading of the regulatory institutions themselves.[119]

Nonetheless, despite potential costs from flows and unintended consequences, increasing access to international capital is on most national policy agendas. Latin American country officials see expanding FDI as a key policy tool for growth. How can countries, particularly those that have not been the largest beneficiaries in the past, attract FDI? How does the policy environment affect the location decision of multinational companies? Policy recommendations for attracting productive new international investments include lowering trade costs, improving export processing zones, investigating the further use of incentives, promoting dialogue with investors on business climate issues, and investing in education.[120] Foreign firms must have some advantage in producing abroad that justifies additional coordination costs and risks in a foreign business climate.

CONCLUSIONS: FINANCING DEVELOPMENT

When domestic savings are insufficient, providing stable access to the financial resources is crucial to promoting stable growth. These resources—bank lending, bonds, equity finance, FDI, remittances, and ODA—all are potential contributors with drawbacks to consider. International capital is a necessary—but at the same time problematic—ingredient in the growth process. The magic mix of stable, predictable financing from both the private and the public sectors is one that takes constant monitoring and accountability from all parties.

Key Concepts

capital controls	official flows	short-term money
capital flight	portfolio bonds	*tesobono*
equity investments	remittances	
foreign direct investment (FDI)	short- and long-term portfolio investments	

Chapter Summary

Capital Flows and Latin America

- In the 1990s, after the debt crisis, there was an influx of foreign capital. The new interest stemmed from changes in international financial markets as well as structural changes within Latin America that have made it a good investment risk.
- Capital inflows into Latin America can be divided into short-term and long-term capital. Short-term capital includes portfolio bonds or equity investments, which are more volatile than FDI. However, FDI has both pros and cons. FDI can represent a source of technology, increase efficiency, and generate employment with higher wages. Yet MNCs have also been responsible for human rights abuses and infringement of sovereignty. Production in enclaves with low levels of linkages to the local economy may do little for long-run growth. Whether a multinational is helpful or harmful is best measured on a case-by-case basis.

- Capital flows can spur growth and, subsequently, savings. However, imperfect information and thin markets may lead to inefficiency. An influx of short-term money, such as portfolio bonds, depresses interest rates, discourages domestic savings, and appreciates the exchange rate, discouraging exports. It may also create inflationary pressures.
- With the liberalization of financial markets, an appropriate institutional framework is needed to provide supervision and oversight. The fragile banking sector contributed to instability after liberalization. Strong institutions are critical to mediate capital inflows.

The Mexican Peso Crisis

- After engaging in a fiscal stabilization, privatization, and the opening of internal markets to international trade, Mexico was perceived as a safe haven for investors. The optimism in the Mexican economy induced high levels of capital inflows and an appreciation of the Mexican peso. The appreciation exacerbated the current account balance, which was already at unsustainable levels, financed mostly by volatile capital inflows. After the uprising in Chiapas and the assassination of presidential candidate Luis Donaldo Colosio, investors panicked. The Mexican government, in its attempt to defend the exchange rate, saw reserves rapidly dwindle. In response to the imminent crisis, the government began to offer *tesobonos,* dollar-denominated treasury bonds, refusing to raise interest rates or devalue the currency. The markets were unconvinced by the attempt, and the Mexican government was forced to let the currency float and, hence, devalue. To bail out Mexico from the crisis, the Clinton administration, along with the IMF and the BIS, provided loan relief. Three main lessons stemmed from the Mexican peso crisis: a sustainable current account balance is important, short-term capital is volatile, and the inflexibility of the exchange rate as an inflation anchor can be dangerous.

Regulating Capital Inflows: Chile

- A strong export-oriented economy such as Chile's is generally rewarded with capital inflows. As capital flows increase, the currency appreciates, choking the export sector. As a response to this dilemma, Chile established reserve requirements, quotas, and fees, as well as engaging in foreign exchange market intervention and the sterilization of the monetary effect of foreign exchange. Its aim was to reduce portfolio inflows and increase domestic saving.

Effects of the Asian and Russian Crises on Latin America

- The Asian economic crisis and the collapse of the Russian ruble had negative repercussions on Latin American economies. The loss of confidence in the

Asian Tigers spread to the Latin American region, leading to significant capital outflows, an increase in interest rates, and a loss of competitiveness for Latin American goods against cheaper Asian goods. The hardest-hit country was Brazil. It was forced to float its currency, abandon the Real Plan established in 1994 as an anchor for inflation, and subsequently experience a large devaluation.

Remittances: The New Source of Latin American Capital and ODA

- The largest source of capital in Latin America is now remittances sent home by Latins working abroad, reaching $45 billion in 2004. Accounting for 10 percent of GDP, 50–80 percent of household income for the 18 percent (Mexicans), 23 percent (Central Americans), and 14 percent (Ecuadorans) who are remittance receivers, the dollars are financing new investment in communities throughout the region.
- ODA plays a role in the poorest of Latin American economies. The United States is the principal donor, primarily financing education, health, and environmental projects.

Lessons for Capital Mobility

- It is clear that capital inflows incur a cost for the domestic economy. The higher interest rates needed to attract investors also represent a higher price for domestic borrowers, hurting investment. They also increase the cost of servicing the publicly held domestic debt and lead to pressure for an appreciation of the currency. Two possible solutions have been suggested to deal with this dilemma. The first is decreasing current consumption in favor of domestic saving, which may reduce the reliance on capital inflows. The second is promoting tradable goods over nontradable goods. On the global scale, a form of international credit insurance corporation has been proposed. All of these have their limitations, especially where they undermine confidence in free markets and raise the cost of capital.

Notes

1. World Bank, *Global Development Finance 2004: Harnessing Cyclical Gains for Development* (Washington, D.C.: World Bank, 2004), 7.

2. The top ten developing country recipients of FDI in descending order are China, Brazil, Mexico, Argentina, Poland, the Czech Republic, Chile, the República Bolivariana de Venezuela, Thailand, and India. Ibid., 79.

3. Lending directly to support trade includes bank letters of credit that provide

financing for exports in transit until the importer pays for the goods as well as commercial bank lending.

4. Barry Eichengreen and Ricardo Hausman, "Original Sin: The Road to Redemption," www.nber.org, revised January 2005.

5. Paul J. Davies, Joanna Chung, and Kevin Allison, "Brazil Raises $1.5bn," *Financial Times,* September 20, 2005, www.ft.com.

6. Depository receipts represent purchases made through another exchange. A depository receipt is a security issued by a U.S. bank in place of the foreign shares held in trust by that bank. Essentially, it is a mechanism for listing on the U.S. exchange. For example, American depository receipts (ADR) could represent shares of Brazilian Telebras bought on the U.S. stock exchange. Each Telebras ADR that is traded on the New York Stock Exchange represents one thousand preferred shares held by the Bank of New York. An advantage of the ADR is that the liquidity and visibility of the stock increase. Some American retail investors by their own rules are not permitted to buy emerging market shares but can purchase an ADR. In some countries, to control capital inflows and outflows, only qualified institutional buyers approved by the central bank can invest in local shares. To qualify for an ADR, the foreign firm must file with the Security and Exchange Commission (SEC) and abide by SEC rules. The costs associated with filing (e.g., registration, lawyers, and investment bankers) are high, and the requirements for listing in terms of transparency and reporting are stringent. However, the gains in increasing market size are often worth the cost.

7. World Bank, *Global Development Finance 2004,* 95.

8. Augusto De la Torre and Sergio Schmukler, *Whither Latin American Capital Markets?* Sponsored by the Office of the Chief Economist, World Bank (Washington, D.C.: World Bank), October 2004.

9. De la Torre, "Developments in Capital Markets," in *Whither Latin American Capital Markets?* 27.

10. World Bank, *World Development Indicators, 1997* (Washington, D.C.: World Bank, 1997), table 5.3, "About the Data."

11. De la Torre, *Whither Latin American Capital Markets?* 8. G-7 includes Canada, France, Germany, Italy, Japan, the United Kingdom, and the United States. East Asia is an average for Hong Kong, Indonesia, Korea, Malaysia, Philipines, Taiwan, and Thailand. Latin America data is an average of Argentina, Brazil, Chile, Colombia, Mexico, Peru, and Venezuela.

12. Ibid., 17.

13. Ibid., 8.

14. Ibid., 14–21.

15. As of October 1992, U.S. authorities approved increasing the number of institutional investors, including pension plans and insurance funds, allowed to invest in privately placed securities. Standardization of legal and accounting practices between the United States and Mexico has also helped.

16. Sebastian Edwards, *Capital Flows into Latin America: A Stop-Go Story?* National Bureau of Economic Research Working Paper No. 6441 (Cambridge, Mass.: National Bureau of Economic Research, 1998), available at www.nber.org/papers/w6441. Edwards cites a 1993 IMF staff paper by Guillermo Calvo and a 1997 World Bank study on capital flows.

17. Adapted from José Angel Gurría, "Capital Flows: The Mexico Case," in *Coping with Capital Surges: The Return of Finance to Latin America,* ed. Ricardo Ffrench-Davis and Stephany Griffith-Jones (Boulder, Colo.: Rienner, 1995), 189.

18. Masood Ahmed, Timothy Lane, and Marianne Schulze-Ghattas, "Refocusing IMF Conditionality," *Finance and Development* 38(4) (December 2001), as accessed at www.imf.org.

19. This is not weighted by the share of a country's GDP in regional GDP; it is a straight

average of FDI taken as a percentage of 1995 GDP. World Bank, *World Development Indicators, 1997.*

20. Several studies, including those by Barry Eichengreen, Joseph Stiglitz, Stephanie Griffith Jones, and William Easterly are summarized in The United Nations, *World Economic and Social Survey 2005, Financing for Development,* chap. 3, "International Private Capital Flows."

21. Ian Katz, "Snapping up South America," *Business Week,* January 18, 1999, 60.

22. Nader Nazmi, "The Internationalization of Capital in a Small and Vulnerable Economy: The Case of Ecuador," in *Foreign Direct Investment in Latin America,* ed. Werner Baer and William R. Miles (New York: Hayworth, 2001), 119–139.

23. Shatz, "Expanding Foreign Direct Investment," 7.

24. Ibid., 11.

25. Zdenek Drabek and Warren Payne, "The Impact of Transparency on Foreign Direct Investment," IMF Staff Working Paper ERAD-99-02 (Geneva: World Trade Organization, 1999).

26. Jacob Stenfeld, "Development and Foreign Investment: Lessons Learned from Mexican Banking," Carnegie Endowment for International Peace, *Carnegie Papers* No. 47, July 2004.

27. ECLAC, slide presentation on the Internet, April 18, 2001.

28. Ibid.

29. Shatz, "Expanding Foreign Direct Investment," 31.

30. Alejandro C. Vera-Vassallo, "Foreign Investment and Competitive Development in Latin America and the Caribbean," *CEPAL Review* 60 (December 1996).

31. Richard E. Caves, *Multinational Enterprise and Economic Analysis,* 2nd ed. (Cambridge: Cambridge University Press, 1996), 230.

32. Mangus Blomström and Edward N. Wolff, "Multinational Corporations and Productivity Convergence in Mexico," in *Convergence of Productivity: Cross-National Studies and Historical Evidence,* ed. William Baumol, Richard R. Nelson, and Edward N. Wolff (New York: Oxford University Press, 1994), 265.

33. Blomström and Wolff, "Multinational Corporations," 228.

34. S. Lael Brainard and David Riker, *Are U.S. Multinationals Exporting U.S. Jobs?* National Bureau of Economic Research Working Paper No. 5958 (Cambridge, Mass.: National Bureau of Economic Research, 1997).

35. Brainard and Riker, *Are U.S. Multinationals Exporting U.S. Jobs?*

36. Blomström and Wolff, "Multinational Corporations," 265. For a general discussion of multinationals, see Thomas J. Biersteker, *Distortion or Development? Contending Perspectives on the Multinational Corporation* (Cambridge, Mass.: MIT Press, 1978).

37. Jorge Blázquez and Javier Santiso, "Mexico: Is It an Ex-Emerging Market?" *Journal of Latin American Studies* 3 (2004): 297–318.

38. David Wheeler, "Racing to the Bottom? Foreign Investment and Air Pollution in Developing Countries" (Washington, D.C.: World Bank, Environmental Division).

39. Aaron Berstein, "Sweatshop Reform: How to Solve the Standoff," *BusinessWeek,* May 3, 1999, 186.

40. Blomström and Wolff, "Multinational Corporations," 276.

41. Paul Harris, "Chile's Copper: Surplus Spells Woe for Exporters," *Financial Times,* May 8, 2006, www.ft.com.

42. James Cypher and James Dietz, *The Process of Economic Development* (New York: Routledge, 1997), cited by Miguel D. Ramirez, "Foreign Direct Investment in Mexico and Chile: A Critical Appraisal," in *Foreign Direct Investment in Latin America,* ed. Werner Baer and William R. Miles (New York: Hayworth, 2001).

43. E. Borenstein, J. De Gregorio, and J. W. Lee, "How Does Foreign Investment Affect Economic Growth?" *Journal of International Economics* 45 (1998): 115–135.

44. ECLAC, *Foreign Investment in Latin America and the Caribbean, 2000,* "Introduction: A Regulatory Challenge," 27–31.

45. Robert Devlin, Ricardo Ffrench-Davis, and Stephany Griffith-Jones, "Surges in Capital Flows and Development: An Overview of Policy Issues," in *Coping with Capital Surges,* ed. Ricardo Ffrench-Davis and Stephany Griffith-Jones (Boulder, Colo.: Rienner, 1995), 234, 243–244; and "Some Mutual Funds Go Back Full Throttle to Emerging Markets," *Wall Street Journal,* November 12, 1996, A1.

46. Devlin, Ffrench-Davis, and Griffith-Jones, "Surges in Capital Flows and Development," 243–244.

47. Comment by Agustín Carstens and Moises Schwartz in *Securing Stability and Growth in Latin America,* ed. Ricardo Hausmann and Helmut Reisen (Paris: OECD Publications, 1996), 128.

48. Comment by Charles Wyplosz in Hausmann and Reisen, *Securing Stability,* 132.

49. Liliana Rojas-Suarez and Steven R. Weisbrod, "Building Stability in Latin American Financial Markets," in *Securing Stability and Growth in Latin America,* ed. Ricardo Hausmann and Helmut Reisen (Paris: OECD Publications, 1996), 140.

50. Walter Molano, *Financial Reverberations: The Latin American Banking System during the Mid-1990s,* Working Paper, SBC Warburg, April 1997, 2.

51. ECLAC, *Foreign Investment in Latin America and the Caribbean, 2000,* table I.12, 65.

52. Ibid., 27.

53. Ethan Kapstein, "Global Rules for Global Finance," *Current History,* November 1998, 358.

54. Robert Wade, "The Asian Crisis and the Global Economy: Causes, Consequences and Cure," *Current History,* November 1998, 362.

55. Comment by Jans Blommestein in Hausmann and Reisen, *Securing Stability,* 171.

56. Stephany Griffith-Jones, "The Mexican Peso Crisis," *CEPAL Review* 60 (December 1996): 156–157.

57. Griffith-Jones, "The Mexican Peso Crisis," 155–175.

58. Sebastian Edwards, "The Mexican Peso Crisis: How Much Did We Know? When Did We Know It?" *World Economy* 21(1) (1998): 1–7. Much of this section follows the argument that Edwards makes in this article. See also James T. Peach and Richard V. Adkisson, "Enabling Myths and Mexico's Economic Crises (1976–1996)," *Journal of Economic Issues* 31(2) (June 1997).

59. Shahid Javed Burki and Sebastian Edwards, *Latin America after Mexico: Quickening the Pace* (Washington, D.C.: World Bank, 1996), 5.

60. If the interest rate in Chile adjusted for risk is higher than in the rest of the world, capital will flow to that higher return. If people expect an appreciation, they will purchase the currency today when it is still cheaper, making money on the transaction when it strengthens. Of course, such expectations are self-fulfilling. If the market believes that a currency will rise in value, it is purchased, and its price, or value, not surprisingly increases.

61. Ricardo Ffrench-Davis, Manuel Agosin, and Andras Uthoff, "Capital Movements, Export Strategy and Macroeconomic Stability in Chile," in *Coping with Capital Surges,* ed. Ricardo Ffrench-Davis and Stephany Griffith-Jones (Boulder, Colo.: Rienner, 1995), 104.

62. Jonathan Friedland, "Their Success Earns Chileans a New Title: Ugly Pan-Americans," *Wall Street Journal,* October 3, 1996, A1; and Ffrench-Davis, Agosin, and Uthoff, "Capital Movements," 114.

63. The inflow of foreign capital increases the supply of, for example, dollars. The price

of dollars falls, and that of pesos rises. Remember as well that dollars coming into Chile are also purchasing Chilean assets—which increases the demand for (and the price of) pesos.

64. Edwards, *Capital Flows into Latin America.*

65. Sterilization involves an offsetting action on the part of the central bank. If, under a fixed exchange rate, foreign capital flows in, thereby increasing the money supply, the central bank can draw money out of domestic circulation to offset the capital flow.

66. Eduardo Aninat and Christian Larraín, "Capital Flows: Lessons from the Chilean Experience," *CEPAL Review* 60 (December 1996).

67. Dan Glaister, "Emigrants Provide Lifeline," *The Guardian,* March 31, 2004, Internet edition.

68. Richard Lapper, "Workers Throw a Lifeline Home," *Financial Times,* March 29, 2004, 1.

69. SELA, "Current Trends in Migrants' Remittances in Latin America and the Caribbean," SP/SRRM-UAALC/Di No. 3, Rev. November 1, 2003.

70. Inter-American Development Bank, "Remittance Flows to Latin America and the Caribbean (LAC), 2004," http://www.iadb.org/mif/.

71. Michael Frias, "Linking International Remittance Flows to Financial Services: Tapping the Latino Immigrant Market," *Supervisory Journal,* FDIC.gov, last updated 12/01/2004; see also Roberto Suro, "Remittance Senders and Receivers: Tracking the Transnational Channels," Joint Report of the Multilateral Investment Fund (MIF) and the Pew Hispanic Center (PHC), Washington, D.C., November 24, 2003.

72. Suro, "Remittance Senders and Receivers."

73. Ibid.

74. John Authers, "Mortgage Scheme Offers a Tiny Piece of Mexico," *Financial Times,* September 1, 2005, 8.

75. Frias, "Linking International Remittance Flows to Financial Services."

76. SELA, "Current Trends in Migrants' Remittances in Latin America and the Caribbean," 17.

77. *IMF Survey,* July 18, 2005, 212.

78. Ralph Chami, Connel Fullenkamp, and Samir Jahjah, "Are Immigrant Remittance Flows a Source of Capital for Development?" *IMF Staff Papers* 52(1) (2005).

79. Glaister, "Emigrants Provide Lifeline."

80. Frias, "Linking International Remittance Flows to Financial Services."

81. SELA, "Current Trends in Migrants' Remittances in Latin America and the Caribbean," 18.

82. Frias, "Linking International Remittance Flows to Financial Services."

83. Lucian Chauvin, "With Money Sent from U.S., Peruvians Buy Homes," *Christian Science Monitor,* July 13, 2005, 4.

84. Authers, "Mortgage Scheme Offers a Tiny Piece of Mexico."

85. Ibid.

86. United Nations, "The Millennium Development Goals: A Latin American and Caribbean Perspective," August 2005, 232.

87. Bárcena as cited in United Nations, "The Millennium Development Goals," table VI.5, 231.

88. United Nations, "The Millennium Development Goals," table VI.5, 231.

89. Ibid.

90. Jeffrey D. Sachs, *The End of Poverty* (New York: Penguin, 2005), 299.

91. Dr. Carol Adelman, *Aid and Comfort,* Tech Central Station, August 21, 2002, as located at www.globalissues.org. Note that these numbers are for worldwide assistance, not simply Latin America.

92. Edwards, *Capital Flows into Latin America.*

93. Felipe B. Larraín, ed., *Capital Flows, Capital Controls and Currency* (Ann Arbor: University of Michigan Press, 2000), 12.

94. Warburg Dillon Read, "The Impact of the Asian Crisis on Latin America," July 14, 1998, 2, fax newsletter.

95. Warburg Dillon Read, "The Impact of the Asian Crisis," 5.

96. Diana Jean Schemo, "Brazilians Fret as Economic Threat Moves Closer," *New York Times,* September 20, 1998, online edition.

97. Paul Lewis, "Latin Americans Say Russian Default Is Hurting Their Economies," *New York Times,* October 6, 1998, online edition.

98. Mac Margolis, "Hat in Hand," *Newsweek,* October 12, 1998, 32B.

99. Lewis, "Latin Americans," A13.

100. Michael Mortimore, Álvaro Calderón, Pablo Carvallo, and Márcia Tavares, "Foreign Investment in Latin America and the Caribbean," ECLAC Unit on Investment and Corporate Strategies, Briefing Paper 2005.

101. Laura Alfaro and Eliza Hammel, "Latin American Multinationals," World Economic Forum: Latin America Competitiveness Report, Geneva, Switzerland, April 2006.

102. "Brazil's Affluent Are Hurt by Crisis," *Washington Post,* January 25, 1999, A18.

103. Remember that a Latin American government—just like the U.S. Fed or the Bank of England—issues domestic debt to finance fiscal expenditures. If the Fed raises the interest rate, the cost of financing the U.S. debt goes up; correspondingly, when a Latin American government raises interest rates, it increases the cost of financing domestically held debt.

104. Diana Farrell, Jaana K. Remes, and Heiner Schulz, "The Truth about Foreign Direct Investment in Emerging Markets," *The McKinsey Quarterly* 1 (2004).

105. Russell Mokhiber and Robert Weissman, "The Ten Worst Corporations of 2004," *Multinational Monitor* 25(12) (December 2004), multinationalmonitor.org.

106. Richard E. Caves, *Multinational Enterprise and Economic Analysis,* 2nd ed. (Cambridge: Cambridge University Press, 1996), 230.

107. Mangus Blomström and Edward N. Wolff, "Multinational Corporations and Productivity Convergence in Mexico," in *Convergence of Productivity: Cross-National Studies and Historical Evidence,* ed. William Baumol, Richard R. Nelson, and Edward N. Wolff (New York: Oxford University Press, 1994), 265.

108. Ibid., 228.

109. Brian Aitken, Ann Harrison, and Robert Lipsey, "Wages and Foreign Ownership: A Comparative Study of Mexico, Venezuela and the United States," *Journal of International Economics* 40: 345–371.

110. S. Lael Brainard and David Riker, *Are U.S. Multinationals Exporting U.S. Jobs?* National Bureau of Economic Research Working Paper No. 5958 (Cambridge, Mass.: National Bureau of Economic Research, 1997).

111. Ibid.

112. Blomström and Wolff, "Multinational Corporations," 265. For a general discussion of multinationals, see Thomas J. Biersteker, *Distortion or Development? Contending Perspectives on the Multinational Corporation* (Cambridge, Mass.: MIT Press, 1978). For an excellent extensive summary of studies relating to FDI, see Michael Klein, Carl Aaron, and Bita Hadjimichael, "Foreign Direct Investment and Poverty Reduction," Policy Research Working Paper No. 2613 (Washington, D.C.: World Bank, June 2001).

113. Ricardo Ffrench-Davis, "Policy Implications of the Tequila Effect," *Challenge,* March–April 1998, 36.

114. Ian A. Goldin and Kenneth Reinert, "Global Capital Flows and Development: A Survey," *Journal of International Trade and Economic Development* 14(4) (2005): 9–11.

115. Economic Survey of Latin America and the Caribbean, 2000–2001, www.eclac.org.

116. This problem is discussed in José María Fanelli and José Luis Machinea, "Capital Movements in Argentina," in *Coping with Capital Surges: The Return of Finance to Latin America,* ed. Ricardo Ffrench-Davis and Stephany Griffith-Jones (Boulder, Colo.: Rienner, 1995), 183.

117. In Richard N. Haass and Robert E. Litan, "Globalization and Its Discontents," *Foreign Affairs* 77(3) (1998): 4.

118. José Antonio Ocampo, "Towards a Global Solution," *ECLAC Notes* 1 (November 1998): 2.

119. Communiqué of ECLAC on the international financial crisis, September 15, 1998, Available at www.cepal.org.english/coverpage/financialcrisis.htm.

120. Howard Shatz, "Expanding Foreign Direct Investment in the Andean Countries," CID Working Paper No. 64 (Cambridge, Mass: Center for International Development at Harvard University, March 2001), 3.

CHAPTER EIGHT

CONTEMPORARY TRADE POLICY

Engine or Brakes for Growth?

Liberalization of trade has encouraged production and processing of nontraditional exports such as Chilean wine. *(Courtesy of Lindsay Snyder)*

Trade liberalization has been at the center of economic reform in Latin America. In contrast to the internal approach of import substitution industrialization (ISI), Latin America now looks to the global market as the source of dynamic growth. This change in orientation was motivated in part by the debt crisis. Without external financing, the internal orientation of ISI was not viable over time. International trade rather than the state has become the engine for growth. Yet even without the financing constraint, many analysts argued that an open trading regime is preferable to a closed model. As globalization of trade, finance, and production came to define the international agenda, an external orientation was widely adopted as the only strategy compatible with global trends. This chapter provides the theoretical framework for the free trade argument. But some of the concerns of the ISI period about the vulnerability of less-powerful nations competing in a trading arena dominated by industrial giants remain. We will consider these objections and analyze policies consistent with an open trading regime that may mitigate some of the costs. To enhance the gains from trade, some policymakers advocate economic integration with other regional partners. We will therefore analyze the benefits of subregional integration as well as the progress toward a hemispheric free trade agreement. Different strategies have different risks and opportunities. Free trade with a large number of partners should be weighed against the possible trade-diverting effects of integration. The effects of trade policy choices on the environment and equitable growth will also be discussed.

The following questions will orient this chapter:

- What are the theoretical benefits of free trade?
- What concerns do some analysts have with the free trade model?
- What has been the record of liberalization in the region?
- Who trades what and why?
- Why and how have countries entered into subregional trading arrangements?
- Is a hemispheric free trade agreement desirable and feasible?

THEORETICAL BENEFITS OF FREE TRADE

Economists have long been enamored with the gains from free trade. In 1776 Adam Smith posited trade as the answer to a central development question: How do nations become wealthy? In contrast to the mercantilist, state-centered policies of the seventeenth and eighteenth centuries in Europe, Smith countered that nations become wealthy through open trade with each other. For Smith, open markets encouraged individuals to pursue greedy self-interest—the surplus of which could be traded for overall gain, generating good for all.

David Ricardo, in the nineteenth century, provided the conceptual underpinnings for the theoretical argument for free trade: the **theory of comparative advantage.** In a classical model, where all factors of production can be reduced to the labor required to produce them, Ricardo showed that if each country produces the good it is relatively best at producing, world output would increase. Even if a country is absolutely better in both growing wheat and producing engines, if in comparison to another country it is relatively better at engine production, it should build engines and leave wheat to be grown elsewhere. The gains derive from the benefits of specialization.

To understand the gains, first imagine that there is no trade. Each country must produce both wheat and engines. Given scarce resources (a fixed supply of labor), a certain quantity of each good can be produced. Because there are only two goods in this hypothetical model, we can create an internal trading price of how much wheat it would take to buy an engine. For example, we might find that each engine costs one hundred bales of wheat, or each wheat bale trades for one–one hundredth of an engine. Now drop our imaginary trade barriers. In another country each engine might cost two hundred bales of wheat or each wheat one–two hundredth of an engine. An engine costs more here, but wheat costs less—one–two hundredth rather than one-one hundredth of an engine. By specializing in the product you are relatively better in, you can produce that product more cheaply than in the other country. Furthermore, your country may produce both goods more efficiently than the other. In this case it should produce the good it is relatively best at; because you are not using scarce labor to produce the good that you are only second best at, your labor can focus on engines, your star performer.

This is analogous to the often-told story of the lawyer who can type faster than her secretary. Should the lawyer type her own briefs? The answer is no, because the secretary can't appear in court to try the cases. With each person doing what she is relatively best at, the law firm will make more money. The same logic is extended to countries. Even if the United States can produce textiles and cars more cheaply than Guatemala, if textiles can be produced relatively less expensively in Guatemala, there are gains from trade.

The **Heckscher-Ohlin theorem** extends the concept of comparative advantage to a two-factor model, incorporating capital with labor. In the Heckscher-Ohlin model, factor proportions determine the direction of trade. A country relatively well endowed with labor should produce and export labor-intensive goods; the country with a larger proportion of capital than labor should focus on capital-intensive products. Relative costs once again drive the two-factor model. In a country where labor is abundant relative to capital, the excess supply of labor will make for lower wages, and the scarcity of capital will exact higher interest rates. Producing labor-intensive products will allow the labor-abundant country to bring the cost advantage of the cheaper labor to the international market.

Two corollaries to the Heckscher-Ohlin theorem extend its range to include distributional implications. The **Stolper-Samuelson effect** indicates that if a labor-abundant country produces cheap labor-intensive goods, over time the increased international demand for these goods will raise their price and by association the price of their key input, labor. The Stolper-Samuelson effect therefore predicts that trade will initially benefit the least well-off—the poor workers. As more people in the world demand Guatemalan textiles, workers should share in the rewards. A second corollary, the **factor price equalization** theorem, suggests that as wages increase in the labor-abundant country (and fall in the capital-rich country), international prices of labor and capital will each converge. Therefore, at least in theory, there should be greater equality of prices for each factor in the international economy:

both wage rates and interest rates should be nearly equal in all markets. Of course, this implies that there may be a social price, including unemployment, in the country where wages are rising. Although consumers will benefit from the cheaper price of imports, trade policy, including worker retraining, might be indicated.

The Critique of Liberalization

Free trade advocates therefore contend that by producing in accord with comparative advantage, global output and income distribution will improve. In May 1978, Carlos Díaz Alejandro, a Cuban economist teaching at Columbia, wrote an article in the *American Economic Review* questioning the theory of free trade in practice.[1] Using the construct of a Martian landing on Earth, he challenged readers to explain why, if the theory of free trade is so compelling, haven't the gains from trade been more apparent in developing countries? Why were countries still so poor? Why were the poor workers in these countries still suffering? Why hadn't the prices of capital and labor equalized?

The results of the free trade model as applied to the real economy motivated ISI. Many economists in the developing world believed that free market trade theory wasn't benefiting the least well-off. Indeed, the theory itself doesn't predict necessarily *which* country will gain from the increased production in trade but simply that there will be gains to global welfare. In practice, developing countries perceived that the gains were accruing to the powerful industrial countries, leaving the periphery further and further behind. In particular, we remember from the discussion in chapter 2 on dependency theory the problem of declining terms of trade; control of technology in the center made it more and more difficult for the periphery countries to export a sufficient quantity of goods to purchase the high-tech products. For the South, trade was therefore impoverishing. Dependence on commodity exports left countries open to export price instability. Furthermore, rather than trade improving the lives of poor workers, the belief was that multinational corporations were exploiting the cheap labor in the periphery and keeping the additional profits for themselves. Export pessimism caused nations to turn inward, developing domestic industrial sectors to attend to the needs of the population.

In addition to the dependency critique, three other negative assessments of the results of trade emerged: the environmental, the gender, and the welfare dimensions. Environmentalists fear that specialization in accord with comparative advantage further encourages countries to base their economies on agricultural export crops such as timber, bananas, soya, or coffee that can be environmentally damaging. Pressures to export create unsustainable burdens on the environment. Environmentalists are also concerned that in an open global trading system, companies seeking to reduce production costs will flee to those countries in the developing world with the lowest environmental standards or lax enforcement. Those concerned about the gender implications of free trade point to the cases of multinational production exploiting a cheap female labor force in the developing world. With double obligations in the home and in the factory, women find it difficult to organize; low wages and poor working conditions result. The gender critique is part of a larger literature questioning the welfare effects on trade. Despite the theoretical predictions of benefiting the least well-off, ~~some contend that trade accentuates poverty and inequality~~. As countries open to trade, jobs may move to the lowest price producer, leaving those least able to compete worse off. Furthermore, the poor lack the assets of education and training that contribute to higher value-added exports. As some in an economy benefit from globalization, other are left behind. Those marginalized are all too frequently women. Box 8.1 illustrates some of the trade-offs between trade in accord with comparative advantage and negative externalities of trade in the case of cut flowers in Ecuador.

BOX 8.1.   FLOWER POWER OR TAINTED COLORS? MANAGING THE EFFECTS OF SOCIAL EFFECTS OF TRADE IN ECUADOR

The flower industry in Ecuador has blossomed. A wide variety of microclimates, the equatorial sun, and the country's cool Andean Valley make for prime growing conditions. The industry got its boost in 1991 when the Andean Trade Preferences Act opened tax-free exports to the United States. Fresh cut flowers went from almost zero to 9 percent of Ecuador's export earnings—third place behind traditional exports of oil and bananas.[2] Ecuador provides 20 percent of U.S. flower imports, a market segment growing as supermarkets and discount stores have brought competitively priced flowers to fill American vases. Niche products of tropical varieties are also giving a boost to biotrade from the Andean region. CAF, the development agency of the Andean Community of Nations, has been working with small- and medium-size growers, rural communities, and indigenous groups to promote sustainable agroexports.[3]

Valentine's Day is the peak of the selling season. Approximately three hundred Ecuadorian growers, many owned by Dutch or Colombian partners, gear up for the homage to love. Crop management is labor intensive, particularly with roses, Ecuador's top floral product. Workers carefully monitor the plant's progress, providing irrigation and protection from disease. The plants are carefully harvested, hydrated, and wrapped and within twenty-four hours are placed on a plane for Miami. There they clear customs, particularly the strict U.S. Department of Agriculture (USDA) animal and plant inspection for pests or disease. Firms such as UPS's Big Brown maintain the "cool cycle" until they arrive to the delighted recipient—"'Nothing would ruin a Valentine moment faster than dried up flowers,' said a company spokesman."[4]

But the reality of the flower industry is far less romantic. Peak harvesting is exhausting, as lax labor legislation and weak unions keep workers in the field for sixty grueling hours a week. Flower workers normally have short-term fixed contracts without job security, pensions, maternity leave, or health insurance.[5] The minimum wage of $145 a month barely covers subsistence—and overtime is not paid. Pushed to work quickly to make production quotas, rose thorns prick workers' hands. ~~Since only edible crops are inspected by the USDA for pesticide residue, intensive chemicals are applied daily~~. Workers are generally not well protected; the International Labor Organization (ILO) found that only 22 percent of workers were familiar with chemical safety techniques. The Pan American Health Organization (PAHO) has documented a nearly sevenfold increase in pesticide intoxication cases since 1990.[6] Pesticide poising raises the rate of spontaneous abortion and premature birth.[7] Pesticides also contaminate rivers and water systems.

The ILO estimates that 20 percent of the seasonal flower workers are children. Approximately 70 percent of the workers are women. Although the flora culture export

continued

continued

sector has opened new off-farm work opportunities for women, harassment and illegal pregnancy testing have been documented in the firms. Flower companies strongly retaliate against attempts at unionization to improve workers' conditions.[8] "The companies are organized among themselves and they have a list on the Internet of the people who have tried to unionize or have unionized," said Olga Tutillo, a labor union leader at one of the four farms that are unionized. "If someone tries to create a union, the company threatens to fire them and says they won't be able to find another job. These are the famous blacklists."[9]

Is the flower trade therefore bad for Ecuadorian workers? Were the workers better off unemployed or in lower-paid jobs? As the Andean Trade Preferences Act expires in 2006, should Ecuador sign a free trade agreement with the United States or let Colombia, which has negotiated an agreement, take this market? Two important lessons can be taken from this case. First, opening up to the international sector without adequate institutions to manage the opportunities and minimize the damage of trade is likely to impose new social costs. For example, the Ecuadorian government is now launching a campaign to reduce child labor and strengthen inspection and monitoring of conditions. Stronger labor legislation and enforcement can help improve the lives of the flower workers.

Second, in markets themselves can also help. Germany, for example, launched the Flower Label Program in 1999 to require growers to sign an International Code of Conduct for the socially and environmentally sustainable production of cut flowers. Life for workers in the 10 percent of Ecuador's companies that are covered by the certification standards has improved.[10] None of these firms use prohibited pesticides, and workers are protected by permanent contracts. But the demand for certification of fair labor standards —or for flowers produced under organic conditions—has been weak in the United States. Until American consumers decide they are willing to pay for "sustainable" romance, Ecuadorian workers are likely to be the ones to suffer.

It is important to focus policy attention on the intersection between trade and economic inequality. As Diana Tussie notes, trade policy is an inherently distributive instrument. That is, employment in import-competing sectors is exchanged for employment in export-oriented sectors—creating both losers and winners. These trade-offs need to be made more explicit within the context of domestic policy-making. Markets are social constructions, embedded in sociopolitical systems, advises Tussie. However, with globalization developing-country governments face less and less flexibility in establishing the domestic parameters within which their markets function. Attention to the effects of trade on poverty and social exclusion is critical in considering policy interventions to improve the position of the losers in the global trading arena.[11]

HAS TRADE PROMOTED GROWTH?

The record of liberalization throughout the world has raised the question of when greater openness has promoted growth. This has been an important policy question without convincing answers.[12] A slew of empirical studies have attempted to measure the effects of openness on growth, but a definitive relationship has not been established. Part of the problem is that the empirical relationship is full of nuances, the data base is imperfect, it is difficult to define just what is meant by openness, and countries whose incomes are high for reasons not related to trade may have high trade ratios.[13] There is a great deal of heterogeneity in the extent to which growth rose after trade,[14] and trade opening is not implemented in isolation but as a part of a package of policy initiatives. Three seminal studies have framed the policy debate on trade and growth. David Dollar found that higher levels of trade distortion were associated with lower levels of growth. His research underscores the theoretical lesson of the free trade argument. Among globalizing developing countries in the period 1970–1990, those with open trade regimes grew at 5.0 percent per capita; nonglobalizing developing countries struggled along at 1.4 percent. The conclusion of this body of work indicates that trade does seem to create higher growth.[15] This protrade stance was confirmed by Jeffrey Sachs and Andrew Warner who, after controlling for other policy variables such as investment and government spending, find their openness index to be related to the growth rate of per capita gross domestic product (GDP).[16]

Francisco Rodriguez and Dani Rodrik criticize the findings that trade brings growth, showing instead that there is no guarantee of faster growth with trade.[17] They suggest that these findings are less robust than claimed due to complexity in measuring openness, statistically sensitive specifications, the colinearity of protectionist policies with other bad policies, and other econometric problems.[18] The results of the Rodriguez and Rodrik studies have focused attention on the complexity of the trade and growth relationship. Simply lowering trade barriers will not increase growth. Rather, as Robert Baldwin concludes, changes in trade policy must be complemented by prudent macroeconomic management and corruption-free, transparent policies promoting growth.[19] Of particular importance is the management of the exchange rate such that appreciation does not choke off export price competitiveness and encourage a flood of imports. This was the case Christoph Ernst reports in Brazil and Argentina, where an emerging specialization in dynamic manufacturing was slowed by exchange rate appreciations driven by primary and semiprocessed exports booms.[20] It is hard to come up with the counterfactual in the modern global economy of closed and insulated economies growing faster than open markets. The giant leaps of the Chinese economy stand as an example of the effects of opening. However, as with the experience of China, it is not trade alone but the set of complementary policies that will shape the long-term growth rate and the welfare implications for the nation.

In addition to the predicted gains in resource allocation from trade in accord with comparative advantage, new protrade arguments began to dominate the liberalization debate. Openness to the international market brings with it better access to technologies and inputs to production and a wider array of intermediate and final goods. An economy producing for the international market is also better positioned to take advantage of economies of scale in production. Also very important is the fact that opening borders to the influx of new products as well as investment by multinational firms encourages competition in the domestic market. Oligopolistic power to set prices enjoyed by large firms in protected domestic markets is pressured by the competition of international markets. Production under conditions of competition not only encourages lower prices but also provides incentives to produce goods more efficiently. The shake-up of domestic industries from the challenge of international competition may create a Schumpeterian effect as firms adapt to the new business environment.[21] Participation in the international market opens firms to new ideas and the transfer of knowledge that define success in the global economy. Indeed, improvements in productivity rates have been correlated with periods of liberalization in Latin America.[22]

HOW SHOULD LIBERALIZATION BE IMPLEMENTED?

No country has grown over time by turning its back on trade and capital flows. However, simply opening up to trade without building institutions to manage its social and environmental costs is a risky approach.[23] Despite the gains from liberalization over time, there are also short-run costs. Tearing down trade barriers can decimate inefficient firms, putting large numbers of employees out of work. The time path of liberalization is therefore important. How quickly should it proceed? Should industries gradually adapt to international price signals, giving them time to modernize or become more efficient? In contrast, does a gradualist approach prolong the agony of adjustment, suggesting that a quick, tough shock, although painful, might be preferable? Some research indicates that a staged process of tariff reduction works best. In the first stage, tariffs might be brought down to a uniform rate of, say, 50 percent. After industries adapt to this structure, tariffs could be lowered to an across-the-board 10 percent rate. However, others suggest that a quick and thorough opening of the external sector is an important element in establishing credibility in the seriousness of the reform process.

In addition to the question of the time path, liberalization should be seen in the context of a package of policies to maximize its benefits. Trade liberalization without an appropriate exchange rate is dangerous. If a currency is or becomes overvalued and trade barriers are low, the country will face an explosion of imports, and exporters will find it difficult to sell goods internationally. Trade liberalization may also need to be accompanied by short-term incentives from the state (perhaps financed through multilateral agencies) for export promotion. The Asian export model does not indicate a pure free market but rather one in which the state selectively promoted the growth of the export sector. In particular, firms that have been producing for domestic consumption need to learn international marketing. They may also need state assistance in the form of trade missions and financing to establish themselves abroad. Finally, trade liberalization works best when it is preceded by fiscal reform. If internal consumption—either public or private—is too high, the surplus for export disappears. Relieving pressures on the internal balance facilitates the generation of an external equilibrium. Without fiscal reform, internal interest rates may become too high, attracting short-term financial capital, leading to an appreciation of the exchange rate, and thwarting export efforts. It is clear that trade liberalization must be seen in the context of overall structural reform.

The Record of Liberalization in Latin America

Despite growth and equity concerns, in the 1990s liberalization was on the agenda of nearly every nation in the region. Why? Economic imbalances had built up under

ISI. The overvalued exchange rates typical of the period resulted in a bias against exports. By 1981, regional current account deficits had reached $42 billion annually. In 1982, no country had a positive current account balance. If you import more than you export, someone has to pay for it. As capital dried up due to the debt crisis, current account deficits became unsustainable without external financing.

In contrast to deteriorating performance in Latin America stood the successful export-oriented growth model in Asia, which was capturing the attention of multilateral agencies as well as governments. Although the Asian model also relied in good part on an active role for the state, the International Monetary Fund (IMF), the World Bank, and the Inter-American Development Bank (IADB) came to promote trade liberalization as an engine of growth. It is also important to note the change in the global context. The process of globalization—the integration of production and trade structures, the expansion of international financial markets, and the information revolution that knows no borders—had transformed the way states and firms participated in the international economy. The world had changed, and Latin America needed to change with it. The game went global.

Average tariff rates in Latin America declined significantly following adjustment to macroeconomic crises in the early 1980s and 1990s. The average tariff for the region was nearly 50 percent in 1985, with rates as high as 80 percent in Brazil and Colombia. By 2002, average tariffs in the region had come down to just above 10.4 percent, a radical transformation in the structure of the economies. There is

Table 8.1.   Average Tariff by Percentage in Latin America, Selected Years (1985–2002)

Country	Mid 80s	Late 80s	Mid 90s	2000–2002	Difference 1985–2002
Argentina	28.0	43.7	14.0	12.2	15.8
Bolivia	20.0	18.6	9.7	9.3	10.7
Brazil	80.0	50.6	12.6	12.3	67.7
Chile	36.0	15.1	11.0	7	29.0
Colombia	83.0	47.6	11.4	11.7	71.3
Costa Rica	53.0	n/a	11.7	6	47.0
Ecuador	50.0	39.9	11.2	11.3	38.7
El Salvador	23.0	n/a	9.2	7.3	15.7
Guatemala	50.0	n/a	10.8	6.9	43.1
Honduras	n/a	41.9	17.9	6.1	35.8
Mexico	34.0	10.6	13.7	16.4	17.6
Nicaragua	54.0	n/a	17.4	5.1	48.9
Panama	n/a	33.0	n/a	8.9	24.1
Paraguay	71.7	19.3	9.4	10.7	61.0
Peru	64.0	67.8	16.3	13.5	50.5
Uruguay	32.0	27.0	9.6	11.4	20.6
Venezuela	30.0	33.8	11.8	12.2	17.8
Latin America	49.98	33.99	12.35	10.43	39.6

Source: Data from IADB. Available online at www.iadb.org.
The tariff history of each country corresponds to different years, depending on the availability of information.

far less dispersion in rates, signaling the consensus view that open economies are more conducive to growth. In table 8.1 we can see the high rates and variability in the tariff structure in the prereform period. Although Argentina, Brazil, Mexico, and Peru retain higher than average tariff rates, they are relatively close to the low tariff countries of Bolivia, Chile, and Paraguay. Most of the reductions were introduced gradually over the period to soften the adjustment effects on industries, but in cases such as Peru, the tariff surgery was radical and swift, with rates falling from 68.05 percent in 1990 to 17.63 percent in 1992.

Lower tariffs and free access of goods to the region without high taxes was accompanied by a surge in growth of exports of goods and services from the region. Figure 8.1 shows the growth of Latin American imports and exports. With liberalization in the mid-1990s, as import barriers came down the goods came pouring in, leading to current account deficits throughout the region. Most recently, the strong demand that China has exerted in international markets has propelled export growth above imports. Table 8.2 shows the dramatic change in most countries of the importance of exports in the overall economy. Argentina has doubled its export weight since 1985; Costa Rica and Mexico have also gone through radical changes. However, figure 8.2 shows us that as remarkable as these changes are, as a region Latin America remains less export driven than Asia or Africa.

Trade Imbalances

Liberalization of trade does not, of course, imply that a country's trade accounts will be balanced. Improvement in exports, if outpaced by an increase in imports,

Figure 8.1. Latin American Trade Trends 1985–2004

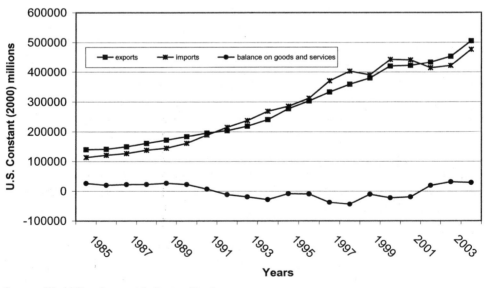

Source: World Development Indicators Database.

Table 8.2.   Exports of Goods and Services (% of GDP)

	1985	1990	1995	2000	2004	Change 1985–2004
Argentina	12	10	10	11	24	12
Bolivia	19	23	23	18	26	7
Brazil	12	8	8	11	22	10
Chile	28	35	31	30	38	10
Colombia	14	21	15	22	19	5
Costa Rica	31	35	38	49	46	15
Ecuador	28	33	26	37	30	2
El Salvador	22	19	22	27	26	4
Guatemala	12	21	19	20	17	5
Honduras	24	36	44	42	35	11
Mexico	15	19	30	31	30	15
Nicaragua	15	25	19	24	22	7
Panama	69	87	101	68	64	−5
Paraguay	22	33	35	21	30	8
Peru	23	16	13	16	20	−3
Uruguay	27	24	19	19	30	3
Venezuela, RB	24	39	27	28	36	12
Latin America & Caribbean	16	17	19	21	27	11

Source: World Development Indicators database, www.worldbank.org and World Bank national accounts data, and OECD National Accounts data files.

Definition: Exports of goods and services represent the value of all goods and other market services provided to the rest of the world. They include the value of merchandise, freight, insurance, transport, travel, royalties, license fees, and other services, such as communication, construction, financial, information, business, personal, and government services. They exclude labor and property income (formerly called factor services) as well as transfer payments.

will result in a deteriorating trade balance. Unless this trade deficit is matched by strong inflow of capital to finance the gap, the country may quickly find itself with balance of payments problems. Throughout the mid-1990s, the strong increase in exports of goods was accompanied by continued demand for the import of services, leaving the region with a negative balance on goods and services. Financial inflows compensated for this balance in 1995 and 2000. By 2002, rising commodity prices pushed exports over imports. Promoting a sustainable global balance that does not draw down reserves or necessitate IMF interventions is a delicate process. External variables, including the performance of the global economy, play havoc with national accounts. One mechanism to attempt to decrease some of the extraregional effects of trade disturbance has been to pursue regional trade integration. However, as we will see below with the effects of the Brazilian currency crisis on **Mercosur,** there may be some unintended effects in the transmission of disturbances within the region.

Chile provides an interesting example of trade liberalization. From an average tariff level of 105 percent at the time of the military coup in 1973—with some tariffs reaching more than 700 percent—Chile unilaterally implemented a 10 percent tariff rate within four years of the start of the Pinochet government. How did such

Figure 8.2.   Exports as a Share of GDP

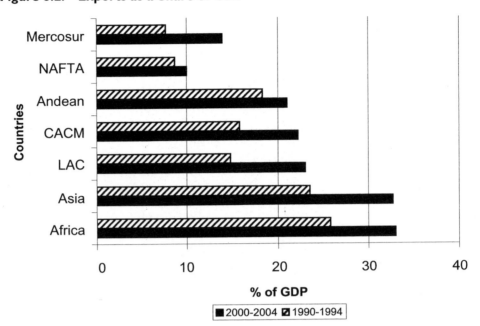

Source: ECLAC: Latin America and the Caribbean in the World Economy 2005 Trends.

a radical and rapid restructuring of the economy take place?[24] Five stages distinguished the Chilean process. After a dramatic reduction of trade barriers as part of a comprehensive stabilization package that included a real exchange rate devaluation in the first period (1974–1979), the second stage (1979–1982) was characterized by exchange rate overvaluation when the peso became the anti-inflationary anchor. During the third stage (1983–1985) Chile suffered through a temporary reversal during a deep economic crisis, while in the fourth (1985–1990) liberalization accompanied recovery. With the transition to democracy in the fifth stage (1991–), Chile began its turn to preferential trading agreements to complement its unilateral liberalization.

Foreshadowing later reform efforts in the region, economic crisis drove the adoption of a new model. Views of economists trained at the University of Chicago—later called the Chicago Boys—gained ascendancy in the Pinochet regime. Criticism of the distributional implications of the open trading model was carefully voiced by economists opposed to the authoritarian regime. Nevertheless, when these economists came to power in the democratic transition in 1990, it became clear that the open trading model would not be altered. The consistency of policy was made possible through a variety of compensation schemes designed to buy off the losers in the liberalization and stabilization process, including owners of import-competing industries, nontradable goods industries, and labor. Export promotion schemes and assistance in export diversification channeled private-sector energies from import substitution toward the external economy. Accompanying financial-sector reforms reduced the prices of credit for domestic entrepreneurs. Repression of labor unions made restructuring easier on firms, albeit at a high political price. Although organizing activity was repressed, by law real wages were maintained in labor contracts. Subsidies eased the transition in the agricultural sector. The Chilean example surprisingly contains some of the elements we discussed in chapter 6 with respect to the role of government in an internationalized economy. Chilean performance confirms Rodrik's proposition of the need for an enhanced role for the state in an open economy.

Composition of Goods

The type of goods that Latin America is exporting to the rest of the world has changed over recent decades. As can be seen in table 8.3, exports vary considerably by subregion. Mercosur has engaged in the greatest degree of diversification, with a mix of primary products such as soy and poultry with manufactured exports in passenger motor cars and aircraft. Natural resources—crude petroleum, gold, and coal—form the base for the Andean nations, with agricultural exports comprising the bulk of their other exports. Likewise, Chile has a very strong concentration in copper and its derivatives; more than half its exports are tied to the commodity. Nonetheless, it has also managed to develop other high-value export markets in fish and wine. Mexico is also concentrated in oil, but its integration into the North American automotive manufacturing market further defines its export list. Panama remains grounded in fish and agricultural products, while the Central American common market countries furthered diversification into light machinery, textiles, and medical supplies.

The historical problems of geographic market concentration and export price instability discussed in chapter 2 continue to plague the region. Latin America sends the bulk of its exports—roughly one-third—to the large North American market. About one-fifth of its trade is with Europe. An increasing amount is being sent to Asia, particularly the voracious Chinese market that grew from 1.8 percent of merchandise exports in 2000 to 5 percent in 2004. This increase came from both the North American and the intraregional shares. Table 8.4 shows the dramatic changes in commodity prices over time. In inflation-adjusted dollars, coffee in 2005 generated about a third as much income as it did in 1980; cocoa fell by half. For small farmers, losing 50–65 percent of income is devastating.[25] Copper has taken the most dramatic ride in prices. Most recently, China has bid up the prices of raw materials and agricultural commodities. In an interesting twist, sugar prices are heading for a twenty-five-year high in 2006—driven by the hot demand for flex fuel cars in Brazil. Sugar is coming to be seen not only as a sweetener but also as an energy crop. The question, of course, is how sugar producers will manage the wide swings in price variation.[26] Even these price booms of copper, soy, and crude oil have the downside of Dutch Disease, sucking resources into these sectors while depleting others.

Table 8.3.   Top Ten Export Products by Trade Group and Their Share in 2003 Exports

Mercosur	%	CACM	%	Andean	%
Soya beans	6.3	Parts of office	12.2	Crude petroleum	46.7
Oil seed cake	5.7	machinery		Gold	4.9
Petroleum products	4.7	Bananas	8.2	Coal	2.9
Crude oil	4.2	Coffee	7.7	Bananas	2.8
Iron ore	3.3	Medical instruments	4.1	Petroleum products	2.7
Passenger motor cars	2.5	Medicaments	3.2	Cut flowers	1.8
Soybean oil	2	Raw sugar	2.3	Coffee	1.5
Aircraft	1.9	Tropical fruit other	1.9	Refined copper	1.5
Poultry	1.8	than bananas		Meat and fish meal	1.4
Internal combustion	1.6	Crude petroleum	1.5	Other ferro alloys	1.1
engines		Misc food	1.5		
		Undergarments	1.3		
		knitted			

Source: ECLAC, "Latin America and the Caribbean in the World Economy, 2005 Trends."

Regional Energy Trade

Despite resource abundance in energy resources, Latin American nations confront frequent deficits in energy supply. Venezuela, Colombia, Ecuador, and Mexico have abundant supplies of petroleum. Gas is in ample supply in Venezuela, Peru, and Argentina; Chile and Colombia have rich sources of coal; and Brazil, Paraguay, Uruguay, Ecuador, Chile, Colombia, and Venezuela have strong hydropower potential. Yet chronic shortages surface. Given abundant supply, the only explanation for energy shortages is weak mechanisms for investment, transmission, and intracountry trade. Energy trade is not like selling bananas or shoes. Instead, it requires very clear institutional rules and coordinated regulatory frameworks governing pricing,

Table 8.4.   Commodity Price Indexes (real dollars deflated by 1990)

	1980	1990	1999	2000	2001	2002	2003	2004	2005 forecast
Crude oil	36.9	22.9	18.1	123.4	106.4	109	126.3	164.9	191.9
Cocoa	260.3	126.7	113.5	71.5	84.4	140.4	138.2	122.4	125.8
Coffee, arabica	346.6	197.2	229.1	97.3	69.6	68.8	71.8	89.9	127.4
Coffee, robusta	324.3	118.2	148.9	77.3	51.4	56	68.9	67.1	72.9
Soybeans	296.2	246.8	201.7	85.8	79.4	86.2	107	124.2	105.7
Bananas	377.3	540.9	373.8	78.4	107.8	97.7	69.3	97	135
Sugar	63.2	27.7	13.8	65.2	68.8	54.9	56.5	57.1	71
Copper	2,182.1	2,661.5	1,572.9	68.1	59.3	58.6	66.8	107.7	110.5

Source: Global Development Finance 2005, Mobilizing Finance and Managing Vulnerability.

Chile	%	Mexico	%	Panama	%
Refined copper	22.3	Crude petroleum	10.2	Fish, fresh	36.1
Ores and concentrates of copper	12	Passenger motor cars	7.6	Bananas	13.3
		Statistical machines	6.1	Crustacea and molluscs fresh	9
Fish	7	Other parts for motor vehicles	4.2		
Sulphate wood pulp	3.7			Other fresh fruit	6
Grapes	3.5	Trucks	4	Fish, salted	2.6
Wine	3.3	Television broadcast receivers	3.9	Crustacea and molluscs	2.4
Methyl alcohol/ methanol	2.2	Insulated wire and cable	3.7	Bovine cattle	2.3
Lumber	2.1			Medicaments	1.8
Petroleum products	2	Apparatus for electrical circuits	31	Raw sugar	1.6
Blister copper and unrefined copper	1.9	Electric power machinery	2.7	Coffee	1.6
		Other telecommunications equipment	2.7		

access, and dispatch systems. Effects may be unintended. For example, when Argentina went through its convertibility crisis in 2001, the government imposed ceilings on energy rates to contain inflation. This created a boom in domestic demand, leaving very little for export to its neighbor, Chile, and precipitating a crisis there. Trade in energy must be predictable and guaranteed by international agreement even at a domestic cost.[27]

An ambitious new project is being launched to build a South American energy ring—a large regional pipeline stretching from Peru through Chile, later expanding to Argentina with Bolivian participation, then building a branch to Uruguay and from there to Porto Alegre in Brazil and Buenos Aires in Argentina. At an initial project cost of $2.7 billion, this might easily double as the interest of the Mercosur governments expands. Loans from the IADB have supported initial project costs, and work is under way to develop a legal framework for trade. Such an endeavor would enhance energy stability but only if the legal framework grew along with the infrastructure. Nevertheless, the resource nationalism exhibited by the Bolivian, Venezuelan, and Ecuadorian governments in levying high taxes on gas and oil extraction is dampening enthusiasm for cross-border investment.

THE NEW GEOGRAPHY OF INTERNATIONAL TRADE: WHERE TO FOCUS TRADE OPENING

Latin American nations have incorporated trade as a central element of their development strategies. In a globalized world, the question is no longer one of inward

Nontraditional export crops have opened new opportunities for women but also added to their burden. *(Courtesy of the Inter-American Development Bank)*

versus external orientation but rather how Latin America will trade with the world. Trade generates winners and losers. How a country pursues the process of liberalization shapes the distribution and the timing of gains and losses. In Latin America, the first stage of opening to the international arena was driven in large part by IMF mandate or the desire to signal a change in the model of development. Chile and Mexico were among the early liberalizers, unilaterally reducing trade barriers to benefit from the inflow of cheaper imports and investment flows. Other countries such as Colombia and Peru were pushed toward liberalization by structural reform packages. But the period of the liberalization drive by policy decree has ended. The new approach engages trade liberalization by negotiation. With average tariff rates hovering at 10 percent, the gains from further liberalization must be achieved not by the benefits of lower-priced imports but rather by gaining market access to other countries' markets. Access is achieved by negotiation on multilateral, regional, or bilateral levels. Trade policy, then, is no longer a simple economic calculation of tariff rates but rather a political balancing act of exchanging domestic opening (which may hurt certain sectors) for access to broader markets (which may help export sectors). Trade negotiations are a complicated calculus of bargaining power and market potential constrained by the bureaucratic capacity for intricate consultation and effective implementation. The key question facing Latin American nations is whether liberalization is most effectively pursued through multilateral negotiations through the World Trade Organization (WTO), hemispheric negotiations through the **Free Trade Area of the Americas (FTAA)**, or bilateral and subregional arrangements. Multiple tracks may be pursued, but Brazil, Argentina, and Venezuela in particular have chosen to strengthen subregional integration to enhance bargaining power at the hemispheric and global levels. Let us consider progress and pitfalls in each arena to assess the potential gains from liberalization for the region.

The Road to Doha: The WTO and the Development Round of Market Opening

In 2001 trade ministers from WTO member countries meeting in Doha, Qatar, began a long and arduous process of trade negotiations with an important central focus: addressing the problems that developing countries face in international trade. The so-called Doha Development Agenda principally aimed to lower the barriers that developing countries face in highly protected agricultural markets in the industrial world—areas where many developing countries should have a comparative advantage—in exchange for opening of markets for investment and services in the South. Some analysts argued that the world would gain between $250 billion and $650 billion (half of which would accrue to developing countries) if high tariffs and subsidies, particularly those on protected agricultural commodities, were reduced. Other analysts have suggested that the gains are more modest, on the order of a one-off increase in world income of between $40 billion and $60 billion.[28]

The road to Doha has been full of disruptions and detours. The power of the 100 developing countries of the 148 participating in this trade round has distinguished it from earlier efforts at trade liberalization. The meeting in Cancun, Mexico, in 2003 to advance the agenda ended in an impasse, with the developing South rejecting the so-called Singapore issues being advanced by the more industrial North—issues of investment protection and services liberalization. The round was nearly scrapped until a compromise in July 2004 brought negotiators back to the table with an agreement to focus on the agricultural issues, putting investment and market access to the side. Key Doha issues for Latin America include increasing the effectiveness of market opening, especially for agriculture; maintaining policy space for development through the WTO convention of the special and differential (S&D) treatment of developing countries to include longer phase-in times for measures; moving ahead with the liberalization of services, particularly the service of labor and movement of persons; and developing a transparent institutional framework to support trade.[29] There are profound differences in priorities and approaches. The Hong Kong Ministerial of December 2005 revealed further the deep divide on reducing agricultural subsidies. Some movement has been made toward resolving these issues, but progress has been bogged down by constituencies protecting vested interests.

Although the Doha efforts to improve the rules for developing countries are faltering, some success has been achieved in cases brought by developing countries pressuring the United States and Europe to uphold existing trade rules. In March 2005 Brazil won an appeal at the WTO against the United States that was ruled as unfairly subsidizing cotton farmers. A month later the WTO found for Brazil, Australia, and Thailand against the European Union (EU) policy of supporting sugar exports. In 2006 the EU was also mandated by the WTO to realign its tariffs on bananas in a move that will improve the standing of Latin American exports, especially Ecuador, against the African and Caribbean Producers, who enjoyed historically preferential treatment by the EU. These cases are encouraging steps for developing countries in achieving greater access to agricultural markets, but there is still a long way to go. The theory of free trade—exporting those goods most efficiently produced—is thwarted by powerful protectionist interests in the North.

The Chinese Challenge—or the Oriental Opportunity?

The most dramatic contemporary change confronting Latin America in international markets is the rise of Chinese trade from 2 percent of the world totals in 2000 to 6.5 percent in 2004. Now the world's third largest exporter and importer, it is a global engine for growth. Table 8.5 shows the main products China imports from its top five Latin American trading partners. China has created a positive net terms of trade for Latin America, bidding up the price of raw materials. From 2002 to 2004, overall commodity prices increased from 1.2 percent in 2002 to a dramatic 29.4 percent in 2004.[30] China accounted for one-third of the upsurge in global demand for petroleum and worldwide oil consumption. For the Latin American exporters of commodities—Brazilian soybeans, Chilean copper, and Venezuelan oil—China has been a great boon to export growth. Large demand has made China an international price maker, placing between first and third in the world as a market for copper, fertilizers, iron and steel, oilseeds, oils, plastics, and electronics and optical,

Table 8.5. China: Main Products Exported from Five Latin American Countries

Main Products	Argentina	Brazil	Chile	Cuba	Peru	Total of 5 LA Exports	World's Exports to China	% 5 LA Share
Soya	2,555	2,619	0	0	0	5,174	8,528	60.7
Copper	12	39	2,787	7	505	3,350	8,490	39.5
Iron	25	3,155	168	0	256	3,604	17,474	20.6
Wood and pulp	53	521	349	0	4	927	4,374	21.2
Fishmeal	17	0	103	0	502	622	764	81.4
Leather	103	300	0	0	0	403	2,783	14.5
Machine parts and accessories	3	101	0	0	0	104	7,305	1.4
Sugar	0	0	0	111	0	111	225	49.3
Tin	0	0	0	0	122	122	437	27.9
Zinc	0	0	8	0	7	15	171	8.8
China's rank as trading partner								
1990	14	18	30	5	16			
2004	4	4	3	4	2			
Percentage of total exports to China								
1990	2	1.2	0.4	4.3	1.7			
2004	7.7	5.6	10.4	8.2	10.2			

Source: ECLAC, "Latin America and the Caribbean in the World Economy, 2005 Trends."

photographic, and medical devices. As a result, commodity prices rose 29.4 percent in 2004; soy oil rose 28.3 percent in 2002, 21.9 percent in 2003, and 11.2 in 2004; soy went from 8.6 in 2002 to 24.1 in 2003 and 16.1 in 2004. Copper fell 1.2 percent in 2002 but rose 14.1 in 2003 and 61.1 in 2004.[31] These are dramatic prices changes that squarely affect Latin American exporters.

If the current trend of integrating the rural people into Chinese cities continues, agricultural exports from Latin America to feed urban dwellers in Beijing or Shanghai will still be needed.[32] China has begun investing in Latin America's infrastructure to facilitate the rapid movement of goods to its markets, partnering to restructure Argentina's railways to reduce transport costs for beef and soya and investing $5 billion in Brazilian infrastructure development. Technological collaboration is beginning; for example, there is a joint venture with Embraer, the Brazilian aircraft producer, to build airplanes in Harbin. In 2004, Latin America, particularly Argentina, Brazil, and Chile, were the hosts to a parade of state visits and trade tours to develop relationships with China.

But the Chinese boom also has its downside. The obvious fear is devastating competition for countries—particularly those in Central America—that compete with China in labor-intensive manufacturing. With a large population of 1.3 billion people, two-thirds of whom remain impoverished in the countryside, there is a large pool of labor willing to work for very low wages. Those countries with labor intensiveness most like China—Mexico, Costa Rica, and Guatemala—may suffer.[33] The average wage in China is lower than the minimum wage throughout most of Latin America. The region simply cannot compete on cheap labor. Furthermore, the Chinese have traditionally invested more in human capital and education and, most recently, have made a strong push on infrastructure development to bring goods to market.

But there are also pitfalls for the countries enjoying the commodity price boom. Students of Latin American history will recall the problems of Dutch Disease, with commodity price peaks sucking resources away from other sectors only to suffer a crash during a trough. The appreciation of Latin American currencies driven by the demand for their soya, beef, metals, and minerals are making manufactured exports less competitive. Association of South East Asian Nations (more commonly known as ASEAN) partner exports to the Chinese market are 50 percent high-tech items; for Latin America, 70 percent are overconcentrated in commodities and natural resource-based manufactures. Finally, the opportunity to market to China's 1.3 billion consumers is made difficult by nontariff barriers of legal regimes forming a labyrinth that many countries have great difficulty in negotiating.[34] Small- and medium-sized enterprises are at the greatest disadvantage in placing goods in China's markets.

There are policies that governments might consider to mitigate the downsides of the China boom. Trade delegations and information-clearing mechanisms for Chinese markets, with special attention to the needs of small and medium enterprises, can be encouraged. The costs of exploring the Chinese market are high; grants to those who propose collaborative projects might generate new opportunities. The Chilean government has begun to tax copper exports and is investing this fund to promote innovation and competitiveness in research and development in nontraditional, agriculture-based exports and industries in which Chile has a comparative advantage.[35] Finally, it is important to recognize Paul Krugman's dictum that countries don't compete with each other—companies do. The growth of China need not be at the expense of Latin America, particularly if Latin governments use this period to build stronger institutions to support market-based growth of their firms.[36]

Subregional Building Blocks or Stumbling Blocks to Liberalization?

Regional integration may assume different forms depending on the penchant for forfeiting national sovereignty in search of synergies and economies of scale in unification. There are four broad categories of trade integration: a **free trade area (FTA)**, a **customs union**, a **common market**, and an **economic union**. In an FTA, trade restrictions are abolished between participating countries, but each country maintains an independent trade policy and separate tariff rates with the rest of the world. In a bit of an ironic play on words, an FTA is actually a step away from pure free trade. Economists define free trade as an open, multilateral system in which countries do not define preferences for partners but simply buy the cheapest goods available in the global market. An FTA negotiates preferential status for member countries, diverging from pure unfettered trade. A customs union takes preferential arrangements a step further, establishing a common external tariff (CET) for the group, and a common market advances cooperation in other policy-making measures, such as agriculture and the social sector. Full economic integration, including a common monetary policy and a common currency, is an economic union. Because trade integration tends to occur on a regional basis to take advantage of geographic proximity, the different forms are sometimes lumped together as regional integration arrangements; **preferential trade agreements (PTAs)** take account of the fact that countries not sharing a geographic space are increasingly interested in opening new avenues for trade.

Why pursue economic integration? Economic integration may create special opportunities to take advantage of economies of scale, allowing export diversification by producing for a larger market. Absent trade restrictions and in the presence of a stable currency, trade might proceed as if it were between Massachusetts and Connecticut. This may be particularly useful in broadening the markets for nontraditional exports, where global markets themselves remain relatively protected. Where labor training, technology, and long-term capital are scarce in developing markets, economies of scale may offer new opportunities to strengthen markets and create new sources of international competitiveness.[37] Regional trading arrangements may also be a means of moving beyond opening markets for goods to promote "deep integration" in trade in services, harmonization of regulatory regions, and the coordination of macroeconomic policies.[38] Regional trade arrangements may also be seen as a protective step toward freer trade. That is, countries gain some of the benefit from a larger market, but if they associate with partners with similar development levels, their industries will not be overwhelmed by more advanced and competitive international providers.

A free trade agreement can work to open protected markets, creating new sales opportunities. In particular, PTAs are pursued where market potential in services such as telecommunications and investment may open opportunities not covered by simply lowering tariffs. Countries with similar tastes and cultural predispositions as well as common language ties may find invigorating marketing opportunities. Opening to trade through regional integration may meet less political resistance than unilateral tariff reductions. The perception of neighborliness and reciprocity may serve to soften the price of sectoral reform. As new competitors emerge in the regional context and as the dislocation that always accompanies the change in the trading rules of the game dissipates, new players may be better positioned in the global economy. The learning curve in terms of international marketing and shipping infrastructure can be extended to the world marketplace.

Free trade agreements have proliferated around the world, accounting for 84 percent of trade agreements. Of the 170 trade agreements globally, 39 involved countries in the Western Hemisphere as of 2005. Table 8.6 shows the proliferation of agreements. With a total of 12 trade agreements involving more than forty countries, Mexico is one of the countries leading the PTA pack. Western Hemisphere PTAs are more diverse than those involving European nations in that they have more different-sized players not sharing similar national objectives.[39] Integration may also have an effect on the expectations of investors, promoting credibility in the permanence of reforms. This is due to the difficulty of rolling back trade liberalization after it has been locked in by a treaty with another country. For example, when Mexico suffered from the 1994–1995 peso crisis, it raised tariffs on 550 products—except for those exported to **North American Free Trade Agreement (NAFTA)** partners. The political costs of abrogating a treaty may exceed the short-term pain of economic adjustment.

The gains or losses from economic integration may be assessed in light of the existing distance from a free trade ideal. If a free trade agreement opens a country further, it is said to have a trade-creating effect. If a country trades more—and in the process makes more efficient use of its own resources—welfare will increase. If, however, the treaty serves to create an economic enclave, it is trade diverting, as purchases are now made from a partner, not the most efficient global producer. Some have suggested that trade integration in the region has diverted trade from its most efficient sources. Traditional suppliers of textiles from the Caribbean countries, for example, may have suffered from Mexico's improved access to the U.S. market under NAFTA.[40] Economists such as Jagdish Bhagwati and Anne Kruger believe that FTAs are by definition discriminatory; the degree of trade diversion is a function of the rules of origin restricting trade. As most FTAs embed domestic content rules to prevent the FTA partner from becoming a backdoor to duty-free access from other countries, they contend that the higher the domestic content requirement, the greater the efficiency loss. For example, with the **Central American Free Trade Agreement (CAFTA)**, proponents of the accord argued that because Central American countries would be restricted in sourcing the fabric for their clothing from U.S. mills, jobs would be gained. Of course, from an efficiency standpoint if the Central American clothing manufacturer could procure cheaper textiles from China, it should. The rules-of-origin requirement creates a tangled spaghetti-like arrangement that could limit the trade-creating potential of the hard-earned PTAs.[41]

Table 8.6.   Regional Trade Agreements

BOL-MEX	Group of Three (COL-MEX-VEN)	CACM	MERCOSUR
Canada-Chile	MEX-EFTA	Andean Community (CAN)	MERCOSUR-BOL
Canada-CR	MEX-EU	COL, EC, PE and VEN (Members of CAN)-Brazil	MERCOSUR-Chile
CARICOM-CR	MEX-Israel	COL, EC, PE and VEN (Members of CAN)-ARG	MERCOSUR-Egypt
Chile-EFTA	MEX-Japan	Central America-Chile	MERCOSUR-ECFramework Cooperation
Chile-EU	MEX-Nicaragua	Central America-D.R.-U.S. (CAFTA)	MERCOSUR-MEX
Chile-Korea	MEX-(ES -GUAT-HON)	Central America-DR	MERCOSUR-MEX Economic Complementation
Chile-MEX	MEX-Uruguay	Central America-Panama	MERCOSUR-Southern African Customs Union
Chile-NZ-Singapore-Brunei	NAFTA (Canada-MEX-U.S.)	CR-MEX	PE-MERCOSUR
Chile-U.S.	PE-Thailand	Panama-Taiwan	Andean Community-MERCOSUR
		U.S.-Panama	COL, EC and VEN-MERCOSUR

Source: Patrice Franko.

Other economists such as Robert Lawrence, Jeffrey Schott, and Fred Bergsten look at FTAs as steps toward liberalization.[42] FTAs can lead to reductions in barriers on services and other activities not covered in multilateral WTO negotiations, creating dynamic welfare effects. Able to address tough trade problems, they can be considered a pragmatic second best when multilateral routes are not working. For many, whether the FTA has a positive or negative effect depends on the design and implementation of the accord. When embedded in a consistent and credible reform strategy, FTAs can lead to positive outcomes. However, their very success may precipitate failure. The proliferation of agreements is leading to a weakened ability by governments for implementation and enforcement. If different agreements have different liberalization schedules and different rules of origin, enforcement becomes a customs nightmare.[43] It is also problematic for business, as each new rule in each PTA represents a new policy for firms to consider in their export, outsourcing, and investment decisions.[44] Genuine free trade avoids these bureaucratic costs.

Despite the complications of FTAs, the free trade ideal may not, however, be

Trade is dependent on export infrastructure such as the Panama Canal. *(Photo by Patrice Franko)*

the most practical benchmark to assess efforts. One of the difficult parts of assessing the impact of regional trading arrangements is figuring out what would have happened in its absence. Would there have been more movement toward the pure trade model or greater protectionism? Analysis of regional economic integration parallels the joke about the economist who is asked "How is your love life?" and replies "Relative to what?"[45] Evaluating integration involves a benchmark: should the benchmark be the free trade ideal or increasing global isolation?

In promoting integration in the area, the Economic Commission for Latin America and the Caribbean (ECLAC) has embraced a concept called **open regionalism.** This concept refers to a coupling of regional integration with overall liberalization of trade barriers to nonmember countries. Countries accompany lower tariffs to integration partners with a general opening of the economy to world trade. Where the old schemes were protectionist and supported state-led development, new regionalism embraces an outward focus, encourages foreign investment, and has encouraged strategic participation in hemispheric and world forums.[46] The new regionalism is market driven and relies on a scaled-down institutional architecture. In this sense intraregional trade may be considered a complement to and not a substitute for an open global trading arena. Let us turn to consider the wide range of integration efforts in the region to evaluate this proposition.

The Community of Andean Nations

The **Community of Andean Nations (CAN)** has a long but uneven history. A modern realization of independence hero Simón Bolívar's vision of unification, the treaty was signed in 1969. It provided for free commerce and a common external tariff among Bolivia, Colombia, Ecuador, Venezuela, and Peru.[47] The hope was that subregional production would overcome the limitation of economies of scale faced under ISI. Problems in the early stages of the Andean Pact derived in large part from political disputes as well as very different domestic economic policies and goals. An ambitious emphasis on industrial planning and joint industrialization was more than the meager sums dedicated to the projects could support, particularly as disputes arose between the more powerful countries and the smaller nations. Policies governing foreign capital were also controversial. International investment disputes led nations to ban foreigners from investing in activities that would compete with existing firms; strict controls were also placed on foreign ownership and profit remittances.[48]

With greater contemporary homogeneity in economic policies, there are improved prospects for the development of subregional trade. Trade in goods between Bolivia, Colombia, Ecuador, and Venezuela is fully deregulated, allowing any goods originating in a partner country to enter duty free; Peru is becoming part of this through a liberalization program. The Andean Community embraces the concept of supranationality, which means that its regulations apply in all member countries and supersede national laws if in conflict. Its institutional structure parallels that of the EU, including a formal Andean Presidential Council, a Court of Justice with supranational powers, and an Andean integration system that incorporates all the Andean integration agencies. Future plans include promoting a customs union, reinforcing dispute resolution mechanisms, establishing joint investment particularly in energy and agroindustry, and providing special support for Bolivia as a poorer partner. **Trade creation** seems to dominate **trade diversion** in an assessment of the impacts of the union. The regional market appeared to play a key role in promoting export expansion. Scale economies in intraindustry trade between Andean partners are preparing firms for competition in the global marketplace.[49] Economic and political setbacks among member nations have occasionally led to the use of unilateral, trade-distorting measures that pressure the system. Nonetheless, the commitment to a common market agenda is widespread, supported by both business and labor.

The biggest challenges for deepening integration within the Andean community at this time appear to be its extrapact trade negotiations. The Andean Mercosur and Peru Mercosur free trade agreements are precursors to the South American community of nations envisaged in the 2004 Cuzco declaration of the South American summit to unite the two trade blocks. Nonetheless, this is complicated by the fact that Colombia and Peru (perhaps with Ecuador on the way) have signed free trade agreements with the United States with deeper and broader commitments than those with Andean or Mercosur partners. Four Andean nations—Colombia, Peru, Ecuador, and Bolivia—currently enjoy duty-free treatment on nearly all their exports into the United States under the Andean Trade Preference Act, designed to encourage alternatives to coca trade, that is due to expire at the end of 2006. Colombia and Peru have opened their agricultural markets to imports from the United States in exchange for continued preferential access to the lucrative U.S. market. This of course introduces tension with President Hugo Chavez of Venezuela, not exactly a huge fan of the United States, as well as Brazil, which is using South-South integration as a bargaining chip in multilateral trade and foreign policy arenas.[50] Chavez has therefore threatened to pull out of CAN, proposing instead a union of Bolivarian nations—that is, those not allied with the United States.

Central American Common Market and CAFTA

The **Central American Common Market,** formed in 1960, has had a rocky history. The treaty signed in 1961 by Guatemala, El Salvador, Honduras, and Nicaragua established a secretariat for Central American economic integration that Costa Rica joined in 1963; Panama now has observer status in some areas. Progress toward integration in the 1970s was set back by geopolitical struggles and civil war in the region. Although by 1970 intraregional trade had reached 26 percent, small market size and social revolutions turned the clock back. The 1990s, however, saw new resolve to exploit the economies of scale offered by integration. Both business and civil society have taken leadership roles in propelling integration efforts forward. Given that most countries in the Central America region have already pursued unilateral trade liberalization, convergence at a low CET between 0 and 20 percent was achieved. Countries have opened their capital accounts, and investment is returning to the region. Nonetheless, progress by middecade was stalled by macroeconomic instability, weak infrastructure, and unskilled human capital. Priorities of the new regional economic integration program include strengthening the legal and institutional framework, instituting joint actions to reduce debt, and promoting cooperation on sectoral issues such as upgrading infrastructure in transport, energy, and telecommunications. Mexico and the Central American countries have announced an infrastructure strategy, the Puebla-Panama Plan, that would also incorporate social and environmental dimensions.[51] Although imperfect, integration has advanced substantially.

In 2003 El Salvador, Guatemala, Honduras and Nicaragua began talks with the United States to pursue stronger integration with the United States via CAFTA; Costa Rica joined the negotiations in January and the Dominican Republic in March 2004. The agreement promises to boost regional GDP by between .8 and 2.3 percent, sending a strong signal to investors of the potential of Central America's forty-five million consumers close to the U.S. border. On both sides of the border the political push to complete CAFTA was framed in terms of competition with China. Central Americans fear job loss to cheaper Chinese labor. The United States wants to remain a Central American supplier of choice; proponents argued that geography matters in the global supply chain. That is, textile producers in Guatemala or Costa Rica are more likely to use yarns and fabrics produced in the United States, whereas the Chinese would source from South East Asia. Support on the U.S. side also came from quarters within U.S. agribusiness—particularly pork, poultry, dairy, and corn—hoping to open key segments of the Central American market and double exports to the region.[52] Other sectoral interests included paper products, chemicals, telecoms, insurance, finance, and government procurement.

Opponents in the United States cited the weak enforcement provisions for legal compliance with ILO standards for freedom of association, collective bargaining, elimination of child labor, and nondiscrimination of employment.[53] The United States has engaged in trade capacity building with the partner countries to enhance the implementation of local law, but funding in the U.S. Bureau of International Labor Affairs is lacking.[54] Opposition also emanates from Central America, where the potential market gains by the United States are translated into local job losses. According to Guatemala's lead negotiator, Guido Rodas, "rice, pork, corn, beer, telecommunications, and generic medicates are among the losers who will pick up the tab of the CAFTA negotiations largely through job loss."[55] CAFTA was designed to come into effect on January 1, 2006; implementation, however, has been delayed, as legislatures are confronting difficulty in passing implementation legislation in areas such as trade union rights and enforcing intellectual property rights. Costa Rica has not yet ratified the agreement. Opposition has also been ignited by local businesses and peasant farmers fearing impoverishment. In the United States, the vote on the treaty was a close 217 to 215, with the Bush administration pushing hard as a symbol of its commitment to international trade liberalization. CAFTA is a telling example of the potential gains and losses in negotiating free trade agreements.

Mercosur

The second-largest trading agreement in the region after NAFTA is Mercosur. The groundwork for Mercosur began with a bilateral program signed in July 1986 between Argentina and Brazil for industrial integration. Extending from Brazil's tropical jungles to the sub-Antarctic zone of Argentina in Tierra del Fuego, Mercosur countries account for approximately half of Latin American landmass and GDP, 43 percent of the population, and 33 percent of regional trade.[56] Because Mercosur countries include some of the world's richest agricultural and mineral resources, there are ample opportunities for growth and production. The 1991 Treaty of Asunción, which includes Uruguay and Paraguay, expanded this bilateral agreement to include progressive, automatic tariff reduction and a CET in eleven tiers ranging from 0 percent to 20 percent with an average level of 13.5 percent and harmonization of macroeconomic policies. Exceptions were made for four years to the free trade in textiles, steel, automobiles, and petrochemicals.

Chile initially did not join the agreement because it wanted to maintain a lower external tariff than the Mercosur countries, although in 1996 it signed a bilateral agreement with the union as an associate member. Bolivia, Colombia, Ecuador, and Peru are also associates, with preferential duty treatment for their products. They do not necessarily abide by the CET. Venezuela acceded as a full member in 2006; Bolivia may follow.[57] Mercosur places fourth among the world's economic blocs, with more than $767 billion in GDP and more than 230 million inhabitants. Since 2000 Mercosur and the EU have held a series of talks that could lead to a free market agreement. The EU's two-way trade with Mercosur totaled 46 billion euro in 2005, and the EU is Mercosur's top market partner. In particular, Europe is active in the infrastructure arena, buying telephone companies and utilities in Brazil, Chile, Peru, and Argentina. Seven of the ten largest private companies in Brazil are European-owned; only two are dominated by Americans.[58] Nonetheless, as sensitive negotiations on agriculture at the WTO Doha round complicate negotiations, the conclusion of an EU-Mercosur trade area is now likely to await the conclusion of the multilateral round.

Administratively, Mercosur is governed by six institutions. Its Council, a political leadership group, is composed of the foreign relations and economics ministers of the four member states and oversees all other Mercosur institutions, with decision-making authority over member state institutions. The Common Market Group, or the executive organization of the community, has both policy-making and administrative responsibilities. The Mercosur Commerce Commission is divided into eleven working groups charged with monitoring the common commercial policy, including the CET and competition policy. The joint Parliamentary Commission is an advisory commission representing national legislatures; the Forum, a consultative body, reflects the views of various sectors such as producers, consumers, workers, and merchants; and a small secretariat with a permanent staff of about thirty professionals headquartered in Montevideo, Uruguay, completes the list. In comparison to the autonomy built into EU institutions, political control in Mercosur resides in the hands of the member states. In the EU, genuinely European delegates are elected; in Mercosur, institutions are staffed by national representatives.

Mercosur is not yet a true common market. Although members have achieved a customs union, full market status awaits progress in the coordination of economic, legislative, environmental, infrastructure, and technology policies. Member countries face the hard task of harmonizing standards and establishing a supranational bureaucracy beyond the national control of member states. Evaluated by the criteria of common market, Mercosur is still a bit thin. Nonetheless, the achievements of Mercosur over the past fifteen years are important, particularly in locking in progress toward free trade in the region.[59] It is also important to remember that economic unions such as the EU have been decades in the making; slow progress in negotiating tough international issues is rather predictable.

Trade within Mercosur quadrupled since 1990, growing from approximately US$4.1 billion in 1990 to more than US$17.3 billion in 2004. Argentina sells more than one-third of its exports—especially agricultural and natural resource products—to Brazil, making Brazil Argentina's largest trading partner after the United States. Brazilian multinationals have set up shop in Argentina. International auto-makers have taken advantage of the new scale economies to expand auto production in the region. Despite this boom, intraregional trade as a percentage of total exports has fallen in the past few years. However, given relatively steady export levels within the Mercosur group, this decline has more to do with the rise in total exports in 2003 and 2004 driven by the boom in China.

Harmonization of monetary and tax policies has had less success, partly due to economic volatility. Common industrial policies to direct resources toward new areas have also lagged. The asymmetrical nature of the economies makes noncompliance difficult to address. Brazil's economy overwhelms that of Argentina—not to mention tiny Uruguay and Paraguay. For example, the increase in output in one year of Brazil's beer giant Brahma was equal to Argentina's entire consumption of brew. Given its size, Brazil can act without much regard for the effects that a policy may have on Mercosur partners. Relatively weak enforcement institutions make unilateral actions on Brazil's part unpunishable.

Macroeconomic instability has rocked Mercosur. Brazil's move to a floating exchange rate in 1999 pressured the already fragile Argentine economy. The collapse of the Argentine Convertibility Plan in 2001–2002, and its ensuing economic chaos has led to a sharp decline in intraregional trade. Mercosur holds promise but also pitfalls for participant countries. In the wake of the Brazilian crisis of 1998–1999 and the Argentine collapse of 2001–2002 Mercosur may be behaving slightly more like an FTA than a common market, turning outward to Chinese, European, and U.S. markets as a source of dynamism. Mercosur countries, pressured by crisis, pushed for reductions on tariffs in industrial countries on agricultural policies, with the hopes of easing recession through traditional export markets.[60] Macroeconomic volatility precipitated renewed protection. Throughout the union there are too many tariff exceptions, the most recent being refrigerators in Argentina. Argentina is also complaining about Brazilian textiles, footwear and televisions hindering its national reindustrialization. For its part, Brazil alleges that Argentine chickens, dairy, wheat, rice, and sugar are derailing domestic production. To address these tensions, Brazil and Argentina set up a bilateral dispute mechanism—contravening the spirit of the multicountry accord. The mechanism for competitive adaptation, integration, and balanced trade expansion will allow the application of protectionist measures in case a productive sector of Argentina or Brazil proves to the state they are affected by lasting damages.[61] Argentine president Néstor Kirchner was able to leverage this concession from Brazilian president Luiz Inácio "Lula" da Silva as a means to protect Argentina's most vulnerable industries, notably car manufacturing, textiles, and shoemaking.[62] In response to the bilateral balancing between the two strongest members of Mercosur, Uruguay has announced its intention to seek a free trade agreement with the United States, signaling a break in Mercosur unity.[63]

Mercosur suffers from a fundamental implementation deficit. The goals are ambitious, but the mechanisms for attaining them are weak. Institutions lack transparent rules for rule making and managing differences.[64] In 2006 Uruguay and Argentina were locked in a dispute over two paper mills being built on the Uruguayan side of the river. Argentine protestors claim that these giant Spanish and Finnish factories will pollute the river, cause acid rain, and hurt local tourism, farming, and fishing. The International Court of Justice at The Hague ruled against Argentina, and a Mercosur arbitration tribunal found that the roadblocks contravened the government to the free movement of goods—but no penalty was assessed.[65]

Internal disruptions in Mercosur have focused the short-term trade strategy on the multilateral stage. But Mercosur has paradoxically also become stronger, or at least more necessary, to its dominant member, Brazil. As countries are looking outward to gain leverage in multilateral negotiations, carrying the clout of a trade union enhances the country's position on the world stage. Gary Hufbauer, a senior fellow at the Institute for International Economics, notes that "Mercosur was already stumbling as an economic agreement. Now Brazil has evidently decided to make the Mercosur first and foremost a diplomatic pact."[66] If Brazil is able to use this weight to leverage concessions from the developed countries in terms of their agriculture policies, space may be created by growth to strengthen the institutional capacity of Mercosur. But this torturous road to trade liberalization has certainly taken unintended (and protectionist) detours.

U.S.-Chile and U.S.-Panama FTAs

When the U.S.-Chile Free trade agreement went into effect on January 2004, Chile joined a select group of only five other countries with an FTA with the United States: Canada, Mexico, Jordan, Singapore, and Israel. The United States is Chile's largest single trading partner, accounting for 20 percent of Chilean exports and 15 percent of its imports. For the United States, Chile's role is smaller, ranking thirty-fourth as a destination for U.S. exports and thirty-sixth in imports. The United States largely sells Chile capital goods and imports copper, fruit, nuts, fish, wood, and wine. The negotiation process that began in 2000 opened market access, with 85 percent of bilateral trade in consumer and industrial products eligible for duty-free treatment immediately and other tariff rates being reduced over time. Other key issues included environment and labor provisions, more open government procurement rules, intellectual property, and the creation of a new e-commerce chapter. For the United States, Chile was seen as a strategic foothold in Latin America supporting U.S. interests. Its economic and political stability, transparency, and steadfast commitment to market economics made it attractive to U.S. business. The Chilean FTA is being considered by some as a template for other negotiations.[67]

Panama and the United States are also working toward a bilateral free trade agreement. Negotiations began in 2004 and were nearly finalized in 2006. Panama's historic relationship with the United States, including the return of the canal to Panamanian control in 1999, sets it apart from other Central American countries. It is a small U.S. trading partner but has benefited from significant preferences through the Caribbean Basin Initiative, which it seeks to make permanent through an FTA. The United States seeks to go beyond WTO standards in advancing its interests in standardized rules for services trade, investment, intellectual property rights, and government procurement. As with CAFTA, U.S. labor groups are challenging Panama's working conditions and enforcement capability.[68] The Chilean and Panamanian FTAs are small treaties for the United States from an economic perspective but have been negotiated to build commitment to the free trade movement between the United States and its southern neighbors.

NAFTA

In 1991 the United States, Canada, and Mexico began negotiating NAFTA, which was then signed in 1994. NAFTA was the first formal regional trading agreement to involve both developed and developing countries. The centerpiece of NAFTA is the gradual elimination of tariffs over a ten-year period, including the elimination of restrictions in textiles and apparel in the United States and Canada.[69] Intellectual property rights were also strengthened. To prevent the abuse of the free trade status by nontreaty countries, the legislation includes tough rules of origin specifying what proportion of the value of a product must be added locally and imposing strict domestic content rules for the purchase of inputs. Computers, for example, could not be assembled in Mexico with imported components from around the globe and qualify for NAFTA trade preferences.

Key elements of the NAFTA accord include changes in agriculture, manufacturing, and services. The accord provided for liberalization of the export of fresh fruits and vegetables from Mexico into the United States and corn and other grains from the United States to Mexico. It promoted lowering of tariffs and quotas on textiles and apparel. It removed tariffs on cars imported into Mexico over a five- to ten-year period, and it opened the Mexican telecommunications and government procurement markets. Finally, it sped implementation of WTO intellectual property rights and provided national treatment to investors of other NAFTA countries.[70] Unlike the EU, NAFTA makes no provision for the free movement of labor within the bloc. It is notable that the only sectors where the new regime explicitly benefits Mexico are concessions in the U.S. markets for fruit, textiles, and clothing. The more industrialized partners realized significant gains in lucrative telecommunications and government markets. In an effort to gain credibility with international investors, Mexico may have given up more than it got in the NAFTA negotiations. Liberalization with industrialized partners came at a relatively high price for Mexicans.

The signing of NAFTA generated a great deal of controversy. In the United States and Canada, opponents were concerned about the potential loss of jobs as manufacturers moved south of the border to take advantage of cheaper labor. Environmental advocates were also fearful of the motives of big business in relocating to avoid tougher environmental regulations in the North. In Mexico there was the apprehension that the *yanquis* would invade again, exploiting Mexican labor and putting Mexican corporations out of business.

Some of these fears were unfounded. It is important to note that Mexico had already engaged in substantial liberalization, such that the decrease in tariff rates was not particularly dramatic, with the exception of changes in agriculture and government services. Those opposing NAFTA failed to point out that international capital was already well dispersed throughout Mexico through the *maquiladora* program. Begun in 1965, for thirty years this twin-plant program has allowed foreign firms to import components without duty so long as the final product was re-exported. Capital that wanted to be in Mexico because of the cheap labor platform largely was already there. As the study at the ten-year anniversary of NAFTA by Daniel Lederman, William Maloney, and Luis Servén points out, the treaty locked in the benefits of trends already taking place pre-1994 and provided incentives for complementary change.[71]

Furthermore, in assessing the effects of cheap labor, it must be remembered that low wages do not magically guarantee a profit. Low wages may be the result of low levels of productivity such that the cost per unit of product is not reduced. In fact, although wages in the United States are roughly 8 times the wages paid in Mexico, U.S. workers produce 8.2 times as much as Mexicans in *maquila* plants. This is not to say that if cheaper Mexican workers can be made more productive with better education and equipment Mexico wouldn't be more of a threat but rather that the claims for the widespread job loss in the United States, given Mexican productivity levels, were somewhat exaggerated. Profit increases only when productive labor is paid less than it is worth.

In the United States, the American Federation of Labor-Congress of Industrial Organizations, an organization of affiliated labor unions, charged that NAFTA helped keep inflation-adjusted average hourly wages of U.S. workers flat, at approximately twelve dollars per hour. What NAFTA may have done is make the threat of plant relocation to Mexico more real to American workers and therefore depress wage demands in collective bargaining. One study found that 60 percent of union organizing efforts after NAFTA were met by the threat of plant closings, compared to 29 percent before.[72] Nonetheless, NAFTA does not change the fact that multinationals could always threaten to move abroad. As we just noted, *maquiladoras* have been around for thirty years—and if it wasn't Mexico, it would be Malaysia or China.

Jobs have also been created through integration. Transportation sector jobs such as trucking have also benefited, as goods are moved over land between the NAFTA countries. In cases such as the U.S. Fisher-Price Corporation, a job-creating effect of NAFTA was relocating production from Hong Kong to Monterey, because firms such as Celadon Trucking, which move goods from Mexico into the U.S. market, must hire drivers.[73] There is the possibility that NAFTA created as many jobs as it may have lost, albeit in different seectors or geographic areas.

Job creation or job loss is difficult to measure, in part because you can't tell which workers are dedicated to "NAFTA production" and which are making goods sold elsewhere. We know that U.S. employment fell during the first eight years of NAFTA, but it is difficult to directly attribute this to the accord. We also know that when workers are laid off from jobs due to firms moving to Mexico, they may register for benefits under the NAFTA Transitional Adjustment Assistance (NAFTA-TAA). Based on the NAFTA-TAA program, about 525,000 jobs were dislocated in import-competing industries through 2002 when the program was consolidated with general TAA—about 58,000 jobs per year. There is probably some understatement in this figure in that not all workers displaced applied for TAA, but this may be balanced by the fact that not all the firms that moved to Mexico or Canada did so explicitly because of liberalization—there may have been other business reasons. To put these numbers in context, every quarter an average of 10.5 million jobs are displaced in the United States. According to the Public Citizen's NAFTA-TAA database, after NAFTA was enacted, 1,351 businesses relocated from the United States to Mexico and 334 to Canada from 1994 to 2002, representing approximately 200 annually or about 4 percent of U.S. business relocations. In the midst of this churning process, the effect of job loss has been small compared to the overall turnover in the U.S. market.[74]

It is difficult to separate out the direct effects of the trade agreement, the unrelated negative macroeconomic effects of the peso crisis and its aftermath, growth cycles in the United States and Mexico, and the historically positive binational atmosphere that NAFTA has generated. Isolating the effects of the trade agreement from a 45 percent devaluation of the peso, a 7 percent drop in Mexican output, and a 22 percent fall in Mexican real wages staggers even the economists' imagination.[75] Given the small size of trade with Mexico relative to the U.S. economy (two-way trade at 3 percent of U.S. GDP), changes in trade patterns did not generate large impacts on the U.S. economy. More surprising, studies of the Mexican economy have found the impact to be modest at best. A World Bank study found unequal effects across regions and income levels but also showed that Mexican per capita GDP would have been 4–5 percent lower, exports 25 percent lower, and foreign direct investment down 40 percent.[76] At the same time, the spirit of NAFTA worked to encourage both business confidence and a willingness to work together on binational issues. Negative effects have also been reported. The opening of the agricultural market in Mexico to the inflow of cheaper U.S. foodstuffs has been good for urban populations, but the rural sector has borne the brunt of the adjustment. Employment in agriculture fell from more than eight million in 1993 to under seven million in 2002—and net job creation in export manufacturing has not been strong enough to keep pace with the loss. Real wages are lower today in Mexico than they were when NAFTA took effect. The causality of this, however, is in dispute, as the 1995 person crisis and competition from China have undoubtedly depressed wages.[77] Given the economic crisis in Mexico and the threat of job loss from China, the Mexican government has been unable to develop sufficient safeguards and social insurance schemes to compensate those hurt by trade opening and to invest in employment and education to improve competitiveness. Although the poverty rate declined from 42.5 percent in 1995 to 26.3 percent in 2000, NAFTA cannot be fully credited with this progress. Even the World Bank concludes that NAFTA alone is not enough to ensure economic convergence among North American countries and regions.

So if NAFTA has had a role in job loss, it is unnoticeably small on a national level.[78] Perhaps Mexican imports are a complement to U.S. production, boosting the competitiveness of U.S. firms as they market their goods around the world. For the most part, it is macroeconomic conditions and not trade agreements that determine the level of employment in an economy.[79] National levels of income determine aggregate demand; changes in the sectoral distribution of which country is producing each item will not determine an overall job loss. Unfortunately, where jobs are lost the damage is geographically concentrated in communities devastated by plant closings. The pain is magnified on a local level.

Another reason the aggregate job loss hasn't been as high as predicted is the domestic content regulations. Prior to NAFTA, firms (particularly those that had set up in the *maquiladora* zones) had imported components from Asia; now they must purchase from American suppliers. Exports to Mexico may have been higher had the peso crisis not sent the Mexican economy into a tailspin.[80] By 1999, Mexico had indeed become the second-largest U.S. export market after Canada, surpassing Japan. By 2005, two-way trade had nearly reached a record $300 billion. As shown in table 8.7, U.S. exports to Mexico reached $120 billion. Imports were $170.2 billion, leaving the United States with a trade deficit with its southern partner. It is

Table 8.7.   Top NAFTA Exports and Imports

U.S. Exports to Mexico		U.S. Imports from Mexico	
2-Digit End-Use Code (in Thousands of Dollars) Merchandise includes all tangible goods—			
End-Use Code	*Value 2005*	*End-Use Code*	*Value 2005*
Total	**120,048,914**	**Total**	**170,197,884**
85—electric machinery etc; sound equip; tv equip; pts	23,527,509	85—electric machinery etc; sound equip; tv equip; pts	39,838,154
84—nuclear reactors, boilers, machinery etc.; parts	20,075,905	87—vehicles, except railway or tramway, and parts etc	26,813,952
87—vehicles, except railway or tramway, and parts etc.	11,322,082	27—mineral fuel, oil etc.; bitumin subst; mineral wax	25,794,311
39—plastics and articles thereof	9,342,339	84—nuclear reactors, boilers, machinery etc.; parts	21,410,931
27—mineral fuel, oil etc.; bitumin subst; mineral wax	5,372,118	90—optic, photo etc.; medic or surgical instrments etc.	6,358,874
98—special classification provisions, not elsewhere specified or indicated	3,993,131	94—furniture; bedding etc.; lamps not elsewhere specified or indicated etc.; prefab bd	5,263,196
90—optic, photo etc, medic or surgical instrments etc.	3,761,816	98—special classification provisions, nesoi	4,576,558
29—organic chemicals	3,712,158	62—apparel articles and accessories, not knit etc.	3,841,732
48—paper and paperboard and articles (inc papr pulp artl)	2,451,266	07—edible vegetables and certain roots and tubers	2,567,676
73—articles of iron or steel	2,427,116	39—plastics and articles thereof	2,432,770
72—iron and steel	1,836,103	61—apparel articles and accessories, knit or crochet	2,388,594
76—aluminum and articles thereof	1,780,862	73—articles of iron or steel	2,366,577
10—cereals	1,636,621	72—iron and steel	2,291,476
02—meat and edible meat offal	1,552,715	22—beverages, spirits and vinegar	2,081,398
40—rubber and articles thereof	1,549,993	99—special import provisions, nesoi	1,945,110

Source: U.S. International Trade Administration, Trade Stats Express, tse.export.gov.

U.S. Exports to Canada		U.S. Imports from Canada	
e.g., manufactures, raw materials, and unprocessed agricultural commodities.			
End-Use Code	*Value 2005*	*End-Use Code*	*Value 2005*
Total	**211,420,450**	**Total**	**287,870,207**
87—vehicles, except railway or tramway, and parts etc.	42,671,015	27—mineral fuel, oil etc.; bitumin subst; mineral wax	65,771,381
84—nuclear reactors, boilers, machinery etc.; parts	38,687,856	87—vehicles, except railway or tramway, and parts etc.	61,722,146
85—electric machinery etc.; sound equip; tv equip; pts	21,723,784	84—nuclear reactors, boilers, machinery etc.; parts	19,705,155
39—plastics and articles thereof	9,806,455	44—wood and articles of wood; wood charcoal	14,188,201
27—mineral fuel, oil etc.; bitumin subst; mineral wax	8,143,865	85—electric machinery etc.; sound equip; tv equip; pts	10,836,724
90—optic, photo etc.; medic or surgical instrments etc.	6,784,993	39—plastics and articles thereof	10,490,855
98—special classification provisions, not elsewhere specified or indicated	5,694,619	48—paper and paperboard and articles (inc papr pulp artl)	10,421,193
73—articles of iron or steel	4,848,265	98—special classification provisions, not elsewhere specified or indicated	9,865,048
72—iron and steel	4,679,389	76—aluminum and articles thereof	6,934,877
48—paper and paperboard and articles (inc papr pulp artl)	4,559,398	88—aircraft, spacecraft, and parts thereof	6,008,164
94—furniture; bedding etc.; lamps not elsewhere specified or indicated etc.; prefab bd	3,537,925	94—furniture; bedding etc.; lamps not elsewhere specified of indicated etc.; prefab bd	5,794,288
29—organic chemicals	3,525,855	99—special import provisions, not elsewhere specified or indicated	4,864,694
40—rubber and articles thereof	3,368,812	73—articles of iron or steel	4,413,411
88—aircraft, spacecraft, and parts thereof	2,857,224	72—iron and steel	3,853,083
30—pharmaceutical products	2,778,312	40—rubber and articles thereof	2,929,731

interesting to note that the top goods traded have a great deal of overlap between imports and exports, indicating a relatively high degree of intraindustry trade, particularly in the automobile sector. Mexico's duty on American goods has fallen from its pre-NAFTA rate of approximately 10 percent to less than 2 percent, allowing 80 percent of U.S. goods to enter duty free. Half of Mexico's job creation is in the export sector; jobs here pay 40 percent more than the national average. U.S. employment supported by exports to NAFTA countries reached 2.9 million jobs, these paying 13–18 percent more than the average U.S. wage.[81]

The overall effects of NAFTA are still unfolding. It is, in a certain sense, a work in progress. Total U.S. trade with NAFTA partners increased significantly over the past eleven years, rising from $293 billion in 1993 to $710 billion in 2004. Canada and Mexico accounted for 31 percent of total U.S. trade of $2.29 trillion in 2004, up from $292.7 billion, or 28 percent, in 1993. From 2001 to 2004, the trade volume has fallen from 33 percent to 31 percent, in large part because of the pull from the Chinese market. U.S. merchandise exports to and imports from Mexico have increased by 166 percent and 290 percent from 1993 to 2004. It is important to note, however, that an increase in trade with NAFTA partners is not in itself evidence of an increase in trade with NAFTA. That is, trade everywhere has grown, even without preferential agreements. Estimates of causality vary greatly—from 5 to 50 percent of two-way trade. Liberalization began before the pact, but the agreement is likely to have extended and deepened the process. Trade in NAFTA is asymmetrical. The United States is Mexico's most significant trading partner; approximately 90 percent of Mexico's exports go the United States, and about 60 percent of its imports come from the United States; Canada is Mexico's far second cousin, with 2 percent of each. To diversify, Mexico has entered into a total of twelve trade agreements with more than forty countries but is still largely dependent on the United States.[82]

Environmental dumping under NAFTA was also a concern for both sides. The border between the United States and Mexico has long suffered environmental deterioration from sewage problems in Tijuana, inadequate waste disposal from *maquilas,* and copper smelting in Sonora and Arizona. NAFTA heightened fears of greater damage. U.S. firms in conformance with environmental regulations did not want to be put at a disadvantage with respect to firms located in Mexico, and Mexicans themselves did not want to breathe dirtier air or drink more polluted water courtesy of multinational capital. As a result of tough lobbying, NAFTA also includes important side agreements concerning labor and the environment. The nations agreed to an upward harmonization of environmental standards but gave no authority to any country to enforce domestic environmental standards beyond its borders.[83] Under the United States–Mexico Border Program, five-year goals were set for achieving a cleaner environment. Nine binational groups were created to work on reducing vehicle emissions at border crossings, tracking transport of hazardous wastes, minimizing the risk of chemical spills, reducing solid waste, monitoring children's health risks from pesticide exposures, and reducing the impacts of growth on fish and wildlife resources. Two institutions were set up under NAFTA to promote sustainable environmental practices: the **Border Environment Cooperation Commission (BECC)** and the trinational Commission for Environmental Cooperation (CEC). An interesting innovation in the international legislation makes it pos-

---

Box 8.2. NAFTA and the Environment

Strengths	Weaknesses
• Establishes a norm of cooperation • Creates new institutions • Prompted consolidation of environmental legislation in Mexico • New initiatives championed • Encouraged public participation by institutionalizing citizen input and making data available • Self-regulation and adoption of voluntary standards • Citizens have a complaint mechanism • Dispute settlement for persistent nonenforcement	• Governments are ineffective outside of geographic jurisdictions • New institutions are underfunded • Enforcement lags, in part due to budget cuts in Mexico • Many promises unfulfilled due to lack of financing • Inefficiencies make NGO use problematic • Compliance is incomplete • Delays and lack of sanctions impede transforming outcomes • Unwieldy dispute mechanism design discourages use

Source: Jeanne M. Logsdon and Bryan W. Husted, "Mexico's Environmental Performance under NAFTA: The First Five Years," *Journal of Environment and Development* 9(4) (December 2000): 370–383; and Gary Hufbauer and Diana Orejas, "NAFTA and the Environment: Lessons for Trade Policy," Institute for International Economics, Speeches & Testimony online at www.iie.com.

---

sible for citizens and nongovernmental organizations (NGOs) to make direct complaints to the CEC.

Unfortunately, dissatisfaction remains as to the efficacy of the environmental agreements in practice. Box 8.2 summarizes some of the strengths and weaknesses. Some have argued that the institutions are underfunded and that the political attention in Mexico given to macroeconomic stabilization took away from progress on the environmental front. One critic noted that only 1 percent of the $2 billion in cleanup funds promised under NAFTA has been spent.[84] Those defending the record argue that the BECC received funds from the U.S. Environmental Protection Agency and the Mexican Ministry of Social Development and has provided more than $30.2 million in aid to the development of 230 water, sewage, and municipal waste projects in 131 communities on both sides of the border. Recent activities can be viewed at the BECC web site, www.cocef.org.[85] The NADBank, or North American Development Bank, that was set up to finance capital requirements of environmental projects, has been slow to review project proposals and has approved funding for only a handful of projects. Environmental conditions along the border are making people sick. Rates of hepatitis, diarrheal diseases, and gastroenteritis are two to six times the Texas state average—and things are worse on the Mexican side. With a doubling of the border population in the past decades, sanitary services are pressed beyond capacity.[86] New mechanisms may be needed to facilitate lending, as the bank's charter limits it to projects viable on commercial terms. It may need a special concessional window to attend to the needs of the poorest and most vulnerable communities, expanding projects to include some of the structural causes of environmental degradation such as housing and poor sanitation.[87] Finally, some analysts are concerned that under NAFTA institutions basic principles such as "polluter pays" are absent. Although a fine may be levied, it is not calculated on the basis of environmental damage, and it is paid by the government as opposed to the industry.[88] Nonetheless, the environmental side agreement within NAFTA can be seen as an accomplishment in that it exists at all; it is the first to go beyond WTO provisions to address ecological interests. Although this first "greening" of a trade agreement is far from coherent and effective, institution building in environmental cooperation is important.[89] Audley, Polaski, Papademetriou, and Vaughan conclude that the fears of the race to the bottom have been unfounded but that the overall $36 billion in annual environmental damages accelerated pressures already inherent in the Mexican growth process.[90]

Toward a Hemispheric Free Trade Agreement?

Given the ambiguous effects of NAFTA and uneven progress toward regional integration, should subregional hemispheric efforts be linked in a regional free trade agreement? Would a hemispheric free trade agreement benefit the United States? Latin America is a growing market for U.S. exports. From the perspective of the United States, the answer in part depends on the economic importance of the hemisphere. Figure 8.3 shows U.S. trade broken down by trading region. Western Hemisphere free trade countries accounted for 44 percent of U.S. trade. The United States sells more to Chile than to India and more to Central America than all of Eastern Europe.[91] Brazil, with its large population, is seen as a huge potential market; the United States currently sells more there than in China. Table 8.8 gives a more detailed breakdown of U.S. trade.

Of particular importance to the United States are oil imports from the region. A strong argument for improving relations in the hemisphere is protecting energy security. As shown in table 8.9, nearly half of U.S. oil imports in 2005 came from the Western Hemisphere. Venezuela was the leading source of foreign crude oil for the United States, with 14.01 percent of U.S. imports; Canada ranked third and Mexico fourth.[92] The oil sector gives the United States a strong incentive for enhanced integration in the Latin American region. OLADE, the Latin American Energy Organization, was formed to promote cooperative efforts for conservation, sales, and development of oil resources in the region. Given the shorter distances to transport oil compared to the East, Latin American oil sources are more secure, with shorter, less-congested routes to travel.

Many other factors contribute to making Latin America a natural market for U.S. business. Although not the largest trade partner, Latin America has recently been the fastest growing trade partner with total trade turnover (exports plus imports) growing by 154 percent from 1992 to 2003 as compared to 88 percent for Asia, 89 percent for the EU, 78 percent for Africa, and 102 percent for the world in general. For Latin America, the appeal is enhanced access to the large U.S. market.

At the Summit of the Americas, held in Miami in December 1994, regional presidents agreed to negotiate a Western Hemisphere free trade agreement by the year 2005. The idea behind the FTAA is the consolidation of the thirty-nine free

Figure 8.3.   Total Two Way Trade with the United States (Sum of U.S. imports and U.S. exports of merchandise trade by region)

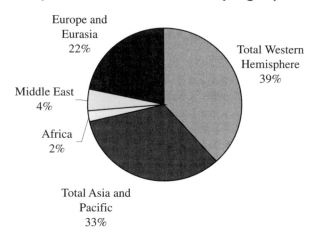

Source: U.WS. trade by geographic regions. dataweb.usitc.gov.

trade pacts already operating in a region of nearly eight hundred million inhabitants and $13 trillion in production of goods and services.[93] Is this a feasible notion? Widely different levels of economic development as well as divergent interests make this process fraught with difficulty. Enrique Iglesias, former head of the IADB, noted that for the FTAA to move forward, a second generation of structural reforms must take place—in areas such as education, pensions, health, modernization of the state, and financial regulation—to promote competitiveness on the part of Latin America. Hemispheric integration should drive structural reform.

Is an FTAA the best approach to deepening trade ties in the region? Some contend that subregional units should be the building blocks. Brazil has been a strong proponent of this approach. Its position, largely shared by Mercosur countries, is that market opening should take place gradually, after South American nations have had the time to build local capacity in import-competing industries. Iglesias rejects the either/or nature of this question. He argues that the process of subregional integration in the formation of subregional blocks is complementary to a hemispheric agreement.[94] Others think that trading blocs—hemispheric or subregional—are trade diverting. On the other hand, proponents of the FTAA suggest that it is "WTO-plus." That is, it moves beyond the issues on the worldwide trade agenda to push barriers in services, intellectual property, and government procurement.[95] The United States sees subregional and hemispheric agreements as a mechanism to achieve greater trade liberalization as well as to advance issues that are not squarely on the table at the WTO through the Doha agenda.

The ambitious free trade goals set forward in 1994 have been thwarted by divergent political and economic interests in the region. In a May 1997 meeting of trade ministers from thirty-four countries, little progress was made, in part due to divergent interests on the part of some Mercosur members. Their position has

Table 8.8. U.S. Trade Balance by Partner Country 2005 (By total turnover = X + M; in million dollars)

		Top 15 Global Trading Partners by Rank				Rest of Latin Partners by Rank			
Rank	Country	U.S. Imports	U.S. Exports	Merchandise Trade Balance	Rank	Country	U.S. Imports	U.S. Exports	Merchandise Trade Balance
1	Canada	287,533.5	183,234.9	−104298.70	31	Colombia	8,770.3	4,962.1	−3,808.10
2	China	242,638.0	38,856.7	−203781.30	33	Chile	6,745.1	4,667.8	−2077.3
3	Mexico	169,216.1	101,666.7	−67549.40	42	Argentina	4,647.7	3,625.5	−1,022.20
4	Japan	137,831.3	51,498.7	−86332.60	45	Ecuador	5,873.9	1,733.2	−4140.80
5	Germany	84,344.6	29,227.0	−55117.60	46	Peru	5,122.6	2,038.0	−3,084.60
6	United Kingdom	50,758.3	34,065.2	−16693.10	48	Honduras	3,758.4	3,155.1	−603.3
7	Korea	43,154.5	26,210.4	−16944.10	49	Costa Rica	3,377.3	3,296.8	−80.5
8	Taiwan	34,574.4	20,527.1	−14047.30	51	Guatemala	3,123.2	2,665.8	−457.4
9	France	33,499.2	20,658.1	−12841.10	56	El Salvador	1,982.4	1,778.4	−204
10	Malaysia	33,694.6	9,472.1	−24222.50	65	Panama	319.9	1,981.9	1,662.00
11	Italy	30,879.9	10,528.4	−20351.50	74	Nicaragua	1,181.6	589.5	−592
12	Netherlands	14,854.4	24,059.3	9204.90	88	Uruguay	727.7	271.9	−455.8
13	Venezuela	32,750.3	6,034.7	−26715.60	91	Paraguay	58.9	828.3	769.4
14	Brazil	24,345.9	13,554.3	−10791.60	107	Bolivia	293.3	185.8	−107.5
15	Ireland	28,384.8	8,702.0	−19682.80	115	Cuba	0.0	361.4	361.4
					121	Belize	98.4	209.8	111.4
					122	Guyana	119.9	166.5	46.6

Source: U.S. International Trade Administration, Trade Stats Express, tse.export.gov.

Table 8.9. U.S. Imports of Crude Oil by Country (in thousand U.S.$)

2005 Rank	Trade Partner	2000	2001	2002	2003	2004	2005	2005 % of U.S. Total Oil Imports
1	Venezuela	12,392,507	10,117,509	10,916,340	12,691,184	18,397,677	25,599,873	14.01
2	Saudi Arabia	13,082,731	12,150,662	12,375,818	16,886,577	19,398,051	24,764,515	13.55
3	Canada	12,715,451	10,145,790	11,225,468	14,195,908	18,966,224	24,359,051	13.33
4	Mexico	11,953,090	9,510,657	11,499,740	14,427,593	17,998,954	23,202,103	12.70
5	Nigeria	10,023,813	8,126,069	5,579,151	9,629,280	15,401,907	22,377,629	12.24
6	Iraq	6,096,738	5,795,728	3,590,343	4,561,534	8,352,349	8,646,923	4.73
7	Angola	3,391,364	2,989,615	2,990,729	4,105,346	4,300,218	8,161,778	4.47
8	Algeria	56	516,977	1,249,549	2,858,437	5,006,789	6,993,762	3.83
9	United Kingdom	2,986,001	2,296,564	3,800,569	4,367,897	3,731,047	4,709,451	2.58
10	Ecuador	1,054,865	860,844	950,090	1,392,762	2,835,239	4,222,752	2.31
11	Kuwait	2,537,412	1,692,234	1,761,920	1,977,132	2,904,481	3,702,214	2.03
12	Colombia	3,402,427	2,416,476	2,400,606	2,239,120	2,586,695	3,276,377	1.79
13	Norway	3,352,735	2,844,265	3,732,919	2,690,347	3,517,084	3,252,339	1.78
14	Gabon	2,144,150	1,622,033	1,558,185	1,937,415	2,421,515	2,759,391	1.51
15	Russian Federation	76,781	0	695,163	1,514,667	1,938,275	2,689,575	1.47
	Additional Western Hemisphere Nations Supplying less than 1% of U.S. oil imports							
16	Brazil	66,556	112,154	513,541	744,183	778,000	1,585,469	0.87
20	Trinidad and Tobago	564,484	481,162	602,918	781,567	840,206	1,205,897	0.66
22	Argentina	556,830	498,908	681,506	608,659	783,889	1,055,972	0.58
34	Guatemala	154,167	100,870	168,423	176,758	179,559	142,340	0.08
37	Peru	36,307	47,572	48,325	110,816	11,911	88,035	0.05
40	Bolivia	0	7,152	0	0	934	44,501	0.02
	Total Western Hemisphere imports	42,896,684	34,299,094	39,006,957	47,368,550	63,379,288	84,782,370	46.39
	Total U.S. imports from world	89,785,632	75,263,362	79,368,165	101,722,159	135,999,308	182,752,137	

Source: Office of Trade and Industry Information, Manufacturing and Services, International Trade Administration, U.S. Department of Commerce.

been that consolidation of Mercosur prior to a hemispheric agreement will strengthen Latin America's bargaining position vis-à-vis the United States. In the United States, trade issues draw strong fire from antiglobalization protestors and union activists who fear job losses with the opening of trade. Protrade was a difficult position for President Bill Clinton to assume; President George W. Bush has likewise encountered divided constituencies on the issue. After slow technical progress in 2002, a new compromise was reached in 2003 to keep negotiating on all issues. However, an accommodation was made to allow those countries who wanted slower commitments to opening in contentious areas to pursue a different track. In July 2003 Brazil made a proposal, dubbed FTAA-Lite, that kept market access issues for agriculture and manufactured goods, market access for services including investment, competition policy, and dispute settlement on the table but moves rules for services, government procurement, rules of investment, intellectual property rights, agricultural subsidies, and trade remedies to the WTO. This did little to appease the United States, which wanted investment issues, governmental procurement, and the hemispheric divide deepened. By February 2004 an impasse was reached as the two-tiered structure failed to resolve the North-South differences. Brazil, which was scheduled to host a meeting to advance the negotiations late in that year, never called the meeting. Talks were suspended, and the scheduled target date to conclude the FTAA passed without agreement.

The anti-FTAA position has gained momentum in Latin America under the fiery rhetoric of President Chavez of Venezuela, who has likened talk about a "balanced and comprehensive FTAA"—the wording at a hemispheric summit in Argentina's Mar la Plata in 2005—to "talking of a kind hearted assassin." At the meeting, Brazil, Argentina, and Venezuela, joined by Paraguay and Uruguay, thwarted the resuscitation of the FTAA; on the U.S. side were the twenty-eight other countries of the region backing the accord.[96] Many see the conclusion of the negotiations to be on hold until the Doha round at the WTO has been completed—a process that has reached its own quagmire. At that point some of the contentious issues in U.S. agriculture—which must be resolved via multilateral bargaining with the EU—will be negotiated, and the hemispheric process might advance. The Mar la Plata meeting underscored how polarized the issue of free trade has become—with smaller countries and Mexico in need of the U.S. market being held off by the stronger bargaining power and maneuvering of the politically more powerful South American countries jockeying for position on the world stage.[97]

From a business perspective, an FTAA with Latin America may bring direct and indirect benefits. In addition to the elimination of tariffs and other restrictions on goods and services and changes in rules governing investment practices, the FTAA provides an opportunity to design mechanisms to ensure that governments do not divert from existing environmental, health, safety, or labor measures to gain competitive advantage in trade or investment. It also aims at increasing transparency in both government policies and practices in areas affecting business, particularly in establishing standards and regulatory requirements, improving intellectual property protection rights, and adhering to Organization of American States and Organization for Economic Cooperation and Development accords to combat corrupt business practices.[98] In this way, the FTAA provides a negotiating forum for issues that are created by the process of globalization of trade and finance but are outside pure market mechanisms for resolution.

FREE TRADE AND TRADE INTEGRATION REVISITED

Latin America has radically reoriented its trade approach in the past two decades. It has gone from a relatively inward-looking to an outwardly oriented development model. Much of this has taken place through unilateral changes in accord with global trading rules. A second wave of trade reform was prompted by the movement to subregional trading arrangements. These arrangements have encouraged countries to negotiate some of the tougher issues of market access and management of externalities. But these issues have created division. Whether the countries of the hemisphere will be able to reverse this momentum to create a regional trading system is uncertain. Neighborliness is somewhat easier at the subregional level, where countries may share common economic characteristics or have a clear incentive to solve common border problems. In the spirit of cooperation, we should also not forget to ask again whether such a regional regime is desirable. Will a hemispheric agreement increase trade or divert trade from other, more efficient suppliers in the world? Nevertheless, in the end it may, like NAFTA, be a story less of pure economic effects and more of the ways in which a genuine trade partnership may open the door to solutions on tough problems facing the region on the social and environmental agendas. After we look at the effects of the new economic model on sources of competitiveness in the industrial and agricultural sectors in chapters 9 and 10, we will turn to these difficult issues of poverty, human capital formation, and environmental degradation that require remediation for the nations of the region to pursue genuinely sustainable and dynamic integrated development.

Key Concepts

Border Environment Cooperation Commission (BECC)

Central American Common Market

Central American Free Trade Agreement (CAFTA)

common market

Community of Andean Nations (CAN)

customs union

economic union

factor price equalization

free trade area (FTA)

Free Trade Area of the Americas (FTAA)

Heckscher-Ohlin theorem

Mercosur

North American Free Trade Agreement (NAFTA)

open regionalism

preferential trade agreements (PTAs)

regional integration

Stolper-Samuelson effect

theory of comparative advantage

trade creation

trade diversion

Chapter Summary

The Theory of Free Trade

- The theoretical underpinning of free trade is the theory of comparative advantage, which states that countries should trade those goods that they can most efficiently produce to maximize global output. Neoclassical trade theory posits that trade will benefit the least advantaged through raising the price of labor in developing countries and will bring factor prices into global equilibrium.

- Critics of free trade contend that, in practice, there are few gains from trade for developing countries. From a dependency, gender, and environmental standpoint, critics believe that free trade can actually damage a country's overall welfare by perpetrating trade in commodities with low value added, produced through exportative means that pressure fragile environments.

- Although Asia prospered from export-oriented growth during the 1980s, Latin America experienced deteriorating current account deficits. Based on Asia's success, trade liberalization was promoted by the international community as a way of improving growth conditions in Latin America.

- Policymakers pursuing trade liberalization should consider an adequate time frame, appropriate exchange rates, trade adjustment assistance, and fiscal reform.

- Reduced tariffs in Latin America have effectively increased the flow of exports and imports in the region. The composition of goods has changed somewhat, although primary products continue to play a dominant role in the export sector.

- China presents both a challenge (to product competing countries) and an opportunity (for those exporters to the huge Chinese market).

Integration: Trade Creation or Trade Diversion?

- There are four ways a country can integrate its markets: by establishing an FTA, a customs union, a common market, or an economic union. Integration encourages economies of scale, opens markets, and promotes credibility within the region. If trade diversion occurs, however, the costs of integration may be high.

- CAN fully deregulates trade between Bolivia, Colombia, Ecuador, and Venezuela; Peru is acceding to full status. However, bilateral negotiations on the part of Colombia, Ecuador, and Peru with the United States threaten pact unity.

- The oldest integration unit in Latin America, the Central American Common Market, has achieved significant liberalization and has been engaged in infrastructure integration through Plan Puebla Panama. Member countries have negotiated a parallel agreement, CAFTA, with the United States to take advantage of free access to the large North American market.

- NAFTA, a regional trade agreement among the United States, Canada, and Mexico, sought to decrease tariffs over a ten-year period and thereby increase trade in the region. The controversy surrounding the agreement was based upon fears that NAFTA would lead to job loss in the North, contribute to environmental degradation, and put domestic corporations out of business in the South.

- Mercosur is a customs union comprised of Brazil, Argentina, Uruguay, Paraguay, and Venezuela with Chile and Bolivia as associate members. Since the inception of Mercosur, trade has increased not only among the member states but with the EU as well. Harmonization of policies has, however, proved difficult, and dispute settlement mechanisms are weak.

- Chile and Panama have negotiated FTAs with the United States. The Chilean agreement has been described as a template for negotiations between richer and less industrialized partners in the region. The Panama FTA (as yet incomplete) is of interest to the United States because of the service trade through the Panama Canal.

- The importance of Latin America as a trading partner for the United States led to negotiations for an FTAA. Divergent interests between many Latin American countries and the United States thwarted the achievement of the pact by its 2005 target date.

Notes

1. Carlos Díaz Alejandro, "International Markets for LDCs: The Old and the New," *American Economic Review,* May 1978, 254–269.

2. Larry Sawers, "Nontraditional or New Traditional Exports," *Latin American Research Review* 40(3) (October 2005): 1.

3. "Ecuadorian 2004 Flower Exports at $314 M," *Latin America News Digest,* January 13, 2005.

4. "On Valentine's Day, Cupid Is Dressed in Brown," *Canada NewsWire,* February 10, 2005.

5. ILRF, "Codes of Conduct in the Cut-Flower Industry," Working Paper, September 2003, www.laborrights.org/projects/women.

6. PAHO Basic Health Indicator Data Base, Ecuador, http://www.paho.org/english/dd/ais/cp_218.htm (accessed March 23, 2006).

7. "Share the Love with Flower Workers," Pesticide Action Network Updates Service (PANUPS), February 7, 2006.

8. "Do We Not Bleed?" *Multinational Monitor* 26(1/2) (January–February 2005): 37–40.

9. "Respect the Rights of Cut-Flowers Workers," http://www.unionvoice.org/campaign/RosasDelEcuador.

10. Stephanie Cuttler, "Valentine's Day Consumer Alert #2: Cut Flowers," *Calvert News,* January 31, 2006, http://www.calvert.com/news.

11. Diana Tussie and Cintia Quiliconi. "The Current Trade Context," HDR Publications, Background Papers, 2005, hdr.undp.org/publications/.

12. Juan Carlos Hallak and James Levinsohn, "Fooling Ourselves: Evaluating the Globalization and Growth Debate," *National Bureau of Economic Research Working Paper,* 10244, January 2004.

13. Robert E. Baldwin, "Openness and Growth: What's the Empirical Relationship?" National Bureau of Economic Research Working Paper No. 9578, March 2003.

14. Romain Wacziarg and Karen Horn Welch, "Trade Liberalization and Growth: New Evidence," National Bureau of Economic Research Working Paper No. 10152, December 2003.

15. David Dollar and Aart Kraay, "Trade, Growth and Poverty," Development Research Group, the World Bank, June 2001, Research paper posted at www.worldbank.org.

16. Baldwin, "Openness and Growth."

17. Ibid.

18. Wacziarg and Welch, "Trade Liberalization and Growth."

19. Baldwin, "Openness and Growth."

20. Christoph Ernst, "Trade Liberalization, Export Orientation and Employment in Argentina, Brazil and Mexico," Employment Strategy Papers 2005–15, International Labour Office, 2005.

21. Schumpeter argued that shocks to an industry, like crises in the life of an individual, might force the sector to grow and adapt. Industries, like people, he suggested, sometimes need to be pushed to try something different.

22. Sebastian Edwards, "The Opening of Latin America," in *Crisis and Reform in Latin America: From Despair to Hope* (New York: Oxford University Press, 1995).

23. Dani Rodrik, "The Global Governance of Trade As If Development Really Mattered," United Nations Development Programme, October 2001, accessed at www.undp.org.

24. This section summarizes the findings of Sebastian Edwards and Daniel Lederman, *The Political Economy of Unilateral Trade Liberalization: The Case of Chile,* National Bureau of Economic Research Working Paper No. 6510 (Cambridge, Mass.: National Bureau of Economic Research, 1998), available at www.nber.org/papers/w6510.

25. Warburg Dillon Read, *The Latin American Adviser,* July 9, 1998, 16 (fax newsletter).

26. "Prices Soar As Brazil's Flexfuel Cars Set the Pace," *Financial Times,* FT News Alerts, March 26, 2006.

27. Inter-American Development Bank, http://www.iadb.org/idbamerica.

28. Sandra Polaski, "Winners and Losers: Impact of the Doha Round on Developing Countries" (Washington, D.C.: Carnegie Endowment, 2006).

29. ECLAC, "Latin America and the Caribbean in the World Economy, 2005 Trends," Santiago Chile, United Nations, 2005.

30. Ibid.

31. Ibid., table I.1.

32. Eduardo Lora, "Should Latin America Fear China?" Inter-American Development Research Department Working Paper No. 531 Bank, May 2005, www.iadb.org.

33. "China Ascendant: A Snapshot of Economic Performance," *Ideas* 6 (January–April 2005), www.iadb.org.

34. ECLAC, "Latin America and the Caribbean in the World Economy, 2005 Trends."

35. "China Ascendant: A Snapshot of Economic Performance."

36. Lora, "Should Latin America Fear China?"

37. Ricardo Ffrench-Davis, comment on L. Allan Winters, "Assessing Regional Integration," in *Trade: Towards Open Regionalism,* proceedings of the 1997 World Bank Conference on Development in Latin America and the Caribbean (Washington, D.C.: World Bank, 1998), 73–74.

38. Sarath Rajapatirana, *Trade Policies in Latin America and the Caribbean: Priorities, Progress, and Prospects* (San Francisco: International Center for Economic Growth, 1997), 15.

39. M. Angeles Villarreal, "Trade Integration in the Americas," Congressional Research Service Report RL33162 Washington, D.C., Library of Congress, November 22, 2005.

40. Jagdish Bhagwati, "The FTAA Is *Not* Free Trade," in *Trade: Towards Open Regionalism,* proceedings of the 1997 World Bank Conference on Development in Latin America and the Caribbean (Washington, D.C.: World Bank, 1998).

41. Antoni Estevadeordal and Kati Suominen, "Is All Well with the Spaghetti Bowl in the Americas?" *Economía* 5(2) (2005): 63–103.

42. William H. Cooper, "Free Trade Agreements: Impact on US Trade and Implications for US Trade Policy," Congressional Research Service Report RL31356, Washington, D.C., Library of Congress, December 6, 2005.

43. World Bank, *Global Economic Prospects 2005: Trade, Regionalism and Development Annual Report,* chap. 3, "Regional Trade Agreements: Effects on Trade," www.worldbank.org.

44. Antoni Estevadeordal and Kati Suominen, "Is All Well with the Spaghetti Bowl in the Americas?"

45. L. Allan Winters, "Assessing Regional Integration."

46. Robert Devlin and Antoni Estevadeordal, "What's New in the New Regionalism in the Americas?" INTAL Working Paper No. 6, Inter-American Development Bank, Integration and Regional Programs Department, May 2001, 7–8.

47. Venezuela joined in 1973; Chile was a member between 1969 and 1976. Peru has had difficulty with adoption of the common external tariff.

48. Devlin and Estevadeordal, "What's New in the New Regionalism in the Americas?" 24.

49. Juan José Echavarría, "Trade Flow in the Andean Countries: Unilateral Liberalization or Regional Preferences," in *Trade: Towards Open Regionalism,* proceedings of the 1997 World Bank Conference on Development in Latin America and the Caribbean (Washington, D.C.: World Bank, 1998), 95.

50. Bruce Odessey, "U.S. Announces Completion of Free-Trade Agreement with Colombia," *Washington File,* http://usinfo.state.gov/wh/Archive/2006/Feb/27-250339.html.

51. Eduardo Lizano and José M. Salazar-Xirinach, "Central American Common Market and Hemispheric Free Trade," in *Integrating the Hemisphere, 1997: The Inter-American Dialogue,* ed. Ana Julia Jatar and Sidney Weintraub (Santa Fé de Bogotá, Colombia: Tercer Mundo, 1997).

52. "CAFTA Accord," *Oxford Analytica,* Latin America Daily Briefs, February 2, 2004.

53. Kimberly Ann Elliott, "Trading Up: Labor Standards, Development and CAFTA," *CGD Brief* 3(2) (May 2004).

54. Elliott, "Trading Up."

55. "CAFTA's Missed Opportunities," *Bulletin of the Washington Office on Latin America,* March 2004.

56. Data do not include new member Venezuela.

57. "Venezuela: Accession Will Not Affect Mercosur's Economy," *Latinnews Daily,* January 26, 2006.

58. John Templeman, "Is Europe Elbowing the U.S. Out of South America?" *BusinessWeek,* August 4, 1997, 56.

59. *Argentina Business: The Portable Encyclopedia for Doing Business with Argentina* (San Rafael, Calif.: World Trade Press, 1995).

60. Diana Jean Schemo, "A Latin Bloc Asks U.S. and Europe to Ease Trade Barriers," *New York Times,* February 23, 1999, online edition.

61. "Argentina, Brazil Agree on Regulating Bilateral Trade," *La Nacion—Argentina,* distributed by Latin America News Digest, February 2, 2006.

62. "Kirchner Gets What He Came For in Brazil," *Latinnews Daily,* January 19, 2006.

63. José Márcio Camargo, "Mercosur: Greater Protection Tends to Hurt Smaller Bloc Members," *Tendencias,* January 19, 2006.

64. Pedro da Motta Veiga, "Mercosur: In Search of a New Agenda," *The Challenges of a Project in Crisis,* INTAL-ITD, July 2004, www.iadb.org.

65. "Mercusor Tribunal Rules on Paper Mills," *Latin News Daily,* September 7, 2006.

66. Alan Clendenning, "From Wine to Washing Machines, South American Trade Zone Faces New Challenges," *Associated Press,* February 15, 2006.

67. J. F. Hornbeck, *The U.S.-Chile Free Trade Agreement: Economic and Trade Policy Issues,* Congressional Research Service Report RL31144, September 10, 2003, www.opencrs.cdt.org.

68. Mark P. Sullivan, *Panama: Political and Economic Conditions and U.S. Relation,* Congressional Research Service Report RL30981, February 15, 2006, www.opencrs.cdt.org.

69. Domestic lobbies in both countries kept the tariffs on textiles high.

70. Arvind Panagariya, "The Free Trade Area of the Americas: Good for Latin America?" *World Economy* 19(5) (1996): 496.

71. Daniel Lederman, William F. Maloney, and Luis Servén, *Lessons from NAFTA for Latin America and the Caribbean* (Palo Alto, Calif.: Stanford University Press, 2004).

72. "NAFTA: Where's That Giant Sucking Sound?" *BusinessWeek,* July 7, 1997, 45. Cites study by Kate Bronfenbrenner of Cornell University.

73. "NAFTA: Where's That Giant Sucking Sound?"

74. Gary Clyde Hufbauer and Jeffrey J. Schott, *NAFTA Revisited: Achievements and Challenges* (Washington, D.C.: Institute for International Economics, 2005), 41.

75. Data from Lustig's comment on Jeffrey J. Schott, "NAFTA: An Interim Report," 125.

76. "Lessons from NAFTA for Latin America and Caribbean," World Bank, 2003.

77. Sandra Polaski, "Jobs, Wages, and Household Income," chap. 1 in John Audley, Sandra Polaski, Demetrios G. Papademetriou, and Scott Vaughan, *NAFTA's Promise and Reality: Lessons from Mexico,* Carnegie Endowment Report, November 2003.

78. "NAFTA: Where's That Giant Sucking Sound?" and Jeffrey J. Schott, "NAFTA: An Interim Report," in *Trade: Towards Open Regionalism,* proceedings of the 1997 World Bank Conference on Development in Latin America and the Caribbean (Washington, D.C.: World Bank, 1998).

79. Employment Policy Foundation, "Open Trade: The 'Fast Track' to Higher Living Standards," *Contemporary Issues in Employment and Workplace Policy* 111(10) (October 1997), Internet publication available at epfnet.org.

80. Sidney Weintraub, "In the Debate about NAFTA, Just the Facts, Please," *Wall Street Journal,* June 20, 1997, A19.

81. USTR, Report, *NAFTA at Eight: A Foundation for Economic Growth,* May 28, 2002, www.ustr.gov/naftareport/nafta8_brochure-eng.pdf.

82. M. Angeles Villarreal, "Trade Integration in the Americas," Congressional Research Service Report RL33162, November 22, 2005, www.opencrs.cdt.org.

83. Claudia Schatan, "Lessons from the Mexican Environmental Experience: First Results from NAFTA," in *The Environment and International Trade Negotiations: Developing Country Stakes,* ed. Diana Tussie (New York: St. Martin's in association with International Development Research Center, 2000).

84. Congressman David Bonior, "I Told You So," editorial, *New York Times,* July 13, 1997.

85. See www.cocef.org/ingles.php.

86. Sam Howe Verhovek, "Pollution Problems Fester South of the Border," *New York Times,* July 4, 1998, online edition.

87. Data from Lustig's comment on Jeffrey J. Schott, "NAFTA: An Interim Report," 127.

88. Schatan, "Lessons from the Mexican Environmental Experience," 178.

89. Ibid., 184.

90. Polaski, "Jobs, Wages, and Household Income."

91. Thomas F. McLarty, "Hemispheric Free Trade Is Still a National Priority," *Wall Street Journal,* May 26, 1995, A11. Facts confirmed in *U.S. Total Exports to Individual Countries, 1991–1997,* available at www.ita.doc.gov.

92. International Trade Administration, "Top 20 Suppliers of Petroleum," www.ita.gov.

93. GAO Free Trade Area of the Americas, "Missed Deadline Prompts Efforts to Restart Stalled Hemispheric Trade Negotiations," GAO-05-166 Report to the Chairman, Committee on Finance, U.S. Senate, and to the Chairman, Committee on Ways and Means, House of Representatives, March 2005.

94. As reported in "The Key Points of the FTAA Agenda," *Latin American Weekly Report,* WR-97-20 (1997), 230.

95. Paulo Wrobel, "A Free Trade Area of the Americas in 2005?" *International Affairs* 74(3) (1998): 547–561.

96. Adam Thomson, "US Latin American Trade Policy under Scrutiny As FTAA Fall Off Summit," *Financial Times,* November 7, 2005.

97. Patrick McDonnell and Edwin Che, "Bush Exits Summit As Trade Talks End in Disagreement," *Los Angeles Times,* November 6, 2005.

98. Robert Mosbacher, Chairman, Council of the Americas, "Trade Expansion within the Americas: A U.S. Business Perspective," remarks at the Chile–United States Issues Round Table, Crown Plaza Hotel, Santiago, Chile, April 17, 1998.

CHAPTER NINE

POLICIES UNDERPINNING GROWTH

Productivity and Competitiveness in the Global Economy

Increasing labor productivity is a key challenge to compete in global markets. *(Courtesy of David Mangurian and the Inter-American Development Bank)*

Every good microprinciples student knows that the key to enhancing the welfare of a population is improving the economy's productivity. More money in an economy will only result in higher prices. If wages rise but output is constant, the price of goods will only go up, and no one is better off. The only way to genuinely improve people's standard of living is to increase the quantity of goods and services produced per unit of input or to decrease the input costs associated with production. Absent aid, people have to be able to make more in order to have more. Improving productivity is fundamental to the elusive quest for growth.

Our basic microeconomics can again be helpful in thinking through the factors associated with rising productivity. We recall that total product, or our production function, is determined by the combination of land, labor, and capital. In this chapter we analyze the contributions of labor and capital to increasing production in Latin America over time; in chapter 10 we will consider some of the issues associated with agricultural change. From the economics literature we know that in addition to our primary inputs of labor and capital, we also need to account for the ways they are combined—or the way technology enhances output growth. Technological change is hard to measure; in much of the econometric literature it is considered the "residual"—the part of the explanation that is left over when we calibrate for the effects of increasing labor or capital in production. Technology is perhaps as difficult to measure as it is important in explaining why some economies are structured to make more with less over time. We also must expand our production function to take into account how differences in the policy environment affect the ability of firms to produce. Do government policies send the correct incentives to firms to produce more efficiently, or do they act as a drag on increasing output? As the work of Daron Acemoglu argues, countries with strong economic institutions sending appropriate signals will invest more in human and physical capital and will use these factors more efficiently.[1] Complementary infrastructure such as roads and telecommunications are also obvious accelerators of growth. This chapter will consider this mix of input conditions—labor, capital, technology, government policies, and infrastructure—as factors in the creation of the wealth of Latin American nations.

Measuring the Immeasurable: A Profile of Microfoundations for Growth in Latin America

The notion that making people better off can only be accomplished by creating more output with fewer inputs is elegantly simple. Creating a profile of how nations stack up in their ability to produce and combine these inputs to promote a prosperous economy is devilishly complex. Although total product is a function of land, labor, capital, technology, and infrastructure, capturing all the factors that affect the quality and quantity of these critical inputs is a tough assignment—but one that has seized the intellectual imaginations of analysts of growth and the business environment.

A central actor in the project to construct indicators to measure conditions promoting productivity has been the World Economic Forum, a Geneva-based foundation whose annual meeting at Davos, Switzerland, attracts both intellectuals and business practitioners. The World Economic Forum's annual Global Competitiveness Report makes a big splash each year as papers around the world cover star performers or bemoan the results for laggards.[2] Its **Growth Competitiveness Index** attempts to capture the collection of factors, policies, and institutions that can determine the level of prosperity of an economy. It is important to note that its use of the term "competitiveness" does not imply a race where a winner captures the gains and excludes the losers. Competitiveness is not defined as a zero-sum game or a dominant share of markets. Rather, by highlighting the quality of key inputs contributing to growth, the index is designed to propel all countries to excel, a win-win proposition for global prosperity. The index attempts to sum up key contributors to productivity.

The Growth Competitiveness Index is based on three pillars: the quality of the macroeconomic environment, the state of public institutions, and the level of technological readiness in an economy. Appreciating that the role of technology in growth in North America or Europe is different from that in developing countries, the index distinguishes between core innovators and those countries better poised to adapt technologies developed elsewhere, providing different weights to measures of innovation in the core versus noncore economies. Each pillar is comprised of weighted contributions of qualitative and quantitative submeasures. Included, for example, are subjective surveys of business executives on the quality of law or level of corruption as well as objective counts of the number of procedures to start a business, real effective exchange rates, and number of computers. In addition to the Growth Competitiveness Index, a second index, the **Business Competitiveness Index,** zeroes in on the microeconomic factors crucial to firm performance. Based on the work of Harvard Business School competitiveness guru Michael Porter, it provides a composite of the effects of factor input conditions, the context for firm strategy and rivalry, the quality of local demand conditions, and the presence of local and supporting industries.

Finally, the World Economic Forum has launched a new index, the **Global Competitiveness Index,** that is designed to assess the gaps in the Growth Competitiveness Index's ability to explain growth. Meant to replace the Growth Competitiveness Index in the future (a quick switch-over defies the logic that consistent benchmarking over time provides an incentive for counties to improve), it incorporates a broader range of factors, including health, education, labor market rigidities, and the sophistication of financial institutions. The Global Competitiveness Index also recognizes that countries at different stages enhance productivity (and therefore output) for different reasons. Although too mechanistic for some analysts, it suggests that at a fundamental level, growth in less sophisticated economies is driven by basic factor conditions. Once countries improve the primary levels of health, education, and infrastructure, in the second stage growth is derived from improving efficiency. Finally, when the gains from efficiency enhancers reach diminishing returns, in order to continue to improve productivity countries in the third stage must focus on the factors that enhance business sophistication and innovation. Although all factors matter to all countries, enhancing productivity in Bolivia or Nicaragua is likely to be more successful by targeting factor policies such as education. Colombia or Peru are in the transition between factor-driven and efficiency-driven competitiveness, while sustained strong growth in Brazil or Chile is most likely to result from efficiency enhancers. Recognizing country differences, the index smoothly weights the factors by a country's place in the stages of development.

The rather dismal results (with the exception of Chile) for all three indexes for Latin American economies are presented in table 9.1. The top four countries in each category are in boldface; the worst four performers are italicized. Globally, Chile ranks 23rd in the Growth Competitiveness Index, leading other Latin American countries by a wide margin. Its 2006 ranking values its remarkably competent macromanagement as well as its public institutions that have achieved transparency and efficiency on the level of the European Union (EU). Indeed, beating countries such as Ireland, Spain, and France, only 8 of the 25 EU countries rank higher than Chile on public institutions. Mexico and Brazil fell in 2006 due to weakness in the quality of public institutions. Brazil was particularly deficient on measures of judicial independence (72nd), wastefulness of government spending (111th of 117), and favoritism in the decision making of government officials (69th). Venezuela tumbled more than 25 places from 2001 to 2006—a huge decline due to budget deficits (despite the oil boom) and high scores for wasteful government spending, inflation, weak protection of property rights, lack of judicial independence, and favoritism in government officials. Venezuela's company in 89th place —just between Nigeria and Mali—may also point to the free market bias in the index construction. Venezuela, pursuing a program of resource nationalism, scores poorly on subindicators of market freedom, creating a downward bias in the overall score.

Comparing the Global Competitiveness Index to the Growth Competitiveness Index, we can see that although Chile still leads Latin America, we observe different strengths. The performance of Costa Rica, Brazil, and Argentina improve, as weighted by factors favoring efficiency enhancement and accomplishments in health and education. In the Business Competitiveness Index, Chile again leads the Latin American pack, with Brazil, Costa Rica, and Colombia trailing in the lead. Nicaragua, Bolivia, Ecuador, and Paraguay again anchor the bottom of the Latin American countries in terms of the overarching business environment. Across the three indices, it is instructive to observe that top performers share high rankings across the three indices, those in the middle do not distinguish themselves in any of the subcategories, and those on the bottom score dreadfully low across the board. Furthermore, there are huge spreads between top performer Chile and the best of the rest as well as between the top and the bottom of the barrel. If nothing else, this exercise underscores the enormous dispersion in technological, institutional, market, and industry conditions across the region. Given this wide range, students of international business would do well to avoid thinking in "Latin American" terms, instead designing country-specific business strategies to take advantage of strengths and minimize the impact of weaknesses. According to the global competitiveness indices, Latin America is dividing itself into groups of higher achievers and laggards in the pursuit of improving productivity and welfare.

Despite the appeal of the indices in the global competitiveness report—after all, who doesn't like a good race—caution should be taken in interpreting the results with respect to answering the important question of why some countries grow faster

Table 9.1. Competitiveness Indexes for Latin America

	Growth Competitiveness Index 2005 components				Business Competitiveness Index	Global Competitiveness Index
	Overall Composite Ranking	Technology Index	Public Institutions Index	Macro Environment Index		
	Collection of Factors, Policies, and Institutions Determining Productivity	*Innovation, ICT, Technology Transfer*	*Contracts, Law, and Corruption*	*Macro Stability, Government Waste, and Country Credit Rating*	*Sophistication of Company Operations and Overarching Business Environment*	*Institutions, Infrastructure, Macro, Health, Education, Market Efficiency, Technology, Innovation*
Chile	**23**	**35**	**22**	**15**	**29**	**27**
Uruguay	**54**	63	**33**	84	70	70
Mexico	**55**	**57**	71	**43**	60	59
El Salvador	**56**	70	**54**	**57**	58	60
Colombia	57	74	**49**	**61**	**56**	58
Costa Rica	64	**56**	58	82	**56**	**56**
Brazil	65	**50**	70	79	**50**	**57**
Peru	68	75	59	70	81	77
Argentina	72	59	74	86	64	**54**
Panama	73	65	75	74	61	65
Venezuela	89	72	*106*	85	92	84
Honduras	93	95	88	89	105	97
Guatemala	97	96	*107*	81	103	95
Nicaragua	99	*102*	82	*110*	*106*	*96*
Bolivia	*101*	*108*	84	*103*	*113*	*101*
Ecuador	*103*	*100*	*113*	80	*107*	87
Paraguay	*113*	*111*	*112*	*102*	*114*	*102*

Top four in each category are boldfaced; worst four performers are italicized.
Source: Global Competitiveness Report 2005–2006.

than others. The index reflects a rich mosaic of data. However, economists grounded in strong economic techniques will take issue with the causal relationships between the data presented and changes in productivity or the rate of growth of output.[3] In an economic model, regression techniques allow us to highlight the contribution of a factor to changes in output—that is, it establishes causality between independent and dependent variables. The Growth Competitiveness Index does not weight its factors—or indeed collect its data—in a controlled environment. The specificity of an index and annual leader-of-the-pack rankings stretch is attractive; more complicated but less glitzy causal models don't sell newspapers. Despite these methodological weaknesses, the index is a useful reminder of the key factors that we need to consider in understanding the foundations for productive growth. Both causal growth models and the indices support the proposition that the quality of inputs matters in promoting productivity. Let us now turn to examine these factors of labor markets, technology, infrastructure, and government policy in greater detail.

WHY IS PRODUCTIVITY GROWTH IN LATIN AMERICA SO LOW?

Although some economists take issue with the construction of competitiveness indicators, few disagree with the fundamental conclusion that, with the exception of Chile, productivity in Latin America is low. Another way of putting this question is, why isn't Latin America growing faster? Despite the years of tough adjustment in the 1980s and 1990s to put macroeconomic houses in order and the attempts at structural reform of the role of the state in the economy, Latin American nations lack a sustainable growth engine. Even the boomlet in 2006, driven by extremely positive external conditions of strong commodity prices and ample capital, have left most countries with relatively unimpressive growth rates in the 4–6 percent range. Why are other developing countries posting stronger performance?

Perfectly solving this puzzle of growth and productivity performance in Latin America is probably the stuff of Nobel prizes and not introductory textbooks, but we can point to the weakness of several conditions in the region that contribute to slow growth. One study, by Mario Gutierrez, looks at the contributions of capital, labor, and productivity over four periods of growth: the 1960s, when growth rates were high under import substitution industrialization (ISI); the accelerated decay of ISI and tough external conditions for non-oil exporters in the 1970s; the lost decade of growth due to the debt crisis in the 1980s; and the new insertion into the global economy in the late 1990s and mid-2000. The study concludes that although physical capital played a role in the process—that is, without accumulating physical capital countries won't grow—capital didn't explain when growth was fast and when it was slow. Mexico, for example, grew at twice the rate of Argentina and Venezuela despite the same average rate of capital. Some fast-growing countries had less capital than slow-growing countries. Human capital, as measured by those enrolled in secondary schooling, was important in the earlier periods but also lost significance after 1980. Instead, the key to understanding when countries grew fast or slow was found in the measure of technology known as total factor productivity.[4] In another study when Andres Velasco asks why growth is so slow, his results point to institutional quality as a predictor of when countries grow. Indeed, one could surmise that good institutions give rise to incentives to invest in technology, guaranteeing at a reasonable cost that the gains from investment in a new product or process will accrue to the investor—making these complementary explanations. Good institutions that promote technological growth matter. But this is still no magic bullet in our productivity growth puzzle. What are good institutions? It is easier, in some sense, to describe bad institutions—those that fundamentally discourage investment. It is a bit like wine. It is pretty evident when a wine is really bad—but tastes for wine vary substantially, creating a range of good wines. As with wine, avoiding bad policies is easier than coming up with a clear metric for policies and institutions that are intrinsically good. Indeed, it might matter where the policies are grown and how they are nurtured.

Labor Productivity: The Key to Making People Better Off

The simplest measure of productivity is a snapshot of how output changes relative to labor over time. This indeed is the measure of average productivity considered in most principles classes. As shown in table 9.2, **labor productivity** for 2002 in Latin America is disappointing for a large number of countries in the region. The Inter-American Development Bank (IADB) report "Good Jobs Wanted" on labor markets in Latin America shows not only low—as in the case of Guatemala, El Salvador, Bolivia, Argentina, Brazil, and Panama—but actually negative rates of growth of productivity for Peru, Honduras, Colombia, Nicaragua, Venezuela, Ecuador, and Paraguay. For the region as a whole, labor productivity growth is flat. Mexico actually topped the United States with its change in labor output—but remember, this doesn't mean that a Mexican worker is more productive than an American, just that from 1995 to 2000 the worker became more productive than he or she was before. The Chilean labor productivity growth rate is also strong, and those of Costa Rica and Uruguay are reasonable—but this is a small head of the class for a large region. Overall productivity in Latin America is roughly the same as it was in the beginning of the 1990s—accounting for much of the poverty in the region. Production per worker grew very slowly between 1990 and 2005—only .21 percent annually. Think for a minute why productivity growth rates for labor would fall. You may remember from principles that labor productivity is determined by the stock of complementary natural and physical capital as well as technology. Wars and natural disasters are prime destroyers of capital; while El Niño (in Ecuador's case) and hurricanes may have a hand in falling labor productivity, it is hard to explain why labor productivity growth is so low in a period of relative peace. Other economic shocks—such as the cutoff of finance during the debt crisis—might explain the slow growth, but 1995 to 2000 was not as shock prone as earlier periods. An excursion into characteristics of labor markets in Latin America may help.

Table 9.2.   Labor Productivity in the Americas

	Labor Productivity	*1995–2000*
	Mexico	3.21
	United States	2.81
	Chile	2.63
	Costa Rica	1.46
	Uruguay	1.45
	Panama	0.89
	Brazil	0.79
	Argentina	0.74
	Bolivia	0.58
	Average LA	0.31
	El Salvador	0.19
	Guatemala	0.14
	Peru	−0.26
	Honduras	−0.84
	Colombia	−1.01
	Nicaragua	−1.49
	Venezuela	−2.79
	Ecuador	−3.10
	Paraguay	−3.19

Source: IADB 2004 Economic and Social Progress Report; Good Jobs Wanted based on data from Alan Heston, Robert Summers, and Alan Bettina, "Penn World Tables Version 6.1," Center for International Comparisons at the University of Pennsylvania, October 2002.

Labor Markets: Good Jobs Wanted

Labor markets in Latin America are not allocating resources well. Unemployment is high relative to historical values and to other regions. Official unemployment rates obscure much of the story of inadequate job creation in Latin America. Open unemployment refers to those officially counted by governments as actively searching for jobs. Imagine the data difficulties in counting the unemployed in poor countries. As shown in table 9.3, unemployment rates rose in the late 1990s and early 2000s but began to moderate slightly in most countries with the 2005 expansion. Unemployment of those ages fifteen to twenty-four who would like to be working is double that of the general population in most countries. Be careful, however, about how much you conclude from intercountry comparisons of unemployment. Higher unemployment in Argentina doesn't necessarily mean that its labor markets are more dysfunctional than those in Guatemala. Low unemployment rates may reflect stronger labor market conditions—or they may simply indicate that the social safety net in that country is so weak that workers desperately take the next available job to keep food on the table. Indeed, there is some indication that workers involuntarily displaced took the first available job, most often one for which the worker was overqualified. Most unemployed workers in the region cannot afford the luxury of waiting in line at the unemployment office. With weak unemployment safety nets,

Table 9.3. Unemployment Rates

Country		Overall Unemployment										Youth Unemployment, 2003–2004 (% of total labor force ages 15–24)
		1996	1997	1998	1999	2000	2001	2002	2003	2004	2005	
Argentina	Urban	17.2	14.9	12.9	14.3	15.1	17.4	19.7	17.3	13.6	11.6	34
Bolivia	Urban	3.8	4.4	6.1	7.2	7.5	8.5	8.7	9.2	8.5	8.0	..
Brazil	Urban	5.4	5.7	7.6	7.6	7.1	6.2	11.7	12.3	11.5	9.9	..
Chile	National	6.4	6.1	6.4	9.8	9.2	9.1	9	8.5	8.8	8.1	19
Colombia	Urban	11.2	12.4	15.3	19.4	17.2	18.2	17.6	16.7	15.4	13.9	..
Costa Rica	Urban	6.6	5.9	5.4	6.2	5.3	5.8	6.8	6.7	6.7	6.9	15
Ecuador	Cuenca, Guayaquil and Quito	10.4	9.3	11.5	15.1	14.1	10.4	8.6	9.8	11	10.9	22
El Salvador	Urban	7.5	7.5	7.6	6.9	6.5	7	6.2	6.2	6.5	7.2	11
Guatemala	National	5.2	5.1	3.8	..	..	..	..	3.1	3.4	3.1	..
Honduras	Urban	6.5	5.8	5.2	5.3	..	5.9	6.1	7.6	8	6.8	8
Mexico	Urban	..	5.4	4.7	3.7	3.4	3.6	3.9	4.6	5.3	4.8	6
Nicaragua	Urban	16	14.3	13.2	10.7	8.3	11.3	11.6	10.2	9.3	5.6	13
Panama	Urban	16.4	15.4	15.5	13.6	15.2	17	16.5	15.9	14.1	12	29
Paraguay	Urban	8.2	7.1	6.6	9.4	10	10.8	14.7	11.2	10	16.0	..
Peru	Metrolima	8	9.2	8.5	9.2	8.5	9.3	9.4	9.4	9.4	9.6	19
Uruguay	Urban	11.9	11.5	10.1	11.3	13.6	15.3	17	16.9	13.1	12.1	38
Venezuela	National	11.8	11.4	11.3	15	13.9	13.3	15.8	18	15.3	12.4	28

Source: ECLAC.

people must find whatever work they can to scrape by. White-collar unemployed take blue-collar jobs. You may be surprised at the level of underemployment, for example, if you ever have occasion to debate politics or philosophy with your over-educated Buenos Aires cab driver. Many are subsisting with jobs for which they are extremely overqualified. The informal sector, the topic of our next section, has also claimed large numbers of the unemployed. As the number trying to eke out a living in this sector increases, many turn to petty street crime and social violence to survive. In the case of Mexico and Central America, low unemployment rates are also masked by those who are working—on jobs in the United States because work with adequate return is not available at home close to their families.

In addition to low unemployment in some countries, a second surprise in the data is that unemployment rates didn't rise more rapidly in the period 1998–2002 when the region largely was in recession. Indeed, a fall in wages was the primary mechanism to adjust to negative economic shocks. These low wages are not enough to cover need. In Honduras, Bolivia, Nicaragua, and El Salvador, more than 50 percent of those working are poor, making less than two dollars a day. These poverty wages reflect the low level of labor productivity among the unskilled and manual workers; wages have moved in the same direction as productivity throughout the region. Furthermore, the evidence suggests that slow rates of growth of technology are behind the wage stagnation. That is, increases in technology do not substitute for labor; rather, technology is a complementary input that raises productivity and wages. Given the huge challenges of incorporating an additional 5 million workers into the 210 million Latin Americans who offer their skills to the labor market each day, improvements in technology that make workers more productive might serve to both decrease unemployment and increase wages.

Workers in all sectors of the economy are confronting conditions of **precarious employment** where, compared to past regimes of labor guarantees and state jobs, employment for some has become less remunerative, less regulated by government, and less subject to collective control of workers.[5] An International Labor Organization (ILO) survey shows that two-thirds of all workers in the region are worried or very worried about losing their jobs.[6] Competition for export assembly in the global arena has decreased worker and community leverage with respect to employment conditions. Economic crises and associated adjustments such as the currency crisis in Mexico have resulted in lower wages and poorer conditions for workers. In 1995 minimum wages adjusted for inflation were 70 percent of their 1980 levels. Imagine if your family income had declined nearly one-third while you grew up. A worsening of formal-sector conditions has contributed to the poor progress on poverty reduction in the region.[7] A weakening of labor rights increased insecurity in the labor market.

Women's participation in the labor force has also changed. Long-term forces including technological changes, advances in educational attainment, decreases in fertility, progress in women's rights, shifts in the structure of households, and intensified consumerism have pushed more women into the workplace. But women have also responded to short-term cyclical changes. Labor force participation by women increased from an average of 28 percent in the 1970s to currently at approximately 40 percent.[8] The good news for the future is that as women have entered the workforce, population growth rates have fallen from 2 percent a year in the late 1980s to 1.6 percent today.[9] There is, however, wide variation as population rates continue to grow in Central America.[10] This means that in the future, there is less pressure for the economy to grow faster than population increases. This demographic window opens the possibility for more productive growth in the future if investments are made in the human capital of youth today.

The growth of female participation is concentrated at the low end of the income structure, indicating that necessity has pushed women into the workplace.[11] Once at the bottom of the labor market, women tend to stay there. Labor market segmentation, or the stereotyping of jobs suitable for women, has a profound impact on employment potential in the region. A World Bank study found that 60 percent of the earnings differential between men and women in a study of fifteen Latin American countries was attributable to cultural aspects segmenting the market and limiting the suitable jobs for women.[12]

In addition to unemployment generated by the legacy of economic crisis, the relatively young age structure of the population in the region requires substantial new job creation. The employment problem is compounded by the need not only to find jobs for existing workers but also to accommodate new members of the economically active population (EAP). Youth unemployment has rocketed. The youth bulge, placing half the population under the age of twenty-five, requires that people entering the workforce, roughly from ages fifteen to twenty-four, make the transition from school to jobs. Varying by country, currently 15–40 percent of those young workers seeking employment are unemployed. One program, called Entra 21, is designed to benefit approximately seventeen thousand unemployed youth across the region by training young job entrants in the information technology field. Set up by the International Youth Foundation, it runs thirty projects in twenty-one countries in a multisector partnership among business, schools, and the civil sector. In El Alto, Bolivia, where four in ten residents are unemployed, Entra 21 teaches infotech skills in areas demanded by the job market such as linking isolated rural communities to the Internet. In addition to financial support, donor partners such as Lucent Technologies and Microsoft may participate through provision of training services, job opportunities, and technical assistance to participating nongovernmental organizations (NGOs).

A growing proportion of workers concentrated in the urban sector further compounds this unemployment problem. The industrial sector must create jobs not only faster than the rate of growth of the population but also fast enough to absorb those fleeing rural poverty and land degradation. New types of growth in Latin America have had a limited effect on job creation. Even Chile, following its first recession after fifteen years, found itself in 1999 with a more than 50 percent increase in unemployment; its unemployment rates have remained stuck at historically high levels through 2001 despite economic recovery. The failure of globalization to deliver jobs has led to social protest and strikes across the region.

Latin America's advantage in the international market does not lie in cheap labor. Wage competitiveness is relative; wages in Latin America will never fall to levels such as those in China. Poised between two worlds, export performance of Latin American manufacturers has lagged. Latin America has an abundance of workers with primary education—and a huge deficit in specialized developed skills. Latin America's comparative advantage isn't in cheap inputs but rather in exports in the midlevel technology range. As an example, Mexico and Costa Rica have broken into export markets based not in natural reserves but in technology and skilled labor. As a percentage of manufactured exports (and allowing what constitutes high technology to vary), Costa Rica has higher high-tech export content than the United States (table 9.4). Rather than low wages, the key to competitiveness is investment in human capital, leading to higher labor productivity. The objective is to create conditions for business development that are better than what might be predicted by the income level of the country. That is, if wages correlate with national income levels, success rides on firms becoming more productive than the average cost of wages. Wages need not be low if exceeded by productivity gains.

Table 9.4. Technology Indicators

	2004 High-Technology Exports (% of manufactured exports)	2002–2004 Households with Television (%)	2004 Information and Communication Technology Expenditure (% of GDP)	2004 Information and Communication Technology Expenditure per Capita (US$)	2002–2003 Technicians in R&D (per million people)
Argentina	8	97	6	224	316
Bolivia	9	..	6	55	6
Brazil	12	90	6	208	..
Chile	5	95	6	340	..
Colombia	6	92	8	180	77
Costa Rica	37	91	8	337	..
Ecuador	7	89	4	83	..
El Salvador	4	..	..	..	..
Guatemala	7	..	..	..	..
Honduras	..	58	5	49	253
Mexico	21	92	3	196	96
Nicaragua	6	..	..	..	39
Panama	2	77	9	400	387
Paraguay	7	..	..	..	113
Peru	2	..	7	166	..
United States	32	97	9	3,595	..
Uruguay	2	..	7	259	50
Venezuela, RB	3	90	4	189	..

Source: World Development Indicators database, www.worldbank.org.
Definition: Information and communications technology expenditures include computer hardware (computers, storage devices, printers, and other peripherals); computer software (operating systems, programming tools, utilities, applications, and internal software development); computer services (information technology consulting, computer and network systems integration, Web hosting, data processing services, and other services); and communications services (voice and data communications services) and wired and wireless communications equipment.

Export success relies on productivity-adjusted labor costs—not on reducing the welfare of the workers.

Labor Policy: Job Security versus Job Creation

High unemployment and underemployment may be attributed to structural rigidity in wage adjustments and job security. Latin American countries have long used labor legislation as a tool of social policy.[13] Minimum wages and measures to protect jobs, such as heavy required severance packages or laws against hiring replacement workers, were seen as political vehicles for income transfers and the protection of the poor. The unintended result, however, was labor market rigidity. **Labor market distortions** in Latin America include government intervention in setting wages, high costs of dismissal, high payroll taxes, and the nature of labor-management relations. There is a long tradition of protecting job security. Workers may contest dismissals in court and may be awarded large severance packages. All these factors reduce the flexibility of management and make restructuring difficult. Studies show that an increase in job security results in a decrease in economy-wide employment.[14] Furthermore, the impact more squarely falls on the employment prospects of young, female, and unskilled workers, contributing to rising inequality. The policy dilemma becomes how to protect income security for the employed—who tend to have political power—and simultaneously open labor markets to new entrants.

Union activity is concentrated in the urban formal sector. The union movement in Latin America has often been the path to political power. Labor unions along with the military have historically been among the few interest-group power centers with the organizational structure, leadership capacity, and defined objectives to affect policy outcomes.[15] However, labor union influence has varied historically. Beginning in the 1920s, many Latin American governments began enforcing workers' rights. Legislation and public controls to address employment issues and resolve labor conflicts fit with the populist political paradigm. Governments were directly involved in collective bargaining, promoting a close alignment between political parties and labor. Through legislative changes, formal-sector employees obtained a number of guarantees, most important among them job security. Ground was lost in the 1970s when military governments restricted labor organizing. The return to democracy in the 1980s was also accompanied by financial austerity, limiting gains on the labor front. Trade liberalization brought global competitors in the 1990s, further constraining labor's bargaining power. Union membership declined in industrial countries from 39.7 percent of the workforce in the 1980s to 31.2 percent in the 1990s; in Latin America the fall was from 24.6 percent to 15.5 percent.

Mexico provides an interesting example of how political change and economic liberalization are affecting the power of unions. For decades union effectiveness through the Confederation of Mexican Workers was tied to the political power of the Mexican Revolutionary Party (PRI), the dominant political party in Mexico. As the power of the PRI was challenged by new political parties in the 1990s, space was created for independent breakaway unions. Changes in labor laws have been proposed by upstart labor foundations such as the National Workers Union, to decrease government's control over the unions. New organizations are also bene-fiting from the North American Free Trade Agreement (NAFTA). U.S. and Cana-dian unions, fearful of being undercut by cheap Mexican labor, have been working to strengthen an independent labor movement in Latin America. International media attention has been called to cases of union bashing in the *maquila* sector. Oddly, internationalization may work to strengthen the hand of labor in the region.

Globalization may transform the role of unions in Latin America. "Reinvent-ing" the labor movement as an inclusionary, democratic movement that promotes accountability is a challenge for the future.[16] Box 9.1 illustrates a productive approach to labor-management relations in the region. In many countries, contract negotia-tions have moved from an industry-wide national level to decentralized collective bargaining at the company level. This allows firms greater flexibility in negotiating contracts that better reflect local conditions and productivity levels. While this of course also decreases the power of the unions to shut down production, greater flex-ibility has created new employment options economy-wide.[17] To deal effectively with the question of unemployment and poverty tied to informal-sector employment, however, unions may no longer be enough. Collective social action that includes measures to improve training, productivity, and work organization is important. NGOs have become active participants in reaching down into the informal market to promote labor reform.[18]

Despite the weakened bargaining power of unions, labor markets remain rigid. In most countries in the region, dismissing a worker after one year carries a sever-ance penalty of more than one month's wages; with ten years' seniority, the cost rises to between six months and one year's salary. Temporary hiring practices have traditionally been constrained in the region in the interest of job security; this inter-feres with firms' ability to meet cyclical global demand. Finally, in the absence of strong social legislation, health, social security, and unemployment compensation schemes have been directly tied to the wage bill. In Argentina, Brazil, Colombia, and Uruguay this tax tops 30 percent of the cost of labor; throughout the rest of the region it ranges between 15 and 30 percent.[19] High social taxes on labor distort whatever advantage abundant labor might confer in the international economy. On average, the costs of mandatory job security provisions in Latin America were nearly three months of wages; this is nearly double the average Organization for Economic Cooperation and Development level.[20]

Formal-sector workers are required to contribute to social security funds, which generally provide workers with pensions, health care, and accident insurance. The difficulties with these funds include their encouragement of early retirement, pay-ments unrelated to individual contributions, and expensive health care packages that exclude the nonworking poor. Pension systems in the region tend to be organized on a pay-as-you-go basis, placing the burden for payments to pensioners today on current workers in the system. In Chile a program of mandatory payments into individual accounts with minimum benefits guaranteed by the government have replaced the pay-as-you-go scheme. Workers may choose among different invest-ment accounts, generating competition in the market. Similar schemes have been adopted in Argentina, Colombia, Mexico, and Peru.[21] Using the market to create the individual incentive for retirement may not only take the burden off firms but also

Box 9.1.   A Seat at the Table: Union Leaders Urge IDB to Include Workers' Concerns in Reform Programs and Free Trade Negotiations

It was the sort of meeting that presumably never takes place.

At the IDB's Washington, D.C., headquarters last February, senior Bank officials spent a day listening to some of their most legendary critics: labor union leaders from Latin America and the Caribbean . . . including John J. Sweeney, president of the American Federation of Labor-Congress of Industrial Organizations (AFL-CIO), Luis Anderson, president of the Inter-American Regional Workers Organization (ORIT), and top union federation officials from Argentina, Barbados, Brazil, Canada, Chile, the Dominican Republic, Mexico, Venezuela, and the United States.

"Much of the mistrust that existed between us before has now disappeared," said ORIT's Anderson. But while he praised the IDB for its willingness to talk with labor leaders, Anderson said most of the region's governments have refused to consult organized labor prior to adopting economic reforms that are promoted by the IDB.

Anderson said this lack of consultation is inexcusable, particularly on issues such as regional integration and trade liberalization, because workers are the first to feel the consequences of these changes. "We've never debated whether or not we agree with economic globalization and integration, because we know it's a reality," Anderson said. "We know that great wealth is being created [thanks to integration], but at the same time we see that poverty is increasing, the number of jobs is decreasing, and the informal sector is growing. So we believe there is a problem in the distribution of the benefits of these reforms."

Anderson and other labor leaders at the meeting said they generally support efforts to open local economies to greater foreign competition, but they warned that governments that fail to address the inequitable distribution of wealth and exclude labor unions from the trade policy debate risk a backlash from voters. . . . As a step in the right direction, Anderson suggested that the IDB promote the creation of a forum for labor consultations as part of negotiations leading to the creation of the Free Trade Area of the Americas (FTAA).

In his remarks at the meeting, IDB President Enrique V. Iglesias agreed that the economic reforms that have swept Latin America in recent years have come at a cost for the regions' workers, and that the problem of unemployment has reached "new dimensions" in many of the region's countries. He also concurred that relations between labor, government, and business have not been as productive as they should, saying there is a need to "improve the quality of the dialogue" between these groups.

Labor participants at the meeting also criticized what they described as a widespread failure to enforce worker rights codified in the various conventions of the International Labor Organization (ILO). The ILO conventions, which most Latin American and Caribbean countries have ratified, set forth a variety of basic workers' rights, including the right to organize and bargain collectively, and protections against child labor and on-the-job discrimination based on gender.

Stan Gacek, the AFL-CIO's assistant director for international affairs, said the failure to enforce labor protections stems from a broader refusal by most governments to link social rights to trade policy. He argued that this refusal is difficult to justify when capital rights, such as those protecting intellectual property and trademarks, are explicitly addressed and defended in trade accords. "Governments that violate copyright protections get harsh treatment," Gacek said, "but what about those who violate labor protections?"

continued

continued

On a different note, other union participants at the meeting acknowledged that labor movement leaders have not always kept up with the changing demands of the market. "We recognize that the trade union movement isn't prepared adequately to deal with new technologies and globalization," said Nair Goulart, a Brazilian who is president of ORIT's Women's Committee. Participants praised an IDB program that paid for selected union leaders to take university courses on labor economics, and they encouraged the IDB to consider additional programs in labor leadership training.

Gustavo Márquez, a labor specialist in the Office of the IDB Chief Economist, said today's union leaders also need to be more understanding of the demands of increasingly specialized and competitive labor markets that require flexible workers to meet evolving production processes. He said many of the labor disputes in Latin America today revolve around outdated work rules that limit the ability of employees to adapt to these changes. He urged new rules that safeguard worker rights while allowing for greater competitiveness and productivity.

"We have different starting points, different jargon, and a different history," IDB Executive Vice President Nancy Birdsall told participants at the conclusion of the meeting. "But we need more of these meetings because it is clear that we also have a great deal in common. We support open negotiations between business and labor. We support social protections, developing better safety nets and better unemployment insurance arrangements."

Source: Paul Constance, www.iadb.org, June 14, 1998, from *IDB América,* April 1998.

raise national savings rates and decrease reliance on capital inflows, a point we made in chapter 7. However, some worry about the future ability of the funds to support the needs of an aging population.

Labor market reforms have not followed a uniform direction in the region. Some countries, such as Colombia, Nicaragua, Argentina, and Venezuela, have worked to increase flexibility. Others such as Chile have traded measures for decreasing the costs of labor to the firm (such as the use of private retirement accounts) for greater protection for workers, including part-time and seasonal workers. Chile pushed through the labor reform bill of 2001, which reduced the workweek and extended labor protection, arguing that Chile must have labor legislation in step with the modern world in order to enter into trade agreements.[22] This tension between labor market flexibility and international standards is a difficult national problem. Nonetheless, despite reforms to enhance flexibility, unemployment and underemployment have remained stubbornly high.

Nations are therefore working to promote job creation rather than job protection. These programs tend toward labor-intensive public works projects or subsidies to private firms to hire more workers. They are financed by central governments and are often executed by local agents, either public or private through NGOs. The difficulty with employment-generating schemes is that unlike unemployment insurance, they are not countercyclical; it is difficult to synchronize spending with an economic downturn. Furthermore, public employment programs such as workfare can distort private labor markets, and supplements to private firms may simply subsidize hires that would have taken place anyway. Training programs are also popular. Chile Joven, a pioneering youth training program, combines scholarships for classroom training with private-sector apprenticeships. In 2006 the Chilean government of Michelle Bachelet proposed a 50 percent subsidy of the salaries of four thousand young workers under age twenty-five as an incentive to incorporate them into the job market. But training programs tend to be expensive on a per-beneficiary basis, and they may in fact attract youth away from continuing formal education. For those who otherwise would be working, scholarships must be set low enough so that they don't discourage job search. Finally, both employment generation and training schemes often don't reach the poorest of the poor—those without the basic requisites for labor market entry.

THE RISE OF THE INFORMAL SECTOR

One result of inadequate job growth in the private sector has been the expansion of the informal sector. Survival strategies have sent workers scrambling for subsistence in a sector not covered by insurance, benefits, or regulations. The informal sector acts as the main source of job creation; 126 million of Latin America's EAP (54 percent) work in the informal sector.[23] Eighty-four out of every one hundred new jobs were in the informal sector, while formal-sector employment shrank from 15.3 percent to 13 percent of total employment.[24] Informal-sector growth has been strongest in Bolivia, Panama, Paraguay, and Venezuela.[25]

Informality can describe any number of jobs, ranging from the street vendor of nail files or the family maid to the small restaurant owner and the corner mechanic. The informal sector has three main areas: microenterprise employment, own-account workers, and domestic service. Microenterprises have been the fastest-growing area, at 5.2 percent per year, accounting for 22.5 percent of total employment in the region. Own-account workers have been increasing at 4.4 percent per year, making up 26.5 percent of the region's total working population. Domestic service employment has increased by 3.9 percent, with workers of this sector making up 7.1 percent of the EAP. Domestic service and own-account work are the lowest productivity occupations, acting as a drag on overall productivity growth.[26]

The lack of a clear definition for the informal sector makes measurement problematic. Some basic guidelines that characterize informality include a low ratio between capital and labor, small-scale worker-owned means of production, family-based operations involving children, and the virtual impossibility of accumulation of capital. The list of informal jobs with these characteristics is extensive, including mobile vendors, taxi drivers, small business owners, artisan manufacturers, maids, subcontractors, other service providers, illegal businesses such as contraband or drug trafficking, and professionals who work for themselves.[27] The informal sector is an easy solution for the unemployed because there is little in the way of money, capital, or qualifications needed to become involved. It is also an important source of employment for women and children. Box 9.2 illustrates the promise and the problems of small firms in export markets.

Informality tends to be associated with unskilled workers. As a large majority of the labor force, the unskilled have difficulty finding formal-sector employment. Limited educational opportunity and an unequal social structure constrain workers

Box 9.2.   The New Entrepreneurs: Preparing the Ground for Small Business

For Eugenia Kleiman and Martha Gámez of Monterey, Mexico, it began as a whim. "We wanted to build something beautiful, something different," said Kleiman, a former shoe shop owner. So in 1990, she teamed up with Gámez, an interior designer, to create Margen Arteobjeto, a workshop that would make home furnishings from wrought iron.

Using personal savings, the two rented a small garage, hired a craftsman and began displaying their plate holders and lamp stands at regional fairs. Buyers were impressed, and orders began to trickle in. The products also caught the eye of an official from Bancomext, Mexico's export promotion bank, who encouraged the pair to show their wares at trade fairs in the United States. Before long, major department stores were placing bulk orders.

"At first our U.S. customers were hesitant, because they had a bad image of Mexican producers," said Kleiman. "But we made it our business to erase that image through quality and service. Now our U.S. customers say, 'Why should we buy from Southeast Asia when you folks are right here?'"

By late 1996, Margen had grown to some three hundred full-time employees operating in three round-the-clock shifts. Annual sales had reached $6 million and are set to top $8 million in 1997, at a time when most of the Mexican economy is still recovering from the effects of the 1995 peso crisis. Most recently, Margen was named one of the four most successful export-oriented companies in Mexico by Bancomext.

THE RIGHT MIX

Margen's story illustrates just how quickly entrepreneurs can germinate when the environment for growth is right. Many economists hoped that this environment would emerge naturally from the structural reforms that have reduced the economic role of the state in the region's countries over the last decade. Indeed, privatization programs, financial reforms, and trade liberalization have opened whole sectors of the economy to competition, and a new generation of political leaders has embraced the notion that private enterprise should be the engine of growth and development. In some countries, most notably Chile, these macroeconomic reforms did have the desired effect, stimulating a flowering of start-up companies and new growth among existing small enterprises. But in many other countries, the benefits of reform have accrued primarily to large, well-established corporations, while activity among the small companies has remained stagnant.

Why have these outcomes been so uneven? The principal reason, according to many observers, is that entrepreneurs need much more than a positive macroeconomic environment to take root and thrive. Indeed, a number of less visible factors, including access to credit, access to nonfinancial services such as market research, and the quality of government institutions that regulate business activity, can ultimately have a much bigger impact on entrepreneurs.

The scarcity of bank credit for small borrowers in Latin America has been a perennial problem. "Small businesses justifiably complain about the lack of access to medium- and long-term financing, high interest rates, the difficulty in finding required collateral, excessive red tape, and a general lack of sensitivity shown by banks toward small firms," says Juan Llisterri, an economist in the IDB's Infrastructure and Financial Markets Division.

Kleiman is a case in point. Like many of the region's small entrepreneurs, she simply assumed that commercial banks would not be interested and didn't even bother seeking credit for the first three years after launching Margen. When Kleiman finally did approach a bank, officials seemed more concerned with her gender than with her ability to offer collateral. "The banks didn't think we knew what we were doing because we are women,"

Kleiman said. Margen's business record eventually persuaded a lender, however, and the company now easily obtains credit.

Although some of the region's commercial banks are in fact beginning to target the small business market segment, the high transaction costs associated with managing multiple small loans still keep most banks from lending to first-time entrepreneurs. As a result, many potential businesses must resort to informal sources of financing at usurious rates that make it difficult to compete.

Even when a start-up enterprise does obtain credit, it often faces additional costs related to official paperwork. In some countries, simply registering a business and obtaining the required government licenses can take months. Moreover, if regulatory institutions are poorly managed and have weak controls, unofficial "service fees" are often necessary to obtain documents and licenses. While large companies can afford to hire intermediaries to navigate bureaucracies and handle paperwork, entrepreneurs can find these transaction costs prohibitive. In fact, as Peruvian economist Hernando de Soto reported in his landmark study *The Other Path,* many small entrepreneurs claim that the cost of dealing with the government is so high that they must operate illegally (in the informal sector) in order to survive.

But entrepreneurs who opt for informality suffer permanent disadvantages compared to their legal counterparts. They cannot request municipal services or utilities, obtain titles to property, apply for credit, or sign enforceable contracts, to name just a few limitations.

Even for entrepreneurs who do operate in the formal sector, the lack of effective legal protections can be crippling. In countries where law enforcement is weak and the judicial system is hampered by inefficiency and corruption, small companies have little recourse against delinquent customers, broken contracts, or other commercial disputes. Large companies compensate for weak legal protections by forging informal agreements with suppliers and partners based on family contacts and friendships. But these closed, inflexible networks make it difficult for entrepreneurs to break into a market.

MANY INGREDIENTS

A strong, open economy, access to financing, transparent and efficient regulations, and effective legal protections: all these conditions must be present for small entrepreneurs to prosper over the long run.

Source: IDB América, 1997, available at www.iadb.org.

from investing in their own human capital. With little education, workers land in low-skill jobs with dismal rates of productivity—jobs that in a vicious circle are associated with limited on-the-job training opportunities. Furthermore, a low-quality and low-skilled labor force can act as a deterrent to investment if investors need an experienced labor force.

Beyond poverty and survival, there are other motives for participation in this sector. Sometimes individuals take advantage of profitable opportunities in market niches waiting to be exploited. This may take place by offering tailored services that large enterprises may not find attractive or possible. Also, the informal sector allows businesses to avoid compliance with regulations. Labor legislation in many countries defines not only basic legal rights but also detailed conditions of employment including wages, job security, the number of vacation days, and employer obligations. In Brazil, for example, taxes and labor laws can add up to 70 percent of the base salary. By law, formal-sector workers are also entitled to large severance packages. Many businesses therefore remain unregistered or unlicensed to avoid costly compliance with regulations. However, there should be a distinction made between those who are capable of paying the cost of regulations and those who cannot because their incomes are too low. Many nonpoor—who could, for example, be paying taxes—also form part of the informal sector.[28]

The large, untaxed segment of the working population in the informal sector creates challenges for fiscal stabilization. Some, such as analysts within the Economic Commission for Latin America and the Caribbean (ECLAC), contend that it has widened the wage gap, increased inequality, and lowered average productivity, hampering competitiveness.[29] Noncompliance places additional burdens on legal firms; prices are higher than on tax- and labor law-evading competitors. However, this may be blaming a symptom and not a cause. According to the ILO, the informal sector arose as a response to the inability of the modern sector to provide sufficient jobs. Urban employment would have to grow more rapidly than the number of new labor market entrants to reduce open unemployment—a daunting objective in the short run. The burden of employment generation therefore falls on the informal sector—not a first best solution.

Some characterize the informal sector as an illegal sector because business are not registered for health and safety inspections, do not pay taxes, and are not bound by labor legislation. Nonetheless, some studies identify up to 50 percent of so-called illegal firms as having some sort of official licensing or tax obligation.[30] In practice, a continuum of legality can be observed in the structure of firms that can be tied to timing or a balancing of costs. Even if a firm wants to be legal, the time involved in filing the appropriate registrations can be up to one year in some countries. There are also registration costs and compliance costs to meet health and safety standards. For example, for a sandwich maker to comply with health regulations including a net to keep insects out, a spring to close a door, and ceramic tiles on the wall and floor, the investment would be five hundred dollars, possibly more than the entrepreneur could afford.[31] This firm by necessity will remain outside the formal sector. We noted the large number of bureaucratic controls on businesses earlier in this chapter; the irony is that these same regulations are also pushing firms into the lower-productivity informal sector.

Given the informal sector's usefulness in absorbing workers, the challenge is to improve sectoral productivity and incomes. There may be hidden opportunities within the informal sector. Job creation was accomplished through microactivity without government subsidy in a hostile policy environment. Informal-sector activity is in fact market-friendly. It provides a wide array of services cheaply and efficiently. For example, many firms are recyclers, collecting and disposing of garbage in cities in a cost-efficient manner. Also, the bulk of low-income housing is produced in the informal sector. These and other arguments indicate that it may be possible to work with and not against the urban informal sector to promote employment and incomes.[32]

Nonetheless, low productivity drags the rest of the economy down. Because the informal sector is by definition capital poor, this is not surprising. Productivity levels in the formal sector, on the other hand, have been advancing, although the increase in the number of jobs has been slow. Thus, the productivity gap between the two sectors has been increasing.[33] Paralleling the productivity gap, the income gap associated with the formal and informal sectors has also been increasing.

Chile stands as an exception to the rising trend in informal-sector activity, with the largest drop in informal-sector activity as a proportion of total employment. Four elements contributed to this decline: rapid growth of the economy; the introduction of private retirement accounts, limiting the burden on the firm for social insurance; increased flexibility in labor legislation; and a strengthening of the legal infrastructure of the state.[34] Consideration of these factors may point to areas of future development in other Latin American countries looking to increase formal-sector engagement. We will return in chapter 11 to the problem of the informal sector as it relates to poverty.

SCIENCE AND TECHNOLOGY POLICY: ACCELERATORS OF PRODUCTIVITY

If growth in a globalized world can't be generated on the backs of low-wage Latin American workers, the key to raising incomes is improving national systems for technology and innovation. Technology improves the productivity of labor. Technology allows companies and ultimately countries to move into a higher value-added world. When confronting the global marketplace, the problem isn't simply producing more but producing something better. Even low-wage Guatemala can't compete with China on wages; it can, however, attempt to identify a market niche where it can innovate, creating a product that is just a little bit different for which people are willing to pay more. For a typical less-developed country, this involves imitating activities that already exist—figuring out how to make t-shirts, coffee, electronics, call centers, or cut flowers better than someone else. Identifying the market niche is a process of self-discovery—but a process that, without the protection of patents, is likely to be imitated by another country or region. The key to sustained growth is creating an environment that continuously favors innovation and adaptation—a tall order for a poor country with competing priorities.

The UN Millennium Task Force on Science, Technology and Innovation has placed technology innovation at the center of its view of growth. Characterizing development as learning,[35] it suggests that economic improvement is largely a result of the application of knowledge in productive activities and the associated adjustments in social institutions. It notes that growth results from interactive learning involving government, industry, academia, and civil society. Learning or continuous improvement in the knowledge base is crucial to growth; technological innovation is not simply a matter of installing devices but also of transforming society and its value systems.[36] Half the growth in rich countries is attributed to technology. How can Latin America appropriate some of this dynamism?

The global competitiveness report shows that Latin America is quite weak on innovation, posting the lowest score for any developing region studied. This reflects low university-industry collaboration, low quality of scientific research institutions, low company spending on research and development (R&D), weak intellectual property protection, low capacity for innovation, and only average scores for the availability of scientists and engineers. Learning requires a culture of openness, criticism, and exploration—institutional qualities often lacking in Latin America's more traditional and hierarchical organizations. Argentina, Brazil, and Chile, the region's leading private technological investors, spent fifty dollars per capita on R&D; this is compared to between two and seven hundred dollars in developed countries.[37] Raising standards of living involves the application of knowledge to transform countries from reliance on the exploitation of natural resources and labor to technological innovation as the basis for development. In Europe, Finland and Ireland are two examples of countries that have made this successful transition; can Latin America do the same?

Innovation engages a wide range of actors in a society who form a system of mutually reinforcing learning activities. Nonetheless, innovative activity in Latin America is segmented. Latin America has traditionally been plagued by a splintering of capacity in science and technology systems. Businesses, universities, research institutes, and state providers of financing do not interact in a smooth technological system. Jorge Sabato conceived of a smoothly functioning technological system as a triangle in which industry, basic educational institutions, and science and technology centers constantly interact. Latin America has been plagued by gaps among these institutions, such that there is little communication between the private sector and the university or even between state-run research institutes and academic researchers. Across much of Latin America, the best scientific minds choose to work in academia over industry—or decide to live in North America or Europe. The connection between the academy and the industrial sector is extremely weak. Most of the limited R&D undertaken in the region is paid for by governments or foreign NGOs and performed by universities—yet much of the university work is unconnected to returns in the private sector.[38] In developed countries, in contrast, 70 percent of R&D activity is supported by the private sector. In Europe 45 percent of researchers and technologists are employed in the private sector; in the United States, private-sector employment in technology-related jobs reaches 80 percent. In Latin America this percentage inverts; 80 percent work in the public sector, leaving only 20 percent in private innovation.[39]

In addition to segmentation, Latin America pursues a linear supply model for science and technology. Because technology and science are seen as public goods, state organizations are given money to develop knowledge. In the linear model, the state develops technology and sends it to the firms. In the United States, while investments are also made in knowledge as a public good, technology is primarily seen as a commodity. That is, information is something that firms buy and sell in the market in response to demand.[40] Market incentives drive investment. This is not to say that there isn't a role for the state in promoting science and technology. The role, however, may be more indirect as a provider or facilitator of risk capital as opposed to a producer in state-sponsored public universities. Demand-driven interactions are nonlinear, engaging a range of actors. States can participate in this dynamic network but are not the primary drivers of technology. An example of this more dynamic model is FINEP, the Brazilian government financier under the Ministry of Science and Technology, that has launched a project called INOVAR to promote the development of small- and medium-sized businesses by providing venture capital. In addition to money, FINEP/INOVAR has acted as a bridge between companies and investors to complete the cycle of technological innovation from research to market.

The need for public financing to promote vibrant technological systems may be explained by market failure. Basic scientific knowledge can be considered a public good that the state must provide to promote new activity. With such a low level of basic science and technology infrastructure, it is expensive for firms to span the gap between basic science and industrial applications. With few firms engaging in R&D, there are limited externalities or synergies created by a core of high-tech firms. It would be as if the high-tech corridor in Silicon Valley were distributed one firm at a time across the poorest counties in the mountains of Appalachia. Not only would low levels of educational attainment hinder innovation, but the clustering of suppliers and skilled labor would disappear. The challenge clearly has become how to overcome constraints of training, size, and geographical dispersion to improve productivity in Latin America.

Beyond linear, state-dominated structures, R&D in Latin America is more heavily weighted toward basic science as opposed to industrial applications where it can help productivity. In most countries in the region, activity has been fragmented and uncoordinated, with players and programs operating in isolation from one another. Table 9.5 summarizes additional statistics with respect to investments in R&D as well as looks at the output of total factor productivity. This proxy for technological change shows us that given the abysmally low levels of investment in R&D, lagging technological change means that it will take Panama fifty-five years, Honduras seventy-nine years, and even our regional leader Chile twenty-five years to catch up to the U.S. level of productivity growth. Although we don't want to make

Table 9.5.   Research, Development, and Total Factor Productivity

	R&D as a Percentage of GDP (1998 or most recent year available)	Company Spending on R&D (% of total)	Researchers per 1,000 Inhabitants	TFP Relative to U.S. Benchmark	Years to Catch U.S. Level	TFP Growth 1990–2000
United States	2.66	68.4	13.94			
Chile	0.55	22.9	1.43	68.9	25	1.9
Mexico	0.43	27.2	0.74	66.4	28	0.5
Panama	0.35	34	0.45	44.2	55	−0.3
Costa Rica	0.27	24.8	1.53	53.4	42	0.1
Guatemala	0.2		0.45	67	27	0.1
Nicaragua	0.13		0.29	n/a	n/a	n/a
El Salvador	0.08	24.6	0.46	62.8	31	0.9
Honduras				31	79	−2.5

Note: Honduras's strong negative TFP growth may have been the result of Hurricane Mitch.
Source: Andres Rodriguez-Clare, "Innovation and Technology Adoption in Central America," IADB Research Department Working Paper Series 525, Inter-American Development Bank, July 2005.

too much of the catch-up metaphor—countries may choose pathways different from that of the United States—it is a rough estimator of the low rate of productivity in the region, a rate that will continue to depress the well-being of its population.

There is also a science and technology gap among countries in the region. Argentina, Brazil, Chile, Mexico, and Venezuela are relatively advanced. Colombia, Costa Rica, and Uruguay have recently generated significant national capacity, but in the rest of the region there is a complete absence of policies and institutions for science and technology development. In technology generation, the number of patents granted ranged from 11 in Guatemala to 2,535 in Brazil.

Meeting the productivity challenge involves a clearer understanding of the nature of technology. Neoclassical theory tends to see technology as exogenous to the production system, a tradable recipe or input that incurs a short-run cost in production. Technological progress is viewed as continuous and cumulative, in a single-track race for dominance. Neostructuralists view technology differently. Relying in part on the views of Joseph Schumpeter, an economist who dedicated much of his work to thinking about technological change, neostructuralists see technology as tacit knowledge not easily transferred, a result of interactive learning and a synergistic process between producers and users. Progress is seen as both continuous and discontinuous, with windows of opportunity for acquisition opening—but abruptly shutting at critical junctions in the process of technological change.[41] The policy ramifications of the different views on technology are complex. Can technology be purchased like any input of production to increase output, or are institutional changes required to promote technological absorption into Latin America economic systems?

No matter what your theoretical perspective, the problem of catching up with the technological frontier involves the question of technological acquisition. Technology is an asset; it must be procured somewhere. Technology may be acquired through foreign direct investment, through licensing or turnkey plants, or through the promotion of national technological parks. Technological acquisition is often asymmetrical. The seller of a technology naturally has more information about the new product or process than the buyer. In the case of hard technologies (incorporated into machinery and equipment) as well as soft technologies (new management techniques, quality control, industrial relations, and just-in-time production), the seller of the technology may be the only agent who knows fully the nature of the commodity.

In a developing country, the next task is the assimilation of technology. Here our question of institutional change comes into play. Simply installing a modern factory does not result in technological acquisition. Technology can remain a black box poorly understood and unsuitable for adaptation and innovation. Improving productivity in an economy involves appropriating information about technological systems, assimilating this knowledge, and disseminating applications beyond the first user. Absorption of technology requires not only obtaining a machine but also training a labor force to run it. Sometimes companies are reticent to make such expensive investments in human capital, as well-trained people often leave the firm. Workers themselves, when poor, may not be able to afford the educational investments to become productive in the international economy. Financing of technological acquisition is also risky—investments often do not pan out. Thin venture capital markets in the developing world make it far more difficult to finance a good idea. Institutions—the set of rules and enforcement mechanisms that shape the behavior of organizations and individuals in society—do not effectively promote technology in Latin America. Poor regulatory quality, weak rule of law, corruption, and ineffective governance contribute to the widening productivity gap between Latin America and the rest of the world.[42] The capabilities of governments to promote technological change are limited not only by financing but also by effective governance. Unfortunately, the challenge of technological development was beyond the capabilities of most states, and most nations in Latin America fell further and further behind in the global arena. The private sector has not risen to fill the technology gap. Incentives must be changed to promote technological change in the region.

Given fiscal constraints, states must focus more on structuring incentives for private-sector investment in technology rather than directly investing in technology. Tax incentives favorable to R&D and strong laws protecting intellectual property rights are crucial in promoting a business environment conducive to the development of a science and technology infrastructure. Regulatory frameworks to encourage firms to finance and undertake more R&D must be designed. The state can also act as an arbiter of information, disseminating information about best practices. Box 9.3 illustrates the way Uruguay's agriculture ministry helped improve farming techniques. It might also work to promote dynamic cooperation among research communities, universities, and the private sector. Collaboration can maximize the use of scarce resources. The state can work directly to redirect public resources in education to improve the quality of human capital. It can take a leadership role in monitoring and assessing the national stock of technological assets.

Attention should be paid to the gender implications of investments in infrastructure and science and technology education. Gender-aware planning in infrastructure might take the location of housing, workplaces, and nurseries into account; it would pay attention to peak and off-peak transportation networks.[43] Good science and engineering indicators are crucial to informed adjustments in science and technology policy.[44] State promotion of investments in science and technology may help transform the problems of economies of scale and limited time horizons that firms face in allocating resources to technological activity. By adjusting incentives, risk may be minimized for these investments, which tend to have uncertain long-term payoffs.

Clearly, with limited resources in the area, incentives toward public-private partnerships might allow for exploitation of economies of scale in technological innovation and adaptation. Costa Rica stands out as an example of a country that has made the transition from a resource-based economy to one that sees itself as pursuing development through technology. The country views "software as the coffee of the new millennium."[45] There are approximately 150 firms in an information technology cluster supporting banking and finance, human resources, health, education artificial intelligence, data migration, communications, tourism, and management. Half these firm export regularly; nearly 85 percent have used the external sector as a means to expand their markets. In addition, multinationals such

Box 9.3. Just-in-Time Fruit: Technology Makes the Difference for Award-Winning Apple Growers in Uruguay

BY CHRISTINA MacCULLOCH

When Felipe Reyes and Osvaldo Moizo formed a partnership in the early 1980s to grow apples and pears in the Melilla region near the Uruguayan capital of Montevideo, they never imagined that they would have to compete with producers around the world.

But with the 1990s came the new era of open markets, when even medium-scale farmers like Reyes and Moizo would have to keep up with the latest technical innovations and consumer demands. If their 39-hectare farm, called Zanja Honda, were to succeed, they would have to learn about the best crop varieties and the latest production systems, and search out buyers at home and abroad.

Luckily, one of the world's premier fruit producing countries was practically next door, so Reyes and Moizo traveled to Chile on a fact-finding mission. Back home they applied what they learned with such success that their operation caught the attention of officials in Uruguay's Ministry of Agriculture who were running a new initiative called the Program for Farm Conversion and Development (PREDEG). The IDB-financed program was established to provide technical assistance and marketing support to small- and medium-size farms, such as Zanja Honda, as well as to agroindustries and nurseries.

That same year, PREDEG awarded Reyes and Moizo a prize for innovation and quality, particularly citing their success in integrating production and marketing. "These producers stand out for their technological capabilities as well as for their business management," declared Carlos Sammarco, PREDEG chief, at the awards ceremony.

Encouraged, Reyes and Moizo set out to change over from the traditional orchards to high-density plantings with quick-growing, early-ripening varieties that would result in higher yields and less damaged fruit. With financing from PREDEG, Reyes and Moizo traveled to Italy, France and Spain to learn about new fruit varieties with the best flavor, color and texture, and get a feel for potential markets. "The trip marked the starting point for a new approach to raising fruit, a trip to the future," recalled Reyes. "The fruit producer of the future is the person who can rapidly adapt to change with new varieties and cutting-edge production systems. It is the only way," he added.

Soon, the two partners had joined a group of other Uruguayan farmers to import 12,000 Australian hybrid apple plants from a supplier in Brazil. Called "Pink Lady," the crisp, flavorful new variety was specifically developed for high-density planting and early maturity.

"Things are changing so fast that in two years we won't have any fruit trees left that we had when we won the PREDEG prize," said Reyes. The full-size apple trees used in years past were spaced the traditional distance apart and would begin producing fruit after five years at the rate of 15 boxes per tree. With the new variety, 15 small, early-maturing trees are planted in the same space that would have been taken by a single tree in the previous production system. Each new tree produces one box of fruit at much lower cost and higher quality in a shorter period of time.

"It is incredible, but the apples that I have on my table today are the first fruit from a tree we planted three months ago," said Reyes. But while the Pink Lady variety is well received by growers and consumers alike, it comes with strings attached. Royalties must be paid to the Australian Ministry of Agriculture for each tree purchased. Further payments must go to the Pear and Apple Export Association of Australia for each apple sold. But by using the latest varieties and production systems, Reyes and Moizo have met the competitive challenge.

The PREDEG program that helped Reyes and Moizo to compete came at a crucial moment for Uruguay. "Our farm sector was lagging," said Sammarco, "and after our domestic producers lost tariff protection, they became vulnerable to competition, particularly from neighboring countries."

PREDEG currently works with some 3,000 farmers organized into 260 producers' groups along with 900 individual fruit producers. It provides the farmers with training and cofinances innovative operations, such as the establishment of new plantings and drip irrigation systems. The program also provides technical assistance and marketing support to some 30 agroindustrial firms and commercial agents and 25 nurseries. In a pilot program that now includes some 200 producers, PREDEG is helping farmers to reduce the use of agrochemicals by introducing alternative disease-control methods.

For more information, contact PREDEG at PREDEG@adinet.com.uy or choose Rural Development under www.iadb.org/sds.

Source: www.iadb.org/idbamerica/Archive/stories/2000/eng/APR00E/e400f5.htm, March–April 2000.

---

as Motorola, Conair, and Sylvania had established plants in the Costa Rican free assembly zone. The sector, dominated by local capital, traces its success back to government initiatives in the 1960s and 1970s that transformed the environment for information technologies. Eliminating debilitating 133 percent taxes on personal computers created the demand for Spanish-language software applications for new imported hardware. The Costa Rican government also invested in two public universities to promote the development of human capital. The centers at the University of Costa Rica as well as the Instituto Tecnológico de Costa Rica created clear rivalry to build computer departments. It also developed a new institution named CENFOTEC, a technical school that didn't duplicate the four-year degree but rather worked with industry to train workers to address the local skills deficit. The people engaged in software development were all at university together; they continue this network at the Costa Rican Chamber of Information and Communication Technologies, a private, not-for-profit business association.

The IADB and the private Costa Rican Foundation in concert with the UN and the United States Agency for International Development promoted computer literacy at the elementary level. Costa Rica supports a science and technology program that funded 239 postgraduate fellowships, many of whose recipients are currently teaching in Costa Rican technical institutions. Such investment in technology was not cheap; Costa Rica leveraged its funds with external financing from the IADB as well as the Canadian Initiative for Industrial Competitiveness in Costa Rica.[46] Partnerships between public institutions and business encouraged firms to develop innovative applications that were not only appropriate for the client but could also be sold externally. Firms were also supported by the Costa Rican trade promotion agency Procomer's "Creating Exporters" program which helped firms with the processes and the search costs of identifying international clients. With more available venture capital as well, firms such as Word Magic Software, a translation software company, have become market leaders in English-Spanish language communications.

Costa Rica's success in building upon this cluster of dynamic firms connected to Intel's 1996 investment in a microprocessor plant; this decision was a function of an ample supply of well-educated workers across the technical, maintenance, engineering, and management levels. As a small country, Costa Rica decided early on to focus on a limited number of technologies: information systems, environmental sciences, and the agricultural and forestry sectors. It has transformed these narrowly defined investments into international comparative advantage in these fields. It has done a good job of balancing investments at the levels of both basic and higher education. In addition to the software sector, Costa Rica has also been aggressive in assisting its firms in financing innovation in other value-added products. Banquete, a food producer, built upon the country's global reputation as a tropical paradise to launch a line of specialized hot sauces in varieties of tropical fruit. Its experience in developing this product line underscored that success wasn't contingent on the acquisition of the physical capital—machines could be purchased at trade shows—but rather on the tacit knowledge involved in innovative product design and international marketing. Costa Rica is seen as an example of the gains of smart, modest investments in the technological arena generating long-term rewards.[47] Box 9.4 provides another successful case of technological development in Brazil. Innovative institutional arrangements supported by strategic financing can promote dynamic technological development in the region.

INFRASTRUCTURE: A CRITICAL COMPLEMENTARY INPUT

Infrastructure is critical to smoothly functioning markets. If you are the most productive coffee farmer or producer of electronic keyboards, it hardly matters if you can't get your goods to market. Given its proximity to the huge U.S. market, Central America, for example, should have a greater geographic advantage in trade than it does; it is blocked from its potential by weak infrastructure linking productive facilities to the world.[48] In addition, intraregional integration is terrible, precluding a vibrant expansion of trade in the Central American Common Market. The weak infrastructure that exists is highly vulnerable to natural disasters of heavy rains, hurricanes, swampy soils, earthquakes, volcanic eruptions, and deforestation. The region historically has responded to destruction after the event—rather than preventative shoring up of areas of extreme vulnerability. In addition to weak technological systems, Latin America faces an infrastructure gap that undermines gains in productivity. Underinvestment, particularly during the 1980s and the debt crisis, led to a need for $60 billion annually in injections in telecommunications, roads, and ports.[49] Latin America spends less that 2 percent of gross domestic product on infrastructure; it needs to invest 4–5 percent simply to keep it on par with countries such as China or the Republic of Korea, countries with which it used to share similar standards. Indeed, if infrastructure in Latin America were brought to Korean standards, it would add 1.4 to 1.8 percentage points to growth a year.

Infrastructure development in Latin America confronts an unfriendly geography. Although long coastlines are a plus, high mountains, dense jungles, dry deserts, and isolated urban centers pose enormous challenges. International rankings of trans-

Box 9.4.   A Scientifc Success Story: Strategic Research Investments in São Paulo

FAPESP, the scientific and research institute of the State of São Paulo, is setting new standards for research in the Third World. The number of citations by Brazilian scientists has grown at three times the global level since 1996, and the institute has been instrumental in promoting a world-class biotechnology industry that has been the first anywhere to decode the genome of a plant pathogen that infests oranges and other citrus fruits. The goal of the institute is to work on the frontier of science—but science with direct social and economic relevance for Brazil. Success has led to international cooperation—including a request from the U.S. Department of Agriculture for work on the sequencing of a gene of a bacterium that afflicts vineyards in California.

What has made FAPESP successful? Funding, autonomy, and strong linkages to the university and the business community are keys to its accomplishments. By law, since 1962, the State of São Paulo allocates 1 percent of total tax revenues to FAPESP to fund scientific and technological research. A quick scan of its website shows the range of projects funded. But FAPESP has few staff. Law prohibits it from assembling its own corps of scientists; instead, it must work through university and commercial labs. Research grants and fellowships strategically target the development of young scientists and new projects. Its administrative costs are limited to 5 percent of its investment in research, and governance is through a twelve-member board with fixed terms. This virtual institute identifies opportunities—and expects accountability. It avoids the brain drain problem of many developing countries by requiring that scientific grantees return to teach in the university for at least four years—or pay back the salary earned. Unlike research in industrial countries, the model among the scientists is more cooperative as opposed to competitive. Although competition among multiple-funded groups may create rapid results, it is not seen as the best use of very limited resources. Private industry is a research partner; for example, it shares the costs in a project to sequence the genomes of the eucalyptus tree, which is cultivated by the paper and cellulose industry.

The approach appears to be working, generating research with a practical return relevant to the Brazilian economy. This niche, often ignored by research institutions in industrialized countries, creates dollars and hope. FAPESP is currently working on a program to identify the genes of the worm that causes a parasitic infection that afflicts millions around the world. The hope is that this research—and other projects—will lead to the development of drugs targeted at tropical diseases such as malaria and Chagas. Given FAPESP's record, success is more than a dream.

Source: Larry Rohter, "Model for Research Rises in a Third World City," *New York Times,* April 24, 2001; and FAPESP's web site, watson.fapesp.br/begin01.htm.

portation infrastructure place Latin America in the bottom seventy-fifth percentile. A movement from the bottom to the top quarter is the equivalent of a reduction of 9,000 miles measured in transportation costs. Traversing the Andes between Santiago and Buenos Aires is equivalent to nearly quadrupling the distance from 1,129 to 4,700 kilometers; transport costs rise as a function of closed passages in winter and the costs of driving at high altitudes. Trucks must detour about 1,500 miles around the Argentine pampas in the worst of winter. The Amazon consumes infrastructure. Intense rains wash out roads; only 30 percent of the jungle roads in which Peru invested in 1980 remain paved today. Overall, the ratio of paved roads in the

Poor roads and mountains such as these in San Jose, Bolivia, create obstacles to transportation. *(Courtesy of David Edelstein)*

region is the lowest in the world, at just 20.2 percent and 13.9 percent for Central America. The global average is 55.3 percent; in the EU 99 percent of the roads are paved.[50] The accompanying photo in this chapter shows just how tough road conditions are in Latin America. For anyone who has traveled in the region, poor roads are an obvious impediment. Only 13.9 percent of roads in Central America are paved; the road density network in Latin America is only one-fourth of U.S. and one-sixth of EU systems. Road systems fail to comply with basic standards for safe and effective traffic patterns. Only 26 percent of the main road network complies with legally required road width; 84 percent of broad secondary networks don't meet standard requirements. Maintenance is unsatisfactory, in part because funding for maintenance has not been prioritized in road-building projects. There is a strong need for self-funding maintenance programs.[51]

El Salvador's road maintenance initiative provides an interesting success story in improving the dismal state of road conditions.[52] Frustrated by the old highway maintenance administration from a bureaucracy of eight thousand employees who inefficiently tried to fix roads, El Salvador created a new agency called FOVIAL, or the Road Conservation Fund. The old ministry was closed down. Workers were given generous severance packages and training in creating their own small businesses in road maintenance, promoting a win-win situation where unemployed workers could be made better off. Created by a twenty-cent (U.S.) tax on gasoline, FOVIAL performs all road maintenance by subcontracting. The organization only has forty-seven employees in charge of planning, proposals, bid execution, and monitoring, leaving 98 percent of the budget to actually fix the roads. Transparency is ensured by audit not only through the government's internal agency but also through scrutiny by NGOs. It shares financial information on its website, and bids are accepted in open-air meetings covered by reporters as well as live Internet access. Contractor performance evaluations create incentives for compliance to contracts if the firm hopes to secure future work, and contractors can be fined for unfixed potholes, rubbish, or unsafe procedures. In the three years since FOVIAL began operation, virtually all major highways have been resurfaced, the huge backlog of repairs has been eliminated, and regular maintenance is being performed.

In addition to inadequate roads throughout the region, railroad infrastructure was designed for requirements at the beginning of the twentieth century—not the global market of the new millennium. Regional integration requires a change in the institutional framework to encourage a long-term vision and promote technical cooperation among countries. Inefficient and lengthy customs and border requirements impede the smooth flow of goods, adding to high operating costs for users. Passenger and cargo regulations overregulate transport of passengers but undersupervise cargo transport. Poor technical expertise, credit limitations, lack of contractual liability, and poor social security benefits compound problems in the rail sector. Marine transport and ports are rendered less efficient by technical problems with fairway depth and the poor availability of equipment to load and unload. Again, the problems are not all with the physical machinery. Given poor roads, travel by sea is the preferred transport mode. Yet the potential of rivers for intra-Latin trade is underrealized due to poorly connected river basins. Latin America has some of the most inefficient ports in the world, better only than South Asia and West Africa. One index of port efficiency places Europe at 5.41 and Latin America at a weak 3.37. Yet Latin ports charge almost twice as much for this poor handling service. Central America's proximity to the huge North American market confers advantage; nevertheless, delays equal to 40 percent of travel time add to costs. In Ecuador it takes 16.4 days to clear customs. Poor customs procedures, lack of electronic data processing, lack of coordination at crossings, confusing documentation, and poorly trained personnel impede trade. Good port performance in Latin America is possible—Chile and Costa Rica, for example, already achieve fast clearing rates to facilitate their export focus.

Investments in infrastructure can support economic growth, reduce poverty, and make development environmentally sustainable.[53] In considering reforms in infrastructure, three policy guidelines emerge: infrastructure should be managed like a business, not a bureaucracy; competition should be introduced; and stakeholders should have a strong voice and real responsibility.[54] In infrastructure reform there is a clear need for a public-private partnership. Profit opportunities create incentives for private participation to increase productivity and reduce costs. But incentives from the public sector are critical in reducing risks that make private-sector activity alone prohibitive.

Throughout the world, public-sector services no longer need to be conceived of

Better roads will facilitate bringing goods to market for peasant farmers. *(Courtesy of David Mangurian and the Inter-American Development Bank)*

as natural monopolies. Revolutions in telecommunications and in provision of electrical and energy services have made a smaller scale possible. Natural monopolies can be opened to the forces of competition, unbundling portions of the service or breaking up service areas geographically. Clearly, this must be done with an eye to equity. Profit-oriented telecoms, not surprisingly, are more interested in servicing high-priced business areas than low-income neighborhoods or rural sectors. Private activity in one area may need to subsidize access for all.[55]

Current shortcomings in transportation that result in high operating costs include limited capacity, poor conditions, and lack of maintenance for roads, airports, railways, and ports.[56] But the problem isn't purely one of physical infrastructure. A key constraint is access to funding. Given the long-term nature and the difficulty, in certain situations, of having users pay for the goods, infrastructure finance usually involves a strong state role. Restrictions in the access to public funding provided by international financial institutions make infrastructure investment in the region problematic. To create the appropriate incentives for infrastructure investment, changes are required in the legal and regulatory framework. Finally, new organizations bridging the public and private sector may be required to build infrastructure deficits. For example, Brazil has changed legislation under its new Public-Private Partnership initiative to allow private providers of port services (under lease agreement with the state) to collect fees—a prohibited activity under prior legislation.

Hydroelectric plant. *(Courtesy of the Inter-American Development Bank)*

In the power and gas sector, population concentrations in urban areas make private investment lucrative. Indeed, Latin America has become a leader in electricity infrastructure privatization. Brazil, Argentina, and Colombia lead the list of developing countries in terms of private investments in the electricity sector. Cost savings are significant. In Bogota, Colombia, the private CODENSA electricity distribution company halved its losses from 24 percent to 12.5 percent, increased customers per employee from eight hundred to nineteen hundred, and reduced the frequency of service disruption 30 percent within two and half years.[57] But other countries such as Mexico and Venezuela have been resistant to privatization and foreign participation in national electricity production.

In transport, possibilities for private road concessions and maintenance are being pursued. In water and waste, public municipalities are accepting bids for lease contracts to private services. However, state activity is critical in providing technical and financial assistance to the solid waste and wastewater disposal firms.

Latin America's information and communications technology (ICT) infrastructure is underdeveloped. This is probably not surprising. Industrial countries roughly spend twenty-five hundred dollars per capita on ICT; in Latin America, where average per capita income is thirty-three hundred dollars, this would mean spending 75 percent of income on information technologies—as opposed to food, housing, or health.[58] Although information and knowledge are considered public goods, the

Table 9.6. ICT in Latin America

	2004 Fixed Line and Mobile Phone Subscribers (per 1,000 people)	2004 Mobile Phone Subscribers (per 1,000 people)	2003–2004 Population Covered by Mobile Telephony (%)	2004 Information and Communication Technology Expenditure (% of GDP)	2004 Information and Communication Technology Expenditure per Capita (US$)	2004 Internet Users	2005 Secure Internet Servers (per 1 million people)	2002–2004 Broadband Subscribers (per 1,000 people)	2004 Personal Computers (per 1,000 people)	2003 Schools Connected to the Internet (%)
Argentina	579	352	95	6	224	5,120,000	11	13	96	..
Bolivia	269	200	60	6	55	350,000	2	..	36	..
Brazil	587	357	68	6	208	22,000,000	14	12	105	50
Chile	799	593	99	6	340	4,300,000	21	30	133	62
Colombia	427	232	74	8	180	3,585,688	4	3	67	50
Costa Rica	533	217	..	8	337	1,000,000	62	..	238	15
Ecuador	472	348	88	4	83	624,579	4	..	56	..
El Salvador	402	271	86	..	..	587,475	5	3	44	..
Guatemala	350	258	78	..	..	756,000	6	..	19	..
Honduras	153	100	49	5	49	222,273	4	..	16	..
Mexico	545	370	86	3	196	14,036,475	8	3	108	60
Nicaragua	177	137	48	..	..	125,000	2	..	37	..
Panama	388	270	87	9	400	300,000	56	6	41	..
Paraguay	344	294	60	..	..	150,000	1	..	59	..
Peru	223	148	75	7	166	3,220,000	5	8	98	..
United States	1,223	617	95	9	3,595	185,000,000	783	129	749	99
Uruguay	465	174	99	7	259	680,000	26	3	125	50
Venezuela, RB	450	322	90	4	189	2,312,683	5	8	82	..

Source: World Development Indicators database, www.worldbank.org.
Definition: Information and communications technology expenditures include computer hardware (computers, storage devices, printers, and other peripherals); computer software (operating systems, programming tools, utilities, applications, and internal software development); computer services (information technology consulting, computer and network systems integration, Web hosting, data processing services, and other services); and communications services (voice and data communications services) and wired and wireless communications equipment.

ability to access these is increasingly tied to hardware, network infrastructure, and software—which have a private cost. Economies of scale define networks, there is a high degree of uncertainty tied to investments, and the need for strong legal and regulatory frameworks to ensure ongoing outlays. Finally, a critical aspect of ICT policy in Latin America is not only the digital divide between rich and poor countries but also the important challenge of promoting social inclusion within countries. Clearly, the wealthy elite in Latin America have the latest in computing and information technologies; it is the large majority of low- and middle-class families who would most benefit from this productivity boost.

As shown in table 9.6, only Chile has half as many phone lines per one thousand people as the United States. The expansion of mobile telephony has improved this number, as mobile phone systems are easier to install in cities than running fixed lines through overcrowded slums; they cost 50 percent less than the equivalent fixed line segment. In addition, mobile phones better suit the payment abilities of the poor, allowing the possibility of pay-as-you-use card systems that can be purchased at kiosks as opposed to the more complicated monthly billing for service rendered in areas where informal housing may mean no fixed address. Access to phones is critically important in securing and maintaining a job. Think about your own process of landing a summer job or internship—or the difficulty of calling in when you are sick—without access to a phone. Mobile phones also have a public safety use; hurricane and disaster warning systems to alert populations will be enhanced with stronger connectivity. Of course, mobile phones are less functional in dispersed or rugged rural areas—as any drive through a mountainous zone in the United States will confirm.

The Internet is another powerful accelerator of growth and productivity. As a medium for information and exchange, it enlarges markets and minds. Although efforts have been made to connect schools to the Internet, providing expanded access to content and online courses, progress is uneven. In eight countries for which data is available, the number of public access centers sponsored by governments increased from fifty in 1996, to forty-nine hundred in 2001, to six thousand in 2002, and to ten thousand between 2003 and 2004.[59] A key problem is annual maintenance costs of information technology systems, sometimes exceeding the initial capital investment. In the poorest countries the number of personal computers is low, and access to fast broadband services (most effective for business) is extremely weak in all countries with the exception of Chile. A new initiative by Microsoft enhances access to computers at the bottom of the economic pyramid—a key contributor to incorporating the marginalized into the modern economy. This is an interesting example of using innovative market mechanisms to attend to a social need while also making money. Nonetheless, to address the huge digital divide both between and within countries, it is likely that the market alone will reinforce existing social gaps and amplify social exclusion.[60]

Public-private partnerships in infrastructure are beginning to provide lessons of how complementary efforts can enhance productivity. In Argentina, with the privatization of the telephone company Entel into two firms, phone service requests can now be met in forty-eight hours, as compared to the five- to ten-year waits common in the 1980s. Overall, privatization has increased the number of main line and mobile phones by about 7 percent and decreased waiting lists for service by 60 percent.[61] But consumers have new complaints: high prices. The cost of local telephone service has risen by about 14 percent. One estimate suggests that consumers are overpaying by about $1 billion per year—with excess profits going into the coffers of Telecom and Telefónica owners in Italy, Spain, and France. Those at the bottom of the market are closed out by an affordability gap. In Brazil the prices of electricity, telephone, and water rose by more than double the increase in general prices from 1995 to 2001.[62] As discussed in private monopolies may need regulation or the introduction of competition policies to restrict price gouging.[63]

There are, unfortunately, unintended consequences to privatization. Private provision of services may be uneconomical in geographically disperse regions. Imagine the cost and difficulty of stringing utility lines in the Amazon. Rural inhabitants are more likely to see their service remain under public ownership, given the higher costs of servicing remote areas. In urban centers, market concentration by a few firms has worked against price decreases. Monopoly rents are accruing to private agents, often based in other nations. Blackouts in Brazil and Chile have raised questions about security of supply and who is ultimately responsible for the delivery of this critical input. Regulatory policies are incomplete at best due to lack of transparency and bureaucratic complication.[64]

The private sector alone may not work; the case of Mexican roads is illustrative. In Mexico, thirty-six hundred miles of highways were built from 1988 to 1994 at a cost of $15 billion. These high costs resulted in government bailouts of forty-eight out of the fifty-two concessions granted.[65] Outrageous tolls scared away traffic, making cost recovery problematic. The tolls from Mexico City to Acapulco were a whopping $63! The government stepped in, cutting average tariffs by 60 percent. In part the lesson of Mexican road concessions concerned the short time frame. Given contract periods of between ten and fifteen years, firms were attempting to recover costs too quickly with exorbitant prices. A longer concession period reduces these pressures, making the concessions more profitable.

Brazilians are looking for productivity gains in the privatization of Telebrás, Brazil's huge telecommunications firm. Telebrás was created as a state enterprise in 1972 under the Ministry of Communications. Although its initial stages registered strong growth, as measured by a 16 percent increase in access lines and a 26 percent fall in the congestion rate, the period of the debt crisis brought underinvestment and dismal performance. It was reorganized in the early 1990s, positioning it for privatization in 1998. International bidders were attracted by the unmet potential of the Brazilian market. As the world's fifth most-populous nation, Brazil had a two-year waiting list for phones in some areas. The total sale—which was split among eight groups of investors paying more than $19 billion—was roughly 13 percent larger than London's privatization of British Telecom in the early 1990s.[66] Competition was later encouraged, initially regulating prices but then moving to free prices as more firms are established in the market. Seven companies, including international capital, now participate in the market: AmeriMovil, Telefonos de Mexico, Telemar, Telesp, Brasil Telecom, Embratel, and Vivo. One benefit of late investments in the industry is the ability to leapfrog over existing technologies to develop a low-cost, high-productivity sector.[67] The market has divided into three segments: fixed line, where growth is rather slow; mobile services, which are booming; and Internet providers. The mobile phone market has grown from 2.7 million users in 1996 to 23.2 million in 2000, now reaching 58 million of Brazil's 187 million residents in 2005. In the Internet sector, Brazil is likely to have 40 million users by the end of 2008, up from 15 million in 2001. Forty percent of the population has access to the Internet through innovations such as placing kiosks in the post office. Seventy-two percent of federal services, including tax filing, procedures for court cases, distance learning, and elementary education registration, are online. The ample provision of statistics on government and economic performance is creating greater transparency and accountability. Info-tech productivity—enhancing the performance of labor, infrastructure, and industry—is clearly the key to raising living standards in the region.

The Business Environment: The Emerging Shape of the Latin American Industrial Sector

Macroinstability and the contractionary effects of the debt crisis had a profound impact on industrial performance in Latin America. High rates of inflation and associated uncertainty thwarted long-term strategic decision making and investments in the capital stock. Capital formation was stalled by the lack of available finance. Survival depended on financial ingenuity, not investments in plant and equipment. During this period, dramatic changes in information technologies transformed the frontiers of business practice, largely leaving Latin American firms behind. The technological lag in automated production and in new inventory systems set firms at a competitive disadvantage. Sluggish domestic demand forced a new orientation toward the export sector as opposed to production for the domestic market, but the focus was on agriculture and natural resource-based products, not higher value-added technological gems. Industries that process raw materials have been more successful than those relying on labor or engineering services. Trade liberalization and associated import competition have had negative effects on textiles, footwear, and the metal and machinery branches.[68] Small and medium-sized enterprises were hard hit, in part because of difficulties in securing bank guarantees critical to exports. Some weathered the crisis by becoming subcontractors to large transnational firms. One study suggests that in the manufacturing sector, the expected dynamic results of liberalization have been muted. As demonstrated at the beginning of the chapter, lagging institutional environments for business—large bureaucracies creating delays in registering businesses—create inefficiencies. Insertion into the international economy as a competitive exporter not only involves sound macroeconomic policies and the change toward export orientation but also depends upon institutional change in domestic markets for labor, technology, and infrastructure.

We began our chapter by presenting in table 9.1 the composite indexes reflecting weakness in the business environment. Table 9.7 and figure 9.1 present additional details on the challenges of doing business in the region. Using the United

Table 9.7.   The Business Environment in Latin America

	2005 Time to Resolve Insolvency (years)	2005 Time to Prepare and Pay Taxes (hours)	2005 Time Required to Start a Business (days)	2005 Time Required to Register Property (days)	2005 Time Required to Enforce a Contract (days)
Argentina	3	580	32	44	520
Bolivia	2	1,080	50	92	591
Brazil	10	2,600	152	47	546
Chile	6	432	27	31	305
Colombia	3	432	43	23	363
Costa Rica	4	402	77	21	550
Ecuador	4	600	69	21	388
El Salvador	4	224	40	52	275
Guatemala	4	260	39	69	1,459
Honduras	4	424	62	36	545
Mexico	2	536	58	74	421
Nicaragua	2	240	42	65	155
Panama	2	424	19	44	355
Paraguay	4	328	74	48	285
Peru	3	424	102	33	381
United States	2	325	5	12	250
Uruguay	2	300	45	66	620
Venezuela, RB	4	864	116	33	445

Source: World Development Indicators database, www.worldbank.org.
Definition: The rigidity of employment index measures the regulation of employment, specifically the hiring and firing of workers and the rigidity of working hours. This index is the average of three sub-indexes: a difficulty of hiring index, a rigidity of hours index, and a difficulty of firing index. The index ranges from 0 to 100, with higher values indicating more rigid regulations.

States as a benchmark in table 9.7, you can see the difficulty that an entrepreneur faces in starting and running a business in the region. Rather than focus on issues of productivity or technology generation, managers' attention is often dragged toward resolving bureaucratic red tape. In addition to regulations and rigidity, managers also must confront social and political problems of corruption, crime, and policy uncertainty that weigh down competitiveness in the region. Given these obstacles, it is perhaps surprising that businesses perform as well as they do. Firms such as Embraer in Brazil or Cemex in Mexico demonstrate the ability to contest the international market. Embraer has become a global leader in the export of medium-range aircraft; Cemex is truly multinational in the production and distribution of cement. Both show that strong technological systems adapted to local markets can create success. Imagine the productivity and creativity within the Latin American business sector if these constraints were reduced!

2005 Time Required to Build a Warehouse (days)	2005 Cost of Business Start-Up Procedures (% of GNI per capita)	2005 Financial Information Infrastructure Index (0 = less developed to 10 = more developed)	2002–2004 Management Time Dealing with Officials (% of management time)	2005 Rigidity of Employment Index (0 = less rigid to 100 = more rigid)	2005 Business Disclosure Index (0 = less disclosure to 7= more disclosure)
288	13	8	..	48	7
187	155	6	..	40	1
460	10	4	9	56	5
191	10	7	..	24	8
150	25	7	..	57	7
120	24	7	..	39	2
149	38	..	18	58	1
144	118	6	9	41	6
294	58	7	17	40	1
199	64	6	14	34	1
222	16	8	..	51	6
192	139	4	17	47	4
128	25	9	..	63	3
273	148	..	..	59	6
201	38	8	..	48	7
70	1	..	..	3	7
146	44	6	..	31	3
276	16	5	..	38	3

Figure 9.1.   Survey of Managers' Complaints about the Business Environment in Latin America

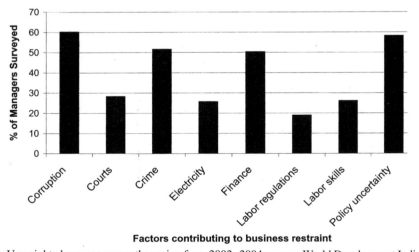

Source: Unweighted average across the region from 2002–2004 surveys World Development Indicators.

Key   Concepts

Business Competitiveness
  Index
Global Competitiveness
  Index

Growth Competitiveness
  Index
labor market distortions

labor productivity
precarious employment

Chapter   Summary

Microfoundations for Growth Are Weak in Latin America

- The competitiveness indices rank the competitiveness of the countries in
  relation to growth, business, and other factors. The Growth Competitiveness Index ranks the quality of the macroeconomic environment, the state of
  the country's public institutions, and the level of technological readiness. The
  Business Competitiveness Index has four interrelated areas: factor input conditions, the context for firm strategy and rivalry, the quality of local demand
  conditions, and the presence of related and supporting industries. The Global
  Competitiveness Index suggests three levels of growth: improvement on
  basic development indicators, increasing efficiency, and business sophistication. However, indexes should be carefully analyzed because of differences
  in data collection.
- Productivity in Latin America is low because of the lack of good institutions;
  capital accumulation alone does not explain the slow speed of growth. Labor
  productivity lags due to the lack of natural and physical capital and weak
  investment in technology. Latin American productivity is roughly the same as
  in the early 1990s, accounting for much of the poverty in the region. Although
  Chile, Mexico, Uruguay, and Costa Rica have reasonable or strong growth in
  productivity, for the majority of the region anemic or even negative productivity growth dominates. Reversing this trend is critical, as per capita productivity growth is essential to making all Latin Americans better off.

Labor Market Rigidities and Unemployment Constrain Growth

- The unemployment problem in Latin America is probably underestimated
  in the official unemployment statistics, given the difficulty in measuring
  those workers who are actively searching for jobs. Furthermore, the weak unemployment safety nets cause workers to take jobs for which they are overqualified. Increasing numbers of women and youth entering the labor force
  increase the need for faster growth to incorporate these new workers.
- Historically, strict labor legislation created a rigid labor market, with high
  social taxes on labor. Higher mandatory job security provisions undermine

cheap labor advantages. The informal sector serves as a safety net for unskilled workers and avoids costly compliance to regulations. The informal sector also acts as a main source of jobs. This sector is divided into three areas: micro-enterprise employment, own-account workers, and domestic service. However, it tends to be a low-productivity sector because of its capital-poor definition, dragging the overall productivity growth.

- Labor market regulation and oversight are falling; remuneration and collective organization of workers are also declining.

Weak Investments in Technology Constrain Enhancing Competitiveness

- Latin America is weak on technological innovation as compared to the developed world. Latin America traditionally has had a fractured capacity for R&D because universities, research institutions, and businesses do not interact. The public sector accounts for an extremely large portion of the funding for research that is normally focused in basic science as opposed to industrial applications, where innovation can enhance productivity. Rather than a direct investment role, state institutions might rethink incentives for technological development, promoting investment and training workers for new global realities.

Infrastructure Gaps Reduce the Capacity for Growth

- Infrastructure in Latin America was underdeveloped in the 1980s. The harsh environment of Latin America creates challenges for the construction of infrastructure. Public private partnerships (PPPs) can enhance productivity with private investment and knowledge. Also, privatization in many sectors has improved the service; nonetheless, private monopolies need stronger regulation to avoid overpricing. Services in uneconomical areas might still be provided or subsidized by the government to attend to the populations in distant rural areas. The privatization of companies can provide a low cost and high productivity by easier acquisition of technology, but the social risks of privatization require careful policy initiatives.

Uncertainty in the Business Environment Retards Investment and Growth

- The crisis of the 1980s led to a reduction in long-term capital investment, leaving Latin American businesses lagging behind. Growth and investment in technology and infrastructure require robust institutions. Bureaucracy, corruption, crime, and policy uncertainty rather than technology or productivity are consistently in the managers' agendas. Institutional reform is required to improve the long-term growth potential of the region.

Notes

1. Daron Acemoglu, Simon Johnson, and James Robinson, "Institutions as the Fundamental Cause of Long-Run Growth," in *Handbook of Economic Growth,* ed. Philippe Aghion and Steven Durlauf (Amsterdam: Elsevier, 2005), chap. 6, accessed at elsa.berkeley.edu/~chad/Handbook.html.

2. Michael E. Porter, Klaus Schwab, and Augusto Lopez-Claros, *The Global Competitiveness Report 2005–2006: Policies Underpinning Rising Prosperity* (New York: World Economic Forum held by WEF at Geneva, Switzerland, published by Palgrave Macmillan, 2005).

3. See, for example, the important article by Sanjaya Lall, "Competitiveness Indices and Developing Countries: An Economic Evaluation of the Global Competitiveness Report," *World Development* 29(9) (September 2001): 1501–1525.

4. Mario A. Gutierrez, "Economic Growth in Latin America: The Role of Investment and Other Growth Souces," United Nations Economic Commission for Latin America and the Caribbean, Santiego, Chile, CEPAL, Economic Development Division, June 2005.

5. Richard Tardanico and Rafel Menjívar Larrín, "Restructuring, Employment and Social Inequality: Comparative Urban Latin American Patterns" in *Global Restructuring, Employment and Social Inequality in Urban Latin America,* ed. Richard Tardanico and Rafel Menjívar Larraín (Miami: University of Miami North-South Center Press, 1977), 244.

6. "Creating Jobs Is Main Headache," *Latin American Weekly Report,* January 5, 1999, 2.

7. Tardanico and Larín, "Restructuring, Employment and Social Inequality," 252.

8. Laís Abramo and María Elena Valenzuela, "Women's Labour Force Participation Rates in Latin America," *International Labour Review* 144(4) (2005): 369–399.

9. Population Reference Bureau, *World Population Data Sheet 2005,* www.prb.org.

10. World Bank, *Labor and Economic Reforms in Latin America and the Caribbean: Regional Perspectives on World Development* (Washington, D.C.: World Bank, 1995).

11. World Bank, *Labor and Economic Reforms in Latin America,* 253.

12. Psacharopoulos and Tzannatos (1992), as presented by Rosemary Thorp, *Progress, Poverty, and Exclusion: An Economic History of Latin America in the 20th Century* (Baltimore: Johns Hopkins University Press/IADB, 1998), 31.

13. Shahid Javed Burki and Sebastian Edwards, *Latin America after Mexico: Quickening the Pace* (Washington, D.C.: World Bank, 1996), 19.

14. James J. Heckman, Carmen Pages, Working Paper 7773, NBER Working Paper Series, www.nber.org/papers/w7773, June 2000, table 2, Summary of Existing Evidence on the Impact of Job Security in Latin America, 15.

15. Sebastian Edwards and Nora Claudia Lustig, eds., *Labor Markets in Latin America: Combining Social Protection with Market Flexibility* (Washington, D.C.: Brookings Institution, 1997), 32.

16. Burki and Edwards, *Latin America after Mexico,* 20.

17. Victor E. Tokman, "Jobs and Solidarity: Challenges for Post-Adjustment in Latin America," in *Economic and Social Development into the Next Century,* ed. Louis Emmerij (Washington, D.C.: Inter-American Development Bank and John Hopkins University Press).

18. Ibid.

19. IADB, *Latin America after a Decade of Reforms: Economic and Social Progress 1997 Report* (Washington, D.C: Johns Hopkins University Press/IADB, 1997).

20. Inter-American Development Bank, *Competitiveness: The Business of Growth 2001 Report,* Economic and Social Progress in Latin America Series (Washington, D.C.: IADB), 113.

21. World Bank, *Labor and Economic Reforms in Latin America.*

22. Mark Mulligan, "Chile Labour Reform Secures Backing," *Financial Times,* September 5, 2001, Internet edition.

23. ILO, *Key Indicators of the Labour Market (KILM),* 2005, www.ilo.org.

24. Economic Commission for Latin America and the Caribbean (ECLAC), *The Equity Gap: Latin America, the Caribbean and the Social Summit* (Santiago, Chile: ECLAC, December 1997), 60–61.

25. Ibid., 61.

26. Ibid., 66.

27. Vanessa F. Cartaya, "El confuso mundo del sector informal," *Nueva Sociedad Marginalidad* 90 (July–August 1987): 81–84.

28. International Labor Organization home page, usa.ilo.org/news.

29. ECLAC, *The Equity Gap,* 65.

30. International Labor Organization home page, usa.ilo.org/news.

31. ECLAC, *The Equity Gap,* 60.

32. Díaz, cited in Tardanico and Larrín, "Restructuring," 249.

33. Hubert Schmitz and José Cassiolato, *Hi-Tech for Industrial Development: Lessons from the Brazilian Experience in Electronics and Automation* (London: Routledge, 1992), 9.

34. IADB, *The Business of Growth,* 3.

35. Calestous Juma and Lee Yee Cheon, *Innovation: Applying Knowledge in Development,* UN Millennium Task Force on Science, Technology and Innovation, Belfer Center for Science and International Affairs, John F. Kennedy School of Government, 2005.

36. Juma and Cheon, *Innovation,* citing Sagasti.

37. Augusto Lopez-Claros, Latin American Competitiveness Review 2006, World Economic Forum on Latin America, 2006.

38. Andres Rodriguez-Clare, "Innovation and Technology Adoption in Central America," Research Department Working Paper Series No. 525, Inter-American Development Bank, July 2005.

39. RICYT, "El Estado de la Ciencia: Principales Indicadores de Ciencia y Tecnología Iberoamericanos/InterAmericanos 2004," Network on Science and Technology Indicators—Ibero-American and Inter-American—(RICYT), www.ricyt.edu.ar.

40. Mario Cimoli, João Carlos Ferraz, and Annalisa Primi, "Science and Technology Policies in Open Economies: The Case of Latin America and the Caribbean," Productive Development Series, No. 165 (Directors Office) October 2005, www.eclac.cl/.

41. Caroline Moser, "Gender Planning in the Third World: Meeting Practical and Strategic Gender Needs," *World Development* 17(11) (1989): 1799–1825.

42. Lauritz Holm-Nielsen, Michael Crawford, and Alcyone Saliba, *Institutional and Entrepreneurial Leadership in the Brazilian Science and Technology Sector,* World Bank Discussion Paper No. 325 (Washington, D.C.: World Bank, 1996).

43. Case taken from Paul Constance, "A High Technology Incubator," *IDB América* (1997), available at the Inter-American Development Bank home page at www.iadb.org.

44. World Bank, *Meeting the Infrastructure Challenge in Latin America and the Caribbean* (Washington, D.C.: World Bank, 1995), 10–11, gives data on infrastructure deficits.

45. Andres Rodriguez-Clare, "Innovation and Technology Adoption."

46. CAMTIC webpage, www.camtic.org/EN/camtic/proyectos_cooperacion/ICCI_en.phtml.

47. Statistics in this section from Jeffery Sachs and Joaquin Vial, "Can Latin America Compete?" in *Latin American Competitiveness Report* (New York: Oxford University Press, 2002).

48. Ricardo Sanchez and Gordon Wilmsmeier, *Bridging Infrastructural Gaps in Central*

America: Prospects and Potential for Maritime Transport, United Nations, Economic Commission for Latin America and the Caribbean (ECLAC), Serie CEPAL, Recursos Naturales e Infraestructura, No. 97, September 2005.

49. World Bank, *World Development Report 1994* (New York: Oxford University Press/ World Bank, 1994).

50. Infrastructure report on Latin America and the Caribbean. Information on the energy sector is available at www.eia.doe.gov/emeu/cabs/argentina.html.

51. Sanchez and Wilmsmeier, *Bridging Infrastructural Gaps in Central America.*

52. "A Smoother Road," *IDB Americas,* March 2006.

53. World Bank, *Economic Growth and Returns to Work* (Washington, D.C.: World Bank, 1995), 17.

54. IADB, *The Business of Growth,* 166.

55. Ibid., 186.

56. Sanchez and Wilmsmeier, *Bridging Infrastructural Gaps in Central America.*

57. Richard Lapper, "Policy under Pressure," *Financial Times,* October 6, 2002, weekend I.

58. ECLAC, Division of Production, Productivity and Management, "Public Policies for the Development of Information Societies in Latin America and the Caribbean," LC/ W.19 Junio 2005, www.eclac.

59. ECLAC, "Public Policies for the Development of Information Societies in Latin America and the Caribbean."

60. Ibid.

61. Juan Manuel Valcarcel, "Calling Someone in Argentina: Dial M for Monopoly," *Wall Street Journal,* August 16, 1996, A11.

62. IADB, *The Business of Growth,* 166.

63. "Tequila Freeways," *The Economist,* December 16, 1996, 66.

64. Seth Schiesel, "Brazil Sells Most of State Phone Utility," *New York Times,* July 30, 1998, D1.

65. McKinsey Global Institute, *Productivity: The Key to Accelerated Development Path for Brazil 1998,* Telecom Case 9 (São Paulo, Brazil: McKinsey, 1998).

66. José Miguel Benavente, Gustavo Crespi, Jorge Katz, and Giovanni Stumpo, "Changes in the Industrial Development of Latin America," *CEPAL Review* 60 (December 1996): 62.

67. A firm will typically secure a bank letter of credit to finance goods in transit. The bank loans the firm money while the goods are in transit, before they arrive, and are paid for by the importer.

68. Benavente, Crespi, Katz, and Stumpo, "Changes," 63.

RURAL DEVELOPMENT

Sowing the Seeds of Equitable, Sustainable Growth in Latin America

Large-scale farms have increased Mexican agricultural exports. *(Courtesy of the Inter-American Development Bank)*

Due to its unique characteristics, the rural sector presents policymakers with some of the most intractable challenges in development. Agriculture is more than coffee and bananas, wheat or cattle. It is a complex, interrelated set of markets for land, labor, capital, and technology embedded in a socioeconomic web of traditional and corporate farming practices producing for both domestic and international consumption. Successful agriculture must paradoxically meet the need for low-cost national food security as well as provide a sufficient income for rural families. It is increasingly an export engine for developing nations in search of comparative advantage, yet it faces relatively high import barriers to agricultural products in the developed world. Agricultural export drives may strain environmental resources, undermining the future productivity of the sector. Agriculture is full of promise yet requires careful tending to maximize the benefits of socially, environmentally, and economically sustainable growth.

In this chapter we will consider the opportunities and constraints in agricultural development in Latin America. We will explore the following questions:

- What are the characteristics of agricultural markets in Latin America? Do agricultural markets behave differently from other markets? Who are the owners of assets in the agricultural sector, and how do incentives condition performance? How are complementary inputs with respect to infrastructure and transportation provided?
- How have past development strategies shaped agricultural performance in Latin America? What is the legacy of feudal land patterns and/or import substitution industrialization (ISI)?
- What is the impact on rural dwellers of trade liberalization? How has opening up to world export markets affected small- and medium-sized farmers as opposed to the corporate agriculture?
- What was the experience with **land reform** to redress some of the inequality in asset distribution in the rural sector? Was it successful?
- What is the appropriate mix of market and economic policy to promote sustainable development in the rural sector?
- What challenges remain for agriculture in Latin America?

RURAL LATIN AMERICA: DIVERSE STRUCTURES AND PERFORMANCE

Agriculture in Latin America spans a wide diversity of crops and climates. From the plains of the Argentine pampas to the hilly Guatemalan highlands, from traditional crops such as cattle and coffee to new boom products such as soya and kiwis, the plurality of agricultural systems in the region presents challenges to understanding agricultural practice. Nonetheless, we can generalize with respect to dominant modes of agricultural production and consider agricultural strategies that will help overcome common constraints of regional production.

The agricultural sector has gone through dramatic changes not only in terms of its relative importance in the economy but also in its internal structure. The share of agriculture in total gross domestic product (GDP) has been slipping over time; in countries such as Brazil and Chile it is less than 9 percent, while in Guatemala and Honduras it remains more than 22 and 17 percent, respectively.[1] In Colombia, for example, twenty-five years ago agriculture accounted for 22 percent of GDP; today it is at 14 percent. As shown in table 10.1, more people depend on agriculture than its share in GDP indicates: in Brazil 22 percent of the labor force is in agriculture, while in Guatemala 44 percent are rural earners. For Mexico the importance of agriculture in GDP is roughly constant at a low 4–5 percent, but the percentage of the economically active population (EAP) in agriculture has fallen from 36 to 19 percent, indicating a replacement of capital for labor in the sector. These represent sizable shifts in economic production. We can also see a substantial difference in some countries between the EAP in agriculture and the rural population. In Ecuador, 38 percent of the population lives in the rural sector, but only 23 percent are active in agriculture. The varied activities of the sector are important when we think through rural development strategies. Our focus must be multidimensional, taking into account those engaged in nonfarm rural activities as well as the unemployed poor.

Agricultural trade matters in Latin America. You may be surprised to note in table 10.2 the relatively strong weight that agricultural imports play in most Latin American import profiles. Many countries are dependent on imports to meet caloric intake requirements, raising questions of food security. Although manufacturing has assumed increased importance in the export profile of the region, agricultural products still account on average for 30 percent of the value of Latin America's exports. Bolivia and Ecuador have increased the importance of agriculture in their export profiles, but in most of the Central American countries, while roughly maintaining the dollar value of agricultural exports, the share has been eclipsed by manufacturing.

Crop production has risen in most countries of the region around 2004, although table 10.3 shows some variability in performance. Given that land use is relatively stable and that the number of workers in agriculture is falling, we can surmise that an increased use of fertilizer and machinery has accounted for much of the rise in productivity in the region. This is of course mixed news. Rising productivity is necessary for feeding urban populations and earning foreign exchange in exports; to the degree that this is substituting workers for more expensive inputs, we need to be especially concerned about displaced small farmers. Furthermore, as seen in table 10.4, even with rising production in the region, Latin American farmers still constitute a small percentage of global production in meat, fruits and vegetables, and world cereals—leaving producers ever subject to competition in global markets.

Traditional and Nontraditional Exports to Global Markets

The primary focus of agribusiness has moved from production for local consumption to nontraditional products for exports. Countries of the region have expanded production beyond traditional crops of sugar, cocoa, bananas, and coffee into high-value products such as fruits, vegetables, flowers, nuts, and oils.[2] Brazil has become one of the world's five food powers through increasing productivity generated by

Table 10.1. Agricultural GDP and Its Share in Total GDP

Countries	Agricultural GDP (Million $ constant 1995 prices)			Share in Total GDP (%)			Economically Active Population (EAP) in Agriculture (1000)		
	1979–1981	1989–1991	2002	1979–1981	1989–1991	2002	1979–1981	1989–1991	2004
Argentina	9,948	10,860	14,821	5	6	6	1,392	1,479	1,455
Bolivia	735	857	1,170	13	16	14	1,063	1,250	1,619
Brazil	35,707	46,709	69,690	7	8	9	17,427	15,315	12,134
Canada	12,715	15,705	14,907	3	3	2	795	503	353
Chile	2,796	4,740	6,429	10	11	8	801	934	989
Colombia	11,400	15,190	13,561	22	20	14	3,757	3,711	3,666
Costa Rica	866	1,174	1,703	12	13	11	289	308	327
Ecuador	3,919	5,890	4,561	27	33	20	1,021	1,199	1,242
El Salvador	1,347	1,161	1,299	18	17	11	699	709	782
Guatemala	2,704	3,067	4,181	25	26	22	1,262	1,568	2,089
Honduras	475	629	829	18	19	17	682	697	789
Mexico	11,846	13,300	16,009	5	5	4	7,988	8,535	8,453
Nicaragua	609	504	644	31	30	24	393	393	392
Panama	423	537	710	8	9	7	200	243	248
Paraguay	1,355	1,973	2,466	24	26	26	513	597	756
Peru	2,846	3,475	5,804	6	8	9	2,192	2,651	3,074
Uruguay	1,262	1,331	1,596	8	8	9	193	193	189
United States	80,112	106,600	165,893	2	2	2	3,888	3,633	2,791
Venezuela	3000	3,761	4,283	5	6	6	763	869	769
World	895,273	1,160,372	1,423,137	5	4	4	1,068,171	1,219,486	1,347,294

Countries	EAP Share In Total (%)			Rural Population (1000)			Rural Share In Total (%)		
	1979–1981	1989–1991	2004	1979–1981	1989–1991	2004	1979–1981	1989–1991	2004
Argentina	13	12	9	4,806	4,236	3,755	17	13	10
Bolivia	53	47	43	2,920	2,963	3,244	55	44	36
Brazil	37	23	15	41,064	37,651	29,643	34	25	16
Canada	7	3	2	5,962	6,481	6,098	24	23	19
Chile	21	19	15	2,093	2,190	2,023	19	17	13
Colombia	40	27	18	10,635	10,942	10,359	37	31	23
Costa Rica	35	26	18	1,247	1,426	1,646	53	46	39
Ecuador	40	33	23	4,223	4,611	4,983	53	45	38
El Salvador	44	36	26	2,562	2,593	2,629	56	51	40
Guatemala	54	52	44	4,269	5,153	6,740	63	59	53
Honduras	57	42	28	2,323	2,908	3,832	65	60	54
Mexico	36	28	19	22,732	22,952	25,503	34	28	24
Nicaragua	40	29	17	1,452	1,797	2,363	50	47	42
Panama	29	26	18	966	1,116	1,353	50	46	43
Paraguay	45	39	33	1,815	2,164	2,539	58	51	42
Peru	40	36	28	6,138	6,763	7,098	35	31	26
Uruguay	17	14	12	426	343	248	15	11	7
United States	3	3	2	60,748	63,102	57,847	26	25	19
Venezuela	15	12	7	3,106	3,124	3175	21	16	12
World	52	49	43	2,698,101	2,990,156	3,271,629	61	57	51

Source: FAO Statistical Yearbook 2004, www.fao.org.

Table 10.2.   Agriculture and the External Sector

Countries	Share of Agricultural Imports in Total Imports (%)			Share of Agricultural Exports in Total Exports (%)		
	1979–1981	*1989–1991*	*2002*	*1979–1981*	*1989–1991*	*2002*
Argentina	6.6	5.4	5.6	69.9	56.7	42.9
Bolivia	14.6	13.5	11.2	8.5	17.9	29.1
Brazil	10.2	11.1	6.5	44.3	26.9	27.7
Canada	7.6	6.0	5.7	10.7	7.2	6.5
Chile	14.1	5.6	6.9	8.6	13.8	19.7
Colombia	10.3	6.7	12.6	74.9	36.7	22.9
Costa Rica	8.9	9.4	7.7	68.5	59.9	30.1
Ecuador	7.9	9.1	9.0	28.2	31.7	34.3
El Salvador	15.7	14.8	16.4	73.9	49.0	15.1
Guatemala	9.7	11.4	13.5	72.5	68.5	54.7
Honduras	15.8	11.6	16.4	74.5	75.5	39.7
Mexico	14.0	14.1	10.6	12.8	11.3	9.3
Nicaragua	16.2	17.9	15.6	83.7	70.0	62.5
Panama	9.3	11.7	13.4	56.7	65.4	32.0
Paraguay	15.7	11.0	8.6	77.4	82.3	36.9
Peru	22.4	17.0	14.2	9.3	9.5	10.1
Uruguay	10.1	8.6	10.5	48.7	44.8	42.9
United States	7.7	5.2	3.7	19.9	11.4	8.0
Venezuela	15.7	11.9	13.1	0.5	1.6	1.2
World	12.0	10.0	7.0	12.0	10.0	7.0

Source: Food and Agriculture Organization 2005, www.fao.org.

investments in mechanization. Brazilian farmers have expanded beyond their own borders, planting 33 percent of the soy in Bolivia and Paraguay and owning 4 percent of Uruguay's land.[3] Mexico's high-value agricultural exports began in the 1960s, promoted by transnational corporations. Strawberry and tomato exports boomed in the 1970s and 1980s, resulting, in conjunction with export of other fruits and vegetables, in more than a doubling of agricultural exports in two decades. Chile and Mexico hold 53 percent of the world share of avocados; Mexico, Brazil, and the Philippines control 62 percent of mangoes; and Costa Rica and Cote d'Ivoire maintain 61 percent of pineapples. Over the past fifteen years, Peru has added nearly four hundred different export crops to traditional staples. Scarcely produced at all a few years ago, paprika is the new darling of Peruvian farming, and artichoke production doubled from 2004 to 2005.[4] Guatemala has become a major supplier of snow peas to the U.S. market, although its pesticide-intensive production has created environmental externalities. Central American melons have become one of its top agroexports. Colombia has become known for its cut flowers, becoming the second-largest exporter of flowers after the Netherlands. Ecuador has also become a cut-flower exporter, increasing sales to 9 percent of nonpetroleum earnings.[5] Overall, **nontraditional agricultural exports** (**NTAEs**) constitute 15 percent of agricul-

Agricultural Exports (US$ million)			Share of World Agricultural Exports (%)		
1979–1981	1989–1991	2002	1979–1981	1989–1991	2002
5,815	6,413	11,022	2.6	2.0	2.5
81	159	383	0.0	0.1	0.1
8,665	8,750	16,725	3.9	2.7	3.8
6,800	8,887	16,474	3.0	2.8	3.7
362	1,187	3,475	0.2	0.4	0.8
2,545	2,413	2,724	1.1	0.8	0.6
672	890	1,591	0.3	0.3	0.4
634	836	1,724	0.3	0.3	0.4
715	298	445	0.3	0.1	0.1
918	793	1,220	0.4	0.3	0.3
588	627	515	0.3	0.2	0.1
1,860	2,873	7,894	0.8	0.9	1.8
442	214	372	0.2	0.1	0.1
216	285	270	0.1	0.1	0.1
239	741	472	0.1	0.2	0.1
336	318	773	0.2	0.1	0.2
496	727	982	0.2	0.2	0.2
41,417	44,667	55,585	18.5	14.0	12.6
81	246	289	0.0	0.1	0.1
224,137	319,341	442,057	100.0	100.0	100.0

tural exports from Latin America. Beyond agricultural products, exports of beef and poultry also make use of pasture land. In terms of land use, 80 percent of the nearly eight hundred million hectares dedicated to agriculture are used for stock breeding.[6] Meat and poultry are competing for scarce land in the region.

Reverse seasons from North America make Latin American agricultural production complementary to the U.S. and Canadian markets. As Americans replace meats with more fruits and vegetables, demand has risen year-round. Mega grocery stores with global reach in sourcing bring new fruits and vegetables to northern tables. Innovations in packaging and refrigerated cargo handling have facilitated long-distance transport. Chilean fruit and wine have become common items on North American tables. Melting Andean snows water rich land in Chile's central zone, supporting new varieties of grapes and pears that are most welcome in northern countries in midwinter. Chilean wines are now winning international competitions. Poor farmlands converted into forest plantations have shown handsome dividends. Agriculture and forestry have contributed to Chile's trade balance to the tune of more than $2 billion per year.

But aggregate growth rates don't tell us who the largest regional producers are or how the value of agricultural production fared. Returning to table 10.2, we see that

Table 10.3. Agricultural Inputs and Output

	Fertilizer Consumption (hundreds of grams of nutrient per hectare)			Agricultural Machinery (tractors per 1,000 agricultural workers)			Land Use, Arable Land (hectares per person)				Crop Production Index (1999–2001 = 100)				
	1979–1981	1996–1998	2000–2002	1979–1981	1996–1998	2000–2002	1980	1990	1995	2002	1980	1990	1995	2002	2004
Argentina	46	330	244	132	190	205	1.03	0.9	0.85	0.9	49.2	64.4	77.4	102.9	104.9
Bolivia	23	53	38	4	4	4	0.36	0.31	0.33	0.34	45.7	60.7	81.9	109.5	119.9
Brazil	915	1,020	1,201	31	58	62	0.37	0.34	0.36	0.34	59.1	75	88.4	111	126.7
Chile	338	2,225	2,386	43	52	55	0.34	0.21	0.15	0.13	51.8	74.8	94.9	106.8	107
Colombia	601	1,077	2,605	8	6	6	0.13	0.09	0.06	0.05	80.6	95.9	100.4	103.5	110.8
Costa Rica	812	2,826	6,455	8	6	22	0.12	0.09	0.07	0.06	45	69.2	84.1	92.7	91.8
Ecuador	471	955	1,531	6	7	12	0.19	0.16	0.14	0.13	60.8	76.6	93.5	95	99.7
El Salvador	1,376	1,619	1,054	5	4	4	0.12	0.11	0.1	0.1	115.8	95.5	97.6	90.1	89.8
Guatemala	726	1,604	1,477	3	2	2	0.19	0.15	0.14	0.11	62.1	75.2	84.9	101.8	103.2
Honduras	163	720	1,193	5	7	7	0.42	0.3	0.28	0.16	81.1	94.6	99.5	110.5	120.1
Mexico	570	658	727	16	20	38	0.34	0.29	0.28	0.25	70	84.1	89.9	100	105.6
Nicaragua	392	198	177	6	7	7	0.37	0.34	0.37	0.36	69.7	72.1	83.5	103.2	117.9
Panama	692	753	545	27	20	32	0.22	0.21	0.19	0.19	110.9	119.7	106.7	97.6	106.2
Paraguay	44	233	319	14	24	23	0.52	0.51	0.55	0.55	49.7	94	96.1	106.1	118.8
Peru	381	498	759	5	3	4	0.19	0.16	0.15	0.14	44.4	53.8	72.9	106.8	94.9
Uruguay	564	1,102	895	171	173	174	0.48	0.41	0.39	0.39	56	66.6	87.2	90.3	122
Venezuela	711	1,058	1,157	50	59	62	0.2	0.14	0.12	0.1	61.7	76.5	83	92.2	93.4

Source: World Bank, World Development Indicators.

in terms of regional output, Brazil, Argentina, Mexico, and Chile have the largest agricultural exports. Although to some degree this is to be expected given endowments of land and population, it is important to remember because as these countries have become players in global agricultural markets, others have fallen further behind. Contrast the agricultural export numbers with the small market shares in table 10.4. Most countries are price takers in agricultural markets. It should be noted, moreover, that strong output does not necessarily translate into healthy revenues. Because revenues are determined by both the quantity produced and the price charged, the gains from agricultural production are highly sensitive to price changes. Agricultural prices of Latin America's major commodities, measured in constant dollars, fell to their lowest level of the century during the 1990s.[7] In part the fall in agricultural prices was driven by a fallacy of composition. As debt-laden countries across the globe adopted the neoliberal focus on agricultural exports, markets were saturated. Excess supply drove prices down. Although the prices of some commodities, especially soybeans, have recovered with trade with nontraditional partners such as China, primary product production still suffers from cyclical swings in prices.

Protectionist measures in the developed world limit export opportunities. Although the current Doha development round of trade talks is supposed to reduce agricultural subsidies in the industrialized world, little concrete progress has been made. As a percentage of production, subsidies remain stubbornly stuck at 40 percent, ranging from lows of 2 percent and 6 percent in New Zealand and Australia to 65 percent in Japan, 73 percent in Switzerland, 24 percent in the United States, and 49 percent in the European Union (EU).[8] According to the World Bank, rich countries support their farmers with $350 billion a year in subsidies, seven times the amount spent on international development aid. The United States and the EU are the biggest subsidizers, providing $50 and $100 million, respectively. High tariffs comprise the competitive advantage of agricultural exports from the region. Subsidies depress global prices by flooding markets with low-priced agricultural products.

Developing countries, led by World Trade Organization (WTO) cases filed by Brazil in sugar and cotton, have made a few dents in the historic preferences enjoyed by first world agricultural producers. Brazil's WTO complaint contested the $3 billion in annual subsidies paid to American cotton farmers, arguing that the measure increased output and depressed global prices. Brazil contended that American cotton exports would fall 41 percent and production would drop 29 percent if Washington eliminated its subsidies, pressuring a 12.6 percent rise in global prices and helping farmers in developing countries. Although the United States argued that the payments were legal under international trade law because they were decoupled from current production, the WTO ruled that they were trade distorting. Some estimates suggest that Brazil could double cotton production with the gap in the U.S. market.[9] Under WTO pressure, the EU has announced plans to overhaul its sugar regime, reversing its behavior of purchasing EU sugar at up to five times the world price. European farmers, responding to distorted price signals, produce more sugar than its domestic sweet tooth demands; the rest is dumped on international markets, depressing price.[10] Reducing such subsidies should promote production and export of sugar from the tropical countries where it is most efficiently grown—but much remains to be done to reduce subsidies and nontariff barriers to trade on other agricultural products. The

Table 10.4. Production and Share in World Meat Market

Countries	Share in World Meat Production (%)			Share in World Fruits and Vegetables (%)			Share in World Cereals (%)		
	1979–1981	1989–1991	2003	1979–1981	1989–1991	2003	1979–1981	1989–1991	2003
Argentina	2.72	1.97	1.64	1.35	1.07	0.77	1.56	1.05	1.65
Bolivia	0.15	0.15	0.17	0.14	0.15	0.14	0.04	0.04	0.07
Brazil	3.84	4.58	7.37	3.65	4.44	3.18	1.96	1.98	3.20
Canada	1.85	1.56	1.68	0.39	0.34	0.23	2.72	2.78	2.42
Chile	0.26	0.28	0.42	0.54	0.56	0.53	0.11	0.16	0.18
Colombia	0.61	0.66	0.57	0.84	0.79	0.63	0.21	0.21	0.19
Costa Rica	0.07	0.08	0.07	0.23	0.30	0.29	0.02	0.01	0.01
Ecuador	0.12	0.14	0.24	0.64	0.59	0.58	0.04	0.07	0.09
El Salvador	0.04	0.04	0.05	0.06	0.05	0.03	0.05	0.04	0.04
Guatemala	0.08	0.08	0.10	0.16	0.22	0.22	0.07	0.07	0.06
Honduras	0.06	0.05	0.06	0.28	0.20	0.14	0.03	0.03	0.03
Mexico	1.86	1.58	1.94	1.88	1.97	1.84	1.30	1.24	1.47
Nicaragua	0.06	0.04	0.05	0.06	0.04	0.02	0.02	0.02	0.04
Panama	0.05	0.06	0.06	0.20	0.16	0.07	0.02	0.02	0.02
Paraguay	0.15	0.19	0.17	0.13	0.10	0.06	0.03	0.04	0.07
Peru	0.26	0.28	0.37	0.35	0.35	0.42	0.09	0.10	0.19
Uruguay	0.30	0.25	0.21	0.07	0.06	0.05	0.06	0.06	0.11
United States	17.86	16.05	15.28	8.24	6.93	5.00	19.16	15.35	16.80
Venezuela	0.49	0.43	0.48	0.39	0.38	0.30	0.10	0.11	0.14

Source: FAO Statistical Yearbook 2004, www.fao.org.

fact that smaller producers of agricultural products have not made the news for cases at the WTO should not be lost on the astute student of international market bargaining power.

In addition to trade restrictions, revenues and production are also sensitive to the exchange rate. Recall that under ISI the overvalued exchange rate biased development against the agricultural sector. Overvalued exchange rates worked against the development of comparative advantage in external markets. Industrial protection distorted the internal terms of trade between the domestic sectors. Very often, agricultural protection of competitive commodities was directly taxed as a means of raising revenue to support industrial expansion. One estimate placed indirect taxation through industrial protection and macroeconomic policies at 22 percent of agricultural output. To offset this drain, politically powerful agricultural elites were sometimes able to garner favors in terms of subsidies or infrastructure support—but rarely did these benefits trickle down to the small producers.[11] More competitive exchange rates under the neoliberal package have helped spur growth in agriculture. In some cases—Brazil in 2005, for example—the foreign exchange earned in the export boom has led to an appreciation of the exchange rate, choking off growth. Maintaining a competitive exchange rate is a delicate balancing act.

Between exchange rate biases, industrialized country tariffs, and subsidies, agriculture faces significant distortions. But simply getting prices right will not work unless adequate rural infrastructure is available, including irrigation, roads, power, and telecommunications as well as credit, market information, research, extension, and farmer education and health.[12] If the farmer—particularly the small producer—does not have the necessary complementary inputs, production and revenues will not rise. Despite the growth in agricultural exports in the region, rural poverty remains stuck at difficult levels. The Economic Commission for Latin America and the Caribbean (ECLAC) suggests that the new wave of modernizing growth in agriculture that is limited to a small range of products such as fruit, soybeans, beef, chicken, and pork and concentrated in a handful of countries is leaving behind the neediest of rural dwellers.[13] Although agriculture has grown at rates of 3 percent a year (surpassing overall GDP growth for the region), growth has not been pro-poor. We now turn to look at why growth in agriculture has failed to deliver equity, focusing on the structural constraints in production that block improvements in both equity and sustainable growth in the region.

The Structure of the Agricultural Market: Inequality in Assets and Outcomes

Liberalization has created larger, more lucrative markets for agricultural exporters from Latin America. Theory would tell us that given rich resources, Latin America might have a relative comparative advantage in the production of agricultural products and that the welfare of the least well-off should be improved. Unfortunately, all producers have not been able to share equally in this boom. Constraints in rural markets prevent all stakeholders from sharing in this growth. A discussion of the multiple imperfections in agricultural markets in Latin America will help us understand why.

Input markets for land are not competitive in Latin America. Two types of land-holdings dominate agriculture in Latin America: relatively small-scale, traditional peasant agriculture and large-scale corporate farming. This pattern of small and large landholdings is a legacy of the colonial latifundia, in which large tracts of land were deeded to Spanish or Portuguese descendants. Although intermediate-sized producers exist, policy has been driven by this **dualistic structure of production** in agriculture. The latifundia or hacienda system has more or less disappeared, but its large scale has been retained by modern capitalist farming. The nature of agri-cultural production has changed. Whereas the large oligarchic estates had a certain socioeconomic cohesion, the divide between modern commercial farmers and peasant producers is huge. Under the latifundia system, labor for coffee, sugar, and cotton production was tied to the estates through sharecropping, credit, and per-sonal obligations to create a framework of paternalistic relations.[14] With the dis-solution of this social structure and flourishing commercial farms, peasants are marginalized from land, labor, and credit markets. In the 1990s land use under cul-tivation for wheat, coffee, and cotton—products grown primarily by small- and medium-sized farms—lost ground with an increase in commercial production.[15] The legacy of the latifundia has resulted in highly unequal holdings of land.

A major shift has taken place in the agricultural labor force. Over the last twenty years, the workforce available to farms fell from 35 percent to 21 percent of the region's total workforce.[16] As machines and fertilizers replace workers, the share of the labor force in agriculture declined in most countries 20–50 percent in terms of agriculture's share of employment—a wrenching change. For anyone who has traveled in Latin America and was amazed at the influx of poor workers from the countryside, perhaps this number is not startling. Landless workers are searching for survival in cities. There is also an increase in the migrant laborers called *volantes*—those who fly between the rural sector and the outskirts of the urban sector as labor demand changes. These are workers without permanent jobs or homes, generally leading lives of misery, contributing to both urban and rural poverty.

Changing structures of production in agriculture have sometimes led to vio-lence. In Mexico, twenty-six villagers were killed in 2002 in a clash over land, a long-standing feud ignited by dwindling resources for survival.[17] Given the tradi-tional homelands of indigenous peoples in the rural sector, the movement to the cities in search of survival has also resulted in a significant loss of cultural diversity. As migrants scratch out an urban existence, traditional ways of living are lost. In Brazil, landless workers suffering from the drought and desperate for survival erupted into violence in 1998, looted stores, and commandeered government buildings in an attempt to call government attention to their plight. Organized by Brazil's land-less movement, Movimento Sem Terra (MST), the group has, with the support of churches and international groups, occupied (or invaded) unproductive ranches to pressure for land reform in a country where 3 percent of the richest farmers own 66 percent of the land. Killings by police defending the land have made land reform in Brazil an international human rights issue. By forging connections between the rural and urban sector, the MST has been able to transform itself into the largest social movement in the region. It has developed an alternative socioeconomic devel-opment model that places people before profits, transforming the face of the Brazilian countryside and its politics.[18] The movement has extended to other countries. Box 10.1 chronicles the incredible obstacles and devastating human cost faced by those struggling for land in Bolivia.

Inequality has been exacerbated by the boom in commercial farming. Table 10.5 presents Gini coefficients for land; these high ratios give Latin America the dubious distinction of topping the global list for land inequality. We can see that for those countries reporting Gini coefficients for land, they are extremely high, reflecting a very skewed distribution. From table 10.5 we can also see that poverty in the rural sector is much higher for all countries than overall national poverty. We will pay closer attention to problems of poverty in chapter 11; for now we should simply focus on the fact that the rural sector reflects more than farming—and it is a very hard life for many of its inhabitants.

As farmers moved into nontraditional crops and as corporate farming has dominated the sector, producers of traditional crops such as wheat, maize, sugar beets, and milk have suffered. In particular, smaller *campesino* producers have been hurt. Recall the story of the Lehmans from chapter 1 who were squeezed by competitive global tobacco companies. Smaller producers find it difficult to overcome credit and finance constraints; economies of scale in marketing, packaging, and transport; import regulations and inspections in foreign markets; and production challenges with respect to pest control, soil management, and pesticide use. Many small landholders risk exclusion from global markets. Imagine how a small potato farmer in the highlands of Peru is going to make contact with your local Wal-Mart Supercenter—not easy, particularly if he is indigenous and doesn't speak Spanish, much less English.[19] Small and medium producers often cannot absorb the transactions costs—the information, negotiations, monitoring, and enforcement costs of international trade contracts. The result has been a bimodal agricultural sector in which the rich agroexport firms are edging out traditional producers. For example, at the beginning of this chapter snow peas were mentioned as a nontraditional agricultural export from Guatemala. However, consolidation in this sector is beginning as the smaller firms find themselves unable to meet U.S. Food and Drug Administration guidelines for pesticide use in agricultural products. As smaller producers are squeezed out, many former farmers now find themselves in orchards and packaging plants. Prospects for peasant farmers are dim unless investments in microtechnologies are promoted by the state to bring peasant farmers into small-scale commercial sectors.[20] Transnational corporations command a large proportion of agroexports. Chiquita (United Brands), Del Monte, and Dole (Standard Fruit) continue to exert substantial influence in Central America, using their base in traditional bananas to capture 25 percent of all nontraditional export production. Three of the four top firms leading the Chilean boom are transnational.[21] Agriculture is big business in Latin America—usually to the detriment of the small farmer.

This difficult change to less labor-intensive means of production has indeed produced gains in output. Several countries—Chile, Argentina, Paraguay, Peru, Uruguay, Bolivia, and Costa Rica—have logged relatively rapid growth in the agricultural sector. A second group of countries—Ecuador, Mexico, and Brazil—roughly matched the change in the world production. Other countries in the region did not fare as well. Not surprisingly, domestic conflict in El Salvador and Nicaragua

BOX 10.1.   BOLIVIAN LANDLESS GIVE BIRTH TO A MOVEMENT

BY PETER LOWE, TARIJA, BOLIVIA

Leading two tired kids by the hand and carrying her youngest in a cloth on her back, Juana Ortega arrived on foot in this southern Bolivian provincial capital, the destination of a 175-mile protest march. "My children are heavy," she said, not even mentioning the one she had been carrying *in utero* for almost nine months. "But I do this out of necessity. We need land."

Ortega, 31, and her children had been riding in a crowded truck or walking in the sweltering sun for six days since leaving their hut in Pananti, one of eight landless settlements on the Chaco, a low-altitude plain east of here. The Ortegas were among 150 families that converged from the settlements for the march, organized by Bolivia's two-year-old Landless Rural Workers Movement (MST), which took its name and many of its tactics from the Brazilian group famous for occupying idle farmland.

In Tarija, the marchers demanded titles to their parcels. But the government ignored them for a week, until they occupied a National Institute of Agrarian Reform office March 6. Officials quickly called the police, who fired tear gas and clubbed protest leaders.

As Ortega ran from the building, she stumbled and fell hard. Four days later, back in her hut in Pananti, her pregnancy ended in a stillbirth.

The death was just the most recent tragedy for the settlement. Last October, Ortega was among 350 women and children who lived along a parched riverbed without food or shelter for three days after dozens of landowners and paramilitary thugs tried to dislodge landless communities in the area. The following month a paramilitary gang massacred six settlers in Pananti. Despite Bolivia's 50-year-old agrarian reform law and recent government promises, Pananti residents don't expect titles for their plots anytime soon, leaving them vulnerable to more attacks.

Conditions are similar in the other landless settlements on the Chaco, the poorest part of South America's poorest country. But the MST is pressing forward. "What we're doing here in Bolivia is not illegal," says Ermelinda Fernández, president of the group's Chaco chapter. "We're struggling together, on the basis of our reality, to recuperate what has always been ours—the land."

Bolivia's landless movement follows a half-century of dashed rural hopes. In 1952 a revolutionary government banned forced labor and gave some land to *campesinos*. Since then, however, most Bolivian regimes have favored export farming and large estates while ushering in transnational firms such as Syngenta, the Swiss seed and chemical giant. Free-market policies have kept most of Bolivia's 8 million inhabitants in poverty.

Former President Gonzalo Sánchez de Lozada's 1993–1997 administration banned large estates that serve no social or economic purpose, attempted to reduce corruption in the agrarian-reform agency and streamlined the legal framework for redistributing abandoned land. Despite the reforms, the Sánchez government did not manage to wrest a significant number of plots from large landholders, known here as *latifundistas* and *patrónes*. His successors, Hugo Banzer Suárez and Jorge Quiroga Ramírez, who assumed the presidency last August, have not done much better. "On the Chaco," Fernández says, "agrarian reform has only strengthened the hold of the *patrónes* and not resulted in the distribution of land to those who work it."

Today 4.5 percent of the nation's landowners own 70 percent of its agricultural acreage, according to the Bolivian Documentation and Information Center, a nongovernmental organization [NGO] based in the central city of Cochabamba. As they wait for the value of their idle parcels to increase, an estimated 100,000 landless agricultural workers live in extreme poverty. "There are still haciendas where 30 peons work from sunrise to sunset for a completely inadequate salary," Fernández says, citing daily pay as low as $1.41. "They have no alternative because they have no land of their own."

Perhaps nowhere in Bolivia is the problem more glaring than in Yacuiba, the municipality that includes Pananti and runs along the Argentine border. Just 25 families own 80 percent of the municipality's land, according to the Permanent Assembly of Human Rights (APDH), a Bolivian nongovernmental organization. Another 3,000 families have no land.

The disparity prompted the Gran Chaco Campesino Federation, the local arm of the Sole Union Confederation of Rural Workers of Bolivia (CSUTCB), to start organizing landless workers to occupy underused plots instead of waiting for government action. In the first takeover, the Ortegas and 140 other landless families occupied Pananti, an abandoned 235-acre property, in May 2000. Most of the families had lived and worked for years on plantations nearby. The MST was formed at a conference the following month in Yacuiba, the municipality's largest town, 25 miles south of Pananti.

Since then, landless workers have founded seven other settlements on the Chaco, and the MST has organized new chapters in the provinces of La Paz, Potosí and Santa Cruz. MST President Angel Durán says another is in the works in Cochabamba.

Headquartered in La Paz, the capital, the MST has coordinated actions with farmers battling U.S.-backed coca eradication programs in the Chapare, a jungle region in central Bolivia. The group also cooperates with trade unions, indigenous organizations and others interested in social justice for *campesinos.*

And the MST is developing ties with Brazil's Landless Rural Workers Movement, the world's largest and most successful agrarian-reform group, which has grown to an estimated 500,000 families since forming in 1984. The Brazilian group is planning to send a delegation to Tarija in June for the Bolivian MST's annual meeting.

Bolivian latifundistas aren't happy about the movement. One of their groups, the Gran Chaco Stockbreeders Association (Asogachaco), has called for violence against landless people.

The Chaco settlers, in turn, have fought off eviction attempts by police and soldiers. Last October about 80 landowners and at least seven masked paramilitary thugs, wearing military uniforms and carrying military weapons, burned down huts in a landless community called Los Sotos. Then they threatened settlers in Pananti. Neither the landowners nor the masked men were punished, says Fernández, the local MST leader. "The authorities did nothing."

That was just a warm-up. Shortly after dawn November 9, as unarmed Pananti settlers walked to their fields to prepare for corn planting, paramilitary gunmen ambushed and killed six of them and wounded 21. The injured included Ortega's husband, Mario. Later that day, some of the survivors fatally beat a man they had identified as a ringleader of the attack.

Responding to the incidents, authorities arrested nine landless *campesinos* and five people linked to area landowners. The five were quickly released, while the landless remained in jail. (Fernández herself was jailed December 18, just three days after giving birth. She was released on bail three days later.)

Bolivia's interior minister, Leopoldo Fernández, ordered an investigation of nearby police and army troops who failed to prevent or stop the violence. And a communiqué from NGOs that work with Bolivian *campesinos* alleged that a variety of government officials and institutions were complicit in the massacre for failing to resolve land conflicts quickly. On November 20, the government promised to release the jailed MST activists and grant landless people titles to 21,000 acres, including Pananti.

But attacks on landless settlers have continued. On December 11 army troops fired on *campesinos* occupying an estate in Santa Cruz Province, just north of the Chaco. Human rights activists say at least two *campesinos* died in the violence.

The terror in Pananti disrupted corn planting, so the community has no harvest this

continued

contributed to low growth rates in agriculture. In most cases the conflict itself had roots in highly unequal patterns of land distribution. The outbreak of fighting was the manifestation of social conflict over control of land, a precious commodity. Policy measures must resolve the underlying unequal conditions of production to generate a sustainable and strong pattern of agricultural growth. Simply improving output without improving the lives of rural residents is not sustainable as a development policy.

Attempts have been made to incorporate the small farmer into higher value-added production. The transition of small landholders to nontraditional, high-value exports has been facilitated by development agencies and governments as part of structural adjustment packages. In particular, the United States Agency for International Development (USAID), has been an active supporter of private incentives in the agricultural sector. The Commonwealth Development Corporation, the World Bank, and the Inter-American Development Bank (IADB) also provide support for agricultural export growth.[22] International aid agencies are promoting restructuring for small farmers, especially in lowland areas, to switch to other crops. The Organization of American States is helping Central American and Colombian farmers experiment with medicinal plants such as sarsaparilla, which can be grown alongside or instead of coffee.[23] Nonetheless, steep hillsides, poor infrastructure, lack of information, and remote villages thwart such a transition. Hopeless farmers in Colombia are increasingly pushed into the illegal coca market.

Despite these efforts to promote **nontraditional exports** by peasant farmers, the successes are due primarily to large corporate farming. The growth in agriculture has been primarily driven by soybean exports in Brazil and Argentina. Indeed, the expansion of agricultural exports often has been at a cost to small farmers and the production of subsistence foods for domestic consumption. Caution must be taken to strengthen local and regional markets as the process of globalization in agriculture continues. Argentine economist Walter Pengue notes that removing subsidies under WTO pressure within a global production context such as the present one could actually hurt small farmers. As corporate farming expands to satisfy global markets, without strengthening of local capacity it is possible that the boom will put additional pressure on small landholders, increase environmental degradation, and further concentrate land ownership and mass migration of small farmers to the cities.[24]

Table 10.5. Inequality and Rural Poverty

| | Gini Coefficient for Food Consumption, Income and Land Distribution and Percent in Poverty | | | | | | | | |
| | Inequality of Dietary Energy Consumption | | Inequality of Income | | Concentration of Land | | Poverty (% of population) | | |
Countries	Survey Year	Gini Coefficient (%)	Survey Year	Gini Coefficient (%)	Survey Year	Gini Coefficient (%)	Survey Year	Total	Rural
Argentina	1970	12	2001	52	1988	83	1980	8.5	19
Bolivia	1990	14	1999	45		n/a	2002	52	79.2
Brazil	1975	17	1998	59	1996	85	2001	34.1	55.2
Chile	1996	12	2000	57	1996	92*	2003	18.6	20.1
Colombia	1972	16	1999	58	2001	80	2002	50.6	52
Costa Rica	1996	12	2000	47		n/a	2002	17.5	24.3
Ecuador	1994	13	1998	44	1999	85*	2002	49	n/a
El Salvador	1995	14	2000	53		n/a	2001	39.4	62.4
Guatemala	1989	15	2000	48		n/a	2002	45.3	68
Honduras	1996	17	1999	55	1993	66	2002	66.7	86.1
Mexico	1990	16	2000	55		n/a	2002	32.2	51.2
Nicaragua	1993	17	2001	55	2001	72	2001	63.9	77
Panama	1991	15	2000	56	2001	52	2002	25.3	48.5
Paraguay	1995	15	1999	57	1991	93	2001	50.1	73.6
Peru	1986	15	2000	50	1994	86	2001	42	78.4
Uruguay	1996	12	2000	45	2000	79	2002	15.4	n/a
Venezuela	2000	13	1998	49	1996/1997	88	2002	48.6	n/a

Source: Food and Agriculture Organization 2005, www.fao.org.
*Gini numbers from Robert Eastwood, Michael Lipton, and Andrew Newell, "Farm Size: Prepared for Volume III of the Handbook of Agricultural Economics."
Note: Poverty data is from ECLAC Annual Yearbook 2004. Poverty is measured the percent of population unable to purchase by twice the cost of a basic food basket; the data include the indigent, those unable to afford a basic food basic.

Is Niche Farming an Answer to the Agricultural Coffee Crisis?

One area of traditional export earnings that has been particularly hit by oversupply and low prices is coffee. International coffee prices hit historic lows in the first half of this decade, having fallen by almost 50 percent since 1999. A production glut—driven in part by new entrants into the international coffee market such as Vietnam —has driven global prices down. World exports were a record 88.7 million bags in 2001, sold at the lowest prices in fifty years. As shown in figure 10.1, from 1980 to 1989 the composite indicator for coffee prices averaged $1.2792 per pound and coffee-producing counties earned an average of $10.2 billion a year in export revenues. From 2000 to 2004 the average price plummeted by more than half to $.5433 per pound, with annual earnings at $6.2 billion.[25] Declining coffee revenues created debt in excess of $100 million.[26] Coffee growing accounts for 8.2 percent of the GDP in Honduras, 7.2 percent in Nicaragua, 4.2 percent in Guatemala, 2.5 percent in El Salvador, and 2 percent in Colombia. Forty-four percent of the region's crop-land is used to grow coffee. In Ecuador, 105,000 coffee-producing families including 800,000 people are involved; prices are not covering harvest costs. The processing sector is working at one-third capacity and has dismissed staff. Producers are migrating to the cities or seeking work abroad, leaving destitute families behind.[27] Indirect activities, including commerce, banking, storage, and transportation, are

Figure 10.1.   International Composite Coffee Prices, Annual Average

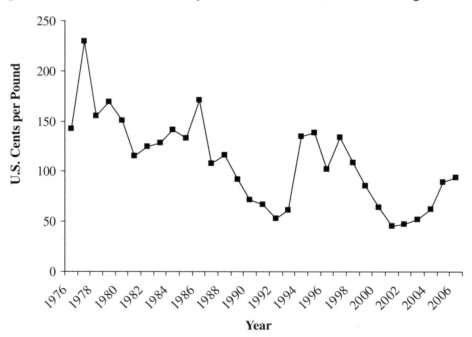

Source: International Coffee Association, www.ico.org.

also affected by the crisis; at the macroeconomic level states must cut back public spending due to lower tax revenues.[28]

It is estimated that 300,000 have lost their jobs in Guatemala due to the coffee crisis; in El Salvador coffee exports are down 40 percent. The world food program distributed emergency rations to 10,000 coffee-growing families.[29] The situation in Central America is made worse by a severe drought in some parts of the region; 220,000 rural Nicaraguan families are estimated to be suffering from food shortages and abandoning their land to search for work in Costa Rica. Coffee farms were seized by banks. Health officials estimate a growing number of Nicaraguans dying from hunger due to the lack of jobs, income, and food created by the coffee crisis. Acute child malnutrition has risen. Beggars from shanty towns lined the roads, pleading for help. It was a desperate time. In September 2002, Nicaraguan protesters held government negotiators hostage in exchange for food, medicine, and debt relief for workers.

Anger erupted across the region against what is perceived as an unjust global market that does not give small farmers a chance. Coffee farmers receive a global average of $.24 cents a pound for their produce; consumers pay $3.60 a pound. In the global commodity chain that produces coffee, there is a high concentration of firms at the buyer end. By 1998 Philip Morris, Nestle, Sara Lee, P&G, and Tchibo controlled 69 percent of the roasted and instant market.[30] This is in contrast to the production which is primarily undertaken by small farmers where the family is the primary source of labor. The coffee sector is dominated by small-scale production, with 70 percent of farms overall and 85 percent of the farms in Central America working as micro-organizations. Ten years ago coffee-producing companies got approximately one-third of every dollar spent on coffee; now they get about $.08.[31]

What can be done? One possibility is to differentiate coffee—that is, to make some brands of coffee more distinctive than the common cup. Small farmers are urged to move into designer coffee; organics have been increasing by 20 percent a year as consumers prefer a pesticide-free shot of caffeine. Certified organic coffee accounts for 3–5 percent of the specialty coffee in the United States. Organic coffee farming is appealing to small-scale producers in the region because of the minimal use of expensive fertilizers and the high prices that organic products obtain in international markets. Global sales of organic fruit and vegetables have been increasing at annual rates between 20 and 30 percent in the last years of the 1990s.[32] Guatemala is using the Internet to auction its specialty beans as an alternative to selling them on the New York market under the supervision of PricewaterhouseCoopers.

Yet organic farming is not problem-free. Small farmers still need to find reliable buyers, be able to meet volume and quality requirements, and find affordable and timely transportation to avoid spoilage. Organic coffee is expensive to produce, requiring three times the labor of a moderately tended plant. One can't simply stamp coffee "organic"—it must be proven that the process was indeed pure. Producers, through international organizations, pay for the costs of certification to northern agents.[33] This is a new kind of nontariff barrier: certification. All organic produce must be certified by an organization such as the Organic Crop Inspectors Association for compliance to strict standards. For an illiterate farmer to provide documentation that a field has been chemical free for at least three years is a daunting task.[34]

Local agricultural organizations help. Cooperatives can create economies of scale in marketing and transportation. In Costa Rica, through a small blackberry farmers' association, APROCAM, berries plucked from mountain bushes at dawn arrive on Miami grocery shelves by that same afternoon. In Guatemala some of the larger farms are selling organic produce directly to supermarket chains such as Fresh Fields. Organic coffees have exhibited more stable (and 20 percent higher) prices due to consumer tastes for designer, chemical-free coffees. In Mexico, a confederation of coffee-producer organizations, UNCAFESUR, through an organization called La Selva, is working with small-scale ejido farmers to switch to organic production.[35]

Organic production not only has a stronger upscale market but also can be better suited to the needs of the small farmer. It rejects the chemical cocktail of expensive fertilizers in favor of labor-intensive natural composting and weeding by hand.[36] La Selva is working to teach terracing techniques, organic composting, intercropping of bananas to provide shade, and developing nurseries for seedlings. The InterAmerican Foundation, in conjunction with a private foundation and a Dutch coffee broker, supported the transition costs. Although nearly half of the initial harvest was lost to the violence in the Chiapas region, marketing efforts exceeded all expectations, with three North American companies—Aztec Harvests Coffee Company, Ben & Jerry's, and United Airlines—featuring coffee grown by La Selva producers. A potential downside is that the more labor-intensive methods of organic farming have drawn women further into agricultural production, adding to their already burdensome dawn-to-dusk routines. Nonetheless, the additional demand for labor has decreased the degree of migration of males and older children in search of work. Furthermore, organic methods are environmentally sustainable, creating an economic incentive to produce without using inputs that interfere with the ecosystem.[37] Box 10.2 provides an example of how, with funding, green methods have boosted yields and markets in El Salvador.

While organic products are certified as not using agrochemicals for production, **fair trade labels** certify the trade process. Fair trade labeling organizations establish standards of production that cover sustainable livelihoods for growers. The product itself is not distinguished as much as the remuneration going to the producer. Fair trade coffee is the response of an international movement that helps businesses buy directly from rural coffee cooperatives, eliminating middlemen and providing double the price to small farmers. Fair trade labels guarantee a price of $1.26 per pound for high grade and $1.06 for more common robusta if market prices are below these levels and a 5 percent premium if they are above. Producers belong to a cooperative or association that is certified as paying a livable wage. Fair trade markets are highly remunerative and certification costs low—rather than verify organic inputs and practices over time, agents only need to certify that workers and small-scale owners are fairly compensated—something nearly automatic in the higher price paid for fair trade products. One drawback, however, is the difficulty for the smallest or most remote farmers to form and maintain producer cooperatives. Fair trade in this sense can leave out some of the neediest producers. Work may need to be done to promote the organizational skills of peasants in forming cooperatives.[38] Fair trade marketing may also have an unintended effect. If one assumes that most coffee drinkers are price sensitive, boosting the price for fair

Box 10.2. Organic Crops Gain Ground in El Salvador: IDB Program Assists Farming Cooperatives That Supply Local Restaurants and Supermarkets

BY CARLOS GONZÁLES, LA PALMA, EL SALVADOR

Organic food, like fancy bottled water, is often portrayed as a luxury for well-heeled people in rich countries. The assumption is that only people with means can afford to buy food produced without chemical pesticides, synthetic fertilizers and other agricultural inputs that have become the mainstay of farmers around the world.

But in El Salvador, a number of forward-looking farming cooperatives have discovered a market for organic fruits and vegetables at their doorstep. Under a project partly financed by the IDB's Multilateral Investment Fund, these cooperatives are selling fruits and vegetables to health-conscious restaurants, hotels and supermarkets right in the capital of San Salvador. Better yet, the cooperatives are generating new, better-paying jobs for rural men and women while helping to protect and restore scarce farmland.

One such cooperative operates out of a large shed in the Salvadoran municipality of La Palma, just a few kilometers from the border with Honduras. On a typical workday, women stand at stations inside the shed, sorting piles of carrots, spring onions, tomatoes, strawberries and passion fruit, all of which has been delivered there by local organic farmers. All the produce is washed, graded, and bagged. Some of the fruit, such as strawberries, is processed and bottled as jam and bar-coded so that checkout machines at supermarkets can identify it.

"We have been working in various localities, and several cooperatives are now implementing expansion plans," says Mario Urrutia, coordinator in El Salvador of the Cooperative League of the United States of America (CLUSA), one of two executing agencies running the project. CLUSA provides technical and marketing assistance to participating cooperatives along with Proexsal (Producers and Exporters of El Salvador), an agricultural marketing company based in San Salvador that is the project's other executing agency. "We come in once the farmers have begun to produce organic crops and want to penetrate the local market," explains Godofredo Pacheco, manager of Proexsal. "Our pitch is simple: high-quality, organically grown Salvadoran products." Together, the two organizations help qualified cooperatives to become financially and ecologically sustainable businesses.

GREEN METHODS BOOST YIELDS

The case for organic farming in El Salvador goes beyond rising consumer demand. One of Latin America's most densely populated countries, it already faces a shortage of high-quality agricultural land. The intensive use of pesticides and chemical fertilizers can often hasten the degradation of land in tropical climates, so farmers who correctly implement organic methods can actually increase yields and lower their production costs over time.

Scarce land is just one of the challenges facing El Salvador's farming cooperatives, however. Many of these were founded 20 years ago, when the government instituted an agrarian reform program in response to long-standing conflicts over land tenure. Most of the farmers who acquired land thanks to the reform had little or no experience managing businesses, and as a result many new cooperatives saw their production decrease. The country's commercial banks have also proved unwilling to finance most cooperatives; even when loans are available, interest rates remain prohibitively high.

The new project aims to help cooperatives deal with all these obstacles. "CLUSA is

continued

continued

helping us with the production of organic cacao and sesame, and strengthening the cooperative," says Rafael Pineda, chairman of La Carrera cooperative. "We are learning about how to run a business and the different types of credit." Proexsal's Pacheco says La Carrera is learning to handle the kind of strategic and planning decisions that all businesses face. "Now they're trying to come up with a brand name for their chocolate bars," he says. "But first, they have to learn about the features of the market and use efficient processing and packaging techniques so that they can compete."

As recent earthquakes and hurricanes have shown, Salvadoran farmers also face a disproportionately high risk of natural disasters. In the Lempa River basin, the river is once again threatening to flood, as it did in 1998 when Hurricane Mitch struck. "Now we are more aware of the danger the Lempa River represents," says José Santos, chairman of the Los Navegantes cooperative, "but our situation has changed a great deal in two years. Even though there were many promises of support for development of the region after Hurricane Mitch, we have not received any significant aid. Since April, CLUSA has been providing us with advisory services," says Santos, "and we have been very encouraged by what we can learn."

"They came to us," says CLUSA's Urrutia, "because they had heard about the progress other cooperatives have been making with the program. So we explained to them that CLUSA and Proexsal could help them, but that they would have to follow the official procedures and commit to the program. In just four months of work, the first farmers are already experimenting with demonstration plots of organic crops and the cooperative members are immersed in institutional and technical training."

One of the more interesting aspects of Los Navegantes is that 56 percent of the cooperative members are women. "Many of us are parents," notes member Sonia Hernández, "and we need a strategy to help us improve our lives. That need motivated many of us women to join the cooperative."

Pacheco and Urrutia say the ultimate proof that organic farming is viable in El Salvador is the fact that several cooperatives are starting to compete effectively with imported conventional food products. They say the market for organic produce also tends to be more stable than the general agricultural market, a factor that helps cooperatives to maintain a steady revenue stream.

Source: www.iadb.org/exr/idbamerica/English/MAY01E/may01e6.html, June 2001.

trade while stigmatizing drinkers of nonspecialty coffee may in fact work to put more growers out of work. For this reason, some critics argue that promoting niche marketing for organics is better than pushing fair trade products.[39] There is perhaps less risk in appealing to people to drink a premium chemical-free blend rather than sip a cup that has been picked by well-paid workers.

Brazil, the world's biggest producer and exporter of the bean, is attempting to add value to current production by doing more of the processing, aiming to roast and grind more beans and produce more instant coffee. Embrapa Café, the coffee research arm of the Brazilian agricultural research agency, is working to make the often delicate bushes more resistant to disease and sharp changes in temperature.[40] The International Coffee Organization, representing fifty producer countries, is launching a quality standard that aims to remove five million bags a year of low-quality coffee from the market. Oxfam, the international NGO, is campaigning to spend $100 million of aid from rich countries to destroy five million more bags of stock.[41] Addressing the coffee crisis will certainly take both local and global solutions.

Extralegal Production: Coca

Despite the gains from crop diversification and organic farming, access by peasant farmers to inputs and good land as well as international market conditions limit widespread benefits. Planting coca is easier, albeit illegal. As an agricultural crop, coca is versatile and lucrative. First synthesized in 1859 from the coca leaf, for centuries the original Andean plant has held an important place in Aymara culture.[42] It grows in a wide range of conditions, may be harvested from three to six times per year, and can have a gestation period as short as eighteen months. Four-fifths of the coca is grown in the Upper Huallaga Valley of Peru and in the Chapare of Bolivia. Earnings for coca range from ten times that of cacao, to nineteen times that of citrus, to ninety-one times that of rice. There are three markets for coca: traditional, for uses in medicine and folk remedies; licit, for markets controlled by governments for production for cola and pharmaceuticals; and illicit production. Before coca is brought to the illicit market, its leaves are mashed and mixed with chemicals to become paste. The paste is then treated with sulfuric acid and potassium permanganate to form a cocaine base that can range in purity from 90 to 92 percent. It is then transported and cut before reaching the $110 billion international market, double the combined profits of all Fortune 500 companies.

Production is extremely mobile; illegal narcotics have become Latin America's true multinational product. The technology is fairly straightforward, low cost, and relatively barrier-free. South American traffickers earn between $5 billion and $6 billion in the U.S. market. It is also labor-intensive, engaging growers, processors, and distributors in the production chain. The value added at higher levels of production graduates from $500 to $1,000 for an average kilogram through $160,000 to $240,000 as it hits the street. Small coca farmers can earn a few thousand dollars a week to pay employees and feed, clothe, and house their families and, unlike with traditional crops, have some left over to buy goods. Former president Paz Estenssoro of Bolivia once remarked that "cocaine has gained an importance in our economy in direct response to the shrinking of the formal economy; it is perhaps the only wealth in our history that benefits an important sector of the Bolivian population." In 1986 the aggregate value of coca production was 20 percent of farm income; in the Upper Huallaga Valley and Chapare, the proportion hit 90 percent. Peru's Alan García once called cocaine "our only successful multinational." For peasants, coca cultivation can be the margin between subsistence and a decent standard of living. It is an interesting example that agriculture can pay—as long as consumers are willing to pay for agricultural products.

Despite the money, coca also brings economic costs to production in imbalanced growth driven by conspicuous consumption, potential inflationary effects from the infusion of money, the displacement of domestic food production as more land is dedicated to coca, and environmental damage, especially through chemical processing. In addition to economic costs, the political price of narcoterrorism, the threat to democratic institutions, and international pressure is relatively high. The governments of the region have tried to promote alternative development by drawing producers toward new crops, but many peasants find the dollar lure of illicit crops irresistible. Furthermore, falling prices for agricultural products have turned back limited progress on alternative development schemes. Said one Colombian *cocaleiro,* "We grow coca for survival, not because we like it."[43]

The United States has attempted to stem trade in cocaine through controversial eradication programs. Plan Colombia provided $4 billion in assistance during 2000–2005 to restrict supply at the source. Contentious spraying programs have arguably failed to reduce the cocaine entering the United States; prices of cocaine, which should have risen with a decreased supply, have fallen or remained steady. Rather than spray, most recently Colombian president Alvaro Uribe has moved to manual eradication of coca.[44] Spraying had moved production from unprotected areas to national parks (where spraying was prohibited), putting pressure on sensitive ecosystems. Manual eradication, according to Uribe, will not have the negative effects of spraying Round-up on healthy plants and is also designed to interrupt the supply of narcodollars reaching guerrilla groups.[45] Even with manual eradication, the balloon effect—squeezing coca in one area only for it to inflate production in another region—is argued to undermine eradication efforts. Critics of eradication suggest that dollars would be better spent in promoting lucrative alternative development schemes for boutique legal agricultural products with high prices as well as in reinforcing demand-side policies in northern states.

CHARACTERISTICS IMPEDING SUSTAINABLE GROWTH IN THE AGRICULTURAL SECTOR

Moving beyond the price volatility of coffee or the illegality of coca is critical to promoting sustainable livelihoods in the agricultural sector. Nonetheless, structural characteristics of the agricultural market create challenges for successful policy. The agricultural sector is often characterized by missing or **incomplete markets** for products, labor, and finance and by high risk, in terms of both crop failure and pricing. Market failures result in inefficient or inequitable outcomes. They often result from inadequate property rights and underpriced or unpriced resources as well as unwise government regulations and subsidies. The rural poor are either landless farmworkers in commercial farming areas or small landholders in areas of low productivity. They lack adequate access to roads, potable water, electricity, communications, secondary schools, and public health. Indeed, it is difficult to think of another market as difficult and complex as agriculture. Let us consider the intersection of the problem of multiple market imperfections with the problem of small- and medium-size stakeholders in greater detail.

Property rights in the rural sector are often poorly defined, with official records frequently incomplete or nonexistent. A lack of computerization, insufficient staffing, or inappropriate storage facilities may contribute to poor record keeping. Conflicts emerge between nationally registered systems and de facto rights of occupancy by local squatters or customary rights of traditional communities.[46] Indige-

Small traditional farmers, many using sustainable techniques, have been squeezed out by large agroenterprises. *(Courtesy of Amanda McKown)*

nous land rights are sometimes mapped but not recognized. Settlers with guns have usurped traditional rights and crudely marked boundaries.[47]

Transferability or sale of rights is limited when land records are absent or conflicting, or when a functioning legal system with enforcement capabilities is missing. Secure land titles are often a prerequisite to obtaining credit. Poor judicial and police enforcement may make it difficult to exercise legal claims to land. Uncertainty in retaining property rights over time promotes underinvestment in the land and reduces the incentives to use land efficiently and sustainably. A farmer facing the possibility of eviction is less likely to invest in reforestation or conservation, because there is great uncertainty about reaping the benefits of the investment. For the farmer with tenuous land rights, environmental irresponsibility is economically rational.

According to the Food and Agriculture Organization, worldwide three of every four people suffering from hunger live in rural areas and depend on natural resources for survival. However, the majority don't have secure access to those resources.[48] In South America, cultivated land area is expected to increase more than 50 percent by 2050, with approximately 70 percent of the new land coming from deforestation and wetland conversion. The pressure for agricultural land in Central America is slightly lower at 40 percent but at a higher cost of 80 percent coming from forests and wetland areas.[49] Agriculture—for both corporate and peasant farmer—is therefore a major cause of forest loss in developing countries.

Developing countries typically have **segmented credit markets** such that different borrowers are charged different prices. Formal credit markets intermediated by state and private institutions generally charge a low rate of interest that is often government subsidized. But lack of access to collateral to guarantee formal-sector loans forces smaller holders to rely on kinship circles, friends, landlords, or professional moneylenders, often at higher than market interest rates. Agricultural lending is more difficult than commercial lending. The seasonal nature of agricultural activity yields products only at harvest season. Because the same adverse weather conditions affect all borrowers, diversification is problematic. Several factors complicate lending: a high cost to serving geographically dispersed customers, frequent deficits of collateral, problems in contract enforcement, and a lack of trained and motivated financial personnel in the rural sector.[50] There is an informational constraint as well, because less is usually known about a large number of little farmers. The typically high rates of interest in the informal sector can be traced to the ways these factors affect different groups of farmers. Small producers with uncertain harvests and a lack of collateral are less likely to find formal-sector lending than large, mechanized farms. Without credit, the investment in orchards that bear fruit years later, or even in vegetable farming with no returns until the end-of-season harvest, is extremely difficult for the small family farmer. In the past, some governments attempted to intermediate to provide cheaper rural credit through agricultural development banks offering rediscount lines at negative interest rates and frequent debt forgiveness. However, following the strict stabilization and adjustment policies of the 1990s, these traditional rural finance mechanisms have been curtailed due to heavy fiscal costs.[51]

Fundamental to agricultural success is **risk management.** Farmers face a range of risks: weather-related factors such as rain, floods, drought, winds, tornadoes, and hurricanes; geological factors such as earthquakes and volcanic eruptions; and biological factors including disease and insect infestations. Small- and medium-sized farmers in most developing countries have little access to formal agricultural insurance. Instead, those who are most vulnerable bear the full burden of risk. With Hurricane Stan in 2005, some communities lost practically all their crops—creating a domestic food crisis as well as a production crisis.[52] ECLAC estimated that Stan damaged 1.7 million acres in Guatemala—acres used for both export and subsistence production. Washed-out roads and bridges meant that coffee or sugar farmers whose crops were salvaged couldn't get goods to market.[53] This also happened after Central America's worst natural disaster, Hurricane Mitch in 1998, that affected 3.4 million people, principally in Honduras and Nicaragua. A U.S. government survey six months later estimated that three hundred thousand migrated to the United States in the storm's wake.[54] Northern Mexico faces continuing drought, the worst in 50 years. This has cost Mexican farmers 10 million tons of grain and the death or forced sale at low prices of 3 million head of cattle since 1992, according to the Confederation of Rural Landowners. Water reservoir levels have plunged below 15 percent. By its very nature agriculture is subject to risk and uncertainty. However, when Texas farmers face weather or disease, private as well as government crop insurance and disaster subsidies provide a safety net. Natural disasters happen to crops in industrialized countries; in the developing world they happen to people.[55]

In addition to credit and risk management, the allocation of **water rights** is another important element of incomplete or inefficient agricultural markets. Typically, surface water rights systems accrue based on seniority. Under this system, there is little incentive for those with first rights to conserve water to increase the availability to others. For groundwater, incentives need to be developed to prompt efficient use today and conservation for the future. In the case of surface water in rivers or streams, a market for water rights could be developed. Under this system, if those with prior rights were given a greater number of shares in a water rights system to head off political opposition, they could trade these shares, also prompting more efficient allocation of this scarce resource.[56]

Rural poverty has clear connections to **environmental degradation.** Those without assets find it hard to invest in the land through sustainable agricultural practices. The lack of attention to environmental considerations in the early stages of macroeconomic adjustment further resulted in a high degree of environmental degradation.[57] The lack of off-farm employment in the most isolated areas leaves households with few options except to pressure the land.[58] The intensification of agriculture has also had environmental costs. Attempts to increase agricultural output through intensive application of fertilizers and pesticides have contributed to environmental and human costs. Illiteracy and poor health training among uneducated workers have resulted in the poisoning of workers who spread pesticides by hand and then ate without washing. One investigation showed that 39 percent of pesticide applications were undertaken without protective clothing, and 18 percent of workers admitted to not washing after completing the chore. Mothers in Nicaraguan cotton regions were found to have DDT in breast milk, and some blame agrochemicals for the region's malaria epidemic.[59] Environmental degradation is a constraint in expanding agricultural output. Box 10.3 on rural electrification in Brazil gives an example of how innovative marketing of solar technologies can address rural poverty while improving the environment in Brazil. Good environmental laws are often not enough in the face of weak enforcement and strong incentives to deforest as a survival strategy. In the Brazilian Amazon, new farmers largely come from outside the

BOX 10.3. RURAL ELECTRIFCATION IN BRAZIL:
USING INNOVATIVE MARKETING FOR SOCIAL TRANSFORMATION

BY MARIAH HUDNUT

One of the most significant contributing factors to rural poverty worldwide is the lack of access to electricity. It is estimated that approximately 30% of the world's population is affected by this problem, which drastically lowers the standard of living and limits potential for development.

In Brazil, one man has taken action to address the need for rural electrification for the 25 million people living in the dark. Through hard work and undying persistence, Fabio Rosa has managed to transform the lives of thousands of Brazilians, using a mixture of appropriate technologies and innovative marketing strategies.

Rosa's work began in the late 1980s in the Southern part of Brazil with a pilot project called "Project Light," designed to provide cheap electricity to rural homes and farms. Rosa's ambition was to raise the quality of rural life in Brazil, and help quell the explosive urban migration draining the Brazilian countryside of human resources. Using inexpensive materials and innovative solar technologies, Rosa and his colleague Ricardo Mello developed a low cost electrical distribution system capable of providing electricity to millions of rural Brazilians. Rosa's system supplies power for a fraction of the cost of government-supplied power, and has far fewer environmental implications than traditional methods of electricity generation.

With electricity privatization in the 1990s, private companies shunned Rosa's project because rural electrification was much less profitable than urban grids. Rosa had to look for a new marketing strategy to continue providing electricity to people at a low cost. He discovered a new, superior way to reach the rural poor: through a rental system. Because the actual purchase of solar panels was prohibitive for most rural Brazilians, Rosa developed a system whereby people could rent solar panels and pay a low per-month fee of US$10–24 for electricity. The rental prices under this "Sun Shines for All" project are much lower than the alternatives.

In addition to the economic savings through rural electrification, the solar energy technologies have important environmental benefits. Program evaluations show that if these decentralized micro-technologies reach 52,000 people, 9 million liters of kerosene, 4.6 million kilos of liquefied petroleum gas, and 23.3 million liters of diesel fuel would be conserved, significantly reducing carbon emissions.

During the 1980s, Rosa spread his system to over 27,000 people, and throughout the 1990s, he has reached hundreds of thousands more. He continues to tirelessly work towards his goal of universal electrification, constantly updating his business strategy to best serve his target clientele. "First," he says, "we will demonstrate results on a small scale, then on a regional scale, then all over Brazil, and then all over the world."

Sources: Ashoka Fellow Profile, http://www.ashoka.org/fellos/viewporile3.cfm?reid=96996, "Utilizing the Market for Environmental Changes," Adapted from essays by Fabio Rosa, Ashoka Fellow, Brazil; http://changemakers.net/journal/01march/rosa.cfm; David Bornstein, "Fabio Rosa: Making the Sun Shine for All," May 2003, http://changemakers.net/journal/03may/bornstein.cfm.

region, bringing skills unsuitable for the region. Soils are generally poor; farmers slash and burn for a one-time transfer of stored biomass to the soil. In subsequent years, without fertilizer the yields decline rapidly. One simulation suggests that despite regulations for small landholders to leave half the land in forest, the archetypical farm will be completely deforested in about ten years—but will have an income above poverty. Causes of tropical deforestation are therefore quite local, tied to struggles to improve welfare in the face of credit, information, and other constraints.[60]

The Gender Dimension and Politics

Agricultural production has a **gendered dimension.** Women are the invisible contributors to agricultural production. Economic activity by women in the rural sector has risen from 16.2 percent to 25.2 percent from 1980 to 2000—yet this number is likely to be statistically underreported.[61] Nicaraguan census data report only 5–12 percent of women involved in farming, yet an IADB study found 50 percent of the labor of corn and bean production being carried out by women. With an expanded regional survey methodology, the IADB shows participation rates of 68–90 percent of rural women. By including the subsistence activities of women—the "secondary" activities assumed by women of maintaining the livestock and kitchen gardens and handling postharvest processing—a more accurate picture of women's contributions to agriculture is emerging.[62] Out of their sixteen-hour daily workload, women usually dedicated an average of four hours to farming. The rural woman's day is consumed by food preparation, collection of water and firewood, care of vegetable gardens and domestic animals, clearing and plowing land, weeding, cultivating, milking cows, processing milk and other foods to sell at market, and acting as business managers for the family enterprise.[63] Unlike men, whose crops tend to be seasonal, they work year-round to provide food for their families. When men migrate to the cities in search of work, women are left completely in charge of the farms. The transition to export crops has also opened up new employment opportunities for women. Large agroindustries employ predominantly female labor forces, because women tend to be more readily available to work on a seasonal basis for lower wages.[64] In eleven of thirteen countries, with Bolivia and Brazil as the exceptions, the majority of active rural women are employed in nonagricultural activities, ranging from 57 percent in Paraguay to 92 percent in Panama. In Central America women largely work in *maquila* production; other activities include the service sector and commerce. Low-productivity activities with low wages such as cloth weaving, street vending, or domestic services help comprise the survival strategy of the household.[65] Older daughters in a household take on additional tasks, releasing women for remunerated labor.[66] This naturally calls into question traditional roles in the rural family. Without changes in the social division of labor in the family, women's increased work in the commercial sector is on top of an already long day in the rural home. Sound agricultural policy must take the problems of rural poverty, its environmental dimensions, and its gendered characteristics into account.

Women's invisibility in agriculture has been perpetuated by a **gender asset gap** in the region. Historically men have been granted preference in inheritance and privilege in marriage and have also benefited from a bias in community, state, or market allocation of land. Legal constraints have impeded gender parity in land distribution. In Mexico, for example, historically the rules of *ejido* membership allowed titles to be held only by one person per household. Although the purpose was to avoid dividing the parcel and creating uneconomical farming units, the un-intended effect was for families to favor sons in distribution. Indeed sons were often made beneficiaries of a father's estate to the detriment of surviving wives.[67] As men were considered heads of the household, women's property rights were largely cir-cumscribed until the mid- to late twentieth century.[68] When decisions were made about community land distribution, the assemblies were comprised of men—who favored patrimonial patterns. Illiterate women found it difficult to contest their rights. Legal changes have now established the principle of joint titling, reinforcing the notion of dual heads of household and allowing women a stronger say in the hereditary pattern of distribution.

Nonetheless, despite more equal treatment under the law, in practice women have yet to achieve parity in landholdings. Under contemporary land redistribution programs in Brazil, for example, eligibility to receive land is contingent on assem-bling an identity card, a registration number, a voter's card, a land reform receipt book, a rental contract, and a work permit—documents that can cost a month's salary for the poorest to obtain. Although some organizations are working to register women as potential beneficiaries, the process can be slow and cumbersome.[69] Rural trade unions are beginning to include representation for women, and the Brazilian national rural women's movement has struggled for great recognition, but women remain underrepresented in asset holdings in the countryside.[70] The argument for greater gender parity in land has larger developmental implications. In Honduras and Nicaragua the amount of land that women own has a significant and positive impact on food expenditure and on educational attainment.[71] Equity in assets is important in promoting overall equity in outcomes.

In addition to market failure arguments we must also consider the **political economy** explanation for the failure of agriculture to generate an adequate income for most rural inhabitants. Politically, governments have viewed agriculture as a declining sector with falling prices. The rural poor have little political power; urban elites have therefore pursued policies that disadvantage agriculture. Past policies on the part of multilateral organizations have been overly centralized, with top-down integrated rural development schemes ignoring the needs of rural inhabitants. Credit was directed to specific crops and often concentrated in the hands of the rural elites. Frontier settlements contributed to environmental degradation, and many large-scale irrigation projects carried unforeseen environmental costs.[72]

In the past, rural development policies may have been too narrowly targeted toward agriculture and failed to address the multiple market imperfections and the heterogeneity of the rural sector. Rural poverty programs must consider three key groups: farmers, the landless agricultural workers, and rural non-farmworkers. It must also take into account the diversity of rural economies. For example, whether a region sits in a **rural exclusive area** with little or no infrastructure, few perma-nent structures, and low population density or whether the rural area is connected to local and international markets is crucial to policy design. Inhabitants of rural exclusive zones suffer the most abject poverty. In northeastern Brazil, for example, among the poorest 20 percent of the population, 75 percent of household heads are illiterate, 27 percent of teachers have incomplete primary education, and 26 percent of schools have no sanitary infrastructure. Options to improve livelihoods are limited by the dearth of human capital and the lack of opportunity for nonfarm employment. Exit strategies for rural poverty must therefore provide a safety net for those trapped in poverty, permit migration of the young from remote low-density rural areas, stimulate the growth of rural nonfarm activities where possible, foster dynamic commercial agriculture in areas connected to markets, and intensify the productivity and income of the small-farm sector.[73] Geography matters. Different topographic, climatic, and sociocultural factors must be taken into consideration. In rural Ecuador, for example, a poorly qualified workforce with 23–27 percent of the small producers having no kind of education, a high degree of concentration in land ownership, availability of credit (even informal) to only 7 percent of agricultural producers, and the poor state of rural roads increasing transactions costs are key factors that must shape policy design.[74] Geography, gender, politics, and incomplete markets present enormous obstacles to change. But surely something can be done. Appreciating constraints, we now turn to policy options.

AGRICULTURAL POLICY OPTIONS: REDRESSING MULTIPLE MARKET FAILURES AND RURAL INEQUALITY

A strategy to spur rural development must take a broad focus, moving beyond the narrow agricultural sector to include the entire rural productive system.[75] The management of natural and human resources, infrastructure development, and social development must be woven into a comprehensive strategy. Past policy mistakes in rural development derive in part from a narrow focus. Rather than simply look at irrigation and drainage, questions of resource allocation and comprehensive watershed management must be addressed. Instead of a focus on crop production, forestry, or livestock management, attention must be given to management of natural resources in a sustainable production system. Human capital development, infrastructure, and community-based decision making form the basis of an equitable, sustainable strategy. Stakeholders must be involved in the development and execution of projects.[76]

The greatest challenge in any agricultural strategy is to create equitable pathways to rising farm productivity. Farmers need incentives to produce more with fewer inputs. Cheap food for burgeoning urban populations is often a key policy objective. Yet if the price of foodstuffs falls without a decrease in the costs to the farmer, farm income is likely to suffer. Maintaining rural incomes while supporting urban populations can best be resolved by either increasing export quantities or decreasing costs through improvements in technology. But export-driven models do not guarantee benefits to the poor, and technological change costs money. If the dynamism in the rural sector is going to extend beyond large corporate farms, a system of peasant credit is necessary to support advances in small-scale farming. Technological change is also risky: if a peasant is living on the margins of subsistence, although change might have a large production payoff, it could also fail dismally, and the family would likely starve. Policies to improve productivity for peasant farmers must acknowledge the risk-averse nature of small-scale producers and provide flexible, extended terms to smooth the potential losses in any one year.

Policy remedies for incomplete markets include securing transferable property rights, creating enforceable contracts, removing subsidies, implementing market-based initiatives as opposed to command and control regulations, adopting green accounting methods and peer monitoring, and cosigning loans to decrease risk. In credit markets, mechanisms have been employed to reduce the risk to lenders of bad loans through relying on local leaders or group-lending schemes.[77] Positive incentives such as interest rebates for timely repayment and access to new benefits including longer time horizons may enhance enforcement of repayment. Negative sanctions such as legal proceedings may be useful, but the large number of small producers makes enforcement tough and costly. Local governance structures, such as cooperative lending to promote repayment, are more promising. Such unconventional rural finance can also facilitate the growth of horizontal civic rural institutions, enhancing the sustainability and equity of rural finance.[78]

The State-Market Mix

Our policy measures can once again be broken down as neoliberal, new institutionalist, and neostructuralist. Pure marketeers will focus on removing governmental restrictions in the agricultural market, eliminating subsidies, and opening markets to free trade. They would also push to strengthen and clarify contractual property rights. New institutionalists would focus on the high transaction costs imposed by incomplete markets and would revamp agricultural credit systems.

Consistent with a mix of neoliberal and institutionalist market approaches, agricultural loans supported by the new integrated rural development strategy of the World Bank are structured to help eliminate price controls, replacing generalized subsidies with targeted interventions. They are geared to develop competitive local markets for inputs and outputs and to reduce state interventions in international trade. In terms of agricultural trade policy, the goals are to replace quantitative restrictions with tariffs and to abolish state marketing boards. Improvements in the legal and regulatory system should include land tenure, export regulations, phyto-sanitary procedures, and the licensing of commerce. Finally, a stronger emphasis on food security might include targeted spending on food and nutrition programs. For example, Mexico was given a World Bank loan to support trade, price, privatization, and other policy reforms and reduce the government's role in the production, planning, marketing, storage, and processing of agricultural products and inputs. In Honduras, support was given to modify the land reform law, improve property rights, permit the development of land markets, and reorient forestry practices toward protection and conservation of the environment.[79]

For neostructuralists, policies designed to improve the functioning of the market that ignore a class and gendered understanding of market actors face likely failure. In Latin America, agricultural reform is about more than markets. It involves the power of elites to influence policy outcomes.[80] In a case of imperfect factor markets, in which different-sized farms face different prices for labor, capital, or technology, the strongest—the largest—are most likely to benefit from policy changes. For example, in the macroeconomic changes accompanying neoliberal reforms in the government of Violetta Chamorro in Nicaragua—a nation that pursued aggressive redistributive land reform—small farmers were shown to fail in tough times, selling between 6 and 13 percent of the land back to large-scale owners or wealthy individuals.[81] Policy must take the market structure into account.

But this doesn't mean that neostructuralists will advocate large size. Although small-scale farmers are more vulnerable to external policy shocks, it is not clear that large farmers are necessarily more productive than small farmers. Evidence suggests that with the exception of plantation crops such as sugar or cotton, or where market imperfections such as access to credit or information about international marketing exist, there are few economies of scale in agriculture for farms larger than a family can operate with its own labor. One historical study contrasted the relatively small landholdings in the United States under the Homestead Act, with limits of 160 acres, to large-scale allocations of land in Brazilian agriculture of plots no smaller than 988 acres. It showed that large size forced Brazilian farmers to rely on wage labor, with the resulting inefficiencies in supervising hired labor, as opposed to the incentives for the family farmer to rely on productive family labor.[82] Furthermore, to supplement meager wage earnings on the large Brazilian farm, a system of sharecropping emerged that later introduced its own fears in terms of evictions in the face of possible land invasions or impending land reform. Large landowners evict poor sharecroppers because they are afraid of land invasions from squatters exercising the right of occupancy.

Where should the state intervene directly in agricultural policy? A state role is critical in dealing with common property and environmental sustainability issues. Public institutions are preferable when benefits are diffuse, when the public policies require change, or when enhanced equity is a central goal. A public-private mix works best when the ability to achieve responsive and flexible management is contingent on political influence. A strictly private provision of services is superior when direct and continuous interaction with users is required.[83] The appropriate mix of state and market is therefore a function of local conditions. The agricultural sector may be an example where the temptation to employ our neat policy prescriptions of neoliberal, neoinstitutionalist, or neostructuralist may lead to policy failure unless we are clear on the characteristics of the market.

Agricultural policy reform has paralleled broader changes in development policy in the 1990s. The broad elements of reform, as captured by a World Bank directive in 1982, combine the use of markets and prices with strengthening property rights and regulatory institutions to promote productivity increases in the agricultural sector.[84] In part the answer to the new mix between state and market in the agricultural sector depends on the type of good or service being delivered. If the good is a plantation product such as sugar, a new tractor, or new seed, the private sector can probably address the need. If, however, the constraint is in practices such as farm management or marketing, some combination of public and private efforts is most likely to bear fruit. Finally, in areas affected by externalities and uses of common resources, government intervention is critical to provide incentives for cooperative voluntary action. In the agricultural sector, the new role for the state is to create enabling environments for private and voluntary action—not to deliver the goods or the technologies, as in the past.[85] Enhancing the voice of farmers in a demand-driven approach may result in a more efficient and equitable agricultural system.

Agricultural Extension Programs: Getting Farmers Involved

The constraints in agriculture suggest that simply getting prices right is clearly not enough. **Agricultural extension programs** must speak to the family and cultural needs of the farmer. Improvements in productivity are driven by encouraging farmers to adopt new agricultural practices. This has historically been accomplished through agricultural extension programs. The World Bank estimates that global extension services have reached one million direct beneficiaries—an unsatisfactory record given the number of rural poor.[86] However, many farmers find agricultural extension programs ineffective. Problems with free extension services included budget pressures, poorly defined objectives, low motivation, a lack of accountability to clients, and little interest on the part of farmers in obtaining quality service. Centralized systems are also costly and inefficient delivery vehicles for services. In an era of fiscal tightening, expensive, centrally directed extension programs are unsustainable. In contrast, demand-driven services operate on the market concept that extension is an economic input that, if effective, may generate additional income that farmers would be willing to pay for. Free services may result in underuse or overuse.[87]

As a measure of their effectiveness, when extension services were cut in Nicaragua in December 1995, no one went on strike. Yet when university financial support was cut, strikes were widespread. In part this had to do with an outdated centralized extension system in which information was delivered to peasants and not developed and appropriated by them. Extension can also have a gendered dimension, because in some cultures it is inappropriate for a male outside the household to work closely with a female. Peasant farmers need to be involved in determining the necessary changes in farming practices to solve local problems. Extension should be thought of not as the transfer of knowledge but rather as the development of agriculture systems to promote innovation and sustainable growth.

One program shows promise in Nicaragua—a demand-driven accountable extension system through the Agricultural Technology and Land Management Project, financed by the World Bank and the Swiss government. Through demonstration of a willingness to pay, farmers shape the services of the extension agent. Providers of extension services compete for contracts; because dissatisfied farmers can cease to be clients of extension agents, this creates a stake on the part of the agents to be more attentive to the needs of the farmers.[88] Despite initial objections, through small group meetings with farmers, extension agents overcame the lack of confidence of clients. In a voluntary pilot test, they were convinced that it was to their benefit to pay for services. An NGO provided credit to purchase the extension services. In addition, half the crop increase would go to the extensionist, with half retained by the farmers. The extension agent was to visit the site at least once a week. Although measurement of output was somewhat suspect, with overreporting of historical yields and underreporting of current production, the success of the program was defined by a uniform willingness to sign new contracts for the following season. Similarly, in a Costa Rican project to address the needs of poorer farmers, government vouchers are awarded for extension services to farmers on the basis of farm type.[89] Farmers will trade vouchers for the services of extension agents, building up a corps of private extension agents accountable to local clients. As farmers see the gains from effective extension services, vouchers will gradually be eliminated and private provision of services will take over.

With limited public resources to provide extension services, private-sector participation in promoting innovation and change in the rural sector has garnered increased attention. From a 2005 survey of Latin American agribusiness, Carlos Pomareda finds that private firms are encouraged to invest in innovation in agribusiness when there is a clear understanding of the costs and benefits of innovating production and market processes, when there is demonstrated demand for a product or services from innovation, when competition spurs innovation, when a favorable investment climate exists, and when intellectual property rights are well established.[90] A new generation of community and commercial organization such as dairy cooperatives in Chile, Costa Rica, and Peru and horticulture and coffee producers in Colombia have sprung up to expand production and processing of agricultural productions. Private corporations are partnering with these and other university or government entities to promote the development of new products and processes. Some of the more successful partnerships have taken place in the diagnosis of pests affecting product quality, development of processing standards for fruits and vegetables, and genetic adaptation of cereal varieties to local conditions. Commitment, technical capacity, economies of scale, strong facilitators, and leadership all contribute to project success.[91]

Other innovative means have been used to raise efficiency in cost and quality in extension services. In Colombia, research extension projects for small landholders are generated on a demand-driven basis. Locally run networks develop ideas for projects that are then submitted to regional review panels. Approximately 17 percent are approved. Forty-six percent of project finance comes from outside the state, relieving pressure on extension budgets. Because the projects are linked to real needs of small landholders, the quality has risen. Cofinancing is also an aspect of the Venezuelan system, where all levels of government and society contribute to extension services. In Ecuador a competitive fund has also been established with cofinancing; it is estimated that the research dollar is stretching 40 percent further as new partners in NGOs and universities are engaged. Alliances with international organizations are also encouraging access to the latest knowledge in the sector.[92]

Participation, Decentralization, and Community Control

In part, the difficult challenge of agricultural policy derives from the fact that farmers are not simply workers or owners but are inhabitants in a rural system with different practices from those in urban commercial markets. Agricultural policy—far more so than industrial policy—must be community based. **Demand-driven rural**

investment funds (**DRIFs**) are an instrument for improving local control of agricultural development. Through DRIFs, central governments transfer funds to local governments and communities to address their own priorities within a carefully constructed set of guidelines. Beneficiaries include neighborhood associations, women's groups, and producer associations or cooperatives. Specific eligibility requirements must be met, including cost limits, and beneficiaries are required to contribute to the project cost either directly or through in-kind work. In Mexico, for example, communities must contribute a minimum of 20 percent of the project costs. Communities decide for themselves what type of technical assistance is required and then receive the funding to pay for it. The Mexican experience with DRIFs has extended to thirty thousand subprojects with average costs 30–60 percent less than traditional centralized funding mechanisms. The economic sustainability of the projects is also higher, because local groups are vested in the project from the start.[93]

State and Market Experience with Land Reform

One of the politically most explosive aspects of agricultural policy is land reform. From an economic perspective, the cost of unequal landholdings may be high. Some evidence suggests that the legacy of unequal landholdings can pose a serious barrier to growth over the long term. One study shows that initial land distribution and associated low primary education for sixteen developing countries explain variation in national growth rates. Other empirical investigations also point to this inverse relationship between land inequality and economic growth.[94] As demonstrated by Southeast Asian nations, small family farmers supplemented by investments in rural infrastructure appear to fare better in terms of long-run growth. In contrast, the unequal land distribution from colonial times in Brazil, Colombia, or Guatemala, as worsened by a policy mix of industrial protection under ISI and agricultural taxation, constrained dynamic growth in the agricultural sector.[95]

Politically, and for the neostructuralist, unequal landholdings correlate with unequal power and unfair access to resources. It is important to consider that existing patterns of landholdings may be suboptimal from both an economic as well as a social standpoint. According to Klaus Deininger, historically discriminatory patterns of landholdings rather than market forces provide justification for land reform.[96] In Guatemala, for example, communal lands were expropriated in 1879 after a declaration giving proprietors (likely illiterate and uninformed) three months to register land titles (which wouldn't exist for communal land) after which the land would be declared abandoned. Most of the abandoned land was then given to coffee growers.[97] Property rights were constructed socially according to the power of the state. Reversing these politically appropriated rights then becomes a politically charged issue. Conflict also affects land boundaries. One Colombian expert estimated that since the 1990s both drug traffickers and paramilitaries in the Colombian conflict appropriated three million to four million hectares of land—more than the state had redistributed in the preceding thirty-five years. The tough political decision was made in 1996 to authorize forcible expropriation of illegally acquired lands without compensation.[98]

Land reform has been used in Latin America to address asset inequality in the rural sector. How reform takes place is quite controversial. Should the government confiscate land? Should compensation be paid for land granted centuries ago? When land is not being productively used, does the state have the right (and at what price) to redistribute property? Can the market be used in land reform efforts? These are some of the many questions informing the debate. The land reform movement in Mexico and Bolivia was revolutionary; throughout the rest of the region it was a legislated process. Extensive land reforms were undertaken in Chile, Ecuador, El Salvador, Nicaragua, and Peru—although they have generally failed to reduce the poverty of the peasantry. Several issues inform the process. What is the optimal size of farms? As farms are broken up, will small peasant farmers have access to credit, technology, and new equipment to increase productivity? If the nation does not have idle land, whose land should be taken, and what kind of compensation should be offered? When the easy stage of capturing idle or uncolonized land is over, how will the confiscation affect the credibility of property rights in the economy? Should the process take place quickly to send signals of resolve, or does a slower, more measured program allow for the development of complementary infrastructure? How nations have resolved these questions defined the nature of their land reforms. We will now consider some of the regional experience in addressing these issues.

Given high inequality, Mexican agriculture was strongly characterized by the bimodal agricultural production system. In response to high inequality, Mexican land reform was a legacy of the Zapatista agitation in 1917. Based on the constitutional recognition of community rights to land, it created a system of small landholdings called ejidos. In practice the ejido was farmed individually, but the land could not be sold. Despite this land reform, some of the best lands remained under the control of wealthy farmers. Today the large-farm sector produces 70 percent of all marketable food and nearly half the exports. The ejidos, poorly integrated into the marketplace, suffer from a lack of roads and marketing networks, producing corn and beans for peasant subsistence.[99] Attempts were made by various administrations to assist peasants. During the 1970s, under the Luis Echeverria administration (1970–1976), state marketing agencies bought peasant commodities at subsidized prices to support small-scale agricultural production. President Miguel de la Madrid (1982–1988) confronted the problem of land fragmentation without complementary resources, and his successor, President Carlos Salinas (1988–1994), called for the modernization of the ejido through privatized joint ventures—without fundamentally altering the *campesino* way of life.[100] Nevertheless, the primary purpose of the policies was, too often, to support the political arm of government, the Mexican Revolutionary Party (PRI), and not to improve the peasants' lives.

Reduction of subsidies under the neoliberal model and the opening of agricultural markets to imports have further impoverished the peasantry. The 1994 Chiapas rebellion in Mexico can be seen as evidence of the rural crisis exacerbated by the opening to international markets.[101] An ECLAC study showed approximately 11 percent of ejido agricultural producers in Chiapas to be commercially viable; 58 percent are diversified producers who barely eke out an existence on the land, earning a surplus of about three hundred dollars per year, and 31 percent are subsistence farmers on the margins of economic life unable to obtain basic necessities from their efforts.[102] In contrast to the ejido farmers is the commercialized private sector. Large commercial landowners control the most productive assets, while Indians and peasants are forced to the margins. Such poverty and inequality create ripe ground for rebellion. Reprivatization of rural institutions of credit and technology and a sharp decline in public investment in the sector have left the Mexican peasantry without access to institutional resources to improve productivity. Small- and medium-sized farmers would benefit from the promotion of producer organizations for self-delivery of services and lowering of transactions costs of bringing goods to market. A transition program orchestrated by governmental agencies, NGOs, and the private sector is necessary to preserve the economic viability of this important sector.[103] The World Bank and the government of Mexico are collaborating on developing decentralized approaches to enhance small-scale social and productive infrastructure.[104]

In Bolivia, land reform was designed to address problems of increasing violence in the countryside due to the unbalanced nature of landholdings. Beginning in 1952, 80 percent of land was affected by the redistribution process. Eighty-two percent of farmers—largely poor—holding 1 percent of the land began to invade large estates and claim property. Often the expropriation was spontaneously undertaken by *campesinos,* without governmental assistance. This later created problems of legal title to the land, and settlement of property rights has taken decades. Furthermore, the process was not accompanied by a program of capital assistance to the peasant farmers. Although the Bolivian reform was a political success, economically it did little to improve the lives of the peasantry. Ironically, a residual of the poorly orchestrated reform process is that cocaine production is easily maintained on a large number of small plots without much in the way of technological assistance.

In Peru, the process of land reform was guided by clear political objectives: to bring social justice to the rural areas, to support an enlargement of the internal market, and to contribute to the capital formation critical for rapid industrialization. The revolutionary military government of General Juan Velasco initiated an ambitious program in 1969 that expropriated 40–50 percent of agricultural land. Land was subject to expropriation if it was between 150 and 200 hectares on the coast and 150 to 330 hectares on the sierra; land could also be expropriated if certain conditions were not met, such as provision of satisfactory living conditions for workers. Workers were also supposed to receive 50 percent of the profit, own 50 percent of the capital, and receive 20 percent of net income.[105] Land was reorganized as agrarian cooperatives. This decision, geared to maintain scale economies and allow cooperative farming, did not translate into improving productivity and incomes.[106] The Peruvian land reform experience was state directed as opposed to spontaneously driven by peasant demands. Problems with compensation for expropriated lands bogged down the process, resulting in delays that undermined legitimacy. Later, revolutionary groups such as Sendero Luminoso in the highlands were better able to provide the support that peasants needed for survival. As in Mexico and Bolivia, failed Peruvian land reform has had a high political cost.

The Chilean land reform process has been reversed to some degree by the effects of the agroexport boom. Data show that nearly half of the *parceleros,* the small-scale farmers given land under reform measures, completely sold their farms between the late 1970s and 1991, leading to a reconcentration of land in medium to large holdings. Forty-seven percent of *parceleros* in the fruit boom region became completely landless by 1990, excluding these smaller farmers from the direct benefits of the agroexport boom. However, this exclusionary model was somewhat offset by an increase in labor absorption of the boom, providing employment for the landless peasants.[107] The experience in Guatemala demonstrates different results with agroexports, with small farmers benefiting from the boom in nontraditional exports. The differences between the Chilean and Guatemalan experiences reflect differential impacts of crop choice on small farmers. Small farmers tend to be more risk averse, fearful that the adoption of new technologies or crops could, if unsuccessful, wipe out their livelihood. They tend to face higher prices for inputs and lower prices for outputs than larger farms that are able to take advantage of economies of scale. In particular, they are poorly connected to marketing and transportation networks. Small farmers often have a difficult time gaining access to credit, and they have been able to invest less in their own human capital. These biases against small farmers interact with crop choice. Orchard crops for fruit exports in Chile require multiyear investments; vegetable crops in Guatemala may advantage smaller producers because they are relatively labor intensive. Small-scale farmers did not find themselves in competition with large-scale producers for land or resources.[108] But this is not to say that the land problem is solved in Guatemala. Two percent of landowners hold two-thirds of the country's land.[109]

Contemporary land reform in Venezuela has generated interesting debate with regard to the definitions of historical title as well as productive land. Land ownership in Venezuela is highly concentrated in great landed estates. According to the government organization that oversees redistribution efforts, 60 percent of arable property belongs to just 2 percent of landowners.[110] The first stage of redistribution under the government of President Hugo Chavez took place from land held by the government. Under the 2001–2003 Land and Agrarian Development Law, the "Return to the Countryside" provision set limits on the size of landholding, taxed unused property as an incentive to spur agricultural activity, and redistributed unused, initially government, land to peasant families and cooperatives with compensation at fair market value.[111] By 2004 with the appointment of the president's brother Adán, distribution accelerated. The shift toward appropriation of privately held land began in 2005 under Mission Zamora. The name of the campaign refers back to a military agitator for land reform in the mid-1800s—a period of civil war during which many landholders expanded their property by fencing in public and communal land. Approximately 3.7 million acres of land (an area larger than the country of England) have been deemed idle and await redistribution by the government. The state is working with "social production companies," essentially cooperatives with state-supported housing, health care, education, and soft agricultural credit, to run agricultural and ranching operations. Two legal issues are in play. The first is the definition of "idle" lands. How, for example, should environmental conservation easements be considered? In one highly publicized seizure of the La Marquesena ranch, questions of buffer lands around a dam complicate the problem. What is the margin for error in classification of productivity? Second, the title must be in question. If the title was issued before 1847, it is relatively safe. Interestingly, part of La Marquesena reportedly belonged to Chavez's great-grandfather, a veteran of the civil wars fought a century ago. The Chavez family property was lost in 1850; as the land became part of La Marquesena after 1847, it is now subject to reappropriation and redistribution.[112] In addition to these legal issues, implementation problems plague the program. Redistribution is to go to cooperatives—yet there are problems in creating sustainable cooperatives among independent farmers who lack adequate training and political education.[113] Furthermore, with the dislocation in agriculture caused by the violent defense of land in the countryside, production has suffered. There is a strong need for food for the 90 percent of the twenty-six million of Venezuela's population who live in the city. Supported by oil revenues, Venezuela is current importing 6,000 metric tons of milk a month and a similar amount of beef, a 20 percent rise since Chavez came to power.[114] Some are also concerned about the effect of the assault on private property rights in promoting a climate for investment in the country.[115]

Several lessons can be distilled from the experience with land reform. First, the easy stages of redistributing unproductive land are over. Land is in short supply, so redistribution now has a clear economic opportunity cost. The goal of increased production may be harmed, because taking land away from large owners may result in less land available for export sectors. Second, land reform has not helped the poorest of the rural poor. Those who were relatively better off were able to take advantage of changes in policy; those on the margins of existence were less adept at working with authorities to transform property rights. Third, land reform works best when accompanied by ample credit and technical assistance. Simply owning land without the complementary inputs does little to raise productivity or incomes. The presumption in some land reform efforts that larger size was more efficient may have really been a proxy for the fact that larger farms had access to credit, not that larger farms are necessarily more efficient. To succeed, land reform therefore requires a comprehensive strategy for rural development. Fourth, policies adopted may have differential effects on small and large landowners. A policy package that reduces biases toward large holders and secures property rights of small peasants may help reduce rural poverty. This package could be supplemented with public investments to develop infrastructure and promote better exchange of information among small farmers to encourage broader-based growth. Picking labor-intensive crops to promote may direct growth toward the small farmer.[116] Fifth, this strategy must incorporate environmental as well as economic dimensions of reform. Environmental deterioration is closely tied to **insecure property rights,** inadequate credit, and poorly designed public infrastructure for water use, waste disposal, or transportation of goods to market.

Toward Sustainable Rural Livelihoods

Agricultural reform is more than land reform. Box 10.4 provides a strategic checklist for rural development. Reform requires changes in law as well as public and private investments. Public resources for an integrated rural development strategy might come from increased taxation of agricultural land, particularly unproductive land. Higher taxation of larger parcels might encourage private market sales to small-scale producers. Revenues from taxation can be used for public infrastructure as well as financing loans to prospective buyers. Multilateral and bilateral international assistance in agricultural reform can help in project lending for infrastructure, and NGOs can facilitate grassroots access to poor farmers to promote extension services well suited to local conditions. In one IADB project in Brazil, rural families are being helped in their efforts to create self-sufficient communities through improving infrastructure, providing social services to settlers, and establishing a set of procedures to transform settlements into economically viable units.[117] Carefully crafted policies with clear results are important to demonstrate the benefits of infrastructure investments as well as gain the confidence of small farmers in new techniques for small-scale production. Technical support for agricultural production should not be restricted to primary production activities but should also emphasize marketing, value added, management, and other aspects.[118]

Concrete achievements will build confidence in the rural reform process. Overall, the key to a strong agricultural policy is to raise productivity while simultaneously including the poor. In doing so it is essential to triage the really poor, providing emergency relief. From there, working with community organizers to resolve land tenure issues, define emergent farmers, and identify technologies appropriate to local practices and conditions will facilitate rural development. A complementary program between the agricultural and nonagricultural sectors will help stem the migration from the farm to the cities. Providing off-farm activities for those unable to make it in farming will also help reverse the demographic tides toward urbanization. Nonetheless, coordination of an agricultural policy with other aspects of reform may require a superministry, or a national coordinator with authority over other ministries, and a great deal of political will. Box 10.4 provides a strategic checklist for government rural development policy. The key to the millennium rural development strategy at the World Bank is a better recognition of the needs of the poor with a focus on the neglected political voice of the rural poor.[119] Addressing these issues will facilitate a balanced development strategy that provides sustainable resources for a greater portion of the agricultural population in the region.

BOX 10.4.   STRATEGIC CHECKLIST FOR RURAL DEVELOPMENT

- Macroeconomic and sectoral policies are stable. The foreign exchange, trade, and taxation regimes do not discriminate against agriculture but are similar for rural and urban sectors.
- The growth of private agriculture is encouraged by minimizing distortions among input and output markets and by market development for agricultural and agro-industrial products, both at home and abroad.
- Public investment and expenditure programs for economic and social infrastructure, health, nutrition, education, and family planning services do not discriminate against rural populations or the rural poor.

continued

continued

- Large farms and large agroindustrial firms do not receive special privileges and are not able to reduce competition in output, input, land, or credit markets.
- The agrarian structure is dominated by efficient and technologically sophisticated family operators who rely primarily on their own family's labor. The rights and needs of women farmers and wage laborers are explicitly recognized.
- Access to and security of land and water rights are actively promoted. Restricting land rentals hurts the poor. Where land distribution is highly unequal, land reform is needed. Decentralized, participatory, and market-assisted approaches to land reform can achieve this much faster than expropriations by land reform parastatals.
- Private and public sectors complement each other in generating and disseminating knowledge and technologies. Public-sector financing is particularly important for areas of limited interest to the private sector such as strategic research, small land-holder extension, and diffusion of sustainable production systems and techniques.
- Rural development programs mobilize the skill, talents, and labor of the rural population through administrative, fiscal, and management systems that are decentralized and participatory and through private-sector involvement.
- Rural development programs are designed so that the rural poor and other vulnerable groups are fully involved in the identification, design, and implementation of the programs. Otherwise, rural elites will appropriate most of the benefits.
- Sustainable rural development requires multidisciplinary and pluralistic approaches to poverty, social and gender equity, local economic development, natural resource management, and governance.
- An agricultural focus is necessary but not sufficient for sustainable rural development; key are integrated approaches to infrastructure, technology, and building institutional capacity.
- Solutions in rural development must be based on participation, empowerment, and rural governance in contrast to earlier programs of top-down, noninclusive approaches.
- A holistic agricultural strategy must also foster growth of the private-sector and market mechanisms for financial sustainability.

Source: Adapted from World Bank, *Rural Development: From Vision to Action,* Environmentally and Socially Sustainable Development Studies and Monograph Series No. 12 (Washington, D.C.: World Bank, 1997), and World Bank Rural Development Strategy: *Reaching the Rural Poor,* draft posted at www.worldbank.org, June 2002.

Key Concepts

agricultural extension
   programs
demand-driven rural
   investment funds
   (DRIFs)
dualistic structure of
   production
environmental degradation

fair trade labels
gender asset gap
incomplete markets
insecure property rights
land reform
nontraditional agricultural
   exports (NTAEs)
nontraditional exports

political economy
property rights
risk management
rural exclusive area
segmented credit
   markets
water rights

Chapter   Summary

Latin American Agriculture: Diverse Structures and Performances

- The agricultural sector in Latin America is characterized by its dualistic nature: corporate farming and small-scale, traditional peasant agriculture. The trend in many Latin American countries has been a shift away from production for local consumption to production for exports. Commercialization for exports has marginalized peasant farmers and increased migration from the rural sector into the cities.
- Although some Latin American countries have experienced slow growth in agriculture, many have seen moderate to rapid growth in production. Nevertheless, falling prices, international trade barriers and subsidies, overvalued exchange rates, and other forms of indirect taxation have placed constraints on the agricultural sector.

Problems for Small Producers

- Agriculture has not been able to generate sustainable incomes for the rural majority. Rural poverty contributes to a number of problems such as environmental degradation or harmful use of pesticides. Women's contributions to agricultural production are often unaccounted for, yet women play a major role in the agricultural sector. Weak capacity in agricultural ministries has led to poor input in integrating agricultural policy with an overall development policy. A fragile private sector cannot fill the gap as governments have moved out to make room for the market.
- The failure of the agricultural sector to generate adequate incomes for the rural poor is due to several factors. Previous policies and incomplete markets have been biased against the peasant farmer and in favor of the rural elite. Ambiguity with property rights, common in the region, has led to underinvestment, barriers in obtaining credit, and inefficiency in the use of land. Peasant farmers face more obstacles in obtaining much-needed credit due to their lack of collateral and the nature of agricultural activity. Policies to remedy the problem must use unconventional forms of allocating credit for the small farmer and address the issue of unequal landholding.

Niche Farming and Organic Production: Potential Solutions for Small Farmers

- In response to the price volatility, some small producers have looked for ways in which to differentiate their products, namely through organic production and fair trade certification. A rising demand for organic products from consumers has led to higher prices on certified coffee beans, making organic farming more profitable for small farmers. In addition, it is ecologically sustainable and poses fewer health risks than large agroindustry. Fair trade is a process by which the middleman is eliminated so that farmers receive a larger percentage of profits from their produce. While organic and fair trade certification have the potential to be very beneficial to small producers, there are some drawbacks as well. Certification processes can be difficult and expensive, especially given language and literacy barriers. However, rising demand for more environmentally and socially responsible products gives niche farming a positive future outlook.

Extralegal Production: Coca

- Because of the difficulties of the agricultural market in Latin America, many small producers have been driven to produce coca rather than traditional food crops. Much of this production is illegal; while some coca is used for the production of medicines and cola, most of it is intended for the production of cocaine. Eradication efforts have largely been aimed at the supply side, through crop-spraying campaigns. Such efforts have been largely unsuccessful, as they have done little to raise the price of cocaine. Government incentives for growing alternative crops and efforts to reduce the demand for cocaine on the global market are more promising policies.

Policy Options and Alternatives to Land Reform

- Historically, many Latin American countries have engaged in land reform to address the issue of inequality. The experience in the region has shown that land reform has done little to improve the quality of life of the rural peasant. Its failure is due to a lack of complementary policies that will address problems such as the biases disadvantaging the poor relative to the elite, the problem of credit, and environmental sustainability.
- Agricultural policy must be multidimensional. Farm productivity must be raised, but policy needs to take into account the concerns and behavior of the poor small farmers, who tend to be risk averse. Policies that consider factors such as migration to urban sectors, infrastructure, credit, and landholding patterns will tend to be more successful in the long run.
- Decentralization through DRIFs has increased local control and participation in agricultural development. Communities must usually meet certain requirements before the funds are distributed. This type of fund allocation allows different groups to set their own priorities and address their own needs.

Notes

1. ECLAC and IICA, Survey of Agriculture in Latin America and the Caribbean, 1990–2000, December 2001 at www.eclac.cl, 36.

2. Johan Bastiaensen, "Non-Conventional Rural Finance and the Crisis of Economic Institutions in Nicaragua," in *Sustainable Agriculture in Central America,* ed. Jan P. de Groot and Ruerd Ruben (New York: St. Martin's, 1997).

3. ECLAC and IICA, 17.

4. "Blooming Desert: Peru." *The Economist,* July 9, 2005.

5. Larry Sawers, "Nontraditional or New Traditional Exports," *Latin American Research Review* 40(3) (October 2005): 1.

6. Diego Cevallos, "Latin America: Farm Exports Grow, but Who Reaps the Harvest?" *IPS-Inter Press Service/Global Information Network,* November 8, 2005.

7. "Worst Ever Coffee Crisis Hits Latin America," *Cepal News* 22(4) (April 2002).

8. T. Christian Miller and Davan Maharau, "Coffee's Bitter Harvest," *Los Angeles Times* Staff Writers, as circulated by CENTAM-L@LISTSERV.BUFFALO.EDU, October 7, 2002.

9. Todd Benson, "Brazil's Big Stake in Cotton Likely to Become Bigger," *New York Times,* June 29, 2004, nytimes.com.

10. Editorial, "Harvesting Poverty: Napoleon's Bittersweet Legacy," *New York Times,* August 11, 2003, www.nytimes.com.

11. Oxford Analytica *Latin America Daily Brief,* Thursday, September 12, 2002, prodept@oxford-analytica.com.

12. "Brazil: Aiming to Add Value," *Latin American Economy & Business,* LAEB-02-03, March 2002, 22.

13. Panorama 2005, "El Nuevo Patron De Desarrollo De LaAgricultura En America Latina Y El Caribe," *Outlook 2005, The New Pattern of Development of Agriculture in Latin America and the Caribbean,* ECLAC, September 2005.

14. *Mugged: Poverty in Your Cup,* Oxfam International 2002, www.maketradefair.com.

15. Lori Ann Thrupp, *Bittersweet Harvests for Global Supermarkets: Challenges in Latin America's Agricultural Export Boom* (Washington, D.C.: World Resources Institute, 1995), 17.

16. James Brooke, "Home, Home on the Range, in Brazil's Heartland," *New York Times,* 26 April 1995.

17. Thrupp, *Bittersweet Harvests,* 18, 58.

18. Ibid., 24.

19. Irini Maltsoglou and Aysen Tanyeri-Abur, "Transaction Costs, Institutions and Smallholder Market Integration: Potato Producers in Peru," ESA Working Paper No. 05-04, Agricultural and Development Economics Division, June 2005, www.fao.org.

20. ECLAC and IICA, 196.

21. Canute James, "Caribbean Banana Producers See Future in Organic Farming," *Financial Times,* November 13, 2001, Internet edition.

22. Jim Adriance, "Living with the Land in Central America," *Grassroots Development* 19(1) (1995): 15.

23. *Ejidos* were created by the Mexican government following the 1910 revolution. The structure adapted a pre-Columbian farming practice of communal landholdings, requiring the Mexican government to cede tracts of land to Mexican peasants. Each *ejido* comprises between twenty and two thousand *ejidatarios* and is governed by a general assembly and an elected administrative council. Although the individual *ejidatario* cannot sell, mortgage, or rent the land, he may pass it on to his spouse, children, or other relatives. The 1992 agricultural law has worked to privatize *ejidos.*

24. Marcela Valente, "Latin America: End to Subsidies Also to End Rural Poverty?" *IPS Terraviva,* December 5, 2005.

25. Nestor Osorio, "International Coffee Council, Impact of the Crisis of Low Coffee Prices," July 14, 2005, www.ico.org.

26. Christopher Bacon, "Confronting the Coffee Crisis: Can Fair Trade, Organic, and Specialty Coffees Reduce Small-Scale Farmer Vulnerability in Northern Nicaragua?" *World Development, Elsevier* 33(3) (2005): 497–511.

27. International Coffee Council, "Impact of the Coffee Crisis on Poverty in Producing Countries," ICC 89-5 Rev. September 1, 2003.

28. "Green, As in Greenbacks," *The Economist,* February 1, 1997, 42.

29. International Coffee Council, "Impact of the Coffee Crisis on Poverty in Producing Countries."

30. Bacon, "Confronting the Coffee Crisis," 497–511.

31. Ellen Contreras Murphy, "La Selva and the Magnetic Pull of Markets: Organic Coffee-Growing in Mexico," *Grassroots Development* 19(1) (1995): 27–34.

32. United Nations Office for Drug Control and Crime Prevention, *World Drug Report 2000,* Oxford University Press, 2000, Annex 1, www.odccp.org/pdf/world_drug_report_2000/report_2001-01-22_1.pdf.

33. Muriel Calo and Timothy A. Wise, "Revaluing Peasant Coffee Production: Organic and Fair Trade Markets in Mexico," *Global Development and Environment Institute G-DAE,* Tufts University, October 2005.

34. Monique Stauder, "Colombian Cocaine Runs through It," *Christian Science Monitor,* June 13, 2001, 12–13.

35. "New Farms for Old," *The Economist,* January 10, 1998, 30.

36. Thrupp, *Bittersweet Harvests,* 67.

37. ECLAC, IICA, 152.

38. B. Lewin, D. Giovannucci, and P. Varangis, *Fair Trade and the Coffee Crisis Coffee Markets: New Paradigms in Global Supply and Demand* (Washington, D.C.: World Bank, 2004).

39. Brink Lindsey, "Grounds for Complaint? Understanding the Coffee Crisis," Report posted at www.adamsmith.org, Adam Smith Institute, London, 2004.

40. ECLAC, IICA, 46. The total number of agricultural workers had flattened at 43.3 million by 1999; the EAP during this period increased from 125.2 million to 210.2 million.

41. Tim Weiner, "16 Arrested in Killings of 26 over Land Disputes in Mexico," *New York Times,* June 2, 2002, Internet edition.

42. "Brazil Boosts Border Surveillance as Bolivia Plans to Up Coca Production," *BBC Monitoring Latin America,* December 22, 2005.

43. James Petras, "The Rural Landless Workers Movement," *Z Magazine* March 2000, on the MST web site at www.mst.org.br.

44. Adam Isacson and John Myers, "Plan Colombia's Drug Eradication Program Misses the Market," Commentary at americas.irc-online.org, International Relations Center, July 18, 2005.

45. Sibylla Brodzinsky, "Pulling Colombia's Coca By Hand," *Christian Science Monitor,* February 24, 2006, 7.

46. John Weeks, "Macroeconomic Adjustment," as noted in "Latin America's Export of Manufactured Goods," a special section of *Economic and Social Progress in Latin America 1992 Report* (Washington, D.C.: IADB, 1992), 68.

47. ECLAC and IICA, 141.

48. "FAO and Brazil Prepare an International Conference," FAO Newsroom, November 24, 2005.

49. Edward Barbier, "Agricultural Expansion, Resource Booms and Growth in Latin America," *World Development* 32(1) (2004): 139.

50. Maurice Schiff and Alberto Valdes, "The Plundering of Agriculture in Developing Countries," 1994 draft paper, available at the World Bank home page at www.worldbank

.org/html/extpb/PlunderingAgri.html. See also Anne Krueger, Maurice Schiff, and Alberto Valdes, *Political Economy of Agricultural Pricing Policy* (Baltimore: Johns Hopkins University Press, 1991), cited in Hans P. Binswanger and Klaus Deininger, "Explaining Agricultural and Agrarian Policies in Developing Countries," *Journal of Economic Literature* 35 (December 1997): 1958–2005.

51. "Trends and Challenges in Agriculture, Forestry and Fisheries in Latin America and the Caribbean," *FAO Regional Review Executive Summary,* July 2005.

52. Hugh Dellios, "Storms Leave Guatemalans in Food Crisis," *Chicago Tribune,* November 18, 2005, http://www.chicagotribune.com, reproduced at www.americas.org.

53. Ibid.

54. Ibid.

55. Pietra Rivoli, *The Travels of a T-Shirt in the Global Economy* (Hoboken, N.J.: John Wiley and Sons, 2005), 56.

56. Jacob Meerman, *Reforming Agriculture: The World Bank Goes to Market* (Washington, D.C.: World Bank, 1997), 38.

57. Michael Redclift, "The Environment and Structural Adjustment: Lessons for Policy Intervention," in *Structural Adjustment and the Agricultural Sector in Latin America and the Caribbean,* ed. John Weeks (New York: St. Martin's, 1995).

58. Miguel Bahamondes, "Poverty-Environment Patterns in a Growing Economy: Farming Communities in Arid Central Chile, 1991–99," *World Development, Elsevier* 31(11) (2003): 1947–1957.

59. Andy Thorpe, "Sustainable Agriculture in Latin America," in *Sustainable Agriculture in Central America,* ed. Jan P. de Groot and Ruerd Ruben (New York: St. Martin's, 1997), 42.

60. Stephen A. Vosti, Evaldo Munoz Braz, Chantal Line Carpentier, Marcus V. N. d'Oliveira, and Julie Witcover, "Rights to Forest Products, Deforestation and Smallholder Income: Evidence from the Western Brazilian Amazon," *World Development, Elsevier* 31(11) (2003): 1889–1901.

61. Carmen Diana Deere, "The Feminization of Agriculture? Economic Restructuring in Rural Latin America," UNRISD Occasional Paper #1, February 2005.

62. Deere, "The Feminization of Agriculture?"

63. IADB, "Invisible Farmers," in *IDB Extra: Investing in Women* (Washington, D.C.: Inter-American Development Bank, 1994).

64. Cristóbal Key, "Rural Development and Agrarian Issues in Contemporary Latin America," in *Structural Adjustment and the Agricultural Sector in Latin America and the Caribbean,* ed. John Weeks (New York: St. Martin's, 1995).

65. Deere, "The Feminization of Agriculture?"

66. Elizabeth G. Katz, "Gender and Trade within the Household: Observations from Rural Guatemala," *World Development* 23(2) (1995): 327–342.

67. Deere, "The Feminization of Agriculture?"

68. Carmen Diana Deere and Magdalena Leon, "The Gender Asset Gap: Land in Latin America," *World Development* 31(6) (2003): 925–947.

69. Julia Guivant, "Agrarian Change, Gender and Land Rights: A Brazilian Case Study," United Nations Research Institute for Social Development, PP SPD, June 14, 2003, www.unrisd.org.

70. "21 anos da morte de Margarida Alves," http://www.mmcbrasil.com.br/noticias/21margarida.htm.

71. Klaus Deininger, *Land Policies for Growth and Poverty Reduction* (Washington, D.C.: World Bank and Oxford University Press, 2003).

72. World Bank, *Rural Development: From Vision to Action,* Environmentally and

Socially Sustainable Development Studies and Monographs Series No. 12 (Washington, D.C.: World Bank, 1997), 33.

73. World Bank, *Rural Poverty Alleviation in Brazil: Toward an Integrated Strategy* (Wadhington, D.C.: World Bank, 2003).

74. Maria Donoso-Clark, "Rural Development," in *Ecuador—An Economic and Social Agenda in the New Millennium,* ed. Marcelo Giugale and Jose Roberto Lopez-Calix Vicente Fretes-Cibils (Washington, D.C.: World Bank, 2003).

75. Karla Hoff, "Designing Land Policies: An Overview," in *The Economics of Rural Organization,* ed. Karla Hoff, Avishay Braverman, and Joseph Stiglitz (New York: Oxford University Press/World Bank, 1993), 231.

76. Michael Richards, "Alternative Approaches and Problems in Protected Area Management and Forest Conservation in Honduras," in *Sustainable Agriculture in Central America,* ed. Jan P. de Groot and Ruerd Ruben (New York: St. Martin's, 1997), 147.

77. Avishay Braverman and J. Luis Guasch, "Administrative Failures in Government Credit Programs," in *The Economics of Rural Organization,* ed. Karla Hoff, Avishay Braverman, and Joseph Stiglitz (New York: Oxford University Press/World Bank, 1993), 53.

78. Fared Shah, David Zilberman, and Ujjayant Chakravorty, "Water Rights Doctrines and Technology Adoption," in *The Economics of Rural Organization,* ed. Karla Hoff, Avishay Braverman, and Joseph Stiglitz (New York: Oxford University Press/World Bank, 1993), 478.

79. Johan Bastianensen, "Non-Conventional Rural Finance," pp. 191–209 in *Sustainable Agriculture in Central America,* ed. Jan P. De Groot and Ruerd Ruben (London: Macmillan, 1997).

80. Ibid., 199.

81. Robert L. Paarlberg, "The Politics of Agricultural Resource Abuse," *Environment* 36(8) (October 1994).

82. Jon Jonakin, "The Interaction of Market Failure and Structural Adjustment in Producer Credit and Land Markets: The Case of Nicaragua," *Journal of Economic Issues* 31(2) (June 1997): 355.

83. Hans Binswanger and Miranda Elgin, "What Are the Prospects for Land Reform," in *Agriculture and Governments in an Interdependent World,* Proceedings of the Twentieth International Conference of Agricultural Economics, August 24–31, 1988, ed. Allen Maunder and Alberto Valdes (Aldershot, UK: Edward Elgar, 1989), cited in Binswanger and Deininger, "Explaining Agricultural and Agrarian Policies in Developing Countries," 1997.

84. D. Roderick, "King Kong Meets Godzilla: The World Bank and the East Asian Miracle," pp. 13–53 in *Miracle or Design: Lessons from the East Asian Experience,* ed. A. Fishlow et al. (Washington, D.C.: Overseas Development Countil, 1994), as described in Carlos Acevedo, Deborah Barry, and Herman Rosa, "El Salvador's Agricultural Sector: Macroeconomic Policy, Agrarian Change and the Environment," *World Development* 23(12) (1995): 2153–2172.

85. Johan van Zyl et al. (1995), cited in Binswanger and Deininger, "Explaining Agricultural and Agrarian Policies in Developing Countries."

86. Michael Foley, "Agenda for Mobilization: The Agrarian Question and Popular Mobilization in Contemporary Mexico," *Latin American Research Review* 26(2) (1991): 66.

87. Ibid., 61.

88. Roger Burbach and Peter Rosset, "Chiapas and the Crisis of Mexican Agriculture," *Food First Policy Brief,* No. 1 (San Francisco: Institute for Food and Development, 1994).

89. Ibid.

90. Carlos Pomareda and Frank Hartwich, "Agricultural Innovation in Latin America: Understanding the Private Sector's Role," IFPRI Issue Brief No. 42, January, 2006.

91. Ibid.

92. World Bank, "Reaching the Rural Poor: A Rural Development Strategy for the Latin American and Caribbean Region," Box A4.1, Public/Private Partnerships in Research and Extension Projects, 2002.

93. Alain de Janvry and Elisabeth Sadoulet, "NAFTA and Mexico's Maize Producers," *World Development* 23(8) (August 1995): 1349–1362.

94. Mexico, "Municipal Development in Rural Areas Project," July 2002, www.worldbank.org.

95. David Lehmann, ed., *Agrarian Reform and Agrarian Reformism: Studies of Peru, Chile, China, and India* (London: Faber & Faber, 1974), 51–59.

96. Klaus Deininger, *Land Policies for Growth and Poverty Reduction* (Washington, D.C.: World Bank and Oxford University Press, 2003).

97. Ibid.

98. Stephen Baranyi, Carmen Diana Deere, and Manuel Morales, "Land & Development in Latin America, Openings for Research, North-South Institute and International Development Research Centre," Processed Document, n.d.

99. Michael Carter and Dina Mesbah, "State-Mandated and Market-Mediated Reform in Latin America," in *Including the Poor,* ed. Michael Lipton and Jacques van der Gaag (Baltimore: Johns Hopkins University Press/World Bank, 1993).

100. Michael Carter and Bradford Barham cite Dina Mesbah in "Level Playing Fields and Laissez Faire: Postliberal Development Strategy in Inegalitarian Agrarian Economies," *World Development* 24(7) (July 1996): 1136.

101. Ibid., 1136–1138.

102. H. Byrnes and B. Spencer, "U.S. Must Aid Guatemala's Shift to Peace," *St. Louis Post-Dispatch,* December 20, 1996.

103. Carter and Barham, "Level Playing Fields," 1144–1148.

104. Nora Lustig and Ruthanne Deutsch, *The Inter-American Development Bank and Poverty Reduction: An Overview* (Washington, D.C.: IADB, 1998), available at www.iadb.org.

105. World Bank, *Rural Development.*

106. Ibid., 17.

107. Julio A. Beredegué and Germán Escobar, "Agricultural Knowledge and Information Systems and Poverty Reduction," World Bank AKIS Working Papers, January 2001.

108. Gabriel Keynan, Manuel Olin, and Ariel Dinar, "Cofinanced Public Extension in Nicaragua," *World Bank Research Observer* 12(2) (August 1997): 230.

109. Ibid., 226.

110. Humberto Márquez, "Chávez to Further Strengthen Social Reform," *Inter Press Service,* August 31, 2002, Americas.org

111. "Venezuela: Blitz of Ranch and Industrial Plant Seizures," *Latin American Weekly Report,* September 13, 2005, lexisnexis.com.

112. Márquez, "Chávez to Further Strengthen Social Reform."

113. Federico Fuentes, "Land Reform Battle Deepens," *Green Left Weekly,* New South Wales, Australia, October 12, 2005, http://www.worldpress.org/Americas/2161.cfm#down.

114. Márquez, "Chávez to Further Strengthen Social Reform."

115. "Venezuela's Chaotic Land Reform," *Economist* 374(8409) (January 15, 2005): 34.

116. Keynan, Olin, and Dinar, "Cofinanced Public Extension," 227.

117. World Bank, *Rural Development,* 83. Excerpted from box 6.10.

118. FAO Regional Review Executive Summary, www.fao.org.

119. Charles Ameur, *Agricultural Extension: A Step beyond the Next Step,* World Bank Technical Paper No. 247 (Washington, D.C.: World Bank, 1994), 12–13.

POVERTY AND INEQUALITY

Addressing the Social Deficit
in Latin America

CHAPTER ELEVEN

Extreme poverty forces children to scavenge at dumps to contribute to meager family incomes—although this does promote sustainable recycling. *(Copyright Pan American Health Organization)*

The social challenges of reducing poverty and inequality constitute the greatest obstacle to sustained growth in the region. Forty-four percent of Latin Americans cannot meet the cost of basic food consumption needs.[1] Poverty constrains human beings from investing in the education and health necessary for productivity. Inequality skews opportunities toward the rich, not those who desperately need it. When people lack the ability to invest in the future, they are forced to deplete natural resources to survive today. Despite this need, programs to address poverty in the region have failed dismally, in part due to the fact that the poor themselves have not been involved in their design or implementation. For poverty programs to do more than simply ward off starvation or malnutrition, people themselves must be involved. As the former president of the World Bank said, "The lesson is clear: for economic advance, you need social advance—and without social development, economic development cannot take root."[2]

Discrimination against women and ethnic minorities limits their full potential as economic actors. Poverty exacts a toll on the environment, as people lack the assets to invest in their future. Poorly nourished children will not grow up to be productive members of the global workforce. Reducing the depth of poverty in the region is key to long-term, sustainable development.

This chapter will focus on the question of development for whom and ask how marginalized groups can more fully participate in the benefits of growth. The following questions will shape our understanding of the issue:

- How do we measure poverty? Is Latin America poor?
- How do we measure inequality in the region? What are trends in inequality?
- How do poverty and inequality define living standards?
- What effects do gender and inequality have on economic well-being in Latin America?
- Why are poverty and inequality in Latin America so intransigent?
- How can intergenerational transmission of poverty and **chronic poverty** traps be addressed?
- What are areas for action to reduce poverty and the social deficit in the region?

A PROFILE OF POVERTY

Is Latin America poor? As measured against the typical North American family, the answer is yes. Compared to the images of starvation from the most destitute countries of the world, Latin Americans are relatively well-off. Poverty is culturally and socially constructed. Beyond income measures, poverty may be experienced as relative deprivation. Poverty in a major metropolis such as Buenos Aires will differ from that in a small remote village in the Andes.

Income Measures of Poverty

How is poverty defined? This is a controversial question. We can begin with an income measure of poverty and somewhat arbitrarily define the poor as the portion of the population not making enough income to meet basic needs such as food, health care, education, and shelter. The **poverty line** is determined as the minimum income needed to purchase socially determined essentials for living.[3] Once a poverty line is established, the **headcount ratio** estimates those who fall below it.

International comparisons of poverty are complicated by cultural differences in defining human needs, the variety of local goods available at different prices, and divergent government policies including transfer payments, exchange rates, and inflation. Cross-country comparisons are also difficult because the notion of poverty may differ between countries. Counting the poor is extremely problematic, especially for those without permanent residences. Unlike the people enumerated in data generated by income tax payments, census takers, or those in formal public support programs, the very poor are often nameless. The data should therefore be interpreted with caution. Setting a dollar benchmark is also controversial. The World Bank uses fifty dollars per month as a rule of thumb; the Economic Commission for Latin America and the Caribbean (ECLAC) uses sixty dollars, categorizing those making less than thirty dollars per month as living in **extreme poverty.** **Moderate poverty** is therefore roughly two dollars per day, with those living in extreme poverty subsisting on one dollar per day.

Table 11.1 shows how Latin America as a region stacks up against other developing country areas. We can see by the two-dollar-a-day count that in 2001, roughly one in four Latin Americans are considered poor (24.5 percent) as opposed to nearly one in two in East Asia and the Pacific and three out of four in Sub-Saharan Africa. Measures that account for national poverty levels, as opposed to one dollar or two dollars a day, generate different results. By ECLAC's count, there are more than 213 million poor in the region, accounting for 40.6 percent of Latin Americans. As shown in figure 11.1, this number is down from a high of 226 million in 2003. (In figure 11.1, add the 98 million for the indigent poor line to the 128 million poor.) Although this fall is encouraging, it is still a far cry from a sustained reduction in poverty of those living in misery. Of particular concern are poverty traps—

Table 11.1. Poverty Headcount Ratios at $1 and $2 a Day (PPP) (% of population)

Region	1996		1999		2001	
	$1 a Day	$2 a Day	$1 a Day	$2 a Day	$1 a Day	$2 a Day
East Asia & Pacific	16.6	53.3	15.7	50.3	14.9	47.4
Europe & Central Asia	4.3	20.7	6.3	23.8	3.6	19.7
Latin America & Caribbean	10.7	24.1	10.5	25.1	9.5	24.5
Middle East & North Africa	2	22.3	2.6	24.3	2.4	23.2
South Asia	36.6	81.7	32.2	78.1	31.3	77.2
Sub-Saharan Africa	45.6	75.1	45.7	76	46.4	76.6

Source: World Bank, World Development Indicators.
Definition: Population below $1 a day is the percentage of the population living on less than $1.08 a day at 1993 international prices. Data is derived from nationally representative primary household surveys conducted by national statistical offices or by private agencies under the supervision of government or international agencies and obtained from government statistical offices and World Bank Group country departments.

Figure 11.1.   Poverty Measures

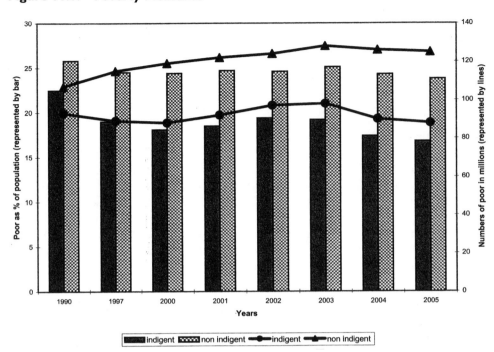

Source: ECLAC: Social Panorama of Latin America 2005.

the intergenerational transmission of poverty that we will discuss later in this chapter. While some are leaving the ranks of the poor, those left behind lack the resources to improve their lives.

Analyzing country experience, we see wide diversity in terms of progress on poverty over the decade of the 1990s. As evidenced by regional totals, poverty rates escalated from approximately 40–48 percent as countries painfully adjusted to the debt crisis from 1980–1990. Measured in or around the end of this adjustment period, those suffering from the greatest poverty lived in Honduras, Guatemala, Nicaragua, and Bolivia. Strong performers in reducing poverty include Chile, Costa Rica, and Uruguay. Indeed, the achievement of Chile in reducing poverty from nearly one in two of the population to less than one in five is an extraordinary demonstration that the lives of those with less in the region can improve. On a regional basis, however, progress is far less encouraging.

We should, however, look at trends in poverty line data with some caution. Although the headcount ratio gives us a sense of the number living in poverty at any point in time, it does not measure the extent of immiseration. A person making forty-five dollars and a person making twenty dollars per month would each count as one poor person despite tragically different lives. A second measure of poverty therefore calculates the size of the income shortfall or the amount of money it would take to raise the person to the poverty line. This **income gap** measures the

Table 11.2.   Poverty Gap Indicators

	Survey Year	Poverty Gap at $1 a Day (%)	Poverty Gap at $2 a Day (%)
Argentina	2001	0.5	4.7
Bolivia	1999	5.4	14.9
Brazil	2001	2.1	8.8
Chile	2000	<.5	2.5
Colombia	1999	2.2	8.8
Costa Rica	2000	0.7	3
Ecuador	1998	7.1	17.7
El Salvador	2000	14.1	29.7
Guatemala	2000	4.6	16
Honduras	1999	7.5	20.2
Mexico	2000	3.7	10.9
Nicaragua	2001	16.7	41.2
Panama	2000	2.3	7.4
Paraguay	2000	7.4	16.2
Peru	2000	9.1	18.5
Uruguay	2000	<.5	0.8
Venezuela	1998	6.9	15.2

Source: World Bank, World Development Indicators 2005, table 2.5.

depth of poverty that a nation faces. In table 11.2 we can see that in Honduras, Guatemala, and El Salvador, on average people's income falls short of the two dollars a day poverty line by 20.2, 16, and 29.7 percent, respectively. This says that in Honduras it would take a 20.2 percent increase in a poor person's income to raise the individual out of poverty. This is in contrast to Uruguay or Chile, where on average the poor are short of the poverty line by .8 or 2.5 percent. The experience of the 1990s was that although growth and macroeconomic instability allowed most countries to make some progress on reducing poverty, those unfortunates remaining poor were poorer than at the beginning of the decade.[4]

The first and most important of the Millennium Development Goals (MDGs) adopted internationally in 2000 is to half the number of those suffering from poverty by 2015 from a 1990 baseline. Figure 11.1 illustrates the regional progress —and the distance to the target. Although the goal doesn't specify the measurement of poverty, we can see that by all measures—one or two dollars a day or local poverty lines—60 percent of the time period has passed, but Latin America hasn't covered 60 percent of the distance between baseline performance and targets. Furthermore, what the data show is that while indigence rates fell from 22.5 percent in 1990 to 19 percent in 1997 and 18.1 percent in 2000, they then got stuck. This is not to deny substantial progress. Poverty declined by 13 million people between 2003 and 2005. New measures indicate that poverty declined in most countries. In 2004, it fell 16 percentage points in urban Argentina, while indigence was down 9.8 points since 2002. In Mexico, poverty has been declining since 1996, and in 2004 it dropped a further 2.4 percentage points from overall levels in 2002, with a decline in indigence of 0.9 percentage points, mainly in rural areas. Likewise, indigence was down 2.8 percentage points in Peru.[5] However, the rate of progress is frustratingly slow for those who suffer; 213 million people (40.6 percent) are still affected by poverty, and 88 million (16.8 percent) of these are indigents.[6] Why, despite significant efforts, have outcomes fallen short? No single explanation suffices, but there is a consensus surrounding the importance of the poverty trap in this outcome. Poverty in the region is transmitted and reinforced across generations of people suffering from exclusion and inequality, creating poverty traps that are difficult to address.[7] Indeed, as Nancy Birdsall notes in her definition of development in chapter 1, these traps may even be difficult to see. Let's turn to consider dimensions of this problem of chronic poverty.

CHRONIC POVERTY

Poverty is not simply about not having enough money. Rather, chronic poverty is multidimensional deprivation—hunger, undernutrition, dirty drinking water, illiteracy, lack of access to decent health services, social isolation, and exploitation.[8] It is not simply low income but the vulnerability and uncertainty that accompanies life on the margins of society. Individuals who experience significant deprivation over a period of five years or more may be considered chronically poor.[9] Chronic poverty is not simply a lack of resources but rather is an absence of entitlements promoted by social exclusion and discrimination. The chronically poor are trapped in low-productivity activities and lack both social protection and opportunities for advancement.

Because it is defined by persistence over time, chronic poverty in developing countries is difficult to measure. Although only 5 percent of the world's chronically poor people live in Latin America, about one in every two or three poor Latin Americans is persistently poor.[10] In Latin America, persistent poverty is intertwined with inequality and a highly unequal distribution of income and opportunity. It is integrally tied to education—or lack of it. Only one in four children of poorly educated parents completes secondary education—a bare minimum in today's globalized world for a ticket out of poverty.[11] The intergenerational transmission of poverty traps roughly three out of four children born into uneducated households. The cycle is vicious. Parents with little schooling and poorly marketable skills begin childbearing early, resulting in stunted children with impaired learning who fail in school. Functionally illiterate and unskilled, they leave school with a high propensity for dysfunctional and antisocial behavior. They then socialize with other out-of-school youth, resulting in early childbearing and becoming parents with little schooling and scant skills.[12] A stunning half of Latin American children have experienced a developmental failure before reaching age eighteen. That is, they have either died before the age of five, have dropped out of school between ages eight and fifteen, or are unemployed and out of school at age seventeen or eighteen.[13] This is a dramatic loss of human capital for a region hoping to compete in the global marketplace.

Even those who are lucky enough to be working find social mobility nearly unattainable. Three-quarters of the employed population don't make enough to surpass the poverty line. High participation in the **informal sector** accentuates the low-wage, low-productivity trap, excluding jobs with mobility. Informality combined with poor social insurance leaves more than 85 percent of the Bolivian, Nicaraguan, and Peruvian workforces without benefits.[14] According to a 2001 study by the Inter-American Development Bank (IADB), the son of a blue-collar worker in Mexico has only a 10 percent chance of making the jump to a white-collar job—one-third the possibility if he were born in the United States.[15] In Latin America, 80 percent believe that connections—not hard work—are the single most important ingredient to success.[16] People trapped in poverty have learned that it is rather hopeless to try to escape.

Social Exclusion by Gender, Ethnicity, and Race

Gender, ethnicity, and race shape one's probability of being poor in Latin America. The systematic and historical denial of access of opportunities to women, people of mixed race, and ethnic origin highly correlates with poverty in the region. In Brazil, 45 percent of the poorest decile is black; 85 percent of the richest tenth is white.[17] In Bolivia, Indians are barred from swimming pools at some clubs and are shunned in the street by whites.[18] Indigenous Bolivian males earn on average 41 percent of the hourly earnings of nonindigenous males; in Brazil, Afro descendents earn about half the hourly wage of whites.[19] Of all Brazilians of African descent, barely 2 percent enter university; only 3 percent of Afro Brazilian women have fifteen or more years of schooling as compared to 12 percent of white women.[20] Table 11.3 provides additional detail on poverty rates by race and ethnicity. In Guatemala, for example, 77 percent of the indigenous population is poor as compared to 44 percent of non-ethnic origin. (With a national poverty ratio overall of 60 percent living on less than two dollars a day, neither statistic is enviable!) Controlling for age, education, employment, and region, being indigenous in Latin America raises your chances of being poor from 13 percent to 30 percent. This is a telling sign that discrimination is at work, keeping even educated indigenous people behind.

Afro Latin Americans, most commonly Brazilians of African descent, are 1.9

Table 11.3.   Poverty, Race, and Ethnicity

		Racial or Ethnic Groups as % of Population		Poverty Rates by Population Group % <$2 a Day		
		National	Urban	Non Ethnic	Ethnic	Total Population
Bolivia (1999)	Indigenous	36.2	16.8	49	81	62
Brazil (1999)	Afro-descendent	46	42.9	29	56	41
Guatemala (1998)	Indigenous	48.6	32.9	44	77	60
Peru (2000)	Indigenous	15	6.8	44	75	49

Source: Suzanne Duryea and Maria Eugenia Genoni, "Ethnicity, Race and Gender in Latin American Labor Markets," in *Social Inclusion and Economic Development in Latin America,* ed. Mayra Buvinic and Jacqueline Mazza (Washington, D.C.: Inter-American Development Bank, 2004).

times as likely to live in poverty as their white counterparts.[21] Colonization patterns laid the foundation for inequality in Latin society. In Brazil and Spanish America in 1825, the early period of independence, roughly one-fifth of the population was white, with black and indigenous people constituting the bulk of the labor force. The white minority controlled agricultural and mining assets, with the rest of the population living on the edge of subsistence. The reverse was true in the United States, where 20 percent of the population were slaves or Native American Indians without assets and distribution was more widely spread among white landowners and mine owners. Wealth was therefore hierarchically configured in Latin America from the very start.[22] These historical patterns have persisted over time. For the indigenous and Afro Latin poor, few gains were made in poverty reduction in recent years. Significant numbers suffer from deep poverty, and have less access to education and health services.[23]

Women are systematically herded into low-paying jobs with few benefits. Women in Latin America have a greater chance of being poor than men, primarily due to the fact that they are segregated in low-income jobs, earning on average 14–53 percent less than men do.[24] Poverty in the region has therefore become feminized, forcing a rethinking of how to reduce misery throughout Latin America. In most low-income households, women face a triple burden: they are responsible for the reproductive work of the home, enter the workplace as secondary income earners, and tend to be the central force in community organizing.[25] Low-income girls are particularly limited in full labor force participation due to high rates of adolescent pregnancy and domestic responsibilities. Overall, 45.9 percent of low-income girls as opposed to 8.6 percent of high-income girls are devoted entirely to domestic unpaid work. Low-income boys' entry into the labor force is four times that of low-income girls.[26] Women are especially vulnerable when elderly. In Mexico, 80 percent of elderly men have an income, as compared to 36 percent of women. Poverty indeed has a gendered dimension in the region.

Life for the Poor in Latin America

The living conditions of the poor constrain their human potential. Poverty and inequality interact to limit the opportunities for the less fortunate. Poverty is a complex, multidimensional phenomenon. How do the realities of their daily lives constrain them from pursuing better options? If you ever have the opportunity to observe life in a poor neighborhood—a *favela* in Brazil, a *villa miseria* in Argentina, or a *callampas* (mushroom) in Chile, where roughly one in four Latin Americans live—you will notice that nearly everyone is working hard to survive. Why aren't these tremendous energies transformed into a better quality of life for people?

Quality of life statistics can give us an appreciation for the standard of living in the region. The UN *Human Development Report* also calculates **Human Development Index (HDI)** as a composite of life expectancy at birth, educational attainment (measured by adult literacy and school enrollments), and income. The Human Poverty Index (HPI) is a proxy for the denial of choices and opportunities in life. The Gender Empowerment Index (GEM) concentrates on economic, political, and professional participation by incorporating variables such as female share of income, access to professional and managerial jobs, and seats in public office. The GEM therefore measures the degree to which opportunities are open to women in society. These indices are further described in box 11.1. It should be noted that they have their drawbacks. Although as composite indexes they take attention away from gross domestic product (GDP) as a measure of human development, the measures of life expectancy, education, and income do not take the distribution of the population around the average into account, covering considerable variation in performance.[27] They give us a sense of how countries stack up by living standards but miss a large amount of intracountry heterogeneity.

Table 11.4 presents the HDI, HPI, and GEM for Latin American countries. Some interesting results appear. The best performers in quality of living include Argentina, Uruguay, Chile, and Costa Rica, although the effects of Argentina's 2001 crisis will likely have it slip considerably as poverty increases with economic crisis. In terms of women's participation in economic and political life, Costa Rica and Argentina top the list. A low score on the HPI indicates greater access to investments in health and education. Overall, Latin American nations perform well as compared to countries in Africa or poorer nations in Asia—note, for example, that no Latin American countries are denoted as low human development. There is, however, a wide range of variation from Chile and Argentina at the top of the list to Guatemala, Nicaragua, and Honduras at the bottom. Furthermore, it is interesting to note a few disparities between the HPI and the HDI rankings. Panama and Colombia indicate more opportunity, while Mexico and Brazil evidence greater exclusion.

Measures such as housing, communications, and basic infrastructure help fill out the picture of poverty in Latin America. Housing in the region is woefully inadequate. Adequate housing is critical to the development of individual capability and to fostering family and community ties. Table 11.5 shows that in some countries between a quarter and a fifth of the population lack access to sanitary sewage facilities. In the rural sector, on average only two in three have access to improved water. These deficits have significant implications in terms of health in that access to running water and appropriate treatment of waste water is critical to reducing disease. In Peru, for example, only 66 percent of rural residents have access to good drinking water and 33 percent to modern sanitation facilities. Throughout the region, the level of rural poverty has led to desperate claims on political resources through strikes, marches, and violent land invasions The failure of the economic model to reach the rural poor has placed these concerns high on the global development agenda for the new millennium.

Poverty has largely become an urban phenomenon. With three of every four residents living in cities, Latin American is one of the most urbanized regions in the world. This transformation has taken place quickly, rising from an urbanization rate of approximately 40 percent in the 1950s. Given that the absolute number of people has increased in the same period, this means that in a place such as Mexico City, in the 1950s approximately 3.33 million lived in the urban area—this number has now reached more than 10 million. Over this time period, Latin American nations have been grappling with growth and crisis—with few sustainable resources to direct at the required upgrades to support the mushrooming population. Rapid urbanization

Box 11.1.   What Is the Human Development Index?

The Human Development Index (HDI) is a summary composite index that measures a country's average achievements in three basic aspects of human development: longevity, knowledge, and a decent standard of living. Longevity is measured by life expectancy at birth; knowledge is measured by a combination of the adult literacy rate and the combined primary, secondary, and tertiary gross enrollment ratio; and standard of living is measured by GDP per capita (PPP [purchasing power parity] US$).

WHY IS GDP PER CAPITA (PPP US$) USED OVER GDP PER CAPITA (US$) IN THE HDI?

HDI attempts to make an assessment of 175 very diverse countries and areas, with very different price levels. To compare economic statistics across countries, the data must first be converted into a common currency. Unlike conventional exchange rates, PPP rates of exchange allow this conversion to take account of price differences between countries. GDP per capita (PPP US$) accounts for price differences between countries and therefore better reflects people's living standards. In theory, at the PPP rate, one PPP dollar has the same purchasing power in the domestic economy of a country as one U.S. dollar has in the U.S. economy.

WHAT IS THE GENDER EMPOWERMENT MEASURE?

The Gender Empowerment Measure (GEM) is a composite indicator that captures gender inequality in three key areas:

- Political participation and decision making, as measured by women's and men's percentage shares of parliamentary seats;
- Economic participation and decision-making power, as measured by two indicators—women's and men's percentage shares of positions as legislators, senior officials, and managers and women's and men's percentage shares of professional and technical positions;
- Power over economic resources, as measured by women's and men's estimated earned income (PPP US$).

WHAT IS THE HUMAN POVERTY INDEX?

Poverty has traditionally been measured as a lack of income, but this is far too narrow a definition. Human poverty is a concept that captures the many dimensions of poverty that exist in both poor and rich countries—it is the denial of choices and opportunities for living a life one has reason to value. The HPI-1—Human Poverty Index (HPI) for developing countries—measures human deprivation in the same three aspects of human development as the HDI (longevity, knowledge, and a decent standard of living). HPI-2—human poverty index for selected high-income Organization for Economic Cooperation and Development (OECD) countries—includes social exclusion in addition to the three dimensions in HPI-1.

For developing countries: deprivations in longevity are measured by the probability at birth of not surviving to age forty; deprivations in knowledge are measured by the percentage of adults who are illiterate; deprivations in a decent standard of living are measured by two variables: the percentage of people not having sustainable access to an improved water source and the percentage of children below the age of five who are underweight.

Source: FAQs on the Human Development Indices, http://www.undp.org/hdr2003/faq.html#21.

Table 11.4. Human Development Index

	Country	HDI Rank among All Countries	HDI Index Value	HPI Rank Among Developing Countries	GEM Rank among All Countries
High Human	Argentina	34	0.863	na	20
Development	Chile	37	0.854	2	61
	Uruguay	46	0.84	1	50
	Costa Rica	47	0.838	3	19
	Mexico	53	0.814	13	38
	Panama	56	0.804	9	40
Medium	Brazil	63	0.792	20	na
Human	Colombia	69	0.785	8	52
Development	Venezuela	75	0.772	14	64
	Peru	79	0.762	26	48
	Ecuador	82	0.759	22	55
	Paraguay	88	0.755	17	65
	El Salvador	104	0.722	34	62
	Nicaragua	112	0.69	40	na
	Bolivia	113	0.687	30	47
	Honduras	116	0.667	39	74
	Guatemala	117	0.663	51	na

Source: United Nations, Human Development Report 2005.

has given rise to precarious conditions for the 44 percent of urban dwellers estimated to live in slums.[28] In poor households, only 24 percent live in housing that
meets minimum service standards of clean water and sewage. Air and noise pollution are health hazards, and crime is a problem for both the rich and the poor. In the
region, 48 percent of cities have areas considered as inaccessible or dangerous
to the police.[29] Housing in the region has been affected by macroeconomic crisis.
Formal housing construction slowed down as government lending dried up, families working longer hours had less time to work on homes, and municipalities trying
to raise taxes pushed more families into informal housing.[30]

Home ownership in urban areas in Latin America is relatively high. Even among
the poor (with the exception of Ecuador and Colombia), it is above 60 percent—
although roughly half of these don't hold formal title to their land.[31] Informal housing
accounts for between 10 percent of urban housing in Buenos Aires and 59 percent
in Bogota. Informal-sector housing makes pragmatic sense, allowing families to
build as resources become available. Rooms are added when there is money to buy
materials. However, informal-sector housing challenges policymakers to provide
appropriate services and weakens the ability of the poor themselves to use their
homes as collateral. Building formal low-income housing is not largely serviced by
construction companies in the region, and in many countries cumbersome regulations deter those who would potentially seek a legally registered route. Where access
by the poor to low-cost mortgages is weak and the regulatory burden is high, companies simply can't make money on the intermittent schedules.

Table 11.5.   Indicators on Water Supply and Sanitation

Country	Access to Improved Sanitation Facilities			Access to Improved Water Source		
	% of Urban Population 2002	% of Rural Population 002	% of Population 2002	% of Urban Population 2002	% of Rural Population 2002	% of Population 2002
Argentina	::	::	::	97	::	::
Bolivia	58	23	45	95	68	85
Brazil	83	35	75	96	58	89
Chile	96	64	92	100	59	95
Colombia	96	54	86	99	71	92
Costa Rica	89	97	92	100	92	97
Cuba	99	95	98	95	78	91
Dominican Republic	67	43	57	98	85	93
Ecuador	80	59	72	92	77	86
El Salvador	78	40	63	91	68	82
Guatemala	72	52	61	99	92	95
Haiti	52	23	34	91	59	71
Honduras	89	52	68	99	82	90
Mexico	90	39	77	97	72	91
Nicaragua	78	51	66	93	65	81
Panama	89	51	72	99	79	91
Paraguay	94	58	78	100	62	83
Peru	72	33	62	87	66	81
Puerto Rico	::	::	::	::	::	::
Uruguay	95	85	94	98	93	98
Venezuela, RB	71	48	68	85	70	83
Latin America & Caribbean	84	44	74	96	69	89

Source: World Bank, World Development Indicators 2005.

Given the housing crisis, ECLAC estimates that 20–30 percent of children in Latin America grow up in conditions of overcrowding, with three or more people per bedroom—a condition closely associated with poor school performance. In Bolivia, Peru, El Salvador, and Nicaragua, 20 percent or more of the dwellings are beyond repair, a threat to health and life. Some rural indigenous workers in Bolivia and in Brazil are kept in a state of virtual slavery, as employers charge them more for room and board than they earn. The most extreme housing deprivation is to be homeless. In Brazil, more than two hundred thousand children are growing up on the streets without the protection that a home affords. Box 11.2 sadly illustrates life

BOX 11.2. STREET CHILDREN: A FACE OF POVERTY IN LATIN AMERICA[32]

BY COURTNEY FRY

Since his parents died seven years ago, José has made his home in the streets of La Paz, Bolivia. He sometimes washes cars or watches them while people are in the market, but he spends a good deal of his time drinking and inhaling. José has no future goals or plans. Forced to struggle to survive on a daily basis, he feels that he is worthless to society.[33]

A phenomenon primarily caused by poverty, street children such as José are a recurrent part of the urban landscape throughout Latin America. One witnesses these children doing any number of things on the street, including begging, selling candy, sleeping, shining shoes, washing cars, selling drugs, and stealing. UNICEF estimates that there are around seven million street children living in Brazil. However, any data regarding street children should be interpreted with caution, since the transient nature of their lives makes obtaining accurate data difficult. Tobias Hecht, an anthropologist who has done field research on street children in Recife, Brazil, estimates that there are around thirty-nine thousand street children in Brazil.[34]

Street children have garnered much attention in the international and regional press over the past two decades, with their portrayal ranging from the innocent victim to the drug dealer or criminal. Most tend to think of street children as a problem that needs to be solved. Some who write about street children make sweeping statements regarding life on the street, but this uniform package hides the complexity of their lives. It is difficult to describe "life in the street," since there are as many different street lives as there are street children. One important distinction made in the literature on street children is children *in* the street versus children *of* the street. Children *in* the street have a home to which they return at night, although many spend a considerable part of their lives in the street. Most children *in* the street use the street as a place to earn money to contribute to their family. Children *of* the street have severed ties with their family, voluntarily or involuntarily, and literally live in the street.[35] However, the unstable nature of life in the street frequently blurs these distinctions. Despite these differences, the one constant in the lives of street children is poverty: the poverty that drives them to the street and the poverty in which they live once in the street.

LIFE IN THE STREET

Children live in the street for a myriad of reasons. Some children run away because they experience physical, emotional, or sexual abuse at home. Others, like José, are orphans

continued

continued

and have nowhere else to go. Still others live in the street because it is closer to where they work or there is less competition for work at night. The lure of freedom entices various children to life in the streets. Some children stay out on the street because they eat better living in the street than at home.[36] When parents cannot provide basic necessities for all their children, some are forced to the streets to earn additional income for the family or for themselves. Some children must face the harsh reality that their parents do not want them at home. When one Brazilian street boy briefly returned home, his mother's first words were, "But I thought you were dead. There's no room for you here."[37] There are other parents, however, who will go to great lengths to drag their children out of the streets and bring them back home. Another Brazilian street boy had run away from home more than twenty times over a period of six years, and no matter where he went, his mother kept searching for him and dragging him home.[38] Many assume that the children are only living on the streets because they have nowhere else to go, but there is a sizable contingent of street children who choose to live on the streets rather than at home.

Even within the category "children *of* the street," time spent actually sleeping in the street varies. Some children spend time in shelters or even jail, while others, like José, spend every day and night in the street. In cities where the temperature fluctuates with the seasons, some children live in the street during the summer and return home or to a shelter during the winter.[39] When children sleep on the street, they tend to sleep in groups for protection and warmth. During the day, most street children also roam in groups, but few are members of formal gangs. Street children typically have an extremely individualistic mentality, which inhibits their forming gangs with responsibilities to others in the group.[40]

There are numerous jobs in which one finds street children working: collecting fares in buses, carrying bags for women at the market, cleaning windshields at a stoplight, and watering flowers in cemeteries, to name a few. José washes cars and watches parked cars when people go inside the market. Since their age forces them to work in the informal economy, street children frequently face labor exploitation, including long hours and extreme physical exertion. Many children beg for money or food. However, as one might expect, younger children are more successful at begging.[41] As a child grows older, he or she must find another way to obtain money, which can drive children to illegal activities such as selling drugs and stealing. Many street children both work and steal to make ends meet. Unfortunately, an occupation in which many street children, especially girls, find themselves is prostitution. According to a study done by Casa Alianza in 2003, around ten thousand children, both girls and boys, were prostitutes in Honduras,[42] many starting in the age range of eleven to fifteen years old. Although not all ten thousand are street children, they all have similar lives of destitution. Because street children must work daily to survive, the vast majority do not have the opportunity to go to school.

Drugs are everywhere on the streets. Although there are some children who do not give in to the temptation of drugs, a child is more prone to use drugs if he or she has been living on the street for several months. The reasons for drug use among street children range from peer pressure to the desire to escape reality. Glue is the most popular drug of choice for street children, given its availability and cheap price. A mixture of paint thinner and gasoline, José's drug of choice, is another frequent option for inhaling. Some children claim that inhaling glue or thinner suppresses their hunger, but others say that inhaling actually makes them more hungry once they come down from their high.[43] More expensive drugs accessible to street children are marijuana, alcohol, cocaine, and prescription drugs. Hecht concludes that those who have spent a considerable length of time on the streets generally start to experiment with prescription medicines. Of forty-nine children he interviewed, thirty-three had used Rohypnol, a sedative popular among street children. Hecht also asked these children whether they spent more money on drugs or on food. Fifty-two percent responded that they spent more on drugs.[44]

Girls typically have a much different life on the streets than boys. Apart from the mentality and maturity differences between girls and boys, girls tend to experience sexual aggression and assault more than boys. Prostitution and sexual violence make street girls more susceptible to sexually transmitted diseases and unwanted pregnancies. Most street girls get pregnant young and often. Many choose painful and life-threatening methods of terminating pregnancies, such as having people kick them in the belly, taking high doses of presciption medications, or having illegal abortions.[45] For those who choose to have their child, pre- and postnatal health care are difficult to obtain, risking the lives of both the mother and the child. José's girlfriend, Ibi, is pregnant for the second time. She continues to inhale frequently, despite expecting a child. She worries about how she will provide for her baby, since she cannot even provide for herself.[46] José says, "The street is bad enough for guys, but for girls it is worse because they are more fragile."

Violence directly affects the lives of all street children. The street forces these children to grow up all too quickly, and many do not make it to adulthood. The violence that characterizes street life can be summarized into two broad types: violence committed against street children and violence committed by street children. In addition to the physical abuse at home that drives some children to the streets, there are several actors of violence against children. A week ago, José wounded his arm as he struggled to escape from the police. His wound is now infected, and his left hand trembles. When asked why the police had tried to grab him, he says, "Because I live in the street." Some police torture and abuse street children. A Brazilian boy describes his most recent arrest. "They hung me upside down, poured water in my nostrils, made me drink Pine Sol and bleach. Then they beat me with a strip of rubber."[47] It is not uncommon for police to beat street children when arresting them, and some police will wake street children up from sleeping with beatings.[48] Death squads or other forms of vigilante "justice" groups have claimed the lives of many street children. Brazil is particularly well known for death squad murders, and the threat of their strikes weighs on the minds of the street children. However, street children are not only victims of violence; they are perpetrators as well. Retribution is a guiding principle in the street, which contributes to a culture of violence and a never-ending cycle of violent acts committed by and against street children. Hecht concludes that more street children die by the hands of other street children than by outside forces, such as the police and death squads.[49] This violence is one reason that societies fear street children and consider them a problem.

Street children, like José and Ibi, are not the problem; they are a symptom of the poverty and inequality that pervades Latin America. One cannot sweep all of the children off the street one day and expect them not to return the next without addressing these key issues. Nongovernmental organizations (NGOs) work to improve the lives of current street children, but Latin American governments and the international community must make significant progress in their fight against poverty to prevent additional children from moving their home to the streets in the future.

for children on the streets in Latin America. The waste of young lives to poverty is a tragic result of slow growth and limited opportunity.

Hunger and food insecurity are not perfectly correlated with poverty. In 2000, extreme poverty afflicted 18.5 percent of the population; those suffering from undernourishment represented 11 percent, or fifty-four million people. There is a high degree of heterogeneity of those going hungry across the region. In Nicaragua, 29 percent of the population was undernourished; other countries at the high end of the spectrum include Guatemala (25 percent), Bolivia (23 percent), and Honduras (21 percent). In contrast, Mexico, Ecuador, Chile, Uruguay, and Argentina all registered rates under 5 percent for the 1998–2000 period.[50] Only four countries, all in Central America—El Salvador, Guatemala, Honduras, and Nicaragua—appear unlikely to fulfill the MDG of reducing child malnutrition and undernutrition by half by 2015. The nature of hunger in Central America is distinctive; it is not caused by a scarcity of food but rather because families lack the resources to buy it. If inequalities in access to food were redressed, countries would meet the MDGs. Structural problems in the delivery of food are exacerbated by natural disasters, including hurricanes and drought, that have severely impacted peasant farming. Hurricane Mitch was followed by two earthquakes in El Salvador in 2001 and a drought that has reduced production by 18 percent and has affected all countries in the subregion.[51] Better planning for natural disasters will help reduce the short-term pain in terms of malnutrition.

Breaking out of poverty involves access to knowledge. Two measures of literacy and the effect of the media on public consciousness are the number of newspapers sold daily and televisions per one hundred people. Table 11.6 gives a sense of the role of the media in shaping people's worldview. It is not surprising that the more affluent nations sell more newspapers. Literacy is correlated with wealth. Furthermore, if a newspaper costs fifty cents, for those making two or three dollars a day it is quite a luxury. During the periods of macroeconomic crisis in Brazil, even upper-middle-class families would get together in a buying group for *Veja,* the Brazilian equivalent of *Time* magazine. Indeed, if you walk the streets in a Latin American city, you are likely to find people standing around the newspaper kiosk reading the headlines of papers for sale because they are too expensive to buy. The number of televisions has exploded in the region, although not quite approaching the industrial country average of one television for every two people. Television transforms culture. Many American TV shows are translated and rebroadcast. The contradiction of walking into a *favela,* or poor *barrio,* and seeing an imported sitcom on the lives of the rich and famous is startling. In countries where functional literacy is not universal, the ability to communicate (or miscommunicate) through the media is a powerful social and political tool. Without widespread literacy, people do not have the opportunity to evaluate competing arguments, and they come to accept pronouncements made on television as truth. Internet penetration remains low, limiting access to important opportunities for e-learning and international communication.

Education is lacking. Despite strong enrollment rates, repetition and dropout rates are high. Income and educational attainment are clearly correlated. In Guatemala, for example, a poor child is likely to complete only one year of schooling, while a wealthy child on average will finish seven. Even in Costa Rica, one of the region's best performers on social indicators, as many as one in three school-age children do not attend school; about 20 percent of those between seven and ten years old are absent, primarily among the poor and the rural communities. This contrast is maintained in the wealthier countries as well. In Chile, a poor child might complete 6.1 years of schooling, while a wealthy one will likely complete 11.6 years. Both cause and effect are at work here. Wealthy individuals have lower opportunity costs for education, and the higher level of education helps improve their income. For the poor, the additional wages of children are important to family incomes.

Table 11.6. Communications Indicators

Country	Daily Newspapers (per 1,000 people) 2000	Television Sets (per 1,000 people) 2003	Personal Computers (per 1,000 people) 2003	Internet Users (per 1,000 people) 2003	Telephone Mainlines (per 1,000 people) 2003	Mobile Phones (per 1,000 people) 2003
Argentina	40	326	82.0	112	219	178
Bolivia	99	..	22.8	32	72	152
Brazil	46	369	74.8	82	223	264
Canada	168	691	487.0	513	629	417
Chile	98	523	119.3	272	221	511
Colombia	26	319	49.3	53	179	141
Costa Rica	70	..	197.2	193	251	111
Cuba	54	251	31.8	11	51	2
Dominican Republic	28	..	..	64	115	271
Ecuador	98	252	31.1	46	122	189
El Salvador	29	233	25.2	84	116	176
Guatemala	33	145	14.4	33	71	131
Haiti	3	60	..	18	17	38
Honduras	55	119	13.6	25	48	49
Mexico	94	282	82.0	118	158	291
Nicaragua	30	123	27.9	17	37	85
Panama	62	191	38.3	62	122	268
Paraguay	43	..	34.6	20	46	299
Peru	23	172	43.0	104	67	106
Puerto Rico	126	339	..	175	346	316
United States	196	938	658.9	551	621	543
Uruguay	293	..	110.1	119	280	193
Venezuela, RB	206	186	60.9	60	111	273
East Asia & Pacific	60	317	26.3	68	161	195
Latin America & Caribbean	61	289	67.4	106	170	246

Source: World Bank, World Development Indicators 2005.

Because the poor complete fewer years of school, their income is likely to be lower. Education is the greatest explanatory variable in both income inequality and the probability of being poor. Differences in educational attainment account for nearly 25 percent of the total income inequality in the region. Improving education will not only improve the distribution of income but will also improve the standard of living of the poor.[52]

Health statistics not only paint a picture of human misery but are also a proxy for the shortfall in resources for investment in human capital. Poor people find it difficult to purchase health care. It is estimated that 130 million people, or one in three Latin Americans, do not have routine access to health services. Maternal and child health programs are deficient. More than 10 million children under age five suffer from malnutrition in Latin America; 12 percent of the total population is under-nourished. The Pan American Health Organization (PAHO) evaluated seventeen hundred lab services and hospitals in eighteen countries and found eighty unsatis-factory. In chapters 12 and 13 we will take up these important issues of health and education in depth.

Spatial Poverty Traps in Latin America

Poverty varies by country and subregion. Much of the poverty is concentrated in Brazil, Mexico, and Peru. Forty-four percent of the region's poor live in Brazil, which is home to 33 percent of the region's total population. Mexico and Peru account for 11 and 9 percent of the poor, respectively; despite their small size, Bolivia, El Salvador, Guatemala, Haiti, Honduras, and Nicaragua together account for an additional 19 percent.[53] Whether you live in the city or the rural sector mat-ters enormously, with rural poverty being twice as high as urban poverty region-wide. A separate HPI was calculated for the poor northeastern region versus the relatively affluent southern region of Brazil. The northeastern region of Brazil shows an HPI of 46 percent, consistent with some of the worst poverty in Asia, whereas the southern and southeastern regions enjoy relatively low rates at 17 and 14 per-cent. This disparity has grown in Brazil, leading to the nickname of "Belindia" for Brazil: a country with luxuries similar to Belgium yet with the misery of India. Diversity of needs within countries makes policy a difficult political issue.

THE QUESTION OF INEQUALITY

Differences by region, gender, and ethnicity give rise to another critical issue: inequality. High inequality is sadly the defining characteristic of the pattern of development in Latin America. Compared to other regions, Latin America contains the most unequal income distribution in the world.[54] The wealthiest 20 percent of the population in Latin America has an average income nearly 20 times higher than that of the poorest 20 percent, compared to 9 times in the United States or 5.2 times in Canada.[55] Since the 1960s, inequality in Latin America has been higher than any other region in the world, and there is no sign that the gap is narrowing. Average incomes such as gross national product (GNP) per capita don't give us a sense of the national range of incomes. Brazil, for example, has a GNP per capita of $7,790 per year or about $650 per month, yet 8.2 percent of its population subsists on less than $1 a day or $30 a month, and 22.4 percent subsists on less than $2 a day or $60 a month.[56] This is due to a highly unequal income distribution in which the top 20 percent of the population makes 24.4 times the income of the bottom 20 percent.

To understand the quality of life, it is therefore important to measure the degree of income inequality in a country using the **Gini coefficient.** The Gini coefficient measures the difference between a hypothetical population with all income divided equally and the actual distribution in an economy. A forty-five-degree line represents the hypothetical situation of perfect equality. If the population is divided into quintiles from lowest to highest, in a perfectly equal society the first 20 percent of the population would hold 20 percent of the income, the next 20 percent for a cumulative 40 percent would hold another 20 percent for a cumulative 40 percent, and so on. However, societies are not equal. The **Lorenz curve** measures the actual distribution. The Gini coefficient is equal to the area between the line of perfect equality and the Lorenz curve, labeled "a," and the whole triangle, or a + b. If a society were perfectly equal, the area "a" would be empty, because the distribution would be the same as the line of perfect equality, and a/(a + b) would therefore be zero. If a society were perfectly unequal, one person would hold all the wealth, so that the area "a" would take up the whole triangle, or a/(a + b) would equal one. Figure 11.2 shows the Lorenz curve for Brazil, a highly unequal country, and Costa Rica, one of the more equal countries in the region.

Figure 11.2. Lorenz Curves and Gini Coefficient

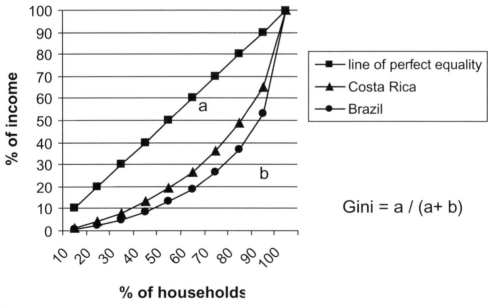

Source: Author.

The average Gini for the region is .537, the highest regional Gini in the world. (Note that sometimes the Gini is written as ".537" and other times it is represented as "53.7." The two forms are parallel.) Latin America's Gini is 19 points higher than the OECD average and 23 points higher than Taiwan's.[57] Table 11.7 shows the distribution of income for Latin American countries. The data lines people up by income, grouping them into deciles. Group 1 relates to the poorest 10 percent of the population, which in Guatemala holds a meager .7 percent of national income. The richest 10 percent, in contrast, control 46.8 percent of the income. Imagine the effect of these different worlds on the perception of fairness and opportunity in Latin American societies. The chasm that separates the haves and the have-nots not only creates social tension, but also acts as a drag on growth.[58]

One's access to basic services—health, education, and safe housing—is clearly shaped by where you might fall on the income spectrum. If you are unlucky enough to be born into the lowest quintile in Latin America, you are 50 percent less likely than average to have a doctor at your birth; a rich baby would be 45 percent more likely to receive this medical attention. Not surprisingly, but sadly, infant mortality rates are 138 percent the average for the poorest segment and 59 percent of the average for the rich. Your chances of being stunted, defined as 2 standard deviations below median height for age, decreases from 175 percent for the poor to 31 percent for the richest quintile. Diarrhea afflicts the rich only 67 percent of the average rate, while the poor suffer at 121 percent of the mean. These indicators paint a picture not of access to expensive cardiac or cancer treatments but rather of the highly un-equal fundamental chances that a kid has to live a healthy, normal life.

The availability of services tracks the inequality in health. If you are wealthy in Honduras, you have a 97 percent chance that your home has running, safe water—but only 79 percent of the poor homes benefit from this sanitary connection. None-theless, there is cause for hope—this number has risen from approximately 43 per-cent over ten years. Electricity has also improved through the region, with roughly 75 percent of the poorest decile in the regional having access—and near complete coverage at the top. Telephones are another metric of service—just try getting a job without one. In Ecuador, only 6 percent of the poorest have access to either a fixed or mobile phone; 56 percent of the top echelon enjoy this luxury. Mexican fixed-line telephone coverage ranges from 6 percent at the bottom to 74 percent in the upper echelon of income. The most connected among the wealthy are the Chileans and the Colombians at 91 percent and 94 percent, respectively.

Inequality in Latin America not only is high but also has worsened in most Latin American countries. Table 11.7 shows the Gini coefficient, a number that usu-ally doesn't vary much, as lower in 1990 for most countries as compared to 2000. Increasing economic polarization is illustrated by changes at the extremes in the income distribution. In 1970, the richest 1 percent of the population made 363 times the amount of the poorest 1 percent. After falling to a multiple of 237 prior to the debt crisis, by 1995 this ratio had climbed to 417. Some suggest that the increase in inequality is because the poor have not benefited from growth as much as the rich.[59] In Argentina, a country that has struggled with macroeconomic crisis, the Gini for the urban greater Buenos Aires area increased from .345 in 1974 to .538 in 2002—an extraordinary change.[60]

Table 11.7. Income Distribution: Percentage Share of Per Capita Household Income

	Year	1	2	3	4	5	6	7	8	9	10	Gini around 1990	Gini around 2000
High Inequality													
Guatemala	2000	0.7	1.7	2.6	3.6	4.7	6.1	7.8	10.4	15.6	46.8	na	0.583
Brazil	2001	0.9	1.7	2.5	3.4	4.5	5.8	7.5	10.4	16.1	47.2	0.585	0.573
Chile	2000	1.2	2.2	2.9	3.7	4.7	5.8	7.4	10	15.2	47	0.55	0.571
Bolivia	1999	0.3	1	2.3	3.6	5.1	6.8	8.9	11.9	17.8	42.3	0.54	0.578
Colombia	1999	0.8	1.9	2.8	3.7	4.8	6.1	7.7	10.3	15.4	46.5	0.57	0.576
Moderate-to-High Inequality													
Paraguay	1999	0.6	1.6	2.7	3.8	5	6.5	8.4	11.2	16.5	43.8	0.57	0.568
Panama	2000	0.7	1.7	2.7	3.8	4.9	6.3	8.3	11.3	17	43.3	0.56	0.56
Ecuador	1998	0.7	1.9	2.9	3.9	5	6.4	8.3	10.8	15.9	44.2	0.56	0.56
Nicaragua	1998	0.8	1.9	2.9	4	5.2	6.5	8.3	11	15.6	43.9	0.57	0.559
Honduras	1999	0.9	3.1	4.1	5.4	6.9	9	12	17.5	38.9	42.2	0.57	0.55
Mexico	2000	1	2.1	3.1	4.1	5.2	6.5	8.2	10.7	16	43.1	0.53	0.54
El Salvador	2000	0.9	2	3.1	4.2	5.5	6.9	8.8	11.4	16.5	40.6	0.51	0.532
Argentina	2001	1	2.1	3.1	4.1	5.4	6.9	9	12	17.5	38.9	0.48	0.52
Moderate Inequality													
Venezuela	1998	1.3	2.7	3.7	4.9	6.1	7.6	9.4	12	16.7	35.6	0.44	0.47
Costa Rica	2000	1.4	2.8	3.9	5	6.1	7.6	9.5	12.2	16.7	34.8	0.46	0.46
Peru	2000	0.8	2.3	3.6	4.8	6.3	7.8	9.5	12	16	36.9	0.46	0.49
Uruguay	2000	1.8	3	4.1	5.2	6.4	7.8	9.5	12.1	16.6	33.5	0.41	0.44
Average Latin America													0.53705

Source: World Bank, *Breaking with History?* (2003), Statistical Appendix A.2.

What Causes Inequality in Latin America?

What factors have shaped the high degree of inequality in the Latin American region? Inequality tends to be driven by the allocation of endowments and by the distribution of natural resources and human capital in society. As we remember from chapter 2, initial endowments based on patterns of colonization in the region were highly unequal. Pathbreaking work by economic historians indicates that land endowments in Latin America lent themselves to commodities featuring economies of scale such as sugar or silver. They posit that commodity endowments are a central determinant of inequality and that in turn inequality promotes bad institutions, weak redistributive policies, and low capital investment. Allocation of commodity endowments predict middle class income; a robust middle-class share raises income and growth.[61] As we discussed earlier regarding poverty, another factor in Latin America was the effect of race. For example, in Brazil's first 250 years, roughly 70 percent of the immigrants to the colony arrived in chains to work sugar plantations in slave gangs. The privileged whites did well, politically guaranteeing their rights over time.[62] Furthermore, in contrast to the values of individualism, materialism, and scientific inquiry that characterized northern European colonialists, Spanish and Portuguese culture tended to transmit values of tradition, order, and spirituality.[63]

Nonetheless, one cannot forever blame the Spanish and the Portuguese for the woes of the region. Even the World Bank (not exactly a radical source) argues that policy making in the almost two hundred years since independence has continued to favor the wealthy elite over the poor. The 15 percent excess of inequality in Latin America versus the rest of the world can be decomposed into different sources. Because scarce capital attracts high returns, the owners of capital have had a premium paid to them that accounts for 1 percent of this excess inequality. Inequality in the distribution in natural resources explains another 5 percent, but the bulk of the excess inequality is driven by underdevelopment of human capital.[64] In particular, growth in the number of years of education has been slower in Latin America than in the rest of the world. As we will see in chapter 13, access to education varies widely by income. The poorest in Brazil or El Salvador are unlikely to finish second grade. Socioeconomic mobility—the opportunity to move up the economic ladder —is also squarely tied to educational attainment. Children with poorly educated parents tend to remain stuck in poverty; socioeconomic success hinges on family background.[65] To lower inequality, countries must focus on building educational opportunities, a topic that we will concentrate on below and in the following chapter.

Does Growth Cause Inequality?

The slow progress on poverty reduction in the region appears tied to inequality. If inequality were not in excess of international levels commensurate with similar GDPs—that is, if excess inequality were eliminated—poverty in Latin America would have been reduced by half. Indeed, if Latin America had an income distribution similar to other middle-income nations, it would be the developing region with the lowest poverty rates.[66] Chile remains an exception to this story, having experienced an increase in inequality in the 1980s and a decline in the 1990s. Poverty in Latin America can be seen as largely a distributive problem. As we will come back to in the conclusion to this chapter, policy programs should therefore be targeted less at an insufficiency of resources and more squarely at improving the access of the poor to the assets in the economy.

In addition to the effect of equality on poverty, economists have long wondered about the relationship between overall growth rates and equality. This is slightly different from changes in poverty. A nation could grow rapidly, with the absolute conditions of the poor not changing but the relative distance between the poor and the rich increasing. Alternatively, growth could improve the position of the poor with respect to the rich, or it could leave the lives at the extremes untouched and encourage the expansion of a middle class. What happens to the relative positions of income groups as countries grow? In turn, how do different levels of inequality affect the possibilities for growth?

Economists have tested the puzzling relationship between economic growth and inequality. In pathbreaking work in the 1950s, Nobel Prize winner Simon Kuznets hypothesized that inequality follows a U-shaped path as economic growth expands. Called the **Kuznets curve,** it shows inequality increasing as countries begin to grow rapidly. As the country continues to develop, however, inequality should decline as more people begin to benefit from the growth process.

The empirical evidence regarding the Kuznets curve is contradictory. Although some studies confirm the pattern, others indicate that inequality does not necessarily have to increase before it lessens. Indeed, some economists argue that the causality might run in the other direction: increasing equality could help to spur growth. If more people had money, they would spend it. Improving income distribution could work to increase domestic demand for goods and services, providing a consumer-led expansion for growth. Furthermore, greater access to assets could improve investment in complementary resources. With greater equality, the poor might find it easier to borrow to invest in human capital. That is, if income were more equally distributed, one might see a stronger demand for investments in human capital such as health and education, improving economic performance. In contrast, unequal income distribution weakens the accumulation of physical and human capital, acting as a drag on productivity growth, the key to economic change.[67] Improving equality would therefore be growth-enhancing.

The inequality and growth puzzle is difficult to resolve empirically because of data limitations. Good census surveys are time-consuming and costly. They are even more problematic in developing countries than in industrial countries. Furthermore, limited observations of slow-moving inequality data versus frequent and volatile macroeconomic growth rates make estimates difficult. Cross-country comparative studies run into trouble because of the different institutional characteristics of economies and different data collection techniques over time. Nevertheless, despite these difficulties, interesting work has emerged. Recent studies at the World Bank indicate that inequality as measured by the Gini coefficient has been relatively stable over periods that include divergent macroeconomic patterns. In a study of eighty-eight cases in which a country's GDP per capita grew for a decade, inequality increased in forty-five countries and decreased in forty-three.[68] This calls into question the Kuznets proposition that growth will initially lead to an increase in inequality. It also raises questions about the ability of growth to reduce inequality. However, it is important to remember that magnitudes of growth rates and time matter. As one Bolivian economist put it, "You don't eradicate centuries of structural inequalities with 4 percent growth rates."[69] Policy conditioning the kind of growth and how it is distributed is apparently an important variable.

Some suggest that economic liberalization has exacerbated inequality because opening to international markets keeps wages low. Globalization has amplified pre-existing inequality in the distribution of assets, especially human capital, and of access to infrastructure and other productive resources.[70] However, not all the evidence on growth, globalization, and inequality confirms the hypothesis that globalization and growth increase inequality and poverty. David Dollar and Aart Kray conclude that growth benefits the poor proportionately with the rest of society and that greater openness of economies has not added to inequality.[71] Liberalization may also introduce more capital to combine with labor, can limit monopoly power, might reduce the bias against agriculture, and can exert greater pressure for efficiency and technical change.[72] The empirical evidence is mixed, with the work leading us to conclude that the relationship between globalized growth and equality may not be a direct one. Growth may enhance equality or, if the rewards from growth are unevenly distributed, may increase inequality. Correlation of inequality and growth may not indicate causation. More research needs to be done in this area.

What research appears to be telling us, however, is that if social or ethical concerns direct policymakers toward reducing inequality, this does not necessarily have to come at the price of economic growth. Indeed, poor growth records may have inhibited improvements in equality. Some studies show that high levels of inequality are statistically linked to weak macroeconomic performance.[73] A vicious cycle of poverty and inequality impeding growth—and low growth accelerating poverty and inequality—dominates regional performance.[74] Growth-dampening political conflict and populist redistributive cycles may be propelled by inequality. Bolivia, for example, has gone through more than 250 rebellions and military coups in its 150-year history. Unequal income distribution may also limit the market size and interfere with human capital accumulation.[75] Political opening with more genuine democratic participation may create incentives toward equity-enhancing policies. High incomes have been maintained by the special privilege and protection enjoyed by economic elites in the region; as the poor exercise greater voting power, there may be political incentives to design policies to improve economic opportunities for them.[76]

This interaction between relatively rapid growth and anemic reduction in poverty rates in the 1990s leads us to an important conclusion: growth is a necessary but not sufficient condition for poverty alleviation. Growth is critical to reducing poverty in the region, but if changes are not made to enhance the ability of the poor to participate in the growth process and its rewards, poverty and inequality will remain a sad fact of life in Latin America. The problem has been that despite renewed efforts on the part of governments to strengthen social programs, poverty rates have been stubbornly high, and inequality has been increasing.[77]

AREAS FOR ACTION: ENHANCING THE ASSETS OF THE POOR

Why Pursue Poverty-Reducing Policies?

Latin America is too rich to perform so poorly on increasing opportunity and reducing poverty for the least advantaged. Although progress has been made, it is puzzling that despite changing economic policies, poverty and inequality remain. Reducing poverty and inequality remains the central development challenge for the region. The design of effective antipoverty policies is a challenge driven by both ethics and efficiency. From an ethical standpoint, people have a basic human right to a life without extreme deprivation. But there is also a huge efficiency loss in terms of human capital. Without the assets to invest in their future, the poor are systematically excluded from working toward a better life. Addressing poverty in Latin America is crucially important for those living in North America as well. In a world linked by globalized trade, travel, and culture, poverty in Latin America can materially affect everyone through unsustainable environmental practices, illegal migration, and the export of violence and political dissatisfaction.

Policymakers are beginning to think through the multidimensional nature of this problem. The adoption of the MDGs in 2000 was an important first step in affirming a global commitment to fight poverty; the financial commitments made at the Monterrey meetings to support ending poverty were encouraging—if as yet unactualized pledges. On a personal level, addressing the moral question of helping those in need may be a reason that you are interested in development. Financially and socially sustainable answers to solving the problem of poverty, however, are difficult to come by. There are no magic bullets to addressing the tough multidimensional problems of poverty and inequality in Latin American—just the need for consistent, hard, politically difficult work.

Policy Approaches to Achieving the MDGs and Reducing Poverty in Latin America

The millennium challenge of reducing poverty in Latin America by half by 2015 is at once daunting and attainable. It is overwhelming when we review past policies and the historical failure of growth to deliver significant poverty reduction in the region. It appears attainable, however, when we analyze best-case evidence and see that lives can indeed be improved and even saved through good policy. The question becomes which policy tools will generate the strongest returns in the struggle to end poverty in Latin America. Our neoliberal, neoinstitutional, and neostructuralist frameworks developed in Chapter 6 may provide some guidance. From these perspectives we may want to choose a policy mix of working with the market (neoliberal), building institutions (neoinstitutional), and strategic investment on the part of the state (neostructuralist). Market-based measures look at where the market has failed to deliver and redress deficits such as access to human or physical capital that prevent the poor from investing in better lives.[78] An institutionalist would likely agree with the need to address market failure but would suggest that this is a necessary yet not sufficient condition for change. For the institutionalist, the structure of institutions, particularly the ways in which history has shaped political access to power, must be redressed before markets can deliver **pro-poor growth.** The neostructuralist would likely take this recommendation even further, pointing to the need for the state to provide quality public goods and address externalities to promote a sustainable and equitable growth path for the region. Like any pragmatic policymaker, you may find yourself not espousing a pure variant of any position but rather considering a judicious mix of all three to address the call of Jeffrey Sachs to end poverty.[79]

Market Magic: Can the Market Be Used As an Instrument to Alleviate Poverty?

A neoliberal purist might argue that the best policy prescription to reduce poverty is to remove regulatory impediments to growth in Latin America and allow the market to deliver returns to the less advantaged in society. Growth, they argue, is the best poverty program. Logically, it is hard to refute the fundamental question: Can you name a country that has redressed poverty over time without growth? As even Dani Rodrik (not a pure neoliberal) agrees, growth is good for the poor. All countries that have experienced sustained growth over a few decades have reduced poverty. Furthermore, he argues, poverty reduction is good for growth.[80] But why have the benefits of growth been so slow to reduce poverty? You may have guessed, given our discussion, that this has to do with the high degree of inequality. In highly unequal societies, it takes higher rates of growth to reduce poverty.[81] Inequality in Latin America perpetuates allocations that are essentially inefficient, preventing the poor from undertaking projects that would have high expected social returns.[82] The appropriate policy mix for the neoliberal, therefore, is to correct the market imperfections that perpetuate inequality, allowing entrepreneurial energies to flourish and thus generating both growth and poverty reduction.

One approach to decrease the role of social welfare bureaucracies is that of **decentralization.** Decentralization moves state activity from the national to the local level. The premise behind decentralization is that local control will decrease costs and increase the effectiveness of each dollar spent on local services. In principle, local authorities are in better touch with the needs of their constituencies and can therefore make better choices in programming. There are four elements to decentralization: deconcentration, delegation, devolution, and privatization. Deconcentration shifts workloads from central ministries to federally paid employees located outside national capitals. Delegation involves the transfer of authority from the central government, whereas devolution genuinely transfers authority. Privatization turns the administration of social programs over to nongovernmental or private-sector agencies.[83] In most cases of decentralization, financing flows through block grants from the central government to equalize revenue across regions. However, decentralization may also include revenue and expenditure decision making.[84]

The experience with decentralization in Latin America has been mixed in terms of improving the quality of services delivered. Success was a function of the ability of local bureaucracies to function more effectively than centralized governments. The tradition of local strongmen in Latin America created opportunities to subvert this process, but in some cases it was overridden by greater responsiveness to local demand. Where social mobilization could work to demand change, decentralization was pro-poor. Where closed political power could exclude less-powerful groups, the policy reinforced inequality and poverty.[85]

One policy approach to reduce bureaucratic entanglements was to pursue the process of contracting out the provision of public services. Private operators, either for-profit or nonprofit agencies, have increasingly been engaged in the provision of public social service delivery. From concessions for delivery of water, electricity, and telecommunications to school concessions and health care services, firms and NGOs are delivering services. Since these organizations are in constant competition for contracts, the incentives are structures for the groups to deliver higher-quality results to ensure contract renewal. Unlike a traditional government ministry with few incentives for effectiveness, private providers must meet goals or be fired. Some worry, however, that the proliferation of contracting out weakens the legitimacy of the state. Clients see the face and the name of the NGO—not their tax dollars at work.

Although the goal of hard-line neoliberals might be to take the federal government out of social assistance, some evidence suggests the need for a central government role in building capacity in local institutions to deliver quality services. Linkage between local and national levels is also important in setting and enforcing national standards and regulations. Administrators in remote areas may not have had the training necessary to manage a variety of social assistance programs; the federal government is important in developing professional local capacity. Although most now agree that huge bureaucracies in state capitals are not the most efficient way to deliver social services, a role for central government in allocation, training, and oversight is largely seen as warranted.

Two policy approaches that essentially take their cue from the neoliberal recommendation to strengthen market-based instruments are microenterprise lending and conditional cash transfers. Investing in microenterprises addresses the lack of financing available to the poor to invest in business projects; conditional cash transfers focus on the gap in resources for the poor to invest in their own human capital, particularly education and health. The diagnosis is that the demand for health and education investments by the poor will rise if they have the money to make these investments. Some suggest, however, that cash transfers are an end run around deeper reforms in institutions to improve the supply of delivery services.[86] We will look at conditional cash transfers in depth in chapters 12 and 13; for now, let's turn our attention to **microcredit** mechanisms.

Microfinance As a Market-Based Solution

Can the market be used to help reduce poverty? One approach toward poverty reduction is to build on the entrepreneurial energies within the informal sector, improving productivity and therefore income. We remember from chapter 9 that the informal sector is a catch-all term for individuals and small firms or microenterprises operating in open, unregulated markets outside the tax base, using local resources and labor-intensive technologies. The objective of activity in the informal sector is basically to guarantee subsistence of the family group.[87] Jobs in the informal sector are often characterized by low productivity (with little associated capital investment) and instability. Although it holds limited promise for advancement, the informal sector does serve as a social net for the poor and unskilled and has therefore helped to rescue families from deprivation. Where there are weak social safety nets and limited unemployment insurance, the informal sector offers employment of last resort.[88] Women are disproportionately represented in the informal sector—in food services, domestic washing and cleaning, tourism, petty trading, dressmaking, companionship, and sex. This may be attributed to the difficulties that women face in accessing formal education and credit as well as technical training.[89] Women tend to be pushed into the informal sector to earn money for family survival.

It is estimated that women in Honduras, Peru, and Colombia comprise 68, 67, and 57 percent, respectively, of informal-sector employees, concentrated in independent labor.[90] The informal sector allows women greater flexibility in terms of hours of employment and child care as well as lower entry barriers. Unfortunately, these jobs are also characterized by low remuneration, with 75–80 percent of those employed in the informal sector earning less than the poverty level. Labor legislation, social security, and minimum wage laws are not enforceable in the informal sector. Labor, benefits, payments into social security funds, and vacations can add as much as 20 percent to the firm's labor bill.

The impetus behind the informal sector is the urban labor surplus created in part by unemployed rural migrants. The International Labor Organization reports that since 1990, 85 percent of all new jobs in Latin America and the Caribbean have been created in the extralegal sector. Neoliberals argue that this growth outside formal employment is exacerbated by excessive government regulation in the labor market, creating rigidities in hiring. High tax rates may also encourage black markets in goods. Neostructuralists contend that the surplus labor is created by technology-intensive production in the formal sector patterned after the industrialized world. Because firms don't use appropriate labor-intensive technologies, arguably fewer workers are hired, and the informal sector is a default survival strategy.

The informal sector is both rich in economic activity and poor in opportunity. In his book *The Mystery of Capital*, Peruvian Hernando de Soto argues that although the poor save and accumulate assets, they are dead assets. That is, their land, their houses, and their businesses do not have legal protection that can be used for collateral against an investment. Indeed, an understanding of the workings of the informal sector has transformed our notion of the relationship between the poor and society. In its infancy development theory tended to describe the poor on the margins of society, outside the reach of the engines of growth. The provision of a bit of fuel—income support—was intended to jump-start the process of growth. Today, researchers see the poor as globally and locally integrated into the productive system. Clearly sputtering rather than zooming, new forms of social organization have emerged as survival mechanisms of the poor in a globalized society. The poor are linked to society—excluded from formal institutions of quality education and health, often violently frustrated by the lack of mobility within systems—but tied to a social system that perpetuates this exclusion.[91]

The addition of capital and technology to the entrepreneurial and survival instincts of the hard-working poor may improve the position of the marginalized. This of course involves investment—a critical constraint in enterprise expansion. Small loans are often not profitable for banks because of their high transactions and monitoring costs as well as low repayment rates. Imagine the reaction of a bank when a poor woman would come in to ask for a seventy-dollar loan to open a pastry business. "They would laugh in my face," said Eulogia Santelices, a Chilean mother of four. Her other alternative was 10 percent monthly interest from money-lenders—but there clearly isn't enough margin in selling cakes to cover those high interest rates![92] Santelices found her financial backing at Fondo Esperanza, a Catholic humanitarian organization in Chile. NGOs and, increasingly, the public sector have begun to attend to this need through microfinance, or microcredit. A microenterprise is defined as a sole proprietorship with fewer than ten employees that lacks the collateral and traditional creditworthiness to borrow money from traditional banks. The IADB reports that the sixty-five million tiny businesses in the region account for employment of roughly half of Latin America's workforce and contribute 40–65 percent of regional GNP.[93] Microfinance organizations allow the poor to convert small savings over time into the needed lump sums for investment as well as insurance against shocks.[94] Box 11.3 shows examples of microcredit enterprises in the region.

How do microfinance organizations work? Microfinance organizations attempt to substitute the traditional financing requirements—collateral and a credit history —with terms appropriate to small businesses and the local social context. Solidarity groups—where members of the group share responsibility for repayment of the loan—have been an effective mechanism for self-monitoring and for maintaining high repayment rates. Lenient payment terms are structured to respond to the challenges of a life of poverty. Normally involving groups of women, more than 700,000 have benefited from microloans in the Latin American region.[95] Microcredit programs are usually accompanied by technical training in such skills as basic bookkeeping. Some also packaged health or nutritional lessons into the required bimonthly meetings. Microfinance is more than simply money; it is designed as a means to leverage cash into a sustained investment. Stanley Fischer, former chief economist of the World Bank and now governor of the Bank of Israel, says that microcredit offers "hope to many poor people of improving their own situations through their own efforts."[96]

In Latin America more than four hundred microfinance institutions provide soft loans to the region's poor. Although the ground for microfinance lending was broken by NGOs such as Accion, commercial institutions increasingly are participants in this arena. A constellation of actors work to support microlending in the region. In addition to private funding through charitable donations, the World Bank, the Andean Development Corporation, the IADB, and foundations have promoted

Box 11.3.   Micro Credit, Macro Hope

BOLIVIA

Fortunata María de Aliaga has sold flowers from a street corner in La Paz, Bolivia, for as long as anyone can remember. When her children were young, she worked long days to give them the opportunity she never had: the chance to go to school. There were days when she barely had enough money to set up shop. Then, fifteen years ago, Fortunata learned about Banco Sol, a bank affiliated with ACCION International. Together with three other women, she qualified for a loan that allowed her to buy flowers in bulk at a much cheaper rate. With a strong repayment record, Fortunata was approved for larger loans and began to borrow on her own. Today, Fortunata is proud to report that she put her savings to good use. "All three of my children finished school," she beams. "And I even had money left to make some improvements to my house!"

NICARAGUA

With a reputation as a strong woman who drives hard bargains and makes tough sales, Emerita Centeno Granada is a street vendor who has lived in Boaco, Nicaragua, for twenty-two years. For much of that time, with profits from her business, she has helped support her seven children, four of whom are female. Growing her vegetable- and fruit-selling business has demanded a keen business sense and a vision for taking full advantage of resources that allow her to eke out as much as possible from her business.

But even with her natural business sense and decades of experience as a street vendor, Emerita has struggled to have enough money to buy produce to sell. In the past, she has often had to resort to moneylenders or to buying produce on credit. Both of these activities eat into her meager profit margins because the interest rates on the loans are so high. This makes it next to impossible for her to get her family above the poverty line, despite all of her hard work.

By providing her with a microloan of sixty dollars at an affordable rate of interest, YMCA Nicaragua is helping Emerita to build both a stronger business and a more stable foundation for her family. A simple sixty-dollar loan has served as an entry point for Emerita and YMCA Nicaragua to develop a relationship of mutual trust and benefit—and allows her the opportunity to disentangle herself from relationships with loan sharks. A hallmark of the Grameen philosophy, Emerita's loan size—and the accompanying capacity to build her business—will increase after she repays her first loan and subsequent loans.

Currently, Emerita is using her sixty-dollar loan from YMCA Nicaragua to buy more popular produce to sell. These days, most of her products are fruits and vegetables—a variety of melons, oranges, bananas, and onions. Emerita also sells honey and pork products. Her most popular sales may come in the morning, though, when she sells corn nacatamales—a kind of steamed corn flour dough that is wrapped in a banana leaf—with a cup of coffee for just five cordobas (approximately fifty cents). When gathering produce to sell, Emerita buys only a little lettuce because it is slow to sell. But her melons, oranges, and bananas move very quickly.

Support for entrepreneurs such as Emerita is important for the whole town of Boaco, as it strengthens not only the lives of the entrepreneurs but also adds economic opportunities and exciting new choices for many members of the community. Emerita knows that the YMCA's program is not just about the sixty-dollar loan. It is about improving the economic and social situation of the people in her community. It may well be that one day her children will take advantage of the YMCA's loans as well, to try to improve their own businesses. Currently, one is a chauffer and another is a welder—when there is work available. Through loans from the YMCA, Emerita is teaching them what stability is.

GENDER EQUITY THROUGH MICROFINANCE IN EL SALVADOR

Las Mélidas is an NGO based in San Salvador, El Salvador, whose mission is to promote gender equality through organization, training, and education programs for women from all sectors of society. One Las Mélidas program is a microfinance initiative set up with support from the Grameen Foundation USA. In this program, borrowers form groups that are federated into centers using the Grameen solidarity group-lending methodology. The centers meet every fortnight for financial transactions (receiving or repaying loans) in their community. In addition, the center meeting is an opportunity for Las Mélidas staff to provide additional educational services to its clients.

In this picture the center chief is accounting for payments that she has received. In the background is some educational material that is used to teach clients about the rights of their daughters and sons. *(Photo by Nigel Biggar)*

Source: "Microfinance and Microcredit: How Can $100 Change an Economy" http://www .yearofmicrocredit.org/docs/MicrocreditBrochure_eng.pdf; Grameen Foundation USA, http:// www.gfusa.org/programs/borrower_profiles/emerita_from_nicaragua/. For more information on Las Mélidas, visit www.lasmelidas.org. For more information on Grameen Foundation USA, visit www.gfusa.org.

microenterprise lending. The International Year of Microcredit attracted a good deal of attention to the potential of as well as the constraints on creating a more inclusive financial sector for the poor.

Microcredit success stories point to the power of this tool. As heralded on the International Year of Microcredit 2005 website, in Bolivia the Global Development Research Center shows that microcredit loan clients doubled their income in two years. Clients were also more likely to seek health care for their families and more likely to send their children to school.[97] An estimated 15.7 million people in Brazil work in the informal economy as microentrepreneurs, outnumbering formal-sector entrepreneurs by more than three to one, according to the World Business Council for Sustainable Development. Of these informal microentrepreneurs, 93 percent run profitable businesses.[98] Becoming a microfinance client has led to increased self-confidence in women and improved status within the community, according to results of Freedom from Hunger studies in Bolivia; participants were more actively involved than nonparticipants in local government.[99]

But some suggest that while microcredit has been an important tool, its long-run potential to contribute to poverty reduction is overblown. The goal of commercial microcredit organizations is profitability. Although international organizations have enthusiastically contributed to this market-based idea, many question the viability of a market-based tool precariously predicated on donor goodwill. If donor preferences change, noncommercial microfinance will dry up. The momentum, therefore, is to wean organizations off external financing and special funding and to encourage the development of a commercial banking system that itself is inclusive of the poor. There are, however, significant challenges to this objective. First, the success of microfinance paradoxically holds the seeds of crisis. The increased number of microlenders drove competing funds to overlend to unviable projects, increasing the likelihood of bankruptcy.[100] Second, there may be a contradiction among greater expansion, long-run profitability, and the personal nature of providing microfinance services. Attending to a large number of small lenders, each needing personal assistance, is a labor-intensive, costly endeavor. But to keep costs reasonable, microlending works best with large economies of scale—that is, in urban centers with a large number of clients per loans officer. This, however, will also bias the development of microfinance away from spatial pockets of poverty, particularly in the rural sector. In addition, if profitability becomes the driver, the culture of the lending environment will change—from charitable organizations to proper businesses.[101] Additionally, there is a not surprising tendency to gravitate toward ever larger microclients. Borrowers who have been able to make a go of their microenterprises are more creditworthy and have needs for larger-sized loans. But as microfinance organizations are drawn to better credit risks, less attention may be given to the poorest of the poor—those who truly need assistance in transforming de Soto's "dead" assets into active capital. Finally, as successful group members developed credit histories, they were less likely to need the meetings or the solidarity contracts, and groups themselves began to fall apart. But as these group members leave, failure rates of those who struggle with their businesses will rise, compromising the viability of the microcreditor.

Despite these obstacles and growing pains, many remain optimistic about the virtues of microfinance. The entry of more competition from traditional banks may help reduce costs. New demand for microservices is also being fueled by the flow of remittance dollars discussed in chapter 7. Migrants working in North America and Europe require banking services to reach poor relatives in underserved rural and urban areas in their home countries. Other nonbank entities have also entered the market, and new products, including savings accounts and insurance, are being provided. In Merida, Mexico, for example, Wal-Mart offers life, automobile, and fire insurance for less than one dollar a month through a marketing agreement with Met Life.[102] The poor live with enormous vulnerability to bad luck; microinsurance programs can help safeguard their extraordinary hard work. Finally, technology—not only bank machines but also mobile phones—offers new avenues for making payments on loans, making deposits, and getting cash. Vodafone and Hewlett-Packard have prototype programs that may eventually make the need for branch banks in small villages—and perhaps even cash—superfluous.[103] Facilitated by technology, funding can efficiently find its way into the hands of the poor.

Studies of the effects of microcredit lending on the intended beneficiaries, the poor, have only begun to appear. Loan impacts appear to be small for the very poor, because they tend to use loans to finance consumption rather than investment; the not-so-poor are better able to transform loans into productive business investments.[104] Moreover, it is important to remember that microcredit lending is not enough. Complementary measures, particularly in infrastructure, health, and education, are necessary to address the problem of poverty. It doesn't matter if a woman has the money to invest in a sewing machine if she cannot market her goods or if the possibilities aren't open for her child to become more than a seamstress. A neostructuralist, for example, would argue that microcredit is useful in providing financial services for the poor but that there is still a necessary role for the state in building roads and schools.

Business and Poverty Alleviation

Are businesses effective partners in poverty alleviation in Latin America? The reflexive response from a pure neoliberal might be to argue that of course businesses are the central actors—businesses create wealth, hiring people and making goods in the process. But can—and should—businesses place social concerns as a core element of their corporate strategy? Given the gap between the resources of the fiscally constrained state and the needs of the 40.9 percent of Latin Americans in poverty, some pragmatists argue that indeed the market can be harnessed to contribute to sustainable development. Advocates for **corporate social responsibility** suggest that the only truly sustainable businesses in the long run are those that invest in their people and their communities. The value proposition for the firm resides in the link between good social and environmental performance and the bottom line for the firm. The urgency of the social question in Latin America and the clear understanding that firms cannot grow in negative, unstable environments motivate the need for clear thinking about the business role in social development.

The study of corporate engagement in development is a new field. Simon Zadek of AccountAbility suggests that there are five levels of engagement. At the most basic level, firms are socially responsible if they are not behaving too badly—that is, they are in legal compliance with labor laws, treating workers decently and creating products that do no obvious harm. Firms may go beyond legalistic good behavior to engage in philanthropy. In Latin America, firms tend to engage at this level, donating money or time to a community. Quite often this commitment is driven by the ethical or religious engagement of a private owner. But genuine corporate responsibility goes beyond giving to involve the strategic positioning of the firm. A commitment to sustainability and the adoption of international benchmarks and behavior as good local neighbors in a community go to the core, strategic values of the firm. Firms can build upon this strategic approach to achieve the fifth level, competitive corporate engagement. Here firms enter into multistakeholder partnerships with NGOs and community actors as well as the state to align actions with goals of national competitiveness. Where public governance is lacking, firms might go even further to create governance structures, ensuring that other corporations are held to high social standards. Box 11.4 illustrates the potential as well as the constraints in a subset of thinking about the role of business in development, a notion known as **bottom of the pyramid marketing.** In this framework, the poor aren't excluded from the market but rather constitute the bulk of the marketing strategy in the developing world.

Corporate social responsibility in Latin America is in its infancy. Although some firms such as CEMEX of Mexico and Natura of Brazil have taken leadership roles, this new paradigm for doing business is in the construction stage. Several drivers are missing. In Europe, for example, the role of consumers in demanding socially responsible products is far stronger than weak consumer consciousness in Latin America. Likewise, pressure from stockholders to maintain good reputations is weaker, as many of Latin America's companies are privately held in close family conglomerates. Multinational firms with offices in Latin America may support community programming to sell soap or soda, but the firms are not normally forced to examine their supply chains to encourage the range of small- and medium-sized corporations to upgrade pay or working circumstances. Finally, national regulatory systems of standards in both employment and product development remain relatively weak.

These constraints notwithstanding, both Latin American firms and multinationals operating in the region do have a role in corporate social responsibility. Huge banks such as Itau in Brazil have taken leadership in education, culture, and literacy. Unilever, a leading international consumer goods producer, is working with the Chileans to ensure that the hake in their Gordon's fish sticks is certified as meeting sustainability standards; in its Mexico office it adheres to good citizenship with its internal public, its workers, by promoting stigma reduction for HIV-positive workers. The Brazilian aircraft producer EMBRAER runs schools in its San Jose dos Campos to contribute to the human capital of its employees' children. CEMEX has a wide-ranging agenda that covers environmental standards, environmental impact assessments for cement-processing plants, and programs to help low-income customers purchase cement in quantities commensurate with available income. CVRD, one of the world's largest mining companies (which happens to be Brazilian), maintains a

Box 11.4.   The Fortune at the Bottom of the Pyramid

Stop thinking of the poor as victims, argues C. K. Prahalad. Opportunities will open to develop new markets as businesses approach the poor as resilient and creative entrepreneurs.[105] In his book *The Fortune at the Bottom of the Pyramid,* Prahalad exhorts big business to start serving the world's 5 billion or so poorest consumers who live on less than two dollars a day. In Latin America, the 300 billion consumers who make up more than 40 percent of the region's population can be a source of profits—if product design and marketing are targeted to overcome obstacles to purchase.

This is not a new concept to Samuel Klein, who, after surviving two years in a Nazi concentration camp, immigrated to Brazil and began selling linens door to door in poor neighborhoods.[106] He learned that poor people do buy goods—just a bit differently than those with money. His approach grew into the largest retail chain in Brazil, Casas Bahia, serving 10 million customers in 330 stores across the country. Klein targeted a key aspect of selling to the poor: lack of credit. Those with few financial resources can't just drop the Visa card to make their dreams come true. Customers without formal-sector income—and often without fixed legal addresses—are tough subjects of credit searches. Instead, Casas Bahia's customers are interviewed by credit analysts right in the store—people looking not for telephone numbers but indicators such as calloused hands that hint at steady employment. In less than ten minutes and based on a set of questions, credit is extended to purchase the new oven or television. Payment is divided into schedules from one to fifteen months—and once an item is 50 percent repaid, another loan may be extended. Such financed sales account for 90 percent of Casas Bahia's volume, and as customers return monthly to the store to make payments the relationship with the store is cemented, leading to a relatively low default rate of 8.5 percent—only 2 percent higher than the general retail sector. There is of course plenty of room for Casas Bahia to grow—the other 166 million Brazilians sitting at the bottom of the pyramid who account for 41 percent of the spending capacity of the economy.[107]

The financial sector is also an important arena to attract low-income customers. In Bolivia, a microcredit institution, Prodem FFP, has installed automatic teller machines with fingerprint recognition that communicates via text to speech technology in three local dialects—accommodating the needs of the illiterate or non-Spanish speakers among the indigenous population.[108] When customers approach the machines they receive verbal instructions in Spanish, Quechua, and Aymara and are instructed to place their smart cards in the machine and touch for fingerprint recognition.[109] Many retailers, such as Compre-Bem in São Paulo, are also offering house credit without interest to attract new customers. Although monthly payments might only amount to $.45 to $.90, retailers are using the free credit terms (interest is only charged when a customer misses a payment) to lure in the half of the population making less than 1,000 reais, or $445 a month. With the highest interest rates in the world, traditional credit card options are simply not viable for Brazil's poor. At the Wal-Mart in southern Rio, one could buy a telephone in twelve monthly installments of 3.57 reais—and even wine and beer in three interest-free installments.[110]

Retail firms in the region are beginning to recognize the profits to be made by marketing to low-income consumers. In addition to providing innovative financing schemes, firms are adjusting products to the needs of the poor. For example, Proctor and Gamble (P&G) has radically shifted its business model to benefit from the growth in emerging markets. Consumer research is a bit different—surveys and focus groups don't work with the busy poor. P&G instead sent researchers to people's homes to study habits. They learned, for example, that the plastic lining in sanitary napkins was uncomfortable in the humid heat in Mexico—and that the women facing long commutes to work without access to bathrooms also couldn't afford more than a few pads a day. P&G developed a

continued

continued

new product, Naturella, that integrated a locally used ingredient of chamomile to sooth the product next to the skin—and it doubled its market share in feminine pads.[111] Cemex, the Mexican multinational cement manufacturer, packages its cement in smaller bags, making it possible for low-income people to work on their homes in stages as money becomes available.

Marketing to the bottom of the pyramid is not limited to basic consumer products. The poor also desire the benefits that technology can bring into their lives. With funding from companies such as Google, Massachusetts Institute of Technology's Media Lab is developing a $100 computer that will be produced by Quanta Computers to be put in the hands of 5–10 million children in developing countries.[112] Microsoft has launched a pilot prepaid business model in Brazil where customers can take home a computer with a small upfront payment. The computer opens with ten hours of preinstalled usage time; to continue using the PC beyond this time, the user purchases additional cards with scratch-off codes for fixed usage hours. Friends and family can buy additional cards for use on the computer, allowing the purchaser to become the full owner of the machine more quickly. There is no fixed time period, allowing customers to pay as their budgets allow; buyers therefore don't risk losing their investment in the machine for nonpayment.[113]

Critics contend that bottom of the pyramid marketing is just one more way of exploiting the poor, preaching the gospel of consumerism to those with less.[114] One might conclude that the poor Argentines stressed by macroeconomic collapse don't need the antiaging hand cream or that Amazonian gold miners don't need the deodorants that Avon ladies sell to door to door in poor areas in Buenos Aires or paddle up the Amazon to promote. But perhaps the poor should be their own judges of their needs and desires.[115]

forest preserve in Linhares, rehabilitating a tract of Brazil's devastated Atlantic forest. Starbucks has been working with the rain forest alliance to promote fair trade coffee. But overall, the progress is relatively weak. A report by the IADB suggests that while many firms practice philanthropy, a unified, strategic approach is lacking, especially among the small- and medium-sized enterprises. Corporate social responsibility has a contribution to make—but thus far it has not approached its potential.

BUILDING PRO-POOR INSTITUTIONS

Change that is sustainable over time usually involves changes in institutions. In both the short and the long terms, the poor must be brought into the process of change so that they become actors in transforming their lives and not passive victims receiving assistance. Short-term measures are critical in alleviating human suffering, but it is the long-term structural changes that create opportunities to transform the lives of the poor. Direct transfers to the poor are best when they simultaneously build assets. For example, scholarships for the children of poor families may help supplement family incomes and also entice kids to stay in school. Compensation for visits to health posts can help balance the family budget while encouraging preventive health care.

To promote sustainable programs, the poor must be involved in the process of planning and implementing poverty-alleviation efforts. They should be thought of as clients rather than recipients, reinforcing the view that they can take action against their human suffering. In addition, programs should be integrated into the broader economy instead of creating enclaves of the poor. The example of infrastructure development in Rio de Janeiro serves to illustrate these points. Rio de Janeiro has embarked on an ambitious project to upgrade its *favelas,* or slum areas. Rather than relocate residents to planned, affordable urban housing with the unintended side effect of destroying the social fabric of a community, the city is working with residents to upgrade the standard of living within the poor communities. The city inaugurated its efforts with a competition for proposals from prominent and budding architects for community designs. The mayor's office then took these proposals to the IADB, which loaned it $300 million for the projects. Two key aspects defined the *favela* projects. First, the *favelas* were to be integrated into the surrounding communities and not reinforced as poverty enclaves. For example, in one of the most famous *favelas* in Rio, Serinha (the home of the samba), housing and workshop space for samba artists, costume areas, after-hours samba instruction facilities, an area for the *macumba* religious ceremony, a cultural center and arena stage, and a tramway to bring visitors into the *favela* were planned alongside a water-pumping station, day care facilities, and tanks of potable water.

The second concept is community engagement. *Favela* residents have been involved in planning changes and must ultimately approve plans before construction begins. The city pays for the improvements in common services, and residents are responsible for improving their own houses. Through another World Bank loan, Rio de Janeiro is using digital technology to remap the entire city, including *favelas.* This is critical to homeowners because previously the squatter settlers had no legal right to the land their homes were on, decreasing the incentive for permanent improvements. Streets will be named and houses numbered so that residents can apply for titles, and perhaps the one million residents of the *favelas* will be able to receive mail. With titles they can also use their homes as collateral for lending. Of course, a less-welcome aspect of the improvement will be that the tax agency will also know where to call![116]

Involving the poor acknowledges the gender dimension of poverty. Poverty programs must include women, as poverty is increasingly wearing a female face in the region. A range of reform measures hold promise. Women need access to economic assets, including credit; incentives to start small businesses; training to upgrade their skills in traditional and nontraditional industries; and mainstreaming into rural development strategies, especially extension services. In the social sector substantial expansion of the access of poor women to family planning and reproductive health services, educational reform agendas designed to increase educational opportunities for girls, and expansion of programs on women's leadership, violence prevention, and legal reform will contribute to improving the lot of women—and their families—in the region. Racial and ethnic discrimination must also be addressed, particularly in transforming education from an instrument of social exclusion to a tool of growth with equity. Changing power and institutions in Latin America will also require chipping away at the legacy of inequality in the region.

High inequality defines the Brazilian economy. The Bella Vista favela (slum) on the sides of the Dois Irmães mountains has a great view of Rio's playground for the rich, Ipanema Beach. *(Photo by Patrice Franko)*

Social-sector institutions have been far more resistant to modernization than institutions such as central banks that manage macroeconomic policy in the region. As opposed to central banking, which is best done by a small core of technocrats, service delivery institutions are highly transaction-intensive and involve a wide range of low-level bureaucrats who are difficult to monitor or control.[117] Although public-sector reform efforts have focused on professionalizing bureaucracies, the legacy of personalistic and clientelistic relations without strong systems of accountability continues to define many organizations. To promote better-quality services, upgrades are needed in administrative systems as well as systems of monitoring and evaluation.

Building effective propoor institutions involves giving clients greater power over providers to prompt stronger accountability. In some sectors this has involved giving clients a choice of providers. Using vouchers, this is an approach more consistent with market-based solutions. Competition has indeed been successful in reforming health, education, and social security in Colombia and Chile. In Chile, results of a voucher system indicate greater educational attainment in the transition to secondary schools for the poor, although questions remain regarding measures of school performance and cream skimming among private schools.

Colombian reform, successful by attainment measures, was discontinued due to pressure from unions.[118] Client participation in the management of services has also shown gains. Community-run schools in El Salvador and Nicaragua evidence the benefits of participation. In Peru, local health administration committees prepare local health plans that become the basis for a contract with providers. Cooperatives throughout Latin America have successfully managed potable water cooperatives, improving the delivery of this important service. If appropriate mechanisms of regulation and capacity building exist on the part of the central government, local demand and empowerment can be a significant force for institutional change. The pressure for accountability, however, must flow up the bureaucratic chain to promote the responsiveness of states to its citizens—a characteristic of democracy still under construction in Latin America. The goal is to create a virtuous cycle of social accountability mechanisms to promote more effective state actions in service delivery. Local report cards soliciting citizen feedback as well as roundtables and participation in the budgeting process can help.[119] Where external donors are involved, pressures to engage clients as conditions for grants as well as mechanisms for monitoring and evaluation can create transparency in the delivery of results. Local characteristics, especially political relations, must be taken into account in the design of heterogeneous delivery options.

THE MANAGEMENT OF POVERTY PROGRAMS: THE ROLE OF THE STATE

Combating poverty in Latin America is very much tied up in the broader question of the role of the state in the economy. The neoliberal approach advocates minimizing the role of the state in meeting the needs of the poor. For the neoliberal, the market should provide the mechanism to improve the standard of living. Neostructuralists, in contrast, argue that the problem of persistent poverty cannot be addressed without a proactive role for the state. Although neostructuralists understand the tight fiscal constraints of contemporary policy making in the region, they contend that investment in people is critical to enhancing long-term growth potential. Nonetheless, the debate on the role of the state versus the role of the market in reducing poverty is not as starkly divided as views on privatization or the role of foreign investment. All agree that the problem of persistent poverty and the social deficit in Latin America must be addressed to promote sustainable growth. The debate centers on how much state participation is optimal in achieving this objective. Box 11.5 presents the findings of the Commission on Economic Reform in Unequal Societies as an example of a comprehensive pro-poor reform agenda for equitable growth that incorporates many of the ideas presented in this chapter.

In his pathbreaking book *The End of Poverty,* Jeffrey Sachs makes the case for why governments should finance schools, clinics, and roads to complement private-sector activities. First, many kinds of infrastructure are defined by economies of scale, which would lead to monopolization of services such as transportation grids. Monopolies, if unregulated, will naturally overcharge, resulting in a loss of welfare. Second, many goods in the social sector are nonrival. A good example is the creation

Box 11.5.   Pro-poor Policy Changes

Pro-poor Policy Reform	How Past Policies Hurt the Poor	Examples of Pro-poor Policy Changes
Rule-based, transparent fiscal discipline	Fiscal deficits invite inflation and debt, a huge burden on the poor	Build stronger budget institutions to lock in decisions across administrations; enhance standards of disclosure at all levels of budgeting
Smooth booms and busts	Poor benefit less during booms and suffer in busts; first to lose jobs or drop out of school	Constrain the political spending game; stabilization funds; countercyclical policy, especially in boom to afford proactive policy in busts; strengthen public-sector debt management
Build automatic social safety nets	Uncoordinated programs tied to clientelism don't reach the poorest of the poor	Targeting, transparent rules, community involvement; countercyclical programs with automatic kick-ins and sunset clauses
Education for the poor, too	Poor distribution of income reduces educational opportunity	Autonomy to schools, presidential leadership, voice to communities; strengthen national standards and measurement; partnerships with the private sector
Tax the rich and spend more on the rest	Regressive tax policy hurts the poor and neglect opportunities to raise revenues from the rich; weak enforcement encourages evasion	Improve administrative capacity, consider progressive property and asset taxes; spend more on poor as opposed to middle-class entitlements such as pensions
Give small business a chance	Political influence of powerful corporate groups, often family owned, biased against small entrepreneurs, yet small- and medium-sized enterprises (SMEs) are 70 percent of new job creation	Expand microcredit through revised regulatory measures; broaden access to finance through legal and regulatory changes that deepen capital market reach to SMEs; streamline bureaucratic measures
Protect workers' rights	Focus on job security prevents workers from negotiating directly with employers; little unemployment insurance	Stimulate rights of association, encourage flexibility in contracts, extend unemployment insurance
Deal openly with discrimination	Race, gender, and ethnic differences lower wages and increase poverty	National leadership including better data on conditions of racial and ethnic minorities; public education to change attitudes toward women; stronger legal protection of women's rights

Pro-poor Policy Reform	How Past Policies Hurt the Poor	Examples of Pro-poor Policy Changes
Repair land markets	Unequal land distribution is connected to income inequality and the evolution of political and social institutions that lock in inequality	Improve land markets through credit and matching grants to land purchases; complementary agricultural extension inputs; engage stakeholders
Infrastructure delivery for the poor	Rural sector and poor neighborhoods least well served by infrastructure services; higher health and occupational risks for the poor; weak regulatory structures permit monopoly pricing	Change to demand-driven culture of delivery; focus on competition and information; target subsidies to poor households; draw on labor of the poor to build infrastructure in their neighborhoods
Reduce rich-country protectionism	Decreasing returns to market liberalization in developing countries without a complementary opening in the industrial world	Job training and trade readjustment benefits in industrialized countries to reduce political opposition to market opening

Source: Nancy Birdsall and Augusto de la Torre, *Washington Contentious: Economic Policies for Social Equity in Latin America,* Findings of the Commission on Economic Reform in Unequal Latin American Societies, sponsored by the Carnegie Endowment for International Peace and the Inter-American Dialogue, 2001.

of knowledge—its consumption by one person doesn't diminish availability to another. Where one doesn't charge for such knowledge creation, however, who but the state will be willing to invest in this sector? Third, the concept of spillovers or externalities is important in considering investment in the social sector. If I want you to be better educated so that you are less likely to rob me or to be vaccinated so that I am less likely to suffer an epidemic, it is easier to encourage you to go to school or a clinic if it is freely provided by the state. Fourth, social-sector investments by the state fall into the category of being merit goods—it is right and just to provide them. Upheld by the Universal Declaration of Human Rights, everyone has a right to a standard of living adequate for health and well-being and for education through fundamental stages. Finally, although governments should not provide capital for private businesses, it may want to consider investments to help the poorest of the poor when the distribution of assets prevents the most disadvantaged from using the market to provide for livelihoods.[120]

Neostructuralists agree that market energies, when harnessed by strong equitable institutions, will promote growth and reduce poverty and inequality—but not without stronger investments on the part of the state. Although village microcredit institutions may relieve some of the capital constraints on the poor and conditional transfer programs may create new incentives to attend schools and utilize health clinics, if these same people now armed with a bit of cash can't get their goods to market, send their kids to a quality school, or get appropriate health care, poverty and inequality will persist in the region. In a subtle way, the adoption of the MDGs reveals a change in paradigm at the international level away from development giving prominence to markets and toward an acknowledgment of the need for public investment in social sectors to address market failures.[121] The new consensus implies a role for government to meet internally agreed targets to reduce poverty through investments in education, health, and infrastructure. The million dollar question in an age of fiscal constraint is where investments should be made to generate the highest social return.

How Much Does the Latin State Spend?

Before asking where states should expand spending, it is useful to have a baseline on spending on social services in the region. There is a fair amount of diversity in the commitment of Latin American states to spending in the social sector. The heterogeneity runs from Cuba, spending 29.2 percent as a percentage of GDP on the social sector, to Ecuador, which only allocates 5.7 percent. Table 11.8 presents this data. Not surprisingly, poorer countries are not able to raise substantial tax revenue to fund programs. Argentina, Brazil, and Uruguay spend more than the 60 percent of total public spending on social investments; given that they have relatively large states, with state spending accounting for more than 30 percent of GDP, this is a substantial investment relative to country size. At the other end of the spectrum, in El Salvador and Peru the state spends less than 20 percent of GDP, and from this smaller pot less than 40 percent of the spending is directed to the social sector.[122] Overall, social spending as a component of GDP grew from 12.8 percent in 1990–1991 to 15.1 percent in 2003; per capita spending rose in real terms 39 percent over this period.[123] But the regional average of 15 percent does not approach the 23.6 percent of GDP that the United States spends—much less the 33.6 percent of GDP that Germany or the 35 percent of GDP that France spends.[124] This is particularly striking when it is noted that defense expenditures (included in central government expenditures) for the region are under 2 percent of GDP, leaving most of the spending in the social and economic arena. We remember from chapter 6 that in part this derives from the limited ability of the Latin American state to raise revenues. Overall, despite increased commitment in the social sector, outcomes have been resistant to change. The quality as well as the quantity of services delivered in Latin America must improve. But this takes money. Reduction of poverty will require a strengthening of the revenue-raising capabilities of the state so that it can become an effective actor. Combined with mechanisms to improve the delivery of services, selective interventions by the state may reduce the suffering of the poor in the region. Finally, given the fact that the state's fiscal capacity to finance social spending is weak, improving services will also entail higher growth rates in the region.

Neostructuralists agree that investment in the social sector will not spontaneously take place through the market. Although the private sector must be incorporated as a partner in social change, investments will be led by the state. Unfortunately, Latin American states have often been characterized as weak and unequal when providing basic public goods.[125] Given the budgetary limitations, however, hard choices must be made. Some structuralists who hold that the state must assume an active

Table 11.8.   Social Spending and Inequality

	Public Social Spending as a Percentage of GDP 2002/3	Public Social Spending as a Percent of Total Public Spending	Per Capita Spending Levels for 2002/3 in Constant 2000 $	Gini 1990	Gini around 2000
High Human Development					
Argentina	19.4	66.1	1,283	0.48	0.52
Chile	14.8	67.6	763	0.55	0.57
Uruguay	20.9	60.6	1,071	0.41	0.44
Costa Rica	18.6	64.5	774	0.46	0.46
Mexico	10.5	59.3	600	0.53	0.54
Panama	17.3	45.1	683	0.56	0.56
Medium Human Development					
Brazil	9.1	59.4	676	0.58	0.57
Colombia	13.5	32.7*	267	0.57	0.58
Venezuela	11.7	38.6	488	0.44	0.47
Peru	8	41.9*	170	0.46	0.49
Ecuador	5.7	25.2	76	0.56	0.56
Paraguay	9	41.6	114	0.57	0.57
El Salvador	7.1	35.9	149	0.51	0.53
Nicaragua	8.8	40	68	0.57	0.56
Bolivia	13.6	33	136	0.54	0.58
Honduras	13.1	52	126	0.57	0.55
Guatemala	6.5	50.4	109	na	0.58

Source: ECLAC, "Social Panorama 2005" (social spending and per capita data), table 43; EC/IDB Seminar Inequality, Exclusion and Poverty in Latin America, Brussels, June 5–6, 2003; World Bank, *Breaking with Inequality;* Brazil data from FGV, Marcelo Neri Miseria em Queda, 2005 (no full publication date).
* data for 1998/9.

role in the improvement of the quality of life in the region offer the concept of **effective selectivity** as a criterion for state intervention. The goal is to identify where the benefits of spending would be greatest and to pursue projects with the highest rates of social return. They see the state holding a twofold role: in the short run minimizing the impact of structural change on the poor, and in the long run investing in human resource development. It is their contention that central-government spending in the social sector in Latin America is not out of control but rather inefficient.

In addition to problems of quality and quantity, social spending unfortunately continues to be largely procyclical. Because of fiscal constraints, when poor economies slow down the government does not have the financial flexibility to intervene with needed safety nets. During a downturn in industrial countries, unemployment insurance and later welfare automatically kick in to stabilize consumption spending. In contrast, in fiscally strapped Latin America, governments are often forced by austerity measures to cut spending when it is most needed. Contraction hits those with fewest means of protection hardest. Governments did somewhat better in protecting the social sector in the 1998–2003 downturn as compared to periods of slow growth in the past, but social spending clearly contracts along with the economy.

Beyond the procyclical nature, social-sector spending in Latin America is squarely concentrated in the middle- and upper-income brackets, reinforcing inequality. The difficulty is that social spending involves spending not only on poverty-level social assistance but also on social security, education, and health programs where the more fortunate have historically had greater access. Redressing the deep-seated inequality in Latin America will involve reversing some of the entitlements, particularly in pensions and education, that the middle and upper classes have come to expect. But this, of course, is a delicate political maneuver.

For the poorest households, social spending nearly doubles the available economic resources of the family, comprising 46.2 percent of income. For the upper-income bracket, it amounts to 8 percent. However, when we look at this from the perspective of the amount of state spending going to each income group, figure 11.3 shows us that more is spent on the top fifth than on the bottom. Some of this imbalance is driven by the fact that state spending includes relatively generous pension accounts that the wealthy and formal-sector workers have paid into. One might question, however, the use of educational dollars for the upper-income groups—a topic we will return to in our education chapter.

Not all state spending has the same impact. Better econometric methods have begun to allow policymakers to track the marginal impact of programs on least-advantaged groups. Although the data remain scarce, studies show that programs that target preschool and primary education, nutrition programs for young children and prenatal women, and upgrades in basic services such as water and sewer con-

Figure 11.3. Composition of Spending by Program and Income Level

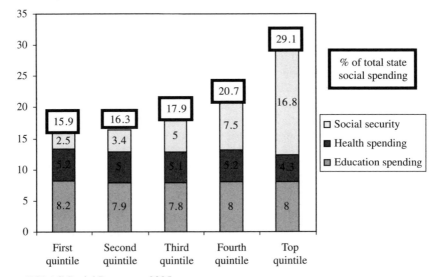

Source: ECLAC Social Panorama 2005.

nections have the strongest redistributive impact on the poor. Social spending on subsidies for milk, tortillas, or electricity (from which all income groups benefit) and investments in tertiary education or strengthening pension programs or defined benefit health plans associated with social security systems do not contribute to reducing pervasive inequality in the region.[126] Rather than broad national food subsidies for milk or tortillas, **targeting** involves identifying eligible recipients to direct expenditures toward those who need them most.[127] Instruments to identify the poor without significant leakage to middle- and upper-income groups include poverty maps to identify neighborhoods where the neediest are concentrated combined with easily collected information on dwelling characteristics, family size, and age.[128] For example, in Ecuador subsidies for electricity and gas together account for 2 percent of GDP, although only 17 percent of the electricity subsidy and 23 percent of the cooking gas subsidy reach the poor. Removing this subsidy and targeting the resources so that all the funds benefit the poor would be a more effective poverty-reduction strategy, although it may not be as politically popular with the other roughly 80 percent of beneficiaries! Although this might sound like common sense, it is not always as easy as it sounds.

Some of the biggest success stories have been in highly targeted programs where participants must qualify by a means test. It sounds logical to test if the poor are really poor, but the expansion of such programs is limited by challenges in implementing nationwide targeting systems that limit leakage of funds to the non-poor. Some worry about constructing large bureaucracies to manage poverty programs. Targeting also suffers from high administrative costs as well as errors of exclusion and errors of inclusion. Bureaucratic challenges notwithstanding, targeting can work. Targeted programs that require registration and verification of means testing are also difficult to ramp up during a sudden downturn in economic activity, reinforcing the procyclical nature of poverty programs in Latin America. For example, when the poverty rate shot up from 30.8 percent to 58.0 percent in Argentina between 1999 and 2002, it would have been harder to create a new register of the poor than to promote broad investment in the social arena.

Targeted dollars should be spent in response to local demand. Despite these difficulties, Mexico has identified an innovative mechanism for targeting food subsidies. Using a two-tiered approach, Mexico's Oportunidades program pays poor families to come to health clinics and attend schools. First, it takes into account spatial poverty and identifies clusters of poor communities. Within each community, local boards identify the most needy. Needy families are given a smart credit card with a food account to replace public tortilla subsidies that also benefited the rich. Families must self-identify by coming into the local health clinic for preventive health care. While they are there for visits they get their food account renewed. Parents who keep their kids in school are given an extra bonus, creating incentives for education. The government is able to identify those who need services the most and not spend money on generalized public assistance programs. The program is defined by three complementary strategies: first, the provision of welfare benefits such as food credits, housing, and sanitation targeted to the poor; second, production programs of rural credit and loans for infrastructure development to raise the investment potential of the poor; and third, regional development programs in road and education infrastructure to improve the social capital of the poorest regions.[129] It is an attempt to meet the short-term needs of the poor while also transforming the structural conditions of poverty. Serving more than twenty million Mexicans, Oportunidades provides more than 20 percent of the income of its customers, which draw substantially from the poorest strata of society.

Targeting works well to ensure that scarce social spending reaches the poor. One mechanism to address the problem that targeting is a rather cumbersome tool is an economic downturn of **social investment funds (SIFs)**. SIFs are targeted toward emergency employment programs, including building or repairing roads, bridges, and schools; social assistance programs such as food aid; and projects that improve productivity through credit, microenterprise development, and worker training. SIFs were characteristically independent of the national bureaucracy, reporting directly to the president. The emergency nature of the funds in the 1980s has evolved into their use as parallel institutions for the delivery of social services. Because they enjoy broad administrative, technical, and financial autonomy, they are able to respond to local demand more quickly and effectively. The main source of financing comes from foreign grants and donations and national public contributions. Their transparency creates public confidence because there is little doubt about how the funds are used.[130] Effects are rapid and demonstrable. Resources are distributed in response to requests from local groups, enhancing the role of NGOs as mediators.[131] Social funds have often shown positive outcomes for the poor; lower operating costs, an agility to work outside traditional government bureaucracies, and stronger ties of accountability improved results.[132]

A model SIF in Bolivia through the World Bank facilitated the process of decentralization by assisting local authorities and communities in managing investment resources as well as building and maintaining social infrastructure. The Bolivian SIF was focused on four areas: economic infrastructure, social infrastructure, social assistance, and credit schemes. In its inception it was targeted at employment generation; it then turned to social assistance and infrastructure creation. In the least, it contributed to the political sustainability of the adjustment process.[133] Reaching between 3.5 and 4 million people, the fund has supported the building or refurbishing of health and educational facilities and rural water supplies. Health indicators as measured by number of severe diseases among children have decreased, vaccinations and birth control dissemination have increased, and teaching performance and school attendance have improved.[134]

Public works programs may have multiple benefits: improving the infrastructure in a community, changing local institutions, and creating employment for residents. Improving infrastructure, including the region's woefully inadequate housing stock, is designed to enhance the physical and emotional well-being of the poor. In the rural sector, the timing of public works projects should be in the agricultural off-season. In both the rural and urban cases, setting the wage below the minimum wage helps to attract the poorest into the program. Public works programs in Chile during the 1980s, for example, set the wage for public works jobs at 70 percent of the national minimum, so that people already employed did not leave their jobs for attractive public works projects. Work projects located close to low-income communities help to decrease transportation costs—a significant factor for a poor person. Programs can be designed to encourage the participation of women by paying attention to child care and school-day issues, and the involvement of local NGOs can help to increase the accountability of the programs to the public and reduce the likelihood of corruption.[135] Social funds can also be designed to target historically excluded groups. For example, the IADB supports the Fund for the Development of Indigenous Peoples.

SIFs also have their drawbacks. Unfortunately, because the most indigent are the least politically able to organize, SIFs do little to help the poorest of the poor. The funds tend to help the new poor—that is, those made temporarily poor through tough economic adjustment policies—as opposed to dealing with the tough issues of helping the chronically poor.[136] A lack of coordination with state bodies has also led to duplication of services. The reliance on foreign finance introduces year-to-year uncertainty. In the case of the Honduran SIF created by the United Nations Development Programme (UNDP) in 1990, the bulk of the spending was directed toward short-term infrastructure, with little reaching the marginalized poor. Nonetheless, policies can be especially targeted to the poor. In the initial stages of combating Chile's 18 percent open unemployment in its early introduction of the neoliberal model, a minimum employment program and an occupational program for heads of households employed close to 11 percent of the country's labor force, in hopes of holding off political opposition to tough economic measures.[137] The employment, however, was often dead end and did little to improve human capital investment. Under the democratic governments, a new approach was taken. The Chilean Solidarity and Social Investment Funds (FOSIS) program has been more successful in combating poverty because of its focus on the long-term, structural causes of poverty. Its priorities include credit, marketing and training of small businesses and small farmers, youth job training, and building self-help capacity in poor communities.[138] Institutionally independent of the state planning ministry, FOSIS is by design flexible and open to local participation. It is therefore able to respond to the heterogeneous and decentralized nature of poverty in Chile. Fostering grassroots participation, it works closely with Chile's relatively well-articulated network of NGOs to reach the poorest of the poor. Nonetheless, it faces the same difficulty as SIFs in other countries: the most destitute are the least well organized to demand government services.[139]

Costa Rica is a case where policy initiatives to reduce inequality led to a decrease not only in the inequality of income allocation but also in the rates of poverty. In 1960 Brazil and Costa Rica had similar levels of inequality; by 1989 the Gini coefficient for Brazil was .6331 and for Costa Rica was .4604. Brazil had 40.9 percent of its population in poverty, and Costa Rica had 3.4 percent. What were the ingredients of success in Costa Rica? The foundation of Costa Rican social policy was state intervention following the 1948 civil war. In part, the ability of the state to use resources to promote equality was due to the weakened position of the coffee oligarchy in the postwar period. In addition, the military was disbanded, and defense spending was redirected to education and social policies. By 1976, 30 percent of the Costa Rican budget was spent on education versus 7 percent worldwide. As defense spending was slashed from 25 percent of the national budget in the late 1940s to 2 percent in 1958, federal spending on health and social services more than doubled from 20 percent in 1938 to 45 percent in 1958.[140] Costa Rica also benefited from a land reform in 1961, redistributing land assets. Investments in social services combined with asset distribution have contributed to the nation's standout perform-ance on poverty reduction in the region.

INTEGRATING GROWTH AND EQUITY

Improving the standard of living of the poor in Latin America must, like the Mex-ican Progressa/Opportunidades program, go beyond temporary food assistance. Attacking the roots of poverty involves changes in the overall pattern of develop-ment. ECLAC advocates an **integrated approach** to poverty reduction. It proceeds from the premise that growth policies have a distributional impact and that social policies affect growth. A strategy for growth with greater equity must therefore include both dimensions in economic and social policy making. Changing pro-duction patterns to compete in a globally integrated economy should involve con-siderations of equity. As we saw in chapter 9, sources of competitiveness for participating in the global economy will require improvements in the quality of the labor force, enhancing the returns to human capital. Otherwise, the poor will not benefit from growth. This should include job retraining as well as investments in education, health, and housing to improve the productivity of labor.

ECLAC is focusing on the positive synergies between human capital invest-ments, economic growth, and improvements in income distribution and standards of living. Macroeconomic reforms in the fiscal and monetary realm should be com-plemented by social-sector investments for long-term stable growth.[141] In particular, greater attention must be paid to the informal sector, technological modernization, the promotion of microenterprises, and rural development facilitated by improved access to land and credit. Complementary reforms in education, health, housing, and social security are needed. Programs to promote social cohesion such as pro-grams for families and children at risk, compensatory or transfer policies for those whom employment can't help, programs to strengthen community life, and instru-ments to protect communities from violence and drug trafficking are also critical to provide the underpinning for stable, long-run growth with equity.[142] Poverty reduc-tion is therefore built into a revisioning of the development strategy.

In a review of why poverty in Latin America is so ingrained, three main lessons in shaping the agenda emerged.[143] First, growth is not enough. Although growth is a necessary prerequisite to making people better off, the character of growth patterns must be considered as part of the poverty-reduction strategy. That is, reducing poverty is central to sustained growth in the region—not a policy at the back end to deal with those left behind. Second, poverty reduction must be approached from a systems standpoint, not simply as an aggregation of well-intentioned policies. Strategies must be at once hard-hearted, making tough distinctions in a tough budgetary environment between what is essential and what is desirable. Priorities must be set, and political feasibility must admitted. What are the fiscal and human resources as well as the political capital on hand to pursue poverty-reduction strategies? Finally, poverty reduction needs to be monitored and evaluated. Although evaluation may appear to be a luxury when children are starving, more money is wasted in the long run by poorly conceived or badly administered policies. Monitoring and evaluation promotes accountability and control. Although some countries have made progress in implementing integrated monitoring and evaluation systems that provide feedback into the following year's budget, progress is uneven. The great need for poverty reduction in the region requires the development not of kind hearts but of a results-oriented culture facilitated by a transparent and efficient monitoring of the use of public resources.

Key Concepts

bottom of the pyramid marketing	Gini coefficient	Lorenz curve
chronic poverty	headcount ratio	microcredit
corporate social responsibility	Human Development Index (HDI)	moderate poverty
decentralization	income gap	poverty line
effective selectivity	informal sector	pro-poor growth
extreme poverty	integrated approach	social investment funds (SIFs)
	Kuznets curve	targeting

Chapter Summary

Defining Poverty

- As defined by income measures, the poor are those unable to meet basic needs from monthly income.
- Roughly one-third of Latin Americans live in poverty, with 15 percent in extreme poverty. Chronic poverty, which is poverty that does not improve over time, is also a serious problem, affecting one-half to one-third of all poor Latin Americans. The high rate of poverty is mostly due to rapid urbanization. Currently, 44 percent of urban dwellers in Latin America are estimated to live in slums.
- Performance varies by country, with Costa Rica demonstrating success in alleviating poverty, while citizens in countries such as El Salvador remain desperately poor.

Life for the Poor in Latin America

- Gender, ethnicity, and race are important contributing factors to poverty. People of African and indigenous descent are systematically denied the same opportunities as whites in most of Latin America. Women are also more likely to be poor in Latin America, as they are still excluded from many jobs and don't make incomes equal to their male counterparts.

- Jobs in the informal sector—characterized by low productivity and instability, low remuneration, and a disproportionate number of women—play a large role in Latin America.
- Poverty is a complex, cyclical phenomenon. The poor in Latin America experience an extremely low standard of living, involving inadequate housing, poor health care facilities, unsanitary water treatment, limited education opportunities, high unemployment, and limited access to utilities.
- Poverty should be examined in conjunction with income inequality. The Gini coefficient and the Lorenz curve help give a quantitative and graphical perspective on the income gap between the rich and the poor.

Inequality and Growth

- Latin America contains the most unequal income distribution in the world, with the wealthiest 20 percent earning an average of twenty times the poorest 20 percent of the population. Brazil, Honduras, and Guatemala take the unfortunate lead. Inequality is primarily caused by policies that have favored the rich and neglected the importance of investment for human capital.
- The relationship between income and inequality is unclear. Simon Kuznets theorized that as a country grows, the gap between the rich and poor will initially widen but eventually narrow. Recent studies show that this relationship is not direct and that other factors may be involved.

Addressing Poverty Reduction

- The adoption of the MDGs was an important first step in affirming a commitment to fighting poverty. To attain these goals, a policy mix of working with the market, building institutions, and implementing strategic public investments should be used.
- One approach to poverty reduction has been microenterprise lending. This form of finance allocation organization targets smaller businesses unable to receive credit through traditional means.
- The business sector can be a partner in reducing poverty by following corporate social responsibility. Unfortunately, although there has been some recent improvement, demand for such practices is still weak in Latin America.
- Change in institutions is necessary for poverty reduction. The poor must be brought into the policy-making process so that they can take an active role in improving their situation.

Lessons in Shaping the Agenda for Poverty Reduction

- Sustained growth, accompanied by integrated policies and institutions that enable the poor to benefit from the growth process, will help reduce poverty.

- Strategies for poverty reduction must be realistic and practical, taking financial feasibility as well as long-term and short-term implications into account. To be effective, progress must be monitored and evaluated.

Notes

1. ECLAC, "The Millennium Development Goals: A Latin American and Caribbean Perspective," Report coordinated by José Luis Machinea, August 2005.

2. James D. Wolfensohn, remarks to the Board of Governors of the World Bank Group, October 1, 1996 (LEXIS-NEXIS database).

3. D. L. Blackwood and R. G. Lynch, "The Measurement of Inequality and Poverty," *World Development* 22(4) (1994): 567–578.

4. Miguel Székely, "The 1990s in Latin America: Another Decade of Persistent Inequality, but with Somewhat Lower Poverty," IADB Working Paper No. 454, June 2001, 9.

5. ECLAC, "Social Panorama 2005," Press release, www.eclac.org.

6. ECLAC, "Social Panorama."

7. IADB, "The Millennium Development Goals in Latin America and the Caribbean: Progress, Priorities and IDB Support for their Implementation," Washington, D.C., August 2005, 20.

8. Chronic Poverty Research Center, "The Chronic Poverty Report 2004–5," University of Manchester, Manchester, UK.

9. David Hulme and Andrew Shepherd, "Conceptualizing Chronic Poverty," *World Development* 31(3) (2003): 403–423.

10. Chronic Poverty Research Center, "The Chronic Poverty Report 2004–5," chap. 8.

11. Ricardo Morán, Tarsicio Castaneda, and Enrique Aldaz-Carroll, "Family Background and Intergenerational Poverty in Latin America," in *Escaping the Poverty Trap: Investing in Children in Latin America,* ed. Ricardo Morán (Washington, D.C.: Inter-American Development Bank, 2003).

12. Morán, *Escaping the Poverty Trap,* 9.

13. Carlos Jarque, "Foreward," in Morán, *Escaping the Poverty Trap.*

14. Jacqueline Mazza, "Social Inclusion, Labor Markets and Human Capital," in *Social Inclusion and Economic Development in Latin America,* ed. Mayra Buvinic and Jacqueline Mazza (Washington, D.C.: Inter-American Development Bank, 2004), 188, table 10.3.

15. David Luhnow and John Lyons, "In Latin America, Rich-Poor Chasm Stifles Growth," *Wall Street Journal,* July 18, 2005, A1.

16. Ibid.

17. Chronic Poverty Research Center, "The Chronic Poverty Report 2004–5."

18. William Powers, "Poor Little Rich Country," *New York Times,* June 11, 2005, www.nytimes.com.

19. Suzanne Duryea and Maria Eugenia Genoni, "Ethnicity, Race and Gender in Latin American Labor Markets," in *Social Inclusion and Economic Development in Latin America,* ed. Buvinic and Mazza.

20. ECLAC, "Social Panorama," 127, citing data from Lais Abramo, "Desigualidades E Deiscriminacao De Genero E Raca No Mercado De Trabalho Brasileiro," ILO, August 2003.

21. Ann Helwege, "Poverty in Latin America: Back to the Abyss?" *Journal of Inter-American Studies and World Affairs* 37(3) (Fall 1995): 99.

22. Joseph Ramos, "Poverty and Inequality in Latin America: A Neostructuralist Perspective," *Journal of Inter-American Studies and World Affairs* 38(2–3) (Summer–Fall 1996).

23. World Bank, "Indigenous Peoples, Poverty and Human Development in Latin America: 1994–2004," http://www.worldbank.org.cn/English/content/805w63341746.shtml.

24. Helwege, "Poverty in Latin America," 99.

25. Caroline Moser, "Gender Planning in the Third World: Meeting Practical and Strategic Gender Needs," *World Development* 17(11) (1989): 1799–1825.

26. World Bank, "Challenges & Opportunities for Gender Equality in Latin America and the Caribbean," World Bank Special Report, Washington, D.C., 2003.

27. Frances Stewart, *Adjustment and Poverty: Options and Choices* (London: Routledge, 1995), 17.

28. ECLAC, "Precarious Urban Conditions," News release "Poverty and Precariousness in the Habitat of Latin America and the Caribbean Cities" study, www.eclac.org.

29. Habitat for Humanity, "Affordable Housing Statistics," http://www.habitat.org/how/intlstats.aspx.

30. Habitat for Humanity, "Causes of Inadequate Housing in Latin America and the Caribbean," http://povlibrary.worldbank.org/files/15210_causes.pdf.

31. World Bank, *Inequality in Latin America & the Caribbean: Breaking with History?* (Washington, D.C.: World Bank, 2003), 340.

32. This box was drafted by Courtney Fry, Colby College, class of 2004.

33. Melissa Rosales, "Education, Vocational Skills, and Active Participation As Vehicles to Empowerment: The Impact of Non-governmental Organizations on Street Children in La Paz, Bolivia," unpublished manuscript, 2004, 65.

34. Tobias Hecht, *At Home in the Street: Street Children of Northeast Brazil* (New York: Cambridge University Press, 1998), 22.

35. Benno Glauser, "Street Children: Deconstructing a Construct," in *Constructing and Reconstructing Childhood: Contemporary Issues of the Sociological Study of Childhood,* ed. Allison James and Alan Prout (New York: Falmer, 1990), 139.

36. Hecht, *At Home in the Street,* 54.

37. Ibid., 12.

38. Ibid., 27–34.

39. Glauser, "Street Children," 140.

40. Hecht, *At Home in the Street,* 42–47.

41. Ibid., 52.

42. Casa Alianza website, www.casaalianza.org.

43. Hecht, *At Home in the Street,* 62.

44. Ibid., 61–63.

45. Ibid., 67.

46. Rosales, "Education, Vocational Skills, and Active Participation As Vehicles to Empowerment," 53.

47. Hecht, *At Home in the Street,* 126.

48. Ibid., 127–128.

49. Ibid., 123.

50. Ernesto Espindola, Arturo Leon, Rodrigo Martinez, and Alexander Schejtman, "Poverty, Hunger and Food Insecurity in Central America and Panama," *CEPAL, Serie Politicas Sociales* 88 (May 2005): 28.

51. Ibid., 56.

52. George Psacharopoulos et al., *Poverty and Income Distribution in Latin America: The Story of the 1980s,* World Bank Technical Paper No. 351 (Washington, D.C.: World Bank, 1997), 116.

53. Rosemary McGee and Karen Brock, "From Poverty Assessment to Policy Change," IDS Working Paper 133, July 2001, Institute of Development Studies, Sussex, UK, www.ids.ac.uk.

54. Diana Tussie, *The Inter-American Development Bank,* Vol. 4, *The Multilateral Development Banks* (Ottawa: North-South Institute, 1995), 80.

55. Nora Lustig, *Coping with Austerity* (Washington, D.C.: Brookings Institution, 1995), 2, 31.

56. United Nations, Human Development Report 2005, *International Cooperation At a Crossroads: Aid, Trade and Security in an Unequal World,* Human Development Indicators, http://hdr.undp.org/reports/global/2005/.

57. Miguel Székely and Marianne Hilgert, "What Is Behind the Inequality We Measure: An Investigation Using Latin American Data," IADB Working Paper No. 409, December 1999.

58. Jere R. Behrman, Alejandro Gaviria, and Miguel Székely, "Intergenerational Mobility in Latin America," IADB Working Paper No. 452, June 2001, 5.

59. Stanley Engerman and Kenneth Sokoloff, "The Evolution of Suffrage Institutions in the Americas," *Journal of Economic History* 65 (September 2005), as summarized by William Easterly, "Inequality Does Cause Underdevelopment: New Evidence," Center for Global Development Working Paper No. 1, January 2002, 4.

60. Wagstaff A. Gwatkin and A. S. Yazbeck, eds. "Reaching the Poor with Health, Nutrition, and Population Services," World Bank, 2005.

61. John Sheahan and Enrique Iglesias, "Kinds and Causes of Inequality in Latin America," in *Beyond Trade-Offs: Market Reform and Equitable Growth in Latin America,* ed. Nancy Birdsall, Carol Graham, and Richard Sabot (Washington, D.C.: Brookings Institution Press/Inter-American Development Bank, 1998), 39.

62. World Bank, *Inequality in Latin America & the Caribbean,* 170.

63. Based on a regression of the Gini coefficient to natural resources, level of physical and human capital, land ownership, and educational assets. Juan Luis Londoño and Miguel Székely, "Distributional Surprises after a Decade of Reforms: Latin America in the Nineties," Paper prepared for the annual meetings of the IADB, Barcelona, March 1997, 10.

64. Behrman, Gaviria, and Székely, "Intergenerational Mobility in Latin America," 34.

65. Benedict Clements, "The Real Plan, Poverty, and Income Distribution in Brazil," *Finance and Development,* September 1997, 46.

66. Juan Luis Londoño and Miguel Székely, *Persistent Poverty and Excess Inequality: Latin America, 1970–1995,* Office of the Chief Economist, IADB Working Paper No. 357 (Washington, D.C.: IADB, 1997).

67. Data for 1985 and 1990 showed a steady climb at 285 and 361, respectively. Londoño and Székely, *Persistent Poverty,* 34.

68. Samuel A. Morley, "Distribution and Growth in Latin America in an Era of Structural Reform: The Impact of Globalisation," OECD Development Centre, Technical Papers No. 184, December 2001, 6.

69. Ibid.

70. Inter-American Development Bank, *Facing Up to Inequality in Latin America: Economic and Social Progress in Latin America, 1998–1999 Report* (Washington, D.C.: Johns Hopkins University Press/IADB, 1998), 21.

71. David Dollar and Aart Kraay, "Growth Is Good for the Poor," *Journal of Economic Growth* 7(3) (2002): 195–225.

72. Klaus Deininger and Lyn Squire study New Ways of Looking at Old Issues: Inequality and Growth? *Journal of Development Economies,* Vol. 57 (1998), 259, 287, as reported in "Slicing the Cake: What Is the Relationship between Inequality and Economic Growth?" *The Economist,* October 19, 1996, 2.

73. Carlos F. Toranzo Roca, as quoted by Clifford Krauss, "When Even an Economic Miracle Isn't Enough," *New York Times,* July 12, 1998, 3.

74. Sheahan and Iglesias, "Kinds and Causes of Inequality," 48.

75. Nancy Birdsall and Augusto de la Torre, "Washington Contentious: Economic Policies for Social Equity in Latin America," Findings of the Commission on Economic Reform in Unequal Latin American Societies, sponsored by the Carnegie Endowment for International Peace and the Inter-American Dialogue, 2001, 7.

76. See, for example, Dani Rodrick, *King Kong Meets Godzilla: The World Bank and the East Asian Miracle,* CEPR Discussion Paper No. 944 (London: Centre for Economic Policy Research, 1994).

77. Birdsall and de la Torre, "Washington Contentious," 11.

78. Strahan Spencer and Adrian Wood, "Making the Financial Sector Work for the Poor," *Journal of Development Studies* 41(4) (May 2005): 657–675.

79. Jeffrey D. Sachs, *The End of Poverty* (New York: Penguin, 2005).

80. Dani Rodrik, "Growth and Poverty Reduction: What Are the Real Questions?" http://ksghome.harvard.edu/~drodrik/poverty.PDF.

81. World Bank, *Inequality in Latin America and the Caribbean,* 170.

82. Ibid., 15

83. Michael Carter and Bradford Barham, "Level Playing Fields and Laissez Faire: Postliberal Development Strategy in Inegalitarian Agrarian Economies," *World Development* 24(7) (July 1996): 1133.

84. Sheahan and Iglesias, "Kinds and Causes of Inequality," 52.

85. Ariel Fiszbein, *Citizens, Politics and Providers: The Latin American Experience with Service Delivery Reform* (Washington, D.C.: World Bank, 2005), 22.

86. Ibid., 27.

87. IADB, *1995 Report: Overcoming Volatility* (Washington, D.C.: Johns Hopkins University Press/Inter-American Development Bank, 1995), 190. Morely estimated an elasticity of poverty to growth of –2; that is, had the annual growth rates been 1 percent higher during the 1980s, the number of people below the poverty line would have been lower by some 20 percent.

88. McKinsey Global Institute, *Productivity—The Key to an Accelerated Development Path for Brazil 1998* (São Paulo, Brazil: McKinsey, 1998), 45.

89. Morley, "Distribution and Growth in Latin America," 30.

90. Roberto Korzeniewicz and William Smith, "Poverty, Inequality and Growth in Latin America: Searching for the High Road to Globalization," *Latin American Research Review* 35(3) (2000): 15.

91. Latin American Research Review Forum, "From Marginality of the 1960s to the 'New Poverty' of Today," *LARR* 39(1) (February 2004).

92. Gustavo Gonzalez, "Microcredit Makes Strong Inroads in Latin America," April 26, 2005, www.ipsterraviva.net.

93. IADB, "The IDB and Micro, Small, and Medium-Sized Enterprises," www.iadb.org/NEWS/DISPLAY/issuebriefs/2003/micro.cfm?Language=English.

94. Spencer and Wood, "Making the Financial Sector Work for the Poor," 658, quoting Stuart S. Rutherford, "Money Talks: Conversations with Poor Households about Managing Money." Finance and Development Research Program Working Paper, Series No. 45, IDPM, University of Manchester (www.man.ac.uk/idpm/), 2000.

95. Gonzalez, "Microcredit Makes Strong Inroads in Latin America."

96. "The Hidden Wealth of the Poor: Microcredit Survey," *Economist,* November 3, 2005.

97. Fast Facts on Microentrepreneurship: International Year of Microcredit 2005, http://www.yearofmicrocredit.org/pages/reslib/reslib_recreading.asp.

98. Ibid.

99. Ibid.

100. IADB, *Latin America after a Decade of Reforms: Economic and Social Progress, 1997 Report* (Washington, D.C.: Johns Hopkins University Press/IADB, 1997), 186.

101. "The Hidden Wealth of the Poor: Microcredit Survey," *Economist,* November 3, 2005.

102. Michael Thomas Derham, "A Less Uncertain World," *LatinFinance,* July 2005, 44.

103. "The Hidden Wealth of the Poor: Microcredit Survey."

104. Karin Stahl, "Anti-Poverty Programs: Making Structural Adjustment More Palatable," *NACLA Report on the Americas* 29(6) (May–June 1995): 32.

105. "Profits and Poverty," *The Economist* 372(8389) (August 21, 2004), accessed through Academic Search Premier.

106. Sami Foguel and Andrew Wilson, *Casas Bahia: Fulfilling a Dream,* Michigan Business School Case Study Series, prepared under the supervision of C. K. Prahalad, December 12, 2003.

107. Ibid., 3.

108. Allen Hammond and C. K. Prahalad, "Selling to the Poor," *Foreign Policy* 142 (May/June 2004).

109. Roberto Hernandez and Yerina Mugica, "What Works: Prodem's FFP's Multilingual Smart ATMS," World Resources Institute Case Study, August 2003.

110. Paulo Prada, "Low Cost Credit for Low-Cost Items," *New York Times,* November 12, 2005.

111. Jeremy Grant, "Switch to the Low-Income Consumer," *Financial Times,* November 14, 2005.

112. Steve Stecklow, "The $100 Laptop Moves Closer to Reality," *Wall Street Journal,* November 14, 2005, B1.

113. "Computador pré-pago já está á venda," *Gazeta Mercantil,* April 19, 2004.

114. Hammond and Prahalad, "Selling to the Poor."

115. Jonathan Franklin, "Paddling for Profits: Despite Hard Times, Avon's Huge, Mostly Female Workforce Is on the Move in Latin America," *Latin Trade,* December 2003.

116. Frances Stewart, *Adjustment and Poverty: Options and Choices* (London: Routledge, 1995), 115.

117. Fiszbein, *Citizens, Politicians and Providers,* 16.

118. Ibid., 31.

119. Ibid., 41.

120. Sachs, *The End of Poverty,* 253–254.

121. Oxford Analytica, "Problems with the Millennium Development Goals," *Latin America Daily Brief,* August 28, 2003.

122. World Bank, *Inequality in Latin America & the Caribbean,* 128.

123. ECLAC, "Social Panorama," 17.

124. *Poverty Reduction and the World Bank: Progress in Fiscal 1996 and 1997* (Washington, D.C.: World Bank, 1998). Available at www.worldbank.org.

125. Fiszbein, *Citizens, Politicians and Providers,* 15.

126. World Bank, *Inequality in Latin America & the Caribbean,* 143–160.

127. These factors were highlighted in *Poverty Reduction and the World Bank,* 26.

128. Martin Valdivia, "Peru: Is Identifying the Poor the Main Problem?" in *Reaching the Poor with Health, Nutrition, and Population Services,* ed. D. R. Gwatkin, A. Wagstaff, and A. S. Yazbeck (Washington, D.C.: World Bank, 2005).

129. Stewart, *Adjustment and Poverty,* 214.

130. Carol Graham, *Safety Nets, Politics, and the Poor: Transitions to Market Economies*

(Washington, D.C.: Brookings Institution, 1994), 33. Chapter 2 describes the employment programs in detail.

131. Stahl, "Anti-Poverty Programs," 32.

132. Fiszbein, *Citizens, Politicians and Providers,* 26.

133. Graham, *Safety Nets,* 1994.

134. "Urban Renaissance," *IDB Extra,* 1997, 134.

135. "Urban Renaissance," *IDB Extra,* 1997.

136. Oficina Internacional del Trabajo (OIT/International Labor Organization), *Panorama Laboral 2001,* table 6-A, 60–62.

137. Marinte Guerguil, "Some Thoughts on the Definition of the Informal Sector," *CEPAL Review* 35 (August 1988): 60.

138. Kate Young, *Planning Development with Women: Making a World of Difference* (New York: St. Martin's, 1993), 85–90.

139. Oficina Internacional del Trabajo (OIT), *Panorama Laboral 2001,* table 6-A, 60–62.

140. Victor Tokman, "Policies for a Heterogeneous Informal Sector," *World Development* 17(7) (1989): 1067–1076.

141. Studies presented in Victor Tokman, *Beyond Regulation: The Informal Economy in Latin America* (Boulder, Colo.: Rienner, 1992).

142. Tokman, *Beyond Regulation,* 10.

143. Jaime Saavedra and Omar S. Arias, "Stuck in a Rut," *Finance and Development* 42(4) (December 2005).

CHAPTER TWELVE

HEALTH POLICY

Investing in People's Future

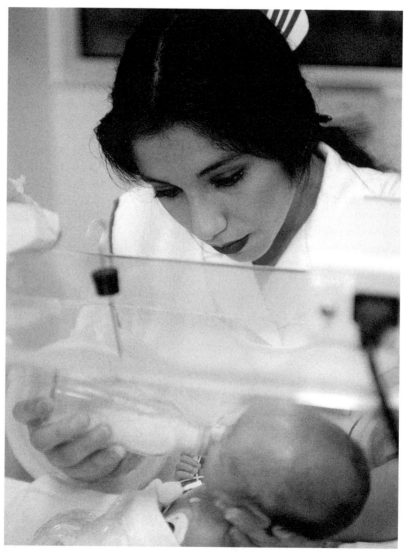

Hard choices sometimes need to be made between hospital-based urban health care and rural needs. *(Courtesy of Willie Heinz and the Inter-American Development Bank)*

Addressing poverty and improving human capital in Latin America rest on progress in health and educational systems in the region. As the World Health Organization (WHO) argues, the promotion of health is the process of enabling people to increase their control over improvements in their environment to reach a state of complete physical, mental, and social well-being. Beyond disease reduction, health promotion is critical not only to maintain a decent quality of life but also to achieve human and social potential. Education is the key to transforming health trends and increasing human capital in the region. Education reform will determine Latin America's competitiveness in the global economy as well as the character of democratic political life and a more just economic distribution within each nation. Without a healthy, well-educated citizenry, Latin America will be left behind.

Our next two chapters consider the health and educational deficits in the region and identify strategies for reform. Chapter 12 begins by analyzing the good news and the bad news in the regional health profile. The good news is that substantial progress has been made, as measured by health indicators. The bad news is that improvement was stalled by the economic crisis of the 1980s and the new fiscal realities in the current period. Smaller public sectors leave less to invest in health and education. Given financial constraints, we then consider ways of organizing health care delivery systems that may be able to do more with less. Efficient and effective delivery of health services is the key to the future well-being of the nearly 510 million residents of the region. Education has faced similar challenges. Chapter 13 will show that although literacy rates in the region measure signs of progress, high rates of repetition and unequal access to education limit the gains from education to society. Innovation in educational policy is critical for Latin American countries to compete in the global arena in the twenty-first century. Both health and education systems are challenged by how to accomplish more with limited resources.

Key questions for exploration in this chapter include the following:

- What is the health profile for Latin America? What health conditions most threaten lives in the region?
- How do health needs of women and indigenous groups differ from those of the broader population?
- How have health challenges changed with globalization?
- What is the structure of health care delivery in Latin America, and how does this affect outcomes? How do health delivery systems differ in the rural and the urban sectors? Are centrally located urban hospitals a better health investment than rural community health providers?
- What is the experience of health care reform in the region?

THE PECULIAR NATURE OF HEALTH CARE AS A GOOD

Health must be seen as integrally linked into the human, social, political, and economic development of a country. The opportunities for human development condition the national health profile. As shown in figure 12.1, health systems develop in a social context and are further shaped by the political environment. Without the

Figure 12.1.   Intersectoral Cooperation: The Health–Development Framework

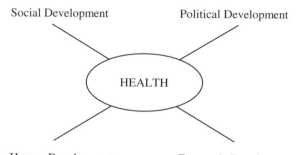

Source: Rosalia Rodriguez-García and Ann Goldman, eds., *The Health–Development Link* (Washington, D.C.: PAHO, 1994), 38.

political will to provide health services as a basic human right, even the wealthiest of countries will have significant health deficits among the poor. Although the right to health care is defined in most Latin American countries in their constitutions or by law, quality delivery of health care impedes growth. The level of economic development in part determines the social resources available for health care as well as individuals' ability to invest in their own well-being. But in Latin America, weakness in the delivery of health care systems contributes to lower than expected performance given per capita gross domestic product (GDP).[1] A poor person has little control over the external environment of open sewage, polluted water and air, or safety from violence. A poor country has limited resources to provide health services and transform the social infrastructure into one that provides basic human needs for all. Avoidable mortality—deaths that could be prevented by improvements in basic health conditions—hover in the 45 percent range in the region. A startling 1.5 million persons under the age of sixty-five are dying each year from avoidable causes. Health care is in crisis in Latin America and, given new challenges on the horizon, will be woefully ill-equipped to provide opportunities for healthy lives to its citizens.

Similar to education, the production of health care has a few peculiarities that we should consider. Health care can be considered a **merit good.** A merit good will be underconsumed in the market because individuals typically ignore the positive externalities created for others in society. Certain diseases, particularly the infectious variety, lead to the classification as a merit good. When people are healthy, the spread of disease is less likely. It is therefore in my interest for you to be vaccinated or taught good preventative health practices. But what if you value health differently? One may also derive some utility from knowing that the basic health needs of a population are met; healthy people are less prone to risky survival behavior such as prostitution or drug dealing that may also have an impact on others. Social returns can therefore exceed the sum of individual returns, meriting a role for government to invest in the provision of public health. But all health care does not have a social benefit. The appropriate mix of public support of health care is a question facing all societies—particularly as costs in health care have skyrocketed. In Latin America this question is even more pressing as the needs for comprehensive access to basic health care overlays with modern disease challenges.

Although all aspects of health care do not meet the two criteria of public goods —nonrivalry and nonexcludability—certain aspects of health provision indeed can be considered a public good. With scarce dollars, consumption of hospital services by one person, for example, may preclude treatment of another person; people are also regularly excluded from health services for an inability to pay. However, the knowledge creation and dissemination critical to public health creates aspects of being a public good. A radio program to promote sanitary hygiene to stem the spread of dysentery does not exhibit rivalry or excludability; likewise, a safe sex campaign to prevent the spread of HIV benefits all. When the externalities of a public good transcend borders, as in the case of HIV, we consider this a case of a **global public good.** The presence of global public goods in health signal the need to strengthen governance for international health risks. Consider the U.S.-Mexican border. The high-risk behaviors and poor treatment options of Mexican laborers who migrate to the United States are a ticking time bomb. Given the lack of health resources, one study shows infection rates among migrants to be three times higher than that in the Mexican population. This international health problem can only be effectively addressed by some form of cooperation between governments.[2]

In addition to having characteristics of a merit good and a global public good, the need for health care is distinguished by the lack of predictability. Unlike education, where it is fairly predictable when the services will be needed, it is more difficult to plan for illness.[3] Given the highly variable nature of demand, the question of insurance arises. Pooling the risk of illness and collecting modest sums to pay for the unlucky who fall ill is a rational response to the unpredictability of health problems. Our key policy question is how the payment for this risk should be organized —through public funds, private contributions, or a mix of both. The design of health care systems therefore breaks out into two central areas: How should health care be financed, and how should it be delivered? Some countries opt for public finance and private delivery, while others rely more heavily on private contributions to insurance accepted at both public and private hospitals. As we will see, in Latin America there has traditionally been a mix of both.

A PROFILE OF HEALTH IN THE REGION

Dramatic Progress . . . and Large Gaps in Coverage

Health care can be seen as a proxy for the dramatic changes in the standard of living in Latin America over the past decades. Since 1960 life expectancy has risen from fifty-four to seventy-two years. In 1927 life expectancy in Costa Rica was about forty years; in the United States at the same time people could expect to live to age sixty. Today Costa Ricans expect to live to age seventy-nine, a year longer than Americans.[4] In 1960, 153 out of every 1,000 children did not make it to their fifth birthday; by 2005, that figure was 27. Unlike other regions, Latin America was able

Table 12.1.   Mortality and Life Expectancy Indicators

	Maternal Mortality Ratio (per 100,000 live births)		Infant Mortality Rate (per 1,000 live births)		Under 5 Mortality Rate (per 1,000 live births)	Life Expectancy at Birth	
	Ratio	Year	Rate	Year	2004	Male	Female
Argentina	43.6	2003	16.5	2003	16.7	71.2	78.7
Belize	n/a	2004	14.3	2004	40.2	69.5	74.2
Bolivia	230	1999–03	54	1993–03	67.6	62.8	67
Brazil	73.1	2002	25.1	2002	33.3	67.5	75.2
Chile	13.4	2003	7.8	2003	9.3	75.2	81.2
Colombia	84	2002	18	2002	30.9	69.9	75.9
Costa Rica	30.5	2004	9.3	2004	11.9	76.2	81
Cuba	38.5	2004	5.8	2004	7.1	76.2	77.9
Ecuador	77.8	2003	22.3	2003	28.2	71.8	77.7
El Salvador	173	1997–02	25	1997–02	n/a	68.3	74.4
Guatemala	153	1997–02	39	1997–02	48.1	64.3	71.6
Honduras	108	1996–00	34	1996–00	46.3	66.5	70.6
Mexico	65.2	2002	19.7	2004	22.9	73.2	78.1
Nicaragua	82.8	2001	35	2001	38	68.1	70.7
Panama	68	2003	15.2	2003	25.7	72.7	72.9
Paraguay	174.1	2003	19.4	2003	43.6	69.2	73.8
Peru	185	2000–05	33.4	2000–05	49.5	68.1	73.3
Uruguay	n/a	2003	15	2003	n/a	72.2	79.5
Venezuela	57.8	2003	18.5	2003	28	70.5	76.4
LA Average	94.7		24.9		33.2	69.5	75.8
United States	8.9	2002	7	2002	8.3	74.9	80.3

Notes: Maternal Mortality Ratios normalize the number of deaths due to pregnancy by the number of live births so that countries with higher birth rates aren't penalized. Likewise, infant and child mortality rates are presented over the number of live births. Care should be taken in cross country comparisons; the methodology of reporting and statistical estimation for missing data can vary from country to country.
Source: PAHO, Health Situation in the Americas Basic Indicators 2005.

to continue to reduce infant mortality by 4 percent a year in the 1990s.[5] In the period 1970–2000, infant mortality fell by 72.42 percent in Brazil. Table 12.1 presents mortality and life expectancy indicators by country. Care should be taken in analyzing the numbers, as each country's reporting and statistical methods vary. Nonetheless, we can roughly correlate poverty with poor performance and see the huge regional diversity on morbidity indicators. Improved sanitation, measured as the greater availability of treated running water and sewerage and additional schooling, particularly by mothers, led to these falls in infant mortality. As shown in table 12.2, countries with incomplete access to water and sanitation have higher morbidity rates.

Huge disparities between the poorer northeastern region of Brazil, where rates stand at 64.25 for every 1,000, as compared to the southeastern region, at 27.46 per 1,000, underscore the challenges ahead. Even for the more affluent southern region,

Table 12.2. Population with Access to Improved Services

| | Socioeconomic Indicators | | | |
| | Water Source (%) | | Sanitation (%) | |
	Urban	Rural	Urban	Rural
Mexico	97	72	90	39
Belize	100	82	71	25
Costa Rica	100	92	89	97
El Salvador	91	68	78	40
Guatemala	99	92	72	52
Honduras	99	82	89	52
Nicaragua	93	65	78	51
Panama	99	79	89	51
Cuba	95	78	99	95
Bolivia	95	68	58	23
Colombia	99	71	96	54
Ecuador	92	77	80	59
Peru	87	66	72	33
Venezuela	85	70	71	48
Brazil	96	58	83	35
Argentina	97	no data	no data	no data
Chile	100	59	96	64
Paraguay	100	62	94	58
Uruguay	98	93	95	85

Source: PAHO, Health Situation in the Americas Basic Indicators 2005.

these rates are high compared to the accomplishments in Chile (of 9.98) or Argentina (at 18.4) in reducing child mortality to rates approximating industrial countries.[6] (The United States is at 6.9.) Problems of malnutrition and preventable diseases are tightly woven into problems of inequality of access. Striking inequalities of access to quality health care between rich and poor, rural and urban residents, and indigenous and nonindigenous citizens care pervade the region. In the Ecuadorian Amazon, life expectancy in 1995–2000 was 59.6 years, and an estimated 21 percent of the population would not survive more than 40 years; in the wealthier Ecuadorian province of Pichincha, life expectancy was 15 years longer—74.5 years—and only 6.8 were expected to die before age 40. In the urban area of Guayaquil, 7 percent of the mothers go without prenatal care; in the remote Amazon, 34 percent have none. Five percent of deliveries in Guayaquil and Quito are at home; 50 percent of the mothers give birth outside medical care in the Amazonia.[7]

Countrywide data should, therefore, be interpreted with caution. Income inequality skews access to health care. If you are an affluent Mexican, for example, the chances of your baby dying in infancy are 13.4 per 1,000 live births; if you are poor, the odds escalate to a tragic 109.76. Rural Peruvian babies are about three times as likely to die as those in Lima. Malnutrition in Ecuador among children under age five ranges from 8 to 42.6 percent, depending on the socioeconomic district. In Peru, a mother with no education is three times more likely to have her child die than a mother with a secondary education or higher. A rural inhabitant in Brazil can expect to live twenty fewer years than a wealthy cousin in the city.[8] Divergent rural and urban standards of living result in widely different health profiles. Health ministries must therefore make tough choices about where to invest the nation's health resources. Should investments be made in cities to confront new challenges to health with technologically sophisticated systems? Or should resources be placed in the poorest rural sectors to address traditional disease threats?

Children who survive but are not properly fed often suffer from stunting, measured by two standard deviations below median height for age of the reference population. Rates of stunting in the countries worst afflicted have fallen from 38 to 26 percent of the age relevant cohort in Ecuador (86–98), from 26 to 15 percent in Colombia (1986–1995), and from 32 to 26 in Peru (92–96). But the decline has tended to bottom out, as nutrition programs have failed to reach the worst-off in society.[9] In Ecuador, stunting continues to afflict 41 percent of the children in the rural highlands. Controlling for differences in education, housing, and economics status, it has been found that discrimination and exclusion of these indigenous children through cultural and linguistic barriers, negative attitudes in health care delivery, and inappropriate educational curriculums are to blame for the retardation in growth.[10] In addition to the effects of stunting, childhood malnutrition severely jeopardizes, reduces, or impairs the prospects for productive social participation into adulthood. Paradoxically, malnutrition exists side by side with obesity—with some of the same causes. Babies from poor social backgrounds who have experienced intrauterine growth restrictions as a result of maternal malnutrition are prone to becoming obese as adults, since they develop thrifty metabolic mechanisms and are exposed to food of poor quality from an early age. The problem of nutrition in Latin America is characterized by the coexistence of excess and scarcity.[11] Progress has been made, but there is still a considerable distance to go in improving the lives of children in the region.

A Demographic Window Is Opening

Gaps not withstanding, improvements in health and living standards have altered the general demographic profile in Latin America. Total fertility rates have fallen from 6 children per woman in the period 1960–1965 to 2.4 in 2005. Children are no longer as valuable as instruments of old age insurance, and as women have entered the workforce the opportunity costs of having children have also increased. As fertility rates have declined, the proportion of the working population aged fifteen to sixty-five has risen. In contrast to this productive group, the older population (6 percent in Latin America) as well as children under age fifteen (30 percent) are net consumers, especially when it comes to health care. In Latin America, this bulge in the working population will peak in the period 2010–2025. This will be a grace period, where the larger percentage of the working population will support fewer dependents. This opens a demographic window for change. Appropriate investments in health care and education complemented by growth-oriented policies can launch a new economic and social transformation.[12] After this, old age will begin to overwhelm the contributions of the working population, and Latin America will begin to look more like Europe, where a 16 percent dependency ratio by both the young and the old severely strains the system. Taking advantage of the demographic dividend will be crucial to the quality of human life in Latin America.

The Unfinished Agenda

Despite advances in the quality of life in Latin America, much work remains to be done. There is a great deal of diversity in health performance in the region. As can be seen back in table 12.1, life expectancy ranges from a low of 62.8 years for Bolivian males to a high of 81.2 for Chilean women. You may be surprised to see that women live longer in Chile and Costa Rica than in the United States. Bolivia and Guatemala are the worst performers on infant mortality, while Chile and Cuba have achieved low child-mortality rates. Hospital beds are scarce relative to high-income countries. In countries with either the political will or the money, significant strides have been made in creating health systems to treat these diseases. Countries such as Cuba and Costa Rica have gone through an **epidemiological transition** where communicable diseases are relatively under control; they have health profiles similar to developed countries. The least-developed countries, such as Bolivia, have truncated transitions and suffer primarily from infectious diseases, such as malaria, and diseases of deficiency, such as malnutrition. The middle- and high-income countries, such as Ecuador and Brazil, have begun their epidemiological transition but still suffer from an accumulation of both the infectious and deficiency diseases found in the less-developed countries while also confronting emerging, chronic, and degenerative diseases as a result of the demographic transition toward a more urbanized and aging society.[13] Known as an **epidemiological backlog,** this double health burden strains social welfare budgets. These systems must solve the problems of poorer countries while also being challenged by the health concerns of the wealthier world. Table 12.3 classifies countries by disease type, underscoring the prevalence of deficiency and infectious diseases in poor countries. This epidemiological mosaic challenges countries to address health challenges on a variety of fronts at once.

The unfinished agenda in resolving the epidemiological backlog in Latin America exacts a high human toll. Despite strides made in reducing child and adult mortality, more Latin Americans are hungry today than in the 1990s, rising from 17 to 21 percent of the overall population.[14] Increasing undernourishment, the condition of people whose dietary energy consumption is continuously below a minimum dietary energy requirement for maintaining a healthy life and carrying out a light physical activity afflicts disproportionate numbers in a region where food is available. Table 12.4 shows how the degree of malnutrition is roughly correlated with achieving other Millennium Development Goals in the region. The Food and Agriculture Organization FAO reports 1.5 million Nicaraguans or 29 percent of the population as undernourished, the highest in the region; 25 percent of Guatemalans are also undernourished, with 49.35 of Guatemalan children not having the caloric intake to maintain normal activity. Yet there is a degree of variation, even within

Table 12.3.   Diseases of the Americas: The Epidemiological Transition

	Poorest Latin American Countries: Bolivia	Middle-Income Latin American Countries: Ecuador	High-Income Latin American Countries: Brazil	Latin American Countries with a Strong Safety Net: Costa Rica/Cuba	Developed Countries: United States/ Canada
Deficiency					
Intestinal disease	X				
Intestinal infections	X				
Malnutrition	X				
Infectious					
Chagas	X				
Malaria	X	X			
Influenza				X	X
Parasitic					
Pneumonia				X	X
Respiratory infections		X	X		
Tuberculosis	X	X	X		
Emerging					
Cancer					X
Heart disease				X	
Malaria			X		
Parasitic		X	X		
Chronic Diseases					
Pulmonary infections					X
Tuberculosis					
Tumors					
Degenerative					
Cancer					X
Cerebrovascular				X	
Malignant tumors					
Strokes					X
Tumors					
Congenital					
Heart Disease		X	X		
Birth defects					X
Congenital anomalies				X	
Diabetes		X	X		
Heart attacks					
Environmental					
Accidents		X	X	X	X
Homicides					X
Parasitic					
Tumors			X		

Source: PAHO, 1989 and 1993 data, and the Ministry of Health, Ecuador.

Table 12.4.   Undernourishment and MDG Indicators

Country	Proportion of Population <$1PPP/Day (MDG1) (%)		Prevalence of Underweight Children <5 (MDG 4) (%)		<5 Mortality Rate/1000 Live Births (MDG 13)		Maternal Mortality Ratio /100,000 Live Births (MDG 16)	
	1990	2004	1990	2004	1990	2003	1990	2000
20–34% undernourished								
Bolivia	6	14	11	8	120	66	650	420
Guatemala	35	16	33	23	82	47	200	240
Honduras	38	21	18	17	59	41	220	110
Nicaragua	48	45	11	10	68	38	160	230
Panama	12	7	6	7	34	24	55	160
10–19% undernourished								
Venezuela	3	14	8	4	27	21	120	96
Colombia	2	8	10	7	36	21	100	130
El Salvador	21	31	15	10	60	36	300	150
Paraguay	5	16	4	5	37	29	160	170
Peru	2	18	11	7	80	34	280	410
5–9% undernourished								
Brazil	14	8	7	6	60	35	220	260
Guyana	8	3	18	14	90	69	na	170
Mexico	8	10	17	8	46	28	110	83
2.5–4% undernourished								
Chile	6	2	2	1	19	9	65	31
Costa Rica	5	2	3	5	17	10	55	43
Ecuador	2	18	17	12	57	27	150	130
Uruguay	2	2	6	na	24	14	85	27
Less than 2.5% undernourished								
Argentina	2	3	na	5	28	20	100	82

Source: FAO, The State of Food Insecurity in the World 2005.

Central America. Malnutrition is at 14 percent in El Salvador and 6 percent in Costa Rica, evidencing the scope for improvement in the worst-off cases. Region-wide, 10 percent of the population is undernourished.[15] Hunger and malnutrition lead to increased poverty; reduced school attendance; weakened immune systems; neo-natal disorders of diarrhea, pneumonia, and malaria; and, of course, death.[16] Reducing the prevalence of underweight children by another 5 percentage points could reduce child mortality by 30 percent.

Poor health is a disease of poverty. Malaria, a life threatening parasitic disease transmitted by the bite of an infected mosquito, breeds in conditions of poverty—particularly stagnant, open sewerage and damp, tropical conditions. About 40 percent of the region's population is at risk of contracting this debilitating disease. This ancient scourge hits indigenous populations harder than other population groups, particularly those living in rural and heavily forested areas.[17] Where malaria is endemic, people are continually reinfected, developing immunity over time. Malaria increases the chance of maternal anemia, stillbirth, intrauterine growth retardation, and low birth weight. A severe episode of malaria can lead to stunting and brain damage, permanently constraining a child's growth and development. Malaria depletes not only the person but also the family, increasing health care expenditures and decreasing income. Outbreaks discourage foreign investment and tourism. Malaria can be prevented by spraying households with insecticide, using insecticide-treated mosquito nets, and eliminating mosquito breeding sites. These are relatively cost-effective measures to combat such a devastating disease but are measures that weigh heavily on the budgets of the poor. Contracted malaria can be treated, but drug therapies that overcome problems of resistance are expensive, excluding their use by most vulnerable populations.[18] The Bill and Melinda Gates foundation has recently donated $168 million in the quest to find a vaccine for this deadly disease; until science advances, however, it is the poor who will suffer.

Another disease of poverty is Chagas' disease. Named after the Brazilian physician Carlos Chagas who first described it in 1909, Chagas' disease is unique to the American continent. The risk of infection is directly correlated with poverty: the blood-sucking triatomine bug that hosts the parasite lives comfortably in crevices in the walls and roofs of poor houses in rural areas and in the peripheral urban slums. The migration from rural to urban areas in the 1970s and 1980s changed the traditional epidemiological pattern of Chagas' disease, transforming it into an urban infection that can be transmitted by blood transfusion. Chagas' disease hits the poorest of the poor in Latin America. This tropical disease affects sixteen million to eighteen million people, fifty thousand of whom die each year. It is estimated that as much as 25 percent of the Latin American population, or ninety million people, are at risk for Chagas' disease; approximately a quarter of those infected will progress to irreversible cardiac, esophageal, and colonic pathology, imposing a heavy socioeconomic burden on countries with weakened or deteriorating economies.[19] Chagas' disease can be addressed; the transmission in most of the Southern Cone has been eliminated. However, with little change yet in Central American and Andean countries, it is a disease of poor resources. Given that it primarily afflicts the poor, it is also a disease that international pharmaceutical firms have tended to ignore.[20]

GENDER, ETHNICITY, AND HEALTH

In addition to biological differences, gender inequalities in health care are driven by differences in men's and women's social roles and in their access to family and community resources. The denial of reproductive rights results in death:[21]

- 23,000 women die each year in Latin America of pregnancy and birth-related causes
- 25,000 die of cervical cancer
- 25 percent give birth without the assistance of a skilled attendant
- 27 percent have no access to prenatal care

Maternal malnutrition is a leading cause of both maternal and infant mortality. Without adequate prenatal care, an infant will not receive important nutrients for growth. Breast-feeding by well-nourished mothers transfers needed antibodies to their children to fight viral and bacterial infections, such as diarrhea and pneumonia; rashes; and allergies. In urban areas, many women, however, have been substituting more modern infant feeding practices for breast-feeding, leading to a decline in infant health.

An important element in health care is a woman's ability to control her own fertility. Table 12.5 presents reproductive health statistics for the region. A Save the Children/Bolivian Mothercare project found that women identified their most urgent health problem as having too many children.[22] All countries in the region are significantly above the high-income fertility ratio of 1.7 children per couple. According to the Inter-American Development Bank (IADB), one-third of all women have their first child before age twenty; in Guatemala, the rate is one-half.[23] As women have entered the marketplace in increasing numbers, the opportunity cost of children has risen. As some market women note, customers want to be waited on quickly and not be distracted by crying babies.[24] Use of contraceptives ranges from 77 percent in Brazil to less than 40 percent in Guatemala; demand (including unmet needs) is between 50 and 80 percent.[25] The most widely used method of contraception in the region has been female sterilization. According to the Brazilian health ministry, 21 percent of women between ages twenty-five and twenty-nine have been sterilized, reflecting a failure to provide other methods of contraception. Family planning, however, remains somewhat controversial, given both religious preferences and the position of some multilateral donor agencies. For some indigenous women, the thought of (mostly male) doctors poking inside them prevents them from seeking medical advice on family planning methods. Traditional men sometimes fear that contraception will encourage promiscuous behavior among their wives and daughters. Tragically, unwanted pregnancies are often terminated with self-induced abortions that threaten the lives of the mother or leave deformities in the child should it be born. Some alliance between ethnomedicine (traditional healers) and biomedical practitioners might help alleviate the difficulties in providing health care to indigenous women. Biomedical practitioners need to better understand the role of patient attitudes and responses in improving the delivery of health services in traditional areas. Husbands need to be included in educational efforts at family planning to dispel widely held myths concerning the negative effects of family planning.

The health and nutritional levels of indigenous communities in Latin America are well below national averages. Viral diseases, including influenza, measles, dengue, and respiratory infections, frequently become epidemics under poor sanitary conditions in indigenous communities. Activities such as mining and oil exploration exact high costs in terms of the health of otherwise isolated indigenous groups. In addition to disrupting the environment, workers introduce diseases for which indigenous communities have not developed immunities. In the Amazon Basin countries, the most important challenges to the health of indigenous communities come from the overexploitation of resources. In Bolivia, indigenous people report more than twice the number of illnesses and injuries and miss twice as many workdays but receive less medical care than the general population. Life

Table 12.5. Gender and Health

	Estimated Total Fertility Rates						Contraceptive Use (women, all methods) (%) Most Recent Data Between 1996–04	Births Attended by Skilled Health Staff (% of total) Most Recent Data Between 2000–2003	Female Adults with HIV (% of population ages 15–49 with HIV) 2003
	1960–65	1970–75	1980–85	1990–95	2000–05	2005–2010 (forecast)			
Argentina	3.1	3.1	3.2	2.8	2.4	2.1	75	99	20
Bolivia	6.6	6.5	5.3	4.8	4.0	2.6	58	67	27
Brazil	6.2	4.7	3.8	2.6	2.3	2.5	77	96	37
Chile	5.4	3.6	2.7	2.6	2.0	3.5	61	100	33
Colombia	6.8	5.0	3.7	3.0	2.6	2.6	77	86	34
Costa Rica	7.2	4.3	3.5	2.9	2.3	2.2	96	98	33
Ecuador	6.7	6.0	4.7	3.4	2.8	3.6	66	::	34
El Salvador	6.8	6.1	4.5	3.5	2.9	2.3	67	92	34
Guatemala	6.5	6.2	6.1	5.5	4.6	2.5	43	41	42
Honduras	7.4	7.1	6.0	4.9	3.7	2.6	41	56	56
Mexico	6.8	6.5	4.2	3.1	2.5	1.6	73	95	33
Nicaragua	7.3	6.8	6.0	4.6	3.3	3.0	69	67	34
Panama	5.9	4.9	3.5	2.9	2.7	2.6	10	93	41
Paraguay	6.6	5.7	5.3	4.6	3.8	3.5	58	77	26
Peru	6.9	6.0	4.7	3.7	2.9	3.2	69	59	34
Uruguay	2.9	3.0	2.6	2.5	2.3	1.9	n/a	::	33
Venezuela	6.7	4.9	4.0	3.3	2.7	4.2	51	94	32
Latin America	6.0	5.1	3.9	3.0	2.6	2.4			

Source: World Development Indicators database, www.worldbank.org, and ECLAC.cl.org/mujeres.

Table 12.6.   Ethnicity and Health

Country	Health Insurance Coverage and Ethnicity		Stunting	
	Non-Indigenous	*Indigenous*	*Non-Indigenous*	*Indigenous*
Bolivia (2002)	19	12		
Ecuador (1998)	12	12	29	59
Guatemala (2000)	18	5	33	58
Mexico (2000)	43	17	14	44
Peru (2001)	47	41		

Source: Gillette Hall and Harry Patrinos, eds., "Indigenous Peoples, Poverty and Human Development in Latin America: 1994–2004" (2005), executive summary at web.worldbank.org.

expectancy for the indigenous in Colombia is about ten years lower than national averages.[26] Cultural differences between health care dispensed in hospitals and traditional practices promoted by healers and midwives in indigenous communities also create a health services gap, particularly in practices such as childbirth that are highly sensitive to custom and tradition. In Guatemala, for example, the maternal mortality rate in the indigenous population is 83 percent higher than the national rate. Access to health care is often poor due to physical isolation as well as a weak relationship to government. The Brazilian government spends just over seven dollars a head on indigenous health care versus thirty-three dollars each for the country as a whole.[27] Table 12.6 provides a few statistics on the lagging quality of indigenous health. Stunting among the indigenous in Mexico, for example, is more than three times the rate in the nonindigenous population. This is likely tied to the weak coverage of health services for the indigenous as well as the lack of income for food.[28] Geographic isolation complicates health care in Guatemala; about 60 percent of the population lives in rural areas, 80 percent of these in remote villages with almost no access to quality health care services. The rural population is comprised predominantly of the Maya, the indigenous people of Central America, most living in conditions of poverty. A dismal fact is that indigenous children exhibit extremely high malnutrition rates, even in countries that have otherwise virtually eliminated this problem. In Mexico, just 6 percent of children nationwide are underweight compared with almost 20 percent of indigenous children.[29]

For the indigenous peoples, humans are inseparable from nature; health care must therefore involve holistic approaches. To be effective, health delivery systems must be sensitive to cultural practices. The 1993 Pan American Health Organization (PAHO) workshop Indigenous Peoples and Health held in Winnipeg, Canada, set out guidelines for health promotion, advocating community participation, preservation of habitat and traditional lifestyles, evaluation and monitoring of the health status and living conditions of indigenous peoples, and formulation of national health policies to address the problems of indigenous communities. Nonetheless, as the communiqué initiating the meeting characterized, the health of indigenous peoples is "perhaps the most technically complex and difficult health issue of the day."[30] Interim evaluation of progress on indigenous health care improvements indicates the need for supplemental funding for nongovernmental organizations (NGOs) to reach indigenous populations, improvement of the database on indigenous health concerns, better preparation of health care workers in multicultural communities to attend to the needs and be respectful of the traditional practices of indigenous peoples, and improved dissemination of program efforts to illustrate best-case practices for other countries.[31] Policy measures will require patience and perseverance for success.

On the Unfinished Agenda: Health for All

The poor are particularly vulnerable to bad health shocks. Economic shocks such as the coffee crisis in Central America have increased malnutrition rates in Guatemala to highs of 35 percent with severe malnutrition and 40–45 percent with significant but less severe food deprivation.[32] Natural disasters cause devastation, displacement, disease, accidents, and death, setting back national development for years.[33] In the competitive global economic scene the poor are most vulnerable; erosion of working conditions, expansion of the informal sector, and the explosion of urban slums make life exceptionally precarious. The deterioration of the physical environment, including the gaps in clean drinking water and basic sanitation, make homes breeding grounds for disease.[34] Poverty not only makes people more vulnerable to health shocks; health shocks also make people poorer. Without adequate insurance, the sick person, and most commonly the whole family, is dragged further into a vicious cycle of decline.

The unfinished agenda to fight preventable disease in Latin America is a battle of resources and political will. It is clearly lodged in providing universal access to basic health services. **Primary health care (PHC)** is the essence of the **Health for All (HFA)** strategy adopted at the 1978 Alma Alta joint WHO-UNICEF conference and endorsed by the WHO Assembly in 1981. This landmark document outlined programmatic health objectives as part of a new model for health care based on comprehensive PHC. These included water, sanitation, food supply, nutrition, mother and child care, family planning, immunization, control of local diseases, essential drugs, and education. Health for All encourages culturally sensitive plans that employ appropriate treatment and technology. Health should be integrated into national development plans to improve the social and economic development of the community. Education and active participation are seen as the keys to the promotive, preventive, curative, and rehabilitative services of PHC. The PHC approach is aimed at mobilizing individuals and communities to improve health systems to provide fair and equitable delivery of needed services. The issue of inequality is particularly important in Latin America; PAHO sees overcoming inequality as the major constraint in meeting the goal of universal access to basic health services for the inhabitants of the region.[35]

The strategies for achieving HFA and the subsequent emphasis on PHC are based on three pillars: participation, equity, and intersectoral cooperation. PHC emphasizes social justice, a broadly defined concept of health that includes lifestyle and environmental components, intersectoral integration, and community participation.

PHC employs a holistic approach, embracing the individual's relationship with community and family. Participation is central to the implementation of effective health plans. It can be viewed as the first step toward the decentralization of local health systems.[36] Equity is threefold: between the first and third worlds, rural and urban areas, and genders. The call for equity is grounded in the fundamental right to health care. Intersectoral cooperation refers to the need to link health and development plans, as seen in PAHO's "health in development" and WHO's "health as a conditionality for economic development" strategies.[37]

Investing in PHC can at times involve tough choices. In Brazil, the Institute Materno-Infantil de Pernambuco (IMIP) faced such a tough trade-off. IMIP, a winner of a UNICEF award for a child-friendly hospital, had to decide whether to maintain its pediatric intensive care unit or engage in community outreach. With 95 percent of its financing coming from the Brazilian Ministry of Health (MOH), it had to match costs to average revenues set by the government. The intensive care unit cost more than the government was willing to pay. Furthermore, the children sent to the unit from all over northeastern Brazil were so sick and malnourished that the mortality rate remained high despite the expensive interventions. A more cost-effective strategy to saving children's lives was pursued: close the intensive care unit and expand the network of small community health posts in slum neighborhoods of the major city of Recife. Indeed, infant mortality declined from 147 to 101 per 1,000 live births in those neighborhoods.[38] Box 12.1 demonstrates another case of effective delivery of preventive health services in Brazil. Local control and local initiative can work to reverse the devastating effects of neglect on children and families in poor rural regions.

Most countries have some elements of PHC in their MOH health care delivery systems and have decreased emphasis on the medicalization of health as well as the engineering model, which saw the body as a machine and good health as a question of getting it tuned correctly. However, due primarily to budgetary and political reasons, selective PHC programs, as opposed to comprehensive PHC programs, have been implemented. Weaker versions, limited to growth monitoring, oral rehydration, breast-feeding, immunization, family planning, food production, and female education, have been the norm. The poor have had an increasing burden of paying for health services out of pocket. With budget cuts, many health posts can no longer provide basic services. In Ecuador, for example, spending on health has come to absorb 12–17 percent of the family budget. Those unable to afford private-sector service are left without critically needed curative care and rarely invest in preventive care.[39] Public and private international donor agencies, led in part by WHO and PAHO, can facilitate a broader adoption of PHC programs through partnerships with state and local governments to bridge the fiscal gap.

Emergent Diseases: The New Agenda

Overlaying problems of malnutrition and attendant diseases such as Chagas' disease or malaria are a host of chronic diseases that are the effect of living in modern societies. Cardiovascular disease, cancer, aids, obesity, mental health, traffic deaths,

Box 12.1.   Preventive Health Care in Ceará: Reversing a Health Nightmare

Prior to decentralization of health care, Ceará, Brazil, had some of the worst health indicators in the region. Fewer than a third of the state's municipal districts had a nurse; most people had never seen a doctor. Infant mortality was twice the Brazilian average, and only one in four children had been vaccinated against measles or polio. A new preventive health care system, the Programa de Agentes de Saúde (PAS), radically transformed the health profile of the state. Infant deaths declined 36 percent, vaccination coverage is nearly complete, and each of the districts has a nurse and a public health program. The program cost was about $1.50 per person served—markedly lower than the $80 per capita cost of Brazil's existing health care system. How was this minor medical miracle—with such tangible gains to so many Brazilians—accomplished?

Starting PAS as an employment-generating program in drought-stricken northeastern Brazil in 1987, the state committed to funding it permanently in 1989. The program supported a small army of public health agents who went from house to house (sometimes, in more distant areas, traveling by bicycle, donkey, or canoe) to teach families good health practices. Agents were paid more than teachers or the wage paid to male agricultural labor, although this sometimes did not amount to the national minimum wage. In an area in which nonagricultural opportunities were rare, the jobs were seen as highly prestigious positions. The work was rewarded by warm public support, as the effects were demonstrable to the community. Standards were high. Unlike many government jobs, these were without tenure, and community members (especially those not selected as agents) were told to report lax behavior on the part of the extensionists. People were told to expect a visit once a month to their homes and for health agents to be a part of the communities in which they worked. Nurse supervisors brought in to train agents and administer the program were, through their success, accorded more control, respect, and admiration than they had received in poorly run city hospitals. Administratively, the program was efficient and cost-effective.

At first agents confronted mistrust from rural inhabitants unaccustomed to government programs and comfortable with traditional medicines and faith healers. Agents used curative tasks such as oral rehydration techniques for a baby seemingly near death to convince mothers of the benefits of modern medicine. With the baby playing happily a few hours after nearly dying, the mother was more amenable to hearing about the benefits of breast-feeding, hygienic food preparation, and water filtration systems. Agents developed a bond of trust with often lonely and overburdened mothers, sometimes helping with cooking or child care. The decentralization of services and the empowerment of seventy-three hundred never-before salaried rural women through training and extension services have truly transformed the health profile in Ceará.

With the completion of the initial phase, the PROQUALI methodology—its accreditation process and its tools—is being institutionalized across the country. In Ceará, the Secretariat of Health has institutionalized the PROQUALI model as its quality improvement approach in providing PHC to children and adults. The Secretariat of Health in Bahia has designated a facility to serve as the Reproductive Health Reference Center from which the PROQUALI model will expand in Bahia and to other states using the Internet and a PROQUALI CD-ROM.

PROQUALI has proven that public-sector clinics can offer quality reproductive health services while inspiring all those involved. During the project, the three cooperating agencies advanced in partnership and technical innovation. The role of the Secretariats of Health in Ceará and Bahia in delivering improved services was strengthened. The participating service providers were empowered to solve health center weaknesses

continued

and violence all place enormous burdens on health systems already buckling under the pressure of addressing traditional infectious diseases. The ability to simultaneously attack both the old and new health agendas calls for a transformation of health systems in the region. "This transformation will require addressing incentives, human resources, information technology, and public needs together in new ways," says Derek Yach, professor of global health at the Yale School of Public Health.[40] Developing country health systems are behind in the diagnosis and treatment of the rising tide of chronic disease; their health financing systems are ill-equipped to support the long-term care and services that those suffering from chronic disease demand.[41] Because of underdeveloped health systems, chronic disease deaths occur at much earlier ages in low- and middle-income countries than in high-income countries.

By 2020 **heart disease** will cause three times the number of deaths as infectious disease; diabetes is higher in Latin America than it is globally.[42] South and Central America have some of the highest cervical **cancer** rates in the world, with incidence rates of 30 per 100,000 in South America and 40 per 100,000 in Central America, four times the U.S. and European rates. This is avoidable; the rates in Costa Rica fell from 45 to 15 from 1992 to 2003 when the Costa Rican government implemented stronger screening initiatives. There are tragic trade-offs, however, in many of the poorer nations of the region with treatment of traditional disease.

Globalization has brought its own disease vector. Approximately 1.8 million people are living with HIV in Latin America; in 2005, 66,000 died of **AIDS** and 200,000 were newly infected.[43] The highest prevalence in the population is in Belize, Guatemala, and Honduras, with approximately 1 percent of adults infected with HIV. Honduras is home to one-third of all HIV cases in the Central American subregion, with infection rates just under 2 percent; AIDS has become the number one cause of death among women of fertile age. The causes of the spread of HIV in Latin America are a combination of unsafe sex and intravenous drug use. In Mexico a man having sex with another man faces a one in three chance that his partner is HIV-positive. The epidemic is concentrated among the poor; 60 percent of those with HIV/AIDS have not completed primary school. IV drug users are another group at risk. In Mexico between 3 and 11 percent are infected; in Brazil and Argentina the rate reaches nearly 50 percent. The epidemic has spread to include women, who now account for one-fourth of all reported AIDS cases.[44]

BOX 12.2. SOCIAL MARKETING

Social marketing uses commercial marketing techniques to influence social behaviors. Playing to the market, it creates important information about the demand for a given product. People appear to value things they must pay for, even if the payment is very modest. Paying customers demand more from services, making providers more attentive to clients. Advertising campaigns can be used to change the tastes of the target audience to promote socially beneficial choices for society. If marketing can sell Pepsi, why not prophylactics?

Social marketing began in the 1970s as public health professionals realized that programs needed to be attentive to the needs and desires of recipient communities. This technique has since been successfully used in international health programs, especially in the areas of contraceptive distribution and oral rehydration therapy for infants. Social marketers follow the four P's: product, price, place (distribution), and promotion. Products can be tangible items (such as condoms or rehydration salts), services (medical exams and education), or practices (breast-feeding). Prices for these products and services are very low, often below production costs, to service the needs of the poor. These low prices are made possible through heavy subsidization. Most programs are funded by organizations such as the United States Agency for International Development (USAID), with as much as 80 percent of the costs covered. These programs, which are often run by private providers, work with or alongside government-run programs to promote social health to a broad portion of the general public.

One example of a successful program in Latin America is in Mexico, which has in recent years had a surplus of doctors. Start-up funding has allowed these unemployed doctors to set up health clinics in previously underserved communities. The Fundacion Mexicana para la Planeacion Familiar (MEXFAM), with support from USAID and the International Planned Parenthood Federation, has helped 175 doctors set up clinics in the past ten years. These clinics provide family planning and child health services in small towns and poor urban areas. With subsidies from MEXFAM, after two years the doctor is able to buy the office and medical equipment from MEXFAM for half of its original setup cost. MEXFAM continues to provide contraceptives and training after the two-year period.

Source: Weinreich Communications, *The Social Marketing Place,* www.members.aol.com/weinreich/whatis.html; and Population Reports, *Johns Hopkins University Population Information* 19(4) (November 1991): 14.

Prevention is inextricably tied to education. Knowledge of AIDS prevention varies by socioeconomic class. In the poorest quintile in Latin America, only 46.8 percent of females have knowledge of AIDS as opposed to 81.8 percent in the wealthiest strata. A 2004 survey in Brazil showed that 36 percent of fifteen- to twenty-four-year-olds had sex before their fifteenth birthday, and only 62 percent knew how HIV was transmitted. Women whose husbands sleep with other men or women are at risk; the culture of machismo in Latin America makes it difficult even for wives to insist on condom use.

Brazil remains unique in providing antiretroviral drugs to all in need via the country's national health system. Beginning in 1996, Brazil implemented what is now considered one of the boldest and most successful AIDS treatment programs in the developing world.[45] Based on a constitutional guarantee, Brazil promises a virtually free HIV drug distribution program.[46] In response to the high price of antiretroviral medicines available largely in the United States, domestic companies in Brazil began the production of generic HIV drugs at low costs. Complementing the antiretrovival treatment is an aggressive education policy. Using a social marketing approach (see box 12.2 for more on social marketing), the Brazilian government's strategy is to provide both education and condoms. During the famous Brazilian revelry of Carnival, for example, volunteers from more than eighteen hundred NGOs handed out more than 11 million condoms paid for by the MOH—in addition to the 20 million normally distributed each month. Prevention through education and condom distribution combined with treatment of those already infected with HIV has shown conclusively that it is possible to curb the HIV/AIDS epidemic in developing countries. The World Bank had predicted that by 2000, 1.2 million Brazilians would be infected; instead, incidence has stabilized at 600,000 people due to widespread educational efforts and universal access to medication. As of September 2005, 170,000 Brazilians were on antiretroviral therapy.

The struggle, however, has not been easy. Given rising costs for the next generation of antiretroviral drugs, it will be a challenge to sustain the program. While many international health agencies have heralded Brazil's treatment program, it has also been the subject of ongoing controversy. The U.S. government has launched legal proceedings against Brazil, claiming that the production of generic HIV drugs breaks international laws on patent production. In 2001, and after months of debate, Brazil and the U.S.-based pharmaceuticals came to an agreement, and the United States withdrew its patent complaint against Brazil. Tensions rose again a few years later when in 2005 Brazil pushed for the right to produce the more sophisticated AIDs drug Kaletra. Without the ability to produce a generic, Brazil would have spent an additional $259 million over six years to maintain patient access to antiretrovirals. A tough bargaining position nevertheless won. Brazil negotiated lower AIDS drug prices by threatening to break patents, without ever actually doing so. Its new strategy is to ally with other developing nations to push for lower-priced products.[47] It is bolstered by the ethical position that if Western governments are to commit themselves to reducing the AIDS epidemic and improving world public health, drug companies must take moral responsibility by providing affordable drugs to the less-developed world.[48]

Brazil has also faced pushback on its condom distribution program. Its cooperative approach between government and the civil sector engages a range of NGO networks to promote safe sex. Its partnership with the Brazilian Network of Sex Professionals drew the $40 million contribution of the U.S. government to its social marketing program under fire. Because the safe sex program extended assistance to commercial sex workers, as of 2006 the money has been withheld because of a requirement in the administration of George W. Bush to condemn prostitution. Nonetheless, this program as well as the deep 45–70 percent discounts negotiated from drug companies reducing treatment costs by more than half has garnered international attention.[49] The nature of AIDS prevention and treatment as a global public good provides a strong rationale for global action.

Violence has risen to become one of the most serious health problems in urban areas of the region. Violence manifests itself in different forms: political (state and

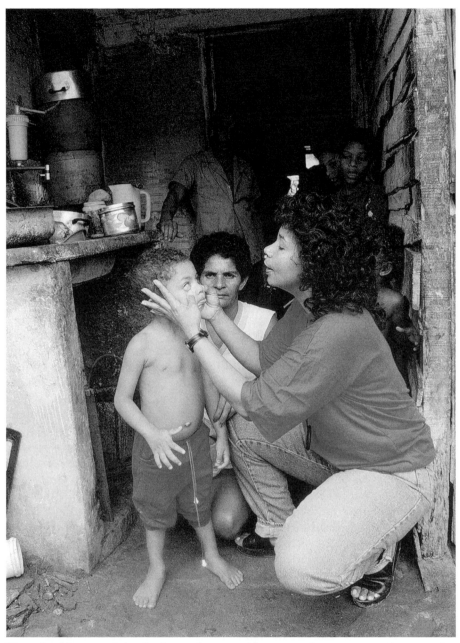

Home health agents bring basic services—and hope—to the very poor. *(Courtesy of David Mangurian and the Inter-American Development Bank)*

nonstate), institutional (lynching, extrajudicial killings by security forces), economic (kidnapping, robbery, drug trafficking, car theft, small arms, trafficking in prostitutes, street theft), economic/social (maras or youth gangs, street children); and social (gender basis, child abuse, intergenerational, bar fights, road rage).[50] Latin America's crime rate is double the world average, taking a huge toll on the region's economic development and public faith in democracy.[51] Compared to the global homicide rate of 5 per 100,000 inhabitants, Latin America's rate of 27.5 is the highest for any region in the world.[52] The leading cause of death in Colombia, for example, is homicide.[53] Gangs proliferate in some Central American countries. According to a study by the United Nations Development Programme, the cost of violence to El Salvador in 2003 was $1.7 billion, equivalent to 11.5 percent of GDP. The IADB is even more pessimistic, estimating that the per capita GDP of the region would be 25 percent higher if the rates of violence were no worse than the world average.[54] The number of homicides in Brazil places it in the UN category of a low-grade civil war.

The explosion of violence sweeping the continent has complex causes. In Colombia and El Salvador it may be linked to historical conflicts over land. Rapid urbanization in the context of huge disparities between rich and poor may exacerbate social violence. Traditional values practiced in the countryside are lost on the new generation of tough urban youth often lured by alcohol and drugs. Rising unemployment associated with globalization may also be a contributing factor. As police capabilities are overwhelmed and judicial systems choked, repression and brutality are more common than prevention and reform. Such violence exacts a high human and economic cost. One World Bank economist estimated that the net accumulation of human capital was cut in half because of the increase in crime and violence since the mid-1980s.[55]

Violence against women is prevalent. A study of select Latin American countries shows rates of ever-married women reporting spousal abuse of 44 percent in Colombia, 42 percent in Peru, and 30 percent in Nicaragua. Perhaps surprisingly, the highest rates of violence occur in moderately wealthy households, not as often assumed among the poorest.[56] Violence against women is a critical concern. The United Nations defines violence against women as an act of gender violence that results or is likely to result in physical, sexual, or psychological harm or suffering to women. The Panos Institute reports that gender violence causes more death and disability among women ages fifteen to forty-four than cancer, malaria, traffic accidents, or war. The costs extend to families; children of abused women in Nicaragua drop out of school four years earlier and were one hundred times more likely to be hospitalized than children of nonabused women. A Costa Rican survey showed that 95 percent of pregnant girls age fifteen or younger were incest victims. According to one Honduran health worker, overburdened health care providers often don't have the time to talk to patients in diagnostic exams; many women will not discuss household violence unless directly asked. A PAHO study ties violence against women in the Americas to a macho culture that reinforces male control over wealth and decision making in the family.[57] **Domestic violence** remains a challenge for countries across the region.

Currently there is a large and widening treatment gap in **mental health** care in Latin America.[58] The number of people with mental disorders in the Americas is forecast to increase from 114 million in 1990 to 176 million in 2010, according to the director of PAHO.[59] Mental health disorders comprise 24 percent of the burden of disease in the Americas, with depression being the principal component of that burden. Nearly 20 percent of children and adolescents suffer from disorders that require the support of or intervention by mental health care services, and those disorders lead to both social stigma and discrimination.[60] Health systems, however, are poorly equipped to gather information on mental health and substance abuse, develop and apply appropriate policies, strengthen services, and improve national legislation in order to enhance systems to prevent and control these problems. Alcohol consumption at rates 50 percent higher than worldwide consumption creates a heavy disease burden, accounting for the fourth largest cause of death in men.[61] Key measures to respond to the mental health needs of the populations of the Americas are to integrate mental health into primary care, develop services in the community, and combat the stigma that mental disorders carry.[62] Addressing the problem of alcohol will involve a focus on the availability of and access to alcohol and implementation and enforcement of these policies, including imposing taxes and putting in place public education campaigns.

As Latin American nations have experienced major transitions in health profiles, **occupational health concerns** have become a leading cause of morbidity among adults in the region. People spend more than a third of each day at work; conditions in the workplace clearly impact health. There are between twenty million and twenty-seven million work-related accidents annually in Latin American and the Caribbean, ninety thousand of which are fatal. Work with hazardous processes associated with international trade is particularly dangerous when workers cannot adequately read warning labels. Despite impacting more than two hundred million workers and their families, occupational safety and health have been largely ignored. The existing data underestimate the problem, and the institutional capacity to address concerns is weak. Heavy physical workloads, hazards such as noise or radiation, dangerous conditions, toxic chemicals, exposure to asbestos or coal dust, risk of cancer, social conditions, and exposure to viruses, fungi, and molds can damage workers' health. In the rural sector, acute pesticide poisoning is a major health problem. Workers do not wear appropriate protective clothing (perhaps because the heavy rubber is designed for colder climates) or follow safety directions. Miners suffer from falls, electrocution, lung disease, and neurological damage from exposure to chemicals such as mercury. Informal-sector employment, accounting for nearly 50 percent of the labor force in the region, increases health risks in that small firms, high turnover, absence of monitoring of conditions, and lack of insurance generate a higher incidence of health problems. Child labor is still widespread in the region, and children are more vulnerable to workplace risk. The fifty-six million women in the workforce face a dual burden: the stress of low-paying jobs and the double duty of their second workday in the evening at home. *Maquila* workers, primarily women, suffer from repetitive stress disorders on the musculoskeletal system. Latin America and the Caribbean's fatality rate in the workplace is approximately twice that of Canada's. This may even understate the data, as reporting in the informal sector is weak as well as the fact that in the formal sector insurance rates in the region are often tied to injuries. The economic cost of occupational health hazards is high; the International Labor Organization (ILO) and WHO estimate the total burden to reach as much as 10 percent of GDP of developing countries, more than three times the estimated occupational health cost of the United States.[63] Despite the enormous burden of occupational health costs, extending regulation is problematic because of the need to create jobs and the weak institutional capacity for enforcement.

Finally, our list of modern disease must include traffic deaths. One study in the Americas of twelve countries showed that traffic accidents were the leading cause of death among boys and girls ages five to fourteen years and the leading cause for women and second leading cause for men between fifteen and forty-four years old. Latin America's narrow, poorly paved streets were simply not designed to accommodate the explosion of cars. Venezuela and Guyana have the highest fatalities at twenty per one hundred thousand inhabitants. In El Salvador, 60 percent of the victims are pedestrians—40 percent of the unfortunate casualties in Mexico, Colombia, and Costa Rica were also on foot.

HEALTH CARE SYSTEMS IN LATIN AMERICA

In addition to choices about the level of sophistication of health care, improvements in health require changes in systems of delivery. The health status of the people of Latin America is affected not only by extant diseases and each country's socioeconomic status but also by institutions and systems established to provide health services for the populations and the environments in which these institutions operate. The challenges to Latin American health care delivery systems are numerous and require a redefinition of the traditional health care system. Old or accumulated challenges include insufficient coverage of the population, poor technical quality, inadequate patient referral, and deficient management of institutions. New challenges to health delivery systems are composed of cost escalation, financial insecurity, and technological expansion in light of their opportunity costs in terms of PHC.

Rural health care poses particular challenges for 25 percent of the hemisphere's population. In some rural areas, health care can be a four- to eight-hour bus ride or a one- to two-hour walk away. Between 50 and 80 percent of all health expenditures go to hospitals located near urban centers. Inaccessible health facilities make prenatal and other types of preventive PHC particularly problematic. Shifting from hospital-based to community-based health systems can help direct resources toward the needs of the local population rather than urban patterns of demand. Although a hospital has the advantage of being a physically distinct unit in which health services can be coordinated under one roof, it can also be a center of power and influence that drains resources from community health systems. Major resources may be tied up in hospitals, equipment, and services that come at an opportunity cost to meeting people's PHC needs. Unless the hospital is integrated into a community health care system, when patients are discharged they may find little continuity of care and suffer from a fragmentation of health services.[64] Health care must extend into the community.

The organization of health care varies across the region. Although each Latin

American country has a unique mixture of social security facilities, private practitioners, and government ministries responsible for health, generalizations can be made. Health care systems have two service dimensions: finance and delivery of service. Financing refers to how and by whom services are paid for. Delivery refers to the actual provision of services. Each factor can be provided either by the public or by the private sector. For example, financing could be public, through universal health insurance, but rely on the services of private practitioners. Alternatively, some financing—especially for the poor—might be public, with a mix of public hospitals and private providers. In Cuba, both financing and provision are public. The Costa Rican model is also largely public with nearly universal state coverage, although private-sector services are available. Paraguay and Argentina are closer to the U.S. model, which is a mixture of private health insurance that includes out-of-pocket expenditures and public resources. The United States is a pure example of this model. In Brazil, public financing is nearly universal, and the services are contracted out.

Moving from financing to delivery of health services, the most common structure in Latin America is a mixed system. Three main health sectors in Latin America are present: the social security institutes (SSI, or Cajas de Seguro Social)[65] for formal-sector employees, the private sector for those who can afford private insurance or those who are uninsured but choose to seek private services, and the MOH for the poor. The formal sector finances and provides health care services to its employees. The MOH is responsible for the coordination of health care service delivery for approximately 70 percent of the population but has only approximately 40 percent of the financing.

There are numerous problems with this common Latin American health care model. Because many institutions provide similar services to different client bases, there is unnecessary duplication of services, especially of costly high-tech items. Services are concentrated in urban areas. There are concerns of quality, especially for the lower classes who utilize the resource-poor MOH facilities. Rising health care costs have thrust the quality and efficiency debate into focus throughout the region. As they stand, funding, personnel, and management systems do not create incentives for efficiency. Doctors, for example, are typically paid a fixed salary irrespective of quality or efficiency of service.[66] Human capital in the sector is poor, as training and support are weak. Health care reflects broader social patterns in the region, defined by a high degree of class inequality. Better use of health resources will require a restructuring of the delivery systems in the region while tackling tough issues of social inequality.

REFORMING HEALTH SERVICE DELIVERY: THE CHALLENGE TO POLICY

Health care policy is determined by a number of critical choices that a nation faces. How much should people pay for health care? How should the trade-off between high-quality, sophisticated treatment and increased access to basic health and nutrition be resolved? Should health services be provided by the public or the private sector? How should governments resolve the tension between hospital-based urban care and comprehensive rural coverage? What kind of health insurance schemes will meet society's goals? Policies to improve health care in Latin America include improving the choices that households face, transforming the pattern of public spending on health, and changing the structure of the health care market.

Latin American governments began addressing these issues in the mid-1990s. After the lost decade of development due to the debt crisis of the 1980s, a better economic climate and the pressures for more responsive government under democracy promoted reform. Increasing international momentum toward health for all accentuated the movement for change.[67] Reform efforts can be broken down into two categories: those fostering efficiency and those promoting equity through enhancing access. Some governments experimented with redesigning incentives to provide new payment and purchaser systems; others promoted hospital or clinic autonomy to make services more responsive to local conditions. There have been attempts to unify aspects of the three segmented sectors of health in the region, bringing the public and social security systems together to reduce duplication and take advantage of economies of scale. Accountability to decrease corruption is being improved by the creation of agencies that separate the purchase of medical supplies from the actual service provider.

It is hoped that decentralization of services will bring health care closer to the needs of the people. Decentralization involves the devolution of previously centralized responsibilities to the local level. In Chile, responsibility for health care was brought down to the municipal level; the budget for PHC and 50 percent of the health staff were transferred from the national health service to local governments. Chilean workers, with a mandatory 7 percent deduction from their paychecks, were given a choice of enrolling in either public or private health insurance plans.[68] Colombia's decentralized contracting system also appears to be a viable model for reforming Latin American health care systems struggling to overcome limited MOH budgets and improve equity, participation, and intersectoral cooperation. Multinational companies such as Aetna and Cigna are entering the Latin American market as partners to local providers of private health insurance. Box 12.3 discusses reforms in Mexican health care in greater depth.

Nonetheless, decentralization carries with it several risks. Some local health systems are deeply penetrated by clientelism and patronage.[69] The political will to implement health reform may vary by the commitment of governors and mayors and the technical capabilities of local service providers.[70] Decentralization can perversely decrease equity and access to a poor state if finance does not follow the responsibility to deliver services. Small may not always be more efficient, particularly when economies of scale affect the purchasing of supplies or equipment. Nonetheless, decentralization need not be an all or nothing proposition.[71] For example, the central government could retain the responsibility for purchasing commodities, saving through economies of scale on items such as contraceptives, while local entities manage personnel and services. Citizen participation in articulating local demands for health care have been quite effective in Peru. Under the Comunidades Locales de Administración de Salud (Local Health Community Administration) system, by the end of 1997 roughly 10 percent of PHC clinics were administered by

Box 12.3.   Reform of Mexican Health Care

While the overall health of the Mexican people has improved significantly, including an increase in male life expectancy from sixty-two to seventy-two years from 1980 to 2004, compared with industrial economies there is considerable room for improvement. Modern health problems of Mexico's NAFTA neighbors coexist with the epidemiological characteristics of low-income countries. Mexicans still face problems of infectious diseases, malnutrition, and concerns related to insufficient mother and infant care while simultaneously confronting the needs of a more urbanized and aging population. Mexico has 1.1 doctors and 2.2 nurses per 1,000 population, as compared to 2.9 doctors and 8.2 nurses per 1,000 in OECD countries. Although Mexico lags OECD countries in health technologies such as coronary artery bypass surgery (only 1 per 100,000 population, whereas no other OECD country performs fewer than 15), improvements in childhood immunization have evidenced great achievements, with coverage for measles, diphtheria, and tetanus surpassing U.S. rates. Challenges to the Mexican health system include extending coverage, particularly in rural areas; reducing disparities in health status among regions; responding to the needs of a more urban and higher-income group; and preparing for the coming needs of an elderly population. Systemic reform is crucial to meeting divergent challenges.

Mexico's health system is segmented into various social security schemes covering insured workers in the formal sector, public health services provided by the MOH, and a private sector that is largely unregulated. Those falling in the public sector are a heterogeneous group including rural inhabitants and those in marginal urban zones. Some in the social security sector overlap, also using private-sector services; provision for the poor is clearly separated from that for the working class and the rich. The weak coverage by insurance leaves nearly all private spending—95.9 percent—coming out of pocket. In reality, some ten million Mexicans have access to little or no health care. Coordination among the different segments of the system is typically low, resulting in a duplication of services. There have been few systemic incentives to improve efficiency or extend coverage.

Improving equity in health services is a goal of the Mexican government. Deficiencies in infrastructure, lack of trained health professionals, long waiting times, large distances to services, lack of medication at clinics, and poor supervision are common complaints. Deficient public health services force the poor to spend meager savings on vital care. As a proportion of their income, the bottom 40 percent of the population spends 5 percent, as opposed to 3 percent in the upper half of the income distribution. Mexico allocates approximately 6.2 percent of GDP on health care, an amount within the normal range given its income level. The problem in Mexico is not necessarily the level of spending but rather the large unmet needs and regional disparities in the health system (table 12.7).

The Mexican health system may exhibit tendencies from the worst of two options in health care, relying on elements of the public integrated model and the private contract model. Much of the population falls under the national health system, and the social insurance schemes are subject to the quasi-monopoly power of providers, with no effective consumer choice. Because the provider of services is also the regulator, supervision and quality control are erratic. The private sector of the market must attend to those dissatisfied with public services.

Systemic reforms aim to increase public access, make service provision more efficient, and contain future cost escalation. One element of the reform is to bring informal-sector workers with prepayment abilities—those in small firms and family businesses—into the social security scheme. A voluntary affiliation scheme will allow unaffiliated individuals to buy into the social security plan. The plan allows for user choice of primary

continued

continued

Table 12.7.   Health Care Spending

Country	Total Spending 2003 per capita PPP dollars	Government Spending 2003 per capita PPP dollars	Total Expenditure on Health as % of GDP	Central Government Expenditure (CGE) as % of Total Health Spending	Health CGE/ Total CGE	Out of Pocket Private Spending as % of All Private Health Spending
United States	5,711	2,548	15.2	44.6	18.5	24.3
Argentina	1,067	518	8.9	48.6	14.7	55.6
Chile	707	345	6.1	48.8	12.7	46.2
Uruguay	824	224	9.8	27.2	6.3	25
Venezuela	231	102	4.5	44.3	6.4	95.5
Brazil	597	270	7.6	45.3	10.3	64.2
Mexico	582	270	6.2	46.4	11.7	95.9

Source: World Health Organization, World Health Report 2006, annex 2 & 3, www.who.org. PPP rates take into account the local buying power of the dollar.

physicians. Regional decentralization is also being pursued to better meet local health demands. It is designed to reduce duplication of services at the national and local levels while addressing equity through a formula for funding that accounts for health needs, poverty, and financial capacity of state governments. Nonetheless, experience shows that decentralization should be phased in gradually to avoid a deterioration of services in poorer regions. Ensuring that local providers meet national standards will be the responsibility of the National Health Council (Consejo Nacional de Salud, CNS) and the MOH. A program targeted to those in extreme poverty financed by federal transfers is focused on twelve primary health services selected for their cost-efficient nature. The federal government will maintain the normative, coordination, planning, and evaluation functions under the new health plan.

The ambitious reform of the health care sector embarked upon by the Mexican government creates the potential for better delivery of health services to millions of Mexicans. In the new health model, preventive strategies dominate over curative approaches, covering the life cycle from reproductive health through aging. Success, however, will depend on the political will to overcome resistance to vested interests in the old, inefficient system of delivery.

Source: The Reform of the Mexican Health Care System, Organization for Economic Cooperation and Development Economic Surveys: Mexico (Paris: OECD, 1998), and Health at a Glance, OECD Indicators 2003 www.oecd.org.

city councils; by 2001 they had expanded to 19 percent, had produced some outstanding clinics, and work better in less-poor urban settings than in rural.[72]

Households are constrained by income and education in the choices they make about health care. Governments should consider pursuing policies that improve choices, particularly among the poor. Health policies to reach the poor include measures to empower users of health services, especially among the poorest in society.

Rather than remain victims of a poor health system, changes to strengthen account-ability to patients by providing information about services quality and rights can be provided along with channels for complaints to be heard. The design of public health systems should respond to the needs of the poor. For example, for many poor (and their families) the costs of a day at the public clinic include the wages foregone in long waits and the need to line up very early in the morning in order to be seen. Improving accessibility and reducing other inconveniences will help the poor address their health care needs.[73]

Propoor health reform includes expanded investments in the link between edu-cation and health, particularly for girls. Girls in the region play important roles in the care of younger siblings. An example of public education is a radio program in Bolivia directed toward eight- to thirteen-year-old children providing lessons on food preparation, sanitation, diarrhea prevention and oral hydration, cholera, and immunizations to improve family health practices. Women are an important target group. The pattern of public spending might be oriented toward the financing of public health interventions and community health services that deliver the greatest improvements in health care per dollar spent rather than toward expensive invest-ments in tertiary care for the wealthy. The use of health promoters—members of the community trained and practicing under a doctor's supervision—can extend the medical reach. Promoters engage in preventive medicine and health education as well as carry small medical kits to deal with wounds, infections, and simple medical problems such as diarrhea. As members of the community themselves, health pro-moters have the trust of their clients, travel to remote areas, and often help bridge the gap between modern medicine and traditional healing practices.

The direction of health policy should in part be shaped by the local demand for health care. The perceived need for medical care—generally determined by medical experts—may diverge from the demand for health care based on a community's assessment of its own health conditions and socioeconomic circumstances. Demand for health care might be influenced by cultural norms, traditional medical practices, income, and prices that include not only monetary fees paid for services but also the travel time and foregone income to seek care.[74] Perception of illness also varies across cultures. If an illness becomes a way of life for a community, fewer members might seek treatment than in a community in which the same disease is rare. Tourists, for example, rarely forget their malaria shots and pills or their diarrhea remedies; inhabitants in some tropic communities may simply find these diseases part of the natural cycle of life—and sometimes death. Education and literacy also condition the demand for health care. Sadly, what people don't know can kill them. Estimating local demand for health services is important to direct funds away from under-utilized services and toward unmet needs. A process of health education at the community level can facilitate grassroots participation in the determination of the demand for health.

PAYING THE BILL FOR HEALTH

Who should pay for health services? Traditionally, public health services in Latin America have been paid for by central governments, although out-of-pocket

Table 12.8.   Health Resources, Access, and Coverage

	Human Resources per 10,000 Population			Hospital Beds per 1,000 Population 2004	National Health Expenditure as a % of GDP	
	Physicians c2001	Nurses c2001	Dentists c2001		Public 2002	Private 2002
Mexico	15.6	10.8	1	1.0[a]	2.8[a,r]	3.2[a,w]
Belize	10.2	12.3	1.3	1.3	4.1[q,k]	1.4[t,k]
Costa Rica	11.5	7.1	3.3	1.4[a]	4.9[q,a]	3.4[t,a]
El Salvador	12.6	8.1	5.5	0.7	2[q,a]	3.8[w,a]
Guatamala	9.5	3.6	1.6	.5[a]	1.4[s,a]	4.8[t,e]
Honduras	8.7	3.2	2.2	1[b]	2[r,d]	2.6[t,e]
Nicaragua	16.4	1.4	2.9	0.9	3.8[r,d]	3.9[t]
Panama	13.8	11.2	2.8	1.8	4.2[q,d]	2[t,e]
Cuba	60.4	71.4	4.9	4.9	n/a	n/a
Bolivia	7.6	3.2	1.2	1	4.3[r]	2.9[t,e]
Colombia	12.7	6.1	7.8	1.2	4[r]	2.6[t]
Ecuador	16.4	5.3	1.7	1.4[a]	2.1[r]	2.9[t]
Peru	11.7	8	1.1	1.1	2.1[q,a]	2[v,e]
Venezuela	20	7.9	5.7	.9[a,p]	1.4[q]	2.7[t,e]
Brazil	20.6	5.2	9.5	2.6	3.6[r,a]	3.6[t,a]
Argentina	32.1[e]	3.8	9.3[e]	4.1[c]	5[r]	3.9[t]
Chile	11.5	6.6	4.4	2.5[a]	2.6[q,a]	3.8[t,a]
Paraguay	5.6	2.2	0.8	1.2[b]	2.9[r,d]	4.1[t,c]
Uruguay	39	8.7	12.4	1.9[a]	2[q,d]	10.4[t,e]

Source: PAHO, Health Situation in the Americas Basic Indicators 2005.
BI 50A, BI 50B: (a) value 2003; (b) value 2002; (c) value 2000; (d) value 2001; (e) value 2004; (f) value 1997; (g) value 1999; (k) value 2001–02; (p) public sector; (q) health, as defined in the Classification of Government Expenditures by Functions of Purposes; (r) health, as defined by the country or author; may

expenses comprise up to 50 percent of health expenditures. Table 12.8 provides data on public and private spending as a percentage of GDP. Although definitions of what is included complicate cross-country comparisons, we see a wide range of public spending, from 4.9 percent of GDP in Costa Rica to 1.4 percent in Venezuela and Guatemala. The table also provides a broad indication of what the money is buying in terms of human resources—the doctors, nurses, and dentists per ten thousand people and the coverage of health care by trained personnel. Given fiscal constraints, some evidence suggests that even the poor can and should pay for at least a part of services rendered. The very poor can be given vouchers to cover expenses, but payment for service sets up greater accountability at the local level. In some areas, user fees have been introduced to stretch scarce public resources in the health field. Some research indicates that even the poor are willing to pay for health services if the introduction of fees is accompanied by an improvement in quality.[75] In cases such as El Salvador, where user fees have been instituted, evidence suggests that cost was an inconsequential factor in determining why rural residents did not seek health care.[76] The additional income can be used to increase the stock and

Health Care by Trained Personnel (%)			Immunization Coverage in Infants Under 1 Year Old (%) 2004				Contraceptive Use (women, all methods) (%) 1996–2004
Prenatal	At Birth	Year	DTP3	OPV3	BCG	Measles/ MMR	
95.8[b]	91.5	2003	98	98	99	96	46
98[b]	87.8	2004	95	95	99	95	56
82	97.5	2002	90	90	90	88	96
45.8	83.7	2004	90	90	94	93	67
84.3	41.4	2002	95	95	98	95	43
85.3	62	2001	89	90	93	92	41
86.2[d]	75.2	2003	79	80	88	84	69
99.2	92.5	2003	99	99	99	99	10[p]
100	99.9	2004	89	99	99	99	77
79	60.8	2002	84	84	86	90	58
90.8[c]	94.5	2003	89	89	92	92[a]	77
83[b]	69	2003	90	93	99	99	66
91.2	71.1	2000	91	91	91	90	69
25.5[f]	99.7	2003	85	82	96	78	51
49.1[b]	96.7	2003	96	98	99	99	77
83.9[g]	99.1	2000	90	96	99	95	75
76.1	99.8	2003	94	94	96	95	61
74.2	85.9	2003	88	88	92	89	58
94	99.4	2002	95	95	99	95	n/a

refer to budgetary-programatic, institutional expenditures; (s) health and social assistance; as defined by the country; (t) health and medical care, excluding health insurance; (v) health without detail; (w) country estimate provided by the Ministry of Health.

variety of effective drug treatments. In contrast to tax-funded "free" health services from the central government, payment at the local level establishes a direct relationship between quality of services delivered and fair compensation. It may encourage cost savings and more efficient delivery of health services.

Nevertheless, some third world medical experts are wary of user fees, especially in very poor areas where barter practices and lack of cash income limits the ability to pay for health services. User fees can also be seen as a form of regressive tax by which the poor pay proportionately more of their income for health than the rich. Unfortunately, there may be few alternatives. With a fixed budget for public health, governments must make tough choices about the allocation of resources. Market-oriented reforms may be needed as a key element of system overhauls. Cost-effectiveness is a criteria that guides many decisions in the health care field.

In addition to user fees, some countries have experimented with the introduction or expansion of insurance schemes. Rather than pay out lump sums to hospitals to provide services, money can be transferred to the patients, creating demand-driven medical services. Colombia was a leader in this reform approach. Prior to the redesign of the Colombian health care system, one-sixth of those who fell ill did not seek medical care because they simply could not pay; other uninsured patients paid dearly out of pocket for services, driving them or their families further into poverty. Prior to reform, only 9 percent of the lowest income quintile and 21 percent of the second lowest group were insured against health problems, creating a huge problem of vulnerability to illness.[77] Colombia's goal was to provide greater access to health care by making it possible to pay for it. There was a widely held view in Colombian society that incorporation into this basic right—health—was critical in stemming social disintegration and building the legitimacy of the state. Under the reform, millions of Colombians became eligible for health insurance and newly increased health purchasing agencies.[78] There were four main elements to reform. First, one had to pass an income test to become eligible for participation. Preference was given to children and single mothers. Second, traditional supply-side subsidies were then transformed into insurance premiums for the poor. Third, the insurance system for the poor was merged into a contributory regime for those working and able to make contributions. Nonetheless, there were two divisions within this unified system, one for the subsidized clients and another for the fund contributors. A 1 percent tax on the contribution plan helped finance the subsidized scheme. Finally, the insurance was designed to purchase services from both the public and private health care sectors.

The effects of the program are impressive. Insurance coverage in the first and second quintiles rose to 49 and 53 percent respectively. Poverty was reduced. Pre-reform, 5 percent of those suffering an ambulatory shock were driven into poverty and 6 percent into indigence (deep poverty); hospitalization pushed 14 percent in poverty and 18 percent into deep poverty. Postreform rates for an ambulatory shock reduced the fall into poverty caused by illness to 4.1 percent (poverty) and 3 percent (deep poverty); for hospitalization the economic costs was reduced to 3 percent (poverty) and 11 percent (deep poverty). The program also reduced the out-of-pocket expenses that the poor had to come up with by 50 to 60 percent. There was a 66 percent increase in child delivery assisted by a physician and a 49 percent increase in prenatal care. The program, however, has not been perfect. Despite the fact that its implementation was part of a national law that guaranteed the right to health care, Colombia has not had the resources to reach universal coverage. Furthermore, the insurance package in the subsidized scheme is not comparable to the coverage obtained by the contributory segment. There are, for example, limited benefits for disease prevention, birth, and basic services, and the quality of hospitals in the system is inferior.[79] Confronting significant political pushback, it has been difficult to transition out many traditional supply-side incentives. The contributory scheme has also been slow to incorporate the self-employed. Other structural changes that were planned to complement insurance reform also lag. Competition is limited due to missing scale economies in small localities or in specialized services.[80] The certification process of participating hospital partners has been slow as well. Some also worry about the sustainability of the program. The revision of the Colombian health care system was accompanied by an influx of resources that cannot be maintained over time. In the 1980s the Colombian government spent 1.2 percent of GDP on health. Between 1993 and 1996 commitments grew 21.6 percent a year, with public money reaching 3.6 percent of GDP in 1998 plus another 4.3 percent of GDP in private funds. In 2000, the total health care spending hovered at 8 percent. Further improvements must be made through efficiency-enhancing measures without the commitment of additional resources. Despite these drawbacks, enhanced insurance schemes are an interesting approach to extending health benefits to the poor. Ecuador is proposing the implementation of a similar insurance scheme targeted at the first and second quartiles. Currently, more than two-thirds of the population has no contributory health insurance, and the public institutions and MOH face severe constraints in providing health care to nearly half the population.[81] Changing the rules of the game to enhance effective demand through insurance, although imperfect, can make a huge difference.

The market, however, is not enough. Market-based insurance schemes are not sufficient allocators of health services. Some services—for example, aerial spraying to reduce dengue-carrying mosquitoes—would simply not take place without government. Without proper state guidance and oversight, the market alone often fails to provide equity and, in many cases, does not yield the expected improvements in efficiency. The market for health services involves a complicated array of interconnected markets, including health care professionals, pharmaceuticals, medical equipment, and education. Market failures in health delivery bedevil sophisticated industrial economies.[82] Marketization of health care may also lead to a fragmentation

Contaminated water is a leading cause of disease and mortality in Latin America. *(Copyright Pan American Health Organization)*

of services.[83] In Chile, for example, as funding chased the quantity of services offered, quality suffered. Decentralization negatively affected the excellent preventive care that had traditionally characterized the Chilean system, in which funding was targeted to curative as opposed to preventive purposes.[84] Furthermore, as workers were given a choice between private and public plans, the healthier participants were drawn to the private sector; those unable to get coverage from risk-averse private insurers were left on the public rolls. Finally, marketization is unlikely to work for those most severely affected by the health crisis in Latin America: the poor, particularly the indigenous, outside the market economy.

The challenge for policy in Latin America is to achieve a workable balance between private-sector participation and public-sector control to address critical health challenges in the region. Given the merit-based nature of investment in health, its dimensions as a public good, and the unpredictable nature of consumption services, state involvement is necessary. Partnerships among governments, multilateral lending agencies, and the nongovernmental community represent the key to health-sector reform. It is important to keep in mind that health care policies must be designed not only for nations but also for multiethnic communities within nations that may have differing health needs. Participation of communities with different traditional practices is critical in the design of health care policies.

Key   Concepts

AIDS	global public good	occupational health
cancer	Health for All (HFA)	concerns
domestic violence	heart disease	primary health care
epidemiological backlog	mental health	(PHC)
epidemiological transition	merit good	violence against women

Chapter   Summary

Latin America's Health Profile: Unequal Access and Quality

- The health profile in Latin America shows suffering from a wide variety of health-related problems, many of which stem from the inequality of access to quality health care and the inability of overburdened governments to provide universal health care services.
- Health care provision and quality vary dramatically with socioeconomic and ethnic status. Those who can afford to pay for it receive excellent care from well-trained medical staff, while those who rely on government services must deal with overcrowded, underresourced, lower-quality services.

Indigenous Groups and Women

- Indigenous groups and women are hit especially hard by health problems in Latin America. Stunting, malnutrition, obesity, malaria and other serious diseases, birth complications, and infant mortality occur with higher frequency in indigenous groups and women than in other sectors of the population.

Policy Reform: Striking a Balance between the Private and Public Sectors

- Inadequate health care institutions are major detriments to health performance in Latin America. Health care is most commonly delivered by a system made up of SSIs for formal-sector employees, private-sector providers, and an MOH for the poor.
- Policies to improve health care in Latin America should include increasing the health care choices made available to households, raising public financing to reflect local demand for health care, and striking a balance between the public and private sectors' roles in health care. Among solutions that have been used in Latin America are insurance schemes, which make health care affordable to the poor while increasing the accountability of health care providers.

Notes

M. Holly Peirce, PhD (Colby College graduating class of 1990), collaborated in the conceptualization and writing of this chapter.

1. Joan Nelson and Robert Kaufman, *The Political Economy of Health Sector Reforms: Cross National Comparisons,* Wilson Center update on the Americas May 2003, Creating Community series.

2. *Eliza Barclay, Mexican Migrant Communities May Be on Verge of HIV/AIDS Epidemic,* September 2005, Population Reference Bureau, http://www.prb.org/Template.cfm?Section=PRB&template=/ContentManagement/ContentDisplay.cfm&ContentID=13000.

3. Joan Nelson, "The Political of Health Sector Reform," in *Crucial Needs, Weak Incentives: Social Sector Reform, Democratization, and Globalization in Latin America,* ed. Robert R. Kaufman and Joan M. Nelson (Washington, D.C.: Woodrow Wilson Center Press and Johns Hopkins University Press, 2004), 27.

4. Population Reference Bureau, Prb.org 2005 World Population Data Sheet.

5. *Unicef Child Survival Report Card,* 2004, http://www.unicef.org/progressforchildren/2004v1/latinCaribbean.php, and Population Reference Bureau, 2005 World Population Data Sheet, Washington, D.C.

6. Denisard Alves and Walter Belluzzo, "Child Health and Infant Mortality in Brazil," IADB Latin American Research Network Working Paper No. R-493, April 2005.

7. World Bank, Government of Ecuador Program Information Document, Health Insurance Project, approved January 19, 2006.

8. Carlos Larrea, Pedro Montalvo, and Ana Ricaurt, "Child Malnutrition, Social Development and Health Services in the Andean Region," HEW 0509011, Economics Working Paper Archive EconWPA, 2005.

9. Ibid.

10. Patrícia Pelufo Silviera, André Krumel Portella, and Marcelo Zubaran Goldani, "Obesity in Latin America," *The Lancet* 366 (August 6, 2005).

11. D. Bloom, D. Canning, and J. Sevilla, "The Demographic Dividend: A New Perspective on the Economic Consequences of Population Change," www.policyproject.com/pubs/generalreport/Demo_Div.pdf, and State of the World Population 2003, http://www.unfpa.org/swp/2003/english/ch1/page3.htm.

12. PAHO, *Strategic and Programmatic Orientations, 1995–1998* (Washington, D.C.: Pan American Health Organization, 1995), PAHO Official Document 269, www.paho.org.

13. Emerging diseases are new diseases such as Lyme's disease. Chronic diseases develop slowly and persist over a period of time and are generally related to lifestyle. Degenerative diseases involve decay of the structure or function of tissue.

14. Jill Replogle, "Hunger on the Rise in Central America," *The Lancet* 363 (June 19, 2004): 2056, citing FAO data.

15. Replogle, "Hunger on the Rise."

16. FAO, *The State of Food Insecurity in the World,* 2005 fao.org.

17. "Latin American Indigenous People More Likely to Die from Malaria, Diarrhea and TB than their Counterparts," November 29, 2005, www.medicalnewstoday.com.

18. Erin Durlesser, Kerry Miller, Olivia Perlmutt, "Malaria in Latin America: A Nutritional Problem," http://www.micronutrient.org/idpas/pdf/1961MalariaInLA.pdf.

19. "Strategic Directions for Chagas Disease Research," www.who.int/tdr/diseases/chagas/direction.htm.

20. Marcela Valente, "Fighting Chagas Disease, Camera in Hand," IPS-Inter Press Service/Global Information Network, August 30, 2005.

21. IADB, "Reproductive Rights," Technical Notes No. 8, in Ana Langer and Gustavo Nigenda, *Sexual and Reproductive Health and Health Sector Reform in Latin America and the Caribbean: Challenges and Opportunities,* November 2001, www.iadb.org.

22. Barbara Kwast, "Reeducation of Maternal and Peri-natal Mortality in Rural and Peri-urban Settings: What Works?" *European Journal of Obstetrics and Gynecology and Reproductive Biology* 609 (1996): 49.

23. *Women in Development,* Technical Note No. 9.

24. Sidney Choque Schuler and Ruth Choque Schuler, "Misinformation, Mistrust, and Mistreatment: Family Planning among Bolivian Market Women," *Studies in Family Planning* 25 (1994): 214.

25. Miriam Krawczyk, "Women in the Region: Major Changes," *CEPAL Review* 49 (April 1993).

26. J. A. Casas, N. W. Dachs, and A. Bambas, "Health Disparities in Latin America and the Caribbean: The Role of Social and Economic Determinants," in *Equity and Health: Views from the Pan American Sanitary Bureau,* Occasional Publication No. 8 (Washington, D.C.: PAHO, 2001), 37.

27. Carolyn Stephens, Clive Nettleton, John Porter, Ruth Willis, and Stephanie Clark, "Indigenous People's Health—Why Are They behind Everyone, Everywhere?" *The Lancet* 366 (July 2, 2005): 11.

28. Gillette Hall and Harry Patrinos, "Indigenous Peoples, Poverty and Human Development in Latin America: 1994–2004," executive summary at web.worldbank.org; Gillette Hall and H. A. Patrinos, eds., *Indigenous Peoples, Poverty and Human Development in Latin America* (Houndsmill, Basingstoke, Hampshire, UK: Palgrave Macmillan), 2005.

29. Gillette Hall and Harry Anthony Patrinos, "Latin America's Indigenous Peoples," *Finance and Development* 42(4) (December 2005).

30. PAHO, *PAHO Resolution V: Health of Indigenous Peoples,* Series HSS/SILOS, 34 (Washington, D.C.: PAHO, 1993). Available at www.paho.org.

31. Anonymous, "Health of Indigenous Peoples," *Pan American Journal of Public Health* 2(25) (1997): 357–362.

32. Replogle, "Hunger on the Rise."

33. PAHO, "Report of the Working Group on PAHO in the 21st Century," August 24, 2005, CD 46/29, www.paho.org.

34. Antonio Giuffrida, William Savedoff, and Roberto Iunes, "Health and Poverty in Brazil: Estimation by Structural Equation Model with Latent Variables," March 2005, http://www.iadb.org/sds/publication/publication_4065_e.htm.

35. Visit PAHO's website at www.paho.org to read more about PAHO's goals and strategic plans.

36. PAHO, *Implementation of the Global Strategy: Health for All by the Year 2000,* Vol. 3 (Washington, D.C.: PAHO, 1993), 10.

37. Also referred to as multisectoral cooperation or collaboration and the health-development link.

38. "Cost Information and Management Decision in a Brazilian Hospital," *World Development Report* (1993): 60.

39. World Bank, *Poverty Reduction and the World Bank: Progress in Fiscal 1996 and 1997.* Available at www.worldbank.org.

40. Heidi Worley, "Chronic Diseases Beleaguer Developing Countries," Population Reference Bureau, prb.org, January 2006.

41. WHO, "Preventing Chronic Diseases: A Vital Investment 2005," www.who.org.

42. PAHO, "Cardiovascular Disease," www.paho.org.

43. UNAIDS Epidemic Update, Prevention Fact Sheet 21/11/2005, http://search.who .int/search?q=cache:AII5Iq27rXkJ:www.paho.org/Spanish/DD/PIN/FS_Prevention_Nov05 _en.pdf+UNAIDS.org+fact+sheet+2005&access=p&output=xml_no_dtd&ie=UTF-8&client=amro&proxystylesheet=amro&oe=UTF-8.

44. WHO, *Report on the Global HIV/AIDS Epidemic, June 1998* (Geneva: UNAIDS, 1998). Available at www.who.int/emc-hiv.

45. Seth Amgott, spokesman for Oxfam, quoted by Barbara Crossette, "US Drops Case over AIDS Drugs in Brazil," *New York Times,* June 26, 2001.

46. This section was authored by Margaret Knight, Colby College graduating class of 2002.

47. Tales Azzoni, "Latin American and Caribbean Nations Vow to Negotiate Price of AIDS Medication Together," Associated Press, January 15, 2006.

48. "South Africa's Moral Victory," *The Lancet* 357(28) (April 2001).

49. Flavia Sekles, "Brazil's AIDS Policies Tightly Link Prevention and Treatment," Population Reference Bureau www.prb.org, March 2005.

50. Caroline O. N. Moser and Cathy McIlwaine, "Latin American Urban Violence as a Development Concern: Towards a Framework for Violence Reduction," *World Development* 34(1) (January 2006): 89–112.

51. Testimony of Adolfo A. Franco, Assistant Administrator, Bureau for Latin America and the Caribbean, United States Agency for International Development, before the Committee on International Relations, U.S. House of Representatives, Subcommittee on the Western Hemisphere Wednesday, April 20, 2005, http://usinfo.state.gov/utils/printpage.html.

52. Moser and McIlwaine, "Latin American Urban Violence as a Development Concern."

53. PAHO, *Strategic and Programmatic Orientations, 1995–1998,* presented at the Inter-American Meeting, Washington, D.C., April 25–27, 1995. Available at www.paho.org.

54. "Out of the Underworld: Criminal Gangs in the Americas," *Economist,* January 5, 2006, www.economist.com.

55. Robert L. Ayres, *Crime and Violence as Development Issues in Latin America* (Washington, D.C.: World Bank, 1998).

56. DHS Report, *Domestic Violence Threatens Health of Children with Lower Immunization Rates, Higher Mortality Rates, Poor Nutrition,* Press release September 9, 2004.

57. Markjke Velzboer-Salcedo and Julie Novick, "Violence against Women in the Americas," *PAHO Perspectives in Health,* 5(2) (2000), available at www.paho.org.

58. Robert Kohn, Itzhak Levav, José Miguel Caldas de Almeida, Benjamín Vicente, Laura Andrade, Jorge Caraveo-Anduaga, Shekhar Saxena, and Benedetto Saraceno, *Revista Panamericana de Salud Pública/Pan American Journal of Public Health* 18(4–5) (October/November 2005): 229–240.

59. "Mental Disorders in Latin America and the Caribbean Forecast to Increase," December 2005, http://www.medicalnewstoday.com/medicalnews.php?newsid=34832#.

60. Ibid.

61. Hnin Hnin Pyne, Mariam Claeson, and Maria Correia, *Gender Dimensions of Alcohol Consumption and Alcohol-Related Problems in Latin America and the Caribbean* (Washington, D.C.: World Bank Publications, 2002).

62. "Mental Disorders in Latin America and the Caribbean Forecast to Increase."

63. William Savedoff, Antonio Giuffrida, and Roberto Iunes, "Economic and Health Effects of Occupational Hazards, IADB, Sustainable Development Department," June 2001, www.iadb.org.

64. WHO, *Integration of Health Care Delivery: Report of a WHO Study Group,* WHO Technical Report Series 861 (Geneva: WHO, 1996), table 5, "The Role of the Hospital in the District Health System."

65. It is important to remember that in most cases we are talking about more than one SSI. Often each public sector will have its own insurance fund and facilities, leading to unnecessary duplication within the sector not to mention across sectors.

66. Nelson and Kaufman, *The Political Economy of Health Sector Reforms.*

67. Ibid.

68. For an overview of the evolution of the Chilean health care system, see Jorge Jimenez de la Jara and Thomas J. Bossert, "Chile's Health Sector Reform: Lessons from Four Reform Periods," in *Health Sector Reform in Developing Countries: Making Health Development Sustainable,* ed. Peter Berman (Cambridge: Harvard University Press, 1995), 199–214.

69. Nelson and Kaufman, *The Political Economy of Health Sector Reforms,* 55.

70. Ibid., 56.

71. Tania Dmytraczenko, Vijay Rao, and Lori Ashford, *Health Sector Reform: How It Affects Reproductive Health,* Population Reference Bureau Policy Brief, June 2003.

72. Joan Nelson, "The Political of Health Sector Reform," in Nelson and Kaufman, *Crucial Needs, Weak Incentives,* citing L. C. Altobelli and J. Pancorvo, *Peru: Shared Administration Program and Local Health Administration Associations (CLAS)* (Washington, D.C.: World Bank and IESE, 2000).

73. D. R. Gwatkin, A. Wagstaff, A. S. Yazbeck, eds., *Reaching the Poor with Health, Nutrition, and Population Services: What Works, What Doesn't, and Why* (Washington, D.C.: World Bank, 2005).

74. PAHO, "Mexico," in *Health in the Americas,* Vol. 2 (Washington, D.C.: Pan American Health Organization, 1998), 370.

75. Harold Alderman and Victor Lavy, "Household Responses to Public Health Services: Cost and Quality Tradeoffs," *World Bank Research Observer* 11(1) (February 1996): 3–22.

76. Ricardo Britan and Keith McInnes, *The Demand for Health Care in Latin America,* Economic Development Institute Seminar Paper No. 46 (Washington, D.C.: World Bank, 1993).

77. Maria-Luisa Escobar, "Health Sector Reform in Colombia Development Outreach," Special Report, May 2005, World Bank Institute www.worldbank.org.

78. Patricia Ramírez, "A Sweeping Health Reform: The Quest for Unification, Coverage and Efficiency in Colombia," in Kaufman and Nelson, *Crucial Needs, Weak Incentives,* 150.

79. Ibid., 144.

80. Ibid., 143.

81. World Bank, Ecuador Public Information Document, www.worldbank.org, 2006.

82. David Swafford, "A Healthy Trend: Health Care Reform in Latin America," *Latin Finance* 83 (December 1996).

83. William C. Hsiao, "Marketization—The Illusory Magic Pill," *Health Economics* 3 (1994): 351–357.

84. WHO, *Integration of Health Care Delivery.*

CHAPTER THIRTEEN

EDUCATION POLICY
The Source of Equitable, Sustainable Growth

Education of rural indigenous children presents special challenges—older girls have responsibilities for siblings and animals. *(Photo courtesy of Emily Hoey)*

Education is the key to promoting equitable, sustainable growth in Latin America. ~~Education raises the level of human capital, enhancing a nation's productivity.~~ Reducing poverty rests upon upgrading basic skills as well as increasing the number of technologically sophisticated workers in the economy. A more informed citizenry is better able to participate in democratic decision making, demanding that government be accountable to the people. A better-educated populace will make wiser decisions about health and family planning, and it can participate more fully in environmentally sustainable development practices.

Few dispute the promise of education in enhancing the quality of life in Latin America, yet the record falls short by nearly any standard. Progress in education is good, but not good enough. Although there have been gains in universal access to education, quality suffers. Segments of the population are excluded from higher education by a primary and secondary school system that encourages repetition and dropping out rather than excellence. Public primary education has been emaciated as dollars are funneled into public university systems. Teachers are poorly trained and managed. Inadequate statistics provide little guidance or incentive for reform. Hard choices must be made between improving education at the primary level, providing quality secondary education to promote competitiveness in a global economy, and promoting the expansion of tertiary education for the poor and middle classes. Education is a catalyst for equitable development. Yet paradoxically, unequal access to education perpetuates exclusion and marginalization of the poor, rural citizens and the indigenous.

This chapter discusses the discouraging state of education in the region and assesses efforts and prospects for reform. Questions we will explore include the following:

- What does Latin America's report card on education look like?
- What are the causes of the **educational deficit** in the region?
- Should the private and the public sector invest more in education in Latin America? What is the balance between the role of the private sector and the state in educational reform?
- Should policies be focused on promoting demand for more (and better) education or on increasing the quantity and quality of the supply of educational opportunities?
- What roadblocks exist in fostering educational reform to promote equitable, sustainable development?

THE RECORD: GOOD BUT NOT GOOD ENOUGH

Advancing Enrollment

Education in Latin America has made great strides in recent decades, increasing access to segments of the population that previously had no formal schooling. More children are in school. As shown in table 13.1, the region has the highest gross primary school enrollment rates among developing countries, with 127 percent of

Table 13.1. Net and Gross Primary School Enrollment

Region	Gross Enrollment						Net Enrollment 2000	Repetition 2000	On-time Enrollment 2000	Grade 4 Survival 1999
	1960	1970	1980	1990	2000					
Sub-Saharan Africa	40	51	80	74	77		56	13	30	76
Middle East/North Africa	59	79	89	96	97		84	8	64	96
Latin America	91	107	105	106	127		97	12	74	86
South Asia	41	71	77	90	98		83	5	—	55
East Asia	87	90	111	120	111		93	2	56	97
East Europe/Former Soviet Union	103	104	100	98	100		88	1	67	97
OECD	109	100	102	103	102		97	2	91	99

Source: Paul Glewwe and Michael Kremer, "School, Teachers, and Education Outcomes in Developing Countries," CID Working Paper No. 122. Prepared as second draft of chapter for *The Handbook on the Economics of Education*, September 2005, Harvard University, based on UNESCO data.

school-age children in classes. This was fueled by the largest increase in the percentage of children entering and completing primary education as compared to any other developing world region.[1] But you may wonder how you can have more than 100 percent of the children enrolled. Gross rates pick up the number of students in primary school divided by the census data for children of that age. To exceed 100 percent, therefore, students above age grade are counted in the gross enrollment numbers. Net enrollment—adjusting out the children who were held back or the late starters—gives a more accurate picture of primary school performance. With high rates of repetition (region-wide averaging 12 percent) and an imperfect record of on-time enrollment, on a net basis enrollment in the region is 97 percent. High repetition, especially in the lowest grades, is mainly an indicator of inadequate learning, prompted in large part by the low quality of inputs into the system.[2] Students cannot reach grade-level norms without sufficient books, pencils, and trained teachers. Rural students often find themselves unable to complete a school year due to harvest seasons and must repeat the same grade in the fall. Reducing repetition rates would release resources for new educational opportunities.

Advances have taken place at the secondary level as well as the primary level. Enrollment rates grew 7 percent annually in secondary school between 1990 and 1998, doubling the number of pupils getting some postprimary education. As shown in table 13.2, secondary gross enrollment rates between 1960 and 2000 soared from 14 to 86 percent. The educational profile of the average Latin American is indeed far different than it was even ten years ago, when secondary enrollments were just under half the relevant age cohort. In measuring secondary enrollment, it is common to use gross figures. Although one should be cautious with intercountry comparisons, table 13.2 shows secondary enrollments on a net basis by country and gender. It is telling that in 1995 half the countries in the region didn't even maintain standardized data on secondary enrollments; for those reporting, we can see significant jumps as well as minimal discrepancies based on gender. Indeed, in most cases of gender imbalance it is the girls who are staying in school longer. But getting kids to school doesn't mean they'll stay. Although most Latin American nations require some secondary schooling by law, enforcement is weak, and those not advancing tend to drop out of the system. Additional enrollments, however, haven't translated into as strong performance in terms of the average years of school held by those more than fifteen years old. Latin Americans have 5.7 years as compared to 6.5 for Asia. In a globalized economy if the productivity of human capital isn't enhanced, gains in enrollment and literacy may barely preserve existing standards of living in Latin America. Workers in Latin America have less education than counterparts in East Asia and Eastern Europe; Latin America is rising, but East Asia is rising faster.[3] The gains from education accrue most pointedly after one finishes high school. Overcoming this secondary education hump can generate increases in wages on the order of 50–70 percent.

Tertiary school enrollment is also rising. Although tertiary education data is not directly comparable over time due to a change in the definition, we can broadly interpret the numbers in table 13.3 to reflect a commitment by students in Latin America to continue with noncompulsory education either in technical fields such as education, nursing, or architecture or traditional theoretical subject areas such as

Table 13.2. Secondary Enrollment and Literacy

	Secondary School Enrollment Gross Enrollment (% of students of secondary school age)					Average Years of School Adults Age 15+					Literacy Rates Adults Age 15+				
Region	1960	1970	1980	1990	2000	1960	1970	1980	1990	2000	1960	1970	1980	1990	2000
Sub-Saharan Africa	5	6	15	23	27	1.7	2	2.3	3	3.4	24	41	54	67	77
Middle East/North Africa	13	25	42	56	66	1.4	2.2	2.9	4.1	5.4	33	54	66	76	83
Latin America	14	28	42	49	86	3.2	3.7	4.4	5.3	6	67	84	90	93	95
South Asia	10	23	27	39	47	1.5	2	3	3.8	4.6	26	43	52	61	69
East Asia	20	24	44	48	67	2.5	3.4	4.6	5.6	6.2	54	83	91	95	97
East Europe/Former Soviet Union	55	64	93	90	88	6.5	7.6	8.5	9	9.7	93	99	100	100	100
OECD	65	77	87	95	107	7.5	7.8	9.1	9.5	10.1	95	98	99	100	100

Source: Paul Glewwe and Michael Kremer, "School, Teachers, and Education Outcomes in Developing Countries," CID Working Paper No. 122, Prepared as second draft of chapter for *The Handbook on the Economics of Education*, September 2005, Harvard University, based on UNESCO data.

Table 13.3.   Enrollment by Education Level and Gender

	Gross Pre-primary				Net Secondary				Gross Tertiary			
	1996		2002		1995		2002		1995		2002	
	M	F	M	F	M	F	M	F	M	F	M	F
Argentina	53	56	60	61	—	—	79	83	32	44	45	67
Bolivia	44	44	47	48	—	—	72	71	29	20	—	—
Brazil	53	54	57	57	—	—	69	74	12	14	16	21
Chile	97	98	49	49	52	57	78	79	30	26	44	41
Colombia	33	34	37	37	42	49	51	56	15	16	23	25
Costa Rica	71	70	60	61	39	13	48	52	33	28	18	21
Cuba	88	87	115	114	52	63	86	86	10	16	29	29
Ecuador	55	56	73	76	—	—	50	51	22	14	—	—
El Salvador	39	42	47	50	21	23	48	49	19	19	16	19
Guatemala	35	34	55	56	—	—	30	29	13	4	19	8
Honduras	13	14	21	22	—	—	—	—	12	10	13	17
Mexico	72	74	80	82	—	—	59	61	16	14	22	21
Nicaragua	23	24	27	28	30	35	36	42	11	12	17	19
Panama	39	37	55	56	—	—	60	66	24	36	35	55
Paraguay	51	71	30	30	37	39	49	51	10	11	16	22
Peru	36	37	57	59	54	52	70	68	28	26	32	31
Uruguay	44	46	63	64	—	—	68	76	25	32	27	48
Venezuela	44	45	52	53	18	27	27	64	30	27	39	42

Source: Preal, Quantity without Quality: A Report Card on Education in Latin America 2006.

history or economics. The diversification of the postsecondary educational network has expanded to include polytechnic training institutes, traditional universities, and new universities (public and private). Through the explosion of the Internet as well as international exchanges, universities have become linked to their international counterparts, spurring internal reorganization of faculties and upgrading of degrees and skill bases. Region-wide networks of private research centers such as the Facultad Latinoamericana de Ciencias Sociales entirely separate from the universities, have also flourished, producing an important body of scholarship on Latin America, in part through funding from international donor agencies such as the Ford Foundation.[4] The number of students in higher education in Brazil more than doubled from 1995 to 2004; in Argentina 62 percent and in Chile 53 percent of young people start university.[5] Although this growth is impressive, Latin America trails many East Asian countries in the commitment to expand tertiary education; worldwide enrollment in tertiary education has risen 50 percent in developing countries. Figure 13.1 illustrates how Argentina, Brazil, and Chile—regional leaders in university education—lag behind global competitors with lower percentages of people receiving at least a two-year college degree. Furthermore, although students are beginning university, graduation rates are low. In Argentina, for example, only 8 percent finish their degree, perhaps driven by the rising need to provide private financing. This low graduation rate might be contrasted to the 27 percent of Thai students

Figure 13.1.   Percentage of People Receiving at Least a Two-Year College Degree

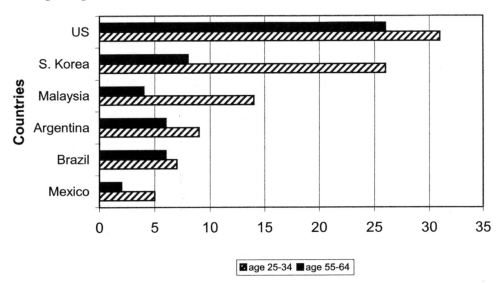

Source: OECD data for 2001/2 presented in David Luhnow and John Lyons, "In Latin America, Rich-Poor Chasm Stifles Growth," *Wall Street Journal* July 18, 2005; page A.

who begin programs and complete the degree.[6] With premiums paid to advanced skills in the global economy, Latin America's progress can be seen as insufficient.

Unequal Education

Rather than promoting opportunity and class mobility, education has perpetuated inequality in Latin America. The paradox of education in Latin America is that the principle of opportunity provided by public schooling has been subverted, resulting in unequal outcomes. Primary and secondary schooling continue to be segregated by class. The wealthy send their children to the best private primary and secondary schools, capturing prized places in competitive public universities. Inequality by class, race, and geography are the strongest variables in explaining income inequality. From childhood, people with different sociogeographic characteristics are treated differently and accumulate different levels of human capital.[7] In Bolivia the poorest fifth of society receive 5.2 years of education as compared to the 12.6 years among the richest fifth. Whereas education as a motor of equality promotes the broadest access to opportunity for the least advantaged, in Latin America the pyramid of opportunity is inverted. Very few from the base economic classes have the chance to achieve advanced education; opportunities accrue most frequently for those already endowed with privilege.

But the news on inequality is not all bad. A larger percentage of poor kids are starting school. In Brazil, enrollment among the lowest quintile rose from 75 to 93 percent from 1992 to 2001.[8] When we measure enrollments, we observe an improvement in the ratios of the poorest to the richest 20 percent of society in six- to twelve-year-old enrollment rates. Brazil evidenced the largest change, from a 26 point spread in 1990 (70 percent of poorest in school versus 96 percent of the rich) to a 6 percent margin (93 percent of the poor and 99 percent of the rich). This is a dramatic change in getting less-advantaged kids into school. The gaps between richest and poorest in enrollment are also largely declining in the thirteen- to seventeen-year-old cohort, although the performance is more heterogeneous. Argentina, for example, cut the gap from 21 to 12 points, but it rose in Bolivia from 38 to 48 points as well as in Uruguay from 24 to 30 points. There is an increase in school enrollment of the poor in the eighteen- to twenty-three-year-old category, but the richest category is rising faster than the poorest. The gaps between the average years of schooling in the richest cohort and the poorest cohort have declined in most countries. In Chile, for example, where the gap among the "older" forty-one- to fifty-year-old cohorts is at 6.2, it is at 5 for the twenty-one- to thirty-year-old cohorts. Nonetheless, the gap is likely to rise again as the better-off pursue more education at the tertiary level.

But the quality of schooling for the poor leaves much to be desired. Despite trends toward equalizing enrollments, poor children perform worse than wealthy kids on national exams.[9] Even for those remaining in school, the gaps are glaring. In Ecuador, indigenous fifth-graders score 20 percent below nonindigenous children in language and math. The difference between the scores of the top and bottom quarters of the income scale taking the PISA (an international test measuring reading literacy) range from 67 in Brazil to 91 in Argentina—as opposed to 34 in Organization for Economic Cooperation and Development (OECD) countries. Interestingly, however, this class difference parallels the top to bottom quintile differences in the United States, whose score is 85. This, of course, is not surprising given academic resources. The poor receive less than a fifth of all education spending. In Nicaragua, the wealthiest quintile receives one-third of public spending on education; the poorest gets a meager tenth. Nicaragua invests seven times more on each university student than it spends on each primary student. This disproportionate investment is not, however, region-wide, as El Salvador and Chile invest equally at the two levels. But given inadequate primary and secondary schooling, poor children rarely get to university, so money spent at that level doesn't reach them.

The good news is that with respect to gender equity, Latin America scores fairly well. With the exception of indigenous communities, there is little difference between boys and girls in their likelihood to attend or complete schooling. Investments in girls' education is critical due to connections between low levels of female education and overall health levels. Box 13.1 illustrates the benefits of education for Daniela, an indigenous Bolivian girl. An increase of between one and three years of a mother's schooling can reduce infant mortality by 15 percent; the comparable rate for men is 6 percent. In Peru, it was shown that an addition of six years of schooling cut infant mortality by a dramatic 75 percent. In addition to having better income-earning capabilities, women with education make greater use of prenatal health

Box 13.1. Gender and Education

by Courtney Fry

Daniela is an indigenous girl striving to overcome numerous obstacles to obtain an education. She is a ten-year-old fifth-grader at the Carmen Guzmán de Mier School, a school in Oruro, Bolivia, supported by the nongovernmental organization (NGO) Save the Children. Daniela resides in an area of Bolivia called the Altiplano, one of the poorest regions of South America. As recently as the previous generation, approximately 70 percent of indigenous girls did not complete primary school.[10] Even now, many girls do not attend school and are working either at home, in the fields, or at some other job. Daniela says, "If I weren't studying, I would have to go to the field to take care of the sheep just like my friend Marlene. She does not go to school and she does not speak Spanish."[11]

BENEFITS OF GIRLS' EDUCATION

The most obvious advantage to improving access to girls' education is the opening of new opportunities in the job market for more women. Numerous studies have shown the correlation between more education and a higher income. At the age of ten, Daniela already understands the importance of education. She says, "If I don't study I will have to work as a household servant in other people's homes. I want my life to be different from my mother's life." Daniela aspires to be either a lawyer or an engineer, and she knows that she will have to continue far in her education to reach this goal.

The benefits of girls' education are not simply limited to the job market. Because the children of educated women have a much better likelihood of attending school, improvements made today in girls' access to education also have a positive effect on the education achievements of children in the future. Only about 20 percent of children of poorly educated parents in Latin America complete secondary education, the amount of education regarded as necessary for a poor person to pull him- or herself out of poverty.[12] Moreover, the mother's education has more than twice the influence on school attendance than the father's.[13] Daniela's education will not only allow her to earn more money, but her children will have a better chance at a more prosperous life as well. She says, "When I have children, they will have better opportunities than I did, because I will educate them."

Health and education are inextricably linked, and mounting evidence suggests that a woman's education has a direct effect on the health of her children. The countries that have yet to close the gender gap in education are among the poorest countries in the region and have some of the worst health indicators. Bolivia by far has the worst infant mortality rate in Latin America at fifty-three deaths per one thousand live births, and Guatemala ranks second with thirty-five deaths per one thousand live births.[14] According to one study, an additional year of girls' education can bring infant mortality rates down by 5–10 percent.[15] Daniela aspires to earn enough money as a professional to be able to pay for health care for herself and her children. A study conducted in Brazil shows that within a family, a woman's resources have twenty times the effect of a man's on the children's health.[16] Women who obtain at least a complete primary education are also more likely to have less children. Having fewer children per family is a factor in determining poverty and the likelihood of children attending school.[17]

COUNTRIES THAT REMAIN BEHIND

Despite rapid progress on improving girls' access to education in much of Latin America, a gender gap persists in some of the least-developed countries, including Bolivia, Guatemala, and Peru. These countries all have substantially lower female literacy rates and

continued

continued

female secondary school enrollment rates than that of males.[18] Many factors contribute to the parents' decision not to send their daughter to school. Some poor parents cannot afford to send all their children to school due to the many direct and indirect costs of obtaining an education. In such cases, poor families tend to choose to send boys to school instead of girls. Girls often must stay at home to complete household chores and take care of younger siblings when both the mother and father work outside of the home. Also, the distance to school or safety concerns may influence a parent's decision. For indigenous communities, there are cultural barriers as well. Indigenous women are among the least educated in Latin American society.[19] The three countries with the largest gender gap in education also have a considerable percentage of the population who are indigenous.

Thanks to efforts by Save the Children and other NGOs and governments throughout the region, many girls like Daniela have the opportunity to go to school and pursue their goals. However, some girls, such as Daniela's friend Marlene, still do not attend school. Improving gender equality in education is a necessary step to addressing the poverty and inequality that plague countries such as Bolivia, Guatemala, and Peru.

services and are generally healthier themselves.[20] Evidence suggests that for countries of similar labor force and capital stock, if the ratio of females to males at given levels of education falls below 0.75, gross domestic product (GDP) growth is likely to be 25 percent lower. Investment in girls' education clearly has public returns. Nonetheless, in terms of income foregone and relatively low levels of economic opportunity, the private costs of educating girls are high. Girls are needed in the home and on the farm to help with chores and to supervise younger siblings. Many families simply cannot afford the indirect costs of schooling.[21] Despite the fact that one out of ten persons in the continent is estimated to have some form of a disability, little attention is paid to the educational needs of the disabled. Rural migrant workers' children are rarely incorporated into educational systems. There is a radical separation between the region's educational systems and its growing development needs in competitive, open democracies. A key challenge for education in the region is not to simply augment schooling for children but also to provide training for those who have traditionally been excluded from opportunity in society.

The Indigenous and Education

The gravity of the educational deficit is greater for the indigenous in Latin America. The direct and indirect costs of education to the poor—the clothes, shoes, books, transportation, or perhaps room and board in the nearest large village for middle or high school as well as the foregone earnings of the child—are compounded by a frequent inability to speak Spanish. Ten percent of Mexicans do not speak Spanish. In Guatemala, 60 percent of the indigenous people have no education.[22] On average, the number of years of schooling for indigenous Guatemalan males is 1.8 years and for females 0.9 years as opposed to their nonindigenous counterparts with 4.5 and 4 years each. The scant evidence available indicates that working-age adults with indigenous or African backgrounds in Peru, Guatemala, Brazil, and Bolivia have three fewer years of education compared to their white counterparts.

Particularly for those in the agricultural sector, the opportunity costs of indigenous children's labor is high. In Bolivia, the incidence of no schooling for monolingual indigenous is 77.9 percent, bilingual indigenous 11 percent, and non-indigenous 2.8 percent, indicating that basic education is not equitably distributed over different ethnic groups.[23] In Peru the difference between indigenous and non-indigenous education levels is narrowing to approximately 20 percent. Nevertheless, when analyzed by gender, indigenous females continue to receive less than half the education of their nonindigenous counterparts, perhaps reflecting the difficult investment decisions that families face with respect to education. Given scarce resources, the indigenous poor may choose to invest in their male children who have a greater probability of remaining in the labor market than in their female children for whom the cultural perception is that they will return to the home.[24]

More education, however, is not the simple answer. Education in the indigenous communities may also have unintended cultural effects. Educational programs may work to obliterate the distinctive languages and customs of the indigenous. Box 13.2 discusses problems and the potential of bilingual education. Participation of indigenous leaders is critical to ensure the transfer of traditional customs and practices as part of the child's educational experience. Bilingual education can facilitate this process of preserving cultural practices. Change should be respectful of local cultures but should open up opportunities for the indigenous poor. Educational policy must be informed by the needs of the target group.

Box 13.2.   Bilingual Education of Spanish with Indigenous Languages

by Courtney Fry

BRIEF HISTORY OF BILINGUAL EDUCATION IN LATIN AMERICA

Rafael Chanchari is of the Shawi people of Peru, one of the forty indigenous groups who live in Peru's Amazon region. Growing up in the 1970s, Rafael experienced firsthand the negative influences that formal education can have on indigenous people, most notably in the alienation of children from their own ethnic customs.[25] Since colonization, the Europeans and their descendants have imposed their own language and traditions on indigenous people. Although the 1900s saw a gradual shift in the government rhetoric toward acceptance of indigenous groups, a gap remains between talk and actions. During the 1970s, Latin American countries began a concerted effort to expand public education into rural areas, including many indigenous communities. Some communities resisted this intrusion of Western ideas into their territory. Many indigenous people, however, welcomed the expansion of the formal education system. Parents believed that their children's best chance of escaping poverty was through formal education taught by nonindigenous teachers. The increasing participation in and dependence on the market economy further entrenched these parents' beliefs that a Western education was more important for their children than their own knowledge and customs. However, the formal education that most

continued

continued

indigenous children received during the 1970s provided them very few useful skills to advance in society. Many indigenous children who finished primary school could barely read, do basic math, or speak Spanish. In addition, Western teachers tended to put down the indigenous way of life in their teaching. As a result, children left school with no way to earn a decent living and with a negative view of their own culture.[26] Rafael observes, "My people lost their freedom when schooling expanded throughout our communities."[27]

Latin American countries gradually accepted the need to incorporate bilingual education into the public education system. However, the lost decade of the 1980s delayed progress. The World Bank, the Inter-American Development Bank (IADB), and other developmental institutions funded various studies that demonstrated that bilingual education for indigenous children improves the quality of learning, reduces repetition rates, and increases the years of schooling.[28] The promotion and financing of bilingual education programs by the development institutions and several countries prompted eighteen Latin American countries to adopt bilingual education by 2004.[29]

THE STATUS OF BILINGUAL EDUCATION AND INDIGENOUS SCHOOLING TODAY

Despite the widespread acceptance and adoption of bilingual education, indigenous children still lag behind in educational achievements. The qualifications of teachers and the quality of education provided indigenous students are generally worse than that provided to nonindigenous students.[30] Mexico spends approximately four times as much on each urban middle-class student than on rural indigenous students.[31] In Bolivia, Guatemala, and Mexico, the average number of years of schooling for nonindigenous children is more than three years higher than that for indigenous children. Indigenous children also have higher repetition and drop out rates than nonindigenous children, and indigenous girls have the worst literacy rates and enrollment rates in the region.[32]

Most indigenous activists promote bilingual education as a way to improve the schooling results of the indigenous population. No one doubts the need to provide bilingual education that values indigenous languages and traditions, but the methodology behind the different programs and the extent of the reforms vary greatly throughout the region. Some programs simply teach the existing curriculum for the first few years of school in the native language, while others overhaul the entire curriculum content as well as the teaching methods. Outside factors such as budgetary constraints, lack of school materials, underqualified teachers, and teacher resistance to change have also impeded progress on implementing many bilingual education programs. In addition to the supply-side constraints, bilingual programs still must overcome parental opposition. Literacy to indigenous parents means reading in Spanish, not an indigenous language. Many indigenous parents want their children to learn Spanish as quickly as possible to improve their standing in the job market.[33] For indigenous children in Guatemala, the average number of years of schooling is about 2.5 years.[34] If the first two years of primary education are taught in the children's native tongue, they will have little exposure to Spanish, if any, before they leave school. Such drawbacks produce wide gaps between the proindigenous rhetoric espoused by governments and developmental institutions and the reality of indigenous education today.

BILINGUAL EDUCATION SUCCESSES

Despite these challenges, there are some programs that are making a positive difference in the lives of indigenous children. In Peru, Juan Carlos Godenzzi, the head of the National Unit of Bilingual Intercultural Education, a division of the National Office of Elementary Education, and his staff of four produced ninety-four teaching manuals in several different indigenous languages between 1997 and 2001. They also joined forces with NGOs and local universities to train more than ten thousand teachers in bilingual education.[35]

Formed in 1988, Formación de Maestros Bilingües de la Amazonía Peruana (FORMABIAP) is one of the NGOs in Peru that specializes in training teachers for effective bilingual instruction. Instead of using the indigenous languages to smooth the transition to Spanish, FORMABIAP uses methods that teach children to value their own language and maintain it. Central to the training is respect for indigenous communities and their way of life. Teachers incorporate into their lessons the knowledge and traditions of the communities in which they teach and also include parents and community leaders in the education of the children. The success of FORMABIAP-trained teachers in improving the quality of education in indigenous communities has even won the support of parents who formerly opposed bilingual education.[36]

Indigenous communities select the teacher they want to send to the FORMABIAP training. Training takes five years to complete, including both scholastic work and fieldwork in the community in which they will teach. There are three major goals to the FORMABIAP training: improve the quality of education in indigenous communities, cultivate understanding of and respect for indigenous knowledge and traditions, and encourage environmental education to promote the sustainable development of their respective communities. Additional programs offered by FORMABIAP include training teachers who already teach without a degree and training in intercultural early childhood education.[37]

Rafael overcame the setbacks of his early education career and is now a teacher who utilizes bilingual education in his classroom. As a result of his FORMABIAP training, he is able to provide a quality education to the children in his community without sacrificing their cultural heritage or identity. Culturally sensitive teacher training, such as that promoted by FORMABIAP, is an important step toward obtaining quality bilingual intercultural education for all indigenous children.

Educational Finance: Who Pays

Improvements in education in Latin America are fueled in part by a growing commitment by the state to funding education. Public spending on education has increased from 2.7 percent of GDP in 1990 to 4.3 percent in 2002–2003—and is above the average for low- and middle-income countries. If private spending is added, this number increases; in Brazil, for example, it rises to 10 percent.[38] Nonetheless, per-pupil spending is still low and variable, from $190 in Nicaragua to $1,400 in Chile as compared to the $4,933 spent in the largely industrial OECD countries. A smaller absolute GDP and a larger cohort of children combine to reflect lower spending per student. The United States on average spends more than $6,000 dollars per pupil on primary and secondary education; Costa Rica, a regional leader in education, only edges over $1,000. This data is already adjusted for the fact that a dollar may go further in Costa Rica. The dismal fact is that at the bottom of the rung, Guatemala, Peru, and El Salvador spend less than $250 per pupil.

In addition to being low compared to OECD numbers, it is inefficient as measured against Asian competitors. When we look at the inflation-adjusted purchasing power parity (PPP) per student expenditures in table 13.4, a curious fact emerges: Latin America is actually spending more than twice as much at both the primary and secondary levels as South and East Asia—yet is barely keeping up with Asian competitors in terms of outcomes. Education finance in Latin America reflects an inverted pyramid. That is, as compared to expenditures in OECD countries, there is

Table 13.4. Educational Expenditures

Region	Expenditure per Student U.S. dollars		Expenditure per Student PPP dollars		Expenditure as a % of GDP		Expenditure per Student as a % of GDP per Capita		Expenditure per Tertiary Student as a Ratio of Expenditure per Student at Lower Levels	
	Primary	Secondary	Primary	Secondary	Primary	Secondary	Primary	Secondary	Primary	Secondary
Sub-Saharan Africa	68	171	338	638	1.9	1.2	10.6	25.8	198.5	81.1
Middle East/North Africa	157	316	429	809	1.8	1.4	15	19.5	5.4	5.3
Latin America	364	504	588	877	1.6	1.6	12.2	14.3	4.3	4
South Asia	34	66	167	322	1	1.2	7.4	22	5.6	3.3
East Asia	66	101	214	347	0.9	0.8	6.6	11.8	12.5	6.5
East Europe/Former Soviet Union	564	555	1,401	1,250	0.2	2.3	21.4	19.1	2	1.5
OECD	4,310	5,655	3,760	4,933	1.2	2.1	18.6	22.8	1.8	1.5

Source: Paul Glewwe and Michael Kremer, "School, Teachers, and Education Outcomes in Developing Countries," CID Working Paper No. 122, Prepared as second draft of chapter for *The Handbook on the Economics of Education*, September 2005, Harvard University, based on UNESCO data.

a higher proportion of public money spent on tertiary education as a ratio of primary or secondary than in more developed countries. As compared to other developing regions, however, this investment in technical and university training on the part of governments is common—if not the optimal expenditure for public dollars.

One indirect measure of the failure of public education systems in Latin America is the prevalence of private education at the lower levels. Officially recognized private education institutions in Latin America teach one out of four students: 26 percent of the preschoolers, 16 percent of the primary grades, 25 percent of secondary education, and 36 percent of those in higher education.[39] Although education is free and compulsory for all through ninth grade in nearly all countries, inadequate quality of schooling pushes families toward private-sector choices, especially at the secondary level. Most private schools are subsidized by the state through student loans, research grants, direct subsidies, **vouchers,** tax exemption for nonprofit training, or skills upgrading for teachers. Private schools are not exclusively for the rich; through subsidies, private institutions also serve some poor or underprivileged clients. Students in private schools tend to perform better on standardized tests, indicating that something is awry in the public sector. The exception to this is university education. Some of the finest universities in the region are public but at a higher cost than private schools. Private schools are able to keep overhead and unit costs at all levels of schooling lower, highlighting potential areas for efficiency gains in public schools. Of course it should be noted that private schools can select students and therefore don't bear the same financial burdens in educating disabled or disruptive students at the primary and secondary levels. They also may not share the same objectives as public schools; for example, a public university may have an objective of developing scientific research in the public interest where the mission of a private institution may be narrower.

Gaps in funding also require that every public school secure private income. Parents are obligated to contribute to public education through student fees, semivoluntary parental contributions, textbooks, exam fees, uniforms, and gifts through parent-teacher associations. Parents contribute 20 percent of the public costs of primary education in Peru, equal to approximately fifty dollars for primary and secondary education. These educational costs in supposedly free public education can be prohibitive for poor families with multiple children, further limiting opportunity through education.

LIFELONG LEARNING

Literacy is recognized as a human right for the set of benefits it confers to make informed decisions, expand personal empowerment, and open opportunities for both passive and active participation in local and global social communities.[40] Literacy is defined as the acquisition and use of reading, writing, and numeracy skills, thereby developing active citizenship and improving livelihoods and gender equality. Literacy development engages a continuous process that requires sustained learning and practice. Despite this broad definition, its measurement is far more basic, focusing in most countries on completing fourth grade in primary school. Literacy has risen in Latin America from approximately two-thirds of the population possessing basic reading skills in 1960 to 95 percent of the population aged fifteen and older being able to read today. Rates for adult literacy (adjusting for the fifteen- to twenty-four-year-old cohort) hover around 90 percent. Nonetheless, there is great variability. Five countries (Honduras, El Salvador, Belize, Nicaragua, and Guatemala) have disappointing rates of illiteracy above 20 percent. In Peru and Bolivia, female illiteracy is almost three times that of males.[41] Although classical illiteracy or the ability to write one's name as a sample message has fallen, many remain functionally illiterate, unable to read and respond to written instructions. Close to 80 percent of low-income students in Latin America cannot understand written messages after six years of schooling. Furthermore, the content delivered by educational systems is isolated from the investments in human capital demanded by global society.[42]

Education As Social Change

Educational reform should not be limited to the walls of the classroom. In developing countries, adult learners play a large role in the educational challenge. Those who support education as a vehicle for social change argue that education should be used to empower the poor to participate in defining their own needs and transforming their physical world. The late Brazilian sociologist Paulo Freire, in his pathbreaking *Pedagogy of the Oppressed,* provided a methodology by which community-based groups, through the identification of common symbols, would become "consciencitized" to the causes of their poverty and empowered through education to change their situation. Freire rejects the "banking concept" of education, in which students are stocked with facts but rarely enter into a dialogue with instructors that is useful in transforming social reality.[43] Instead, Freire advocates the communal problematizing of local conditions and using education as a means of change and empowerment through a process of community-based culture circles. Based upon Freire's concepts, an adult literacy movement was launched in Brazil in the 1990s utilizing partnerships between community-based organization and cities such as São Paulo to recruit and train adult learners and facilitators. With a cost per learner of sixty-two dollars, the program was expanded in 2003 under Literate Brazil, funding government agencies and NGOs to support training, snacks, textbooks, and evaluation of literacy programs.[44] A more contemporary example of using problem solving to spur individual investments in education can be seen in the computer-driven learning initiatives sponsored by the Brazilian telecommunications firm Telemar. Through its foundation, Telemar underwrites hardware and software needs to help young community members solve local problems. Grants have helped create web pages to promote social programs ranging from safe sex to recycling.

Ivan Illich, an Austrian-born social critic, in the 1960s and 1970s made Cuernavaca, Mexico, his home. He argued for "deschooling," or the breakup of the formal (and expensive) educational system in favor of creating mechanisms at the local level to transform the lives of the poor.[45] Nonformal education based on mass media, the distribution of printed materials, and group sessions animated by a local contact may cost a third or a fifth of the unit cost in primary education.[46] Adult education is a central element of the goal of Universal Access to Education for 2010 adopted by the Miami summit. Simply reforming the school will leave generations of the economically active population without the skills to compete in the global environment. Adult education and empowerment will contribute to human capital development in the region. Lessons from a mass literacy campaign in Ecuador demonstrated that broad participation of society is possible, that acceptable learning results can be achieved with a concrete pedagogical plan, that young students can be engaged as effective literacy facilitators, and that the public opinion and participation can be garnered through demonstration of good practices.[47]

WEAK OUTPUTS

Latin America nations have improved on basic quantitative educational measures —more kids are sitting at desks throughout the region. However, despite increasing the number of students in the system—or perhaps because of them—outputs are weak. Students may be coming to school in greater numbers, but completion rates are inadequate and uneven between the urban and rural sectors. Twelve percent of the 50.5 million young people between fifteen and nineteen years old in the region have not been able to finish primary school.[48] In Guatemala, fewer than half of those in the rural sector finish primary school. In Nicaragua, Honduras, and Guatemala, less than 50 percent of the poorest quintile complete primary school; only six countries (Argentina, Chile, Uruguay, Venezuela, Ecuador, and Mexico) show completion rates of above 80 percent for all socioeconomic groups.[49] Although primary education repetition rates have declined from 29 percent in 1988 to 11 percent in 2002, they still hover at more than double the world average of 5.6 percent.[50] This repetition, reflective of the poor quality of educational inputs to allow students to advance, costs the region more than $11 billion a year, according to UNESCO. Brazil pays the bulk at $8 billion a year; rates are also high in Mexico and Argentina. With 27 percent of students overage for grade levels, teaching resources are wasted in regurgitating the same material that was not assimilated the first time through.

Only three countries in Latin America (Argentina, Peru, and Chile) have at least 60 percent of the twenty- to twenty-four-year-old population finishing secondary schooling; in three (Guatemala, Honduras, and Nicaragua) it is less than 30 percent.[51] In the rural sector, only Peru, Venezuela, and Chile have high school completion rates above 30 percent. The regional average (unweighted by population) is a dismal 20.5 percent; for a rural person to have completed secondary school in Guatemala, Honduras, or Nicaragua, the student would have had to defy nearly insurmountable odds as the completion rates in these countries are 8.9 percent, 4.8 percent, and 7.3 percent, respectively.[52] It is no wonder that agricultural productivity in the rural sector is low and poverty is pervasive; the complementary human capital is clearly lacking.

More nuanced qualitative metrics are lacking region-wide. Despite agreeing to the goal of evaluating educational outcomes in the Summit of the Americas process, no system has implemented a comprehensive national standard for education.[53] As much as most students and teachers dread national exams, without some form of standardized testing it is difficult to measure the quality of learning over time. Benchmarks are necessary in measuring progress. Existing national education statistics are largely weak, further complicating the evaluation process.[54] Latin American education systems lack a culture of assessment, have a limited financial and staffing commitment to testing, and confront obstacles in the transparent reporting of results. Some countries are beginning to value the information they can provide in improving education by developing national tests to measure learning, and more countries are participating in global tests. There are pockets of progress and some good best case examples, but change is uneven and incomplete. In some areas teachers are given a curriculum but are not shown how to evaluate progress. Even where testing does take place, there is little accountability for the results or consequences for the schools to promote change.

Beyond national testing, few countries participate in international assessments to measure learning. One might guess that those willing to risk international scrutiny are among the better educational systems in the region, but even they perform poorly on global tests.[55] In the 2003 Program for International Students Assessment, only three Latin American countries participated—Brazil, Mexico, and Uruguay—and they scored near the bottom in reading, math, and science among the forty-one countries testing. Half of Latin American students had serious difficulties using reading to extend knowledge and skills, and three-quarters of Brazilian children, two-thirds of Mexicans, and half of the Uruguayans could not consistently apply basic mathematical skills to explore and understand an everyday situation—as compared to one of five in OECD countries. Results from the Trends in International Mathematics and Science Study were similarly discouraging. Chilean eighth-graders scored between 50 and 70 points lower than its GDP would have predicted; despite investment in education, scores remained unchanged between 1999 and 2003. Something has surely been going wrong.[56] Teaching materials are poor (when they even exist), and some teachers haven't even graduated from high school themselves. Rural students are most deprived, with unprepared teachers, scarce resources, and limitations on the number of grades offered.[57] Teachers are often underpaid, resulting in frequent strikes as well as low morale.[58] Incentives are not structured to encourage retention or job excellence. Low salaries make it more difficult to recruit young talent into education, depressing future educational opportunity. Despite additional expenditures region-wide, why are educational outcomes lagging the inputs? Questions of inefficiency arise. Is education spending in Latin America wasteful? Can Latin America generate stronger outcomes while maintaining expenditure levels?

WHY POOR PERFORMANCE?

The Nature of Education

The fundamental challenges that Latin American educational systems face are not unique but rather are related to the type of good it is. Education is considered a **merit good.** The direct benefits of education may be worth more to individuals than they themselves are aware. Purchasers of education may estimate the benefits in terms of a better job, for example, but may not be able to anticipate the effects on family health and nutrition. As a result, they might demand less education than the whole family's return on the investment would indicate. Given long gestation times, the signals for increasing educational investments may be slow to reach the buyers. Due to the fact that individuals may not correctly value education and the benefits it provides for society, as a merit good education is likely to be undersupplied by the private sector. It is clearly being underprovided in Latin America.

Improving literacy also creates **externalities** in lowering the transactions costs between individuals in society. Instructions at work can be written, not only spoken; social and environmental campaigns can take place in the print media. Literacy may contribute to improving the health profile and fertility control because health education is often disseminated in print. With positive externalities, one person's welfare is enhanced by increasing the educational status of another. Essentially, this position argues that the social rate of return to education, particularly at the primary level, exceeds the individual's investment. Given the externalities of education—the fact that it is better for me to have fellow citizens who can make an informed judgment at the polls, make change in the grocery store, or create the science to saves lives from cancer—there is general agreement that some amount of government investment in public education is necessary. The private market will underprovide when positive externalities exist. The critical question for many, however, is how much. Neoliberals might argue that too much government intervention in educational systems smacks of paternalism—why should the government know more about educational needs than a family? Neostructuralists would contend that education systems mirror political systems. Education will therefore mirror the power and inequality inherent in society; redressing inequality will require significant changes in educational systems.

In addition to its character as a merit good and as possessing externalities, the delivery of education suffers from principal-agent problems. A principal-agent problem exists when there is asymmetry of information between contracting parties such that the contractor can't directly observe the agent's ability to meet goals. Given the lack of observability, the agent will maximize his or her own goals rather than the principal's contract.[59] We can see this problem when individual schools are asked to implement centralized education plans without the availability of quality output metrics. Results are weakly observed. Likewise, if teachers are not held accountable to the instructions of principals, they will pursue their own self-interested agendas. Parents delegate authority to teachers as they deliver their children each day but cannot easily measure results. In a situation where a good such as the education of a child is difficult to measure, the incentives are twisted to individual gain. It is in the teacher's self-interest to maximize pay and minimize days worked, creating incentives for pervasive absenteeism in the region. For an institutionalist, the key question becomes how to design contracts such that schools and teachers are made responsible for their results but also given the flexibility to achieve ambitious educational goals.

Existing structures and incentives in Latin American education systems distort outcomes. Unlike the United States, where education is lodged in local districts and supported by property taxes, Latin American systems are largely centralized and bureaucratic. Central governments maintain substantial discretionary authority over funding, textbooks, teaching materials, and curriculum. Politicians manipulate educational investments for electoral gain. The power of the central government is countered by equally powerful unions that control the hiring and assignments of teachers and principals. One could characterize the Latin American educational system as a dysfunctional monopoly with little history of civic engagement.[60] Unlike the local parent-teacher association demanding accountability, the product is provided with little consumer input. School systems are broadly typified by a lack of accountability, by limited space for innovation or experimentation at the local level, and by perverse incentives for local principals or teachers not to improve pedagogical practices.[61] Public education is captured by interest groups, where parents have little information or influence, elites send their children to private schools, and politicians are reluctant to relinquish control over pork barrel opportunities of doling out political patronage in buildings and jobs.[62]

The management of educational systems in Latin America has led to inferior outcomes. Education has traditionally been managed by central governments insulated from local demands. Teachers have normally been employed by state governments rather than municipalities or individual schools. In Venezuela, for example, the Ministry of Education is the country's largest employer. Bureaucratic educational machines become overly involved in their own interests to the detriment of the student. Often geographically distant and powerless, families have little effective involvement in educational policy at the ministerial or school level.[63]

With policy efforts focused on expanding access to schools, quality suffered enormously. This was acutely felt in the qualifications and training of teachers in the region. National systems of pay, put in place by powerful teachers' unions, leave principals little recourse in local-level administration. Political and administrative obstacles impede much-needed reform. Teachers' unions have resisted **decentralization** and enhanced parental choice. Salaries absorb more than 90 percent of the total educational budget in fifteen of twenty-one countries for which data was available.[64] Politicians fear the loss of control over patronage jobs they can offer, and university students and their families have been able to defend their subsidies for higher education. Politicians would rather channel funds to a new building than contend with reforms in teacher training and performance. As a leading analyst of education in Latin America noted, "You don't see primary-school students protesting in the streets, like university students do."[65] Teachers and elites present a formidable coalition of interests for a poor community to come up against. This intersection of weak demand and inferior supply comes at a high cost to the development of human capital in the region.

Benefits of Educational Reform and the Role of the State

Political roadblocks explain poor outcomes and sluggish reform in education in Latin America. Globalization may, however, be creating a new set of conditions. International competitiveness demands a highly skilled, educated workforce. The educational deficit in Latin America has a high social cost. Education is by far the main factor in determining whether a working individual is poor.[66] There is a strong correlation between national investment in education and economic growth. A better-educated workforce will be more productive and competitive in the global economy. As noted by Alejandro Foxley, "The issue of a well trained labor force is critical to maintaining a path of economic development that is sustainable."[67] Education strongly influences farmer productivity, encourages a reduction in fertility, and results in improved health and nutrition.

No country has made significant economic progress without a strong educational infrastructure. A study of economic returns by education level in fourteen Latin American and Caribbean countries showed that the social rate of return of primary education averaged more than 17 percent—a high rate of return for any social investment.[68] It has been estimated that an increase of one year in Latin America's average educational level of the workforce over current trends would increase long-term economic growth by 1 percent on average in the next decade. An additional year increases productivity by 0.8 percent annually. Evidence from Honduras, Guatemala, and El Salvador shows that an additional year of education translates into a 5–10 percent increase in informal-sector earnings. Another study in the case of Brazil dramatically shows an additional year of education adding 5–20 percent to real output.[69] In a world in which competitiveness is increasingly defined by technology, well-skilled workforces are critical to managing growth. Increasing the educational attainment in the region, with its associated gains in productivity, would bring the region in line with East Asian levels.[70] Education is estimated to account for 40 percent of the divergence in growth rates between Latin America and East Asia.[71] Women with a secondary education are three times as likely to attend political meetings. Global interests have created new incentives for elites to demand better public education systems. The new coalition of interests driven by global competition may have broken the logjam on educational policy change. The million dollar question is how this should be done.

Pressures created by a globalized society may increase the need for a state role in education policy.[72] As the flow of technology and information has increased across borders, there are greater possibilities of coordination failures between the optimal mix of demand and supply skills.[73] **Coordination failures** exist when the effects of actions by one firm or sector depend on activities by other sectors so that a coordinated approach is required. The education and training needed by firms, for example, may not have organic feedback loops into education systems. As discussed in our chapter on competitiveness, gaps between industry needs and educational institutions prevent a free flow of market signals. To develop skills consistent with the needs of industry that will be rewarded with higher pay in the market, the state can play an important role in facilitating education consistent with labor force demand. The challenges in Latin America are enormous. Much like the epidemiological backlog in health where preventable disease measures compete with advances in combating cancer for scarce health care dollars, in education the state must at once bring along those left behind without the most rudimentary educational skills while at the same time encouraging the development of advanced educational opportunities to compete in the global arena. The state clearly needs to leverage resources to accomplish more within limited budgets. The Partnership for Educational Revitalization in the Americas (PREAL) has characterized this as a "smart state"—one that is committed to education over time; specifies objectives; oversees perform-ance; disseminates information on how schools are doing; promotes equity by allo-cating funds to those who need them most; provides resources; is accountable to parents, employers, and society; and links autonomy and accountability.[74] This is a tall order but a necessary one for educational reform in the region.

EDUCATION REFORM: MEETING EDUCATIONAL NEEDS IN LATIN AMERICA

The Momentum toward Change

Although the public generally favors educational reform, politics mitigates against effective change.[75] While stakeholders such as unions are strongly organized, educational reform is plagued by problems of collective action in organizing and sustaining involvement by parents—particularly when these parents may be poorly educated people struggling to make ends meet. Elites—and those with the luxury of time to volunteer for school boards or political lobbying—demand a type of education suited to future lives of privilege that is implemented at the national, centralized level. Public funds have flowed disproportionately to the upper class, reflecting elite political power. Wealthy Latin Americans wanted world-class uni-versities. Private producers could not meet this need, because university systems require costly investments in faculties, libraries, and laboratories. In response to powerful constituents' demands, governments chose to expand secondary and higher education, leaving little left over for the primary level. The best universities in the region are public (and often free), but it takes a high-priced private education to pass the matriculation tests for admission.[76] Educational reform must take into account the vested interests and political power of stakeholders, engaging these participants in the reform process to promote change. Although unions and elites have logically been resistant to losing control over education, packaging change in a way that cre-ates win-win opportunities is crucial for advancement.

External pressure can help to accelerate change. The 1990 World Declaration on Education for All (EFA) set the broad goal that every person—child, youths, and adults—shall be able to benefit from educational opportunities to meet basic learning needs. Latin America appears on track to meet this global goal of universal access to primary education.[77] The Dakar Framework in 2000 reaffirmed this com-mitment to EFA. Through regional meetings leading up to Dakar, a Latin America framework for action was adopted to expand and improve comprehensive early childhood care and education, especially for the most vulnerable; ensure that by 2015 all children, particularly girls, children in difficult circumstances, and those belonging to ethnic minorities, have access to complete, free, and compulsory pri-mary education of good quality; ensure that learning needs of all young people and adults are met through equitable access to appropriate learning and life skills pro-grams; improve levels of adult literacy by 50 percent by 2015; eliminate gender dis-parities in primary and secondary education by 2005; achieve gender equality in education in 2015; improve all aspects of quality of education; and ensure excel-lence so that recognized and measurable learning outcomes are achieved by all.[78]

Box 13.3 gives an example of early childhood education in Brazil. These goals
were reaffirmed in the Millennium Development Goals declaration, which states
that by 2015 all children will complete primary education, achieve equal access to
all levels of education, and eliminate by 2005 gender disparities in primary and secondary education. Given relatively strong progress on the primary school front and
acknowledging the need for secondary education for global competitiveness, at the
second Summit of the Americas in 1998 regional leaders targeted achieving 75 percent of young people having access to a quality secondary education by the year
2010, with increasing percentages of young people completing secondary studies.
The Economic Commission for Latin America and the Caribbean (ECLAC) has
consolidated this long list of international commitments to four key goals, summarized in table 13.5. The good intentions exist. Can the region deliver?

As regional and global momentum swings behind the achievement of these
targets, national policymakers may be pressured toward action. Success in educational reform normally takes a champion—either interest by a strong president or a
powerful minister of education. Box 13.4 illustrates the benefits of leadership in
the case of Brazil. It is also more likely to succeed when linked to a broader agenda
of policy goals such as improving national competitiveness to broaden the coalition

Table 13.5.   ECLAC's Regional Educational Goals

	Additional Resources to Meet Goal (constant U.S. $ 1995)	Percent of Total Additional Resources Required
Universal attendance in preschool education by 2015	64,602	43.09
Universal completion of primary education while reducing repetition	19,082	12.73
Raise coverage of secondary to 75% by 2015 w/ net enrollment of 75%	59,314	39.56
Eradicate adult illiteracy by providing training of population 15 years and over until 2015	6,933	4.62

Source: ECLAC.org.

BOX 13.4.   THE ROLE OF POLITICAL LEADERSHIP: THE CASE OF BRAZIL

Brazil provides an example of what can be accomplished with strong political will that engages educational stakeholders and draws upon the interests of the public sector to improve a highly unequal and ineffective educational system. Since 1934 universal primary education has been the law for children ages seven to fourteen, yet Brazil has one of the highest illiteracy rates in the region. National adult literacy stood at 20 percent in the 1990s, with levels twice as bad in the poor northeastern region. During the 1970s, the government invested lavishly in education, expanding on educational infrastructure. Schools popped up everywhere, but without funding for books, supplies, and teacher training, educational outcomes were dismal. Except in the richest of systems, not every pupil had a book; in most schools books were kept in the school office. Most of the spending went to universities.

Brazil was a striking outlier in terms of the weakness of its primary school system. The educational attainment of upper-income compared to lower-income children was highly divergent. The issue is not the amount of money being spent. From 1980 to 1988 expenditure on education as a proportion of gross national product doubled, and it also increased as a percentage of total federal government expenditure, from 6.1 to 8.2 percent. Despite these real increases in total expenditure, resources directed to primary education were reduced by 39 percent between 1986 and 1989, whereas those to higher education increased 59 percent over the period. The Brazilian education system is asymmetric. Rich students go to private primary and secondary schools and then attend free public universities. The poor attend public primary and secondary schools. Poorly prepared, few pass the tough exams to get into the strong government-funded university system.[79] In 1996 the Brazilian Congress approved an amendment that mandated 25 percent of state and municipal revenues be spent on education, with at least 60 percent of the total money to be allocated to raising teachers' salaries. But funding to federal universities, which receive 80 percent of all federal spending, was preserved, as Congress was unwilling to touch such middle-class entitlements.[80] As a percentage of GDP, Brazilian spending on public education is the highest in the world; it also ranks among the most expensive higher education systems.[81] Because of unequal distribution of educational opportunity, Brazil has spending levels in education comparable to middle-income countries and educational outcomes similar to those in very poor countries. The problem is not a lack of resources but uneven distribution of educational spending.

The results of the skewed spending on education in Brazil are startling. The average worker in the São Paulo area has only a fourth-grade education. As shown in figure 13.2, less than 20 percent of the population has some high school, in contrast to more than 40 percent in Chile, 35 percent in Mexico, 65 percent in Japan, and 90 percent in the United States. In the poorest regions in the northeastern region, public school teachers earn less than $50 a month—drawing in the least talented in the society, many without secondary education themselves.[82]

Despite the difficulties in educational policies, some progress has been made. Figure 13.3 shows the gains in education since the 1970s. It also highlights, however, the unequal distribution by gender, region, and race. The Brazilian educational deficit in the face of global competitiveness was enormous. Radical changes in educational policy were implemented under the Fernando Henrique Cardoso administration. Under the astute political leadership of education minister Paulo Renato de Souza, responsibility for education was decentralized to the local level. Financing was devolved to the local level as well, where the demand for education could address local school board needs. A new role was set for the central government: establishing standards and assessing progress. Efforts are being made at computerization, installing one hundred thousand computers in the

Figure 13.2.   Percentage of Population with Some High School Education

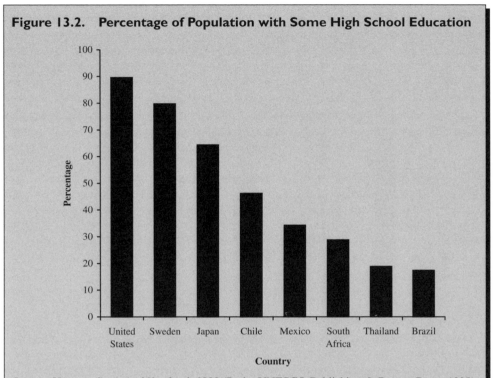

Source: Unesco, *Statistical Yearbook 1998* (Paris: UNESCO Publishing & Bernan Press, 1998), 1-44–1-S4.

schools. Textbook distribution increased 83 percent over 1995, and there was an increase in school lunch programs as well as improvements in the TV school system for distance learning. One innovative program pays children to stay in school. In a suburb of Brasilia, twenty-four thousand children draw a minimum wage of $110. A deposit is made each year that the student stays in school and can be touched only after four successful years of schooling. Enrollments are up and dropouts rare. The historical repeat rate in this district was 17 percent; it has now fallen to 8 percent.

In the Brazilian state of Minas Gerais, decentralization has improved efficiency and educational outcomes. The philosophy is that the school belongs to the community. Before decentralization, if a rural school wanted to buy a few new chairs, it would have to send a requisition to the state capital. Now local schools receive four quarterly payments for supplies and educational materials. School boards were formed to make personnel decisions, and competency exams for teachers were instituted. To overcome problems of patronage, principals are elected by the community among prequalified candidates using secret ballots.[83] The state has seen dramatic improvements in student scores: math scores have doubled, primary school graduation rates increased 47 percent, and repeaters fell from 29 to 17 percent.[84] Surprisingly, participation has been strongest among poor communities.

The overall results of educational reform have been dramatic. Illiteracy is down 15 percent, and test scores are rising. National teacher standards are improving, with nine out of

continued

continued

Figure 13.3.   Average Years of Schooling in Brazil, 1970 versus 1990

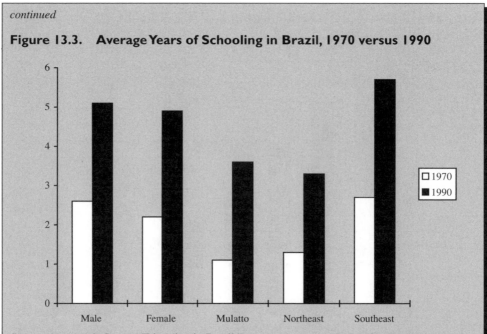

Source: Amaury de Souza, "Education in Brazil," paper presented at IADB Conference, November 1997.

ten teachers attaining a high school education or better. Nonetheless, high repetition rates continue to plague the system.

What lessons can be drawn from educational reform in Brazil?[85] First, there was strong leadership from the top that was complemented by action from the bottom. Programs engaged stakeholders, bringing parents and the private sector together in the battle to keep kids in school. The leadership created a shared perspective on what needed to be done to reach common goals and engaged various levels of society to make it possible. The central government function performed well in producing and disseminating information, while the local level had enough leeway for innovation and local experimentation. Much remains to be done in Brazil, but the educational future looks brighter.

of potential winners from reform.[86] A strong leader can overcome the collective action problem, galvanizing change. But it will also take additional resources and key changes in the supply and demand for education to change outcomes in the region.

Financing the Education Deficit

Educational reform, particularly among the poorer developing countries, will take additional resources. ECLAC estimates that the financing gap to meet these goals by 2015 is approximately $149 billion. This represents an additional outlay of ap-

Housing in Latin America is woefully inadequate, leading to construction solutions that make ingenious use of scarce supplies and limited space. *(Courtesy of Helena Tubis)*

proximately $13.5 billion per year, or roughly 16 percent over current additional expenditures. In the poorest countries the additional spending would raise expenditures 40–70 percent, underscoring the need for external assistance in these cases. Greater efficiency is incorporated into the cost tallies. Brazil, for example, can meet its portion of the goal by reducing repetition to 5 percent in 2015—the savings in reteaching would compensate for the additional coverage. In addition to expanding secondary schooling in the region, ECLAC advocates for the expansion of preschool training. Although this may indeed seem something of a luxury, by getting kids to school earlier it is more likely that students will proceed through primary school on schedule, reducing repetition and enhancing the likelihood of transition and completion through secondary programs.[87]

Table 13.6.   Private Spending for School As a Percentage of Total Public and Private Spending

Country	Preschool, Primary, Secondary	Total, Including Tertiary	Difference
Bolivia	7.3	10.9	3.6
Argentina	11.1	23.7	12.6
Mexico	14.8	17.4	2.6
Peru	22.8	28.4	5.6
Colombia	27.4	38.4	11.0
Paraguay	29.4	31	1.6
Chile	30	46.2	16.2
Ecuador	48.5	51.1	2.6
LA Average	23.9	30.9	7.0
Canada	7.7	16.8	9.1
United States	9.9	31.8	21.9

Source: ECLAC, *Financing and Management of Education in Latin America and the Caribbean,* July 2004.

Private spending must also be tapped and reallocated to expand educational quality in the region. Table 13.6 shows private spending as a percentage of total public and private spending on education in the region. The contrast between most Latin American countries and the United States is striking. Ecuadorian families pay for nearly 50 percent of preschool, primary, and secondary educational expenses out of pocket as opposed to 9.9 percent in the United States. On average in the region, 25 percent of spending before university comes from private resources. When tertiary spending is factored in, however, the ratios are nearly identical. In this case, where most Americans attend public primary and secondary schools—but put family money into either public or private universities—in Latin America the best universities have traditionally been free. Unfortunately, since entrance is guarded by tough matriculation exams, those who have been better prepared by elite private schools not surprisingly receive admission. Meeting the needs of all students will require reallocating some of the educational expenses targeted at higher education toward preschool and secondary—a tough political battle.

Private resources may also be secured in partnership with the private business sector. As businesses have worried about global competitiveness, the private sector has also assumed a role in education in the region. In Brazil, employees of Rigesa, a Brazilian subsidiary of Westvaco, a New York-based paper company and a blue jeans factory owned by a large Brazilian textile manufacturer, sponsor basic literacy classes after hours. A major Brazilian Bank, Bradesco, finances roughly fifty primary and secondary classes around the nation. The need to operate more sophisticated equipment drives the company programs.[88] A São Paulo cosmetics firm called Natura donated more than $3 million to train public school teachers. Embraer, Brazil's successful aircraft exporter, runs a technology institute to encourage young scientists. In Venezuela, a widow of a wealthy industrialist funded a school adjacent to the factory she owned to improve her workers' children's education. Another Venezuela-based firm, the Cisneros Group, is working with IBM and Microsoft in a project to use its Direct TV satellite to beam programs for teachers into 120 schools across the region.[89] Microsoft is working with the IADB in a program called Informatics 2000 to promote computer skills at the elementary and high school levels. To meet the skills gap to compete in the global economy, Mexico's private sector has taken steps by creating a National Commission of Normalization of Job Skills. Patterned on a Japanese program, it provides workers with a certification of job skills or knowledge level, regardless of how or where the skills were obtained. These are but a few of the many examples of corporate contributions to education. Box 13.5 illustrates a successful private initiative that has partnered with public institutions to provide opportunities to children in a Rio de Janeiro favela.

BOX 13.5.   PARA TI: EDUCATING RIO'S POOREST CHILDREN

BY MARIAH HUDNUT

In an unassuming white building nestled in the heart of a slum called Vila Canoas lies a beacon of hope amidst the otherwise violent, poverty-stricken world of the *favelas* in Rio de Janeiro. Para Ti Amizade e Solidariedade (Friendship and Solidarity for You), a school for the poor that started as the philanthropic project of an Italian family, has grown to become part of a citywide initiative to help break the cycle of urban poverty by educating Rio's poorest children.

The project began in the 1970s as a partnership between an Italian NGO called Come Noi (Like Us) and the Uranis, an Italian family living in Rio. When the Vila Canoas slum sprang up near the Urani family's home, the family asked for support from Come Noi to assist in the provision of education for the children living in the slum. At the time, statistics reported that 50 percent of slum children were failing in school, and only 5 percent completed the fifth grade. The Uranis and Come Noi joined forces to help give these children an opportunity for a better future through education. The first initiative was a sponsorship program that started in 1993. The program asked Italian families to fund the educational costs of poor children in the Vila Canoas. This program provided about two hundred dollars to each sponsored child and reached about 350 children in need.

In 1995, the project expanded its quarters to a 250-square-foot building next to the Urani household. During this year, the project gained international attention for its success. The Daniel Agostino Foundation in New York, the Rotary International Club, and Rio's Favela/Bairro programs all became supporters of the newly named Para Ti Amizade e Solidariedade initiative. The funding allowed for the birth of another initiative, called the Bairrinho program, that currently works to directly assist the two hundred thousand inhabitants living in Rio's two hundred small slums. The cost for these programs is divided between the municipality of Rio, foreign investors, and the Come Noi NGO.

Today, the Para Ti School assists hundreds of children by providing quality education in a community setting. The school consists of a nursery, a social area and entertainment center, a health center, a community center with public Internet access, and a public library with more than three thousand books, including courses for university admission. In addition, the school offers professional courses for sixty adults in the slum as well as employment for about fifty members of the community. Para Ti Amizade e Solidariedade is an inspiring example of a public-private partnership that has truly been effective in provoking social change.

Source: www.parati.inf.br.

Public-sector provision of early childhood programs may also be complemented by private-sector initiatives. Partnerships of governments, NGOs, and communities should be encouraged. Informal programs such as the *hogares comunitarios* in Colombia have much lower salary and investment costs than formal programs. Public financing of preschool should start with the most deprived children in the urban and rural slums, and governments should resist middle-class pressures for general support of preschooling until the needs of the poor are met.[90] In Mexico, under the National Solidarity Program, also known as PRONASOL, a poverty reduction program, the residents complemented state investments by providing half the funds and the labor for the building and refurbishing of schools. Local businesses contributed materials. Schoolchildren voted on which classmates were most deserving of funds to help their families while the children attended school.[91] Community participation matters in improving educational outcomes. Nonetheless, there is a long way to go in private participation in social efforts. With different sets of tax laws in the region, there is a limited tradition of corporate philanthropy in Latin America.

International organizations provided approximately $1 billion per year to the region to finance education.[92] The largest donors were the World Bank and the IADB, which granted between $4,000 and $1 billion per year for education. The poorest countries that have become eligible for debt cancellation under the highly indebted poor country initiative may see further benefits as resources are redirected from debt reduction toward investments in the social sector. External assistance represents 2–3 percent of total educational expenditures for the region as a whole, although the volume reaches 6 percent in poorest countries. This is low compared to other regions, but Latin America is viewed as relatively developed and not in as great need of assistance as regions such as Sub-Saharan Africa. Bilateral external assistance in education is somewhat problematic in that one country rarely gets the credit for improving the outcome. Unlike selling a fighter aircraft or building a road, educational benefits are built into human capital and are hard to count or feel.

International resources may also be made available on an emergency basis for unexpected economic crisis. Spain, for example, packaged an emergency response to the crisis in Argentine educational systems with the 2001–2002 peso crash. When household income fell by one-third in real terms and the proportion of the population characterized as poor grew by 15 percent with a doubling of the number of indigent doubled, families decreased their demand for education. The wealthier opted for less expensive private school, the middle class moved from the private to the public sector, and all reduced the purchases of school materials.[93] In response, Spain cancelled $100 million in debt payments in 2004. The savings were earmarked for a special education account to be disbursed over four years to two national scholarship programs. It will help 215,000 students in the three poorest parts of the country to complete lower secondary education by cash transfers of approximately $140 per student per year for three years payable directly to families. Although $100 million is a small amount relative to the overall Argentine debt (it owes $1.3 billion to Spain alone) and to the overall education budget ($3.3 billion), the $100 million is a significant addition relative to total nonsalary elements of education budget.[94]

Proequity Reforms

With equity as a goal, education is seen as an instrument to improve social mobility. Equity-driven reforms tend to focus on acquiring basic literacy skills, increasing school supplies in the poorest areas, and reaching groups such as women and the indigenous populations that have lagged behind in educational performance. To improve equity considerations, the state must assume a central role. Given the complementary goal of increasing competitiveness under fiscal constraints, the private sector has been increasingly involved. Competitiveness-driven reform can be facilitated by market-based mechanisms.

To improve equity, educational reform must attend to the constraints on the most disadvantaged. In particular, the high opportunity costs of sending children to school must be addressed. The Colombian Escuela Nueva program offers an innovative approach to formal education. Working from the assumption that children in rural areas need flexible schedules to accommodate agricultural work, it operates under a multigrade, independently paced framework. Using problem solving rather than rote learning, semiprogrammed modules allow students to work alone when necessary to catch up with the class. Because the modules are relevant to the problems that students are facing at home, academic learning is reinforced by practical application.[95] Pilot studies indicate that Escuela Nueva students have performed better and stayed in school longer than students attending traditional institutions.[96]

As an example of how the private sector might assist in promoting equity, Mayan girls in Guatemala are offered a small scholarship—six dollars per month financed by a small private international organization—to provide pencils, notebooks, and shoes as well as cover some of the money that the girls may have provided to their families. A small but inspiring result of this program was the achievement of two girls in a small mountain village entering the fifth grade: the first ever in the community to do so.[97] A discussion of educational efforts in Guatemala is presented in box 13.6. In Mexico, two million very poor families in Chiapas and other rural areas receive twenty-five dollars monthly from the government if children attend classes, are promoted, and get regular medical checkups.[98]

Supply-Side Approaches

Educational reform in Latin America should encompass policies to address both the supply and the demand for education. On the supply side, structural reforms are warranted to reconsider the relative balance between school autonomy and accountability, creating institutions that will promote accountability but provide room for local input and experimentation. Supply-side reforms will be most effective if accompanied by changes in demand—changes, discussed below, that may pressure schools to offer higher-quality educational services and promote more egalitarian outcome.

Supply-side reform in education in Latin America is a tough political sell. To create the set of incentives that will encourage teachers, principals, and districts

BOX 13.6.   WILL SHE MAKE IT? GUATEMALA FINDS NEW WAYS TO KEEP GIRLS IN SCHOOL

BY CHRISTINA MACCULLOCH

In a cramped two-room house in Villa Nueva, a working-class district south of Guatemala City, seven-year-old Gabriela González Hernández is getting ready for her first day of school. Although she probably does not consider herself a child of privilege, Gabriela is already part of an elite, because slightly less than half of all Guatemalan girls do not enroll in elementary school at all. If she perseveres in her studies, Gabriela could join an even more select group: the one out of eight Guatemalan girls who complete sixth grade.

Gabriela's chances are relatively good. Her mother is herself an elementary school graduate, and her father completed high school. Though their home has but a zinc roof, bare cement floors and no running water, Gabriela's parents are determined to keep her in school because they are convinced that education represents her best chance to escape poverty. Gabriela is also lucky because she lives near a city that offers relatively good access to roads, schools and income-generating work for her parents.

But for girls in Guatemala's rural areas, the outlook is much bleaker. Simply walking to and from a distant school each day can challenge a young girl's endurance and threaten her safety. In households where both parents must do full-time agricultural work, school can seem like a questionable luxury. Most girls end up staying home to care for younger siblings, cook and help wherever else they are needed. The pressures are such that even among girls in rural Guatemala who do enroll in first grade, 66 percent drop out before reaching third grade. And when families feel they can afford to send a child to school, they generally send a boy. In 1991, some 500,000 girls between 7 and 15 were estimated to be missing school in Guatemala, compared to only 300,000 boys. Overall, 60 percent of Guatemalan women are illiterate, and 80 percent of these are from the country's rural indigenous regions, according to official figures compiled early this decade.

Guatemala is hardly alone in this respect. Mayra Buvinic, chief of the IDB's Social Development Division, cites global literacy statistics showing that in 1990, there were only 74 literate women for every 100 literate men worldwide. "The same studies estimated that globally there were 77 million girls between the ages of 6 and 11 who were not attending school, compared to 52 million boys, and that does not take into account repetition, absenteeism and dropout rates that make the gap even wider," says Buvinic.

Although the bias against educating girls has complex social and cultural roots, it is almost universally exacerbated by poverty. The nations of Latin America and the Caribbean are a case in point. In the region's most developed countries and in its largest cities, the education gender gap is either small or nonexistent. But among the tens of millions of Latin Americans who live in acute poverty, even in the richest countries, the problem is pronounced.

HIDDEN COSTS

Societies pay a high price for the failure to educate girls. While investing in boys' education is obviously beneficial, there is evidence that the same investment in female education yields higher returns for society as a whole. Why? Because although both men and women who went to school are more likely to earn better wages and improve a country's productivity, education tends to affect aspects of women's lives that don't apply to men.

Educated women are more likely to obtain prenatal, delivery and postnatal care, which leads to lower rates of infant and maternal mortality. Indeed, a World Bank study of twenty-five countries found that an increase of one to three years in a mother's schooling reduced infant mortality in the first year of life by 15 percent. Among fathers, the same increase in schooling resulted in only a 6 percent reduction in infant mortality rates. Likewise, better-educated women in almost all societies wait longer before they get married and tend to have fewer children—two factors that lower the risk of birth-related health problems for both infants and mothers.

The children of women with as little as three to six years of formal education tend to be better nourished, and they are more likely to enroll and stay in school than the children of uneducated mothers. Educated women also tend to be more active and effective participants in local government, particularly in issues involving social services. In short, because of their multiple roles in the marketplace, the community, and the home, educated women can have a higher impact than educated men on the development and well-being of their societies.

NATIONAL CONCERN, LOCAL APPROACHES

In Guatemala, concern about girls' limited access to education has led to a unique effort to confront the problem head-on. Starting in 1991, a diverse group of educators, researchers, business leaders, civic groups, and donor organizations formed what would later become the National Association for Girls' Education. The association immediately began working with the Ministry of Education to develop a girls' education strategy within the ministry's broader program to strengthen elementary education.

In 1992, with support from the United States Agency for International Development and local foundations, the association commissioned a detailed diagnostic study that for the first time showed the extent of the shortfall in girls' education in Guatemala. The study identified the regions and municipalities where the problem was most severe and proposed a plan of action that included outlines of thirty-seven potential projects.

Soon thereafter, the Ministry of Education launched the Girls' Education Program, a multifaceted effort to develop and test practical ways of increasing enrollment and retention of girls through the sixth grade. The program included projects in four broad areas: technical assistance for the Ministry of Education, the National Association for Girls' Education and individual schools working to implement girls' education programs; training for government officials, teachers and parents; conducting original research on the problem of girls' education; and developing motivational books and other didactic materials in Mayan languages for use by rural schoolgirls.

From the outset, the program's organizers realized that a successful intervention would require coordinating the activities of students, parents, teachers, community leaders and high-level government officials who supported the effort. To find effective approaches, the program launched a pilot "Educate Girls Project," that tested different combinations of initiatives such as training teachers, offering scholarships to individual students, forming parents committees and providing supplementary curricula to schools. The project also hired indigenous women to work as education aides to provide special support to schoolgirls and their families.

The pilot project yielded a number of lessons. For example, project leaders discovered that although teachers were generally receptive to new ideas, they needed training on the theory and practice of reaching girls in the classroom, as well as appropriate teaching aids and materials.

Gabriela Núñez, a sociologist who coordinated the pilot project, believes the training sessions were important because they boosted teachers' sense of their importance in the process. "We found it was crucial to reinforce teachers' assessments of their own value as people, because only with a positive self-image can they transmit a sense of self-worth and recognition to their girl students," she says.

The pilot project also found that even modest scholarship grants, amounting to the

continued

continued

equivalent of around five U.S. dollars per month, were a very cost-effective way of encouraging attendance because they helped compensate for the loss of a girl's labor around the house. Although scholarships were also found to improve long-term retention, project officials concluded that financial support would have to be complemented by a variety of other strategies to encourage girls to return to school year after year.

Núñez argues that efforts to improve educational opportunities for girls invariably benefit boys as well. "When boys see girls becoming more active in class and in school organizations, they get more involved themselves, because they don't want to be left out." Likewise, parent committees formed as part of the pilot project increased the parents' engagement in the education of all their children, regardless of gender.

Although it is hard to quantify the success of Guatemala's girls' education efforts to date, one fundamental accomplishment is clear. "The need to improve girls' access to education is now understood and considered a priority among policymakers at the national level," says Isabel Nieves, lead author of the Guatemalan diagnostic study and now a social development specialist at the IDB.

This new awareness became evident during the drafting of the 1996 Peace Accords that brought an end to Guatemala's civil war. The accords included specific mandates to end gender inequalities in education, a goal that was also specifically addressed in the Guatemalan government's 2000 action plan. Indeed, that plan set an ambitious target of 80 percent primary school enrollment for girls by the year 2000 as part of educational reform programs.

Now, the IDB is supporting that program through a $15 million loan approved last year for Guatemala's Ministry of Education. The funds will be used to pay for training teachers and supplying schools with bilingual and Spanish-language materials, implementing programs to reduce first **grade repetition,** consolidating community participation and replicating successful innovations from the Girls' Education Program.

"The IDB support is arriving at a crucial time," says Nieves. "These funds are allowing the Guatemalan government to mainstream many of the lessons learned during the girls' education pilot project into its overall educational reform program."

The IDB is supporting innovative girls' education efforts in other countries as well. In Bolivia, where illiteracy among women averages 67 percent and girls spend only 60 percent as much time in school as boys, a recent educational reform program partly financed by the Bank set out specifically to reduce dropout rates among girls. The program included a variety of incentives, including scholarships and day care centers where girls could drop off younger siblings in order to attend classes.

In Mexico, an IDB-funded program to assist up to three million children in extreme poverty is testing a different approach to easing the child-care duties of school-age children: letting them bring their younger siblings into the classroom. Though it is too early to judge the effectiveness of this concept, the aim is both to keep girls in school and to offer a more stimulating environment to preschool children.

The ultimate success of these kinds of programs depends, of course, on the perseverance of girls like Gabriela González Hernández and the commitment of parents, teachers and community leaders. But as the progress achieved in Guatemala illustrates, governments can help to create an environment where perseverance and commitment can bear fruit in the lives of individual girls.

Source: Reproduced from *IDB América,* April 1998, pp. 4–7.

to be accountable for failure and be rewarded for success involves changing the way education has been delivered in Latin America. This will create winners as well as losers who will generate significant backlash. Our discussion of educational systems in Latin America highlights key deficiencies: centralized bureaucratic policies inappropriate to local conditions, low-quality teaching driven by ineffective incentives, and a lack of information and accountability by schools and educational ministries to their clients, the students themselves, and outcomes that perpetuate inequality over generations.

Considerations of supply-side reforms in Latin America involve an evaluation of the role of the market in promoting the best set of incentives to encourage both quality and equity in reform. One might consider borrowing the best attributes of the market (the ability to absorb disaggregated bits of information to deliver a good) and marry it with the strengths of a state (the ability to appropriate market externalities to overcome delivery gaps and redress inequality). One might consider building a quasimarket—an approach advocated by the structuralist A. O. Hirschman to encourage the generation of information and incentives for reform.[99] Market-driven public schools, for example, might provide transparent information on the quality of education, including success and failure rates to users, clients, and other stakeholders. As in a market, those responsible for success or failure should be rewarded or penalized. This will necessarily involve stronger evaluations of teachers and administrators, a tradition that has been weak in Latin America.[100] Indeed, Chile is the only country in Latin America to systematically evaluate public schools and their teachers, providing monetary rewards to schools and teachers whose performance is evaluated as excellent.[101] Awards are made on a schoolwide basis so as to encourage cooperation rather than competition among teachers, in support of a local culture of building community.

Salary incentives may promote the buy-in by teachers. In most Latin American countries, there is very little room for merit in teacher salaries. Although starting at a relatively high level compared to other nations (90 percent of per capita GDP), Peru, for example, has no increase in base salaries throughout the teaching career. In Chile and Uruguay the ratio between beginner and experienced teachers is one to two. If you believe that people respond to material incentives, the lack of opportunity to make more money for your own family is naturally a deterrent to investing more time and energy in your classroom. Teachers may require incentives to even show up—or penalties for not doing so. Nazmul Chaudhury reports survey results of surprise visits to primary schools around the world that found 19 percent of teachers absent; absence was not typically concentrated among a small number of frequently absent teachers but appeared to be a widespread phenomenon.[102] It is, indeed, rational not to show up for work if it is unlikely that you will be fired or suffer a monetary penalty. Teachers also need to be provided with better training. Standards are currently set too low for entry into the profession; in Argentina, for example, one doesn't need to complete college to teach primary or lower school. In Brazil, Paraguay, and Uruguay, teachers need less than 3.5 years of postsecondary education to teach primary school. Providing positive incentives as well as penalties to teachers may make them more responsive to their students.

Decentralization: A Balance of Autonomy and Accountability

Community involvement in educational reform is critical. One of the trends in educational reform in the region has been decentralization of educational policy to the local level. This doesn't necessarily mean less government but rather a different combination of levels of government. Local input and control can reduce educational inefficiency.

Public schools should be freed from excessive regulation. The inability to hire or fire teachers at the local level subverts accountability. Decentralization of management will enhance autonomy. Currently, only in El Salvador can the principal hire or fire teachers. In Brazil, a radical provision of school reform in the state of Minas Gerais was the election of school principals for fixed terms by school councils, choosing from a short list of candidates who had passed a qualifying test and prepared plans of statement for their schools.[103] Decentralization of decision making facilitates the expression of local demand for education. It appeals to those who value the deepening of democracy as well as those who believe that locally made, transparent decisions will be more efficient. It is important, however, to ensure that money follows authority down the educational hierarchy. If decision making is decentralized but the ability to tax or raise resources to pay for educational change still resides with the central government, it is likely to result in weakened structures. EDUCO in El Salvador is an interesting example of educational decentralization. In EDUCO schools, local education committees monitor teacher performance, hire and fire teachers, manage school equipment, and oversee maintenance.[104] Program success generated expansion in the rural areas and the reduction of student absences by three to four days per month. Nonetheless, it is difficult to evaluate the EDUCO program systematically because selection was not random.[105] Regionally, we observe a devolution of power to local levels, but implementation has been partial or slow. Decentralization does not mean abandonment by the central government; rather, local policies should be accompanied by smart state oversight.[106] The impact of decentralization will vary by the local environment and capacities.[107] Overall, the impact of decentralization is unclear.[108]

Decentralization of education works best when it is supported by the following factors: political will at all levels of government, explicit guidelines delineating which functions of the educational system will be decentralized or provided by the private sector, an implementation timetable and strategy with clear operational guidelines, continuous training for educational administrators provided at the local level, development of performance indicators to measure outcomes, and adequate financial, human, and physical resources to sustain the process.[109] Incentives should be built into the system to encourage good management and discourage corruption at the local administrative level. Clear lines of responsibility should be defined to encourage accountability for poor standards and failed systems. Decentralization is a process that will take time to alter the rules of financing and delivery systems; it must be carefully monitored for efficiency and effectiveness. Decentralization may confront political obstacles as centralized ministries lose power. Some countries might choose to decentralize particular components of the education system rather than institute a frontal attack. Decentralization that takes place too quickly could simply transfer the inefficiencies from central bureaucracies to the local level.[110]

Decentralization does not mean the abdication of responsibility for education at the national level. PREAL recommends in its task force report, *The Future At Stake,* that governments establish clear standards for education, introduce national tests, and use results to revise programs and reallocate resources. Local governments should have the authority to run schools, but central administration of funds, standards, equity assurances, and monitoring of results is crucial. Better measures of assessment of educational outcomes must be developed to evaluate new directions in policy. Without effective assessment of outcomes, it is difficult to set clear goals. The few assessments that exist focus on inputs such as spending and the number of teachers rather than on indicators of educational performance.[111] Assessment data should be disseminated to the local level to direct resources to the greatest need.[112] In Chile, for example, assessments were used to target schools at greatest educational risk. High- and medium-risk schools were eligible to apply for additional resources for reform. Decentralization does not necessarily mean less state involvement. Instead, it redefines responsibilities for different levels of government.

The Need for Standards

To achieve supply-side objectives of promoting quality education, both public and private schools need coherent standards, means to achieve the standards, rules, and incentives to encourage meeting the standards and feedback on performance.[113] Standards must apply to both public and private schools in the region and provide both oversight as well as flexibility in meeting goals. Some suggest that it is effective to further fund private schools, given that education can be seen as a quasi-public good with clear spillovers for society. Public loans to attend private schools and the support of knowledge creation in the universities may accelerate reform in education. Consideration should be given to expanding mixed educational systems. Chile, for example, has three educational networks: 9 percent of students attend fully private schools, 35 percent are enrolled in private schools that are subsidized by the states, and the balance, 56 percent, attend municipal schools. Purely private fee-paying institutions are the traditional schools of the middle class and elite. If pursued with a careful eye to **equity concerns,** subsidization of private schools can create competition and pressure to upgrade both private as well as public education.

Techno Options

New technologies offer new opportunities for education that both national governments and multilateral agencies are exploiting. The Internet brings a wide range of materials into even the most remote classroom. Students in rural classrooms can read the more than one thousand national and international newspapers on the Internet. Wiring schools, even in remote areas, vastly enhances educational resources—and students often find it fun. Satellite classrooms and videotapes can work around the limitations of teacher training. In Brazil, Telecurso 2000 offers a basic high school equivalency program by television for young adults, with lessons broadcast at different times of day to accommodate work schedules. The workbook to accompany the course can be purchased at newsstands. Brazil is now moving to Internet-based courses to complement televised distance learning opportunities.

Nonetheless, technical solutions must be carefully evaluated for cost-effectiveness. Putting computers in classrooms is an expensive venture. Appropriate software must also be procured. If teachers are not adequately trained in the use of computers, their potential is wasted. Simply providing the hardware and software without clear plans to integrate computers into the classrooms increases the likelihood of failure

Most supply-side changes are hard. They involve rewarding some but punishing others. They may allocate resources to some schools but take them away from underperformers. Although they may create monetary incentives for some teachers to perform, they take away the flexibility of others to be selectively absent without penalty. Although some traditional supply-side changes such as building more schools or buying more textbooks are not controversial, it is not clear that adding resources without addressing dysfunctional incentives will produce better quality, more equitable education in the region. This is not to say that increasing traditional resources is not a welcome complementary input. The Basic Education Development Project (PAREIB) covering 32 percent of all those enrolled in elementary schools in Mexico, for example, is making an important difference in upgrading the school buildings from inadequate palapas—open-sided structures of palm leaves—to well-built classrooms that allow teaching in the rainy season. Interestingly, however, PAREIB pairs building upgrades with performance incentives for teachers, money for pencils or notebooks, involvement of the community, and opportunities to study indigenous languages and cultures.[114] Adding more resources to a system with distorted incentives will not produce the dynamic change critical for growth. Instead, providing a set of complementary resources such as PAREIB may provide the catalyst for change.

Demand-Side Programs

The educational deficit in Latin America is the result of ineffective demand by poor families intersecting with a deficient quantity and quality of the supply offered by school systems. With clear positive returns to education, why don't families elect to invest in more years of schooling? Why is educational reform not demand-driven? One response to this question is to focus not on the desire for education but on the ability to pay for it. Unfortunately, in addition to the direct costs of clothing, books, and other supplies, for many families the opportunity costs of education are high. In many parts of the region, children's income is an important contribution to the family's survival. School calendars often do not accommodate children's work schedules, particularly around harvest times in the agricultural sector. In the urban sector, one estimate places children's participation in the informal sector between

20 and 30 percent of family income.[115] Families found it even harder to give up earnings from children—often amounting to a third of household income—during the periods of macroeconomic instability, causing a slowdown in education accumulation since the 1980s.[116] When survival is at stake, education appears to be a luxury. The demand for education must be seen in the context of the price of day-to-day living. Improving incentives to supply higher-quality, more equitable education may be complemented by initiatives that promote the demand for such programs. Two instruments are central to demand-side policies: vouchers and **conditional cash transfers** (**CCTs**). Vouchers enhance choice among schools, promoting competition and efficiency; CCT programs strive to improve equity and the accumulation of human capital among the less-advantaged members of society.

Chile and Colombia have substantial experience with voucher programs. Implemented back in 1981, vouchers are available to and used by a wide range of families. The use of vouchers was accompanied by the decentralization process, driving educational decisions down to the local level. Intended to generate competition and lower running costs, vouchers were designed to improve educational outcomes.[117] The demand registered by users is supposed to create a quasimarket in which the buyers of the good, education, can direct educational outcomes. After twenty years of the program, a fairly heterogeneous system has emerged. Although public municipal schools are largely populated by those in the lowest three income deciles and the highest two income deciles comprise the population of the fee-paying schools, the private subsidized schools encompass a socioeconomic range of students.[118] The composition of private subsidized schools themselves vary, based in large part on location. Econometric results evaluating the performance of the schools deliver interesting results. Students in private-fee schools score highest on exams irrespective of their income status. Within the publicly subsidized private schools, the average socioeconomic background of the students in the school is more important than an individual's income in explaining student achievement. That is, an average kid will do better than average if placed in a school where classmates are from a more advantaged economic status.[119]

The results of the voucher program in Chile, however, don't fully address the question of equity in education. Markets for education developed only in large towns and in less poor neighborhoods in which private subsidized schools were able to turn a profit. Municipal schools in less-advantaged areas found it difficult to raise funds, contributing to budget pressures.[120] Travel is a key opportunity cost in the use of vouchers; while students can choose schools (subject to meeting admissions criteria), families are reluctant to send children, especially the youngest, across the city to a better school.[121] Poorly educated parents appeared more concerned with things like school appearance, whereas wealthier families demanded qualitative changes in curriculum. Many low-income families were not able to take advantage of access to schools in more affluent areas; the costs of transportation, uniforms, and the commuting time away from home or market work precluded participation.[122] The market may be a useful tool under certain socioeconomic circumstances, but it may have a high price in terms of equity under unequal conditions.

Colombia's results with vouchers indicate that the choice model has merit but also limitations. Vouchers were offered to more than 125,000 students from poor neighborhoods. Demand for vouchers, however, exceeded supply, so a natural experiment could be run on the effects of those who won the voucher lottery versus those who did not have the chance to attend private schools. Data was collected three years later from 1,600 applicants for vouchers—half winners, half losers. Lottery winners were 15–20 percent more likely to be in private schools, were 10 percent more likely to complete eighth grade, and scored two standard deviations higher than losers on standardized tests, equivalent to a full grade level. Winners had greater incentive to work hard and stay in school, since poor grades meant losing the voucher. Kids therefore spent less time working in the labor market than losers and were less likely to marry or cohabit as teens. Interestingly, the net cost of the voucher was twenty-four dollars per winner over the cost of places in the public school.[123] Vouchers, nonetheless, also have their drawbacks. There may be a negative effect on those remaining in the public school as the more motivated are skimmed off to private institutions.[124] It should also be noted that vouchers are limited by the physical availability of private schools—overcrowding the private provision of education would generate many of the same problems prevalent in public schools. Furthermore, quality private schools are not frequently available in rural areas or in the poorer sections of town, limiting the ability of poor children to attend. The use of voucher programs may help in urban areas with safe, inexpensive transportation but will not be a magic fix for many of the problems confronting educators in Latin America.

The second innovation in demand-side education programs are CCTs. After well-publicized programs in Mexico and Brazil, nine countries currently employ CCTs, including Nicaragua, Honduras, and Colombia. CCTs are designed as a demand-side intervention to break the intergenerational transfer of poverty. In addition to the incentive to invest in a child's education, CCTs change accountability in that the central government directly pays families for keeping kids in school and investing in their health and well-being. CCTs work best when paired with supply-side incentives for improved quality; in Nicaragua, for example, teachers receive a bonus for each child participating to be used for school materials. CCTs can cover direct costs such as school fees, supplies, and transportation as well as cover indirect costs of children being in school—the often critical income that the child might lose from not working during school hours.

There are several design issues critical to building an effective CCT program. First, one must establish criteria for who gets the money. Assuming that funds are constrained, how should a child be selected to participate in the program? One clearly wants to use this money to its greatest effect, encouraging students who would otherwise drop out of school to stay on. How should a program be designed to minimize errors of **exclusion**—not awarding cash to kids who really need it—and maximize **additionality** or minimize errors of unwarranted inclusion by awarding money to kids who would stay in school without the funds? How should the rules be established such that they are perceived as fair and open to all, while minimizing the administrative costs of the program? The Opportunidades program in Mexico and Bolsa Família in Brazil provide contrasting answers to these problems.

Opportunidades has its roots in a 1997 program called Progresa. It was designed to increase Mexican school enrollments and performance by paying cash grants to mothers conditional on children's school attendance as well as regular participation in preventative health measures including nutritional supplements, health care visits, and health educational programs.[125] Children had to have 85 percent school attendance records, and the program required health center visits. The payments varied by grade, rising as kids passed the crucial turning points to secondary school, and provided an additional stipend for books. On average, eligible families were awarded fifty-five dollars a month, or an average increase in income of 22 percent dispersed through an electronic cash withdrawal card.[126] Girls were given a 15 percent premium because they were more likely to drop out.[127] Replacing food subsidies as a poverty program, by 2004 Opportunidades reached more than five million households in all thirty-one Mexican states, assisting 20 percent of the population.

Families were chosen in a three-step process.[128] Communities were targeted by a composite measure of deprivation from census data—basically identifying geographical pockets of poverty. Within the target communities, beneficiary households were identified based on household surveys. Before a family was actually included, the list of selected households was presented to a community meeting to review the accuracy of selection. At its inception, 506 communities participated, half randomly selected. The randomized implementation has allowed for systematic evaluation. Progresa/Opportunidades has kept 3.4 percent more kids in grades one through eight,[129] with the largest increase (14.8 percent) in girls completing grade six. Results show increased educational attainment by .66 years, with the largest impact on enrollment in the transition from primary to junior high school—a rise of 20 percent transition for girls and 10 percent for boys. Participation reduced the probability of working among those aged eight through seventeen by 10 to 14 percent, and beneficiaries aged birth to five years had a 12 percent lower chance of illness than nonparticipants. Infants participating in Progresa increased growth by 30–60 percent; the average consumption of Progresa households increased by 14 percent, and median food expenditures were 11 percent higher.[130]

Bolsa Escola, later expanded and renamed Bolsa Família, was designed differently in Brazil. Unlike the complicated selection criteria employed in Progresa, Bolsa pays monthly transfers of $30 to poor households (falling under the $30-a-day poverty line) with children aged six through fifteen years old in grades one through eight so long as they attend 85 percent of school without variation by age, gender, or geography.[131] In this sense, Brazil has opted for a lower payout with minimal administrative costs while risking the error of including families with less need. Local practice may vary as local governments shape programs to their own needs. Bolsa also uses a magnetic card, reaching approximately 5 million families in 2003. Initiated out of domestic resources, by the end of 2003 it had a $500 million loan from the IADB and another $500 million from the World Bank to improve targeting, implement impact evaluation, and enhance institutional organization and management. Renamed Bolsa Família by President Luiz Inácio "Lula" da Silva in 2003, it is targeted to reach the goal of 11.2 million families by 2006. The cash disbursements in Bolsa Família are seen by some as a citizenship right to a basic income, although greater oversight and verification were implemented after signs of corruption were uncovered by the media. Community review boards are designed to provide an element of oversight and transparency.

Given that the Bolsa program was not implemented through a randomized design (and some suggest that indeed it was broadly promoted to put cash in the hands of voters before an election) evaluation of specific outcomes is problematic. Nonetheless, its advantages are clear. Families have more discretionary money to invest in human capital. Since the payment is made to mothers, seen to have their children's best interest at heart, women are empowered to make decisions about household expenditures, and the transactions costs are limited. That is, rather than subsidies for milk, for example, families can choose how they want to spend the money. No large bureaucracy is needed to disburse the subsidy, and more families are pulled into the electronic financial system, where they can also begin the habit of saving. Other studies note that the dropout rate was reduced from 10 to .4 percent, employment rates of children aged ten to fourteen fell by 31.2 percent, the number of street children in Brasilia fell by 36 percent, and ten thousand families were rescued from acute poverty.[132]

But the results are not perfect; several difficulties have been raised with CCTs. We already mentioned the design difficulties of erroneous inclusion or exclusion leading to leakage of funds or undercoverage of families. In addition, it is difficult to enforce conditionalities. It is not impossible to cheat on attending health classes, and it may be that teachers are inflating attendance records under pressure from families and schools. Community reviews are frequently weak. CCTs face a series of administrative challenges. The incentives in a CCT system are largely to report compliance, even if students are not in attendance or families are not using required medical services. How can cost-effective mechanisms for monitoring compliance be designed that are at the same time accurate and timely?[133] As with any social services program, there is a need to establish graduation rates from the program. Once people are in the program, how do you move them out of the program when the need of others is greater? Recertification is an issue, especially because it is easier to bring someone into a program than to kick them out of it. Refinements are warranted to identify and correct errors of inclusion and exclusion, redressing the perception that some selections are unfair.[134]

CCTs are not a magic bullet to solve some of the toughest pockets of poverty. There is a clear need for coordination with service providers so that the program isn't simply mandating that the poor waste valuable time using inferior quality services.[135] They do not serve remote rural areas not attended by health and education services. People without children in school are excluded, and street kids fall through the cracks. CCTs are not effective without complementary supply-side measures. Encouraging kids to attend overpopulated and poorly staffed schools might increase enrollments but is unlikely to do much for the quality of schooling necessary to break the cycle of poverty. CCTs in some sense are an easy political sell—everyone wants more kids in school—but can be used to avoid some of the tougher structural supply-side issues discussed above. Seen as an add-on—especially if funding can be obtained by external resources—they can be used to avoid some of the hard problems of reform.[136] Nonetheless, when judiciously combined with oversight and compassion and complemented by strong supply-side initiatives, CCTs are an important tool in creating incentives to keep kids in school past critical turning points and encouraging them to acquire the human capital to break the inter-generational transfer of poverty and inequality.

Key Concepts

additionality	decentralization	externalities
conditional cash	educational deficit	grade repetition
transfer (CCT)	equity concerns	merit good
coordination failures	exclusion	vouchers

Chapter Summary

Education in Latin America: Deficits and Inequalities

- In comparison to other regions of the world, Latin America suffers from a severe education deficit.
- There is a marked education gap between socioeconomic groups. Those who can afford to send their children to private school benefit from a greater share of public educational expenditures along with higher-quality facilities and resources. The public school system is severely underfunded and deficient in resources and qualified teachers. As a result, poor children tend to have weaker performance, higher dropout rates, and higher repetition rates than children with higher socioeconomic status.

Indigenous Difficulties

- Although Latin America has made progress on gender bias in education, these benefits do not broadly extend to indigenous communities. In addition to the gender bias still apparent among indigenous communities, language, cultural barriers, and high opportunity costs hinder indigenous groups from attending school.

Continuing Education

- Education should not be limited to younger students and formal classrooms. Adult education is an important aspect in reducing the education deficit in Latin America. Informal education programs that allow marginalized groups who are unable to attend school to define their own educational needs have proven to be effective measures in empowering these sectors of the population.

Education Reform: Increasing Both Quality and Access

- Reform should be both supply and demand oriented. On the supply side, measures should be taken to hold schools and teachers accountable for the quality of the education that is being provided. Teacher qualifications should be made more rigorous, and absence or poor performance from teachers and administrators should be punished.
- On the demand side, initiatives from private, nongovernmental, and public institutions should be implemented to encourage families and students to demand better access and a higher quality of education. Vouchers, scholarship programs, and CCTs are all ways in which governments and other institutions can encourage families to send their children to school and help cover the high opportunity costs incurred by education as well as involve communities in the decision-making process.

Notes

Thanks to Kristin Saucier, Colby Class of '04, currently at the Inter-American Dialogue, for her comments on this chapter.

1. Partnership for Educational Revitalization in the Americas (PREAL), *Quantity without Quality: A Report Card on Education in Latin America,* 2006, www.thedialogue.org/publications/2006/winter/preal_quantity.pdf.

2. Laurence Wolff et al., *Improving the Quality of Primary Education in Latin America and the Caribbean: Toward the 21st Century* (Washington, D.C.: World Bank, 1994), 2.

3. PREAL, *Quantity without Quality.*

4. Statistics from Jeffrey M. Puryear, "Education in Latin America: Problems and Challenges," Partnership for Educational Revitalization in the Americas [PREAL], May 7, 1997, Presented to the Council of Foreign Relations, February 27, 1996, for the Latin America program study group Educational Reform in Latin America, New York, www.preal.cl. Key "FLACSO" into your favorite search engine to get a sense of the broad range of activity in the region.

5. "Tertiary Education Soars in Middle-Income Countries," OECD Press Release No. 2005-120.

6. Ibid.

7. David De Ferranti et al., *Inequality in Latin America and the Caribbean: Breaking with History?* World Bank Latin American and Caribbean Studies (Washington, D.C.: World Bank, 2004), chap. 3.

8. PREAL, *Quantity without Quality.*

9. Ibid.

10. Save the Children, "Studying for a Better Future: Daniela in Bolivia," www.savethechildren.org.

11. Ibid.

12. Ricardo Morán, "Introduction: Early Childhood Investment and the Intergenerational Transmission of Poverty," in *Escaping the Poverty Trap: Investing in Children in Latin America,* ed. Ricardo Morán (Washington, D.C.: IADB, 2003), 2.

13. Ricardo Morán, Tarsicio Castañeda, and Enrique Aldaz-Carroll, "Part One: Intergenerational Transmission of Poverty," in *Escaping the Poverty Trap,* 27.

14. World Bank, *World Development Indicators 2005* (Washington, D.C.: World Bank, 2005).

15. Barbara Herz and Gene B. Sperling, *What Works in Girls' Education: Evidence and Policies from the Developing World, Executive Summary* (New York: Council on Foreign Relations, 2004), 4.

16. Ibid., 6.

17. Morán, Castañeda, and Aldaz-Carroll, "Part One: Intergenerational Transmission of Poverty," 25.

18. UNICEF, "The State of the World's Children 2005: Childhood under Threat," Annual Report, 2004.

19. IADB, "Estrategio para el Desarrollo Indígena," www.iadb.org, 2005, 27.

20. IADB, *Women in the Americas: Bridging the Gap* (Baltimore: Johns Hopkins University Press, 1995).

21. M. Anne Hill and Elizabeth M. King, "Women's Education in Developing Countries: An Overview," in *Women's Education in Developing Countries: Barriers, Benefits, and Policies,* ed. M. Anne Hill and Elizabeth M. King (Baltimore: Johns Hopkins University Press, 1993), 19.

22. Diane Steele, "Guatemala," in *Indigenous People and Poverty in Latin America,* ed. George Psacharopoulos and Harry Anthony Patrinos (Washington, D.C.: World Bank, 1994), 104.

23. Bill Wood and Harry Anthony Patrinos, "Urban Bolivia," in *Indigenous People and Poverty in Latin America,* 63.

24. Donna Macisaac, "Peru," in *Indigenous People and Poverty in Latin America,* 170.

25. Lucy Trapnell, "Identity Crisis," *Developments* 22 (2003), www.developments.org.uk/data/Issue22/identity-crisis.htm.

26. Lucy A. Trapnell, "Some Key Issues in Intercultural Bilingual Education Teacher Training Programmes—As Seen from a Teacher Training Programme in the Peruvian Amazon Basin," *Comparative Education* 39(2) (2003): 168.

27. Trapnell, "Identity Crisis."

28. IADB, "Estrategia para el Desarrollo Indígena," 7.

29. Ibid., 27.

30. Ibid., 5.

31. Mary Ann Zehr, "Bilingual Education in One Tongue," *Education Week* 21(27) (March 20, 2002).

32. IADB, "Estrategia para el Desarrollo Indígena," 27–28.

33. María Elena García, "Rethinking Bilingual Education in Peru: Intercultural Politics, State Policy and Indigenous Rights," in *Bilingual Education in South America,* ed. Anne-Marie de Mejía (North Somerset, UK: Multilingual Matters Ltd., 2005), 26.

34. IADB, "Estrategia para el Desarrollo Indígena," 28.

35. García, "Rethinking Bilingual Education in Peru," 23.

36. Trapnell, "Identity Crisis," 11.

37. www.formabiap.org.

38. PREAL, *Quantity without Quality.*

39. Laurence Wolff, Juan Carlos Navarro, and Pablo González, *Private Education and Public Policy in Latin America* (Washington, D.C.: PREAL), 2005.

40. UNESCO, *Education for All, Literacy for Life,* 2006, Education for all Global Monitoring Report, citing Nelly P. Stromquist, "The Political Benefits of Adult Literacy," Background paper, 2005, http://www.unesco.org/education/GMR2006/full/chapt5_eng.pdf, 137.

41. UNESCO Santiago, *Educational Panorama 2005: Progressing toward the Goals,* Regional Education Indicators Project, Summit of the Americas, November 2005, www.unesco.cl.

42. Marcela Gajardo, "Reformas Educativas en América Latina—Balance de una década," PREAL Working Paper No. 15, September 1999, 9.

43. Paulo Freire, *Pedagogy of the Oppressed* (New York: Seabury, 1970).

44. UNESCO, *Education for All, Literacy for Life,* 233.

45. John A. Britton, ed., *Molding the Hearts and Minds: Education, Communications, and Social Change in Latin America* (Wilmington, Del.: Scholarly Resources, 1994), xxiv. For more on social change, see Carlos A. Torres, *Education and Social Change in Latin America* (Albert Park, Australia: James Nicolas, 1997).

46. Wolff et al., *Improving the Quality of Primary Education,* 4.

47. UNESCO, *Education for All, Literacy for Life,* 232.

48. UNESCO, *Educational Panorama 2005.*

49. Ibid.

50. PREAL, *Quantity without Quality.*

51. UNESCO, *Educational Panorama 2005.*

52. Ibid.

53. PREAL, *Quantity without Quality.*

54. Ibid.

55. Ibid.

56. PREAL, *Lagging Behind: A Report Card on Education in Latin America,* 6, www.thedialogue.org/publications/preal/lagging.pdf.

57. PREAL, *The Future at Stake: Report of the Task Force on Education, Equity and Economic Competitiveness in Latin America and the Caribbean,* 7, www.thedialogue.org/publications/preal/future.pdf.

58. Wolff et al., *Improving the Quality of Primary Education,* 5.

59. Wolff, Navarro, and González, *Private Education and Public Policy in Latin America.*

60. Jeffrey Puryear, "Quantity without Quality: A Report Card on Education in Latin America," Powerpoint presentation at Education in Latin America IDB Social Development Week, October 2005.

61. Robert Kaufman and Joan Nelson, "The Political Challenges of Social Sector Reform," in *Crucial Needs, Weak Incentives: Social Sector Reform, Democratization, and Globalization in Latin America,* ed. Robert R. Kaufman and Joan M. Nelson (Washington, D.C.: Woodrow Wilson Center Press and Johns Hopkins University Press, 2004).

62. Puryear, "Quantity without Quality."

63. Puryear, "Education in Latin America."

64. IADB, *Facing Up to Inequality in Latin America* (Washington, D.C.: Johns Hopkins University Press, 1998), 129.

65. Katherine Ellison, "Latin Summit's Focus: Education of Kids," *Miami Herald,* April 13, 1998, A1. Available online at www.alca-cupula.org.

66. A. Fiszbein and G. Psacharopoulos, *Income Inequality in Latin America: The Story of the Eighties,* Technical Department for Latin America Working Paper (Washington, D.C.: World Bank, 1995), as cited in IADB, *IDB Annual Report: Making Social Services Work* (Washington, D.C.: IADB, 1996), 245.

67. "Skills Gap May Be Biggest Trade Barrier," *Journal of Commerce,* April 20, 1998. Online edition available at www.alca-cupula.org.

68. Wolff et al., *Improving the Quality of Primary Education,* 1.

69. Lawrence J. Lau, Dean T. Jamison, Shucheng Liu, and Steven Rivkin, "Education and Economic Growth: Some Cross-Sectional Evidence," in *Education in Brazil,* ed. Nancy Birdsall and Richard H. Sabot (Washington, D.C.: IADB, 1996), 83–116. The large variation, between 5 and 20 percent, is a function of the existing educational infrastructure. If initial levels are low, large returns accrue after four years. The authors estimate that after this jump, the relationship will smooth out, with each year adding 5 percent in output.

70. Eduardo Lora and Felipe Barrera, "A Decade of Structural Reform in Latin America: Growth, Productivity, and Investment Are Not What They Used to Be," Document for discussion at the IADB Barcelona seminar "Latin America after a Decade of Reform: What Next?" on March 16, 1997.

71. PREAL, *Future at Stake,* 10.

72. Wolff, Navarro, and González, *Private Education and Public Policy in Latin America.*

73. ODI briefing paper, *Globalization and Education,* October 2005.

74. PREAL, *Quantity without Quality.*

75. Kaufman and Nelson, "The Political Challenges of Social Sector Reform."

76. Paul Glewwe and Michael Kremer, "School, Teachers, and Education Outcomes in Developing Countries," CID Working Paper No. 122, Prepared as second draft of chapter for *The Handbook on the Economics of Education,* September 2005, Harvard University, 42.

77. Unesco, *Education for All Year 2000 Assessment,* Preparatory document for the World Education Forum, Dakar, Senegal, April 2000.

78. ECLAC, *Financing and Management of Education in Latin America and the Caribbean,* July 2004, LC/G2249.

79. Eduardo Amedeo, José Márcio Camargo, Antônio Emílio S. Marques, and Cândido Gomes, "Fiscal Crisis and Asymmetries in the Education System in Brazil," in *Coping with Crisis: Austerity, Adjustment, and Human Resources,* ed. Joel Samoa (New York: UNESCO/ILO, 1994), 48.

80. Amaury de Souza, "Redressing Inequalities: Brazil's Social Agenda at Century's End," in *Brazil under Cardoso,* ed. Susan Kaufman Purcel and Riordan Roett (Boulder, Colo.: Lynne Rienner, 1997), 76.

81. Claudio de Moura Castro, "Education: Way Behind but Trying to Catch Up," *Daedalus* 129(2) (Spring 2000): 304.

82. Diana Jean Schemo, "The ABC's of Doing Business in Brazil," *New York Times,* July 16, 1998, D7.

83. PREAL, *Future at Stake,* 12.

84. Mary Anastasia O'Grady, "A Brazilian State Shows How to Reform Schools," *Wall Street Journal,* August 16, 1997, A17.

85. Summarized from presentation of Juan Carlos Navarro, IADB conference, Washington, D.C., November 12, 1997.

86. Kaufman and Nelson, "The Political Challenges of Social Sector Reform," 489.

87. ECLAC, *Financing and Management of Education in Latin America and the Caribbean.*

88. Schemo, "The ABC's," D7.

89. Ellison, "Latin Summit's Focus."

90. Wolff et al., *Improving the Quality of Primary Education,* 8.

91. David E. Lorey, "Education and the Challenges of Mexican Development," *Challenge* 38(2) (March–April 1995): 52.

92. ECLAC, *Financing and Management of Education in Latin America and the Caribbean.* Data was for 1990–1994; no more recent data available.

93. UNESCO, *Education for All, Literacy for Life,* citing Ariel Fiszbein, *Argentina's Crisis and Its Impact on Household Welfare* (Washington DC: World Bank, 2002).

94. UNESCO, *Education for All, Literacy for Life,* citing Carlos Aggio, "A Case Study on Debt Conversion, Spain and Argentina" (2005).

95. Rosemary T. Bellew and Elizabeth M. King, "Educating Women: Lessons from Experience," in *Women's Education in Developing Countries: Barriers, Benefits and Policies,* ed. Elizabeth M. King and Rosemary Bellew (Baltimore: Johns Hopkins University Press, 1993), 305.

96. George Psacharopoulos, Carlos Rojas, and Eduardo Velez, "Achieving Evaluation of Colombia's Escuela Nueva: Is Multigrade the Answer?" *Comparative Education Review* 37(3) (1993).

97. Molly Moore, "Mayan Girls Make Fifth Grade History," *Washington Post,* June 20, 1996, A19.

98. Gary S. Becker, "Bribe the Third World Parents to Keep Their Kids in School," *BusinessWeek,* November 22, 1999, 15.

99. Wolff, Navarro, and González, *Private Education and Public Policy in Latin America.*

100. Ibid.

101. UNESCO, *Education for All, Literacy for Life.*

102. Glewwe and Kremer, "School, Teachers, and Education Outcomes in Developing Countries," 41.

103. Kaufman and Nelson, "The Political Challenges of Social Sector Reform," 276.

104. Glewwe and Kremer, "School, Teachers, and Education Outcomes in Developing Countries," 10.

105. Glewwe and Kremer, "School, Teachers, and Education Outcomes in Developing Countries," 44, citing Emmanuel Jiminenz and Yasuyuki Sawada, "Do Community-Managed Schools Work? An Evaluation of El Salvador's EDUCO Program," *World Bank Economic Review* 13(3) (1999): 415–441.

106. PREAL, *Quantity without Quality.*

107. Glewwe and Kremer, "School, Teachers, and Education Outcomes in Developing Countries," 45, citing Edward Miguel and Mary Kay Gugerty, "Ethnic Diversity, Social Sanctions, and Public Goods in Kenya," *Journal of Public Economics* 89(11–12) (2005): 2325–2368.

108. ECLAC, *Financing and Management of Education in Latin America and the Caribbean.*

109. Juan Prawda, "Educational Decentralization in Latin America: Lessons Learned," *International Journal of Educational Development* 13(3) (1993): 253–264.

110. Council on Foreign Relations, "Reforming Education in America," Study group on reforming education in Latin America, "The Second Wave of Reform," directed by Allison L. C. de Cerreño, New York, February–October 1996.

111. PREAL, *Future at Stake,* 11.

112. For a review of educational assessment instruments, see Laurence Wolff, "Educational Assessments in Latin America: Current Progress and Future Challenges," *Partnership for Educational Revitalization in the Americas,* June 1998, 11. Online publication available at www.preal.cl/index-i.htm.

113. Wolff, Navarro, and González, *Private Education and Public Policy in Latin America.*

114. World Bank, "Mexico: Schools without Leaks," www.worldbank.org, external news.

115. William Myers, ed., *Protecting Working Children* (London: Zed, 1991); and Anthony Dewees and Steven Klees, "Social Movements and the Transformation of National Policy: Street and Working Children in Brazil," *Comparative Education Review* 39(1) (1995).

116. Jere R. Behrman, Suzanne Duryea, and Migúel Szekely, "Schooling, Investment and Aggregate Conditions: A Household Survey-Based Approach for Latin America and the Caribbean," IADB Working Paper No. 40, November 29, 1999, 27.

117. Alejandra Mizala, Pilar Romaguera, and Carolina Ostoic, "Equity and Achievement in the Chilean School Choice System," Center for Applied Economics, Universidad de Chile, April 2005.

118. Mizala, Romaguera, and Ostoic, "Equity and Achievement in the Chilean School Choice System."

119. Ibid.

120. Emmanuel de Kadt, "Thematic Lessons from the Case Studies," in *The Public-Private Mix in Social Services,* ed. Elaine Zuckerman and Emanuel de Kadt (Washington, D.C.: Inter-American Development Bank, 1997), 131–143.

121. Mizala, Romaguera and Ostoic, "Equity and Achievement in the Chilean School Choice System."

122. Carol Graham, *Private Markets for Public Goods: Raising the Stakes for Economic Reform* (Washington, D.C.: Brookings Institution Press, 1998), 45.

123. Glewwe and Kremer, "School, Teachers, and Education Outcomes in Developing Countries," 48, citing Joshua Angrist, Eric Bettinger, Erik Bloom, Elizabeth King, and Michael Kremer, "Vouchers for Private Schooling in Colombia: Evidence from a Randomized Natural Experiment," *American Economic Review* 92(5) (2002): 1535–1558.

124. Glewwe and Kremer, "School, Teachers, and Education Outcomes in Developing Countries," 48, citing Joshua Angrist, Eric Bettinger, and Michael Kremer, "Long-Term Consequences of Secondary School Vouchers: Evidence from Administrative Records of Colombia," BREAD (Bureau for Research in Economic Analysis of Development) Working Paper No. 79, 2004.

125. Glewwe and Kremer, "School, Teachers, and Education Outcomes in Developing Countries," 10.

126. Laura B. Rawlings, "A New Approach to Social Assistance: Latin America's Experience with Conditional Cash Transfer Programmes," *International Social Security Review* 58(2–3) (2005); and Alain de Janvry and Elisabeth Sadoulet, "Making Conditional Cash Transfer Programs More Efficient: Designing for Maximum Effect of the Conditionality," UC Berkeley (processed), May 2005.

127. Tatiana Britto, "Recent Trends in the Development Agenda of Latin America: An Analysis of Conditional Cash Transfers," Ministry of Social Development, Brazil, tatib@brturbo.com.br, February 2005, 8.

128. Britto, "Recent Trends in the Development Agenda of Latin America," 9.

129. Glewwe and Kremer, "School, Teachers, and Education Outcomes in Developing Countries," 10.

130. Rawlings, "A New Approach to Social Assistance," 150.

131. Britto, "Recent Trends in the Development Agenda of Latin America," 11.

132. Christian Andrew Denes, "Bolsa Escola: Redefining Poverty and Development in Brazil," *International Education Journal* 4(2) (2003). To present these results, Denes cites Caccia Bava and S. Bolsa-Escola, "A Public Policy on Minimum Income and Education" (Leeds, England: Pólis-Research, Formation and Social Policies Consultancy Institutel, 2002), and C. H. Araújo and E. P. Nascimento, *Bolsa-Escola: Effects and Potential,* Paper presented at the Twenty-fourth General Population Conference International Union for the Scientific Study of Population for Salvador and Bahia, Brazil, August 18–24, 2001.

133. Britto, "Recent Trends in the Development Agenda of Latin America," 19.

134. Ibid., 17.

135. Rawlings, "A New Approach to Social Assistance," 152.

136. Kaufman and Nelson, "The Political Challenges of Social Sector Reform," 479.

CHAPTER FOURTEEN

ENVIRONMENTAL CHALLENGES

Internalizing the Costs of Development

Automobiles are a major source of urban pollution. *(Courtesy of the Inter-American Development Bank)*

Understanding environmental issues in Latin America is very much about understanding the broader pattern of development that has shaped the region. The environment is inextricably linked with past economic performance and social conditions as well as local and global policy choices. In the context of our understanding of the history of the region, the import substitution model, the challenge of the debt crisis, and the transformations of the neoliberal model, we now turn our focus specifically to the environment.

The following questions inform our discussion:

- How do countries, grappling with problems of economic growth and stability and burdened by poverty, address environmental concerns?
- Is there a trade-off between a brighter economic future for the millions of impoverished in Latin America and the health of the environment?
- How should countries weigh the pressing needs of present generations against a clean environment for the future?

Such environmental concerns have challenged and transformed the core of development economics. Traditional economic models neglected to account for externalities in the growth process or the finite nature of natural resources. Today, development economics is being redefined by the concept of **sustainable development.** A simple definition of sustainable development offered by the World Commission on Environment and Development is that current generations should "meet their needs without compromising the ability of future generations to meet their own needs."[1] This vision has inspired local, national, and international organizations to work to define a development model that balances economic growth with environmental sensibility. The 1992 United Nations Conference on the Environment and Development held in Rio de Janeiro was a turning point for the region and the world in revisioning the development process. Ten years later, nations revisited the accomplishments and challenges in international environmental policy in Johannesburg, South Africa. The 2002 meetings highlighted that although much has been accomplished in raising environmental consciousness, financing for sustainable development remains a huge obstacle to measurable progress. But progress can be made through public-private partnerships. At a March 2006 meeting in Curitiba, Brazil crafted a road map to reduce biodiversity loss by 2010 with significant participation of business and civil society.

Implementation of a development strategy that weighs the needs of current generations against the requirements of the future is complicated in practice. Difficult policy questions arise:

- How should competing needs of the present and the future, the economy and the environment, be prioritized?
- How can we think systematically about the complex interrelationships between social, economic, and ecosystems in the region?
- What are the elements of an economically sound and politically viable environmental policy?
- How should global institutions promote financing for sound international environmental policy?

After exploring the concept of sustainable development in greater detail, we will consider its application in the region. Latin America is geographically diverse, ranging from deserts to rain forests, mountains to plains, from the most rural settlements to the most densely populated and extensive megacities in the world. Each area itself contains a huge variety of plants, animals (including humans), and minerals. The complexity of social and ecosystems adds to the challenge of environmental management in Latin America. Priorities in environmental management vary from country to country, as does the institutional capacity to meet the challenge of sustainable development. This chapter will describe the diverse environmental concerns that Latin America faces in terms of human standards of living as well as ecological conditions. It will then turn to consider the best policy mix and the options for financing to meet the standard of sustainable development in the region.

Is Development Sustainable?

The 1987 Brundtland Report of the World Commission on Environment and Development defined environmentally sustainable development as meeting the needs of the current generation without compromising the ability of future generations. Perhaps like all great ideas, it is a deceivingly simple concept. Meeting the needs of a current generation involves integrating economic, social, environmental, and political concerns.[2] Sustainable development promotes the efficient use of resources in the service of a stable growth path. The growth pattern, however, is very much shaped by social conditions. Without attention to poverty and inequality, the basic needs of the current generation are not met. Attention must be paid to the ways that gender shapes access to environmental assets. The Brundtland Report notes that a "world in which poverty is endemic will always be prone to ecological and other catastrophes."[3] All people, including marginalized groups, must be vested in the development process. How can people living in absolute poverty support the hard choices that sometimes must be made to postpone present consumption to favor future sustainability? Postponing consumption while living on the margins of existence threatens survival. Without participation of all segments of the population, a social consensus cannot be achieved to balance present and future needs.

For development to be sustainable, economic and social changes must be set against the capabilities of the physical environment to support human activity. Achieving sustainability therefore must delicately balance a growing population and the ability of the physical environment to absorb the waste of human activity.[4] Technical fixes are one way out of this bind. The capacity of the physical environment to support human life can be transformed by technological changes allowing people to do more with less. However, betting sustainability on potential technological change is fraught with uncertainty. We might hope that new (and cheap) technologies are developed to provide energy, recycle solid and hazardous wastes, purify sewage and industrial wastes before they hit the sea, and reduce emission from motor vehicles. But can we count on it?

Sound environmental policy involves hard choices. Who makes them? Identifying whose needs are met in the present and the future involves political decisions—

This Colombian recycling project contributes to urban cleanup and generates jobs.
(Courtesy of Willie Heinz and the Inter-American Development Bank)

Figure 14.1.   The Complexity of Environmental Decision Making

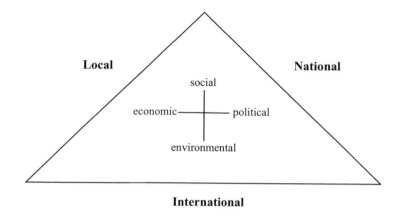

decisions in Latin America that historically have been made by male elites. As can be seen in figure 14.1, economic, environmental, political, and social factors influence policy at the local, national, and international levels. The priorities at each level might be in conflict. Although global concerns for biodiversity or the greenhouse effect might dominate the agenda of the more industrialized nations, the interaction of poverty and the environment is likely to be of greater concern at the local and national levels.

When the problems of current generations are so pressing, it is tough (especially for elected officials) to postpone meeting today's needs in favor of the future. As one Salvadoran said, "There is no point in having a beautiful environment if there is nothing to eat."[5] Furthermore, it is difficult for governments to assess the well-being of present generations. How do we measure environmental quality? Is it measured by homes with sewer connections, clean air, the number of endangered species, or the acreage in protected national parks?[6] An accurate measure of environmental quality involves much better data collection and estimation of current and future resource stocks.[7] Better data would permit a more consistent estimation of the present value of future resource use. This tough calculation of society's willingness to pay today for future access to a sustainable environment is at the core of strong policy recommendations.

To assess the bundle of social and environmental capital that one generation should pass on to the next, some environmental economists promote the concept of a **safe minimum standard.**[8] The safe minimum is seen as a social compact that, in the face of high ecological uncertainty, provides a basis for sustainable growth. Of course, the differing priorities of the industrialized North and the developing South make such a compact on global issues precarious. To a large degree, natural capital or biodiversity finds its home in the South, whereas social capital, including scientific and technical knowledge to preserve natural capital, is largely lodged in the North. Different valuations placed on the need to employ natural capital today versus desires to preserve ecological diversity for the future suggest that the North, having already depleted much of its natural stocks, will have to compensate the South to preserve biodiversity. But how much, and on whose terms?

The **Global Environment Facility** (**GEF**) was formed after the 1992 Earth Summit Rio to address financial and technological transfers. Following the conference, the concept of sustainable development found expression in five basic agreements: the Rio Declaration, which articulated political principles for revisioning development models; **Agenda 21,** a comprehensive agenda for action; the Convention on Biological Diversity; the Convention on Climate Change; and the Declaration of Principles on the Management, Conservation, and Sustainable Development of Forests. The 2002 **World Summit on Sustainable Development** in Johannesburg has underscored the patchy record in reversing environmental degradation while the South struggles under financial constraints. Despite clear goals, there has been an implementation gap, driven by limited resources, policy incoherence, and a fragmented approach in connecting the environment to development. We will return to consider shared global responsibilities later in this chapter.

Globalization has increased the negative externalities created by an integrated production structure. Direct environmental effects are generated by new agricultural and industrial techniques, the exploitation of hitherto untapped nonrenewable resources, and the release of new substances into the environment. Indirect effects are created by the social, economic, political, and demographic adjustments to globalization that have resulted in new forms of organizing work and new consumption patterns and the location and nature of human activities and settlements.[9] New technologies and sustainable social planning are necessary to manage increasing pressures on ecosystems, especially in fragile and remote areas.

Achieving sustainable development is therefore complicated by problems of measurement, the uncertainty of future technological change, and political will on local, national, and international levels to make and pay for hard choices. Yet for all its limitations, it is an extremely useful policy principle. Meeting the needs of the present for a better life without compromising the stock of assets available to future generations is an important criterion that can be applied to policies addressing industry, infrastructure development, or poverty. The accomplishment of the past decade has been to insert sustainable development as a clear frame of reference in macro, poverty, health, and industrial policy. How to bring this principle into the policy arena in a way that minimizes the economic costs and maximizes the environmental benefits will be addressed at the end of the chapter. But before we design policy, we must first better understand the nature of the environmental problem in the Latin American region.

Environmental Priorities in Latin America

What is the most pressing environmental problem in achieving sustainable development in Latin America? In fact, this is not a very good question. There is a broad array of environmental issues in the region that vary in importance based upon who you are, where you live, and what economic resources are available to you. The priority list depends on whether you are rich or poor, urban or rural, male or female. A middle-class resident of Santiago, Chile, is likely to complain most about air quality, while someone living in a shack along the Tiete River in São Paulo might be most affected by problems of water sanitation. A rubber tapper might ally with an international rain forest activist in arguing that tropical deforestation is the most pressing issue, but for very different reasons. Problems in maintaining fishing stocks off the coast of Argentina might seem a long way from the concerns of the Indians in Peru's Altiplano. Women might worry about the ways that communities struggle to overcome deficits with water or sewage. As Latin America is diverse, so are its environmental concerns.

Poverty As an Impediment to Sustainable Development

Throughout Latin America—urban or rural, tropical or polar—it is clear that sustainable development is not possible without making progress toward alleviating poverty. The poor are both agents and victims of an unsafe environment. Lacking resources to invest in cleaner water or waste removal or the assets necessary in agriculture to reinvest in soil quality, the poor can promote environmental degradation in their struggle to survive. But they are also the worst victims of unhealthy water and air quality, and they are often financially unable to flee the worst zones of pollution.

Poverty, and its associated social and economic conditions of malnutrition, underdeveloped human capital, disease, and lack of savings, is linked to environmental damage. Biodiversity loss, deforestation and desertification, soil erosion and nutrient depletion, and water pollution are in part caused by resource constraints of land scarcity, receding fuel wood and water supply, reduced agricultural productivity, and unhygienic sanitation.[10] Unable to postpone present consumption or invest in the future, the poor scrape to survive.

Poverty can be exacerbated by population growth. If the economic pie is not growing, more inhabitants leave fewer people with the ability to sustain themselves today and invest in their futures. Population growth increases the demand for goods and services, introducing more pollutants into the waste stream. In Latin America the population grew 2.4 percent from 1970 to 1980 and approximately 2 percent from 1980 until 1995. Over the lost decade of the 1980s, as gross domestic product (GDP) rose only 1.1 percent, population growth rates far outpaced the economy, leaving little for environmental progress. Over the next twenty years Latin America's population will increase from 559 million to 702 million, multiplying the demands on the carrying capacity of its fragile environmental infrastructure.[11]

But reducing poverty alone will not be sufficient to reduce the stress on environmental resources. Inadequate resources to meet basic human needs may induce destructive survival strategies. More than meeting basic dietary requirements is necessary to promote sustainability. The capacity of households to invest in sustainable strategies depends on having access to adequate assets that permit investment in human and physical capital. Moreover, even when capital is in sufficient supply, people must perceive the incentives to invest in sustainable growth. The nonpoor, for example, contribute to deforestation through illegal logging when the expected return on lumber is greater than the punishment and probability of getting caught compared to the returns in legal and sustainable activities. Simply having enough money does not dissuade them. Policies to induce sustainable strategies must engage a careful blend of regulations and incentives to change behavior.[12]

MEGACITIES BRING ENORMOUS ENVIRONMENTAL CHALLENGES

Population growth rates outpaced the economy in the 1980s, but as the region has recovered in the 1990s, the environmental dividend has been far from evident. Why? In part this is due to the fact that population growth has taken place disproportionately in the urban sector. In 1965, 55.9 percent of the population in South America lived in cities; by 2005 this number reached 82 percent for South America and 68.7 percent for Central America; the U.S. ratio is 77.2 percent. Rates of **urbanization** of 90.6 percent in Argentina, 84.2 percent in Brazil, 88.1 percent in Venezuela, 93 percent in Uruguay, and 87.7 percent in Chile challenge the folkloric picture of a peasant in a small village or an Indian in the rain forest that many hold as typical of Latin America.[13] It is estimated that by 2025 Latin America will have the highest rate of urbanization in the world at approximately 85 percent.[14] The rate of transformation of urban centers has overwhelmed the capacity of municipalities to provide clean air and water or rapid and reasonable transportation and telecommunications infrastructure to their inhabitants. You may have vacationed in Cancun. As its population mushroomed from a small town of 20,000 to a city of 340,000, only 60 percent of its urban zone had running water; those with piped access didn't have a steady twenty-four-hour supply. Waste water was worse; only 30 percent of the urban zone was connected to sewerage systems.[15] The development of this fragile infrastructure has now been further weakened by Hurricane Stan in 2005.

As UN secretary-general Kofi Annan noted in the UN's State of the World's Cities,[16] cities are hubs of dynamism, change, and opportunity but also places of exploitation, disease, and unemployment. Urbanization in Latin America is compressed in a few megacities. In the United States, 41.7 percent of urban dwellers live rather evenly spread over forty-three cities with at least 750,000 inhabitants; in Latin America the pattern, with the exception of Brazil, typically is one megacity per country. Forty percent of all Chileans live in Santiago, 25 percent living below the poverty line; 30 percent of Peruvians inhabit Lima. In 2006, Gran São Paulo and Mexico City had populations of 18.61 million and 19.24 million, respectively, putting them in the top five megacities with Tokyo and Mumbai.[17] As anyone who has lived in or visited New York or Los Angeles knows, the air, water, and transportation problems of the city overpower even the best of intentions. Imagine trying to solve the same set of problems with even fewer financial resources.

The 75 percent of the population living in cities concentrates solid waste and disposal problems. Region-wide, Latin America generates an estimated seventy-four million tons of waste per year—and safe disposal is woefully inadequate. Guatemala City collects only 65 percent of its municipal waste; the rest is disposed of in "unofficial" locations. Garbage collection is seen as outside formal-sector services or inaccessible through narrow, unpaved streets.[18] In Argentina, for example, only 40 percent of solid waste is disposed of in an acceptable manner. Sixty percent lands in open dumps without sanitary controls, breeding disease and promoting surface and groundwater contamination. An estimated thirty thousand families called "cartoneros" are informal paper recyclers in the street, separating and sorting cardboard and other materials. One in two is a child. Miguel Carabagal and his teen son Lucas support nine other children at home by collecting recyclable trash. The city of Buenos Aires recognizes the benefits of these informal recyclers who reduce the amount of solid waste going into landfills by 25 percent. When other city residents protested against the smells that these scavengers brought with them as they boarded city trains for work, a special train was set up to bring the night shift of garbage pickers into the city. Organized leaders of the garbage pickers also won subsidies and special tutoring for the child workers who all too often are too tired to study by day.[19] Others leave the streets to pick in the dumps themselves, exposed to intermingled health wastes and other refuse. Where regulations on safe solid waste management exist, enforcement is weak. The government of Argentina has acknowledged the public good nature of solid waste management and is working with World Bank assistance to stimulate construction of environmentally acceptable final disposal facilities. This is costly—and an even greater challenge for some of the poorer countries in the region.

Ironies abound. If Latin Americans produced as much garbage as those who live in the United States, the result would simply be unbearable. For example, each person in Quito, Ecuador, produces about 281 kilograms of solid waste a year. In São Paulo per capita solid waste generation stands at 352 kilograms—low compared to the average resident in Washington, D.C., who produces 1,246 kilograms of solid waste.[20] Complicating solid waste management even further is the fact that the composition of waste has changed in the past thirty years from largely organic materials to nonbiodegradable refuse with a high percentage of toxic substances. Disposal facilities are little more than garbage dumps rather than sanitary landfills to manage problems of urban waste. Table 14.1 illustrates the dimensions of solid waste per capita, wastewater treatment, and households with waste collection service in selected Latin American cities.

The size of urban cities makes environmental problems extraordinarily complex. Poverty is concentrated in urban areas, with poor urban dwellers living in substandard housing within informal settlements with limited or no access to basic services. Unsustainable human settlements, often in dangerous locations, generally lack basic municipal services such as safe drinking water, sanitation, public transport, schools, and clinics. Of the more than four hundred million urban dwellers in the region, roughly one in four Central Americans and one in three South Americans live in city slums. In Guatemala and Peru, two in three urbanites live in substandard dwellings. Lima, Peru, is home for approximately seven million of the country's inhabitants living in what the government euphemistically refers to as "emergency dwellings." The lack of running water, electricity, and sanitation encourages the spread of infectious disease such as cholera.[21] Of course, aggregate statistics mask the environmental health concerns in the slums. When only 65 percent of waste is collected or 20 percent of the people lack an improved water source, this is not neatly spread out among families in luxury condominiums and neat middle-

Table 14.1.   Solid Waste Production, Wastewater Treatment, and Waste Collection in Selected Latin American Cities

City	Solid Waste per Capita (kg/year)	Wastewater Treated (percentage)	Households with Waste Collection Service (percentage)
Brasilia	182	54	95
Havana	584	100	100
La Paz	182	0	92
San Salvador	328	2	46
Santiago	182	5	57
Toronto[a]	511	100	100

Source: United Nations Environment Program and ECLAC, "The Sustainability of Development in Latin America and the Caribbean: Challenges and Opportunities," prepared for the Preparatory Conference of Latin America and the Caribbean for the World Conference on Sustainable Development (Johannesburg, South Africa, 2002), 81, table IV.12.
[a]For purposes of comparison.

class homes. Instead, in many cities half of those living in slums lack sanitation or a third live without safe water supplies, creating environmental health emergencies.

Poor urban residents in Latin America struggle to cope with a host of these societal shortfalls, making daily life an environmental battle. These deficits may be the result of inadequate urban planning under pressure from population changes, lack of investment in infrastructure, or indifference to the needs of the poor in elite-controlled political systems. Market criteria have dominated development planning, compounding weaknesses of environmental institutions and the lack of formal mechanisms for effective civil society participation.[22] Investments in the poor *favelas* or *barrios* in the region are critical to achieving environmental sustainability.

The costs of urban environmental problems are enormous. The World Bank estimates that the welfare costs of illness and death due to dirty air and water in the region range between $1 billion and $3 billion. Premature death and illness caused by environmental health risks account for one-fifth of the total burden of disease in the developing world, comparable to that of nutrition, and larger than all other preventable risk factors and groups.[23] Brazilians calculate that 70 percent of all hospital admissions are due to diseases related to lack of sanitation. The leading source of death among children under age five in most Latin American countries is traceable to water-transmitted diseases such as cholera and diarrhea;[24] waterborne diseases are estimated to cause 60 percent of child mortality in the Latin America and Caribbean region.[25] Failing to prevent disease costs money. One study estimated that the cost of water pollution in Mexico in terms of the incidence of diarrheal diseases and premature death was US$3.6 billion—nearly 2 percent of total Mexican GDP in 1988.[26] The cost to Peru of the cholera epidemic was US$1 billion, more than three times what it invested in water supply and sanitation during the entire 1980s. The urban environmental challenge in Latin America is a pressing health issue with overwhelming economic and human costs.[27]

Water and Air Quality

Water quality is problematic in both the rural and the urban areas. Overall, 89 percent of Latin Americans have access to improved water sources, leaving 57.8 million people vulnerable to contracting diarrhea, intestinal worms, trachoma, schistosomiasis, and cholera. In Brazil and Chile, just under 60 percent of rural dwellers are drinking from protected and reliable sources. As shown in table 14.2, only 23 percent of rural Bolivians or 33 percent of rural Peruvians have access to improved sanitation to properly dispose of waste water. Region-wide, 116 million people don't have access to sanitation services.[28] Most widespread contamination of water is from disease-bearing human waste, but in the rural areas agroindustrial effluent, especially fertilizer use, is particularly damaging. Toxic chemical buildup in rivers, including lead and mercury, lowers oxygen levels and also threatens fish and aquatic culture. Rapid urban growth will add more than 140 million people to the region's inadequate urban infrastructure.[29]

Box 14.1 illustrates how simple solar technologies can be used to address some of the water problems in the rural sector. Access to safe water is seen as a public good and a basic right. However, cash-strapped governments have found it difficult to provide universal access to this precious commodity. Some governments have relied on the private sector as partners in the provision of water services. In Chile, this has been relatively successful in expanding access in the urban sector. With large distances, nevertheless, rural water delivery suffers from economies of scale. Even in the cities, water provision has become a hotly politicized issue. In Argentina, the private water provider Aguas Argentinas controlled by the French firm Suez became embroiled in a dispute with the government, who had frozen its capacity to raise water tariffs during the 2001 convertibility crisis; it has since pulled out of the country. Violence erupted in Bolivia over water rights. Also involving a Suez subsidiary, Aguas del Illimani was blamed by the citizens of El Alto for not supplying sufficient water and charging exorbitant rates. The company was one of the reasons for the protests in Bolivia in October 2003 during which the former president Gonzalo Sanchez de Lozada was ousted.[30] The Bolivian government rescinded the contract.[31] In Mexico, private contractors provide water in some cities; the best cases are those where there is a strong regulatory framework to provide efficient oversight and control of private provision. As Miguel Solanes, regional advisor for legislation on water and public services for the Economic Commission for Latin America and the Caribbean (ECLAC), notes, "In and of itself, privatization is as good or as bad as the economy in which it occurs, the care with which it is done, and the society around it."[32] The private sector may be able to contribute to increasing access to healthy water, but only in partnership with good government.

It has been estimated that more than eighty million dwellers, or 27 percent of the urban population and 19 percent of the total population, are exposed to air pollution levels exceeding World Health Organization (WHO) guidelines.[33] In a study of twenty-six Latin American cities, 85 million of the 100 million residents in the study group were exposed to particulate concentrations above internationally accepted levels—most at twice the U.S. level. Reducing concentrations will save

Table 14.2. Water Resources and Freshwater Ecosystems: Water and Sanitation

Region/Country	Rural Access to an Improved Water Source (%)		Urban Access to an Improved Water Source (%)		Rural Access to Improved Sanitation (%)		Urban Access to Improved Sanitation (%)	
	1990	2002	1990	2002	1990	2002	1990	2002
Central America	58	76	91	97	32	47	82	87
South America	58	64	94	95	37	42	83	83
Argentina	73	..	97	97	47	..	87	..
Belize	..	82	100	100	..	25	..	71
Bolivia	48	68	91	95	13	23	49	58
Brazil	55	58	93	96	37	35	82	83
Chile	49	59	98	100	52	64	91	96
Colombia	78	71	98	99	52	54	95	96
Costa Rica	..	92	100	100	97	97	..	89
Cuba	..	78	95	95	95	95	99	99
Ecuador	54	77	81	92	36	59	73	80
El Salvador	47	68	88	91	33	40	70	78
Guatemala	69	92	88	99	35	52	71	72
Guyana	..	83	..	83	..	60	..	86
Honduras	78	82	89	99	31	52	77	89
Mexico	54	72	90	97	20	39	84	90
Nicaragua	42	65	92	93	27	51	64	78
Panama	..	79	99	99	..	51	..	89
Paraguay	46	62	80	100	46	58	71	94
Peru	42	66	88	87	15	33	68	72
Suriname	..	73	98	98	..	76	99	99
Uruguay	..	93	98	98	..	85	95	95
Venezuela	..	70	..	85	..	48	..	71

Source: World Resources Institute online database, Earthtrends www.earthtrends.wri.org.
An improved water source includes any of the following types of drinking water sources: household connections, public standpipes, boreholes, protected dug wells, protected springs, rainwater collection. Improved sanitation includes any of the following excreta disposal facilities: connection to a public sewer, connection to a septic tank, pour-flush latrine, simple pit latrine, and ventilated improved pit latrine.
Safe water provides health and economic benefits to households and individuals; nearby access to this water allows women and children to spend less time fetching water and more time on other tasks. A poor water supply and sanitation system can lead to a number of diseases, including diarrhea, intestinal worms, trachoma, schistosomiasis, and cholera. Examples of unimproved water sources include: unprotected wells and springs, vendor-provided water, tanker-provided water, and bottled water. These last examples are considered "unimproved" because they are not consistently available in sufficient quantities.

between 10,500 and 13,500 premature deaths in the study areas, or between 2 and 2.6 percent of the residents of the study group.[34] In the cities, a larger percentage of the population lives in the open air, with greater exposure to toxic pollutants.[35] Indoor pollution through poorly ventilated biomass stoves and the use of unprocessed solid fuels for cooking and heating expose people—mostly women and children in

Box 14.1. How Two Nonprofit International Development Organizations are Using Solar Energy to Improve People's Quality of Life in Rural Latin America

ENERSOL

Enersol, a nonprofit international development organization, uses clean solar energy to improve the quality of life of Latin Americans while protecting the global environment. Specifically, Enersol assists rural communities with the application of solar electric technologies to improve health and education. In its models, the organization seeks to utilize local institutional and private-sector resources and to contribute to the global transition toward sustainable societies.

More than three million Dominicans and Hondurans currently live without access to clean water. Imagine always having to cook, wash, and drink with unsafe water. To combat the problem, Enersol has established solar-powered pumping systems in thirteen communities of the Dominican Republic. In 2000, the first solar-powered community water system was completed in Honduras. Clean Water for Health has effectively made clean water available to thousands of people. Families within each community pay into a fund for maintenance of their water systems, and Enersol trains members within each community to care for them. By training locals to care for their own clean water delivery and by establishing a financial reserve for maintenance of the system, sustainable water projects are created. El Fortin, Honduras, is five kilometers from the nearest electric line and more than half a kilometer walk from its previous water source. Through a collaborative effort between Enersol, ADESOL-Honduras, Accion Contra el Hambre, and community residents, a community water system was installed, with service to each residence. The system runs from eight solar modules that deliver water daily to a fifteen thousand-gallon tank.

Enersol has also begun using solar energy to power computers in rural community schools that lack electricity and own very few books. Through the Information Technology for Education program, solar-powered laptops and educational software are bringing problem-solving skills and knowledge to both teachers and students. In Laguna del Rincon, Honduras, in partnership with the Honduran Ministry of Education's Educatodos Program, two solar electric systems were installed. The first powers a large television and VCR used for a Telebasica distance-learning program aimed at seventh- and eighth-grade students. The second powers lights and audio equipment used for the Ministry of Education's Educatodos program, which provides primary and secondary education to youth and adults. As in the case of providing clean water, family members within the community pay into a maintenance fund, and Enersol provides community training to ensure that the new solar-powered technology can be cared for. Enersol has enabled children who have very little knowledge outside of their own communities to gain skills and knowledge that they perhaps had never dreamed possible.

THE MESOAMERICAN DEVELOPMENT INSTITUTE

If you had a cup of coffee this morning, you are likely responsible for clearing a patch of the rain forest the size of your mug—unless the coffee you sipped was solar dried. Café Solar uses renewable energy rather than conventional firewood equipment. During the coffee harvest throughout Latin America, coffee beans are shipped to centralized facilities where they are dried using wood or diesel-fired burners. This drying process contributes to the deforestation of the region. In Honduras, for example, an estimated 1,885

continued

continued

acres of forest (or 16 percent of the industrial consumption of wood) are cleared annually for coffee processing. In Central America, furthermore, an estimated 16,086 acres of forest are cleared for firewood to be used in coffee production. To combat or at least partly curb this destructive process, the Mesoamerican Development Institute (MDI), founded by University of Massachusetts-Lowell alumni Richard Trubey and Raúl Raudales, developed solar coffee-drying systems for use by small coffee farmers in Latin America. The new drying system uses a lower temperature for drying, which effectively preserves the quality of the coffee bean as well as allows small growers to dry their own beans without outsourcing. Because the coffee can be dried at the farm where it was grown and not mixed with other varieties at centralized processing facilities, the coffee can be characterized according to variety, altitude, plantation, etc. Such production techniques not only contribute to goals of sustainable agriculture in the region but also allow for a higher-quality coffee that can be sold in niche markets. With World Bank and GEF support, the MDI provides training and the development of new financing mechanisms to promote the adoption of this sustainable process.

Source: Information on Enersol has been extracted from the Enersol website at www.enersol.org. Information on the MDI has been extracted from the Solar Energy Engineering, University of Massachusetts, Lowell, website at energy.caeds.eng.uml.edu/coffee.html.

rural areas and slums—to high levels of suspended particulates. The frequency of burning such fuels is likely to increase, as oil and gas prices have risen.[36] Environmental risks account for approximately 4–5 percent of the total disease burden in higher-income Latin American countries and 7–9 percent for lower-income countries in the region. This gives environmental risks the dubious honor of a disease burden roughly equal to childhood and maternal undernutrition and puts it ahead of sexual and health risks.[37] Pollution affects the health of more than 80 million Latin Americans, resulting in the loss of 65 million working days and causing 2.3 million cases of chronic breathing difficulties among children and more than 10,000 cases of chronic bronchitis in adults.[38]

A primary cause of poor air quality is motor vehicles. Concentrated in a few large cities, they account for 80–99 percent of carbon monoxide emissions.[39] Half the Mexican fleet operates in Mexico City, and a quarter of Brazilian cars are registered in São Paulo. In Santiago, cleaner buses decreased emissions of carbon monoxide, volatile organic compounds, and nitrogen oxide by 25 percent.[40] More than in industrialized countries, motor vehicles are a significant source of airborne toxic pollutants; older cars, trucks, and buses (especially diesel) as well as inadequate engine maintenance and poor driving patterns of excessive acceleration and sudden stops increase emission. And it could get worse. Imagine the damage if instead of 158 cars per 1,000 residents in Mexico, the 779 per 1,000 rate of the United States were matched. Rising real incomes could result in an explosive growth in cars; in Santiago, Chile, the number of cars is doubling every five years, contributing negatively not only to pollution but also to declining urban productivity and quality of life.[41] Achieving sustainability may involve changing consumption patterns in both the North and the South. Table 14.3 illustrates both the growth over time in emissions per capita in Latin America as well as the wide dispersion among

Table 14.3. Climate and Atmosphere in Latin America

Region/Country	Air Pollution: Carbon monoxide emissions (Thousand metric tons)		Emissions per Capita (Metric tons of carbon dioxide per person)					Cumulative Percent Change 1985–2002
	1990	2000	1985	1990	1995	2000	2002	
Central America & Caribbean	23,566.5	34,528.90	2.82	2.82	2.76	3.04	3.07	8.87
North America	106,913.5	93,198.30	18.87	18.86	18.98	19.99	19.59	3.82
South America	104,827.8	189,179.50	1.9	1.96	2.14	2.33	2.19	15.26
Argentina	4,392.8	11,684.90	3.33	3.49	3.64	3.84	3.29	−1.20
Belize	81.8	668.10	1.17	1.67	1.76	3.23	3.11	165.81
Bolivia	6,931.2	16,558.80	0.83	0.87	1.3	1.47	1.21	45.78
Brazil	66,104.5	122,231.00	1.41	1.46	1.65	1.94	1.92	36.17
Canada	12,475.2	12,050.50	15.85	15.57	15.74	17.15	16.54	4.35
Chile	2,996.9	2,579.00	1.7	2.43	2.89	3.52	3.39	99.41
Colombia	7,052.7	9,296.90	1.47	1.5	1.64	1.5	1.4	−4.76
Costa Rica	666.5	554.50	0.82	1.01	1.34	1.35	1.31	59.76
Cuba	953.8	1,483.60	3.21	3.15	2.38	2.84	3.22	0.31
Ecuador	3,166	1,044.70	1.59	1.5	1.6	1.85	1.99	25.16
El Salvador	409.2	553.80	0.44	0.52	0.92	0.93	0.94	113.64
Guatemala	1,993.9	4,099.70	0.46	0.51	0.66	0.9	0.94	104.35
Guyana	271.2	608.00	1.86	1.55	2.01	2.15	2.15	15.59
Honduras	1,447.7	1,717.10	0.44	0.52	0.75	0.77	0.88	100.00
Mexico	12,987.1	20,595.10	3.74	3.66	3.57	3.86	3.84	2.67
Nicaragua	1,820	1,639.00	0.54	0.59	0.61	0.73	0.75	38.89
Panama	854.5	726.70	1.36	1.12	1.64	1.94	2.38	75.00
Paraguay	1,502.4	6,679.40	0.41	0.5	0.78	0.65	0.68	65.85
Peru	3,874.8	3,501.20	1.08	0.91	1.05	1.09	0.99	−8.33
Suriname	245.2	421.70	4.23	4.57	5.26	4.95	5.18	22.46
United States	94,435.1	77,706.70	19.19	19.22	19.33	20.29	19.92	3.80
Uruguay	242.9	391.50	1.18	1.38	1.55	1.92	1.4	18.64
Venezuela	7,967.7	14,136.50	6.04	5.82	5.79	5.7	5.21	−13.74

Source: World Resources Institute online database, Earthtrends www.earthtrends.wri.org.
Carbon monoxide (CO) is a precursor gas of ground-level ozone, which can trigger serious respiratory problems. In addition, when CO enters the bloodstream it reduces the delivery of oxygen to the body's organs and tissues. Exposure to elevated CO levels can cause impairment of visual perception, manual dexterity, learning ability, and performance of complex tasks. CO is formed when carbon in fuel is incompletely burned and it is a component of motor vehicle exhaust. Other sources of CO emissions include industrial processes (such as metals processing and chemical manufacturing), residential wood burning, stoves, and natural sources such as forest fires.

hemispheric emitters. From 1985 to 2002, cumulative changes in per capita emissions rose 45 percent in Bolivia and 75 percent in Panama, yet the number of metric tons of carbon dioxide emitted remains on the order of one-twentieth of those in the United States. The policy scope includes consideration of new emissions standards for fixed and mobile sources, low sulfur diesel fuels, street cleaning to contain dust, and an emissions cap-and-trade program.

Geographic characteristics compound the environmental problems of some cities. Mexico City sits in a basin surrounded by mountains. Ventilation is poor, and during winter thermal inversions occur up to twenty-five days per month. More than thirty thousand industries and twelve thousand service facilities are located in the valley, and 2.5 million motor vehicles—buses, minibuses, taxis, trucks, vans, private cars—operate in the area. WHO guidelines are exceeded regularly, especially during the morning rush hour when low temperature, atmospheric stability (inversion), and heavy traffic occur simultaneously.[42] Sadly, one should not be surprised that more than 25 percent of newborns had toxins in their blood at levels high enough to impair neurological and motor-physical development.[43]

Natural Disasters

Environmental fragility compounds the damage of natural disasters. Table 14.4 provides a historical list of natural disasters in Latin America. Over the past three decades, on average natural disasters have killed about five thousand people and caused $43.2 billion in annual economic losses and damages—and this doesn't take into account the small-scale events that undermine development efforts. This is equivalent to half the lending volume of the Inter-American Development Bank (IADB).[44] "Natural" disasters may be precipitated by a climatic event, but the magnitude of the disaster most often resides in human failure.[45] Poverty, environmental degradation, crowding in high-risk areas, fragile infrastructure, and a lack of preparedness heighten regional vulnerability to natural shocks. Migration to the cities has compounded fatalities as the poor crowd into limited spaces often at risk for natural phenomenon. Hurricane Mitch (1998) was the most destructive disaster in the hemisphere's recorded history. Nine thousand deaths were reported in Central America, and three million people were left homeless. The destruction of social and economic infrastructures such as transportation routes, villages, schools, and crops resulted in an overwhelming $8 billion in damage. In 2005 Hurricane Stan produced $1 billion worth of damage. Generations of deforestation contributed to mud slides that covered dozens of villages and buried their inhabitants.[46] The effects of climate change are likely to increase the negative effects unless better planning and prevention promote stronger risk management. On average, coping with natural disasters costs 2 percent of Central America's GDP per year—many of these damages avoidable. Hurricanes Mitch and Stan are perfect examples of how a physical phenomena can destroy years of development progress. Meeting relief and reconstruction needs must take priority over long-term development goals, setting back progress on environmental sustainability.[47] ECLAC notes that preventing natural disasters constitutes one of the region's main challenges. The return is substantial; a dollar spent on prevention can save seven in resulting damages. Prevention can deter damage escalation; the fire that results from dead material following a hurricane need never begin.[48]

THE ENERGY PROBLEM

Energy Consumption and Efficiency

Migration to the cities also pressures the efficient provision of energy to the population. Energy consumption packs a double environmental whammy. Not only is raw energy a scarce natural resource, but the consumption of energy also generates significant externalities. Table 14.5 dramatically portrays the North-South imbalance in per capita energy consumption. Bolivia only uses 8.55 percent of the U.S. consumption per capita of oil and 3.15 percent of electricity. These data give us a small clue as to the dramatically different life that a person in La Paz may have compared to a person in Los Angeles—far fewer gadgets and comforts!

Low rates of growth of energy consumption are not unambiguously a good thing but may simply reflect a low level of economic development. The use of energy will naturally increase as a country is growing. Growth may result in electrical access for more homes, more appliances for the middle class, and greater industrial requirements. The World Bank projects increased demand for energy in less-developed countries due to growth of populations and per capita incomes, migration to urban areas (substituting energy for fuel wood), and adoption of energy-intensive products (such as fertilizers, petrochemicals, cements, vehicles, appliances, and motors), as well as poor energy efficiency.[49] Higher growth rates of energy consumption are expected at higher income levels.

Energy planning for efficient use of resources is clearly indicated—perhaps most for the United States! The last column in table 14.5 indicates the percentage of energy that a person in each country uses as a proportion of the individual energy use in the United States. On a per person basis, a Brazilian uses approximately 13.12 percent of the electricity of someone living in the United States. Imagine if the Brazilians' appetite for energy continued to grow to emulate their northern neighbors. The demands on the Brazilian balance of payments, not to mention global resources, would be enormous. Conversely, imagine if those living in the United States were able to conserve even a portion of the apparent excess consumption of energy. Energy sustainability requires changing global consumption patterns.

Table 14.6 shows that Latin Americans on average consume roughly a fourth of the energy of people living in Organization for Economic Cooperation and Development (OECD) countries and 22 percent of the world average. They also produce 8.8 fewer carbon monoxide units per inhabitant than OECD residents, creating a basis for potential trades in the greenhouse gas offset market. In total, Latin America accounts for 5.6 percent of world carbon monoxide gas emissions, with the largest share attributed to Mexico and Brazil. What is dismaying is the proxy for energy efficiency, the amount of GDP generated per unit of energy use. Although Latin America has the highest ratio of output of goods to energy input, we see that rather than becoming more energy efficient from 1980 through 2002, the ratio declined from 6.3 to 6.1.

Table 14.4. Latin America Natural Disasters between 1972 and 2005

Country and Year	Type of Disaster	Number of Persons Affected		Total Damage
		Deaths	Directly Affected	Millions of 1998 Dollars
Nicaragua, 1972	Earthquake	6,000	300,000	2,968
Honduras, 1974	Hurricane Fifi	7,000	115,000	1,331
Guatemala, 1976	Earthquake	23,000	1,550,000	2,147
Nicaragua, 1982	Floods	80	70,000	599
El Salvador, 1982	Earthquake, droughts and flooding	600	20,000	216
Guatemala, 1982	Heavy rains and drought	610	10,000	136
Nicaragua, 1982	Floods and drought			588
Bolivia, Ecuador, and Peru 1982/1983	El Niño		3,840,000	5,651
Mexico, 1985	Earthquake	8,000	150,000	6,216
Colombia, 1985	Eruption of Nevado del Ruiz volcano	22,000	200,000	465
El Salvador, 1986	Earthquake	1,200	520,000	1,352
Ecuador, 1987	Earthquake	1,000	82,500	1,438
Nicaragua, 1988	Hurricane Joan	148	550,000	1,160
Nicaragua, 1992	Eruption of Cerro Negro volcano	2	12,000	22
Nicaragua, 1992	Pacific tsunami	116	40,500	30
Costa Rica, 1996	Hurricane Cesar	39	40,260	157
Nicaragua, 1996	Hurricane Cesar	9	29,500	53
Costa Rica, 1997–1998	El Niño		119,279	93
Andean Community, 1997–1998	El Niño	600	125,000	7,694

Location, year	Event	Deaths	People affected	Cost (millions)
Central America, 1998	Hurricane Mitch	9,214	1,191,908	6,008
Colombia, 1999	Earthquake	1,185	559,401	1,580
Venezuela, 1999	Torrential rain	. . .	68,503	3,237
Belize, 2000	Hurricane Keith	10	57,400	265
El Salvador, 2001	Earthquakes	1,159	1,412,938	1,518
Bolivia, 2001	Flood	41	357,250	121
Peru, 2001	Earthquake	145	222,400	200
Mexico, 2001	Hurricane Juliet	3	3,000	400
Brazil, 2002	Floods	14	221,842	200
Mexico, 2003	Earthquake	29	177,530	116
Argentina, 2003	Floods	23	140,000	1,028
Mexico, 2003	Hurricane Marty	2	6,000	100
Brazil, 2004	Hurricane Catarina	4	150,000	350
Cuba, 2005	Hurricane Dennis	16	545,000	500
Mexico, 2005	Hurricane Emily	2		27
El Salvador, 2005	Volcano			
Central America, 2005 Guatemala (1513 killed), Nicaragua, Mexico, El Salvador, Costa Rica	Hurricane Stan	1,600	millions	$988 million for Guatemala; $355 million for El Salvador
Total		84,543	15,604,428	54,703

Source: United Nations Environment Programme and Economic Commission for Latin America and the Caribbean, "The Sustainability of Development in Latin America and the Caribbean: Challenges and Opportunities," Prepared for Preparatory Conference of Latin America and the Caribbean for the World Conference on Sustainable Development (Johannesburg, South Africa, 2002), 99, table V.2; and "Em-Dat," the OFDA/CRED International Disaster Database, www.em.dat.net.

Table 14.5. Energy and Resources

Region/Country	Residential Energy Use per capita (kg oil equivalent per person)				Electricity Consumption per capita (kilowatt-hours, kwH, per person per year)			
	1990	2000	2001	% of 2001 U.S. Value	1990	2000	2001	% of 2001 U.S. Value
Central America & Caribbean	183.1	182.4	180.6		1024.6	1,405.9	1,408.6	16.28
North America	843.6	935.3	894.9		12,132.5	13,993.9	13,415.7	3.15
South America	146.9	145.1	143.3		1,288.3	1,701.7	1,639	13.74
Argentina	194.2	250.5	239.7	27.01	1,307.7	2,129	2,125.5	128.61
Bolivia	127.8	81.5	75.9	8.55	274.9	390.6	410.8	20.29
Brazil	121.8	120.9	116.4	13.12	1,471.1	1,939	1,793.6	5.99
Canada	1,043.2	1,004.6	963	108.51	16,158.1	16,974.5	16,787.1	12.24
Chile	229.9	307.3	314.9	35.48	1,254.1	2,520.8	2,648.2	8.84
Colombia	158	105	113.8	12.82	819.3	792	781.2	5.01
Costa Rica	213.3	83	118.9	13.40	1,096.8	1,564.8	1,598.2	4.44
Cuba	115.4	79.6	78	8.79	1,209.2	1,131.5	1,153.3	2.80
Ecuador	126.3	104.4	105.7	11.91	479.2	635.9	654.2	4.02
El Salvador	196.3	210.3	209.3	23.58	368	644.4	579.4	13.86
Guatemala	318.1	307.5	300.1	33.81	227.3	338.2	365.3	2.57
Honduras	267.1	199.2	192	21.63	311.3	502.1	524.4	10.40
Mexico	177	175.1	172.5	19.44	1,308.6	1,812.9	1,809.3	6.44
Nicaragua	235.6	231.8	232.3	26.17	319	339	335.3	5.39
Panama	180.8	187.5	184.6	20.80	858.2	1,344.8	1,357.6	
Paraguay	328.5	235.5	239.1	26.94	505.1	882.5	841	100.00
Peru	167.2	137.2	138	15.55	552.9	679.6	703.8	14.86
United States	822	927.8	887.5	100.00	11,696.5	1,3672.1	13,052.6	20.91
Uruguay	192.2	216.6	211.5	23.83	1,246	1,968.8	1,939.9	
Venezuela	132.5	144.5	147.3	16.60	2,494.3	2,669.5	2,729.3	

Source: World Resources Institute, Earthtrends online database, Earthtrends www.earthtrends.wri.org, derived from data from International Energy Agency, 2004, and Population Division of the Department of Economic and Social Affairs of the United Nations Secretariat, 2004.
Residential energy use per capita is defined as the average amount of primary energy used for residential purposes by each person living in a specified country. Consumption equals indigenous production plus imports minus exports plus stock changes minus energy delivered to international marine bunkers. Energy losses from transportation, friction, heat, and other inefficiencies are included in these totals. Residential use includes all consumption by households, excluding fuels used for transport.
Electricity consumption per capita is defined as the average kilowatt-hours (kwH) of electrical power generated per person in a particular country or region. Public electricity plants, private electricity plants, and combined heat and power (CHP) plants are all included. Electricity output from crude oil and natural gas liquids is not included here.

Table 14.6.   Selected Energy and Carbon Dioxide Emission Indicators

Region	Traditional Fuel Consumption (% of total energy requirements) 2002	Electricity Consumption per Capita (kilowatt-hours) 1980	2002	GDP per Unit of Energy Use (2000 PPP US$ per kg of oil equivalent) 1980	2002	Carbon Monoxide Emissions Per Capita (metric tons) 1980	2002	Share of World Total (%) 2000
World Total	7.6	1,573	2,465	3.8	4.6	3.4	3.6	100
OECD	4.1	5,761	8,615	3.9	5.1	11	11.2	51
Middle East	18	626	1,946	5.8	3.5	3.1	4.1	4.5
Central and Eastern Europe	4.1	3,284	3,326	. . .	2.4	10.1	5.9	12.2
Africa	70.6	434	536	3.3	2.7	1	0.8	1.9
China	5.3	307	1,484	1.2	4.6	1.5	2.7	12.1
Latin America	19.8	1,019	1,927	6.3	6.1	2.4	2.4	5.6

Source: Human Development Report 2005, table 22, "Energy and the Environment."

In the developing world there are important opportunities for enhancing energy efficiency. Energy sectors in developing countries have been characterized by pricing below costs; concentrated, often inefficient state-held enterprises; companies acting as a direct extension of government, with little distinction between ownership, regulation, and management; high information costs; weak management expertise; and the need for a more transparent regulatory process.[50] Pricing energy to market cost, promoting efficiency at the enterprise level, and increasing transparency in regulatory agencies should, as in Chile, encourage economic growth while holding down energy consumption and costs. There are also opportunities for small-scale changes. Nongovernmental organizations (NGOs) such as Enersol promote grassroots introduction of renewable energy technologies. Encouraging the use of solar-electric systems through financing and technical assistance, Enersol helps local organizations install energy systems that are economically and environmentally sustainable over time.[51]

Energy Producers

Some countries in the region are energy exporters. In 2003, Latin American producers accounted for 14 percent of all oil exports, with Mexico at 5.11 percent and Venezuela providing 4.15 percent.[52] The development patterns of Mexico, Ecuador, and Venezuela have clearly been shaped by their oil sectors. In 2006, Venezuela produced approximately 2.6 million barrels of oil per day and Mexico 3.7 million.[53] Measured by known reserves, Mexico ranked fourteenth and Brazil sixteenth in the world in 2006, and Venezuela, a member of the Organization of

Petroleum Exporting Countries (more commonly known as OPEC), ranked seventh. Together they account for more than 8 percent of the world's reserves of oil.[54]

High oil and gas prices are creating development opportunities and dilemmas for producer countries. Energy-rich countries in the region are using their new-found bargaining power to extract a higher price for foreign participation in energy production. As a barrel of oil traded above sixty dollars in the beginning of 2006 and natural gas doubled its price in the last five years, governments are tightening contract terms for royalties, profits, and taxes. Where sweet deals were offered for exploration in Venezuela in the early 1990s as companies only paid a 1 percent royalty, in October 2005 President Hugo Chavez increased royalties to 16.6 percent and plans to raise the tax rate from 34 to 50 percent. In Ecuador, President Alfredo Palacio signed legislation to impose a 50 percent windfall profits tax on revenues above a reference price. Oil provides 40 percent of the national budget and 60 percent of exports. In Ecuador, private companies account for 60 percent of daily output. Petroecuador produces the rest—but operates at a loss (interestingly equal to the amount of money that the legislation is likely to generate). Oil companies believe that the increased tax is an abrogation of contract rights; no new contracts have been signed since 1996, despite government efforts to attract new investment. There has, however, been some interest on the part of the Chinese in providing the necessary technology and capital for exploration of Ecuador's heavy crude, which is difficult to refine. As long as prices remain high, countries will retain significant bargaining power.

In Bolivia, antiglobalization activists are protesting against foreign control of national resources. Nonetheless, there are limits to pushing energy giants' profits down. Like Ecuador, Bolivia does not have the technology to develop its reserves. Repsol YPF, a Spanish energy conglomerate, is considering legal action for unfair contractual changes due to the new 50 percent tax on gas. Some fear a pullout of investors in the face of uncertainty of potential nationalization. Investor skittishness may also carry over to other sectors that could benefit from multinational technology. Although high oil prices have enhanced bargaining power, multinationals do retain access to key technologies for exploration.

Brazil has enhanced energy independence through a judicious mix of state ownership in the oil sector while encouraging foreign competition. Petrobras retains 55.7 percent of voting shares in government hands; the other shares are openly traded.[55] Soaring profits have made it the largest publicly traded firm in Latin America. In 2006 it was producing an average of 1.9 million barrels a day, just over domestic consumption. Under the last president of Brazil, Fernando Henrique Cardoso, Petrobras was nudged to perform more like a private company; exploration during that period grew 12 percent a year. Despite strong revenues, with the Lula government looking to promote its social agenda, output has fallen to 5 percent a year. The government has held gas price increases below international levels to avoid the burden of fluctuations on the poor. However, some in the financial sector criticize this approach as missing opportunities for growth within Petrobras during the current boom. The firm is foregoing revenues of 7.8 billion reais by limiting prices in the period. Petrobras provides a 30 percent discount below international prices for cooking gas, a big budget item for the poor, and it hasn't been raised since December 2002—the month before President Luiz Inácio "Lula" da Silva took office.[56]

Brazil, though responsible for a sizable percentage of the world's carbon dioxide emissions because of its high rate of deforestation, has emerged as a leader on the renewable energies front. Brazil's energy mix is among the cleanest in the world due to its heavy dependence on renewable sources. As of 1998, fossil fuels accounted for only 38 percent of total energy use in Brazil, while hydropower accounted for 33.4 percent of energy use and biomass combustion (a carbon-neutral process) accounted for 23 percent.[57] The 2005 World Development Indicators reported that 24.3 percent of Brazil's total energy production in 2002 came from renewable sources. This is impressive, especially compared to the United States, where renewables account for a measly 3 percent of total energy production.[58] Brazil continues to invest in alternative energies, making it a leader in clean technologies in Latin America.

Oil production can have devastating environmental costs. One analyst estimates that since oil production began in Ecuador in 1972, the trans-Andean pipeline has spilled one and a half times the oil spilled in the *Exxon Valdez* disaster and discharged 4.3 million gallons of toxic waste daily. There has been an increase in skin and intestinal disease, headaches, and fever, with contaminants in drinking water reaching one thousand times the safety standards set by the U.S. Environmental Protection Agency. This is not to mention the cultural conflict of oil versus indigenous people in the region.[59] Box 14.2 discusses the oil and environment dilemma in Ecuador.

Alternative Energy

Given problems with the high cost and environmental impacts of oil consumption and production, increasingly countries have turned to harness the enormous hydroelectric power in the region. But more needs to be done to offset the environmental costs of energy production and consumption. A strategy to minimize costs and consumption on a global level is critical to sustainable development. The contemporary case of Brazil's ethanol program may be seen as an example of how renewable energy sources can be used to substitute for fossil fuels. The sugar that Brazil has cultivated since the sixteenth century is now fueling flex engine cars. A result of a program of state investment in its Proalcohol program in 1975, the fuel source now yields eight times more energy than corn-based options. Although the program almost died when energy prices subsided in the 1990s, the current boom has made the program economic. Brazilian producers of flex-fuel cars provide 70 percent of the automobiles sold in the country. Consumers love the fact that they won't incur the risk if relative fuel prices change again—they will simply pull up to a different pump. Anticipating this, producers are working to increase the efficiency of turning sugar cane into ethanol, keeping it competitive even if oil drops below thirty dollars a barrel.[60]

Biofuels are produced from agricultural and forestry wastes and are considered carbon-neutral because the amount of carbon dioxide emitted in combustion is equal to the amount that would naturally be emitted through decomposition.[61] In

Box 14.2.   Who Is Responsible for Oil Spills in the Ecuadorian Rain Forest?

As Latin America proceeds with the privatization of natural resource development, crucial questions emerge with respect to responsibility for ensuring environmentally safe and sustainable practices.

Ecuadorians in Shushufindi fear the black slime that forms in pools in their backyards and schools. Florinda Balla's cows have died from drinking the sludge thick with arsenic and other toxic wastes. Crops have been lost, and rivers used for drinking, bathing, and fishing have been contaminated by spills and poor extraction practices. The soil is contaminated, its salty crust crumbling when poked with a stick. Trees are defoliated, branches brittle. Roughly seventeen million barrels of oil were spilled as seventeen billion were extracted from Ecuador's rich petroleum reserves.

Residents are trying to make Texaco accountable for the damage to their ecosystem. The U.S.-based company began operations in Ecuador in 1964 but became a minority partner after the contract in 1977 with Petroecuador, the state-owned company. Lawyers for the community group allege that although Texaco was not the lead company, all extraction technologies were under the supervision of the U.S. firm. The case is being filed in U.S. court, for more than $1 billion in damages and cleanup costs, because the maximum fine for environmental damage in Ecuador is $12,500.

Texaco vehemently denies wrongdoing, claiming that it met all environmental and health regulations at the time, consistent with prevailing international practice. Furthermore, it signed a cleanup agreement with the Ecuadorian government in 1995, although activists charge that treatment has not taken place. Texaco pledged more than $1 million for reforestation, new schools, and medical dispensaries, but improvements have not yet materialized. Other pools with oil spills are not covered by the agreement.

Environmental officials in Ecuador contextualize the damage as a legacy of a pre-environmentally conscious age and Petroecuador's involvement as following Texaco's instructions.

Texaco, which pulled out of Ecuador in 1990, argues that the responsibility for the remaining problems falls in the government's lap. Policy mistakes, including drawing settlers into the region to strengthen its border with Peru, remain the burden of the government.

The losers appear to be the people of Shushufindi, in the Oriente rain forest. Although Ecuador depends on oil and related products for 44 percent of its national budget, less than 3 percent returns to the region. In the town, fewer than 0.2 percent of the homes have tap water. Oil has done little to alleviate their poverty and immiseration.

How should Ecuador balance the need for foreign investment to develop its natural resources with its obligation to protect the environment? What options do Ecuadorians have when they believe that their government is not acting in their best interest? Should environmental standards differ for U.S. citizens and Ecuadorians? Should responsibility for meeting international standards be imposed retroactively in a country?

Source: Adapted from Diana Jean Schemo, "Ecuadorians Want Texaco to Clear Toxic Residue," *New York Times,* January 31, 1998. Available at LatinoLink, www.latinolink.com.

addition, in some cases croplands and forests used for the production of biofuels can be counted as carbon sinks under the Kyoto Protocol, providing countries with tradable carbon credits. Argentina passed a law to provide tax incentives to produce biofuels, with a goal of offering gasoline that includes 5 percent ethanol from sugar cane, corn, or soya. However, biofuels themselves have environmental costs.[62] Activists worry that the expansion of crops, especially soybeans, will negatively impact sustainable agriculture. Soyification, as it has become known, and its pressures on deforestation are potential indirect costs of energy independence.[63] Argentina has become the world's third largest soya producer, after the United States and Brazil. But this "green gold" is competing with other, traditional land uses. As the land occupied by soya has expanded from 6 million hectares to 15.2 million hectares, accounting for about half the agricultural land in use, it pressures forests, encourages pesticide application, and displaces cattle from grazing ground in the pampas to less fertile pastures.[64]

PROTECTION OF RICH FOREST RESOURCES

Forest covers 47 percent of the land area in Latin America, extending from the Mexican dry forests to the southern temperate forests of Chile and Argentina, including the Amazon Basin. Among issues relating to the natural environment, perhaps the most well-known and visible problem is the deforestation of the rain forests. A tropical rain forest is defined as an evergreen or partially evergreen forest located in an area that receives no less than four inches of precipitation per month for two out of three years. The mean annual temperature exceeds 24 degrees Centigrade with no frost.[65] The Amazon rain forest covers 7 percent of Earth, has 15–20 percent of the unsalted water on the planet, and is home to more than half the world's biological wealth.[66] In addition, rain forests take carbon dioxide out of the atmosphere and are a source of food and medicines as well as recreation.[67]

The approximately 7 million square kilometers of the Amazon territory cover eight sovereign states with 42,000 kilometers of highways, river networks, and airports.[68] Its expanse houses a great heterogeneity of climates, geological formations, soils, flora, fauna, and cultural history unparalleled in the world. Between 5 million and 30 million existing species are estimated to inhabit the Amazon, of which 750,000 insects, 40,000 vertebrates, 250,000 plants, and 360,000 microbiota have been identified. Of these, more than 2,000 species of plants have been found as useful for medicinal and nutritive properties and as producers of oils, greases, waxes, varnishes, aromas, tannins, saponin, latex, rubber, condiments, and toxins.

The Amazon River, longer than the Nile, is the most powerful river in the world, with considerable hydroelectric potential. Its many rivers, lakes, lagoons, and swamps contain varieties of mammals, birds, reptiles, fish, and invertebrates. It is estimated that the Amazon River supports twenty-five hundred to three thousand fish species, ten times the number found in the great Mississippi.[69] Although there is some dispute as to whether the Amazon is truly the lungs of Earth, it carries approximately one-sixth of the fresh water flowing into the seas from all the rivers of the world.[70]

The Amazon's roughly 20 million human inhabitants are likewise diverse—the Indians, rubber tappers, woodland societies engaged in logging and mining, and riverbank people, all with rich cultural traditions. Between 1 and 1.25 million indigenous people of approximately 400 ethnic groups remain after the ravages of disease and displacement of centuries of colonization. Twenty percent of the Amazonian population is dedicated to farming, and 50–60 percent live in cities. Some of the Amazonian cities have suffered a more than fiftyfold increase in population since

1940, overwhelming local infrastructure.[71] The basin contains rich oil reserves as well as bauxite, gold, manganese, copper, and iron. *Garimpeiros,* or gold miners, roughly 30 percent of the basin's population, have attracted a good deal of environmental and social attention for the questions they raise about poverty and wealth and their conflicts with the indigenous peoples and the environment. The good news is that approximately 90 percent of the Amazon forest and its affiliated ecosystem are in a good state of preservation; nonetheless, they are subject to increasing risk and an accelerated pace of deforestation.

Despite its importance, the Amazon is not the only forest area under threat in the region. As shown in table 14.7, the fastest rates of deforestation are occurring in Central America; in this area, the third largest among global biodiversity hot spots, total forest cover was reduced 10.8 percent from 1990 to 2000. Over this period El Salvador' forest cover declined 37.3 percent and Nicaragua's 26.3 percent. Mexico's annual deforestation rate is among the highest in the world, threatening a plant diversity that is currently greater than the United States and Canada combined.[72] In the Mesoamerican region, the dry forests have been drastically reduced to only 4 percent of their original area.[73] In contrast to the Amazon basin, where larger commercial interests dominate, land degradation in Central America is tied to the desire of small landholders to obtain property rights under uncertain economic conditions. Throughout the region, forest conservation policies have concentrated almost exclusively on tropical rain forests, ignoring highly degraded areas where the value, potential, and possible extinction of species urgently needs evaluating.

The rich resources of the Amazon are also threatened by deforestation. In the twelve-month period ending August 2004, farming and logging—principally the illegal variant—destroyed ten thousand square miles, an area roughly the size of Massachusetts.[74] This is the largest loss since 1995—startling in light of the environmental efforts in the region. In addition to loss of forest cover and biodiversity, including certain large leaved mahogany trees, it has also contributed to an increase in carbon emissions with the loss of the carbon sink and tree burning to clear land.[75] The Amazon is also suffering its worst drought in four decades, dropping the water level by several feet. Its tributaries are drying up, and fish are dying by the millions.[76] Some new evidence suggests that the loss may be underestimated by 60 to 123 percent.[77] New satellite imaging techniques have allowed scientists to detect small patches in the forest made by selective logging as opposed to clear-cutting. When a tree is selectively logged, thirty more can be severely damaged, with the vines connecting them pulling down neighboring trees. The additional destruction from selective logging adds approximately one hundred million tons of carbon to the four hundred million already entering the atmosphere from traditional deforestation.

Causes of environmental degradation in the Amazon are complex, multidimensional, and often tied to the incentives and survival techniques in local communities. Economic pressures have long been at odds with sustainability. Expanding livestock production is a primary driver of rain forest loss in Latin America.[78] The number of heads of cattle in the Amazon has increased 144 percent in the last ten years.[79] Farmland for soybean exports is also exacting an environmental price. In the state of Matto Grosso, where about half the deforestation occurs, land dedicated to soybean production has expanded by 400 percent in the last ten years. Soybean production has doubled in a decade, driven by surging worldwide demand for soy-

Table 14.7.   Forest Extent in Latin America

Region/Country	Total Forest Area (thousand hectares)		Total Forest Area, Average Annual Percent Change, 1990–2000	Total Forest Area, Cummulative Percent Change from 1990 to 2000
	1990	*2000*		
Central America & Caribbean	88,315	78,737	−1.1	−10.8
North America	466,684	470,564	0.1	0.8
South America	922,731	885,618	−0.4	−4
Argentina	37,499	34,648	−0.8	−7.6
Belize	1,704	1,348	−2.3	−20.9
Bolivia	54,679	53,068	−0.3	−2.9
Brazil	566,998	543,905	−0.4	−4.1
Canada	244,571	244,571		0
Chile	15,739	15,536	−0.1	−1.3
Colombia	51,506	49,601	−0.4	−3.7
Costa Rica	2,126	1,968	−0.8	−7.4
Cuba	2,071	2,348	1.3	13.4
Ecuador	11,929	10,557	−1.2	−11.5
El Salvador	193	121	−4.6	−37.3
Guatemala	3,387	2,850	−1.7	−15.9
Guyana	17,365	16,879	−0.3	−2.8
Honduras	5,972	5,383	−1	−9.9
Mexico	61,511	55,205	−1.1	−10.3
Nicaragua	4,450	3,278	−3	−26.3
Panama	3,395	2,876	−1.6	−15.3
Paraguay	24,602	23,372	−0.5	−5
Peru	67,903	65,215	−0.4	−4
Suriname	14,113	14,113		0
United States	222,113	225,993	0.2	1.7
Uruguay	791	1,292	5	63.3
Venezuela	51,681	49,506	−0.4	−4.2

Note: Total forest area, as defined by the Food and Agriculture Organization of the United Nations, includes both natural forests and plantations.
Source: World Resources Institute online database, Earthtrends www.earthtrends.wri.org.

beans as animal feed—especially from China. It is perhaps telling that Matto Grosso has the most lenient reserve limits on land—only 50 percent as opposed to 80 percent of land must be held in reserve. This may have something to do with the fact that the state's governor, Blairo Maggi, is the world's top individual soya producer. In 1999 he planted fifty thousand hectares of soybeans on his family's Mato Grosso farms; a single Maggi plantation can be bigger than some U.S. states. Indeed, in 2005 Maggi received the dubious honor of the first Greenpeace Golden Chainsaw Award, bestowed on the person whose action or inaction has been most decisive in the destruction of the Amazon.[80]

The Food and Agriculture Organization estimates that some 5.8 million hectares of forests are lost in the region every year, with a yearly rate of .75 percent. However, in most cases agricultural use of these lands is not sustainable due to the generally nutrient-poor soils. The results include erosion and water pollution (especially

Box 14.3.   Chico Mendes

On December 24, 1988, the *New York Times* reported the murder of Francisco "Chico" Alves Mendes. At the time of his death, he was the president of the Xapuri Rural Workers' Union and a committed spokesperson for the defense of the Amazon rain forest in Xapuri Acre in northwestern Brazil. Chico Mendes became a martyr in the plight to prevent the deforestation of the Amazon forest.

Since the eighteenth century and through World War II, the Amazon was a major source of rubber. It is home to a species of trees from the genus *Havea,* which produces the best rubber in the world. Ninety-five percent of world rubber production comes from these trees, of which there are an estimated three hundred million scattered throughout the Amazon and Orinoco river basins.

Until the 1960s, the rubber industry was based on rubber estates operating in a system of debt bondage. Rubber tappers, who were kept illiterate and innumerate, were obliged to sell their product at artificially low prices to the estate owners. Hence, as a son of a rubber tapper, Chico Mendes first went to school in the forest, where he learned the basic plant-animal relationships and the unique method of extracting rubber from *Havea* trees. It was not until the age of twenty that he began to read and write.

In the 1960s, the Brazilian government began to promote the settlement and development of Xapuri Acre by opening the BR-364 road. Incentives were given to cattle ranchers, and estate owners were bought out. The result was the eviction of many rubber tappers and a constant harassment of those who remained. Very often, the tappers were forced to labor for the cattle ranchers, engaging in clear-cutting and slash-and-burn techniques to adapt the land for cattle grazing. Western Brazil became like the American West of the nineteenth century, lawless and without order. Arguments of manifest destiny were used to justify the taking over of the land and the exploitation of its inhabitants.

To protect the rubber tappers and their lifestyle, the Rural Workers' Union was founded in the mid-1970s. As the clear-cutting intensified and the evictions increased, the union actively began to stop the destruction of the forest. It assembled tappers and their families as human walls to prevent clear-cutting by cattle ranchers. This classic form of passive resistance was called an *empate,* frequently translated as a stalemate or draw. The *empates* became so successful by 1979 that the ranchers arranged for the murder of the union's founder, Wilson Pinheiro, leaving Chico with the leadership.

In 1985, the National Rubber Tappers Congress assembled in Brasilia to work out alternative development proposals for the protection of the Amazon and the rubber tappers. Chico wanted to justify the *empates* by providing an alternative development strategy for the forest. He came up with the idea of extractive reserves. In the same manner that the Indians' traditional habitat and living style were protected, Chico proposed the creation of reserves to preserve the rain forests and continue rubber tapping.

Chico's proposal was the weapon that international environmental groups needed to persuade the Brazilian government to slow down the burning of the Amazon. These groups realized that the government might approve because it was not simply another U.S. proposal but instead was a native initiative undertaken by grassroots groups who wanted to preserve their habitat. Thus, Chico was taken to testify before the IADB board of directors. He also met informally with members of the U.S. Senate Appropriations Committee to obtain funds for the protection of the rain forests in Xapuri Acre. In 1987, Chico was awarded the Global 500 Prize from the United Nations and the medal from the Society for a Better World for his fight to preserve Amazonia.

In 1988, the first extractive reserve was put in place in Xapuri Acre. This reserve fell on the land claimed by a prominent cattle rancher who previously had many encounters with the union's *empates.* On December 22, 1988, the embittered son of this cattle rancher assassinated Chico Mendes in the doorway of his home. His death did not quiet the union but strengthened it by attracting more international attention. Chico Mendes's legacy is the expansion of extractive reserves in Brazil to protect the rain forest and the lifestyle of rubber tappers.

REFERENCES

Mendes, Chico. *Fight for the Forest*. London: Latin American Bureau, 1990.
Shoumatoff, Alex. *The World Is Burning*. Boston: Little, Brown, 1990.

More on Chico Mendes and the Amazon is available at the Environmental Defense Fund website at www.edf.org/programs/international/chico/chicotimeline.html.

through pesticide use), leaving behind nonproductive land, and a depleted resource base. The costs of deforestation are not limited to plant life. Of the six to nine million Indians who once called the Amazon home, only remnants of their tribes remain. The twentieth century saw ninety tribes go out of existence.[81] Box 14.3 describes the terrible clash of needs and cultures as local rubber tappers came in contact with the force of ranchers and loggers in the Brazilian Amazon.

In addition to these pressures from largely corporate farming, small landholders use nonrenewable resources in the Amazon to simply survive. Natural resources, particularly forests, are being utilized beyond their regenerative capacity. This presents particular problems for the poor, with limited access to a resource basis. For small landholders, the returns to alternative uses of forested land exceed those tied to tradition extractive forestry by a seven to one margin. That is, it is seven times more profitable to chop down trees and to farm than it is to extract sustainable forestry products.[82] Conversion of forest to farmland is hardly a surprising outcome. Inadequate property rights and unequal asset distribution contribute to the destructive human activity in the rain forest region. In the past, unintended policy outcomes were also to blame. For example, in Brazil during the late 1960s and early 1970s, government regional development programs provided incentives to ranchers and other farmers to move into Amazonia to relieve pressure on overcrowded cities. In addition, mining projects such as the Grande Carajas Program accelerated deforestation.[83]

The construction of roads through the Amazon also contributes to damage. Secondary destruction results from road construction and the equipment necessary to sustain distant settlements. Three-quarters of deforestation occurs within thirty miles of paved roads. Logically, it is easier to get the timber out—and to get any goods to market. Road building creates tough ethical dilemmas in environmental protection. Although the relationship between road construction and deforestation is well documented, roads are lifelines to escape poverty for the poor living in remote areas. Brazil is moving forward with its controversial BR-163, a highway connecting the farms and ranches of southern Brazil to overseas markets via Santarém, a deep water port that feeds into the Atlantic. Said one peasant farmer along this strip, "We used to have to leave here by bus at 2 A.M. to reach Santarém by 5 P.M. in the rainy season," he said. "Now in two hours we can travel to the city to sell our produce. It would be great if they would pave it all the way south to open more opportunities for us poor people."[84]

Roads raise the ethical dilemma between conservation and livelihoods. One can attempt to stem the deforestation from road building and pressures from agriculture and deforestation through strong conservation measures. Indeed, the Brazilian government has recently passed a series of conservation laws; it has long had laws which set aside land for conservation purposes.[85] In 2006 President Lula signed a presidential decree putting six million hectares of Amazon rain forest under governmental protection in an attempt to control illegal cutting.[86] Again, however, economic realities constrain good policy. Nilson Samuelson, a former mayor who acknowledges breaking the law, argues that economic necessity justified his actions. "We're just trying to survive," he said. "Who is going to give me the money to pay my employees and educate my children? What are you trying to do, have Ibama [Brazil's environmental ministry] wipe me out and leave 250 families without jobs? Who cares about the law? What am I supposed to do, go hungry?"[87] Illegal logging is rampant. During a moratorium on issuing permits to log in 2004, Brazilian timber exports increased nearly 50 percent in value. With permits suspended, it does not take a rocket scientist to suspect illegal logging; even the government estimates that approximately 60 percent of the exports are illegal.[88] The regulatory arm of Ibama is chronically understaffed, its employees are regularly threatened, and local police lack the capacity to enforce fines. It is also subject to strong political pressure. Licenses to log were restored in 2005 when loggers and allies blocked major roads, burned buses, and threatened to pollute waterways. A leader of the loggers association threatened that "blood will flow" unless activity resumed.[89] Forest policy is well-intentioned but ineffective. The good intentions of forest policy unfortunately fall victim to economic and political realities.

Forests are not the only ecosystem suffering under the weight of population pressures. Coastal habitats, one of the richest sources of marine biodiversity and a vital source of food supply, are threatened by the so-called progress of development. In South America, 50 percent of the coastlines are under moderate or high potential threat.[90] Coastal development, overfishing, increased waste disposal, industrial pollution, oil spills, and population density have led to dramatic changes in habitat. A 97 percent increase in the use of fertilizers from 1980 to 1999 has contaminated rural water supplies.[91]

Environmental concerns in Latin America are clearly broad. From city sewage to mangrove swamps, from air pollution alerts to the felling of trees, questions of sustainability abound. Without change in current practice, future generations will not be as well-off. The environmental deficit in the region requires changes in policy formation, institutional capacity, and financing to promote sustainable development. Let's turn to these implementation issues.

POLICY FORMULATION:
PROMOTING SUSTAINABLE GROWTH

Given the wide range of problems as well as limited resources, what policy measures would have the greatest returns in promoting sustainable growth in Latin America? How can different groups with widely varied interests be brought together in the service of environmental sustainability? Who should pay for a cleaner environment in the region?

Environmental goodwill has been part of the political platform of Latin American governments since the 1990s. In some cases significant progress has been made. Table 14.8 shows the ranking of countries in the Western Hemisphere on a composite set of indicators that reflect strong environmental policy. Two key components include decreasing stress on environmental health and promoting sound ecosystem vitality and sound natural resource management. Costa Rica, Colombia, and Chile perform better than the United States. Mexico is toward the bottom of hemispheric performers with Bolivia and El Salvador, illustrating that wealth is a significant but not determinate predictor of environmental performance. Indeed, as Daniel Esty, author of the Environmental Performance Index, notes, policy choices indeed matter.[92] Yet progress has sometimes been frustratingly slow. Despite an expansion of proenvironmental legislation in the region and a broader participation by civil society, Latin America remains environmentally vulnerable. Why do policies fail? Policy failures, certainly not limited to the Latin American region, may be attributed to undervaluation of forest resources, inadequate understanding of affected

Table 14.8.   Environmental Performance Index (EPI)

EPI Global Rank among 133 Countries	Country	Composite Score
8	Canada	84
15	Costa Rica	81.6
17	Colombia	80.4
26	Chile	78.9
28	United States	78.5
30	Argentina	77.7
34	Brazil	77
37	Panama	76.5
40	Ecuador	75.5
44	Venezuela	74.1
48	Suriname	72.9
52	Honduras	70.8
56	Nicaragua	69.2
58	Guatemala	68.9
62	Paraguay	66.4
65	Peru	65.4
66	Mexico	64.8
71	Bolivia	64.4
73	El Salvador	63

Source: Daniel Esty, Tanja Srebotnjak, Christine Kim, Marc Levy, Alexander de Sherbinin, and Bridget Anderson, "Pilot 2006 Environmental Performance Index" (New Haven: Yale Center for Environmental Law & Policy, 2006), www.yale.edu.
The EPI ranks 133 countries on 16 tracking indicators in six policy areas: Environmental Health (mortality, indoor pollution, drinking water, adquate sanitation), Air Quality, Water Resources, Biodiversity and Habitat, Productive Natural Resources, and Sustainable Energy. It focuses on policy impact, weighting less environmental destruction of past.

groups, difficulty in analyzing policy impacts, administrative corruption, the lack of synergy among global environmental organizations, and operational difficulties.[93] Ineffective policies, or policies that do not achieve their objectives, most often result from a poor match between ends and means. The policy goal may have been too broad given available resources and institutional capacity. Inefficient policies are policies that could have been achieved at a lower cost. Effectiveness and efficiency gains are necessary to achieve sustainability.

Environmental policies have to make good economic sense to continue over time. Other policy failures have occurred because the goal was unidimensional, focusing on the environment to the exclusion of the economy or the social base. Ignoring gender issues—particularly the ways in which the division of labor by sex, the inequality between men and women in access to productive resources, and the political restrictions on public power that bar women—has limited the positive contributions that women can make to sustainable development.[94] Environmental policies must consider the linkages between social, environmental, and economic objectives for success. Intersectoral linkages are also critical; infrastructure, mining, energy, trade, monetary, fiscal, and agricultural policies are linked. In analyzing potential policy outcomes, these complex linkages must be taken into account. Such environmental accounting is extremely tough but vitally important. Although it is difficult to assign monetary value to natural resources, estimate the effects on a variety of social groups, predict direct and indirect linkages, and account for administrative and operational weaknesses, not doing so will further compromise achievements in the environmental arena.

Types of Environmental Policy

The focus of environmental policy might differ in the rural and the urban sectors. Rural priorities include fuel plantations; tree nurseries; sapling distribution; fuel wood quasi self-sufficiency; southern carbon sink forests fully paid for by the North; alternative small-scale energy systems such as solar, wind, and biogas; intensification of food production through terraces, fish ponds, and small livestock; perennial crops; wood processing from plantation forests; improved water supply with wells and low-technology pumps; and social organizations and collective action by the poor to improve resource management. Possible policy measures in the urban sector include low-technology sanitation; drinking water loss reduction for slums; promotion of cleaner slum fuels (methanol versus charcoal); solar stove and cooker efficiencies; garbage and biogas/methane digesters; garbage prevention; promotion of slum cooperatives and "fair price" shops; health, hygiene, breast-feeding, and family planning education campaigns; and pro bono medical aid for vaccines and oral rehydration, supported by social organizations for the urban poor.[95]

Environmental policy can be broken down into three broad and complementary tools: market-based mechanisms, CAC measures, and capacity-building initiatives. Combining these instruments is usually the most effective way to promote sustainable development.

A market-based initiative involves the sale of environmental services to change

Box 14.4.   Organizing Forest Communities in Mexico

Forest policy must respond to local conditions. In Mexico, communally held land through ejidos and indigenous communities accounts for 70 percent of the 55.2 hectares of forested land.[96] This communal form of commercial ownership presents challenges for the implementation of market mechanisms because market policies primarily attend to individual incentives. Moreover, many of the forest communities are very poor, lacking the assets to invest in sustainable development policies. Imposing change through **command and control (CAC) measures** was not politically feasible or likely to be successful. Some new mix of incentives plus capacity building was in order.

Change began at the local level. In the early 1980s, indigenous communities in the poor, mountainous southern states of Mexico—angered by watching their forests degraded by outside loggers—formed a regional organization and succeeded in stopping the government from renewing timber concessions. Government assistance then facilitated the development of local organization. Many of these communities went on to establish their own community forest enterprises. In 1997, the Proyecto de Conservación y Manejo Sostenable y Recursos Forestales (PROCYMAF, or Community Forest Project), cofinanced by the Mexican government and the World Bank, began to operate in the pine-oak forests of the state of Oaxaca.

The project works on a demand basis, assisting 256 communities to become more organized and build capacity. Communities that are not actively engaged in commercial forestry first develop land-use plans and evaluate their land governance systems. Communities that are already engaged in forestry activities use project funds to develop new management plans, establish new community-protected areas, or explore new business or marketing options. Training courses regularly provide information about silviculture, management, and marketing of wood and nonwood forest products. The project has a separate component that involves private-sector consulting services for communities.

Since the project's start, the area under forest management has expanded from 500,000 to 650,000 hectares, and total wood production has increased from 400,000 to 660,000 cubic meters annually. These communities sell their sustainably forested timber to a local door manufacturer at a premium of 15 percent. This new volume generates at least an additional $10 million in value annually. About 1,300 new permanent jobs in forest management and processing have resulted, and an additional 175 jobs have been generated in nontimber forest product activities, including mushroom production and freshwater bottling. As a result, the State of Oaxaca is taking in an additional $1 million a year in tax revenue, and communities' social expenditures, apart from salaries and wages, have increased at least $1 million a year. Forests are also better managed. Some 13,500 hectares of permanent old-growth reserves have been established. Some 90,000 hectares have already been certified by the Forest Stewardship Council.[97]

Although it supported timber production, PROCYMAF I was primarily a project that built individual and social capacity to improve the economic and well-being of the poor. Despite some success, this approach was incomplete. Markets for new, diversified products did not develop for the poorest communities in the absence of capacity and connections. Small ejidos needed to learn to define and place products in external markets. One lesson from the program was the underlying heterogeneity in the ability of communities to manage forest plans as they move through various stages of development. There were inefficiencies in the management of enterprises such as sawmills and bottlenecks in moving up the production chain to increasing the value added in forest products. For example, after defining resin extracted from pine trees as important supplemental income, a feasibility study was in order to bring the processing of the enterprise to the community, creating additional jobs in the nontimber forest products sector. Government regulation

continued

continued

was inefficient, with the joint roles of oversight and promotion of forest activities falling to one agency. As a result, PROCYMAF I also suffered from inefficiencies and market failure.

PROCYMAF II builds on the success of the first community forest program, expanding it geographically and investing in greater institutional capacity to manage forest resources. A new agency with a strong track record, CONAFOR, was created under the environmental agency, SEMARNAT, to promote markets for environmental services. It targets an improvement in the quality of life of forest owners in six states, reducing migratory labor by increasing employment 30 percent in communities. It hopes to impact sustainable forestry practices with a 20 percent increase in the net value of forest goods and services through technical support. Skilled service providers trained in working with local communities will facilitate local discussions of land-use zoning, provide support for market studies for product diversification, help undertake feasibility studies to expand nontimber forest products, and promote human capital development. The program aims to build social capital through 150 participatory exercises, 48 intercommunity seminars leading to the drafting of new community statutes, and providing travel money and per diems so that communities can learn from each other.

Roughly one-fourth of the world's poor depend fully or in part on forest resources for subsistence needs. However, many environmental policies designed to preserve the world's forests pose barriers for small, low-income producers. Prices are kept low, effectively limiting their ability to acquire capital and technology and therefore their income opportunities and livelihoods. PROCYMAF II is an example of a new strategy designed to ensure that small forest communities are able to capitalize on their forest assets. Without such strategies, forest communities, which own some 25 percent of the world's forests, will have little incentive to protect them for future generations. Strengthening producer organizations, as illustrated in the southern states of Mexico, and establishing business services within Amazon communities can make markets work for local producers while simultaneously promoting sustainable forestry.

the incentives of agents; some initiatives are also implemented to generate resources to finance conservation efforts.[98] **Market-based incentives** encourage or discourage certain behaviors. For example, taxes have been used effectively to reduce industrial wastewater in Brazil by almost half, and gasoline taxes can reduce the consumption of energy. Environmental income might be earned from the sale of carbon credits, payments by downstream users for conservation by upstream users of watersheds, rewards to forest landholders for conservation services, and the fares of ecotourists for participating in scenic and cultural beauty. The Clean Development Mechanism (CDM) is one such market-based incentive that arose from a Brazilian initiative and has become an important part of the Kyoto Protocol on Climate Change. The concept behind the CDM is that Annex 1 countries (those countries with emissions-reductions obligations under Kyoto) can implement emissions-reducing projects in non-Annex 1 countries (developing countries with no commitments under Kyoto) and gain Certified Emissions Reductions (CERs) for the cut in emissions that is achieved as a result of the project. The CDM aims to help Annex 1 countries comply with Kyoto while at the same time helping non-Annex 1 countries by providing valuable technology transfer as well as environmental benefits.[99] So far Brazil has been the most proactive participant in CDM projects. According to the United Nations Framework Convention on Climate Change website, as of September 2006 Brazil has sixty-six registered CDM projects, which is nearly a quarter of the world's total.[100] The revenues from sales of CERs will be put toward environmental protection in Brazil.[101] In Costa Rica, a leader in payment for environmental services programs, the town of Heredia (outside the capital city of San Jose) pays environmentally adjusted water tariffs to finance conservation efforts upstream.[102] In Guatemala, communities are given exclusive rights to log in exchange for commitments to sustainable standards,[103] and in Ecuador, ecolodges such as one called the Black Sheep, brings income to local residents of the mountain town of Chugchilán.[104]

Payment for environmental services (PES) rests on several economic principles. First, the approach recognizes that environmental problems are linked to human incentives and capacities to act. Pricing environmental services fundamentally asks how to design the financial incentives for good stewardship and sustainable natural resource management. Unless incentives are altered, economic agents will focus on direct returns and outlays, ignoring social benefits and costs. A farmer clearing the forest will factor in the benefits from agricultural sales and the costs of clearing the land but will ignore the effects of deforestation and clear more land than is socially optimal.[105] In many applications of market-based tools, the **polluter pays the cost**—that is, the agent is charged for the cost of the environmental externality. A plant discharging emissions in the Netherlands that buys credits from Colombia under the clean development mechanism therefore is paying for its contribution to global warming. Where environmental services are created, the **beneficiary pays for the gain.** Purchasers of lumber products certified to have been produced using sustainable logging practices pay a premium over destructively harvested wood. It is important in evaluating the potential of payment for environmental services that the full **opportunity costs** of alternative activities be calculated. That is, ecotourism might be attractive, but to preserve a forest area, community members must be compensated at a level at least equal to the sale price of timber. Potential risks should be explored. Only 17 percent of ecotourism programs make at least a 20 percent return on their investment—and half have less than 30 percent occupancy in the off season.[106] How will families survive in a community if land is not planted and the ecotourism enterprise dies? Or less dramatically, how will families manage the risk of little income during the down season? Unintended outcomes might also be taken into account. Although market-based mechanisms are appealing in that agreements are voluntary, and we can assume that people largely enter into contracts because they believe that doing so is good for them, sometimes asymmetries of information or power might lead to bad decisions. For example, if land values increase due to payments for environmental services, it is conceivable that the poor will be pushed off the land by higher bidders. Risk and information failures may make the poor and the environment worse off.

Launching a PES scheme raises a series of implementation issues. First, if a market-based mechanism is to be employed, a careful market analysis is in order. Is the market for the environmental services local or global in scope? Are buyers willing to pay enough to compensate providers for alternative uses of natural resources? Is the market reasonably efficient? It is appealing to think that promoting the use of natural cosmetic ingredients from the Amazon will help prevent defor-estation, but hardheaded questions need to be asked about how the small indige-nous gatherer in Peru will make contact with the product development folks for the Body Shop, particularly under its new giant corporate parent L'Oreal cosmetics. How might an illiterate peasant on a Mexican ejido put together a business plan to deliver bottled water or resin, used in the production of paints? (For the answer to this question, see box 14.4.) This is not to say that market mechanisms should be ignored; rather, they may need nurturing. Markets may not spontaneously develop in the absence of capacity and connections.

Markets for environmental products may take time to develop. Think for a moment about the conceptual parallels between a stock market and a market for carbon credits. In setting up the Brazilian Carbon Market, the two partners—the Brazilian Mercantile and Futures Exchange and the Brazilian Ministry of Develop-ment, Industry and Foreign Trade—need to construct the same kind of confidence-building elements that you expect from an efficient stock exchange. That is, you aren't likely to plunk down cash for stock on someone's word. Instead, you would like a certified accounting of a business's track record and some assurance that there will be sufficient liquidity in the market should your portfolio preferences change. You would only invest in a market with clear transparent rules to prevent insider trading and other corrupt practices. Carbon markets also need to develop these characteristics of certification, liquidity, and credibility—and this takes time. The question of credibility is central to the debate on avoided deforestation. Employing carbon mitigation strategies by paying agents not to log or cut timber for farming raises the challenge of guaranteeing that **additionality** as well as verification exist. That is, can it be shown that the trees wouldn't be left standing in any case, and how do you know if the forest remains intact for the specified period of time?

A key consideration in designing payment for environmental services is their impact on equity. Who will be the beneficiaries of such initiatives? Given trans-action costs, there is a danger that payment in communities will accrue to the better-off. If, for example, landowners are compensated to maintain natural reserves as opposed to farming, it is much easier to compensate large landholders. Gathering one hundred small landholders incurs significant **transaction costs** of separate nego-tiations as well as monitoring and enforcement of multiple environmental contracts —and of course ignores completely the fact that the poorest of the poor are unlikely to be landholders in the first place.[107] In fact, significant economies of scale in nego-tiating with large landowners may be the most efficient approach from an environ-mental standpoint; governments will need to weigh environmental priorities with improving the lot of poor. An evaluation of a PES scheme in Costa Rica showed that of 110 landowners paid in the Virilla watershed, 6 percent went to properties under thirty hectares and 80 percent to properties of seventy hectares or more.[108] Indeed, attaching too many objectives—conservation and equity—to market-based tools may render them less effective. But a balance between equity and environ-ment is not impossible. The proposed National Environmental Management Project in El Salvador explicitly links poverty-reduction goals with market-based natural resource management, targeting small farmers to benefit from this strategy.[109] Ac-tivities such as agroforestry, forest management and conservation, reforestation, afforestation (the planting of trees for commercial purposes), and sustainable agricultural production will be promoted in very poor areas, generating valuable environmental benefits such as improving water quality, regulating groundwater and surface flows, maintaining or enhancing biodiversity, and increasing carbon sequestration.[110]

Markets usually focus on incentives to individuals to maximize profit, yet sustainable development most often engages communities. As box 14.5 underscores,

---

BOX 14.5. MARKET-BASED INSTRUMENTS IN LATIN AMERICAN ENVIRONMENTAL POLICY

BACKGROUND

Market-based instruments (MBIs), policies designed to reduce environmental degradation at the lowest possible social cost, are gaining wider attention in developing countries. Hundreds of individual instruments exist, ranging from fines or sanctions that are linked to traditional command-and-control mechanisms to laissez-faire approaches that depend on consumer advocacy. More commonly used mechanisms include tax-and-subsidy approaches. Latin American countries have demonstrated relatively wide experimentation with MBIs. In Brazil, Colombia, and Mexico, credit subsidies are offered for abatement investments in the industrial sector. In Ecuador, taxation and tariff relief is offered for investments on mercury recovery in artisinal mining. Deposit-refund systems for consumers are well established throughout the region as well. Informal collection of beverage and beer cans in exchange for flat fees paid out by recycling operations are growing increasingly popular in Brazil and Venezuela, where beverage-packaging plants are common. Resource-use charges, including forestry taxation, as well as water charges for use and pollution are in place in the region as well.[111]

VENTURE CAPITAL FIRM BUILDS SUSTAINABLE INDUSTRY WITH AMAZON COMMUNITIES

Small- and medium-sized Latin American companies are earning competitive profits while increasing biodiversity with the help of the venture capital fund Terra Capital, a partnership between Axial RR (A2R) of Brazil and GMO-RR of Boston. Investment areas include organic agriculture, sustainable forestry, nontimber forest products, ecotourism, and bioprospecting. Several Terra Capital investments involve community-based forestry in the Brazilian Amazon—including a processing plant for hearts of palm, a company for processing babacu palm, and a large production and processing enterprise for certified sustainable softwood. A2R is committed to improving local livelihoods and conserving forest resources as part of its core business strategy. An interdisciplinary team of financial and technical specialists from A2R visits the enterprises frequently to provide business support.

For example, A2R acquired a financial interest in a heart of palm processing plant on a remote island in Marajo, in the state of Pará, that was suffering from unreliable raw material supply and poor management. A2R helped to resolve local land conflicts and to secure local rights for growing palm fruits, thereby ensuring a regular and secure source for the processing plant. Within three years, the enterprise achieved sales of US$4 million, supporting one hundred factory employees and increasing incomes and assets for five thousand families in one of the poorest parts of the Amazon. A2R also has helped local people produce the palm fruits more sustainably. They have begun to seek Forest Stewardship Council certification, which would establish the first certification for heart of palm in Brazil.[112]

payment for environmental services can be designed to support community as opposed to household decision making. The scope of projects may also need to be broadened beyond natural resources. Taking into account a range of economic activities, including those income-generating options not related to forestry, facilitates sustainable development. Diversification of opportunities derived from the boom in wine making in Chile relieved pressure on overgrazed land and provided additional income for investments in sustainable agricultural practices. The lesson in this case was that focusing on nonnatural resource sector activities to provide remuneration was as important as forest-based activities.[113]

Market-based mechanisms are not a magic bullet promoting sustainable development. They are most effective when complemented by our second category of policy, a strong regulatory framework grounded in clear property rights that are predictably and consistently enforced. This is a tall order. By its very nature—access to a commodity—natural resource management is open to corruption. The power to grant access to land, minerals, or natural products can corrupt, particularly at lower levels of government. The primary difficulty in Latin America is not the design of laws and regulations but their implementation. The 80 percent forest reserve requirement on privately owned land in the Amazon is regularly flouted, and forest management plans for concessions are notoriously weak or fraudulent.[114] As noted above, one of the primary reasons for increased deforestation is illegal logging activity. Indeed, in the absence of bureaucracy effectiveness, creating the pressures for legal compliance from new economic stakeholders is a positive synergy between law and markets. If prices are high and the probability of getting caught and significantly fined is low, it is economically rational to log illegally. Says one farmer of illegal timbering in the Amazon, "You can make 10 times the price of the fine with one year of soya cultivation—and that's if they catch you. So, it's worth the risk."[115] This is the same argument you might use when you calculate just how fast you are going to drive on an underpoliced stretch of highway when you are running late. If the benefit to you is greater than the fine multiplied by the probability of getting caught (discounted again if you think you can buy off the policeman or the judge), you will clearly speed. If other drivers—think of these as the nontimber product producers—were to start calling the state police complaining that you were endangering their lives by reckless speeding, you might slow down. Other stakeholders in nontimber forest product activity may promote accountability to laws.

Market-based instruments (MBIs) may enhance the efficiency of CAC measures, but clear rules and regulations may create the opportunities for a market in the first place. If nations (minus the United States) had not agreed to the Kyoto Treaty, the market for emissions credits would be less robust. The legally binding cap creates the incentive to find more flexible and cost-effective measures for compliance. Limiting natural park land to sustainable uses can create a market for sustainable services if the alternative, more lucrative option—degrading the environment—is not (legally) on the table.

Market-based measures grounded in a strong and transparent regulatory framework are most successful when communities have the assets to manage natural resources. A critical role for national and international government engagement is therefore building local capacity. Governments may choose to invest in public goods. The government may invest directly in infrastructure projects such as waste treatment plants or sewage lines to improve environmental quality. In Chile, for example, investment in irrigation helped raise incomes and decrease pressure on common range land.[116] In addition to infrastructure, strengthening social capital is critical. A key outcome of decentralized resource management in Honduras was building local capacity to make decisions regarding the environment.[117] The wide availability of reconstruction funds following the conflict in El Salvador also had the upside effect of augmenting social capital.[118] International NGOs partnered with local groups to introduce new ideas on environmental sustainability and new technologies to achieve them. Government investment in individual human capital through education and health programs can also facilitate better environmental decision making. Clearly the largest constraint on **direct government investments** to improve the environment are financial. The 2002 Monterrey, Mexico, summit underscored the need to develop mechanisms for financing sustainable development. Although polluter-pays programs can generate their own revenues, investments in public goods can be more problematic to finance.

These three tools—market-based mechanisms, state-mandated CAC measures, and investments by governments into infrastructure and human as well as social capital—are complementary measures. By using each in judicious measure, a virtuous cycle of sustainable growth may be promoted. Regulations, or CAC measures, are most effective when the risk to public health is severe and when the number of polluters is relatively limited.[119] When the regulatory arm is used, it is important that legislation be matched by institutional capacity for enforcement. Lofty environmental goals without the ability to implement and enforce regulations only contribute to a lack of credibility in government. A practical, pragmatic policy mix of government investment, CAC, and MBI gradually implemented will better serve long-run environmental interests. Payments for environmental services have the advantage of limiting fiscal impacts on cash-strapped governments.

Addressing the problem of air pollution involves a mix of regulatory and market policies. Mexico City has a contingency program restricting vehicles and activity of highly polluting industries, including PEMEX refineries, on bad air days. This long-run strategy to substitute low- for high-polluting industries will, however, take time. Using outdated technology, domestically assembled automobiles in Latin America are half as fuel efficient as best practices in the United States and Japan. Based on Latin American experience, the most cost-effective programs include inspection and maintenance programs to comply with emissions standards; the use of reformulated and alternative fuels (with fuels modified to accommodate seasonal geographical variations); traffic management, including bus policy regulations and liberalization, route restructuring, rationalization of truck and bus sizes, traffic signal improvements, area traffic bans, car pooling, and bikeways; road construction (paving decreases dust) and creating high-occupancy vehicle lanes; fuel pricing; and a vehicle emissions tax.[120]

The Chileans used an innovative mix of regulation and market incentives to reduce air pollution levels in Santiago that were reaching critically unhealthy levels about once a week. Ironically, part of the problem had originated in an effort to make transportation more competitive. When bus routes were deregulated, thousands of cheap, old, and polluting buses were imported. In 1991, twenty-six hundred buses with pre-1972 engines, or 20 percent of the fleet, were banned. More stringent emission standards for new buses and limits on the kinds of buses permitted on downtown routes were implemented. The market came into play through the auction of bus transit rights in the city center. Routes were awarded based on fares to be charged and the type of buses to be operated. In this way, private firms could make money through the exclusive right to operate in the downtown area, pollution was to be reduced by regulating the kinds of buses in the downtown area, and low fares would favor the use of public transportation. The result was a reduction in the number of winter days with critical pollution levels by approximately one-third. Although the number of buses permitted in the downtown area was limited, fleets needed fewer vehicles because each bus could make more round trips with reduced congestion. Average fares were reduced by 10 percent, and the auction yielded revenues to finance improvements in dust-reducing paved roads.[121]

Policies to promote sustainability of small farming in the Amazon likewise involve a mix of the market, direct investment, and regulation. Zoning and promoting settlements only where land is sufficiently productive, taxing capital gains to reduce speculative land sales, placing a stumpage tax on deforestation, diffusing appropriate technology, improving market and storage systems to help small farmers, and establishing credit and other institutions have been found to promote good farming frontiers and to help farmers stay where they are without pressuring virgin areas.[122] As described in box 14.6, a controversial example of private initiative arises in the case of Pumalin Park in Chile, where an American businessman proposed the set aside of Chilean lands. Environmental policy requires a partnership between the public and the private sectors.

TOOLS FOR TOUGH ENVIRONMENTAL DECISIONS

Environmental policy has made great strides in Latin America, but much remains to be done. How should this long list of policy options be prioritized? **Cost-effectiveness** is an important criterion to evaluate alternative policies. For example, water-related illness and death, the largest health impact of urban pollution, can be addressed at a reasonable cost. In contrast, although sewage and sanitation services are often demanded, they may have to be postponed until more vital needs are met. As the technology is available, solid waste problems may be solved by additional resources— but this might come at an opportunity cost to more pressing needs. Cost matters for policies to be sustainable over time. Governments might have the greenest of intentions, but without long-term financing, little of enduring value will be accomplished.

A critical step toward good environmental policy is incorporating **environmental assessments** into development policy making. Environmental problems are most often the by-product of the development process. Encouraging environmental accounting before the damage is done will promote the goal of future sustainability. There are three steps in conducting an environmental assessment: data collection, the identification of the problem, and a **cost-benefit analysis** (**CBA**). Box 14.7 discusses the CBA technique and its limitations. Data collection is useful

Box 14.6.   Public-Private Partnerships in Conservation: The Case of Pumalin Park, Chile

With the tenacity of hardheaded businesspeople and the passions of deep ecowarriors, Douglas Tompkins and his wife Kristine McDivitt battled for fourteen years to overcome deep distrust of personal environmental philanthropy in Chile. Tompkins, the founder of Espirit and The North Face, and McDivitt, a former chief executive officer of the Patagonia retail chain who is wealthy in her own right, made a simple proposition in 1991: donate a nearly three hundred thousand-hectare privately owned park bisecting Chile as it extends from the Argentine border to the Chilean coast as a nature preserve. The ecosystem in the region is characterized by snow-capped mountains, crystal-blue glaciers, and meandering fjords and is home to four-thousand-year-old alerce trees, the Andean condor, and the world's smallest deer, the southern pudu. As the world's largest private reserve, Pumalín would encourage scientific research and benefit local communities through ecotourism and apiculture, a low-impact higher return agriculture appropriate to the environment. Tompkins would invest $30 million of his personal fortune to promote sustainable tourism in the park.[123] He shared the vision of Chile's Nobel Prize-winning poet Pablo Neruda, who once claimed, "Anyone who hasn't been in the Chilean forest doesn't know this planet."[124]

Thompkins wanted to bring the forest to Chileans and the world but met incredible pushback from various interest groups unfamiliar with the tradition of personal philanthropy. Among the rumors were accusations that Tompkins was harassing and underpaying local farmers for their land, building a nuclear base, planning a Jewish colony (he is a buttoned-down, gray-haired WASP),[125] developing a secret gold mine, and financing political opposition. Opponents argue that the project will jeopardize national interests and the rights of Chilean entrepreneurs. The Chilean armed forces have claimed that the park could be a threat to national security because it could divide the country in half and that the project would make Chile overly vulnerable due to the unpredictability of foreign direct investment. Meanwhile, industries such as forestry, fishing, agriculture, and mining, which consider Pumalin their primary industrial territory, predicted that the park will affect them adversely. Chile's minister of national property, Adriana Delpiano, challenged the natural sanctuary by arguing that the land ought to be used for industrial economic development.

The long-term, sustainable development plans for the land is Douglas Tompkins's fundamental concern. Knowing that Chile's "free-market economy is 90 percent based on the export of natural resources," he is particularly concerned with the overexploitation and destruction of Chile's native forest. Instead of wasting its four-thousand-year-old alerce trees on wood chip exports, Tompkins aspires to preserve and profit from these rare species through ecotourism.

In August 2005, Thompkins and McDivitt's doggedness paid off. Pumalin Park was designated a nature sanctuary, a special status conferring additional protection to the land. The Pumalin foundation will administer the preserve with full public access to this private park. Moreover, the attention garnered by the much-debated Pumalin project has attracted other important players, both Chilean and international, to private land conservation efforts. Chilean entrepreneur Sebastain Pinera has purchased a large tract of land in southern Chiloé for ecotourism. Over the next five years, he plans to invest $20 million in the conservation of Chiloé and in the development of ecotourism.[126] He wants his park to cover its running costs, estimated at $500,000 a year, with income from tourism. Investment banking powerhouse Goldman Sachs has donated thousands of acres of forested property in Tierra del Fuego that it acquired through a debt default of Trillium logging to the Wildlife Conservation Society of New York to run the Karukinka reserve.

continued

continued

Goldman Sachs hopes to restore the ecosystem, control rampant beaver overpopulation (beavers were introduced from Canada in the 1950s for fur farming and are damming rivers and causing damage to trees), and preserve the area's unique fungi and lichen. Environmental groups are wary of the firm's involvement, but a shift in political culture toward globalization has opened spaces for partnership. The government has a pragmatic need for international cooperation: Chile's National Forestry Service, which manages some 150,000 square kilometers of protected areas—more than fifty times the size of either Karukinka or Pumalín—does so on an annual budget of a mere $5 million. Public-private partnerships in conservation are the only financial alternative.

in establishing priorities for rational decision making in the environmental area. It is important when identifying the problem that both direct and indirect costs and benefits are included. For example, in assessing the Carajas project in Brazil, the Brazilian mining firm CVRD did a good job of working with FUNAI, the Brazilian Indian Protection Agency, to identify the direct effects on Indian lands. What was not accounted for, however, were the indirect costs. New roads led to squatter settlements that encroached on Indian property and brought new diseases into the region. These indirect costs were the greatest source of environmental damage.

Environmental assessments are not cheap and are not always simple. It may be difficult to forecast the benefits of a project. How can one estimate all the benefits of a virgin forest or cleaner air? One approach that attempts to address this problem is called the contingent valuation method. A survey is undertaken asking people's willingness to pay for a given policy. In São Paulo, for example, it was found that people were three times more willing to pay for sewage treatment than for a park.[127] Contingent valuation helps policy planners assess and measure the benefits of a given environmental project.

An alternative method to a CBA would be a cost-effectiveness analysis (CEA). A CEA approach gets around the problem of estimating willingness to pay for future programs by simply ranking projects on the basis of many environmental indicators rather than estimating a dollar benefit. This qualitative assessment, combined with environmental and conventional costs, is a useful, less-expensive tool for decision makers. Difficulties in identifying full costs and benefits should not prevent policymakers from insisting on the best possible estimates of environmental impacts. Limited information is better than none at all in accounting for the environment.

Selecting the appropriate combination of policy instruments is a function of the **institutional capacity** of each country.[128] Policies are not implemented in a vacuum. Different instruments place different demands on the public sector to define a problem, design an instrument, and impose unpopular policies. It is important that agencies develop the technical skills for monitoring ambient conditions and the activities of regulated parties. Accurate data and record keeping are an important basis for the formulation of policy and midcourse corrections. The legal system must be sufficiently sophisticated to cover the forms of pollution discharge, renewable resource damage, and overharvesting that might be the target of policy. Institutions

Box 14.7.   Cost-Benefit Analysis:
A Tool for Policy Effectiveness

THE GOAL OF COST-BENEFIT ANALYSIS

Cost-benefit analysis (CBA) is intended to improve public policy decision making. Used to rank policies on the basis of their potential improvements relative to likely costs, this tool helps policymakers select the option that best achieves a specified goal. It encourages decision makers to evaluate alternatives, making the best possible choice for the money. CBA encourages transparency. The enumeration of potential gains and losses versus alternatives encourages open consideration of various options. The framework relies on consistent data collection and helps identify gaps in knowledge. Ignorance revelation is not an inconsequential outcome in policy making! CBA encourages comparability, encouraging the aggregation of dissimilar effects through the metric of money into one measure of net benefits.

THE FORMULA TO ARRIVE AT A CONSISTENT MEASURE

To arrive at a measure of the costs and benefits of a potential policy, one must list all potential benefits and costs, measured in currency units. This is not an easy task; sometimes it involves imputing a dollar cost on nonmonetized outcomes such as the willingness to pay for clean air. It is especially difficult to impute future gains from policies such as biodiversity, particularly when the true risk of not pursuing a policy is unknown. Nonetheless, mathematics lends probability tools and other methods to calculate contingencies for policy outcomes. Risk assessment is a subset of CBA. Statistical techniques can help quantify risks such as the quantitative relationship between pollution exposure and human response. It is important to enumerate not only the direct effects of a program (for example, building a road) but also indirect effects (such as bringing disease to indigenous communities).

Once benefits and costs are established in money units, the sum of all the benefits minus the costs, discounting these for future value as well as social gain is calculated. The value of the future gains must be reduced by the fact that their benefits may not accrue until some further point in time; there may also be a social discount rate that emphasizes the collective gain from pursuing a public good. The formula is:

$$NPV = \sum(\text{benefits} - \text{costs})/(1 + r)^t$$

In the formula, r represents an interest rate (such as a prime rate) adjusted, perhaps for social gain, and t is time or the number of years that the project will produce benefits and costs.

PROBLEMS WITH THE CBA TECHNIQUE

Several problems arise with CBA. Some question the ability to express social well-being as a summation of individual welfare. Individual welfare—based upon the ability of agents to rationally assess preferences—is controversial in itself. Others worry about quantifying economic value when the outcome in question—such as the environment—is a public good. How can this value be measured? Solutions such as willingness to pay or **contingent valuation** measures are imperfect estimates. Nonetheless, if agencies are clear about the guesses employed in a calculation and estimates are subject to peer

continued

continued

evaluation such as through something like the U.S. General Accounting Office, cost-benefit estimates can help policymakers through the very tough task of decision making, especially in the difficult arena of environmental preservation.

AN EXAMPLE: SANTIAGO SEWAGE

CBA was used to evaluate whether or not the Chilean government should build sewage treatment plants in Santiago. It was proposed as a costly endeavor—and the investment would have to come from other social-sector investments. To decide if the investment was worth the reduction in waterborne disease, health benefits in terms of mortality (wage compensation and foregone earnings of those dying from cholera and typhoid), morbidity (the cost of illness, including medical outlays, pain and suffering, and averting behavior), production and consumption costs (including the effects on crops, forests, fisheries, and the municipal water supply), valuation of economic assets (such as materials and property values), and environmental assets (recreational use, visibility, biodiversity) were assessed against not only the direct investment costs of the sewage plant but also versus the cheaper alternatives of strict regulation and monitoring of runoff by farmers using untreated water in fertilizing fields. It was concluded that the direct costs of investing in the sewage plant were not compensated for by an estimation of benefits (leaving the option of tough regulation and education as more cost-effective). Nonetheless, when the uncertainties of the indirect reputational effect on sales of Chilean fruits and vegetables in the international market were factored into the formula, the Chileans chose to move ahead with the pricey investment of full treatment of sewage in Santiago.

must be financially and technologically capable of turning laws into enforceable rules, with skilled people to monitor compliance. The political will must be available to impose costs on sometimes powerful agents. The residual of import substitution industrialization and the *latifundia* agricultural system is a legacy of powerful, concentrated firms in both the industrial and agricultural sectors. Is the government willing to take on these dominant interests in exchange for returns that are likely to be diffuse and to spread into the future? Is the government capable of monitoring the urban and rural informal-sector participants contributing to environmental degradation? Strong and independent media are necessary both to present information to the citizenry on environmental costs and to act as a watchdog against corrupt government and business practices. The institutional capacity of government and public institutions in the face of commercial and agricultural interests is a binding constraint on good environmental policy. The use of market-based instruments, for example, is limited by the degree to which efficient market transactions have permeated all levels of economic activity. Countries may need to begin with simpler mechanisms and gradually phase in more complicated mixtures of incentives and tax-based instruments as the institutional capacity to enforce and monitor develops.

ENVIRONMENTAL POLICY AND THE ROLE OF THE STATE

Among our three schools of thought there is general consensus that when negative externalities from growth contribute to environmental degradation, market inter-

Ecotourism, well managed, can provide local income and contribute to sustainability. *(Courtesy of E. Drew McKechnie)*

vention by the state is warranted. The debate revolves around how much governments should deal with pollution given fiscal, institutional, and technical and monitoring constraints.[129]

Neoliberals would suggest limited intervention, relying principally on the concept of do no harm. That is, the state should reverse harmful subsidies that promote inefficient energy use, revise resettlement initiatives that pressure fragile lands and promote deforestation, revoke agricultural supports that encourage the overuse of fertilizers and pesticides, or redesign policies that result in overexploitation of extractive resources or coastal life.

MBIs such as expanding markets for renewable forest products (perhaps Ben & Jerry's Rainforest Crunch or Body Shop natural products) or encouraging tradable permits through the Kyoto Protocol's Clean Development Mechanism (where, for example, the Spanish petrochemical group Repsol YPF is acquiring ten thousand tons of carbon dioxide emission rights from an energy project undertaken by the Anglo-Dutch petrochemical giant Royal Dutch Shell in Brazil)[130] might also be encouraged by neoliberals. Neoliberals would also suggest that consumer advocacy measures and stockholders voting with their feet would drive away big polluters. MBIs carry the advantage of being cost-effective and creating profit incentives for sustainable development.

Neoinstitutionalists would point to deficiencies in institutional capacity in managing environmental problems. Regionally, the implementation of environmental laws in Latin America has outpaced the institutional capability to enforce them. Latin

American countries have set up the Forum Ministers of the Environment; its work is supported by the Inter-Agency Technical Committee, created in 1999 by ECLAC, the United Nations Development Programme (UNDP), the United Nations Environment Programme (UNEP), the World Bank, and the IADB. Subregional trade agreements have incorporated environmental provisions to promote the sustainable use of shared natural resources. The Border Environmental Commissions under the North American Free Trade Agreement is an example.

Nonetheless, on a national and regional basis environmental institutions are often ineffective. Despite a proliferation of divisions of global institutions following the Rio Earth Summit such as the UNEP or World Bank's Sustainable Development Unit, institutional governance is fragmented and weak. One controversial proposal is to create a world environmental organization with powers of sanction like those of the World Trade Organization. Neoliberal opponents of this idea criticize the effectiveness of global megainstitutions; other critics worry about widening the gap between the environment and economic and social policy.[131]

Neoinstitutionalists would also point to the power of good information in improving market outcomes. They would applaud the developments on the Internet that allow the sharing of best practices—and of negative publicity surrounding polluters. Corporate environmental reports, often encouraged by NGOs and citizen groups, can help in encouraging responsible corporate behavior. Information gaps also persist in providing technical knowledge to firms desiring regulatory compliance. In Mexico, for example, the information gap is being addressed through increased technical assistance and environmental training targeted at noncompliant enterprises.

Neostructuralists would argue for a stronger role for direct investment on the part of the state to improve environmental outcomes. Pointing to market failures to deliver clean water, breathable air, or sustainable agricultural practices, neostructuralists would allocate larger outlays to improving government provision of infrastructure services. Although they would not necessarily reject MBIs, the neostructuralists' distrust of the power of large corporations would lead them toward stronger oversight and investment by the state. The constraint, of course, is financing. Environmental spending competes with other priorities such as health and education. Environmental protection expenditure in the region rarely reaches 1 percent of GDP, well below the European average of 2.3 percent.[132] Administrative decentralization has resulted in a devolution to provinces or states; municipalities must struggle with the direct costs of water and waste services. One possibility to reconcile budgetary constraints with environmental investments would be through taxes to prevent environmental damage and internalize the social cost of activities, levying charges for the use of natural resources to generate revenues, and designing tax reforms to encourage optimum use of natural resources.[133] Greater implementation of these polluter-pays principles may help finance policies.

GLOBAL RESPONSIBILITY FOR A CLEAN ENVIRONMENT

The biggest constraint on good environmental policy in Latin America is financial. As countries struggle to reduce government budgets, it is difficult to legislate new programs of environmental action. Because the benefits of a clean environment accrue not only to Latin Americans but also to the global community, this raises the question of how the burden should be shared.

Global financing must be used to strengthen local institutions. Improving the environment in Latin America means changing the behaviors of people—people who live in poor rural communities and in mushrooming megacities. Change must take place in the northern industrial countries as well as in the southern countries. To be sustainable, environmental action must empower localities and provide incentives for change.

Environmental policy making involves a wide range of local, national, and international actors, often with conflicting priorities. Addressing local problems will begin to contribute to global solutions. Where such local actions benefit global concerns (such as biodiversity), the developed world should pay. This ought not be perceived as aid but rather as a responsible policy of paying for environmental change.[134] The responsibilities for sustainable development should be shared by North and South, as both will share in the gains.

Given budget constraints of most governments of the Latin American and Caribbean regions, there are limited resources for conservation projects with more global than local significance. The GEF, established in 1991, facilitates environmental project financing for developing countries. This financial mechanism works in collaboration with the UNDP, which hosts technical assistance for the GEF; the UNEP, which provides the secretariat; and the World Bank, which is responsible for implementation.[135] More recently, regional development banks such as the IADB have been managing project lending through the GEF as well. Countries have access to GEF funds if they are eligible to borrow from the World Bank or receive technical assistance grants from the UNDP; they may apply through one of these implementing agencies. Through 2005, the GEF has funneled $18.8 billion to 1,700 projects in 140 countries. It has made 6,000 small grants to communities, and leveraged its projects three to one by raising additional money through cofinancing. Latin America has attracted 21.2 percent of funding, supporting 367 projects promoting biodiversity, climate change, international waters, and ozone layer depletion throughout the region.

As described in box 14.8, the most ambitious GEF biodiversity project in Latin America draws nine Central American countries together in an effort to consolidate the Mesoamerican biological corridor, a proposed network of protected areas and their buffer zones. In another effort, the GEF Honduras Protected Areas project is working with indigenous communities, particularly focusing on the role of women's groups. Its goal is to address the link between natural resource management and women's double workload in the home and in the market. In Argentina a GEF grant is supporting rural electrification through photovoltaics, wind power, and minihydroelectric schemes as sustainable sources of energy. A Brazilian program has invested $40 million through the GEF to pioneer the commercialization of electricity-generating technology that uses wood chips from plantation forests for fuel.[136]

Lessons from the first years of GEF project experience indicate that stakeholder participation, especially by affected communities, is essential to changing behaviors. NGOs play key roles in conducting participatory appraisals in projects designed to minimize conflicts as land-use patterns change. It is also important to engage local

Box 14.8. Mesoamerica: Reviving Nature While Making a Living

BY FRANK A. CAMPBELL

Imagine a forest cover starting in South America, passing through Central America, and continuing all the way to North America, and you've just imagined the way things used to be. Today, unfortunately, this rich manifestation of nature has been reduced to a large number of disconnected forests facing the ongoing threat of destruction.

Just in Mesoamerica—southern Mexico and the seven countries of Central America —44 hectares of forest are lost every sixty seconds, mostly to satisfy the demand for firewood. If this were to continue unabated, the area would be virtually without forest in a decade and a half. At least 42 species of mammals, 31 species of birds, and 1,541 species of higher plants (not counting algae and mosses, for example) are believed to be en route to extinction.

This is a potential loss of biodiversity that neither the region nor the global community can afford. Although measuring only 768,990 kilometers, accounting for just about half of 1 percent of emerged lands, this area accounts for about 8 percent of Earth's biodiversity and is numbered among the greatest riches of the world.

Panama alone has 929 species of birds—more than Canada and the United States put together. Belize is only 22,965 square kilometers in area but is home to more than 150 species of mammals, 540 species of birds, and 151 species of amphibians and reptiles. Costa Rica, with a smaller landmass than Denmark, comprises more than 55 distinct biotic units—communities of plants and animals with similar life forms and environmental conditions. It houses more than 365,000 species of arthropods (a large group of invertebrates, ranging from tiny mites to large crabs). Yes, that's 1,000 species for every day of the year! There are more than 800 species of orchids in Nicaragua. Some 70 percent of the vascular flora of the high mountains of Guatemala are endemic to that country.

Central America alone has 20,000–25,000 vascular plant species. That's as many as in Peru, which is four times as large, or in the United States, which is fifteen times as large. Moreover, the principal archaeological sites and remains of the Mayan civilization are located within the Mesoamerican Biological Corridor.

The bad news is that the conservation status of a third of Mesoamerica's thirty-three ecoregions is judged as critical and another third is regarded as endangered. That leaves only one-third of the area in an acceptable state of ecological health.

Fortunately, a major Mesoamerican Biological Corridor program has been launched to help save the biodiversity of this important corner of Earth's surface. "Today," says an April 11, 2000, note from the program's communications unit, "commences one of the most ambitious environmental and social program to be carried out in the Central America and Southern Mexico region." The goal of the program, the note adds, is the recovery of "the chain of forests that up to a few years ago united South and North America and which at this time appears as a series of barren patches threatened by indiscriminate felling."

This program, headquartered in Nicaragua, does more than project new hope in the environmental area. It projects a new Central America in the political realm. At the formal April 11 launching, Nicaragua's minister for the environment and natural resources, Roberto Stadthagen, declared, "This initiative reintroduces the Central American region in the world scene as a region of progress and sustainable development. After having been known for conflicts and wars, it emerges now as a brilliant example of international cooperation for peace, democracy and the environment."

Indeed, the Mesoamerica Biological Corridor program represents a study in international cooperation at the wider level. In his speech at the launching, Nicaraguan president Arnoldo Alemán expressed special recognition and appreciation to the GEF, the UNDP, and the German government for their support for the program. GEF, for example, is contributing almost $11 million, and this investment is being overseen on the ground by the UNDP. Among other sources of support for the effort are the World Bank and DANIDA, the Danish government aid agency.

The need for such an international collaboration for the rescue of nature in the region became more and more evident over the years as each country developed institutions, usually at the ministerial level, in a valiant effort to meet the twin challenges of economic poverty and environmental degradation. In the course of the last thirty years, the governments of Mesoamerica established 461 separate protected areas. These covered as much as 31 percent of the territory (in Belize) and as little as 2 percent (in Honduras, Nicaragua, El Salvador, and Mexico).

Regionally, these protected areas totaled 18 million hectares. Only half of the protected areas had any kind of staffing. Some 88 percent were without any management plans. Most are not even well demarcated. Only about 40 of the 461 have been host to research programs. Few have at their disposal the institutional and legal frameworks to facilitate either biodiversity conservation or the sustainable production of goods and services to meet the region's development needs.

Moreover, 270—over half—are too small to make a meaningful impact on biodiversity without links to other protected areas. Hence the importance of the new approach to regional cooperation in Mesoamerica. This approach actually goes back at least as far as 1989, when Central American presidents signed the Central American Environmental Protection Agreement and established the Central American Commission on Environment and Development (CCAD). Since then, a culture of cooperation has characterized the work of environment ministries in the region. That the region speaks with one voice on environmental matters has been obvious from the development of the Central American Environmental Agenda. This agenda formed the basis for joint regional positions at the 1992 Rio Summit.

CCAD, elevated to an environmental secretariat within the Central American Integration System, a revived regional integration movement, has been instrumental in strengthening the united regional voice at international forums. It has also helped strengthen the countries' environment ministries and has been the prime mover behind a number of regional activities, including the Mesoamerican Biological Corridor initiative.

While directed toward revitalizing the natural corridor from Mexico in the north to Panama in the southeast, the initiative, according to its website, "is by no means focused exclusively on protecting the animals, plants and microorganisms which inhabit the tropical forests, but will provide benefit on a priority basis to the people who live there, to all Mesoamericans and, by extension, to the entire world."

To achieve all these things, the program is being built upon two main pillars. The first and better known is biodiversity conservation. This includes strengthening the existing protected areas and building links among them.

The second pillar is the sustainable use of the resources of the region. Rather than focusing on a policing role by telling people what they cannot do with the forests, for example, the program will educate them on what they can do and how they can do it without causing ecological harm. Environmentally friendly agricultural pursuits—including organic food production—as well as ecotourism, pharmaceutical prospecting, and reforestation have been identified as possible areas of activity and investment.

The region's governments hope that through the revival of the forests, they will contribute their "grain of sand," to borrow the words of Minister Stadthagen, to help reverse the trend of global warming.

In summary, the supporters and managers of the program hope that by their efforts to

continued

continued

re-create the future, they will make it easier to imagine it. The UNDP's Carmelo Angulo sought to capture this vision of the future for the benefit of participants at the launching of the program.

"Personally," said Angulo, "I wish to imagine many of those here present, within six years, when the evaluation of the successes and advances achieved by this great regional program is being carried out. I am completely certain that in that moment the region will have changed for the better, the panorama of human development will be clearer, and new opportunities will have opened so that a lasting and worthwhile life will be accessible to all."

Source: Global Environment Facility, www.gefweb.org.

scientists, contributing to national scientific capacity. Village-based community projects give local leaders the authority to design and implement successful biodiversity and conservation programs, encouraging self-sufficiency. Recognition of the trade-offs in difficult livelihood choices of communities is important to their resolution in culturally and economically acceptable ways. Finally, lessons indicate that bureaucracies are in need of reform to streamline national environmental policymaking.[137] As the GEF continues to evolve institutionally, its objective is to meet the enormous environmental needs of the developing world with financing from the global community in pursuit of the common goal of sustainable economic practices.

But the GEF is not enough. Global institutions must work with national environmental agencies to protect the environment. Care must be taken to respect national sovereignty. Some Brazilians, particularly in the military, find the insistent zeal of international environmentalists a threat to national autonomy.[138] They maintain that Brazilians have as much right as did the settlers of the Wild West to claim natural resources in the service of growth. Long-run change in the service of sustainable development must take local attitudes and political institutions into account or else it will certainly fail over time.

Sustained financing for development is an essential ingredient for sustainable development. The new Millennium Development Goals create additional resources for the implementation of Agenda 21, the comprehensive plan of action of the Rio Declaration on Environment and Development, but more is needed to reach the target of .7 percent of GDP for official development assistance from developed countries. More innovative and efficient mechanisms for financing environmentally sound development strategies are critical to global health. There is a clear need to develop win-win solutions—for communities, nations, and the global system. Institutional deepening to develop an enabling framework for sustainable development is required, built upon consistent and transparent regulatory regimes. A clean environment is an international public good with global benefits; developing countries can only fulfill sustainable development goals with adequate financing, debt relief, technology transfer, and poverty eradication—a tall order but a necessary one.

Key   Concepts

additionality
Agenda 21
beneficiary pays
   for the gain
command and control
   (CAC) measures
contingent valuation
cost-benefit analysis
   (CBA)

cost-effectiveness
direct government
   investments
environmental
   assessments
Global Environment
   Facility (GEF)
institutional capacity
market-based incentives

opportunity costs
polluter pays the cost
safe minimum standard
sustainable development
transaction costs
urbanization
World Summit on
   Sustainable Development

Chapter   Summary

Sustainable Development

- Sustainable development requires the recognition of environmental, economic, social, and political concerns. Problems of measurement, the uncertainty of future technological change, and political will on local, national, and international levels complicate the implementation of sustainable policies.

Environmental Problems in Latin America

- Poverty perpetuates environmental degradation. The poor are both agents and victims of unsafe environments. Urbanization in Latin America exacerbates environmental problems, including insufficient garbage collection, increasing air pollution, and inadequate water supply.
- High energy consumption can be environmentally unsustainable. While energy is scarce and produces negative externalities, it is crucial for economic growth. Pricing energy at market cost, promoting efficiency at the enterprise level, and increasing transparency and regulatory agencies should encourage economic growth while holding down energy consumption and costs.
- The alarming rate of deforestation is caused by conversion of land to agriculture, commercial logging, firewood gathering, and cattle ranching.

Environmental Policy

- The most effective environmental policies are those that combine direct government investment, MBIs, and CAC measures. Environmental policymakers should recognize the differences between rural and urban environmental concerns. Governments should evaluate the cost-effectiveness of alternative environmental policies and make choices accordingly. Furthermore, when formulating sustainable development policies, environmental assessments should be used to analyze the environmental implications of projects before they are implemented. Sustainable development policies can be costly. Cooperation among local, national, and international organizations is needed to attain the goal of sustainable development.

Notes

1. World Commission on Environment and Development, *Our Common Future* (Oxford: Oxford University Press, 1987), 43.

2. Adapted from Mohan Munainghe and Wilfrido Cruz, *Economy Wide Policies and the Environment: Lessons from Experience* (Washington, D.C.: World Bank, 1995).

3. World Commission on Environment and Development, *Our Common Future,* 8.

4. Dennis Pirages, "Sustainability as an Evolving Process," *Futures* 26(2) (1994): 197–205.

5. Salvadoran representative to the PrepCom for the World Summit on Sustainable Development; Wendy Jackson, "ECLAC Final Summary," *Earth Negotiations Bulletin,* published by the International Institute for Sustainable Development (IISD), 22(06) (October 27, 2001), available at www.iisd.ca/linkages/2002/wslac.

6. John M. Antle and Gregg Heidebrink, "Environment and Development: Theory and International Evidence," *Economic Development and Cultural Change* 43(3) (April 1995): 604.

7. Jerry Taylor, "The Challenge of Sustainable Development," *Regulation* 17(1) (1994): 35–50.

8. Michael A. Toman, "Economics and 'Sustainability': Balancing Trade-offs and Imperatives," *Land Economics* 70(4) (November 1994): 399–413.

9. ECLAC, *Globalization and Development,* Report of the 29th Session, Brasilia, Brazil, May 6–10 (Santiago, Chile: ECLAC Distribution Unit, 2002), 260. Available at www.eclac.cl.

10. Robert Goodland and Herman Daly, *Poverty Alleviation Is Essential for Environmental Sustainability,* World Bank, Environment Department, Divisional Working Paper No. 1993-42 (Washington, D.C.: World Bank, 1993).

11. Population Reference Bureau, "World Population Data Sheet 2005," www.prb.org.

12. Scott M. Swinton, Germán Escobar, and Thomas Reardon, "Poverty and Environment in Latin America: Concepts, Evidence and Policy Implications," *World Development* 31(11) (November 2003): 1865.

13. Population Division of the Department of Economic and Social Affairs of the United Nations Secretariat as found at the World Resources Institute website, earthtrends.wri.org.

14. World Resources Institute, *World Resources, 1996–7* (New York: Oxford University Press, 1997), 3.

15. Gustavo Merino-Jaurez, "Cancun, Mexico: Water System Privatization," Kennedy School of Government Case CR14-00-1593.0, August 1, 2000, www.ksgcase.harvard.edu.

16. United Nations Centre for Human Settlements (Habitat), State of the World's Cities, 2001, www.un.org/ga/Instanbul+5/statereport.htm.

17. Data from World Resources Institute, *World Resources 1994–5* (New York: Oxford University Press, 1995).

18. World Resources Institute, *World Resources, 1996–7*, 23.

19. Nicole Hill, "Lives Recycled in Argentina," *Christian Science Monitor,* January 25, 2006, www.csmonitor.com

20. World Resources Institute, *World Resources, 1996–7*, 70.

21. "Latin America Struggles to Find Solutions to Megacity Woes," *Agence France Presse,* June 2, 1992, available online in the LEXIS-NEXIS database.

22. Report of the Preparatory Meeting of the Southern Cone for the World Summit on Sustainable Development, Santiago, Chile, June 14–15, 2001, UN, ECLAC, and UNEP, September 14, 2001.

23. "Toward an Environment Strategy for the World Bank Group," Progress Report/ Discussion Draft, April 2000, available online at lnweb18.worldbank.org/essd/essd.nsf/ GlobalView/Consultationdraft.pdf/$File/Consultationdraft.pdf.

24. John Dixon, *The Urban Environmental Challenge in Latin America,* LATEN Dissemination Note No. 4, World Bank Latin America Technical Department, Environment Division (Washington, D.C.: World Bank, 1993), 8.

25. "Environmental Protection in an Era of Dramatic Economic Growth in Latin America," Hearing before the Subcommittee on Western Hemisphere, Peace Corps, Narcotics, and Terrorism of the Committee on Foreign Relations, United States Senate, 106th Congress, 2nd Session, July 25, 2000 (Washington, D.C.: GPO, 2001), frwebgate.access.gpo.gov.

26. Dixon, *The Urban Environmental Challenge,* 9.

27. Dixon, *The Urban Environmental Challenge,* 19.

28. "Too Much or Too Little Water Can Spell Disaster in the World's Poorest Nations," World Bank, March 17, 2006, http://web.worldbank.org

29. Dixon, *The Urban Environmental Challenge.*

30. "French Lyonnaise des Eaux Agrees to Close Unit in Bolivia," *Latin America News Digest,* March 28, 2006.

31. "Diego Cevallos, "Foreign Corporations Backing Off," *Tierramérica,* March 16, 2006.

32. Ibid.

33. Asif Faiz, Surhid Gautam, and Emaad Burki, "Air Pollution from Motor Vehicles: Issues and Options for Latin American Countries," *The Science of the Total Environment* 169 (1995): 303–310.

34. A. Cifuentes, R. Krupnick, M. Ryan, and P. Toman, "Health Benefits of Reducing Air Pollution in Latin America," Universidad Católica de Chile, *Resources for the Future,* Universidad de Chile, Inter American Development Bank, lac@ing.puc.cl.

35. World Bank, *Energy Efficiency and Conservation in the Developing World: The World Bank's Role* (Washington, D.C.: World Bank, 1993), 66.

36. Thalif Deen, "The Pros and Cons of Rising Oil Prices," *IPS Terraviva* April 21, 2006.

37. Cifuentes, Krupnick, Ryan, and Toman, "Health Benefits of Reducing Air Pollution in Latin America," 2.

38. ECLAC and UNEP, "The Sustainability of Development," 79.

39. Faiz, Gautam, and Burki, "Air Pollution," 303–310.

40. Cifuentes, Krupnick, Ryan, and Toman, "Health Benefits of Reducing Air Pollution in Latin America," 9.

41. ECLAC and UNEP, "The Sustainability of Development," 78.

42. "Mexico City: A Topographical Error," *Environment* 36(2) (1994): 25–26.

43. World Resources Institute, *World Resources, 1996–7*, 47.

44. Inter-American Development Bank, "Natural Disasters," Background papers, March 13, 2006, www.iadb.org

45. PAHO, "Was 2005 the Year of Natural Disasters?" January 9, 2006, www.paho.org.

46. Ginger Thompson, "In Guatemalan Town Buried by Mud, Unyielding Hope for a Little Girl," *New York Times,* October 9, 2005.

47. "Environmental Protection in an Era of Dramatic Economic Growth in Latin America," Hearing before the Subcommittee on Western Hemisphere, Peace Corps, Narcotics, and Terrorism of the Committee on Foreign Relations, United States Senate, 106th Congress, 2nd Session, July 25, 2000 (Washington, D.C.: GPO, 2001), frwebgate.access .gpo.gov.

48. "Challenges and Opportunities for Sustainable Development," *CEPAL News* 21(11) (November 2001): 3. Available at www.eclacwash.org.

49. World Bank, *Energy Efficiency.*

50. ECLAC and UNEP, "The Sustainability of Development in Latin America and the Caribbean: Challenges and Opportunities," 38.

51. Visit Enersol's website at www.enersol.org to learn about some of its projects. Following Hurricane Mitch, for example, Enersol worked to install ultraviolet water disinfection systems to provide clean water.

52. Earthtrends, Environmental Information, www.earthtrends.org.

53. "Industry at a Glance," World Oil Production, www.worldoil.com.

54. Energy Information Administration, World Proven Reserves of Oil and Natural Gas, Most Recent Estimates, Table posted January 18, 2006 http://www.eia.doe.gov/emeu/ international/reserves.xls.

55. Geraldo Samor, "Brazil's Petrobras Self-Reliant or Pliant?" *Wall Street Journal,* April 21, 2006, A7.

56. Ibid.

57. Ken Johnson, "Brazil and the Politics of Climate Change Negotiations," *Journal of Environment & Development* 10(2) (June 2001): 185.

58. World Bank, www.devdata.worldbank.org.

59. Judith Kimmerling, cited by Suzana Sawyer, "Indigenous Initiatives and Petroleum Politics in the Ecuadorian Amazon," *Cultural Survival* (Spring 1996): 27.

60. Larry Rohter, "With a Big Boost from Sugar Cane, Brazil Is Satisfying Its Fuel Needs," *New York Times,* April 10, 2006.

61. Stephen H. Schneider, Armin Rosencranz, John O. Niles, eds., *Climate Change Policy: A Survey* (Washington, D.C.: Island Press, 2002), 425.

62. Marcela Valente, "Argentina: The Environmental Costs of Biofuel," *IPS Terraviva,* April 21, 2006, www.ipsteriaviva.net.

63. Ibid.

64. Benedict Mander, "Darker Side to Argentina's Soya Success," *Financial Times,* June 7, 2006, www.ft.com.

65. John Vandermeer and Ivette Perfecto, *Breakfast of Biodiversity: The Truth about Rain Forest Destruction* (Oakland, Calif.: Institute for Food and Development Policy, 1995), 19.

66. Commission on Development and Environment for Amazonia, *Amazonia without Myths* (Washington, D.C.: IADB, 1992), xii.

67. Vandermeer and Perfecto, *Breakfast,* 3.

68. The countries and the percentage held of the Amazon are as follows: Bolivia (11.20 percent), Brazil (67.79 percent), Colombia (5.52 percent), Ecuador (1.67 percent), Guyana (0.08 percent), Peru (13.02 percent), and Venezuela (0.72 percent). Suriname and the territory of French Guiana are considered to be part of the "greater Amazon," not countries of the hydrographic watershed (Commission on Development and Environment for Amazonia, *Amazonia without Myths*).

69. Goulding, in Bradley Bennett, "Plants and People of the Amazonian Rainforests: The Role of Ethnobotany in Sustainable Development," *BioScience* 42(8) (1992): 599.

70. Commission on Development and Environment for Amazonia, *Amazonia without Myths,* 6.

71. Ibid., 37.

72. Jennifer Alix-Garcia, Alain de Janvry, and Elisabeth Sadoulet, "A Tale of Two Communities: Explaining Deforestation in Mexico," *World Development* 33(2) (February 2005): 219–235.

73. CIAT 1998 in the Global Environmental Outlook 2000, Latin American and the Caribbean, www.grida.no/geo2000.

74. FAO, "Deforestation Rate 'Alarming,' but Net Loss Slowing," *Agence France-Presse,* November 14, 2005, Reprinted at the World Business Council for Sustainable Development, www.wbcsd.org.

75. Indira A. R. Lakshmanan, "Amazon Highway Is Route to Strife in Brazil," *Boston Globe,* December 27, 2005; Lisa Naughton-Treves, "Deforestation and Carbon Emissions at Tropical Frontiers: A Case Study from the Peruvian Amazon," *World Development* 32(1) (January 2004): 18, 173.

76. Gautam Naik, "Studies of the Amazon Rainforest Intensify Climate Change Debate," *Wall Street Journal,* Oct 20, 2005.

77. World Press Review, "Brazil's Amazon Rainforest Twice as Deforested as Estimated." October 21, 2005, newsbureau@worldbank.org; "Selective Logging Doubles Amazon Forest Loss," *SciDev.Net,* October 21, 2005.

78. Erwin Northoff, "Cattle Ranching Is Encroaching on Forests in Latin America Causing Severe Environmental Degradation—FAO Model Predicts Land Use up to 2010," June 8, 2005. www.fao.org.

79. "Amazon Suffers the Worst Drought in 50 Years," *Latinnews Daily,* October 19, 2005.

80. Jen Ross, "Brazil's Disappearing Jungle," *Toronto Star,* August 6, 2005.

81. Commission on Development and Environment for Amazonia, *Amazonia without Myths.*

82. Stephen A. Vosti, Evaldo Muñoz Braz, Chantal Line Carpentier, Marcus V. N. d'Oliveira, and Julie Witcover, "Rights to Forest Products, Deforestation and Smallholder Income: Evidence from the Western Brazilian Amazon," *World Development* 31(11) (November 2003): 1889.

83. Braga, "Tropical Forests," 178.

84. Lakshmanan, "Amazon Highway Is Route to Strife in Brazil."

85. Philip M. Fearnside, "Conservation Policy in Brazilian Amazonia: Understanding the Dilemmas," *World Development* 31(5) (May 2003): 757.

86. Haider Rizvi, "Biodiversity: Brazil's Lula Lashes Out at Rich Nations," *IPS Terraviva,* March 28, 2006.

87. Larry Rohter, "Loggers, Scorning the Law, Ravage the Amazon," *New York Times,* October 16, 2005.

88. Ibid.

89. Larry Rohter and Elizabeth Johnson, "Brazil Deforestation: Pioneer Loggers Suffer a Setback," *FT News Alerts,* October 7, 2005, www.ft.com.

90. World Resources Institute, *World Resources, 1996–7,* 250.

91. ECLAC, *Statistical Yearbook for Latin America and the Caribbean 2001,* table 357, p. 684, accessed at www.eclac.org.

92. Daniel Estey, Marc Levy, Tanja Srebotnjak, and Alexander de Sherbinin, "2006 Environmental Sustainability Index," Yale Center for Environmental Law and Policy, www.yale.edu.

93. Hernán Cortés-Salas, Ronnie de Camino, and Arnoldo Contreras, *Readings of the Workshop on Government Policy Reform for Forestry Conservation and Development in Latin America,* June 1–3, 1994 (Washington, D.C.: Inter-American Institute for Cooperation on Agriculture, 1995).

94. Maria Nieves Rico, "Gender, the Environment and the Sustainability of Development," Women and Development Unit, ECLAC discussion paper, Serie mujer y Desarrollo No. 25, October 1998.

95. Goodland and Daly, *Poverty Alleviation,* 28.

96. Updated Project Information Document, Report No. AB415, MEXICO—Community Forestry II (PROCYMAF II) Region, November 18, 2003, www.bancomundial .org.

97. Ibid.

98. Simon Zbinden and David Lee, "Paying for Environmental Services: An Analysis of Participation in Costa Rica's PSA Program," *World Development* 33(2) (February 2005): 255–272.

99. Ken Johnson, "Brazil and the Politics of Climate Change Negotiations," *Journal of Environment & Development* 10(2) (June 2001): 178–206.

100. United Nations Framework Convention on Climate Change, www.unfccc.org.

101. Patricia Rojas, "IDB Welcomes Creation of Brazilian Carbon Market," April 2, 2006, www.iadb.org.

102. Stefano Pagiola, Augustin Arcenas, and Gunars Platais, "Can Payments for Environmental Services Help Reduce Poverty? An Exploration of the Issues and the Evidence to Date from Latin America," *World Development* 33(2) (February 2005): 237–253.

103. Bob Davis, "Guatemala Logs Progress." *Wall Street Journal,* November 25, 2005, A9.

104. Oliver Balch, "Growth in Ecotourism—Take the Green Road," January 4, 2006, www.ethicalcorp.com.

105. Maryanne Grieg-Gran, Ina Porras, and Sven Wunder, "How Can Market Mechanisms for Forest Environmental Services Help the Poor? Preliminary Lessons from Latin America," *World Development* 33(9) (September 2005): 1511–1527.

106. Roger Hamilton, "Tourism's Green Frontier: How to Protect Nature and Make a Profit," *IDB America,* January 2002, www. iadb.org.

107. Grieg-Gran, Porras, and Wunder, "How Can Market Mechanisms for Forest Environmental Services Help the Poor?"

108. Ibid.

109. Pagiola, Arcenas, and Platais, "Can Payments for Environmental Services Help Reduce Poverty?"

110. "El Salvador Environmental Services Project," Project Appraisal Document, Vol. 1, April 22, 2005, www.wds.worldbank.org.

111. Excerpted from Scherr, White, and Kaimowitz, "Making Markets Work for Forest Communities," Original source PROCYMAF (2000), Proyecto de conservación y manejo sostenible de recursos forestales en México, Informe y avance 1998–2000, Misión de evaluación de medio terino, SEMARNAP, Mexico; B. DeWalt, F. Olivera, and J. Betancourt Correa, *Mid-term Evaluation of the Mexico Community Forestry Projects* (Washington, D.C.: World Bank, 2000).

112. Excerpted from Scherr, White, and Kaimowitz, "Making Markets Work for Forest Communities," Original source Moles, P, A2R, personal communication, 2000.

113. Swinton, Escobar, and Reardon, "Poverty and Environment in Latin America," 1865.

114. Oxford Analytica, "Sustainable Forestry," *Latin America Daily Brief,* March 23, 2006.

115. Ross, "Brazil's Disappearing Jungle."

116. Swinton, Escobar, and Reardon, "Poverty and Environment in Latin America," 1865.

117. Anja Nygren, "Community-Based Forest Management within the Context of Institutional Decentralization in Honduras," *World Development* 33(4) (April 2005): 639–655.

118. Susanna B. Hecht, Susan Kandel, Ileana Gomes, Nelson Cuellar, and Herman Rosa, "Globalization, Forest Resurgence, and Environmental Politics in El Salvador," *World Development* 34(2) (February 2006).

119. World Bank, *Environment and Development in Latin America and the Caribbean: The Role of the World Bank* (Washington, D.C.: World Bank), 21.

120. Faiz, Gantam, and Burki, "Air Pollution," 303–310.

121. World Bank, *Environment and Development.*

122. Anna Luíza Ozório de Almeida and João S. Campari, *Sustainable Settlement in the Brazilian Amazon* (Oxford: Oxford University Press, 1995), 75–80.

123. "Armed Forces Oppose Tompkins Sanctuary," *Santiago Times,* June 20, 2001; "Natural Preserve," *Geographical Magazine* 73(4) (April 2001): 65; "Tompkins Gets Green Light Pumalin Park to Become Natural Sanctuary," *Santiago Times,* July 3, 2001; "Tompkins Angers Local Politicians Opponents Respond to Allegations," *Santiago Times,* June 28, 2001; and Camus, Pablo, and Ernst R. Hajek, "Douglas Tompkins: El empresario/ecologista y su polemico proyecto de instaler en Chile el 'parque ecologico privado mas grande del mundo,'" Ecology and Environment in Chile, 1998, available online at www.hajek.cl/ecolyma/doc03k.htm.

124. Dominic Hamilton, "Doug Tompkins' Pumalin Park," March 1999, Planeta.com.

125. Larry Rohter, "An American in Chile Finds Conservation a Hard Slog," *New York Times,* August 7, 2005.

126. "Saving the Ends of the Earth," *Economist* 378(8468) (March 11, 2006): 74.

127. World Bank, *Environment and Development.*

128. The argument for this paragraph is distilled from Clifford S. Russell and Philip T. Powell, *Choosing Environmental Policy Tools: Theoretical Cautions and Practical Considerations,* No. ENV-102 (Washington, D.C.: Inter-American Development Bank, June 1996).

129. Ibid.

130. "Spain's Repsol YPF Buys Emission Rights from Shell," *Financial Times,* April 13, 2006.

131. ECLAC, "Globalization and Environmental Sustainability," in *Globalization and Development,* 29th Session Report, Brasilia, May 6–10, 2002, 281.

132. ECLAC/UNDP, *Financing for Sustainable Development in Latin America and the Caribbean,* Joint document prepared for the World Summit on Sustainable Development, August 2002.

133. ECLAC, "Globalization and Environmental Sustainability," 281.

134. World Bank, *Environment and Development.*

135. More on the GEF is available at www.gefweb.com.

136. Mohamed T. El-Ashry, *Statement to the Fourth Session of the Conference of the Parties to the United National Framework Convention on Climate Change,* Buenos Aires, November 11, 1998 (Washington, D.C.: Global Environment Facility, 1998). El-Ashry is CEO and chair of the Global Environment Facility.

137. "Participation Means Learning through Doing: GEF's Experience in Biodiversity Conservation and Sustainable Use," GEF Lessons Notes 12, July 2001, 1–4. Available at ww.gefweb.org.

138. Margaret E. Keck, "Dilemmas for Conservation in the Brazilian Amazon," Environmental Change and Security Project Report, Woodrow Wilson International Center for Scholars, Issue 7:33.

CHAPTER FIFTEEN

LESSONS LEARNED

Cycles in Latin American Development

The devastation of Hurricane Mitch underscored the fragility of life, especially for the poor. *(Courtesy of David Mangurian and the Inter-American Development Bank)*

Nearing his seventy-second birthday, Colombian Nobel laureate Gabriel García Marquez bought a newspaper company, *El Cambio*. He jokingly noted that after his 1982 Nobel Prize, no one would employ him as a journalist because he was too expensive. His reentry into journalism has promoted a greater spirit of open press in his native country, a critical component of accountable government policy. Unfortunately, the magical realism of his novels finds stark parallels in contemporary life in Latin America, giving him much to write about. As he said in a *New York Times* interview describing his political activism as a writer, his engagement in critical issues is driven by the fact that "underdevelopment is total, integral, it affects every part of our lives."[1] Life has imitated art in Latin America.

Many of the political obstacles to underdevelopment that concerned Marquez at the time of his award have changed. Most importantly, the region has gone from one dominated by repressive military regimes to one of open democracy. The economic model was radically altered from state-centered import substitution industrialization (ISI) to a market-driven approach, and a new hybrid model is now evolving. But political and economic openness have not yet transformed the devastating landscape of underdevelopment in the region. The cycle of poverty and oppression in Marquez's literature and his contemporary world remain a sad reminder of unresolved developmental challenges. Social protest and strikes mark the degree of dissatisfaction that many Latin Americans feel regarding the lack of improvement in their material lives. Sixty percent of Latin Americans think that the economy is in trouble, and 70 percent see no hope for improvement in the near future. Seventy-five percent perceive themselves as poorer today than five years ago, and 86 percent believe that income distribution is unjust. Two out of three are dissatisfied with the results of democracy.[2] Such dismal views complicate the generation of confidence in the future of the region. At the turn of the century, social protest and strikes across Latin America registered the level of dissatisfaction with the neoliberal development model. Regional output contracted in the first half of 2002 by 2.5 percent, and financial conditions were extremely fragile. In 2004 and 2005, regional gross domestic product per capita grew by 4.3 percent and 2.8 percent, but the engines of growth vary throughout the region. Many countries remain precariously dependent on the global commodity boom—rising, as in prior historical periods, with the explosion of growth in China or riding the tide of rising energy prices. Some remain dependent on the United States and on their ability to serve as low-cost producers in an era of competing with even lower Asian wages.

As an example of the cycles of poverty, consider the challenges facing Honduras and Argentina as they moved into the twenty-first century. Honduras, along with its Central American neighbors, was ravaged by Hurricane Mitch late in 1998. Decades of development were turned back by this powerful storm. Schools and hospitals were decimated, and the loss of life was staggering. Swelling rivers washed away homes, farms, and factories. Honduras lost export crops such as bananas, coffee, shrimp, and melons; its small farms have no arable soil left to grow sources of domestic sustenance, including rice and corn.

Honduras was terribly unlucky to be in the path of Mitch, but its own development path had made it more vulnerable to the destruction of the storm. Its fragile ecosystem, weakened from overfarming, overlogging, and overpopulation, left little resistance to wind and water. As noted by Edwin Mateo Molina, a Honduran sociologist specializing in environmental issues for the Inter-American Development Bank (IADB), "Everyone realizes that the damage was magnified by the misuse of resources. It will happen again, and will be even worse unless we look for a way to use the land in a more responsible manner."[3]

In Argentina the damage came from political and economic forces as opposed to those from nature. Argentina went from the darling of international capital markets to a financial pariah. Successive economic shocks from the Asian, Russian, and Brazilian crises of 1998–1999 combined with the devaluation of the Brazilian real took their toll on a banking structure riddled with debt. A fall in the terms of trade of Argentina's exports further pressured external adjustment. Unsustainable domestic public sector finances—particularly pension commitments by the powerful provinces—compounded the crisis. Argentine credibility evaporated, and capital markets closed as political risk escalated. Last-ditch efforts to cut public sector wages and reduce government expenditures were insufficient to generate confidence in the Argentine economy. In November 2001 the government announced a restructuring of debt, but this was not enough to forestall default on $140 billion of bonds to private investors. Argentina was forced to break its 1991 convertibility law linking the peso to the dollar after high unemployment and negative growth sent protestors to the streets. Argentina faced enormous political and economic challenges in reconstructing what had once been among the most prosperous economies in the world.[4] Its output contracted at twice the level of the Great Depression; investment fell sharply, and unemployment reached a staggering 25 percent. Argentina suffered an economic contraction unprecedented in its economic history.[5] Although by mid-decade healthy rates of growth resumed, the price of volatility is extraordinary. The government of Nestor Kirschner has reverted to using price controls as a way to allocate scarce commodities such as beef in an economy pumped up by agricultural exports to China.

The news is not all bad. After a decade of economic reform, Latin America is more squarely following a sustainable development path. Decentralization has placed more power in the hands of local governments. Women and indigenous groups have achieved greater recognition in the design of development strategies, although many tangible gains will accrue only over time. Environmental projects have sprung up throughout the region to support sustainable practices. Macroeconomies are better balanced, and the region is integrating through bilateral and regional accords. Cycles have persisted, but Latin America may have reversed some of the practices promoting downward cycles and replaced them with new directions in its unfolding development story. A new pragmatism is emerging in the region, an approach to political economy that respects fiscal constraints and embraces global markets but recognizes the need for investments in health, education, and infrastructure to promote a more equitable, sustainable growth pattern. Pursuit of such a "policy of the possible" is differentiating economies in the region.[6] Governments elected on the recognition of the need for social investments such as those of Luiz Inácio "Lula" da Silva in Brazil and Michelle Bachelet in Chile are balancing these demands with the realities and rigors of fiscal restraint. In contrast, other governments, including those of Evo Morales in Bolivia and Hugo Chavez in Venezuela are responding to the popular demand for rapid change in the social sector—a reasonable response to historical marginalization but fraught with difficulties of sustainability once resource-based revenues peter out.

CHALLENGES FOR DEVELOPMENT POLICY IN LATIN AMERICA REVISITED

In thinking about the progress and the prospects of development in Latin America, we will find it useful to recall the five critical issues for development policy in Latin America introduced in chapter 1:

- How can a balance be achieved between internal and external constraints on development?
- How can change be promoted even as stability is encouraged?
- Whose interests should economic policy serve—the needs of the poor or the investment requirements of the industrialists?
- What role should the state play in promoting a development agenda? What are the appropriate roles for the market?
- How should the needs of people today be addressed while leaving future generations as well-off?

We noted that it is important to understand how economies have resolved these issues to avoid negative historical cycles. What have we learned from our study of Latin American economic development with respect to how these issues have been dealt with across the different periods of development? What lessons can we bring to bear on understanding whether the future of economic development in the region will reflect the cycles of the past?

THE ECONOMIC LABORATORY OF LATIN AMERICA

Latin America has been a virtual economic laboratory to analyze imbalances across the domestic and international sectors. Our study of ISI showed that an internal focus was implemented because of the dissatisfaction with the primary product export model in the late 1880s and early 1900s. Despite comparable starts, it appeared that the region was falling behind relative to Europe and North America. The surprising progress of Latin America as it was isolated during World War II from the international economy led analysts to believe that international capitalism was a cause of the underdevelopment of the region. According to the dependency theorists, powerful industrial countries were draining Latin America of its wealth. Alliances between elites in the center and the periphery perpetuated a model that privileged a few but immiserized the masses. Patterns of asset distribution in large *latifundia* or estate production determined by colonial decree were reproduced in industrial circles. Internal dynamism was lacking, with weak linkages between the export-oriented agricultural sector and the fragile and thin industrial sector. Technological prowess was building in the North, to the exclusion of the South. The perception was that the international economy was strangling dynamic domestic development.

To move beyond dependent development, ISI constructed the state as the defined agent of change. Employing planning tools and the aggressive arm of state-led firms, governments opened new sectors to industrial activity. A focus on linkages and breaking down bottlenecks of production led the state to target key sectors. High tariffs kept multinational firms at bay, unless special technological licensing agreements or local production were negotiated to provide critical inputs of production. Monetary policy was essentially passive, with central banking authorities accommodating the expansionist thrust of the model. An initial euphoria surrounded the ability to promote development in the region. The ambitious plan to build Brasilia, moving it inland as a heartland capital to integrate diverse regions, was a symbol of the unbounded power of state energy. New light and heavy manufacturing sectors developed to meet the needs of domestic consumers. The labor movement strengthened as unions promoted workers' rights. Public utilities were expanded, providing electricity and telephone services throughout the region. Ambitious projects such as the trans-Amazonian highway and the Itaipu Dam were begun with financing from capital markets bullish on Latin America. Latin American nations were transforming their economic landscape.

Unraveling ISI

But signs of disequilibrium began to surface. Balance of payments accounts were pressured by the need to import costly intermediate machinery for final goods production. As import bills surged, the exchange rate bias worked against exports. The state's attempt to do too much too fast resulted in an inflationary tendency in the economy. Rapid change meant frequent supply shortages, and state-led megaprojects required high levels of public finance. Powerful firms and powerful unions passed cost increases around. It was not a total coincidence that as the economies began to twist and crack, militaries around the region were called by industrial elites to govern and maintain order and progress. Stability was threatened by an uneven and unbalanced development process.

Given highly unequal income distributions and a model that had promoted a new urban privileged class, it was risky to begin tinkering too much with the internal and external balance. Rapid structural change made the management of economic outcomes unpredictable. Populist policies to buy off labor and business without strong regard for external constraints dominated the region. Corruption was encouraged by the ability of agents within the state to control economic property rights. Many abused privileges for personal gain in protected state jobs. Quotas on foreign exchange or technology import licenses led to under-the-table payments to grease the economic wheels. Sadly but predictably, the poor were largely neglected, the rural sector was nearly abandoned, and the environment was devastated.

International price shocks dislodged the inward-looking system of ISI. Global interest rate hikes to restrain worldwide inflation triggered a massive debt crisis across the region. Countries faced default in adjusting to high real interest rates after the artificial luxury of low to negative rates over several years. External constraints became overwhelming when the price of international capital rose. Consumption or investment imports could no longer be cheaply financed. Countries could no longer support living beyond their means. A radical reorientation of the development model was required.

NEOLIBERAL REFORMS

ISI was replaced by variants of the neoliberal model throughout the region. The state itself was delegitimized as the economic guardian. Instead, markets became the primary allocators of resources. State spending was slashed to maintain fiscal balance, and state firms were privatized to promote profit and efficiency as the way to provide goods and services in the market. Privatization created enormous profit potential, which enticed international capital back to the region. Tariff walls came tumbling down, exposing firms to competition in the international market. Openness to international competition rooted out inefficiencies in production, and formerly protected firms scrambled to find new market niches. Nontraditional exports penetrated new markets. Agriculture and agroindustries got a boost from international demand. Cheaper imports from the global market provided consumers with new choices of goods at lower prices. Multinational firms established local production to meet the needs of consumers with real purchasing power for the first time in years. As countries looked outward and a democratic revolution swept the hemisphere, subregional integration efforts gained momentum. The external sector was again seen as the engine of development.

Latin American nations once again became darlings of international capital. With inflation in retreat throughout the region and democratic governments installed in all nations except Cuba, stability encouraged investor confidence. Money flowed back to the region, this time through bond and stock markets rather than commercial bank lending. Foreign direct investment blossomed because multinationals were enthusiastic about long-term development prospects. Not every country, however, benefited equally. Larger countries attracted the bulk of capital, while smaller and poorer economies struggled. Nonetheless, the experiences of countries such as Costa Rica demonstrate that small countries that have invested in technology and workforce development can indeed succeed.

THE COMPELLING SOCIAL AND
ENVIRONMENTAL AGENDA

Opening to the external economy also exposed weaknesses in the domestic political economy. Global attention to environmental and social issues promoted by new actors on the global stage, the nongovernmental organizations (NGOs), directed some attention to issues of sustainable development and labor standards. Protests on the negative social and environmental effects of International Monetary Fund (IMF) and World Bank types of conditionality packages led to a rethinking of the sustainability of short-term stabilization measures. Short-term export targets for the release of funds resulted in further deforestation; sweatshops started to spring up throughout the region as multinationals took advantage of cheaper, often female labor. In response to international outcries, new units were set up in multilateral organizations to safeguard environmental concerns and promote the interests of the least advantaged in society. Greater attention was paid to issues of gender and ethnicity in development. Recognition of the economic and social contributions of women and indigenous peoples began to inform decision making. But institutional change is slow and incomplete, and the intermediate environmental and social costs have been high.

There was an extraordinary degree of financial dislocation in the process of rapid transformation from closed to open economies. Some governments have been better able to manage this process than others. Mistakes such as the Mexican management of the 1994 peso overvaluation were made, with devastating financial costs. Brazil weathered its 1998–1999 crisis after a bungled devaluation, fiscal imprudence, and political infighting that shook market confidence. The Argentine economy has collapsed under the weight of external debt that was unmatched by increases in international competitiveness. Changing policies and outcomes have challenged the ability of governments to maintain credibility with their citizens and with international investors. Citizens have placed Left-leaning politicians in Brazil, Argentina, Uruguay, Chile, Bolivia, and Venezuela to address the perceived social deficits—although the implementation of social policy in each country is strikingly different. Social protest has gripped Ecuador, Argentina, and Guatemala. Pleasing one segment of society has sometimes come at a cost to another. Labor-market reform hasn't moved quickly for fear of upsetting domestic labor coalitions. Privatization may have taken place too rapidly, allowing some firms to be sold for less than market value. Appropriate regulatory measures were not always in place to protect consumer and environmental interests in the face of newly privatized monopolies. Finance ministers have had to manage not only money supplies but also extensive public relations efforts with the major brokerage houses around the world. Increasing transparency and credibility in policy making has been critical to maintaining confidence in Latin American markets.

ADDRESSING THE SOCIAL DEFICIT

At the same time that the economies have grappled with both the costs and the benefits of globalization, the Latin American state has had to figure out how to do more with less. The accumulated social and environmental deficits are huge impediments to sustained future growth. Radical structural change shook up the system, energizing productive potential. Realizing this potential in the long run, however, is a function of enhancing investments in human capital. Health and education systems must be revamped. Latin America must contend with its epidemiological backlog, eradicating traditional diseases linked to poor living conditions and inadequate nutrition as well as making headway against the ills of modern society such as violence, AIDS, and heart disease. Quality improvements in the supply of educational services, including better teacher training, appropriate texts, and computer-based learning, are critical to compete in the global economy. Environmental decision making must be systematically incorporated at the local level because people themselves demand it. The complex host of environmental problems born of insufficient infrastructure and unmanaged economic expansion must be reconciled with communities' needs today and for the future.

Yet with the exception of governments riding resource booms, states are not able to spend their way out of these challenges; the money just isn't there. Instead, with diligent attention to the fiscal bottom line, states are attempting to create incentives for the market to pull some weight in the social arena. Public-private partnerships to improve delivery of health and educational services are being employed to reinvigorate moribund systems. Decentralization of social services allows for more local ownership of projects. Local governments are partnering with businesses in communities that have a vested interest in the development of better-educated, healthier workforces and cleaner work environments. Nonetheless, the market is not a substitute for good policy or hard choices, particularly in the areas of public goods provision. It can complement good governance, but it cannot replace it.

The Balancing Act of the State

In balancing between global demands and local needs, the tricky policy issue is deciding just how much government is enough. We have devoted a great deal of attention in this text to discussing the positions of neoliberals, new institutionalists, and neostructuralists. The latter two groups might argue that the pendulum may have swung too far toward the market in light of the weakness of market institutions in guaranteeing property rights, overseeing competition policy, and promoting social welfare. Although public-private partnerships are useful to attend to unmet needs, the invisible hand of the market may not work its magic when economic agents are unable to make rational, self-interested decisions because they simply don't have the minimal level of social assets to invest in themselves. States must be vigilant in their attempts to promote incentives for the formation of a domestic economy oriented not necessarily toward short-term consumption but rather to long-term investments in social and environmental systems. Incentives must be structured to change time horizons to preserve choices in the future. Nonetheless, democracy makes this process problematic, as the electoral cycle is poorly matched to the long-term investments required by genuine, balanced development.[7]

In addition to political contraints, the economic feasibility of long-term decision making may be legitimately questioned. Orientation to the international arena drives countries to focus on short-term macroeconomic performance variables: prices, exchange rates, and fiscal and current account balances. The room to maneuver is extremely limited. Once international investors get a sniff of disequilibrium or social discontent, they quickly shift to another, more stable investment. One of the downsides of the broadening of the stock market to include a large number of smaller players is that the day trader or the middle American investors' circle is unlikely to have a profound understanding of the complexity and the diversity of

Latin American economies. An increase in the current account can mean many things, some of which threaten stable growth (such as luxury consumption) and others that may promote change (business investment). Sorting out the causes of imbalances and placing them in a historical context requires information unavailable to many small investors.

Development is not a process of harmonious equilibrium. Much like people, economies may grow in fits and starts, taking new and unintended directions. Yet the costs today of short-term disequilibrium are loss of investor confidence and instantaneous capital flight. We may have arrived at a kind of MTV international economy with an attention span that is limited to sixty-second sound bites. Economic policymakers have to learn tools of international marketing to sell information about the national product in the global marketplace. The message must be clear and consistent. But the message in Latin America won't be a pleasant one unless the problems of inequality and poverty are resolved. Unfortunately, short-term policy making doesn't encourage the necessary social investments to reverse the plight of the poor, reduce inequality, and promote sustainable development. Latin America is precariously poised with one foot in the fast-moving international arena and the other stuck in a complicated web of unequal social relations that act as a drag on productivity and change. Economic policymaking in the region is a delicate art of selling pragmatic, often muted responses to intense need. Particularly given the historical track record of elitism, few politicians are up to the task of convincing electorates that incremental change will, over time, make the less advantaged better off. Nonetheless, big social programs are only viable in booming resource economies—and only for as long as it is favored by commodity lottery.

MULTILATERAL SUPPORT

As the world has become more tightly integrated and the ability to make economic mistakes has become more circumscribed, there may be a stronger role warranted for multilateral institutions. In the wake of the Asian, Russian, and Brazilian currency crises, there have been calls for a revisioning of the IMF to become more than an institution of last resort. Multilateral development banks such as the World Bank and the IADB can also play important roles in promoting systematic attention to investments in the social and environmental agendas. The Global Environment Facility is an innovative financial mechanism to transfer funds from North to South and share responsibility for global sustainability. NGOs are key not only in raising awareness of issues but also as local conduits between bilateral or multilateral organizations and the local community.

As a consumer of goods produced in the international economy, you too have a role in articulating your social preferences. Public attention is directed not only to governments; the international media and the Internet provide important devices to articulate demands for socially and environmentally sound production. In the least, it is hoped that by reading this book you have become more aware of the problems facing people in other parts of the world, better able to interpret and contextualize the enormous challenges of development, and better prepared, should you so choose, to participate in this arena as a more informed manager, policymaker, activist, or consumer in the international economy.

REVISITING OUR FIVE ISSUES

We can perhaps conclude that because development is a continuous but not smooth process, the five factors we have considered will be found in constant tension. As firms expand when markets are incomplete, they are likely to require imported components. Consumers, facing strong employment prospects in expanding markets, euphorically accelerate purchases with a consumption boom. With relatively weak domestic macroeconomic tools to fine-tune the economy, external disequilibrium mounts, pressuring the exchange rate. Capital flees, creating an external crisis that is resolved by painful domestic austerity.

Economic change can be disruptive, challenging stability. It can also threaten ruling elites if formulated to attend to the marginalized masses. Ironically, if policy does not include those most needy of government attention to raise living, health, and education standards to a level consistent with human dignity and self-empowerment, the development prospects will confront a human capital deficit that is unsustainable in the modern global economy. Rising inequality exacerbates social tension as the marginalized make claims on the state for redress. State intervention in promoting human development is circumscribed by the domestic constraints of financing as well as by the role of the state as an institutional actor. Recent changes in Latin America have shifted this debate to question the appropriate role of state participation at various levels of governance. Centrally funded and monitored local action plans can reduce inefficiency and benefit from local entrepreneurial partnerships. As decentralization plays out, however, it would not be surprising to see a swing back in the activity of the state in certain arenas. As priorities in environmental management shift from locally based sewage and sanitation to industrial pollutants that are not bounded by municipalities, the locus of action might shift as well. Changing development problems require dynamic solutions.

STAGES OF ADJUSTMENT

The resolution of the key issues of internal and external balance, development for whom, confidence and stability in the face of change, the role of the state, and future sustainability has varied with the different stages that countries have passed through in their economic adjustment processes. Development, as we defined it in chapter 1, is a process of meeting the basic human needs of the population while enhancing options for how economic resources will be allocated today and in the future to increase the choices that citizens have in their daily lives. As we have investigated issues of stabilization, adjustment, and growth, we can identify three contemporary stages that countries have passed through on this development journey. The first stage, immediately following the debt crisis, was characterized by often **severe stabilization** measures designed to bring macrofundamentals into line. Macroeconomic stabilization efforts were shaped by the financial constraints of the debt crisis as well as the historical legacy of asset distribution and policy making that constrained policy options. Restraining internal spending to achieve external balance became the dominant concern. Without external finance, countries no longer had the option of pursuing expansionary, inward-looking development strategies. Yet the earlier experience with export orientation left lingering doubts as to the social and environmental effects of active participation in the global economy.

But these questions were of necessity tabled. At the time of the crisis, macroeconomic considerations were primary. In the second phase, **structural transformation** was initiated. The shape of the economy changed with respect to the relative balance of internal and external orientation as well as the roles of the state and the market. Trade reforms, financial liberalization, integration, and privatization have changed the economic rules of the game in the region. The international market has been placed at the center of the development process. International capital flows, both short-term portfolio as well as long-term foreign direct investment, have become important arbiters of international growth. Liberalization of trade and the accompanying process of economic integration have become the drivers of change. With the exception of resource-based economies such as Venezuela, state ownership in the economy has been severely curtailed, with local and multinational firms providing not only traditionally traded products but also many of the services, such as transportation and power, that had been the purview of public utilities. The goal of international competitiveness has prompted countries to think differently

Capacity building at the local level can promote more equitable and efficient use of resources. *(Courtesy of the Inter-American Development Bank)*

about labor relations, the generation of technology, and the provision of infrastructure. The agricultural sector has been infused with market-based policies, including the use of profit incentives for the provision of extension services and water. The structure of economies across the region has been radically altered over the past decade.

Having readjusted the orientation of the economy and the roles of key actors, the challenge of stage three is a long-term process of **capacity building** of human capital, improving productivity, and promoting sound use of natural resources, including land.[8] In short, stage three seeks to enlarge the options each society faces in allocating scarce resources as well as to promote economically and environmentally sustainable development. These are no easy tasks. These reforms profoundly shape the ways people interact within institutions. **Institutions** are the rules that shape the behavior of organizations and individuals. **Formal rules,** such as constitutions, laws, and regulations, or **informal rules,** such as values and norms, condition and are conditioned by the process of economic change.[9] Old or brittle institutions may collapse under the weight of new economic challenges. The private sector has demanded changes in the quality and efficiency of financial and public services and judicial reform as it now perceives competitiveness to hinge on strong social, financial, and legal institutions. Institutional reform may also promote changes in the way economic agents behave. Increased **transparency** in judicial systems, for example, will encourage accountability in business dealings and foster international confidence in economic transactions. Institutional reform poses significant political and technical challenges. Losers in the political systems must somehow be convinced that the long-run gains are worth the cost. It is clear that new models of institutional reform are difficult to implement in economies struggling with a range of unresolved social and economic issues. It is easier to address efficiency-enhancing mechanisms than strengthen the tools to redistribute assets and decrease inequality. Particularly among the poorest economies of the regions, multilateral assistance is critical. The ability to reach the new millennium goals, established by the 2000 UN Millennium Summit, of reducing world poverty by half by 2015 rests on the ability to provide the technical assistance to countries to overcome the institutional obstacles to sustainable development.[10]

As governments move away from crisis management and radical economic restructuring toward the hard, slow process of deepening market institutions and their political environment, they must simultaneously balance issues of credibility and fairness in reform. Given the globalization of international capital, markets must be assured that macrofundamentals remain in place. Confidence is the name of the game.

At the same time, economic actors are beginning to sort out the welfare implications of the radical structural changes of economies. When economies were in crisis, people were willing to make sacrifices. There seemed to be little choice but to reform. As tariff walls came down, international capital found new opportunities, and private capital began to provide the water, telecommunications, and productive services of the region. There have been winners and losers. As growth has accelerated in some sectors, others have felt left behind. As different sectors of society have the opportunity to understand the effects of reform, new claims will likely be

Unfulfilled promises of economic growth and political reform have led to social protest—such as this strike blocking roads in Guatemala—as people desperately search for just recourse. *(Photograph by Patrice Franko)*

made on the political and economic systems of the region. Inequality has remained stubbornly high. In many countries these systems are newly democratized, with evolving practices.

Changes in the economy necessarily call into question the perceived fairness of the results for citizens of the region. Balancing competing demands in newly consolidating democracies is a tricky act. Several questions define policy approaches to emerging concerns:

- As Latin America continues to move forward in the consolidation of economic and political reform, what are likely to be the pressure points constraining the evolution of a model of sustainable economic development?
- How can policymakers balance the need for confidence and credibility against the sometimes dislocating process of promoting dynamic growth?
- How can political momentum be maintained if outcomes are moderate at best or, at worst, when crisis rocks the hard-won gains of stabilization? Will economic frustrations burst the seams of democratic society?
- Can Latin American nations define a social compact on the responsibilities of the state and the market to resolve the deep inequalities in the region, or are the social divisions simply too great?
- Can the enthusiasm for outward-looking development be maintained and the landscape of integration be practically and pragmatically defined beyond this first, relatively easy state of integration? Can and should the commitment to free trade be realized? What will the costs be if it is not?
- Can the fledgling environmental movement in the region be sustained through an era of thin financing? Can a kind of cost-effective environmentalism be promoted in Latin America that will be supplemented by the energies of public-private partnerships?

The first stage of reform was crisis driven. Emergency measures were taken to address short-term goals of inflation stabilization and external balance. There was little choice but to take a deep breath and move ahead with macroeconomic stabilization as economies spun out of control. Stage two has largely changed the structure of the game. The private sector now controls a larger portion of the economy, and internationalized production and finance regimes shape outcomes. But changes in the rules with respect to who plays in the international arena are more easily implemented than the long-term qualitative changes necessary in social systems of health and education or in information. It is simpler to pass a law reflecting lower tariff rates, open the doors to international capital, or put a state enterprise on the auction block than to engage in the painfully slow process of building institutions to promote social fairness. We know less about changes in social systems and how to gauge results. Reforms in health care, education, and environmental management are less clear-cut, and the results take longer to materialize. Yet without this third stage of capacity building and institutional deepening, Latin America is doomed to repeat the cycle of unstable growth that has characterized its economic performance for centuries.

Key Concepts

capacity building

formal rules

informal rules

institutions

severe stabilization

structural transformation

transparency

Chapter Summary

- Cycles of development have persisted in Latin America, calling into question the resolution of internal and external constraints, the problem of stability in the face of change, the target of economic policy, the role of the state, and the tension between current needs and sustainable future development.
- The periods of primary product exports, import substitution development, and the neoliberal model have addressed these issues differently. The economic contradictions of one period cause the pendulum to swing to a different degree of openness and state intervention.
- In analyzing periods of adjustment, three stages can be identified: severe adjustment, structural transformation, and institutional capacity building. The ability of Latin American countries to promote equitable growth hinges on progress in the third stage, creating stronger and more transparent institutions to support equitable, sustainable growth.

Notes

1. Marlise Simons, "A Talk with Gabriel García Marquez," *New York Times,* December 5, 1982, sec. 7, p. 7, available at www.nytimes.com/books/97/06/15/reviews/marquez-talk.html and in the LEXIS-NEXIS database.

2. IADB, "Is Growth Enough?" *Latin American Economic Policies* 14 (April–June 2001), www.iadb.org.

3. Dudley Althaus, "Deforestation Contributed to Tragedy by Mitch in Honduras, Experts Claim," *Houston Chronicle,* December 30, 1998, A1, as found in the LEXIS-NEXIS database.

4. IADB, "The Argentine Saga," *Latin American Economic Policies* 16 (October–December 2001), www.iadb.org.

5. IMF, *World Economic Outlook 2002,* www.imf.org.

6. Javier Santiso, *Latin America's Political Economy of the Possible* (Cambridge, MA: MIT Press, 2006).

7. Santiso, *Latin America's Political Economy of the Possible,* 207–223, makes this point of the mismatch of political and economic aims.

8. Alejandro Foxley uses these three stages in his preface to *The New Economic Model in Latin America and Its Impact on Income Distribution and Poverty,* ed. Victor Bulmer Thomas (New York: St Martin's, 1996).

9. World Bank, *Beyond the Washington Consensus: Institutions Matter,* Regional Brief (Washington, D.C.: World Bank, 1998), available at www.worldbank.org.

10. Carol Graham, "Strengthening Institutional Capacity in Poor Countries," *Brookings Institution Policy Brief* 98 (April 2002), at www.brookings.edu.

A SAMPLING OF INSTITUTIONAL ACTORS IN LATIN AMERICAN ECONOMIC POLICY

As we move forward in our study of the region, it is useful to have a guide to the key governmental and nongovernmental actors in the region. What follows is a sampling of both multilateral and U.S.-based organizations. You are encouraged to visit their websites (at which much of this information was garnered) for further exploration. This is a sampling, not a comprehensive list, to give you an idea of the multilateral, governmental, and nongovernmental policymakers in the region.

REGIONAL MULTILATERAL ORGANIZATIONS

Inter-American Development Bank (IADB or IDB)

Headquarters: Washington, D.C.
www.iadb.org

The IADB, the largest regional multilateral institution, was established in 1959 to accelerate social and economic change in the region. Its membership is composed of forty-six nations, including the United States, Canada, twenty-six Latin American and Caribbean countries, and eighteen nonregional countries. Its mission is to raise funds in financial markets for development in Latin American and Caribbean member countries, to supplement private investment where private capital is not available, and to provide technical assistance for the preparation, financing, and implementation of projects. Its first loan was made in 1961 to improve the water and sewerage systems of Arequipa, Peru. In 1994 the Multilateral Investment Fund was created to assist investment reforms and promote private development throughout the region. The $7.1 billion in IADB loans and guarantees approved in 2005 will help to finance projects involving a total investment of more than $15.5 billion. IADB loans cover only a part of the total cost of the projects being carried out by the borrowing countries. The balance comes principally from the Latin American and Caribbean countries.

United Nations Economic Commission for Latin America and the Caribbean (ECLAC or CEPAL)

Headquarters: Santiago de Chile
www.eclac.cl

The Economic Commission for Latin America was established by the UN Economic and Social Council in 1948 and was redesignated as the Economic Commission for Latin America and the Caribbean (ECLAC) in 1984. It disseminates economic and social information and has little decision-making power but provides a second opinion for governments' economic and social policies. The functions established by its mandate are to promote economic and social development through regional and subregional cooperation; gather, organize, interpret, and disseminate economic and social development information; provide advisory services to governments; plan and advocate development assistance activities; organize intergovernmental conferences, seminars, workshops, and expert group meetings; and help bring a regional perspective to global problems. ECLAC's influence is best known for the import substitution industrialization (ISI) strategy and the dependency theories of its first secretary-general, Raúl Prebisch. Today, the commission has adopted a more centrist approach.

The Organization of American States (OAS)

Headquarters: Washington, D.C.
www.oas.org

The OAS is the oldest regional organization in the world, finding its roots in the first International Conference of American States, held in Washington, D.C., in 1890. The OAS charter was signed in 1948. Its members include all thirty-five states of the Americas. The function of the organization is to strengthen the peace and security of the region; ensure the peaceful settlement of disputes among member states; promote and consolidate representative democracy; provide common action on the part of a member state in the case of aggression; seek the solution to economic, juridical, and political problems that may arise among the states; and promote through cooperative action the economic, social, and cultural development of member states. The OAS's most important roles have been to promote the pacific settlements of disputes among and within member states and to actively participate in democratization.

Pan American Health Organization (PAHO)

Headquarters: Washington, D.C.
www.paho.org

PAHO is an international health association that provides a forum for the consolidation and cooperation of health efforts by countries within the Americas region. Together, the thirty-five member countries work to promote physical and mental health, lengthen life, and fight diseases within their countries. PAHO dates back to the 1902 establishment of the International Sanitary Bureau. Since then the association's name has been changed several times. PAHO operates under a budget consisting of member quotas and other outside extrabudgetary funds.

GLOBAL MULTILATERAL ORGANIZATIONS

International Labor Organization (ILO)

Headquarters: Geneva, Switzerland
www.un.org/Depts/ilowbo

The ILO is an independent agency in the UN system with a mandate to improve working conditions, create employment, and promote human rights around the world. It has 178 member countries, of which 70 percent are less-developed countries. It is the only UN agency in which the private sector works actively with government in decision making. Its activities involve setting international labor standards, carrying out technical assistance and training programs, and providing information on products and services.

World Bank

Headquarters: Washington, D.C.
www.worldbank.org

The World Bank, a product of the 1944 Bretton Woods Conference, provides capital, technical assistance, and policy advice to developing countries. Like the IADB, the World Bank raises funds from capital markets to help finance development where private capital is not available. All of its monetary assistance comes in the form of loans. There are two forms of loans. The first type is for countries able to pay near-market interest rates. Money for these loans comes from private investors who purchase World Bank bonds. The second type of lending is for the poorest countries and is issued by the International Development Association, a World Bank affiliate. Money for these loans does not come from capital markets but rather from thirty donor countries. There is no interest on these loans except for a 0.75 percent administrative charge, and they have thirty-five- to forty-year terms. In addition to providing loans, the World Bank has become one of the most important sources of development information and publications.

International Monetary Fund (IMF)

Headquarters: Washington, D.C.
www.imf.org

The IMF, a result of the 1944 Bretton Woods Conference, was formally established in 1945 as an institution dedicated to the supervision of international monetary systems. It works to coordinate efforts and to encourage cooperation among its 184 voluntary member countries in the creation of economic policies. Acting as a forum for international monetary exchange, the IMF oversees transactions between countries to ensure that they occur smoothly and quickly. Additionally, through often very large loans, the IMF provides access to the different international capitals made available through their quota subscriptions, or membership fees.

United Nations Development Programme (UNDP)

Headquarters: New York
www.undp.org

Working on the ground in 166 countries, the UNDP works to create and develop sustainable development through sound governance and market development. Priorities are placed on poverty elimination, job creation, the advancement of women, and environmental regeneration. The UNDP does not represent any one approach to development; rather, its commitment is to assist partner governments in finding their own approaches, according to their own unique national circumstances. The UNDP maintains a long-term presence in almost all developing countries, and with its extensive networks at the national, regional, and global levels, it is an impartial broker, convener, and facilitator.

U.S.-BASED GOVERNMENTAL AND QUASI-GOVERNMENTAL ORGANIZATIONS

Inter-American Foundation (IAF)

Headquarters: Washington, D.C.
www.iaf.gov

The IAF is a public-private bipartisan U.S. agency supporting programs in Latin America that promote grassroots development, self-reliance, and popular empowerment. It responds to requests for grants by indigenous nongovernmental organizations (NGOs) that provide assistance to peasant cooperatives, small enterprises, trade unions, women's collectives, human rights organizations, and cultural groups. Established in 1969, it was created as a small organization with no overseas staff to reduce costs and maximize program returns. It is viewed by many as a risk taker and groundbreaker for development assistance with its focus on supporting innovative and experimental programs. Between 1972 and 2002, the IAF approved more than forty-four hundred grants totaling $538 million to support more than thirty-five hundred organizations. Many grants went to grassroots organizations such as agricultural cooperatives or small urban enterprises; others were awarded to larger intermediary organizations that provided community groups with credit, technical assistance, training, and marketing assistance. The largest portion of IAF funding has been invested in enterprise development, followed by food production and agriculture, education, training, and ecodevelopment.

United States Agency for International Development (USAID)

Headquarters: Washington, D.C.
www.usaid.gov

USAID is an independent government agency established by President John F. Kennedy in 1961 to respond to the threat of communism and help poorer nations. In the post–Cold War era its mission is to ensure U.S. national security by promoting economic, political, environmental, and social development of developing nations. USAID views underdevelopment as a major threat to global stability. It aids participatory development with the aim of building indigenous capacity, enhancing participation, and encouraging transparency, decentralization, and the empowerment of communities and individuals. USAID is an independent federal government agency that receives overall foreign policy guidance from the secretary of state.

NGOs and Advocacy Groups

Inter-American Dialogue

Headquarters: Washington, D.C.
www.iadialog.org

Started in 1982, the Inter-American Dialogue is a distinguished U.S. center for policy analysis, study, and commentary on Western Hemisphere affairs. Membership consists of one hundred leading citizens throughout the Americas who together seek to promote economic and political cooperation and communication through informed policy issue debate. The Inter-American Dialogue is noted for its influence in shaping the agenda of inter-American relations.

Latin American Working Group (LAWG)

Headquarters: Washington, D.C.
http://www.lawg.org

LAWG is a coalition of activist groups that dedicates its efforts to lobbying the U.S. Congress on Latin American issues. Since 1983 LAWG has worked to craft common policies through public education.

Woodrow Wilson Center Latin American Program

Headquarters: Washington, D.C.
www.wilsoncenter.orgics.si.edu

The Woodrow Wilson Center Latin American Program was established in 1977 to encourage academic-style research and discussion on inter-American issues facing the region as well as specifically Latin American topics. The center provides the opportunity for research and writing on issues of concern to Washington policymakers.

Center for Strategic and International Studies (CSIS)

Headquarters: Washington, D.C.
www.csis.org

The CSIS, founded in 1962, is a prominent institution dedicated to effective analysis and recommendations of policies worldwide. The Americas Program focuses efforts on Latin American policy impact as well as U.S. and Canadian influences throughout the Americas. Policy study is considered from a variety of viewpoints covering such prominent Latin American issues as market integration, threats of narcotics trafficking, and political and economic reform.

Washington Office on Latin America (WOLA)

Headquarters: Washington, D.C.
www.wola.org

WOLA is an advocacy group with particular interests in human rights and counter-narcotics policy. Funded in 1974, it facilitates dialogue between governmental and nongovernmental actors and monitors the impact of their policies and programs.

ACCION International

Headquarters: Boston, Massachusetts
www.accion.org

ACCION International, established in 1961, is a nonprofit organization dedicated to providing microentrepreneurs with critical access to working capital in the form of credit and training. Through short-term loans, solidarity group lending, and technical business support, self-employed poor people throughout Latin America are able to expand their businesses, which indirectly leads to the creation of more jobs. ACCION works with affiliates in fourteen countries and in 1998 disbursed nearly $577 million in loans, with about 447,000 small business recipients receiving an average of nearly $1,300 per loan.

Council of the Americas

Headquarters: New York
www.counciloftheamericas.org

Founded in 1965 under the leadership of David Rockefeller and other business-people, the Council for the Americas encourages free markets and private enterprise throughout the Americas according to the belief that these policies encourage economic growth. The council acts in strategic ways through the advocacy of public discourse as well as through collaboration with private-sector organizations in hopes of achieving economic prosperity. Membership consists of more than 240 firms that share an interest in Latin American investment.

GLOSSARY

absorption   Absorption is domestic consumption of goods both produced at home and imported from abroad. The IMF promoted the absorption approach, or the reduction of domestic utilization of resources to release them for export to earn hard currency to finance a country's debt.

adverse selection   A situation where one side of a deal has more information than another, leading to the selection of an undesirable outcome.

Agenda 21   A comprehensive agenda for environmental action established at the 1992 United Nations Conference on the Environment and Development held in Rio de Janeiro.

agricultural extension programs   Programs to introduce new agricultural practices to peasant farming communities.

Austral plan   Argentina's Austral plan, named after the new currency put in place in 1985, was designed to combat inflation. The Austral plan was labeled as heterodox but also included some orthodox measures. To attack the inertial component of inflation, the administration declared a price freeze in June of 1985, froze wages, and implemented exchange-rate controls. These measures were taken to convince the population that prices would not increase, but the plan fell apart after people lost confidence in the ability of the government to manage the economy.

backward linkage   As industry A grows, demand for inputs to produce industry A's product will increase. This increase in demand can spur investment in a new industry B that will produce inputs for industry A. Central to the thought of A. O. Hirschman, investing in industries with strong backward linkages on the supply chain should promote growth.

Bresser plan   A follow-up to the *Cruzado* plan, the Brazilian use of heterodox policy to combat inflation in 1987. Wages were frozen, mini-devaluations were used to manage the exchange rate, and interest rates were targeted above the rate of inflation. Citizens were deputized as price inspectors. Despite initial success, shortages and external balance problems caused by excess consumer spending reignited inflation once again.

Business Competitiveness Index (BCI)   A composite index using the context for firm strategy and rivalry, the quality of local demand conditions, and the presence of local and supporting industries, the BCI highlights the microeconomic factors crucial to firm performance.

caciques   Spanish word for the landlords of large agricultural estates prevalent in the Latin American colonial period.

607

capacity building   Refers to investments in human capital, improvements in productivity and system design, and greater efficiency in the use of resources within economic, political, and social institutions.

capital controls   Mechanisms such as licensing of foreign exchange used to limit imports or reduce capital flight, or taxation on short-term foreign investments to reduce the volatility of short-term capital flows.

capital flight   Large outflows of domestic capital into safer or more stable foreign banks and foreign stock markets to protect the value of that capital. This phenomenon is associated with countries suffering from severe inflation or the likelihood of devaluation. Individuals opt to invest abroad when they lose confidence in their country's currency.

Central American Common Market   Formed early in the 1960s, this attempt at integration among Central American countries to take advantage of economies of scale in production was set back in the 1970s and 1980s by political strife. The 1990s saw new commitment to strengthening the legal and institutional framework, joint actions to reduce debt, and cooperation on sectoral issues.

Central American Free Trade Agreement (CAFTA)   A comprehensive trade agreement among Costa Rica, the Dominican Republic, El Salvador, Guatemala, Honduras, Nicaragua, and the United States. CAFTA was signed in August 2004, and as of 2006 all but Costa Rica have ratified the agreement. It creates the second largest free trade zone for the United States after NAFTA.

Chicago School   This free market school of thought, a precursor to the neoliberal model, advocated a hands-off role for the state. Adherents believe that the market and open international trade are the main engines behind development.

Collor plan   Economic policy engineered by Brazil's president, Fernando Collor de Mello in 1990 to address inertial inflation through orthodox and heterodox measures. Assets were frozen and a thirty-day price freeze instituted. These measures initially restrained inflation, but pressures such as increasing oil prices and shortages of goods, in addition to a lack of credibility in the government, caused an acceleration in inflation soon afterward.

command and control measures   Government regulations and penalties used to reduce environmental pollution.

commodity lottery   A term used by Victor Bulmer-Thomas that describes the export-oriented pattern of the late 1800s, when most Latin American countries were dependent on one export good, such as nitrates in Chile, coffee in Brazil, and tin in Bolivia.

common market   A form of integration in which countries coordinate policy-making measures in such areas as agriculture and the social sector, along with establishing a common external tariff.

Community of Andean Nations (CAN)   Signed in 1960, the CAN treaty allowed for free commerce among Bolivia, Ecuador, Colombia, Venezuela, and Peru with a common external tariff.

conditionality   A term associated with the prerequisites necessary for disbursal of IMF funds to developing countries. Countries seeking loans from the IMF must first implement tough stabilization policies such as a decrease in fiscal spending, tight monetary policy, and strict trade policies. Conditionality is strongly debated because it forces a government to contract its economy and imposes social costs.

contingent valuation   A form of environmental assessment that asks people to assign a value to their willingness to pay to preserve a natural resource.

convertibility plan   Introduced in 1991 in Argentina, this policy to combat inflation tied the Argentine peso to the U.S. dollar and used a currency board to constrain monetary policy by law. The money supply could not increase unless there was a parallel increase in dollar reserves. Inflation was almost eliminated, but at a high cost in terms of recession and unemployment.

cost-benefit analysis   An important technique for project appraisal, the tool helps value direct and indirect costs adjusted for the time value of money against potential gains.

cost-effectiveness   A criterion used to decide among competing priorities, especially in the environmental arena. Programs with broad impact and low cost are more desirable than programs of limited scope and high cost.

cost-push elements   Certain conditions or external shocks such as food shortages or increasing oil prices that will fuel inflation through the interaction with powerful labor organizations or a concentrated industry structure. Rising costs are seen as pushing up prices.

Cruzado plan   Based on a structural diagnosis of inflation, the first Cruzado plan in Brazil, in 1986, focused on the inertial component of inflation and implemented heterodox measures by freezing prices, wages, and exchange rates. Brazilians were deputized as *fiscais,* or price inspectors, to police the price freeze in supermarkets and shopping malls. Indexation of contracts with less than one year's duration was prohibited. A new currency, the cruzado, was created at a value of 1,000 cruzeiros. After a devaluation, the cruzado was fixed at 13.84 cruzados to the dollar. A neglect of tough fiscal adjustments combined with passive monetary policy that accommodated domestic deficits resulted in the re-eruption of inflation.

customs union   A form of regional trade integration in which a common external tariff is established for the group.

debt-for-equity swap   A win-win method used by firms, banks, and indebted countries to reduce exposure to the debt crisis. A firm wishing to invest in a particular country would buy the country's debt at a discount from a bank through the secondary market. Owing the firm and not the bank, the country could pay the firm in local currency, as opposed to dollars, which the firm then used to buy local supplies and pay workers. Banks got risky loans off their books, countries were released from the need to earn hard currency to service the debt, and firms were repaid the full value of the loan bought at a discount. The plan was limited, however, by inflationary risk and the demand for equity investments.

debt-for-nature swap   An environmental twist on debt-for-equity swaps, in which international organizations buy a country's discounted debt from the secondary market. Debts are reduced or canceled in exchange for a country establishing nature preserves or otherwise protecting the environment. A financial commitment to long-term management of the parks, sometimes through a trust fund, was an important element of success.

debt trap   When long-term projects are financed through short-term debt issues, countries may find themselves paying more in interest and principal than they are receiving in new money. Initially, the borrower is able to finance the project as well as pay the principal and interest with new lending each year. With each coming year, new lending available for investment dwindles because some of the money from new loans is used to pay the principal and interest on previous loans. The debt trap sets in when the new lending is not enough to pay for the principal and interest and the project is not yet generating significant returns to make up the difference.

decentralization   A devolution of governmental responsibilities from centralized bureaucracies to state and local levels. The ability to raise revenues is sometimes also moved to the local level, although systems of fiscal accountability need to be tightened to improve internal balance.

declining terms of trade   Terms of trade are the price of exports relative to the price of imports, mathematically expressed as Px/Pm, an index of export prices divided by an index of import prices. Declining terms of trade are reflected in a decrease in the ratio, meaning that the price of imports is increasing relative to the price of exports. Under these conditions, countries must export increasing amounts of their own goods (often agricultural goods or commodities) to pay for imports (more likely to be machinery and high-tech items).

demand-driven rural investment funds (DRIFs)   The allocation of central government funds to local governments or communities to promote local control of agricultural development. Certain eligibility requirements must be met, and beneficiaries must contribute to the cost of the projects, often through volunteer labor.

dependency theory   Despite different emphases by scholars, the central theme behind dependency is the proposition that a country does not develop because of its natural endowments; its growth is constrained by centers of power in the international system. Industrialized countries (the center) advance at the expense of the third world (the periphery), causing underdevelopment in the region through exploitation of cheap labor and extraction of resources. Underdevelopment was seen as linked to the relationship between the elite of Latin America and the center in their search for short-term profits as opposed to long-term growth.

development   The process of meeting the basic needs of the population and enhancing options for how economic resources will be allocated today and in the future to increase the choices citizens have in their daily lives.

direct government investment   In addition to command and control measures and market-based initiatives, this is a third policy option available to states to promote sound environmental practices. Governments might choose to invest in infrastructure such as sanitation or water projects to promote a cleaner environment.

dualism   The simultaneous existence of modern and traditional economies, usually characterized by an expanding industrial sector and a large self-subsistence agricultural sector. Dualistic models tend to benefit the elite and marginalize the poor.

dualistic structure of production   A bimodal pattern of agricultural production in which large corporate farming practices crowd out peasant farming, lowering employment and the production of basic foodstuffs in favor of lucrative export crops.

Dutch disease   Named after Holland's experience with natural gas, the term describes a country's inclination to concentrate its financial resources into a few profitable sectors. This behavior was prevalent throughout Latin American history with investments in oil and sugar, and it contributed to the unbalanced development of the region as other important sectors were ignored.

economic populism   Economic populism is patterned after the behavior of many charismatic Latin American leaders, such as Juan Perón in Argentina, whose programs were symbolically designed to attend to the needs of the poor. Industry was pacified with large subsidies. The welfare of future generations is sacrificed for the welfare of current generations through excessive current spending to satisfy pressure groups. In a desire to increase the standard of living today, this kind of behavior ignores external balance of payments constraints and large fiscal deficits, conditions that make inflation nearly inevitable.

economic union   A group of countries that have moved beyond a common market to embrace common sectoral policies. Common monetary policies and a common currency constitute an additional step toward an economic community. Mercosur is therefore an economic union, whereas the European Community has moved a step beyond.

educational deficit   The gap between Latin America and the rest of the world in educational attainment and years of schooling. The 4.2 years of schooling Latin American children receive is roughly half of that of counterparts in the United States, Japan, and Germany, and two-thirds those in the Asian newly industrialized countries.

educational performance index   Measure developed by the international NGO Oxfam using weighted values of school enrollment, gender equity, and completion rates.

effective rate of protection   The nominal tariff adjusted for the tariff on intermediate goods. If the garment industry faced a 10-percent tariff and the sewing machines to make clothing faced a 5-percent tariff, the effective rate of protection (adjusted for the importance of the machine in production) would be 15 percent.

effective selectivity   A policy approach advocated by the neostructuralists that promotes prioritizing and allocating limited government funds to areas that will produce the highest social returns.

ejidos   Land that had been held communally for centuries before the introduction of private property. This is the predominant form of peasant landholding in Mexico.

empowerment   The full participation of beneficiaries in their own development process.

enclaves   Industries, in isolation from the rest of the economy, that fail to spur domestic investment, employment, and income.

encomienda   Land received by conquistadors or other Spanish settlers from the Spanish Crown that was accompanied by the deeding of Indian labor to work this land.

Engel's Law   When the increase in the demand for agricultural goods is slower than an increase in income (that is, there is a low income elasticity of demand), exporters of agricultural goods lose ground to producers of manufactured goods. When a low income elasticity for agricultural products exists, this means that if individuals experience an increase in their income, they will not increase their consumption of food or commodities by the same proportion. There is, for example, only so much coffee or sugar one will consume, no matter the increase in income. Engel's Law was used by economists such as Raúl Prebisch to explain why the developing world, which tends to export agricultural commodities, experiences declining terms of trade.

environmental assessment   An impact statement identifying the likely environmental effects of a development policy. Most new development projects today require environments assessments prior to approval.

epidemiological backlog   The simultaneous health challenge of addressing traditional diseases (such as cholera or dysentery tied to inadequate infrastructure and malnutrition) and the diseases of modern society (such as cancer and heart disease).

epidemiological transition   The transition from a focus on fighting traditional diseases such as cholera to a focus on more modern concerns such as heart disease.

equity   The access to equal opportunities within a nation. Although growth may increase inequality, models of growth with equity attempt to promote a more equal distribution of income. Equity also refers to ownership of capital—a very different use of the same term.

equity investments   The purchase of stock by foreigners.

expenditure switching   Changes in the prices of products, most often through an exchange-rate adjustment, that make imports more expensive and exports cheaper. The higher price of imports switches people away from them, helping to balance trade.

export pessimism   A term associated with the Prebisch–Singer thesis, stating that exports alone cannot be the engine of growth because of the effect of declining terms of trade.

externalities   A cost or a benefit that results from an activity or transaction that is imposed on parties outside the transaction. Pollution is a negative externality of production; reducing the spread of disease is a positive externality of education.

extreme poverty   Although levels vary by the local cost of living, those subsisting on roughly less than $1 a day are considered to be living in extreme poverty. Moderate poverty is roughly $2 per day, or between $50 (World Bank benchmark) and $60 a month (ECLAC level).

factor price equalization   As a country opens up to trade, the demand for its products, made with its most abundant (and cheap) factor, should in theory over time result in an increase in the price of this factor to world levels. Global factor prices should therefore become more uniform.

fazenda   Large feudal estates, similar to the *hacienda* in Spanish America, during the colonial period in Brazil.

fiscal austerity measures   Policy initiatives such as decreasing government spending, privatization, increasing tax revenues, and reducing subsidies to relieve pressure on domestic budgets. The IMF often recommends fiscal austerity measures.

fiscal covenant   A term coined by ECLAC to reflect a socioeconomic agreement between a government and civil society. This fiscal covenant incorporates consolidation of the ongoing fiscal adjustment, increases in the productivity of public management, transparency of fiscal activity, promotion of social equity, and development of democratic institutions.

foreign direct investment (FDI)   Describes the investment by foreigners through ownership of equity shares or setting up production facilities within a country. The most common type of foreign direct investor is the multinational corporation.

formal rules   The constitutions, laws, and written regulations that structure economic activity and guarantee property rights.

forward linkage   The production of a good that is complementary to another industry may spur the development of that new sector; such development is called a forward linkage. As opposed to a backward linkage, which calls for the production of critical inputs, a forward linkage moves ahead in the production chain. Roadside restaurants might be a forward linkage to automobile production, whereas tires would be considered a backward linkage.

free trade area   A form of regional integration in which trade restrictions are abolished between participating countries, but each country maintains an independent trade policy and separate tariff rates with the rest of the world.

Free Trade Area of the Americas (FTAA)   The FTAA effort to unite the thirty-four democracies economies of the Americas into a single free trade area in which barriers to trade and investment will be progressively eliminated began at the Summit of the Americas, which was held in December 1994 in Miami and missed its targeted completion date of 2005.

gender development index (GDI)   The GDI discounts the human development index for gender inequality in life expectancy, educational attainment, and income, by assigning a penalty for inequality. The greater the gender disparity, the lower the GDI.

gender empowerment index (GEM)   The GEM concentrates on economic, political, and professional participation by incorporating variables such as female share of income, access to professional and managerial jobs, and seats in public office. The GEM therefore measures the degree to which society's opportunities are open to women.

Gini coefficient   A measure of income inequality that gauges the difference between a hypothetical society where income is perfectly equal and the actual income distribution. It is derived from the Lorenz curve. The higher the Gini coefficient, the more extensive is income inequality.

Global Competitiveness Index   Expanding on the Growth Competitiveness Index, this measure incorporates a broader range of factors, including health, education, labor market rigidities, and the sophistication of financial institutions.

Global Environmental Facility (GEF)   Assists developing countries in funding projects and programs to protect the global environment and promote sustainable development. Established in 1991, GEF is the designated financial mechanism for international agreements on biodiversity, climate change, and persistent organic pollutants. GEF also supports projects that combat desertification and protects international waters and the ozone layer.

global public goods (GPGs)   GPGs transcend national boundaries, are difficult to exclude people from consuming, and the consumption by one does not diminish the good for another. A good example is clean air.

golden age of primary product exports   The period in Latin American history from the late 1800s to the early 1900s, when primary product exports boomed and contributed to the economic growth of the region.

grade repetition   A pervasive problem of educational systems in Latin America. Nearly one third of all school children repeat their grades annually, primarily because of poor educational inputs.

growth   A simultaneous gradual increase in quantities such as GDP, population, saving, and wealth. If the benefits of growth are not widely shared, it may not be considered development.

Growth Competitiveness Index   This composite index attempts to capture the collection of factors, policies, and institutions that can determine the level of prosperity of an economy by weighting the quality of the macroeconomic environment, the state of public institutions, and the level of technological readiness in an economy.

headcount ratio   The proportion within a country's population falling below the poverty line.

Heckscher–Ohlin theorem   A key theoretical construct in international trade that suggests that a country should trade the good that uses relatively intensively that country's most abundant factor.

heterodox policies   Monetary and fiscal policies grounded in the belief that one of the primary components of inflation is the inertia built into an economic chain, with wages increased in anticipation of future price increases, making inflation a self-fulfilling prophecy. Heterodox policies attempt to combat inflation by neutralizing expectations through price and wage freezes.

HFA   A program promoted by the World Health Organization mobilizing efforts to provide basic health services for all by the year 2000.

highly indebted poor country (HIPC) initiative   Through the HIPC initiative, nominal debt service relief of more than US$59 billion has been approved for twenty-nine countries, reducing their net present value of external debt by approximately two-thirds. Of these countries, nineteen have reached the completion point and have been granted unconditional debt service relief of more than US$37 billion.

Human Development index (HDI)   The United Nations Human Development Report calculates the HDI as a composite of life expectancy at birth, educational attainment (measured by adult literacy and school enrollments), and income.

illiquidity   A condition in which cash flow does not match financial obligations. As opposed to insolvency, when an economic entity cannot and will not ever likely meet its obligations, illiquidity may be a temporary condition in which revenues do not cover costs of debt service. In the first stage of the debt crisis, countries were thought to have temporary liquidity problems; it was later seen that fundamental restructuring and debt relief were called for.

import substitution industrialization (ISI)   ISI was the dominant economic policy in Latin America during the 1950s, 1960s, and 1970s as a response to dependency and structuralist theories. It represented a shift away from the outward orientation of export promotion, to an inward-looking orientation. ISI was designed to replace imports with domestic production under the guiding hand of the state. Governments used activist industrial, fiscal, and monetary policy to achieve growth.

income gap   A measure of poverty that captures the difference between actual incomes and incomes at the officially designated poverty line.

incomplete markets   Markets in developing countries may be incomplete in the sense that they do not efficiently convey price signals to buyers or sellers. This may be due to lack of information, a limited number of participants, or the market infrastructure. When markets do not adjust smoothly, transactions costs rise and economic activity is compromised. Neostructuralists and new institutionalists suggest a role for the state in supplementing economic activity where markets are incomplete.

indexation   Under a system of indexation, countries will revise wages and financial prices upward by taking into account expected as well as past inflation. When indexation occurs, countries have embraced inflation and it becomes a part of daily life. Because incomes are protected, the inflation is less painful.

inertial inflation   Implies that inflation is not driven solely by an increase in the money supply, but by expectations as well. As individuals anticipate inflation, they will demand higher wages or set prices accordingly, which will push prices upward.

inflationary expectations   The expectations of a society, based on past experience, of future rates of inflation. When they anticipate future price increases, economic actors demand higher wages or set prices higher to cover the inflation they expect in the future, making the expectations a self-fulfilling prophecy. Inflationary expectations are a large part of inertial inflation.

informal rules   Values and norms that condition and are conditioned by the process of economic change.

informal sector   Small-scale business operations such as selling goods on street corners or providing cleaning services in homes. The informal sector operates outside the official, taxed economy. It is characterized by a low capital-labor ratio, family-intensive production, and worker-owned means of production. The informal sector can be divided into three areas—microenterprise employment, own-account workers, and domestic service.

insecure property rights   When owners of property are not sure of their rights to use or dispose of their property. When institutions guaranteeing land titles are inefficient or nonexistent, farmers may underinvest in developing property because there is a good chance that the returns from efforts will be appropriated by another. Insecure property rights are an important cause of environmental damage, because economic actors may exploit land and natural resources now if they assume that they will not, or may not, continue to have access to these inputs in the future.

institutionalist tradition   A vision of development policy that accords a strong role for nonmarket institutions. Institutionalists assume that markets are not perfect; that people are not purely rational, self-interested maximizers; and that economic power rather than efficiency will shape outcomes. For institutionalists, access to and control over technology is an important ingredient of dynamic (or sluggish) growth.

institutions   Rules that shape the behavior of organizations and individuals engaged in economic activity.

integrated approach   Addressing poverty by means of growth policy and social policy, as suggested by the Economic Commission for Latin America and the Caribbean (ECLAC).

integrated rural development   A holistic approach in the rural sector that takes into account the multidimensional nature of rural poverty, focusing on the well-being of rural people by building their productive, social, and environmental assets.

involuntary lending   During the debt crisis, involuntary lending described the process of rolling over the principal and interest payments due on a loan into new (usually more expensive) loans to give countries breathing room to meet their financial obligations. It was believed that after their economies became more productive through the tough measures required by the IMF, these countries would then be able to pay off their debt. Banks preferred to package the interest and principal due into a new loan because it kept the loan in the "performing" category rather than having a past-due amount trigger a classification of this asset as nonperforming and therefore worth less.

Kuznets curve   A graphical, U-shaped representation that illustrates income inequality initially increasing with economic growth, but later decreasing after economic growth has reached a certain level. At first economies may be equal but poor; equality may fall during rapid growth, but as economies mature, equality should rise again.

labor market distortions   Movements away from free labor markets, these include government intervention in setting wages, high costs of dismissal, high payroll taxes, and the contentious nature of labor-management relations.

labor productivity   A measure of output produced by workers. The productivity of workers, conditioned by their education, health, and access to complementary inputs such as machinery and technology, is an important ingredient of growth. If productivity is rising faster than prices and population, a society will have more goods to distribute and welfare should improve.

land reform   Given unequal patterns of landholdings created by colonial patronage, some governments have attempted to redistribute land. These movements have been revolutionary at times, taking tracts of land from the rich and giving them to the poor, as well as progressive, where only land that has been idle or unproductive is reassigned to those who might use it more intensively.

latifundia   Feudal estates in Spanish Latin America, which stood in great contrast to the small parcels of land (known as *minifundias*) used by peasant farmers. The *latifundia* also served as a form of political, social, and economic organization and later contributed to a pattern of concentrated landholdings and power.

Lorenz curve   A graphical representation of income distribution. The population is sorted by income, usually deciles, and the percentage of income that each portion of the population holds is plotted. For example, in the Lorenz curve for Latin America, the first 20 percent of the population holds 2.5 percent of the income, and the first 40 percent a cumulative 8.6 percent. Altogether, the bottom 60 percent accounts for 19.6 percent of income, with the top 20 percent holding nearly two-thirds of the total.

mandamiento   A system by which communities, most often indigenous, were forced to provide workers for harvest when there were labor shortages, often under brutal working conditions.

market-based incentives   In addition to command and control measures and direct government investment, one of three types of tools used in environmental policy. Instruments such as tax incentives are used to encourage market investments in such areas as recycling and use of solar power as a means of promoting sustainable development. The premise behind market-based initiatives is that if someone can profit from doing environmental good, the policy is more likely to endure over time.

market failure   Neoclassical economic theorists believe that when left on its own, the market will promote economic growth. When the market fails to promote growth, primarily because of information constraints or ineffective price signals, market failure occurs.

Mercosur   The South American common market comprising Argentina, Brazil, Uruguay, Venezuela, and Paraguay as well as associate members Chile and Bolivia.

merit good   Investment in public goods such as education and health that have benefits for society in general.

microcredit   Banking services that reach down to the small-scale entrepreneur. Collateral for loans is often provided by an investment circle that guarantees repayment of members. Microlending makes investment over time possible for the poor, but some question whether, because of the amounts involved and the repayment structure, microcredit makes a significant difference in people's lives.

minifundia   The small parcels of land used for subsistence farming by Latin American peasants during the colonial period and whose remnants can still be seen today.

moderate poverty   A standard of living corresponding to income of about $50–$60 a month, or $2 a day. Roughly 40 percent of the population of Latin America lives in moderate poverty.

moral hazard   A situation that occurs when borrowers have more information than lenders about their own likely behavior after the sale. If sufficient collateral is not secured prior to the loan, the borrower has an incentive to pursue high-risk behavior because the gains will be high if the project succeeds but will be shared by the lender if it fails. Can also be applied to other situations when agents are not forced to internalize costs.

NAFTA   The North American Free Trade Agreement was signed by the United States, Canada, and Mexico in 1994. It sought to reduce tariffs within a ten-year period, increase trade in the region, promote cross-border investment, and introduce environmental and labor standards across the region.

neoclassical tradition   Belief among some economists that rational, self-interested maximizers, if left alone by governments to operate within markets, will generate the greatest quantity of goods for society.

neostructuralists   Adherents of this school of economic thought do not believe that the market alone will spur development; the state should intervene in those areas where there has been market failure. Concentration of economic power in both the domestic and international arenas requires selective intervention to promote equitable development. The principal difference between structuralists and neostructuralists is that the latter group places a greater emphasis on outward-looking export development as opposed to the inward-looking policies that defined import substitution industrialization.

new institutional economics   New institutionalists argue that culture matters in defining the ways the economy provides for society. New institutionalists claim that certain institutional arrangements are necessary to reduce transaction costs that arise in imperfect markets. The arrangements may include improving property rights, providing effective and impartial judicial systems, and instituting transparent regulatory frameworks.

new political economy   The new political economy grounds its assumptions in the material self-interest and rational calculus of economic actors. Intervention by the state will serve only to interfere with market signals and the allocation of resources. The state should, therefore, play a minimal role in the market.

nontraditional export production   Policies such as agricultural extension training or preferential credit to promote goods that are not in the traditional export profile. By diversifying exports, countries are able to capture new markets and be less dependent on price swings in traditional commodities.

Olivera–Tanzi effect   The process by which inflation erodes the true value of tax receipts because of the time lag between assessment of tax liability and actual collection.

open regionalism   Promoted by ECLAC, this policy encourages the formation of regional and subregional trading units without excluding trade initiatives with other parts of the world.

orthodox theory of inflation   For the orthodox theorist, inflation is a monetary phenomenon. Too much money chasing too few goods increases the overall price level. This phenomenon is usually the result of governments trying to finance their budget deficits in one of three ways: raising money domestically, borrowing from abroad, and/or seignorage (printing money). To reduce inflation, the orthodox economists would attack not only the increase in the money supply but also large budget deficits. For the orthodox school, letting the markets work and limiting government intervention is the key to reducing inflation. The purpose behind tight monetary policy and a decrease in expenditures is to reduce aggregate demand that would otherwise lead to higher prices and not higher output.

overvalued exchange rates   Under a fixed exchange rate system, a rate is overvalued when inflation has eroded the true value of the money but a new par or official rate has not been established. For example, if inflation in country A is 25 percent a year higher than in country B and their currencies are fixed in terms of each other, the country experiencing inflation will have a currency that is 25 percent overvalued at the end of one year. Overvaluation of a currency is not sustainable because it encourages imports and discourages exports. If it is not corrected by contracting the economy, people will expect a devaluation, or adjustment in the currency price. As reserves to pay for the current account imbalance are drawn down, people will begin to vote with their feet, moving capital to currencies without the risk of devaluation.

Pact for Economic Solidarity   Also known as *El Pacto,* this was an agreement between the Mexican state, business, and labor to limit price increases as a way to combat inflation.

planning model   A vision of development policy that accords a strong role to a nation's government to jump start economic change.

portfolio bonds   Short-term financial instruments held in emerging market portfolios that make a country vulnerable to quick movements of international capital flows.

portfolio investors   Refers to certain types of investors, such as mutual funds or insurance companies, that generally invest with a short-term outlook.

poverty line   The minimum income required to purchase the goods necessary for subsistence. Although this varies by location, $2 per day is the global benchmark for moderate poverty and $1 a day for extreme poverty.

precarious employment   Describes a state of workplace vulnerability where employment for some has become less remunerative, less regulated by government, and less subject to the collective control of workers.

preferential trade agreements   Trade agreements such as free trade arrangements or customs unions that promote economic activity within a region by favoring trading partners within that region over those outside it.

primary health care   Health care that promotes basic sanitation and nutrition practices to increase people's control over improvements in their environment so as to maintain a decent quality of life and achieve human and social potential.

productivity   A measure of output in relation to inputs. Rising productivity is a key to economic growth.

provisioning   A response by banks to the debt crisis whereby they would set aside profits (before dividend payments) against risky loans so as to reduce their exposure to debt.

purchasing power parity   A good sold in two markets should sell for the same price, adjusted for the exchange rate, in both locations. If it does not, this suggests that one currency is overvalued.

quality primary education by the year 2010   The goal of 100 percent primary-school completion rates and 75 percent secondary-inscription rates agreed to by the presidents of the region at the 1994 Miami summit; action items to promote this goal were elaborated at the 1998 Santiago summit, including targeting vulnerable groups through compensatory programs, preschool education, and distance learning.

Real plan   Introduced by Brazilian president Henrique Fernando Cardoso when he was minister of the economy, the Real Plan redenominated wages, prices, taxes, and the exchange rate in a new accounting unit called the *urv.* Later, a new currency, the real, was introduced. Contractionary monetary policies were undertaken. Unlike many previous attempts, the Real Plan proved to be successful, neutralizing inflationary expectations and curbing inflation.

regional integration   Regional integration is the matching of economic and other policies within a region. The simplest form of integration is a free trade area (FTA) covering goods, with lower (or no) tariffs on goods exchanged within the region. The next level would include an FTA with services and perhaps regulations in other areas such as the environment or social concerns. A customs union deepens the commitment with a common external tariff. A common market permits the movement of factors of production among member countries, and an economic union expands on this to cede sovereignty over commercial, fiscal, and monetary policy to a supranational authority. Regional integration may make the liberalization process politically palatable through playing on sentiments of reciprocity of neighbor markets, and it may improve the confidence of investors because policies of openness have been locked in by treaty.

repartida   Monopoly control over mines and land in the New World was accorded through the *encomienda* system, which gave land rights to colonists, with a share of the output or *repartida* owed in return back to the home country.

returned value   Revenue earned through exports that is retained by a country.

safe minimum standard   The highest level of pollution that a society can safely tolerate with the reasonable expectation that future generations will not be made worse off by the choice.

secondary market   A market for a financial instrument that separates the initial debt issuer from the eventual lender. During the debt crisis, many banks were pessimistic about the ability of Latin American countries to repay loans. In particular, small- and medium-sized banks wanted to unload risky loans and offered them for resale below their face value in the secondary market. Larger banks (with a greater likelihood of being repaid) or multinational corporations interested in operating in a foreign market might choose to assume this credit risk at a discounted price. The larger bank or firm might, for example, pay 50 cents for a piece of paper saying that the borrowing country owed it a dollar. The greater the risk of default, the lower the secondary market price. Buyers of the debt could earn a substantial profit if a Latin American country paid off its debt in full, or in any proportion higher than what the debt was bought for.

segmented credit markets   Different groups of borrowers are assigned different prices for loans, and barriers between the groups prevent arbitrage from evening out the spread in interest rates. These barriers might be geographic distances or may be cultural or social differences that keep one group—perhaps poor minority women—separated from another portion of the population.

seignorage   An increase in the money supply by the mere printing of more currency, usually for the purpose of financing government spending. A government can profit from such an operation because it results in inflation. The government then is able to repay its debts in currency that is worth less than the currency that was borrowed. The result of monetary expansion might be short-run expansion of output, but eventually the increase in money will mean only an increase in prices.

severe stabilization   The first and often very painful stage of macroeconomic adjustment designed to bring macroeconomic fundamentals into line.

short-term money   This includes the "hot" capital flow of portfolio bonds and stocks that may be moved from country to country in an internationally linked global financial system with the stroke of a keyboard.

social investment funds   Targeted emergency aid for poverty reduction.

sovereign guarantee   The backing of a national government (collateralized by national assets) in the extension of a loan.

Stolper–Samuelson effect   As the price of the more abundant (and cheaper) factor rises after an opening of trade, the owners of this factor—in the case of the developing countries, labor—will accrue the largest gain. Trade should therefore make owners of the cheapest factor better off.

structural adjustment programs   Often supported by the World Bank and the IMF, these programs are designed to address internal and external balance by decreasing domestic expenditure, enhancing revenue collection, promoting exports, and limiting luxury imports. These programs changed the shape or structure of economies from the inward-oriented import substitution model to an externally oriented export promotion program, simultaneously privatizing state industries, decreasing government expenditures, and encouraging inflows of foreign capital.

structuralists   Drawing on the work of the Economic Commission for Latin America (ECLA) under Raúl Prebisch, structuralists begin from the assumption that the underlying structure of developing economies differs from that of more industrialized nations. Macro policy for structuralists rests on the premise that relatively concentrated industrial elites can pass on price increases, resulting in inertial inflation. Structuralists tend to downplay the importance of fiscal balance in favor of an activist state policy to redress production bottlenecks. Structuralists and their intellectual descendants, the neostructuralists, have little faith in the ability of the market to generate spontaneous or equitable growth. Borrowing from dependency analysts, structuralists believe that the position of countries in the international system, especially their access to technology, limits possibilities for autonomous growth. Although neostructuralists appreciate the benefits of international trade and finance, they caution that states should intervene to mitigate the social and environmental costs of openness.

structural transformation   The second stage of economic adjustment designed to change the shape of the economy, particularly with respect to decreasing the active role of the state and increasing the economy's orientation to the international market.

sustainable development   Development strategies that will meet today's needs without sacrificing the ability of future generations to meet their own needs.

targeting   A method of allocating social expenditures by identifying and distributing funds to those most in need. Targeted policies have often replaced general programs such as price subsidies on tortillas or milk that could not distinguish between the needy and the well-off. An example of a targeted policy would be a food debit card that is replenished when a mother brings a child to a clinic for preventive child care.

technological change   The key to economic development, technological change allows for new combinations of capital and labor to create more efficient production.

tesobono   A dollar-denominated treasury bond offered by the Mexican government during the Mexican financial crisis. The bonds were structured to convince investors to keep their capital in Mexico by eliminating exchange risk. After a series of political events that deepened the crisis and scared capital away, the *tesobono* led to a further depletion of dollar reserves because the Mexican government had to cover its dollar-based obligations.

theory of comparative advantage   This theory states that to maximize global output, each country should apply its resources to producing those goods that it can produce relatively most efficiently.

trade creation   A benefit of economic integration whereby a trade agreement leads to an increase in overall trade. An integration agreement has positive effects if trade creation exceeds trade diversion.

trade diversion   An effect of economic integration, when trade with a more efficient global producer is discontinued in favor of products from a regional trading partner.

transnational corporations (TNCs)   Transnational corporations, also known as multinational corporations (MNCs) and transnational enterprises (TNEs), are firms with central offices located in one country but with operations abroad. Transnational corporations are the primary form of foreign direct investment. TNCs bring capital, expertise, and jobs but also may thwart the growth of local industries and have been accused of exploiting low-wage workers.

transparency   A policy principle that encourages governments to implement effective anticorruption laws and policies, promotes reform through international organizations, and raises public awareness of the business of governance.

urbanization   The growth of large cities. The high levels of urban living in Latin America, with rates in Argentina, Brazil, Venezuela, Uruguay, and Chile higher than that of the United States, create enormous environmental difficulties.

value added tax (VAT)   A consumption tax levied on the value added at each stage of production. The advantage of the VAT over other tax instruments is its self-regulating mechanism. Each producer requires a receipt from its supplier to demonstrate that taxes already have been paid on the earlier levels of production.

velocity of money   The amount of national output supported by the money supply; mathematically, it is expressed as GDP/M, or gross domestic product divided by the money supply. Velocity is higher when a small stock of money supports a higher level of output. The higher the velocity, the larger the effect of any increase in the money supply.

water rights   A critical element in agricultural policy. Access to water rights, if accrued on the basis of seniority or local power, often interferes with the efficient allocation of resources in an agricultural community.

World Summit on Sustainable Development (WSSD)   In Johannesburg during 2002, the WSSD brought together tens of thousands of participants, including heads of state and government, national delegates and leaders from NGOs, businesses, and other major groups to focus global attention and direct action toward meeting difficult development challenges, including improving people's lives and conserving our natural resources in a world that is growing in population, with ever-increasing demands for food, water, shelter, sanitation, energy, health services, and economic security.

BIBLIOGRAPHY

Abdelal, Rawi. *The State*. Harvard Business School case #9-701-077. Boston: Harvard Business School, 2001.

Abramo, Laís, and María Elena Valenzuela. "Women's Labour Force Participation Rates in Latin America." *International Labour Review* 144(4) (2005): 369–399.

Acemoglu, Daron. "Root Causes: A Historical Approach to Assessing the Role of Institutions in Economic Development." *Finance & Development* (June 2003): 27–30.

Acemoglu, Daron, Simon Johnson, and James Robinson. "Institutions as the Fundamental Cause of Long-Run Growth." Chapter 6 in *Handbook of Economic Growth*, ed. Philippe Aghion and Steven Durlauf. Amsterdam: Elsevier, 2005.

Acevedo, Carlos, Deborah Barry, and Herman Rosa. "El Salvador's Agricultural Sector: Macroeconomic Policy, Agrarian Change and the Environment." *World Development* 23(12) (1995).

Action Plan for Universal and Quality Basic Education by the Year 2000, Summit of the Americas. Available online at www.summit-americas.org.

Adelman, Carol. "Aid and Comfort." Tech Central Station, August 21, 2002, www.global issues.org.

Adelman, Irma, and Cynthia Taft Morris. "Development History and Its Implications for Development Theory." *World Development* 25(6) (June 1997): 841–840.

Adriance, Jim. "Living with the Land in Central America." *Grassroots Development* 19(1) (1995).

Agarwala, A. N., and S. P. Singh, eds. *The Economics of Underdevelopment*. New York: Oxford University Press, 1963.

Aggio, Carlos. "A Case Study on Debt Conversion, Spain and Argentina," May 2005. Background paper prepared for the Education for All Global Monitoring Report 2006, Literacy for Life, unesdoc.unesco.org.

Alderman, Harold, and Victory Lavy. "Household Responses to Public Health Services: Cost and Quality Tradeoffs." *World Bank Research Observer* 11(1) (February 1996): 3–22.

Alfaro, Laura, and Eliza Hammel. "Latin American Multinationals." In *Latin America Competitiveness Report* (Geneva, Switzerland: World Economic Forum, April 2006).

Alix-Garcia, Jennifer, Alain de Janvry, and Elisabeth Sadoulet. "A Tale of Two Communities: Explaining Deforestation in Mexico." *World Development* 33(2) (February 2005): 219–235.

Althaus, Dudley. "Deforestation Contributed to Tragedy by Mitch in Honduras, Experts Claim." *Houston Chronicle,* December 30, 1998, A1, as found in the LEXIS-NEXIS database.

Alves, Denisard, and Walter Belluzzo. "Child Health and Infant Mortality in Brazil." IADB Latin American Research Network Working Paper No. R-493, April 2005.

Amann, Edmund, and Werner Baer. "Anchors Away: The Costs and Benefits of Brazil's Devaluation." *World Development* 31(6) (June 2003): 1033–1046.

"Amazon Suffers the Worst Drought in 50 Years." *Latinnews Daily,* October 19, 2005.

Amedo, Eduardo, José Márcio Camargo, Antônio Emilío S. Marques, and Cândido Gomes. "Fiscal Crisis and Asymmetries in the Education System in Brazil." In *Coping with Crisis: Austerity, Adjustment, and Human Resources,* ed. Joel Samoff. New York: UNESCO/ILO, 1994.

Ameur, Charles. *Agricultural Extension: A Step beyond the Next Step.* World Bank Technical Paper No. 247. Washington, D.C.: World Bank, 1994.

Anayiotos, George, and Jaime de Piniés. "The Secondary Market and the International Debt Problem." *World Development* 18(2) (1990): 1655–1660.

Anderson, Sarah, and John Cavanagh. *The Rise of Corporate Global Power.* Institute for Policy Studies, December 2000.

Anderson, Sarah, and Karen Hansen-Kuhn. *America's Plan for the Americas.* Washington, D.C.: Alliance, February 2001.

Aninat, Eduardo. "Growth and Stability in Latin America and the Caribbean: Challenges for the Epoch of Globalization." Lecture presented for the IMF in Port of Spain, May 26, 2000.

Anonymous. "Health of Indigenous Peoples." *Pan American Journal of Public Health* 2(25) (1997): 357–362.

Antle, John M., and Gregg Heidebrink. "Environment and Development: Theory and International Evidence." *Economic Development and Cultural Change* 43(3) (April 1995).

"Argentina, Brazil Agree on Regulating Bilateral Trade." *La Nacion—Argentina,* distributed by Latin America News Digest, February 2, 2006.

Argentina: Selected Issues and Statistical Annex. Report No. 00/160. Washington, D.C.: IMF, December 2000.

Argentina Business: The Portable Encyclopedia for Doing Business with Argentina. San Rafael, Calif.: World Trade Press, 1995.

"Argentina's New Struggle for Confidence and Growth." *The Economist,* November 18, 2000.

"Argentine Leader Races to Prop Economy." The Associated Press. *New York Times,* July 16, 2001.

Arriagada, Irma. "Unequal Participation by Women in the Working World." *CEPAL Review* 40 (April 1990): 83–98.

Audley, John, Sandra Polaski, Demetrios G. Papademetriou, and Scott Vaughan. "Jobs, Wages, and Household Income," in *NAFTA's Promise and Reality: Lessons from Mexico and the Hemisphere.* Carnegie Endowment Report, November 2003.

Authers, John. "Mortgage Scheme Offers a Tiny Piece of Mexico." *Financial Times,* September 1, 2005, 212.

"Auto Industry Delivers Vote of Confidence in Brazil and Mercosur." *Latin American Weekly Report,* February 3, 1998.

Ayres, Robert L. *Crime and Violence As Development Issues in Latin America.* Washington, D.C.: World Bank, 1998.

Azzoni, Tales. "Latin America and Caribbean Nations Vow to Negotiate Price of AIDS Medication Together." *The Associated Press,* January 15, 2006.

Bacon, Christopher. "Confronting the Coffee Crisis: Can Fair Trade, Organic, and Specialty Coffees Reduce Small-Scale Farmer Vulnerability in Northern Nicaragua?" *World Development* 33(3) (March 2005): 497–511.

Baer, Werner. "Changing Paradigms: Changing Interpretations of the Public Sector in Latin America's Economies." *Public Choice* 88 (1996): 365–379.

———. "Latin America and Europe in the Nineteenth Century: The Impact of an Unequal Relationship." In *Development and Underdevelopment in America,* ed. Walther Bernecker and Hans Werner Tobler. New York: Walter de Gruyter, 1993.

Baer, Werner, and Melissa Birch, eds. *Privatization in Latin America.* Westport, Conn.: Praeger, 1994.

Baer, Werner, and Annibal V. Villela. "Privatization and the Changing Role of the State in Brazil." In *Privatization in Latin America,* ed. Werner Baer and Melissa Birch. Westport, Conn.: Praeger, 1994.

Bahamondes, Miguel. "Poverty-Environment Patterns in a Growing Economy: Farming Communities in Arid Central Chile, 1991–99." *World Development* 31(11) (November 2003): 1947–1957.

Baker, Gerard. "Argentina Awakens US Pragmatism." *Financial Times,* August 7, 2001.

Balch, Oliver. "Growth in Ecotourism—Take the Green Road." Ethical Corporation Conferences, January 4, 2006, www.ethicalcorp.com.

Baldwin, Robert E. "Openness and Growth: What's the Empirical Relationship?" National Bureau of Economic Research Working Paper, No. 9578, March 2003.

Baran, Paul A. "On the Political Economy of Backwardness." *Manchester School* 20(1) (1952). Reprinted in *The Economics of Underdevelopment,* ed. A. N. Agarwala and S. P. Singh. New York: Oxford University Press, 1963; and *Political Economy of Development and Underdevelopment,* ed. Charles K. Wilber. New York: Random House, 1973.

Baranyi, Stephen, Carmen Diana Deere, and Manuel Morales. "Land & Development in Latin America, Openings for Research." North-South Institute and International Development Research Center, www.idrc.ca.

Barbier, Edward. "Agricultural Expansion, Resource Booms and Growth in Latin America." *World Development* 32(1) (January 2004): 139.

Barclay, Eliza. "Mexican Migrant Communities May Be on Verge of HIV/AIDS Epidemic." September 2005, Population Reference Bureau, www.prb.org.

Barro, Robert J. "The Dollar Club: Why Countries Are So Keen to Join." *BusinessWeek,* December 11, 2000.

———. "From Seattle to Santiago, Let the Dollar Reign." *Hoover Digest* 3 (1999).

Bartlett, Christopher A., and Sumantra Ghoshal. "Going Global: Lessons from Late Movers." *Harvard Business Review* (March–April 2000).

Bastianensen, Johan. "Non-Conventional Rural Finance and the Crisis of Economic Institutions in Nicaragua." In *Sustainable Agriculture in Central America,* ed. Jan P. de Groot and Ruerd Ruben. New York: St. Martin's, 1997.

Bate, Peter. "Dollars for Everyone?" *IDB América* (May–June 1999).

———. "Education: The Gordian Knot." *IDB Today.* Online edition available at www.iadb.org/idbamerica.

Bauer, P., and B. Yamey. *The Economics of Underdeveloped Countries.* New York: Cambridge University Press, 1967.

Bellew, Rosemary T., and Elizabeth M. King. "Educating Women: Lessons from Experience." In *Women's Education in Developing Countries: Barriers, Benefits and Policies,* ed. Elizabeth M. King and Rosemary Bellew. Baltimore: Johns Hopkins University Press, 1993.

Bellos, Alex. "Ronaldo's Fame Hasn't Hit Home." *Minneapolis Star Tribune,* July 10, 1998, C6.

Benavente, José Miguel, Gustavo Crespi, Jorge Katz, and Giovanni Stumpo. "Changes in the Industrial Development of Latin America." *CEPAL Review* 60 (December 1996).

"The Benefits and Risks of Short-Term Borrowing." *Global Development Finance.* Washington, D.C.: World Bank, 2000.

Bennett, Bradley. "Plants and People of the Amazonian Rainforests: The Role of Ethnobotany in Sustainable Development." *BioScience* 42(8) (1992).

Benson, Todd. "Brazil's Big Stake in Cotton Likely to Become Bigger." *New York Times,* June 29, 2004.

Berg, Andrew, and Eduardo Borensztein. "The Dollarization Debate." *Finance & Development* (March 2000).

———. "Full Dollarization—The Pros and Cons." *International Monetary Fund Economic Issue* 24 (December 2000).

Berger, Marguerite. *Microfinance: An Emerging Market within the Emerging Markets.* Draft. Washington, D.C.: IADB, 2000.

Bergsten, Fred C. "American Politics, Global Trade." *The Economist,* September 27, 1997.

Bernstein, H., ed. *Underdevelopment and Development.* Harmondsworth, UK: Penguin, 1973.

Berstein, Aarn. "Sweatshop Reform: How to Solve the Standoff." *BusinessWeek,* May 3, 1999.

Bertola, Luis, and Jeffrey Williamson. "Globalization in Latin America before 1940." NBER Working Paper, No. W9687, May 2003, 4.

Bhagwati, Jagdish. "Fast Track to Nowhere." *The Economist,* October 18, 1997.

———. "The FTAA Is *Not* Free Trade." In *Trade: Towards Open Regionalism,* Proceedings of the 1997 World Bank Conference on Development in Latin America and the Caribbean. Washington, D.C.: World Bank, 1998.

Biersteker, Thomas J. *Dealing with Debt.* Boulder, Colo.: Westview, 1993.

———. *Distortion or Development? Contending Perspectives on the Multinational Corporation.* Cambridge, Mass.: MIT Press, 1978.

Binswanger, Hans P., and Klaus Deininger. "Explaining Agricultural and Agrarian Policies in Developing Countries." *Journal of Economic Literature* 35 (December 1997).

Birdsall, Nancy, and Augusto de la Torre. "Washington Contentious." Commission on Economic Reform in Unequal Latin American Societies, sponsored by the Carnegie Endowment for International Peace and the Inter-American Dialogue, 2001.

Birdsall, Nancy, and Carlos Lozada. "Prebish Reconsidered: Coping with External Shocks in Vulnerable Economies." *CEPAL Review* (October 2000).

———. "Recurring Themes in Latin American Economic Thought: From Prebisch to the Market and Back." In *Securing Stability and Growth in Latin America,* ed. Ricardo Hausmann and Helmut Reisen. Paris: OECD Publications, 1996.

Birdsall, Nancy, and John Nellis. "Winners and Losers: Assessing the Distributional Impact of Privatization." *World Development* 31(10) (October 2003): 1626–1643.

Bitran, Eduardo, and Pablo Serra. "Regulation of Privatized Utilities: The Chilean Experience." *World Development* 26(6) (1998): 945–962.

Blackwood, D. L., and R. G. Lynch. "The Measurement of Inequality and Poverty." *World Development* 22(4) (1994): 567–578.

Blazquez, Jorge, and Javier Santiso. "Mexico: Is It an Ex-Emerging Market?" *Journal of Latin American Studies,* 36 (2004): 297–318.

Blomström, Magnus, and Ari Kokko. *Regional Integration and Foreign Direct Investment.* National Bureau of Economic Research Working Paper No. 6019. Cambridge, Mass.: National Bureau of Economic Research, 1997.

Blomström, Magnus, and Edward N. Wolff. "Multinational Corporations and Productivity Convergence in Mexico." In *Convergence of Productivity: Cross-National Studies and Historical Evidence,* ed. William Baumol, Richard R. Nelson, and Edward N. Wolff. New York: Oxford University Press, 1994.

Bloom, D., D. Canning, and J. Sevilla. "The Demographic Dividend: A New Perspective on the Economic Consequences of Population Change." 2003, www.policyproject.com/pubs/generalreport/demo_div.pdf.

Bloomberg Latin America. "Argentine Markets Climb after IMF, Banks Move to Shore Up Confidence." Retrieved July 14, 1999, from www.quote.bloomberg.com.

"Blooming Desert: Peru." *The Economist,* July 9, 2005.

Blumenstein, Rebecca. "GM to Build a Low-Priced Car in Brazil." *Wall Street Journal,* 19 March 1997.

Blustein, Paul. "Currencies in Crisis." *Washington Post,* February 7, 1999.

"Bolivia: Getting Kids Back in School." *IDB América* (November 1997): 14. Available at www.iadb.org/English/projects/projects.html.

Bonior, Congressman David. "I Told You So." *New York Times,* editorial, July 13, 1997.

Bordo, Michael, and Christopher Meisner. "Financial Crises 1880–1913: The Role of Foreign Currency Debt." In *Growth Institutions and Crises: Latin America from a Historical Perspective,* ed. Sebastian Edwards. Washington, D.C.: National Bureau of Economic Research, 2005.

Borenstein, E., J. De Gregorio, and J. W. Lee. "How Does Foreign Investment Affect Economic Growth?" *Journal of International Economics* 45 (1998): 115–135.

Bowman, Kirk, and Jesus Felipe. *Convergence, Catch Up, and the Future of Latin America* (Atlanta: Georgia Institute of Technology). Unpublished paper, October 17, 2000. Access at pro.harvard.edu/papers/020/020015BowmanKirk.pdf.

Bowman, Kirk S. "Should the Kuznets Effect Be Relied on to Induce Equalizing Growth?" *World Development* 25(1) (1997): 127–143.

Boyd, Stephanie. "A Natural Weapon for Preventing Malaria in the Peruvian Amazon." *Science from the Developing World,* January 19, 2001.

Bradford, Colin, Jr. "Future Policy Directions and Relevance." In *The Legacy of Raúl Prebisch,* ed. Enrique V. Iglesias. Washington, D.C.: IADB, 1994.

Braga, Carlos Alberto Primo. "Tropical Forests and Trade Policy: The Case of Indonesia and Brazil." In *International Trade and the Environment,* ed. Patrick Low. Washington, D.C.: World Bank, 1992.

Brainard, S. Lael, and David Riker. *Are U.S. Multinationals Exporting U.S. Jobs?* National Bureau of Economic Research Working Paper No. 5958. Cambridge, Mass: National Bureau of Economic Research, 1997.

Braverman, Avishay, and J. Luis Guasch. "Administrative Failures in Government Credit Programs." In *The Economics of Rural Organization,* ed. Karla Hoff, Avishay Braverman, and Joseph Stiglitz. New York: Oxford University Press/World Bank, 1993.

"Brazil: Domestic Debt Dynamics and Implications." *ING Barings Emerging Markets Weekly Report,* March 5, 1999, 1–3.

"Brazil Boosts Border Surveillance as Bolivia Plans to Up Coca Production." *BBC Monitoring Latin America,* December 22, 2005.

"Brazil's Affluent Are Hurt by Crisis." *Washington Post,* January 25, 1999.

"Brazil's Iron King." *Financial Times,* June 29, 1998.

"Brazil's Neighbors Are Very Nervous." *BusinessWeek,* November 17, 1997.

Britan, Ricardo, and Keith McInnes. *The Demand for Health Care in Latin America.* Economic Development Institute Seminar Paper No. 46. Washington, D.C.: World Bank, 1993.

Britto, Tatiana. "Recent Trends in the Development Agenda of Latin America: An Analysis of Conditional Cash Transfers." Brazilian Ministry of Social Development, February 2005, tatib@brturbo.com.br.

Britton, John A., ed. *Molding the Hearts and Minds: Education, Communications and Social Change in Latin America.* Wilmington, Del.: Scholarly Resources, 1994.

Brodzinsky, Sibylla. "Pulling Colombia's Coca by Hand." *Christian Science Monitor,* February 24, 2006, 7.

Brooke, James. "Home, Home on the Range, in Brazil's Heartland." *New York Times,* April 26, 1995.

Brookings Institution, World Bank, and IMF. *Emerging Market Economies Recover, but Debt Restructuring Problems Linger On.* News Release, 2001. Available at www.brookings.edu/com/news/0004WBIMF.htm.

Bruton, Henry. "Import Substitution." In *Handbook of Development Economics,* vol. 2, 3rd ed., ed. Hollis Chenery and T. N. Srivivasan. New York: Elsevier, 1996.

———. "A Reconsideration of Import Substitution." *Journal of Economic Literature* 36 (June 1998).

Bulmer-Thomas, Victor. "The Brazilian Devaluation: National Responses and International Consequences." *International Affairs* 75(4) (1999).

———. *The Economic History of Latin America since Independence.* New York: Cambridge University Press, 1994.

Buntin, John, and Christine Letts. *Accion International: Where Latin America Meets Brooklyn.* Cambridge, Mass.: John F. Kennedy School of Government, 1996.

Burbach, Roger, and Peter Rosset. "Chiapas and the Crisis of Mexican Agriculture." *Food First Policy Brief,* No. 1. San Francisco: Institute for Food and Development, 1994.

Burki, Shahid Javed, and Sebastian Edwards. *Dismantling the Populist State.* Washington, D.C.: World Bank, 1996.

———. *Latin America after Mexico: Quickening the Pace.* Washington, D.C.: World Bank, 1996.

Burns, Bradford E., ed. *Latin America: Conflict and Creation: A Historical Reader.* Englewood Cliffs, N.J.: Prentice Hall, 1992.

Burns, Tom. "Telefonica Moviles Expands Its Latin American Empire: Mexican Purchase Sharpens Interest Ahead of Listening." *Financial Times,* October 5, 2000.

Buvinic, Mayra, and Andrew Morrison. "How Can We Measure Violence?" *Social Development* (July 2000).

———. *Women in Poverty: A New Global Underclass.* Washington, D.C: IADB, Women in Development, N WID-101, July 1998, p. 2. www.iadb.org/sds/doc/767eng.pdf.

Byrnes, H., and B. Spencer. "U.S. Must Aid Guatemala's Shift to Peace." *St. Louis Post-Dispatch,* December 20, 1996.

Caballero, Ricardo J. *Macroeconomic Volatility in Latin America: A View and Three Case Studies.* Working Paper 7782. Massachusetts: National Bureau of Economic Research, July 2000.

"CAFTA Accord." *Oxford Analytica,* Latin America Daily Briefs, February 2, 2004.

"CAFTA's Missed Opportunities." *Bulletin of the Washington Office on Latin America,* March 2004.

Calcagno, Alfredo, Sandra Manuelito, and Gunilla Ryd. *Proyecciones Latinoamericanos 2000–2001.* Santiago, Chile: United Nations and ECLAC, January 2001.

Caldwell, Laura. "Swapping Debt to Preserve Nature." *Christian Science Monitor,* September 11, 1990.

Calo, Muriel, and Timothy A. Wise. "Revaluing Peasant Coffee Production: Organic and Fair Trade Markets in Mexico." Global Development and Environment Institute, Tufts University, October 2005.

Camargo, José Márcio. "Mercosur: Greater Protection Tends to Hurt Smaller Bloc Members." *Tendencias,* January 19, 2006.

Camdessus, Michel. "The Private Sector in a Strengthened Global Financial System." Remarks at the International Monetary Conference, Philadelphia, June 8, 1999. Available at www.imf.org/external/speeches.

CAMTIC. "Cámara Castarvicense de Technología de Información y Comunicación." Projects web page, www.camtic.org/EN/camtic/proyectos_cooperacion/ICCI_en.phtml.

"CANTV in 1994." *Harvard Business School Case Studies,* February 28, 1996.

"Capital Controversies." *The Economist,* May 23, 1998.

Cardoso, Eliana. "Brazil's Currency Crisis." In *Exchange Rate Politics in Latin America,* ed. Carol Wise and Riordan Roett, 70–92. Washington, D.C.: Brookings Institution Press, 2000.

Cardoso, Fernando Henrique. Interview on the occasion of the second anniversary of the Real Plan, as reported in FBIS-LAT-96-129 (Foreign Broadcast Information Services, Latin America), July 3, 1996. Originally appeared on the Rede Globo website, July 1, 1996.

Carnegie Endowment for International Peace. *Working Papers—Breaking the Labor-Trade Deadlock,* No. 17. Washington, D.C.: Inter-American Dialogue and the Carnegie Endowment for International Peace, February 2001.

Carnoy, Martin. "Structural Adjustment and the Changing Face of Education." *International Labor Review* 134(6) (1995): 653–673.

Cartaya, Vanessa F. "El Confuso mundo del sector informal." *Nueva Sociedad* 90 (July–August 1987): 81–84.

Carter, Michael, and Bradford Barham. "Level Playing Fields and Laissez Faire: Postliberal Development Strategy in Inegalitarian Agrarian Economies." *World Development* 24(7) (July 1996).

Carter, Michael, and Dina Mesbah. "State-Mandated and Market-Mediated Reform in Latin America." In *Including the Poor,* ed. Michael Lipton and Jacques van der Gaag. Baltimore: Johns Hopkins University Press/World Bank, 1993.

Case, Brendan M. "Mexican Tariff on U.S. Beef Ignites Trade Dispute." *Dallas Morning News,* August 3, 1999.

Castañeda, Tarsicio. "Combating Poverty." In *Reforms in Education.* San Francisco: International Center for Economic Growth, 1992.

Catán, Thomas. "Argentina Looks to $6bn IMF Injection." *Financial Times,* August 6, 2001.

Caves, Richard E. *Multinational Enterprise and Economic Analysis,* 2nd ed. Cambridge: Cambridge University Press, 1996.

Center for International Health Information. *Country Health Profile/Bolivia.* Arlington, Va.: Center for International Health Information, December 1996. Available at www.cihi.com.

Central Intelligence Agency. *The World Fact Book.* Available at www.odci.gov/cia.

Cevallos, Diego. "Environment-Mexico: Toxic Waste, a Dirty Problem." Inter Press Service, August 11, 1995. Available on the LEXIS-NEXIS database.

———. "Foreign Corporations Backing Off." *Tierramérica,* March 16, 2006.

———. "Latin America: Farm Exports Grow, but Who Reaps the Harvest?" *IPS-Inter Press Service/Global Information Network,* November 8, 2005.

Chami, Ralph, Connel Fullenkamp, and Samir Jahjah. "Are Immigrant Remittance Flows a Source of Capital for Development?" *IMF Staff Papers* 52(1) (2005).

Chauvin, Lucian. "With Money Sent from the US Peruvians Buy Homes." *Christian Science Monitor,* July 13, 2005, 14.

Chile Facts on Demand. (via fax: 1-888-821-2424, Doc. ID#260) as found at www.american .edu/initeb/dc4388a/TI.html.

"China Ascendant: A Snapshot of Economic Performance." *Ideas* 6 (January–April 2005), www.iadb.org.

Chipman, Andre. "U.S., Latin-American Oil Companies Build Alliance As Mideast Clout Fades." *Wall Street Journal,* March 9, 1998.

Choque Schulter, Sidney, and Ruth Choque Schulter. "Misinformation, Mistrust, and Mistreatment: Family Planning among Bolivian Market Women." *Studies in Family Planning* 25 (1994).

Chronic Poverty Research Center. "The Chronic Poverty Report 2004–5." Manchester, UK: University of Manchester, www.chronicpoverty.org.

"Chronology of FTAA Process." Free Trade Area of the Americas.

Cifuentes, A., R. Krupnick, M. Ryan, and P. Toman. "Health Benefits of Reducing Air Pollution in Latin America." Society for Risk Analysis Annual Meeting 2004, lac@ing.puc.cl.

Cimoli, Mario, João Carlos Ferraz, and Annalisa Primi. "Science and Technology Policies in Open Economies: The Case of Latin America and the Caribbean." *Economic Commission for Latin America and the Caribbean,* Productive Development Series, No. 165 (Directors Office), October 2005, www.eclac.cl/.

"Citizen's Guide to Dollarization." Committee Documents Online—106th Congress. Senate Banking Committee, 2000. Available at www.banking.senate.gov/docs/reports/doillar.htm.

Clements, Benedict. "The Real Plan, Poverty, and Income Distribution in Brazil." *Finance and Development* (September 1997).

Clendenning, Alan. "From Wine to Washing Machines, South American Trade Zone Faces New Challenges." *Associated Press,* February 15, 2006.

Coatsworth, John. "Notes on the Comparative Economic History of Latin America and the United States." In *Development and Underdevelopment in America,* ed. Walther Bernecker and Hans Werner Tobler. New York: Walter de Gruyter, 1993.

Coatsworth, John H., and Jeffrey G. Williamson. "Always Protectionist? Latin American Tariffs Independence to the Great Depression." *Journal of Latin American Studies* 36(2) (May 2004): 205–232.

Coes, Donald V. *Macroeconomic Crises, Policies, and Growth in Brazil, 1964–90.* Washington, D.C.: World Bank, 1995.

Colclough, Christopher. "Education and the Market: Which Parts of the Neoliberal Solution Are Correct?" *World Development* 24(4) (1996): 589–610.

Colitt, Raymond. "Banking and Telecom Sectors Lead the Way: Brazil's New IT Markets." *Financial Times,* November 1, 2000.

"Coming Up Roses." *Latin American Economy & Business,* Intelligence Research Ltd., October 25, 2005.

Comision Económica Para América Latina. *Indicadores Económicos.* Santiago, Chile: Comision Económica Para América Latina, 1997.

"Commercial Debt Restructuring." *Global Development Finance.* Washington, D.C.: World Bank.

Commission on Development and Environment for Amazonia. *Amazonia without Myths.* Washington, D.C.: IADB, 1992.

"Competitiveness Is Vital." *Financial Times,* December 14, 2000.

Conger, Lucy. "A Fourth Way? The Latin American Alternative to Neoliberalism." *Current History,* November 1998.

Constance, Paul. "A High Technology Incubator." *IDB América,* 1997. Available at www.iadb.org.

———. "Lousy Deal." *IDB América,* May–June 2000.

———. "The New Referees." *IDB América,* January–February 1998.

———. "A Seat at the Table: Union Leaders Urge IDB to Include Workers' Concerns in Reform Programs and Free Trade Negotiations." *IDB América,* April 1998. Available at www.iadb.org.

———. "A Smoother Road." *IDB Americas,* March 2006, www.iadb.org/idbamerica.

Contreras Murphy, Ellen. "La Selva and the Magnetic Pull of Markets: Organic Coffee-Growing in Mexico." *Grassroots Development* 19(1) (1995): 27–34.

Cooper, William H. "Free Trade Agreements: Impact on US Trade and Implications for US Trade Policy." Congressional Research Service Report RL31356, Washington, D.C., Library of Congress, December 6, 2005.

Corbo, Vittorio. "Economic Policies and Performance in Latin America." In *Economic Development: Handbook of Comparative Economic Policies,* ed. Enzo Grilli and Dominick Salvatore. Westport, Conn.: Greenwood, 1994.

Cortés-Salas, Hernán, Ronnie de Camino, and Arnoldo Contreras. Readings of the *Workshop on Government Policy Reform for Forestry Conservation and Development in Latin America,* June 1–3, 1994. Washington, D.C.: Inter-American Institute for Cooperation on Agriculture, 1995.

"Cost-Cutting Takes a Private Road." *Euromoney,* September 1996.

"Cost Information and Management Decision in a Brazilian Hospital." In *World Development Report 1993.* New York: Oxford University Press/World Bank, 1993.

Council on Foreign Relations. "Reforming Education in America." Study group on reforming education in Latin America, "The Second Wave of Reform," February–October 1996.

"Creating Jobs Is Main Headache." *Latin American Weekly Report,* January 5, 1999.

"Crime Could Drive Sony from Mexico." *Gazette,* May 10, 2000.

Cuddington, John T. *Capital Flight: Estimates, Issues, and Explanations.* Princeton Studies in International Finance No. 58. Princeton, N.J.: Princeton University Press, 1986.

Cypher, James, and James Dietz, *The Process of Economic Development* (New York: Routledge, 1997), cited by Miguel D. Ramirez, "Foreign Direct Investment in Mexico and Chile: A Critical Appraisal," in *Foreign Direct Investment in Latin America,* ed. Werner Baer and William R. Miles. New York: The Hayworth Press, 2001.

Dadus, Uri, Dipak Dasgupta, and Dilip Ratha. "The Role of Short-Term Debt in Recent Crises." *Finance & Development,* December 2000.

Davies, Paul J., Joanna Chung, and Kevin Allison. "Brazil Raises $1.5 Billion." *Financial Times,* September 20, 2005.

Davis, Bob. "Guatemala Logs Progress." *Wall Street Journal,* November 25, 2005, A9.

"Deal of the Year 2005: Core Transformation." *LatinFinance,* February 2006, 24.

"Debt Relief for Poor Countries (HIPC): What Has Been Achieved?—A Factsheet." *International Monetary Fund* (April 2001).

"Declaration and Action Plan for Latin American Economic Recovery." *UN Chronicle* 21(3) (March 1984): 13–17.

Deen, Thalif. "The Pros and Cons of Rising Oil Prices." *IPS Terraviva,* April 21, 2006.

Deere, Carmen Diana. "The Feminization of Agriculture: Economic Restructuring in Rural Latin America." UNRISD Occasional Paper No.1, February 2005.

Deere, Carmen Diana, and Magdalena Leon. "The Gender Asset Gap: Land in Latin America." *World Development* 31(6) (June 2003): 925–947.

———. "Institutional Reform of Agriculture under Neoliberalism." *Latin American Research Review* 36(2) (2001).

de Ferranti, David, Guillermo Perry, Francisco H. G. Ferreira, and Michael Walton. *Inequality Latin America & the Caribbean: Breaking with History?* Washington, D.C.: World Bank, 2003.

De Gortari, Carlos Salinas, and Roberto Mangabeira Unger. "The Market Turn without Neoliberalism." *Challenge* 42(1) (January–February 1999).

Deininger, Klaus. *Land Policies for Growth and Poverty Reduction,* Washington, D.C: World Bank and Oxford University Press, 2003.

De Janvry, Alain, and Elisabeth Sadoulet. "Making Conditional Cash Transfer Programs More Efficient: Designing for Maximum Effect of Conditionality." *World Bank Economic Review* 20(1) (2006): 1–29. Available at www.wber.oxfordjournals.org.

———. "NAFTA and Mexico's Maize Producers." *World Development* 23(8) (August 1995): 1349–1362.

———. "Rural Development in Latin America: Relinking Poverty Reduction to Growth." In *Including the Poor,* ed. Michael Lipton and Jacques van der Gaag. Washington, D.C.: World Bank, 1993.

De la Torre, Augusto, and Sergio Schmulker. "Whither Latin American Capital Markets?" Working Paper, Office of the Chief Economist, The World Bank, October 2004.

della Paolera, Gerardo, and Alan Taylor. *Finance and Development in an Emerging Market: Argentina in the Interwar Period.* National Bureau of Economic Research Working Paper Series No. 6236. Cambridge, Mass.: National Bureau of Economic Research, 1997.

Dellios, Hugh. "Storms Leave Guatemalans in Food Crisis." *Chicago Tribune,* November 18, 2005.

Delovitch, Emanuel, and Klas Ringskog. *Private Sector Participation in Water Supply and Sanitation in Latin America.* Washington, D.C.: World Bank, 1995.

Delph, Yvette M. "Health Priorities in Developing Countries." *Journal of Law, Medicine, & Ethics* 21(1) (1993).

Denes, Christian Andrew. "Bolsa Escola: Redefining Poverty and Development in Brazil." *International Education Journal* 4(2) (2003).

DePalma, Anthony. "Free Trade's Promise in Latin America; the Poor Survive It All. Even Boom Times." *New York Times,* June 24, 2001.

———. "Passing the Torch on a Chile Trade Deal." *New York Times,* January 7, 2001.

Derham, Michael Thomas. "A Less Uncertain World." *LatinFinance,* July 2005, 44.

De Souza, Amaury. "Redressing Inequalities: Brazil's Social Agenda at Century's End." In *Brazil under Cardoso,* ed. Susan Kaufman Purcell and Riordan Roett. Boulder, Colo.: Rienner, 1997.

Devlin, Robert, and Ricardo Ffrench-Davis. *Toward an Evaluation of Regional Integration in Latin America in the 1990s.* Working Paper No. 2. Buenos Aires: INTAL and ITD, 1998.

Devlin, Robert, Ricardo Ffrench-Davis, and Stephany Griffith-Jones. "Surges in Capital Flows and Development: An Overview of Policy Issues." In *Coping with Capital Surges,* ed. Ricardo Ffrench-Davis and Stephany Griffith-Jones. Boulder, Colo.: Rienner, 1995.

Dewees, Anthony, and Steven Klees. "Social Movements and the Transformation of National Policy: Street and Working Children in Brazil." *Comparative Education Review* 39(1) (1995).

DHS Report. "Domestic Violence Threatens Health of Children with Lower Immunization Rates, Higher Mortality Rates, Poor Nutrition." Press release, September 9, 2004.

Diáz Alejandro, Carlos. "International Markets for LDCs: The Old and the New." *American Economic Review* (May): 254–269.

Diaz Bonilla, Eugenio, and Hector E. Schamis. *The Political Economy of Exchange Rate Policies in Argentina, 1950–1998.* Working Paper #R-379. IADB, April 1999.

Dietz, James L., and James H. Street, eds. *Latin America's Economic Development: Institutionalist and Structuralist Perspectives.* Boulder, Colo.: Rienner, 1987.

Dijkstra, Geske. "The PRSP Approach and the Illusion of Improved Aid Effectiveness: Lessons from Bolivia, Honduras and Nicaragua." *Development Policy Review* 23(4): 443–464.

Dillin, John. "Crime Down, but Many Still Edgy." *Christian Science Monitor,* June 19, 2001.

Dixon, John. *The Urban Environmental Challenge in Latin America.* LATEN Dissemination Note No. 4, World Bank Latin America Technical Department, Environment Division. Washington, D.C.: World Bank, 1993.

Dmytraczenko, Tania, Vijay Rao, and Lori Ashford. "Health Sector Reform: How It Affects Reproductive Health, Population." Reference Bureau Policy Brief, June 2003, www.prb.org.

Dollar, David, and Aart Kraay. "Growth Is Good for the Poor." *Journal of Economic Growth* 7(3) (2002): 195–225.

"Dollarization: Fad or Future for Latin America." IMF Economic Forum. Washington, D.C.: International Monetary Fund, June 24, 1999.

Donoso-Clark, Maria. "Rural Development." In *Ecuador: An Economic and Social Agenda in the Millennium World Bank,* ed. Marcelo Giugale, Jose Roberto Lopez-Calix, and Vicente Fretes-Cibils, 369–387. Washington, D.C.: World Bank, 2003.

Dornbusch, Rudiger. *Stabilization, Debt, and Reform: Policy Analysis for Developing Countries.* Englewood Cliffs, N.J.: Prentice Hall, 1993.

Dornbusch, Rudiger, and Sebastian Edwards. "The Political Economy of Latin America." In *The Macroeconomics of Populism in Latin America* (A National Bureau of Economic Research Conference Report), ed. Rudiger Dornbusch and Sebastian Edwards. Chicago: University of Chicago Press, 1991.

Dos Santos, Theodoro. "La crisis de la teoría del desarollo y las relaciones de dependencia en América Latina." *Boletin de CESO* 3 (1968). English translation in H. Bernstein, ed., *Underdevelopment and Development.* Harmondsworth, UK: Penguin, 1973.

Drabek, Zdenek, and Warren Payne. "The Impact of Transparency on Foreign Direct Investment." IMF Staff Working Paper ERAD-99-02. Geneva: The World Trade Organization, 1999.

Druckerman, Pamela. "Argentina Wants to Speed or Boost Aid." *Wall Street Journal,* August 3, 2001.

———. "Argentine Bank Depositors Hold Reins of Nation's Fate. *Wall Street Journal,* July 17, 2001.

Druckerman, Pamela, Michael Phillips, Jonathan Karp, and Hugh Pope. "IMF Acts to Pre-empt Emerging-Market Crisis." *Wall Street Journal,* August 6, 2001.

Durlesser, Erin, Kerry Miller, and Olivia Perlmutt. "Malaria in Latin America: A Nutritional Problem." http://www.micronutrient.org/idpas/pdf/1961malariainla.pdf.

Duryea, Suzanne, and Maria Eugenia Genoni. "Ethnicity, Race and Gender in Latin American Labor Markets." In *Social Inclusion and Economic Development in Latin America,* ed. Mayra Buvinic and Jacqueline Mazza. Washington, D.C.: Inter-American Development Bank, 2004.

Dyer, Geoff. "Brazil Markets Maintain Boost from IMF Deal." *Financial Times,* August 7, 2001.

———. "Brazil's Star Pupil Status Gets a Caning." *Financial Times,* August 5, 2001.

Eakin, Ken. "Monitoring and Evaluating Poverty Alleviation Programs in Peru. *Science from the Developing World,* September 4, 2001.

Earthtrends. "Environmental Information" database, www.earthtrends.org.

Eberlee, John. "Agenda Peru: Charting a Shared National Vision for the Future." *Science from the Developing World,* March 23, 2001.

Echavarría, Juan José. "Trade Flow in the Andean Countries: Unilateral Liberalization or Regional Preferences." In *Trade: Towards Open Regionalism,* Proceedings of the 1997 World Bank Conference on Development in Latin America and the Caribbean. Washington, D.C.: World Bank, 1998.

ECLAC. "Balance preliminar de las economías de América Latina y el Caribe." www.eclac .cl/publicaciones/desarolloeconomico/3/LCG2153PE/lcg2153sur.pdf.

———. "El nuevo patron de desarrollo de la agricultura en América Latina y el Caribe." *Outlook 2005, The New Pattern of Development of Agriculture in Latin America and the Caribbean,* September 2005.

———. "Financing and Management of Education in Latin America and the Caribbean." July 2004, www.eclac.org.

———. "Latin America and the Caribbean in the World Economy, 2005 Trends." Santiago, Chile, United Nations, 2005.

———. "The Millennium Development Goals: A Latin American and Caribbean Perspective." Report Coordinated by José Luis Machinea, August 2005.

———. "Precarious Urban Conditions." Press release on study "Poverty and Precariousness in the Habitat of Latin America and the Caribbean Cities," January 18, 2005, www. eclac.org.

———. "Public Policies for the Development of Information Societies in Latin America and the Caribbean." June 2005, www.eclac.org.

————. "Social Panorama 2005." Press release, www.eclac.org.

ECLAC/UNDP. *Financing for Sustainable Development in Latin America and the Caribbean,* Joint document prepared for the World Summit on Sustainable Development, August 2002.

Economic Commission for Latin America and the Caribbean. *Communique on the International Financial Crises.* September 15, 1998. Available at www.cepal.org.english/coverpage/financialcrisis.htm.

————. *Economic Survey of Latin America and the Caribbean.* Santiago, Chile: ECLAC, various years.

————. *The Equity Gap: Latin America, the Caribbean, and the Social Summit.* Santiago, Chile: ECLAC, 1997.

————. *The Fiscal Covenant: Strengths, Weaknesses, Challenges.* Santiago, Chile: ECLAC, 1997.

————. *Foreign Investment in Latin America and the Caribbean, 2000,* table I.12, 65.

————. *Indicadores Económicos.* Santiago, Chile: ECLAC, 1997.

————. *Notes* N. 12, September 2000.

————. *Notes* N. 13, November 2000.

————. *Panorama de la Insercion Internactional de América Latina y el Caribe, 1996.* Santiago, Chile: ECLAC, 1996.

————. *Policies to Improve Linkages with the Global Economy.* Santiago, Chile: ECLAC, 1995.

————. *Preliminary Overview of the Economies of Latin America and the Caribbean, 1999.* Santiago, Chile: United Nations and ECLAC, December 1999.

————. *Statistical Yearbook for Latin American and the Caribbean, 1996.* Chile: ECLAC, 1996.

————. *Strengthening Development: The Interplay of Macro- and Microeconomics.* Santiago, Chile: ECLAC, 1996.

"Ecuador Drifts between Opportunity and Deadlock." *The Economist,* December 23, 2000.

Edwards, Sebastian. *Capital Flows into Latin America: A Stop-Go Story?* National Bureau of Economic Research Working Paper No. 6441. Cambridge, Mass. National Bureau of Economic Research, 1998. Available at www.nber.org/papers/w6441.

————. *Crisis and Reform in Latin America: From Despair to Hope.* New York: Oxford University Press, 1995.

————. "The Mexican Peso Crisis: How Much Did We Know? When Did We Know It?" *World Economy* 21(1) (1998).

————. "The Political Economy of Inflation and Stabilization in Developing Countries." *Economic Development and Cultural Change* 42(2) (January 1994): 235–266.

Edwards, Sebastian, and Daniel Lederman. *The Political Economy of Unilateral Trade Liberalization: The Case of Chile.* National Bureau of Economic Research Working Paper No. 6510. Cambridge, Mass.: National Bureau of Economic Research, 1998. Available at www.nber.org/papers/w6510.

Edwards, Sebastian, and Nora Claudia Lustig, eds. *Labor Markets in Latin America: Combining Social Protection with Market Flexibility.* Washington, D.C.: Brookings Institution, 1997.

Eichengreen, Barry. "When to Dollarize." Presented for the ITAM Dollarization Project Meeting in Mexico City, December 3, 1999.

Eichengreen, Barry, and Ricardo Hausman. "Original Sin: The Road to Redemption." *NBER,* January 2005.

El-Ashry, Mohamed T. *Statement to the Fourth Session of the Conference of the Parties to the*

United Nations Framework Convention on Climate Change. Buenos Aires, November 11, 1998. Washington, D.C.: Global Environment Facility, 1998.

Elliott, Kimberly Ann. "Trading Up: Labor Standards, Development and CAFTA." *CGD Brief* 3(2) (May 2004).

Ellison, Katherine. "Latin Summit's Focus: Education of Kids." *Miami Herald,* April 13, 1998, A1. Available at www.alca-cupula.org.

"El Salvador Environmental Services Project." Project Appraisal Document, 1, April 22, 2005.

"Emerging-Market Indicators." *The Economist,* November 4, 2000.

Emmott, Robin, "Bribery Costs Mexicans Up to 14% of Income." *Financial Times,* October 31, 2001.

Employment Policy Foundation. "Open Trade: The 'Fast Track' to Higher Living Standards." *Contemporary Issues in Employment and Workplace Policy* 111(10) (October 1997). Internet publication available at epfnet.org.

Energy Information Administration. *Petroleum Supply Annual, 1995.* Washington, D.C.: U.S. Department of Energy, 1995.

———. "World Proven Reserves of Oil and Natural Gas, Most Recent Estimates." Table posted January 18, 2006, http://www.eia.doe.gov/emeu/international/reserves.xls.

"Energy in Latin America: Even Oil Is Growing Less Sacred." *The Economist,* June 1, 1996.

Engell, Alan. "Improving the Quality and Equity of Education in Chile: The Programa 900 Escuelas and the MECE-Basica." In *Implementing Policy Innovation in Latin America: Politics, Economics and Techniques,* ed. Antonio Silva. Washington, D.C.: IADB, 1996.

The Equity Gap—A Second Assessment. Prepared by ECLAC Secretariat for the Second Regional Conference. ECLAC, 2000.

Ernst, Christoph. "Trade Liberalization, Export Orientation and Employment in Argentina, Brazil and Mexico." Employment Strategy Papers 2005-15, International Labour Office, 2005.

Escobar, Maria Luisa. "Health Sector Reform in Colombia Development Outreach." *World Bank Institute,* World Bank Special Report, May 2005, www.worldbank.org.

Espindola, Ernesto, Arturo Leon, Rodrigo Martinez, and Alexander Schejtman. "Poverty, Hunger and Food Insecurity in Central America and Panama." *CEPAL Serie Políticas Sociales* 88 (May 2005): 28.

Esquivel, Gerardo, and Graciela Marquez. "Some Economic Effects of Closing the Economy: The Mexican Experience in the Mid-Twentieth Century." In Sebastian Edwards, ed., *Capital Controls and Capital Flows in Emerging Economies: Policies, Practices and Consequences.* NBER, 2005, papers accessed at www.nber.org/books.

Estache, Antonio, and Danny Leipziger, "Utilities Privatization and the Poor: Lessons and Evidence from Latin America." *World Development* 29(7) (2001): 1181.

Estevadeordal, Antoni, and Kati Suominen. "Is All Well with the Spaghetti Bowl in the Americas?" *Economía* (Spring 2005): 63–103.

Estey, Daniel, Marc Levy, Tanja Srebotnjak, and Alexander de Sherbinin. "2006 Environmental Sustainability Index." New Haven: Yale Center for Environmental Law and Policy, www.yale.edu.

Evans, Peter. *Dependent Development.* Princeton, N.J.: Princeton University Press, 1979.

———. "The Eclipse of the State? Reflection on Stateness in an Era of Globalization." *World Politics* 50 (October 1997).

———, ed. "State-Society Synergy: Government and Social Capital in Development." *World Development* 24(6), special edition (June 1996).

Faiz, Asif, Surhid Gautam, and Emaad Burki. "Air Pollution from Motor Vehicles: Issues and Options for Latin American Countries." *The Science of the Total Environment* 169 (1995): 303–310.

Fajnzylber, Fernando. "Education and Changing Production Patterns with Social Equality." *CEPAL Review* 47 (August 1992).

Fanelli, José María, and Roberto Frenkel. "Macropolicies for the Transition from Stabilization to Growth." In *New Directions in Development Economics: Growth, Environmental Concerns, and Government in the 1990s,* ed. Mats Lundahl and Benno J. Ndulu. London: Routledge, 1996.

Fanelli, José Maria, and José Luis Machinea. "Capital Movements in Argentina." In *Coping with Capital Surges: The Return of Finance to Latin America,* ed. Ricardo Ffrench-Davis and Stephany Griffith-Jones. Boulder, Colo.: Rienner, 1995.

FAO. "Deforestation Rate 'Alarming,' but Net Loss Slowing." *Agence France-Presse,* November 14, 2005. Reprinted at the World Business Council for Sustainable Development, www.wbcsd.org.

———. "FAO and Brazil Prepare an International Conference." FAO Newsroom, November 24, 2005.

———. "FAO Regional Review Executive Summary," www.fao.org.

———. "The State of Food Insecurity in the World 2005," www.fao.org.

———. "Trends and Challenges in Agriculture, Forestry and Fisheries in Latin America and the Caribbean." *FAO Regional Review Executive Summary,* July 2005.

Farber, Daniel. *Environment under Fire.* New York: Monthly Review Press, 1993.

Farrell, Diana, Jaana K. Remes, and Heiner Schulz. "The Truth about Foreign Direct Investment in Emerging Markets." *McKinsey Quarterly* 1 (2004).

"Fast Facts on Microentrepreneurship: International Year of the Microcredit 2005." http://www.yearofmicrocredit.org/pages/reslib/reslib_recreading.asp.

Fauriol, Georges A., and Sidney Weintraub. "The Century of the Americas: Dawn of a New Century." *Washington Quarterly* 24(2) (Spring 2001).

Fearnside, Philip M. "Conservation Policy in Brazilian Amazonia: Understanding the Dilemmas." *World Development* 31(5) (May 2003): 757.

———. "Deforestation in Brazilian Amazonia: The Effect of Population and Land Tenure." *Ambio* 22(8) (December 1993).

Federal Reserve Bank of Atlanta. "Imbalances in Latin American Fiscal Accounts: Why the United States Should Care." *EconSouth* 2(4) (2000).

Federal Reserve Bank of San Francisco. "U.S. Inflation Targeting: Pro and Con." *FRBSF Economic Letter,* May 29, 1998, 98–118.

Fernández-Arias, Eduardo. "The New Wave of Capital Inflows: Sea Change or Tide?" Presented at the Annual Meeting of the Board of Governors, IADB and Inter-American Investment Corporation, March 26 2000.

Fernández-Arias, Eduardo, and Ricardo Hausmann. *Getting It Right: What to Reform in International Financial Markets.* Working Paper #428. Presented at the Tenth International Forum on Latin American Perspectives in Paris. IADB, November 1999.

———. *International Initiatives to Bring Stability to Financial Integration.* IADB, March 1999.

———. *What's Wrong with International Financial Markets?* Working Paper #429. Presented at the Tenth International Forum on Latin American Perspectives in Paris. IADB, November 1999.

Ffrench-Davis Ricardo. Comment on L. Allan Winters, "Assessing Regional Integration." In *Trade: Towards Open Regionalism,* Proceedings of the 1997 World Bank Conference on Development in Latin America and the Caribbean. Washington, D.C.: World Bank, 1998.

————. "Policy Implications of the Tequila Effect." *Challenge.* March–April 1998.

Ffrench-Davis Ricardo, Manuel Agosin, and Andras Uthoff. "Capital Movements, Export Strategy and Macroeconomic Stability in Chile." In *Coping with Capital Surges: The Return of Finance to Latin America,* ed. Ricardo Ffrench-Davis and Stephany Griffith-Jones. Boulder, Colo.: Rienner, 1995.

"Fifty Years On." *The Economist,* May 16, 1998, 22.

"Firms Now Pay Higher Gas Taxes to Bolivia." Associated Press LA PAZ, Bolivia, June 8, 2006, www.businessweek.com.

"The Fiscal Mire." *The Economist,* May 4, 1996.

Fisher, Stanley. "Reforming World Finance." *The Economist,* October 3–9, 1998. Reproduced at www.imf.org.

————. "Remarks to the Argentine Bankers Association." Presented at the 2001 Argentine Bankers Association Meeting. Buenos Aires: IMF, available at www.imf.org.

Fiszbein, A., and G. Psacharopoulos. *Income Inequality in Latin America: The Story of the Eighties.* Technical Department for Latin America Working Paper. Washington, D.C.: World Bank, 1995.

Foley, Michael. "Agenda for Mobilization: The Agrarian Question and Popular Mobilization in Contemporary Mexico." *Latin American Research Review* 26(2) (1991): 39–74.

Food and Agriculture Organization of the United Nations. *The State of Food and Agriculture.* Rome: Food and Agriculture Organization of the United Nations, 1994.

Foxley, Alejandro. "Preface." In *The New Economic Model in Latin America and Its Impact on Income Distribution and Poverty,* ed. Victor Bulmer-Thomas. New York: St. Martin's, 1996.

Fraga, Arminio. "Monetary Policy during the Transition to a Floating Exchange Rate: Brazil's Recent Experience." *Finance & Development* 37(1) (March 2000).

Franco, Adolfo A. Assistant Administrator, Bureau for Latin America and the Caribbean, United States Agency for International Development. Testimony before the Committee on International Relations, U.S. House of Representatives, Subcommittee on the Western Hemisphere, April 20, 2005, www.usinfo.state.gov.

Frank, Andre Gundar. *Capitalism and Underdevelopment in Latin America.* New York: Monthly Review Press, 1967.

Free Trade Area of the Americas. "Free Trade Area of the Americas Declaration of Ministers Fifth Trade Ministerial Meeting." Canada: Free Trade Area of the Americas, November 4, 1999.

"Free Trade Area of the Americas Sixth Meeting of Ministers of Trade of the Hemisphere." Ministerial Declaration in Buenos Aires. Argentina: Free Trade Area of the Americas, April 7, 2001.

Freire, Paulo. *Pedagogy of the Oppressed.* New York: Seabury, 1970.

"French Lyonnaise des Eaux Agrees to Close Unit in Bolivia." *Latin America News Digest,* March 28, 2006.

Frias, Michael. "Linking International Remittance Flows to Financial Services: Tapping into the Latino Immigrant Market." *Supervisory Journal,* December 1, 2004.

Frieden, Jeffrey, and Ernesto Stein. *The Currency Game: Exchange Rate Politics in Latin America.* Washington, D.C.: Johns Hopkins University Press for the IADB, 2001.

Friedland, Jonathan. "Argentina's Tax Collector Names Names." *Wall Street Journal,* April 13, 1995.

————. "Their Success Earns Chileans a New Title: Ugly Pan-Americans." *Wall Street Journal,* October 3, 1996.

"From Marginality of the 1960's to the 'New Poverty' of Today." Latin American Research Review Forum. *LARR* 39(1) (February 2004).

"From Sandals to Suits." *The Economist,* February 1, 1997.

From Santiago to Quebec City—Report on the Achievements of the Inter-American System. Washington, D.C.: Summits of the Americas Information Network, Office of Summit Follow-up, March 2001. Available at www.summit-americas.org.

Fuentes, Federico. "Land Reform Battle Deepens." *Green Left Weekly,* New South Wales, Australia, October 12, 2005, www.worldpress.org/Americas/2161.cfm#down.

Fuerbringer, Jonathan. "Economic Troubles Worsen in Argentina." *New York Times,* July 11, 2001.

———. "Trouble in Argentina May Help Other Emerging Markets." *New York Times,* July 15, 2001.

"Funds for Farmers Needed for Future." *Financial Times,* December 14, 2000.

Furtado, Celso. *Development and Underdevelopment.* Translated by Ricardo W. Agruar and Eric Charles Drysdale. Berkeley: University of California Press, 1965.

Gagné, Gilbert. "North American Free Trade, Canada, and the US Trade Remedies: An Assessment after Ten Years." *World Economics* 23(1) (January 2000).

Galal, Ahmed, Leroy Jones, Pankaj Tandon, and Ingo Vogelsang. "Divestiture: Questions and Answers." In *Welfare Consequences of Selling Public Enterprises.* Washington, D.C.: World Bank, 1994.

Gallup, John Luke, Alejandro Gaviria, and Eduardo Lora. *Is Geography Destiny?* Washington, D.C.: Inter-American Development Bank, 2003.

García, María Isabel. "Forecast Bright for 'Clean' Agriculture." *Tierramérica,* July 24, 2001.

Garfield, Elsie, Maurizio Guadagni, and Daniel Moreau. "Colombia—Decentralization of Agricultural Extension Services." In *Agricultural Extension: Generic Challenges and Some Ingredients for Solutions,* ed. Gershon Feder, Anthony Willett, and Willem Zijp. Washington, D.C.: World Bank, 1999.

"A Gathering Twilight." *The Economist,* July 14, 2001.

Gavin, Michael. "Hearing on Official Dollarization in Latin America." Presented to the Senate Banking Committee, July 15, 1999.

———. "Surviving Economic Surgery." *The IDB* (December 1996): 4–5.

Gavin, Michael, Ricardo Hausmann, Roberto Perotti, and Ernesto Talvi. *Managing Fiscal Policy in Latin America and the Caribbean: Volatility, Procyclicality, and Limited Creditworthiness.* IADB, Office of the Chief Economist Working Paper No. 326. Washington, D.C.: IADB, 1996.

Gelbard, Alene H. *An Action Plan for Population, Development, and the Environment: Woodrow Wilson Center Spring 1996 Report.* Washington, D.C.: Woodrow Wilson Center, 1996.

Gereffi, Gary, and Peter Evans. "Transnational Corporations, Dependent Development, and State Policy in the Semiperiphery." *Latin American Research Review* 16(3) (1981): 31–64.

Giuffrida, Antonio, William Savedoff, and Roberto Iunes. "Health and Poverty in Brazil: Estimation by Structural Equation Model with Latent Variables." IADB Working Paper, March 2005, www.iadb.org.

Glaister, Dan. "Emigrants Provide Lifeline." *The Guardian,* March 29, 2004.

Glewwe, Paul, and Michael Kremer. "Schools, Teachers and Education Outcomes in Developing Countries." CID Working Paper No. 122, prepared as second draft of chapter for *The Handbook on the Economics of Education* (Cambridge: Harvard University, September 2005).

Global Development Finance 2001, Washington, D.C.: World Bank Publications, 2001, 186, table A42.

Global Environmental Fund. "Participation Means Learning through Doing: GEF's Experience." In "Biodiversity Conservation and Sustainable Use," *GEF Lessons Notes,* July 12, 2001, 1–4. Available at ww.gefweb.org.

"Globalization and Education." ODI Briefing Paper, October 2005.

"Gloom over the River Plate." *The Economist,* July 14, 2001.

"Going Too Far in Support of Trade." *The Economist,* December 16, 2000.

Goldin, Ian A., and Kenneth Reinert. "Global Capital Flows and Development: A Survey." *Journal of International Trade and Economic Development* (2005): 9–11.

Gómez, Ricardo. "The Hall of Mirrors: The Internet in Latin America." *Current History* 99(634) (2000).

Gonzalez, David. "Gaining Dollars, Town Is Losing Its Folkways." *New York Times,* January 1, 2001.

Gonzalez, Gustavo. "Microcredit Makes Strong Inroads in Latin America." Inter-Press News Service Agency, www.ipsnews.net, April 26, 2005.

Goodland, Robert, and Herman Daly. *Poverty Alleviation Is Essential for Environmental Sustainability.* World Bank, Environment Department, Divisional Working Paper 1993-42. Washington, D.C.: World Bank, 1993.

Gori, Graham. "Mexicans Wait More for a Phone." *New York Times,* January 24, 2001.

———. "Mexico's Heavy Industries Threatened by Natural Gas Costs." *New York Times,* January 5, 2001.

Goulet, Denis. *The Cruel Choice: A New Concept in the Theory of Development.* New York: Atheneum, 1971.

Government Accountability Office. "Missed Deadline Prompts Efforts to Restart Stalled Hemispheric Trade Negotiations." *GAO Free Trade Area of the Americas.* GAO-05-166 Report to the Chairman, Committee on Finance, U.S. Senate, and to the Chairman, Committee on Ways and Means, House of Representatives, March 2005.

Graham, Carol. *Private Markets for Public Goods: Raising the Stakes for Economic Reform.* Washington, D.C.: Brookings Institution Press, 1998.

———. *Safety Nets, Politics, and the Poor: Transitions to Market Economies.* Washington, D.C.: Brookings Institution Press, 1994.

———. "Strengthening Institutional Capacity in Poor Countries," *The Brookings Institution Policy Brief,* No. 98, April 2002, www.brookings.edu.

Graham, Edward, M. and Erika Wada. *Domestic Reform, Trade and Investment Liberalisation, Financial Crisis, and Foreign Direct Investment into Mexico.* Washington, D.C.: Institute for International Economics, 2000.

"Green, As in Greenbacks." *The Economist,* February 1, 1997.

Greig, Alan, Michael Kimmel, and James Lang. *Men, Masculinities & Development: Broadening Our Work towards Gender Equality.* UNDP Gender in Development Monograph Series #10, May 2000.

Grieg-Gran, Maryanne, Ina Porras, and Sven Wunder. "How Can Market Mechanisms for Forest Environmental Services Help the Poor? Preliminary Lessons from Latin America." *World Development* 33(9) (September 2005): 1511–1527.

Griffith-Jones, Stephany. "The Mexican Peso Crisis." *CEPAL Review* 60 (December 1996).

Grilli, Enzo, and Dominick Salvatore, eds. *Economic Development: Handbook of Comparative Economic Policies.* Westport, Conn.: Greenwood, 1994.

Grosh, Margaret E. *Administering Targeted Social Programs in Latin America.* Washington, D.C.: World Bank, 1994.

"Guadalajara Takes High-Tech Route." *Financial Times,* December 14, 2000.

Guerguil, Marinte. "Some Thoughts on the Definition of the Informal Sector." *CEPAL Review* 35 (August 1988).

Guivant, Julia. "Agrarian Change, Gender and Land Rights: A Brazilian Case Study." United

Nations Research Institute for Social Development, PP SPD, June 14, 2003, www. unrisd.org.

Gunnarsson, C., and M. Lundahl. "The Good, The Bad, and the Wobbly." In *New Directions in Development Economics: Growth, Environmental Concerns, and Government in the 1990s,* ed. Mats Lundahl and Benno J. Ndulu. London: Routledge, 1996.

Gutierrez, Luish H., and Sanford Berg. "Telecommunications Liberalization and Regulatory Governance: Lessons from Latin America." *Telecommunications Policy* 24 (December 2000): 865–884.

Gwatin, Wagstaff A., and A. S. Yazbeck, eds. *Reaching the Poor with Health, Nutrition, and Population Services.* Washington, D.C.: World Bank, 2005.

Haass, Richard N., and Robert E. Litan. "Globalization and Its Discontents." *Foreign Affairs* 77(3) (1998).

Haber, Stephen. *How Latin America Fell Behind.* Stanford, Calif.: Stanford University Press, 1997.

Habitat for Humanity. "Affordable Housing Statistics." http://www.habitat.org/how/intlstats. aspx.

———. "Causes of Inadequate Housing in Latin America and the Caribbean." http://povlibrary.worldbank.org/files/15210_causes.pdf.

Hall, Gillette, and Harry Patrinos. "Indigenous Peoples, Poverty and Human Development in Latin America: 1994–2004." Hampshire, UK: Palgrave Macmillan, 2005. Executive summary at www.worldbank.org.

———. "Latin America's Indigenous Peoples." *Finance and Development* 42(4) (December 2005).

Hall, Susan E. A. "Conoco's Green Strategy." Harvard Business School Case #9-394-001, October 4, 1993.

Hallak, Juan Carlos, and James Levinsohn. *Fooling Ourselves: Evaluating the Globalization and Growth Debate.* National Bureau of Economic Research Working Paper, 10244, January 2004.

Hamilton, Roger. "Tourism's Green Frontier: How to Protect Nature and Make a Profit." *IDB America,* Inter-American Development Bank, January 2002, www.iadb.org.

Hammergren, Linn. "The Development Wars: Analyzing Foreign Assistance Impact and Policy." *Latin American Research Review* 34(2) (1999).

Hanshaw, Margaret. "Venture Philanthropist." *Harvard Business Review* (July–August 2000).

Hanson, Simon. *Economic Development in Latin America.* Washington, D.C.: Inter-American Affairs Press, 1951.

Harris, Paul. "Chile's Copper: Surplus Spells Woe for Exporters." *Financial Times,* May 9, 2006.

Harriss, John, Janet Hunter, and Colin M. Lewis, "Introduction: Development and Significance of the NIE." In *The New Institutional Economics and Third World Development,* ed. John Harriss, Janet Hunter, and Colin M. Lewis. London: Routledge, 1995.

Harriss-White, Barbara. "Maps and Landscapes of Grain Markets in South Asia." In *The New Institutional Economics and Third World Development,* ed. John Harriss, Janet Hunter, and Colin M. Lewis. London: Routledge, 1996.

Hartshorn, Gary S. "Natural Forest Management by the Yanesha Forestry Cooperative in Peruvian Amazonia." In *Alternatives to Deforestation: Steps toward Sustainable Use of the Amazon Rain Forest,* ed. Anthony B. Anderson. New York: Columbia University Press, 1990.

"Harvesting Farming's Potential." *The Economist,* September 9, 2000.

"Harvesting Poverty: Napoleon's Bittersweet Legacy." *New York Times,* editorial, August 11, 2003, www.nytimes.com.

Hasan Khan Mahmood. "Rural Poverty in Developing Countries—Implications for Public Policy." *IMF Economic Issues* 26 (March 2001).

Hausmann, Ricardo, and Helmut Reisen, eds. *Securing Stability and Growth in Latin America.* Paris: OECD Publications, 1996.

Hausmann, Ricardo, and Ernesto Stein. "Searching for the Right Budgetary Institution for a Volatile Region." In *Securing Stability and Growth in Latin America,* ed. Ricardo Hausmann and Helmut Reisen. Paris: OECD Publications, 1996.

"Heading Off Contagion." Editorial comment. *Financial Times,* August 7, 2001.

Hecht, Susanna B., Susan Kandel, Ileana Gomes, Nelson Cuellar, and Herman Rosa. "Globalization, Forest Resurgence, and Environmental Politics in El Salvador." *World Development* 34(2) (February 2006): 308–323.

Helleiner, Gerald K. "Toward a New Development Strategy." In *The Legacy of Raúl Prebisch,* ed. Enrique V. Iglesias. Washington, D.C.: IADB, 1994.

Hellinger, Daniel. "Understanding Venezuela's Crisis—Dutch Diseases, Money Doctors, and Magicians." *Latin American Perspectives* 27(1) (January 2000).

Helwege, Ann. "Poverty and Inequality in Latin America and the Caribbean." *CEPAL Review* 47 (August 1992).

———. "Poverty in Latin America: Back to the Abyss?" *Journal of Inter-American Studies and World Affairs* 37(3) (Fall 1995).

Hemispheric Social Alliance. *Alternatives for the Americas.* Prepared for the 2nd Peoples Summit of the Americas. Canada: Hemispheric Social Alliance, April 2001.

Henriot, Peter J. "Development Alternatives: Problems, Strategies, Values." In *The Political Economy of Development and Underdevelopment,* 2nd ed., ed. Charles K. Wilbert. New York: Random House, 1979.

Hey, Jeanne A. K., and Thomas Klak. "From Protectionism towards Neoliberalism: Ecuador across Four Administrations (1981–1996)." *Studies in Comparative International Development* (Fall 1999).

"The Hidden Wealth of the Poor." Microcredit Survey, *The Economist,* November 3, 2005.

Higgins, B. *Economic Development: Problems, Principles, and Policies.* New York: Norton, 1968.

Hikino, Takashi, and Alice Amsden. "Staying Behind, Stumbling Back, Sneaking Up, Soaring Ahead: Late Industrialization in Historical Perspective." In *Convergence of Productivity: Cross-National Studies and Historical Evidence,* ed. William Baumol, Richard R. Nelson, and Edward N. Wolff. New York: Oxford University Press, 1994.

Hill, M. Anne, and Elizabeth M. King. "Women's Education in Developing Countries: An Overview." In *Women's Education in Developing Countries: Barriers, Benefits, and Policies,* ed. M. Anne Hill and Elizabeth M. King. Baltimore: Johns Hopkins University Press, 1993.

Hill, Nicole. "Lives Recycled in Argentina." *Christian Science Monitor,* January 25, 2006.

Hinds, Manuel E. "Hearing on Official Dollarization in Latin America." Presented to the Senate Banking Committee, July 15, 1999.

Hirata, Helena, and John Humphrey. "Workers' Response to Job Loss: Female and Male Industrial Workers in Brazil." *World Development* 19(6) (1991): 671–682.

Hoff, Karla. "Designing Land Policies: An Overview." In *The Economics of Rural Organization,* ed. Karla Hoff, Avishay Braverman, and Joseph Stiglitz. New York: Oxford University Press/World Bank, 1993.

Hoff, Karla, Avishay Braverman, and Joseph Stiglitz. "Introduction." In *The Economics of Rural Organization,* ed. Karla Hoff, Avishay Braverman, and Joseph Stiglitz. New York: Oxford University Press/World Bank, 1993.

———, eds. *The Economics of Rural Organization.* New York: Oxford University Press/World Bank, 1993.

Holmes, Michael. "TDA Urges Mexico to Reconsider Beef Tariffs." *AM Cycle,* August 4, 1999.

Holm-Nielsen, Lauritz, Michael Crawford, and Alcyone Saliba. *Institutional and Entrepreneurial Leadership in the Brazilian Science and Technology Sector.* World Bank Discussion Paper No. 325. Washington, D.C.: World Bank, 1996.

"Hope for the No-Hopers." *The Economist,* December 23, 2000.

Hornbeck, J. F. "The U.S.-Chile Free Trade Agreement: Economic and Trade Policy Issues." Congressional Research Service Report RL31144, September 10, 2003, www.opencrs. cdt.org.

Hsiao, William C. "Marketization—The Illusory Magic Pill." *Health Economics* 3 (1994): 351–357.

Huber, Richard M., Jack Ruitenbeck, and Renaldo Serra De Motta. "Market-Based Instruments for Environmental Policy Making in Latin America and the Caribbean: Lessons Learned from Eleven Countries." World Bank Discussion Paper No. 381. Washington, D.C.: World Bank, 1998.

Hufbauer, Gary. *NAFTA in a Skeptical Age: The Way Forward.* Washington, D.C.: Institute for International Economics, 2000.

Hufbauer, Gary, and Diana Orejas. *NAFTA and the Environment: Lessons for Trade Policy.* Speech delivered at the International Policy Forum organized by the Bildner Center. Washington, D.C.: Institute for International Economics, February 28, 2001.

Hufbauer, Gary, and Jeffrey J. Schott. *NAFTA Revisited: Achievements and Challenges.* Washington, D.C.: Institute for International Economics, 2005.

Hulme, David, and Andrew Shephard. "Conceptualizing Chronic Poverty." *World Development* 31(3) (March 2003): 403–423.

"Human Development Index." In *Human Development Report, 1997,* ed. United Nations Development Program. New York: Oxford University Press, 1997.

Idelovitch, Emanuel, and Klas Ringskog. *Private Sector Participation in Water Supply and Sanitation in Latin America.* Washington, D.C.: World Bank, 1995.

"IFC: Making a Positive Difference for Sustainable Development." Washington, D.C.: The World Bank Group.

"If Not for NAFTA, When?" *The Economist,* October 28, 2000.

Iglesias, Enrique V. "The Search for a New Economic Consensus in Latin America." In *The Legacy of Raúl Prebisch,* ed. Enrique V. Iglesias. Washington, D.C.: IADB, 1994.

———, ed. *The Legacy of Raúl Prebisch,* Washington, D.C.: IADB, 1994.

Ignatius, David. "'Dollarization' in Latin America." *World News,* April 28, 1999, A26.

"IMF Completes Brazil Fifth Review." IMF News Brief No. 00/33. Washington, D.C.: IMF, May 31, 2000.

"IMF Concludes Article IV Consultation with Argentina." Public Information Notice No. 00/84. Washington, D.C.: IMF, October 3, 2000.

"IMF Lending to Poor Countries—How Does the PRGF Differ from the ESAF?" Washington, D.C.: IMF, April 2001.

"IMF Managing Director Köhler Welcomes Argentine Senate Action." News Brief No. 01/67. Washington, D.C.: IMF, July 30, 2001.

"IMF Press Conference on Exchange Rate Regimes in an Increasingly Integrated World Economy." Washington, D.C.: IMF, April 14, 2000.

"The IMF's Poverty Reduction and Growth Facility (PRGF)—A Factsheet." *International Monetary Fund,* March 2001.

"Indigenous Peoples, Poverty and Human Development in Latin America: 1994–2004." http:// www.worldbank.org.cn/english/content/805w63341746.shtml.

"Industry At a Glance," *World Oil Production,* www.worldoil.com.

Inter-American Development Bank. *Annual Report 2001,* www.iadb.org.

————. "Argentina—Country Paper."

————. "The Argentine Saga." *Latin American Economic Policies* 16 (4th Quarter 2001).

————. "Completion Point under the Heavily Indebted Poor Countries Initiative." www. iadb.org, March 8, 2004.

————. *Disaster Prevention Sector Facility.* Document GN-2085-5, March 2001.

————. *Economic and Social Progress in Latin America 1995 Report: Overcoming Volatility.* Washington, D.C.: IADB, 1995.

————. *Economic and Social Progress in Latin America 1996 Report: Making Social Services Work.* Washington, D.C.: IADB, 1996.

————. *Facing Up to Inequality in Latin America: Economic and Social Progress in Latin America, 1998–1999 Report.* Washington, D.C.: Johns Hopkins University Press/IADB, 1998.

————. *Group Support to the Microenterprise Sector (1990–2000).* IADB, February 2001.

————. "The IDB and Micro, Small and Medium-Sized Enterprises." Small and Medium-Sized Enterprises Unit, IDB News, www.iadb.org.

————. *Intra-Hemispheric Exports by Integration Group.* July 12, 1997. Available at www.iadb.org.statistics/notaest.htm.

————. "Invisible Farmers." In *IDB Extra: Investing in Women.* Washington, D.C.: IADB, 1994.

————. "Is Growth Enough?" *Latin American Economic Policies* 14 (2nd Quarter 2001).

————. *Latin America after a Decade of Reforms: Economic and Social Progress, 1997 Report.* Washington, D.C.: Johns Hopkins University Press/IADB, 1997.

————. "The Millennium Development Goals in Latin America and the Caribbean: Progress, Priorities and IDB Support for Their Implementation." www.iadb.org, August 2005.

————. "Natural Disasters." Background papers, March 13, 2006, www.iadb.org.

————. "Reform Fatigue." *IDEAS* 3 (January–April 2004), www.iadb.org.

————. "Remittance Flows to Latin America and the Caribbean." www.iadb.org, 2004.

————. "Why Geography Matters." *Economic and Social Progress in Latin America* (2000): 21.

————. *Women in the Americas: Bridging the Gap.* Baltimore: Johns Hopkins University Press, 1995.

International Coffee Council. "Impact of the Coffee Crisis on Poverty in Producing Countries." ICC 89-5, Rev. September 1, 2003.

"International Cooperation At a Crossroads: Aid, Trade and Security in an Unequal World United Nations." United Nations Human Development Report 2005, www.undp.ord.

International Labor Organization. *World Employment Report 2001: The World Employment Report 2001; Life at Work in the Information Economy.* Geneva, Switzerland.

International Monetary Fund. *Bolivia—Interim Poverty Reduction Strategy Paper.* Prepared by the Bolivian Authorities.

————. *IMF Survey,* 2005. Available at www.imf.org.

————. *International Financial Statistics, 1997.* Washington, D.C.: IMF, 1997.

————. *Key Features of IMF Poverty Reduction and Growth Facility (PRGF) Supported Programs.* Prepared by the Policy Development and Review Department, August 16, 2000.

————. *World Economic Outlook 2002,* www.imf.org.

International Trade Administration, U.S. Department of Commerce. *U.S. Foreign Trade Highlights, 1995.* Washington, D.C.: U.S. Department of Commerce, 1995.

"In the Gap and Sweatshop Labor in El Salvador." *NACLA Report on the Americas* 29(4) (January–February 1996): 37.

"Involving the Private Sector and Preventing Financial Crises." *IMF Survey* 28(12) (June 21, 1999).

Isacson, Adam, and John Myers. "Plan Colombia's Drug Eradication Program Misses the Market." International Relations Center, www.americas.irc-online.org, July 18, 2005.

"It's Time to Bite the Bullet." *Euromoney,* September 1996.

Jallade, Lucila, Eddy Lee, and Joel Samoff. "International Cooperation." In *Coping with Crisis: Austerity, Adjustment, and Human Resources,* ed. Joel Samoff. New York: UNESCO/ILO, 1994.

Jameson, Kenneth P. "Dollarization in Ecuador: A Post Keynesian Institutionalist Analysis." University of Utah Department of Economics Working Paper 2004-5.

———. "The Financial Sector in Latin American Restructuring." In *Privatization in Latin America,* ed. Werner Baer and Melissa Birch. Westport, Conn.: Praeger, 1994.

Jarque, Carlos. "Foreward." In *Escaping the Poverty Trap: Investing in Children in Latin America,* ed. Ricardo Morán. Washington, D.C.: Inter-American Development Bank, 2003.

Jenkins, Rhys. "Car Manufacture in East Asia and Latin America." *Cambridge Journal of Economics* (October 1995): 625–646.

———. *Transnational Corporations and Industrial Transformation in Latin America.* New York: St. Martin's, 1984.

———. *Transnational Corporations and the Latin American Automobile Industry.* Pittsburgh: University of Pittsburgh Press, 1987.

Jessen, Anneke, et al. *Integration and Trade in the Americas.* Washington, D.C.: IADB, 1999.

Jewett, Dale. "Magna Touts Lower-Cost Navigational System." *Automotive News,* October 23, 2000.

Jimenez de la Jara, Jorge, and Thomas J. Bossert. "Chile's Health Sector Reform: Lessons from Four Reform Periods." In *Health Sector Reform in Developing Countries: Making Health Development Sustainable,* ed. Peter Berman. Cambridge: Harvard University Press, 1995.

Johnson, Brian. *The Great Fire of Borneo: Report of a Visit to Kalimantan-Timur a Year Later, May 1994.* London: World Wildlife Fund, 1991.

Johnson, Ken. "Brazil and the Politics of Climate Change Negotiations." *Journal of Environment & Development* 10(2) (June 2001): 185.

Jonakin, Jon. "The Interaction of Market Failure and Structural Adjustment in Producer Credit and Land Markets: The Case of Nicaragua." *Journal of Economic Issues* 31(2) (June 1997).

Juma, Calestous, and Lee Yee Cheon. "Innovation: Applying Knowledge in Development." UN Millennium Task Force on Science, Technology and Innovation, Belfer Center for Science and International Affairs, John F. Kennedy School of Government, 2005.

"Just Don't Call It Downsizing." *IADB América* (September–October 2000): 10–11.

Kadt, Emanuel de. "Thematic Lessons from the Case Studies." In *The Public-Private Mix in Social Services,* ed. Elaine Zuckerman and Emanuel de Kadt. Washington, D.C.: IADB, 1997.

Kahn, Joseph. "Congressional Leadership Agrees to Debt Relief for Poor Nations." *New York Times,* October 18, 2000.

Kaltenheuser, Skip. "Fitting Microcredit into a Macro Picture." *Christian Science Monitor,* February 5, 1997.

Kapstein, Ethan. "Global Rules for Global Finance." *Current History,* November 1998.

Karp, Jonathan. "Brazilian Central Banker Plays It Cool." *Wall Street Journal,* July 18, 2001, A12.

Kate, Adriaan ten, and Robert Bruce Wallace. "Nominal and Effective Protection by Sector." In *Protection and Economic Development in Mexico,* ed. Adriaan ten Kate and Robert Bruce Wallace. Hampshire, UK: Gower, 1980.

Katz, Elizabeth G. "Gender and Trade within the Household: Observations from Rural Guatemala." *World Development* 23(2) (1995): 327–342.

Katz, Ian. "Snapping up South America." *BusinessWeek,* January 18, 1999.

Kaufman, Robert, and Joan Nelson. "The Political Challenges of Social Sector Reform." In *Crucial Needs, Weak Incentives: Social Sector Reform, Democratization, and Globalization in Latin America,* ed. Robert R. Kaufman and Joan M. Nelson. Washington, D.C.: Woodrow Wilson Center Press and Johns Hopkins University Press, 2004.

Kay, Stephen J. "Privatizing Pensions: Prospects for the Latin American Reforms." *Journal of Interamerican Studies and World Affairs* 42(1) (Spring 2000).

Keen, Benjamin. *Latin American Civilization,* 3rd ed. Boston: Houghton Mifflin, 1974.

Kepp, Michael. "Refining Mining." *Latin Trade* (April 2002): 30.

Key, Cristóbal. "Rural Development and Agrarian Issues in Contemporary Latin America." In *Structural Adjustment and the Agricultural Sector in Latin America and the Caribbean,* ed. John Weeks. New York: St. Martin's, 1995.

"Key Indicators of the Labour Market (KILM)." International Labor Organization, 2005, www.ilo.org.

Keynan, Gabriel, Manuel Olin, and Ariel Dinar. "Cofinanced Public Extension in Nicaragua." *World Bank Research Observer* 12(2) (August 1997).

"The Key Points of the FTAA Agenda." *Latin American Weekly Report,* WR-97-20, 1997.

"Kirchner Gets What He Came for in Brazil." *Latinnews Daily,* January 19, 2006.

Kliksberg, Bernardo. "Public Administration in Latin America." *International Review of Administrative Sciences* 71(2) (2005): 325.

Klitgaard, Robert. "Subverting Corruption." *Finance & Development* (June 2000).

Knight, Alan. "Populism and Neo-Populism in Latin America, Especially Mexico." *Journal of Latin American Studies* 30 (1998): 223–248.

"Köhler Says IMF Management to Recommend Accelerated Disbursement of US $1.2 Billion for Argentina." News Brief No. 01/17. Washington, D.C.: IMF, August 3, 2001.

"Köhler Says IMF Management to Recommend US $15 Billion Stand-By for Brazil." News Brief No. 01/72. Washington, D.C.: IMF, August 3, 2001.

Kohn, Robert, Itzhak Levav, José Miguel Caldas de Almeida, Vincente Benjamín, Laura Andrade, Jorge J. Caraveo-Anduaga, Shekhar Saxena, and Benedetto Saraceno. Special issue of *On Mental Health. Revista Panamericana de Salud Pública* 18(4–5) (October/November 2005): 229–240.

Krauss, Clifford. "Argentina's Austerity Plan Provokes Nationwide Strike." *New York Times,* July 20, 2001.

———. "Argentina to Hasten End of a Phone Monopoly." *New York Times,* March 11, 1998.

———. "Argentine with a Headache: The Economy." *New York Times,* July 18, 2001.

———. "Bolivia Wiping Out Coca, At a Price." *New York Times,* October 23, 2000.

———. "Economy Aide to the Rescue, As Argentina Fights Default." *New York Times,* March 30, 2001.

———. "Poll-Whipped and Pilloried, Chief Endures in Argentina." *New York Times,* July 8, 2001.

———. "When Even an Economic Miracle Isn't Enough." *New York Times,* July 12, 1998.

———. "Where the Coca Trade Withers, Tourism Sprouts." *New York Times,* November 2, 2000.

Krawczyk, Miriam. "Women in the Region: Major Changes." *CEPAL Review* 49 (April 1993).

Kroll, Luisa, and Allison Fass, eds. "Billionaires by Rank." Special Report. *Forbes* (2006), www.forbes.com.

Kronish, Rich, and Kenneth S. Mericle. "The Development of the Latin American Motor

Vehicle Industry, 1900–1980: A Class Analysis." In *The Political Economy of the Latin American Motor Vehicle Industry,* ed. Rich Kronish and Kenneth S. Mericle. Cambridge, Mass.: MIT Press, 1984.

Krueger, Anne O. *NAFTA's Effects: A Preliminary Assessment.* Oxford: Blackwell, 2000.

Krugman, Paul. "A Latin Tragedy." *New York Times,* July 15, 2001.

———. "Other People's Money." *New York Times,* July 18, 2001.

Krugman, Paul R., and Maurice Obstfeld. *International Economics: Theory and Policy,* 3rd ed. New York: HarperCollins, 1994.

Kuttner, Robert. "What Sank Asia? Money Sloshing around the World." *BusinessWeek,* July 27, 1998.

Kuznets, Simon. "Modern Economic Growth: Findings and Reflections." *American Economic Review* 63(3) (June 1973).

Kwast, Barbara. "Reeducation of Material and Peri-natal Mortality in Rural and Peri-urban Settings: What Works?" *European Journal of Obstetrics and Gynecology and Reproductive Biology* 609 (1996).

Lains, Petro. "Before the Golden Age: Economic Growth in Mexico and Portugal, 1910–1950." In *Growth Institutions and Crises: Latin America from a Historical Perspective,* ed. Sebastian Edwards. Washington, D.C.: National Bureau of Economic Research, 2005.

Lakshmanan, Indira A. R. "Amazon Highway Is Route to Strife in Brazil." *Boston Globe,* December 27, 2005.

Lall, Sanjaya. "Competitiveness Indices and Developing Countries: An Economic Evaluation of the Global Competitiveness Report." *World Development* 29(9) (September 2001): 1501–1525.

Lamb, James J. "The Third World and the Development Debate." *IDOC-North America,* January–February 1973.

"Land for the Landless." *The Economist,* April 13, 1996.

Lanjouw, Peter. "Nonfarm Employment and Poverty in Rural El Salvador." *World Development* 29 (3) (2001).

La Porta, Rafael, Florencio Lopez-de-Silanes, and Andrei Shleifer, 1999, as summarized in William Megginson and Jeffry M. Netter, "From State to Market: A Survey of Empirical Studies of Privatization," *Journal of Economic Literature* 39 (June 2001).

Lapper, Richard. "Policy under Pressure," *Financial Times,* October 6, 2002, weekend I.

———. "Workers Throw a Lifeline Home." *Financial Times,* March 29, 2004, 1.

Larner, Monica, and Ian Katz. "It's Ronaldo's World." *BusinessWeek,* June 22, 1998, 204.

Larraín, Felipe B., ed. *Capital Flows, Capital Controls and Currency* Ann Arbor: University of Michigan Press, 2000.

Larraín, Felipe B., and Luis F. López-Calva, "Privatization: Fostering Economic Growth through Private Sector Development." Chapter 13 in *Economic Development in Central America,* Vol. 2, *Structural Reform.* Cambridge: Harvard University Press, 2001, 68.

Larraín, Felipe B., Luis F. López-Calva, and Andrés Rodriguez-Clare. *Intel: A Case Study of Foreign Direct Investment in Central America.* CID Working Paper No. 58. Center for International Development at Harvard University. December 2000.

Larrea, Carlos, Pedro Montalvo, and Ana Ricaurte. "Child Malnutrition, Social Development and Health Services in the Andean Region." HEW 0509011, Economics Working Paper Archive, March 2004.

"Latin American Indigenous People More Likely to Die from Malaria, Diarrhea and TB Than Their Counterparts." November 29, 2005, www.medicalnewstoday.com.

Latin America Research Review 35(3) (2000).

"Latin America's Car Industry Revving Up." *The Economist,* April 27, 1996.

"Latin America Sees Progress." *Washington Times,* August 9, 2005, www.washington-times.com.

"Latin America's Export of Manufactured Goods." Special section of *Economic and Social Progress in Latin America 1992 Report.* Washington, D.C.: IADB, 1992.

"Latin America Struggles to Find Solutions to Megacity Woes." *Agence France Press,* June 2, 1992. Available on the LEXIS-NEXIS database.

Latin America Weekly Report. May 26, 1998.

Latin Watch. Banco Bilbao Vizcaya Agentaria, December 2000.

Lau, Lawrence J., Dean T. Jamison, Shucheng Liu, and Steven Rivkin. "Education and Economic Growth: Some Cross-Sectional Evidence." In *Education in Brazil,* ed. Nancy Birdsall and Richard H. Sabot. Washington, D.C.: IADB, 1996.

Lederman Daniel, William F. Maloney, and Luis Servén. *Lessons from NAFTA for Latin America and the Caribbean.* Palo Alto, Calif.: Stanford University Press, 2004.

Leff, Nathaniel H. "Economic Development in Brazil." In *How Latin America Fell Behind,* ed. Stephen Haber, 1822–1913. Palo Alto, Calif: Stanford University Press, 1997.

Lehmann, David, ed. *Agrarian Reform and Agrarian Reformism: Studies of Peru, Chile, China, and India.* London: Faber & Faber, 1974.

Lepziger, Danny, Claudio Frischtak, Homi J. Kharas, and John F. Normand. "Mercosur: Integration and Industrial Policy." *World Economy* 20(5) (1997).

Lewin, B., D. Giovannucci, and P. Varangis. "Fair Trade and the Coffee Crisis, Coffee Markets: New Paradigms in Global Supply and Demand." World Bank, 2004, www.worldbank.org.

Lewis, Colin M. "Industry in Latin America." In *Dependency and Development,* ed. Fernando Henrique Cardoso and Enzo Faletto, translated by Marjory Mattinglly Urguidi. Berkeley: University of California Press, 1979.

Lewis, Paul. "Latin Americans Say Russian Default Is Hurting Their Economies." *New York Times,* October 6, 1998, A13. Online edition.

Lindsey, Brink. "Grounds for Complaint? Understanding the Coffee Crisis." London: Adam Smith Institute, 2004. Available at www.adamsmith.org.

Lippert, John. "'Going Zunion' Is the Buzz at Magna Auto Parts Giant Pays Wages Half the Big Three's." *Toronto Star,* August 15, 1998.

Lizano, Eduardo, and José M. Salazar-Xirinach. "Central American Common Market and Hemispheric Free Trade." In *Integrating the Hemisphere, 1997: The Inter-American Dialogue,* ed. Ana Julia Jatar and Sidney Weintraub. Santa Fé de Bogotá, Colombia: Tercer Mundo, 1997.

Lizondo, S., et al. Chile: Selected Issues. IMF Country Report No. 01/120. Washington, D.C.: IMF, July 2001.

"Loan 'Club' Is a Useful Model." *Financial Times,* December 14, 2000.

Londoño, Juan Luis, and Miguel Székely. "Distributional Surprises after a Decade of Reforms: Latin America in the Nineties." Paper prepared for the annual meetings of the IADB. Barcelona, March 1997.

———. *Persistent Poverty and Excess Inequality: Latin America, 1970–1995.* Office of the Chief Economist. IADB Working Paper No. 357. Washington, D.C.: IADB, 1997.

López, Ramón. *Policy Instruments and Financing Mechanisms for the Sustainable Use of Forests in Latin America.* No. ENV-16. Washington, D.C.: IADB, 1996.

Lora, Eduardo. *Should Latin America Fear China?* Inter-American Development Research Department Working Paper No. 531, May 2005, www.iadb.org.

Lora, Eduardo, and Felipe Barrera. "A Decade of Structural Reform in Latin America: Growth, Productivity, and Investment Are Not What They Used to Be." Document for discussion at the IADB Barcelona seminar, "Latin America after a Decade of Reform: What Next?" March 16, 1997.

Lora, Eduardo, Carmen Pagés, Ugo Panizza, and Ernesto Stein. "A Decade of Development Thinking." Washington D.C.: Inter-American Development Bank Research Department, 2004, 26.

Lora, Eduardo, Ugo Panizza, and Myriam Quispe-Agnoli. "Reform Fatigue: Symptoms, Reasons, Implications." Paper presented at Rethinking Structural Reform in Latin America, Federal Reserve Bank of Atlanta, October 23, 2003.

Lorey, David E. "Education and the Challenges of Mexican Development." *Challenge* 38(2) (March–April 1995): 51–55.

Loser, Claudio M. "The Long Road to Financial Stability." *Finance and Development,* March 2000.

Loser, Claudio M., and Jesús Seade. *Second Review under the Stand-by Arrangement and Request for Augmentation.* Report No. 01/26. Washington, D.C.: IMF, January 2001.

———. *Staff Report for the 2000 Article IV Consultation, First Review under the Stand-By Arrangement, and Request for Modification of Performance Criteria.* Report No. 00/164. Washington, D.C.: IMF, December 2000.

Loungani, Prakash, and Philip Swagel. "Source of Inflation in Developing Countries." IMF Working Paper 01/198, Washington, D.C., International Monetary Fund, December 2001.

"Lousy Deal." *IDB América* (May–June 2000): 2.

Loyola, Gustavo. "Elusive Tax Reform: 'President Must Lead the Way.'" *UNICEF—Info-Brazil,* September 2001.

Luhnow, David, and John Lyons. "In Latin America, Rich-Poor Chasm Stifles Growth." *Wall Street Journal,* July 18, 2005, A1.

Lustig, Nora. *Coping with Austerity.* Washington, D.C.: Brookings Institution, 1995.

———. *NAFTA: Setting the Record Straight.* Brookings Policy Brief No. 20.

Lustig, Nora, and Ruthanne Deutsch. The *Inter-American Development Bank and Poverty Reduction: An Overview.* Washington, D.C.: IADB, 1998. Available at www.iadb.org.

MacCulloch, Christina. "Will She Make It? Guatemala Finds New Ways to Keep Girls in School." *IDB América* (April 1998): 4–7.

Macisaac, Donna. "Peru." In *Indigenous People and Poverty in Latin America,* ed. George Psacharopoulos and Harry Anthony Patrinos. Washington, D.C.: World Bank, 1994.

Maddison, Angus. "Economic and Social Conditions in Latin America, 1913–1950." In *Long-Term Trends in Latin American Economic Development,* ed. Miguel Urrutia. Washington, D.C.: IADB/Johns Hopkins University Press, 1991.

———. *Monitoring the World Economy, 1820–1992.* Washington, D.C.: OECD Publications and Information Center, 1995.

"Magna Auto Parts Boss on $33m a Year Roll." *Canadian Press Newswire,* April 10, 2000.

"Magna Forms Mexican Joint Venture." *Canada Newswire,* August 20, 1997.

"Magna International Inc.—Online Earnings Conference Call Notification." *Canada Newswire,* August 17, 2000.

Mahon, James E., Jr. "Was Latin America Too Rich to Prosper? Structural and Political Obstacles to Export-Led Industrial Growth." *Journal of Development Studies* 28(2) (1992).

"Making Money from Microcredit." *IDB América,* June 1998.

Malpass, David. "Hearing on Official Dollarization in Emerging-Market Countries." Presented to the Senate Banking, Housing and Urban Affairs Committee, July 15, 1999.

Maltsoglou, Irini, and Aysen Tanyeri-Abur. "Transaction Costs, Institutions and Smallholder Market Integration: Potato Producers in Peru." ESA Working Paper No. 05-04, Agricultural and Development Economics Division, www.fao.org, June 2005.

Mandel-Campbell, Andrea. "I Bet the Ranch, and I Won—Absolutely." *BusinessWeek,* June 22, 1998, 64–65.

Mander, Benedict. "Darker Side to Argentina's Soya Success." *Financial Times,* June 7, 2006.

"The Man from Whom Miracles Hang." *The Economist,* October 28, 2000.

Mangurian, David. "Against the Odds: How a Seemingly Hopeless Energy Project Became a Model for Investors." *IDB América,* March 1998. Available at www.iadb.org.

Margolis, Mac. "Hat in Hand." *Newsweek,* October 12, 1998.

Márquez, Humberto. "Chávez to Further Strengthen Social Reform." *Inter Press Service,* August 31, 2002, www.americas.org.

Martinussen, John. *Society, State, and Market: A Guide to Competing Theories of Development.* London: Zed, 1997.

Maxwell, Kenneth. "Latin America: Sustaining Economic & Political Reform—A Working Conference on the Underlying Realities." Conference Overview. The Council on Foreign Relations, May 18, 2000.

Mayer-Serra, Carlos Elizondo. "Tax Reform under the Salinas Administration." In *The Changing Structure of Mexico,* ed. Laura Randall, Armonk, N.Y.: Sharpe, 1996.

Mayorga, Román. *Closing the Gap.* IADB Working Paper SOC97-101. Washington, D.C.: IADB, 1997.

Mazza, Jacqueline. "Social Inclusion, Labor Markets and Human Capital." In *Social Inclusion and Economic Development in Latin America,* ed. Mayra Buvinic and Jacqueline Mazza, 188, table 10.3. Washington, D.C.: Inter-American Development Bank, 2004.

McDonnell, Patrick, and Edwin Che. "Bush Exits Summit As Trade Talks End in Disagreement." *Los Angeles Times,* November 6, 2005.

McKee, Colin. "Realizing the Potential of the Internet in Latin America." Unpublished paper, Colby College, Waterville, Maine, 2001.

McKinsey Global Institute. *Productivity: The Key to an Accelerated Development Path for Brazil 1998.* São Paulo: McKinsey, 1998.

McLarty, Thomas F. "Hemispheric Free Trade Is Still a National Priority." *Wall Street Journal,* May 26, 1995.

McQuerry, Elizabeth, Michael Chriszt, and Stephen Kay. "Patterns in Latin American Public Sector Accounts." Federal Reserve Bank of Atlanta, 2001. Available at www.frbatlanta.org/econ_rd/larq/fiscal_policy/public_sector/patterns/htm.

Meerman, Jacob. *Reforming Agriculture: The World Bank Goes to Market.* Washington, D.C.: World Bank, 1997.

Meier, Gerald M. *Leading Issues in Economic Development,* 6th ed. Oxford: Oxford University Press, 1995.

Meier, Gerald M., and Dudley Seers. *Pioneers in Development.* Oxford: Oxford University Press, 1984.

Meller, Patricio. "IMF and World Bank Roles in the Latin America Foreign Debt Problem." In *The Latin American Development Debate: Neostructuralism, Neomonetarism, and Adjustment Processes,* ed. Patricio Meller. Boulder, Colo.: Westview, 1991.

"Memorandum of Economic Policies." International Monetary Fund. Public Information Notice No. 00/84. Washington, D.C.: IMF, 1999.

Mendez, Chico. *Fight for the Forest.* London: Latin American Bureau, 1990.

"Mental Disorders in Latin America and the Caribbean Forecast to Increase." December 12, 2005, http://www.medicalnewstoday.com/medicalnews.php?newsid=34832#.

Mercosur Consulting Group Limited. "Recent Developments Affecting the Mercosur Economic Integration Project." *Thunderbird International Business Review* 42(1) (January–February 2002): 1–7; www.mercosurconsulting.net.

"Mercosur Survey." *The Economist,* October 12, 1996.

"Mexico City: A Topographical Error." *Environment* 36(2) (1994): 25–26.

"Mexico Domestic Sales Rise Sharply." *Reuters Financial Service,* June 4, 1997. U.S. Department of State, "Mexico FY 2000 Country Commercial Guide," July 1999. Available at LEXIS-NEXIS.

"Mexico FY 2000 Country Commercial Guide." Washington, D.C.: U.S. Department of State.

Mezzera, Jaime. "Abundancia como efecto de la escasez. Oferta y demanda en el Mercado laboral urbano." *Nueva Sociedad* 90 (1997): 106–117.

Miller, Eric. *Financial Services in the Trading System: Progress and Prospects.* Washington D.C.: IADB, 1999.

Mishkin, Frederick. "Understanding Financial Crises: A Developing Country Perspective." In *The Annual World Bank Conference Report on Development Economics, 1996.* Washington, D.C.: World Bank, 1997.

Mizala, Alejandra, Pilar Romaguera, and Carolina Ostoic. "Equity and Achievement in the Chilean School Choice System." Center for Applied Economics, Universidad de Chile, April 2005.

Moffett, Matt. "Deep in the Amazon, an Industrial Enclave Fights for Its Survival." *Wall Street Journal,* July 9, 1998.

Mokhiber, Russell, and Robert Weissman. "The Ten Worst Corporations of 2004." *Multinational Monitor* 25(12), multinationalmonitor.org.

Molano, Walter. *Financial Reverberations: The Latin American Banking System during the Mid-1990s.* Working paper, SBC Warburg. April 1997.

Monteiro, Viviane. "Fiscal Resolve Is Crucial to the Economy Says Finance Minister Palocci." *Noticias Financieras/Group de Diarios America InvestNews,* Brazil, September 13, 2005.

Moody-Stuart, Mark. *Putting Principles into Practice: The Ethical Challenge to Global Business.* Presented at the World Congress of the International Society of Business, Economics and Ethics in São Paolo, Brazil, July 19, 2000.

Mooney, Elizabeth. "South American Economic Crisis Hits Telecom Operators." *RCR Wireless News,* April 2002, 25.

Moore, Mick. "Toward a Useful Consensus." In *The Bank, the State, and Development: Dissecting the World Development Report, 1997. IDS Bulletin* 29(2), special issue (1998).

Moore, Molly. "Mayan Girls Make Fifth Grade History." *Washington Post,* June 20, 1996.

Morales, Juan Antonio, and Jeffrey Sachs. "Bolivia's Economic Crisis." In *Developing Country Debt and the World Economy,* ed. Jeffrey Sachs. Chicago: University of Chicago Press, 1989.

Morán, Ricardo, Tarsicio Castaneda, and Enrique Aldaz-Carroll. "Family Background and Intergenerational Poverty in Latin America." In *Escaping the Poverty Trap: Investing in Children in Latin America,* ed. Ricardo Morán. Washington, D.C.: Inter-American Development Bank, 2003.

Morandé, Felipe G. "Savings in Chile: What Went Right?" *Journal of Development Economics* 57(1) (1998).

Morris, Valerie, and Donald Van De Mark. "Magna Auto Parts Ceo." *Cable News Network Financial,* March 11, 1998.

Mortimore, Michael, Álvaro Calderón, Pablo Carvallo, and Márcia Tavares. "Foreign Investment in Latin America and the Caribbean." ECLAC Unit on Investment and Corporate Strategies, www.ec.as.org, May 2006.

Mosbacher, Robert, Chairman, Council of the Americas. "Trade Expansion within the Americas: A U.S. Business Perspective." Remarks at the Chile-United States Issues Round Table, Crown Plaza Hotel, Santiago, Chile, April 17, 1998. Available at 207.87.5.23/sr.html; accessed July 12, 1999.

Moseley, Paul, and David Hulme. "Microenterprise Finance: Is There a Conflict between Growth and Poverty Alleviation?" *World Development* 26(5) (1988): 783–790.

Moser, Caroline. "Gender Planning in the Third World: Meeting Practical and Strategic Gender Needs." *World Development* 17(11) (1989): 1799–1825.

Moser, Caroline O. N., and Cathy McIlwaine. "Latin American Urban Violence as a Development Concern: Towards a Framework for Violence Reduction." *World Development* 34(1) (January 2006): 89–112.

Moser, Titus. "MNCs and Sustainable Business Practice: The Case of the Colombian and Peruvian Petroleum Industries." *World Development* 29(2) (2001).

Mulligan, Mark. "Argentine Opposition Backs Government Austerity Package." *Financial Times,* July 18, 2001.

———. "Honeymoon Over for Cavallo." *Financial Times,* July 19, 2001.

———. "Protests Flare over Argentina Austerity Plan." *Financial Times,* July 18, 2001.

Munainghe, Mohran, and Wilfrido Cruz. *Economy Wide Policies and the Environment: Lessons from Experience.* Washington, D.C.: World Bank, 1995.

Myers, William, ed. *Protecting Working Children.* London: Zed, 1991.

"NAFTA: Where's That Giant Sucking Sound?" *BusinessWeek,* July 7, 1997, 45.

"NAFTA Key Provisions." NAFTA Facts Document #3001.

Naik, Gautam. "Studies of the Amazon Rainforest Intensify Climate Change Debate." *Wall Street Journal,* October 20, 2005.

Naim, Moises. "Fads and Fashion in Economic Reforms: Washington Consensus or Washington Confusion?" *Foreign Policy Magazine,* October 26, 1999.

Nasar, Sylvia. "The Cure That Can Sometimes Kill the Patient." *New York Times,* July 19, 1998.

"National Trade Estimate Reports—1998 Country Report." Trade Compliance Center.

"National Trade Estimate 2000—Mexico." Trade Compliance Center.

Naughton-Treves, Lisa. "Deforestation and Carbon Emissions at Tropical Frontiers: A Case Study from the Peruvian Amazon." *World Development* 32(1) (January 2004): 173–190.

Nazmi, Nader. *Economic Policy and Stabilization in Latin America.* New York: Sharpe, 1996.

———. "The Internationalization of Capital in a Small and Vulnerable Economy: The Case of Ecuador." In Werner Baer and William R. Miles, *Foreign Direct Investment in Latin America,* 119–139. New York: Hayworth, 2001.

Nellis, John, Rachel Menzes, and Sarah Lucas. *Latino barómetro poll 2001 and 2002,* as cited in "Privatization in Latin America." Center for Global Development Policy Brief 3(1) (January 2004).

Nelson, Joan. "The Political of Health Sector Reform." In *Crucial Needs, Weak Incentives: Social Sector Reform, Democratization, and Globalization in Latin America,* ed. Robert R. Kaufman and Joan M. Nelson. Washington, D.C.: Woodrow Wilson Center Press and Johns Hopkins University Press, 2004.

Nelson, Joan, and Robert Kaufman. "The Political Economy of Health Sector Reforms: Cross National Comparisons." Wilson Center update on the Americas May 2003, Creating Community series.

Nelson, Richard R. "Schumpeterian Competition." In *The Sources of Economic Growth.* Cambridge: Harvard University Press, 1996.

"The New Entrepreneurs: Preparing the Ground for Small Business." *IDB América* 1997. Available at www.iadb.org.

"New Era Dawns with Great Expectations." *Financial Times,* December 14, 2000.

Newfarmer, Richard S. *Profits, Progress, and Poverty.* South Bend, Ind.: University of Notre Dame Press, 1984.

"New Farms for Old." *The Economist,* January 10, 1998.

"A New Risk of Default." *Euromoney,* September 1996, 283.

"Nicaragua Expects $1.018 Billion Debt Write-Off." *Latin American News Digest,* October 21, 2005.

Noll, Roger G. *Telecommunications Reform in Developing Countries.* Working Paper 99-10. AEI-Brookings Joint Center for Regulator Studies, November 1999.

North, Douglass C. *Understanding the Process of Economic Change.* Princeton, N.J.: Princeton University Press, 2005.

North, Douglass C. "The New Institutional Economics and Third World Development." In *The New Institutional Economics and Third World Development,* ed. John Harriss, Janet Hunter, and Colin M. Lewis. London: Routledge, 1995.

"The North American Free Trade Agreement Is Good for US Agricultural Trade." *World Food Chemical News,* July 23, 1997.

"North Is North and South Is South." *The Economist,* October 28, 2000.

Northoff, Erwin. "Cattle Ranching Is Encroaching on Forests in Latin America Causing Severe Environmental Degradation: FAO Model Predicts Land Use up to 2010," June 8, 2005, www.fao.org.

"Nuts in Brazil." *The Economist,* October 9, 1999.

Nygren, Anja. "Community-Based Forest Management within the Context of Institutional Decentralization in Honduras." *World Development* 33(4) (April 2005): 639–655.

"Obstacles to Business Development." *Latin American Economic Policies* 13(1) (2001).

Ocampo, José Antonio. "The Pending Agenda: A Decade of Light and Shadow." *ECLAC Notes* 20 (March 2001).

———. "Rethinking the Development Agenda." Presented at the American Economic Association Annual Meeting Panel "Toward a Post-Washington Consensus on Development and Security" in New Orleans, January 5, 2001.

———. "Towards a Global Solution." *ECLAC Notes* 1 (November 1998).

Odessey, Bruce. "U.S. Announces Completion of Free-Trade Agreement with Colombia." *Washington File,* http://usinfo.state.gov/wh/Archive/2006/Feb/27–250339.html.

OECD. "Tertiary Education Soars in Middle Income Countries." Press release No. 2005-120.

"Of Cranes, Aid and Unintended Consequences." *The Economist,* October 5, 1996.

"Official Debt Restructuring." *Global Development Finance.* Washington, D.C.: World Bank.

O'Grady, Mary Anastasia. "A Brazilian State Shows How to Reform Schools." *Wall Street Journal,* August 16, 1997.

———. "What Argentina Needs." *Wall Street Journal,* July 17, 2001.

"Oil Chief & Leading Candidate Breach Taboo on Privatisation of PDVSA." *Latin American Weekly Report,* WR-98-30, August 4, 1998.

Olpadwala, Porus, and William Goldsmith. "The Sustainability of Privilege: Reflection on the Environment, the Third World City and Poverty." *World Development* 20(4) (1992).

Ónis, Ziya, and Ahmet Faruk Aysan. "Neoliberal Globalisation, the Nation-State and Financial Crises in the Semi-Periphery: A Comparative Analysis." *Third World Quarterly* 21(1) (2000).

Ortega, Emiliano. "Evolution of the Rural Dimension in Latin America and the Caribbean." *CEPAL Review* 47 (August 1992).

Osorio, Nestor. "International Coffee Council: Impact of the Coffee Crisis on Poverty in Producing Countries." ICC 89-5, Rev. September 1, 2003, www.ico.org.

Ostrovsky, Arkady. "Mexico Bucks Trend and Issues $1bn Bond." *Financial Times,* August 6, 2001.

Otteman, Scott. "Trade Policy Today." *Latin American Advisor,* July 2, 2001.

"Out of the Underworld: Criminal Gangs in the Americas." *The Economist On-line,* January 5, 2006.

Overhold, Catherine, and Margaret Saunders. *Policy Choices and Practical Problems in*

Health Economics: Cases from Latin America and the Caribbean. Economic Development Institute Resources Series. Washington, D.C.: World Bank, 1996.

Oxford Analytica. "Problems with the Millennium Development Goals." *Latin America Daily Brief,* August 28, 2003.

———. "Sustainable Forestry." *Latin America Daily Brief* 23 (March 2006).

Ozório de Almeida, Anna Luiza, and João S. Campari. *Sustainable Settlement in the Brazilian Amazon.* Oxford: Oxford University Press.

Paarlberg, Robert L. "The Politics of Agricultural Resource Abuse." *Environment* 36(8) (October 1994).

Pagiola, Stefano, Augustin Arcenas, and Gunars Platais. "Can Payments for Environmental Services Help Reduce Poverty? An Exploration of the Issues and the Evidence to Date from Latin America." *World Development* 33(2) (February 2005): 237–253.

PAHO. "Report of the Working Group on PAHO in the 21st Century," August 24, 2005, CD 46/29.

———. "Was 2005 the Year of Natural Disasters?" January 9, 2006, www.paho.org.

Palma, Gabriel. "Dependency: A Formal Theory of Underdevelopment or a Methodology for the Analysis of Concrete Situations of Underdevelopment?" *World Development* 6(7–8) (July–August 1979): 881–924.

Palmer, Ingrid. "Public Finance from a Gender Perspective." *World Development* 23(11) (1995).

Panagariya, Arvind. "The Free Trade Area of the Americas: Good for Latin America?" *World Economy* 19(5) (1996).

Pan American Health Organization. *Implementation of the Global Strategy: Health for All by the Year 2000,* vol. 3. Washington, D.C.: PAHO, 1993.

———. "Mexico." In *Health in the Americas,* vol. 2. Washington, D.C.: PAHO, 1998.

———. *PAHO Resolution V: Health of Indigenous Peoples.* Series HSS/SILOS, 34. Washington, D.C.: PAHO, 1993. Available at www.paho.org.

———. *Strategic and Programmatic Orientations, 1995–1998.* Presented at the Inter-American Meeting, Washington, D.C., April 25–27, 1995. Available at www.paho.org.

"Panel Finds Mexican Antidumping Order Violates WTO Rules." Press Release, January 27, 2000. Office of the United States Trade Representative, WTO, Washington, D.C.

Panizza, Ugo. "Financial Contagion in Latin America: Measuring Morbidity." *Latin American Economic Policies* 6(1) (1999).

Pánuco-Laguette, Humberto, and Miguel Székely. "Income Distribution and Poverty in Mexico." In *The New Economic Model in Latin America and Its Impact on Income Distribution and Poverty,* ed. Victor Bulmer-Thomas. New York: St. Martin's, 1996.

Parker, David, and Colin Kirkpatrick. "Privatization in Developing Countries: A Review of the Evidence and the Policy Lessons." *Journal of Development Studies* 41(4) (May 2005): 514.

Parry, Taryn Rounds. "Achieving Balance in Decentralization: A Case Study of Education Decentralization in Chile." *World Development* 25(2) (1997).

Partnership for Educational Revitalization in the Americas. *The Future at Stake: Report of the Task Force on Education, Equity and Economic Competitiveness in Latin America and the Caribbean.* Santiago, Chile: PREAL, in conjunction with the Inter-American Dialogue and CINDE, 1998. Available at www.preal.cl/index-i.htm.

———. *Quantity without Quality: A Report Card on Education in Latin America,* 2006, www.thedialogue.org.

Pastor, Robert A. *Lessons from the Old World for the New: The European Union and a Deeper, Wilder American Community.* HEL-Excerpts, May 5, 2000.

"Patience Runs Out in Bolivia." *The Economist,* April 21, 2001.

Patterson, Allen. "Debt for Nature Swaps and the Need for Alternatives." *Environment* 21 (December 1990): 5–32.

Peach, James T., and Richard V. Adkisson. "Enabling Myths and Mexico's Economic Crises (1976–1996)." *Journal of Economic Issues* 31(2) (June 1997).

Pereira Leite, Sérgio. "International Capital Flows: A Challenge for the 21st Century." *Revista ILO,* July 1, 2001.

Perez-Aleman, Paola. "Learning, Adjustment and Economic Development: Transforming Firms, the State and Associations in Chile." *World Development* 28(1) (2000).

"The Permanent Crisis in Argentina." *Latin American Weekly Report* 24 (June 21, 2001).

Perry, Guillermo, and Ana Maria Herrera. *Public Finance, Stabilization, and Structural Reform in Latin America.* Washington, D.C.: Johns Hopkins University Press/IADB, 1994.

Peterson, Jim. "Commentary: Don't Buy into the Import Hype." *A Monthly Journal from the Lemhi Mountains* (September 2000).

Phillip, Michael. "South American Trade Pact Is under Fire." *Wall Street Journal,* October 23, 1996.

Picciotto, Robert. *Putting Institutional Economics to Work: From Participation to Governance.* World Bank Discussion Papers No. 304. Washington, D.C.: World Bank, 1995.

Picciotto, Robert, and Jock Anderson. "Reconsidering Agricultural Extension." *World Bank Research Observer* 12(2) (August 1997).

Pirages, Dennis. "Sustainability As an Evolving Process." *Futures* 26(2) (1994): 197–205.

Pleskovic, Boris, and Joseph E. Stiglitz, eds. *Annual World Bank Conference on Development Economics, 1997.* Washington, D.C.: World Bank, 1998.

Polaski, Sandra. *Winners and Losers: Impact of the Doha Round on Developing Countries.* Washington, D.C.: Carnegie Endowment, 2006.

Pomareda, Carlos, and Frank Hartwich. "Agricultural Innovation in Latin America: Understanding the Private Sector's Role." *IFPRI* Issue Brief No. 42, January 2006.

Population Reference Bureau. "World Population Data Sheet 2005," www.prb.org.

Porter, Michael E., Klaus Schwab, and Augusto Lopez-Claros. *The Global Competitiveness Report 2005–2006: Policies Underpinning Rising Prosperity.* New York: Oxford University Press, 2005.

Pou, Pedro. "Argentina's Structural Reforms of the 1990s." *Finance & Development* (March 2000).

Poverty Reduction and the World Bank: Progress in Fiscal 1996 and 1997. Washington, D.C.: World Bank, 1998. Available at www.worldbank.org.

"Poverty Reduction Strategy Papers and the HIPC Initiative." Statement of U.S. Treasury Secretary Lawrence H. Summers at the Joint Session of the International Monetary and Finance Committee and the Development Committee, Washington, D.C., September 24, 2000.

Powell, Robert. "Debt Relief for Poor Countries." *Finance & Development* (December 2000).

Powers, William. "Poor Little Rich Country." *New York Times,* June 11, 2005.

Prados de la Escosura, Leandro. "Colonial Independance and Economic Backwardness in Latin America." GEHN Working Paper Series, No. 10/05, February 2005, www.lse.ac.uk.

Prawda, Juan. "Educational Decentralization in Latin America: Lessons Learned." *International Journal of Educational Development* 13(3) (1993): 253–264.

"Prices Soar as Brazil's Flexfuel Cars Set the Pace." *Financial Times,* FT News Alerts, March 26, 2006.

"Pride before the Fall." *The Economist,* October 28, 2000.

"Privatization." *Euromoney,* September 1996.

PROCYMAF. 2000. Proyecto de conservación y manejo sostenible de recursos forestales en México. Informe y avance 1998–2000. Misión de avaluación de medio terino.

SEMARNAP, Mexico; B. DeWalt, F. Olivera, and J. Betancourt Correa *Mid-term Evaluation of the Mexico Community Forestry Projects.* Washington, D.C.: World Bank, 2000.

"Progress in Privatization." *Global Development Finance.* Washington, D.C.: World Bank, 2001.

Psacharopoulos, George, and Harry Anthony Patrinos, eds. *Indigenous People and Poverty in Latin America.* Washington, D.C.: World Bank, 1994.

Psacharopoulos, George, Carlos Rojas, and Eduardo Velez. "Achieving Evaluation of Colombia's Escuela Nueva: Is Multigrade the Answer?" *Comparative Education Review* 37(3) (1993).

Psacharopoulos, George, et al. *Poverty and Income Distribution in Latin America: The Story of the 1980s.* World Bank Technical Paper No. 351. Washington, D.C.: World Bank, 1997.

Puder, Don. "U.S. Bill Would Country-of-Origin Labeling for Beef." *Times,* April 17, 2000.

Puryear, Jeffrey M. "Education in Latin America: Problems and Challenges." Presented to the Council of Foreign Relations, February 24, 1996, for the Latin American Program Study Group, "Educational Reform in Latin America," New York. Available at www.preal.cl/index-i.htm.

———. "Quantity without Quality: A Report Card on Education in Latin America." Power-Point Presentation at Education in Latin America, IDB Social Development Week, October 2005.

"Putting 'Missed' Chances Behind." *Financial Times,* December 14, 2000.

Rajapatirana, Sarath. *Trade Policies in Latin America and the Caribbean: Priorities, Progress, and Prospects.* San Francisco: International Center for Economic Growth, 1997.

Ramírez, Patricia. "A Sweeping Health Reform: The Quest for Unification, Coverage and Efficiency in Colombia." In *Crucial Needs, Weak Incentives: Social Sector Reform, Democratization, and Globalization in Latin America.* ed. Robert R. Kaufman and Joan M. Nelson. Washington, D.C.: Woodrow Wilson Center Press and Johns Hopkins University Press, 2004.

Ramos, Joseph. "Poverty and Inequality in Latin America: A Neostructuralist Perspective." *Journal of Inter-American Studies and World Affairs* 38(2–3) (Summer–Fall 1996).

Randall, Laura, ed. *Changing Structure of Mexico: Political, Social and Economic Prospects.* Armonk, N.Y.: Sharpe, 1996.

"Rate of Growth Moves Up a Gear." *Financial Times,* December 14, 2000.

Rawlings, Laura B. "A New Approach to Social Assistance: Latin America's Experience with Conditional Cash Transfer Programs." *International Social Security Review* 58(2–3) (2005).

Reardon, Thomas. "Rural Nonfarm Employment and Incomes in Latin America: Overview and Policy Implications." *World Development* 29(3) (2001).

Redclift, Michael. "The Environment and Structural Adjustment: Lessons for Policy Intervention." In *Structural Adjustment and the Agricultural Sector in Latin America and the Caribbean,* ed. John Weeks. New York: St. Martin's, 1995.

The Reform of the Mexican Health Care System. OECD Economic Surveys: Mexico. Paris: OECD, 1998.

"Regional Overview of Foreign Investment in Latin America and the Caribbean." *Chapter I of the 2000 Report on Foreign Investment in Latin American and the Caribbean.* ECLAC, United Nations, April 18, 2001.

"The Regulation of Foreign Capital Flows in Chile." Report by *Innovative Experiences.* Available at www.undp.org.

Reimers, Fernando. "Educacion para todos en América Latina en el Siglo XXIL. Los desafíos de la estabilización, el ajuste y los mandatos de Jomtien." Paper presented at UNESCO workshop, Peru, December 1990.

———. "The Impact of Economic Stabilization and Adjustment on Education in Latin America." *Comparative Education* 35(2) (May 1991).

Rennhack, Robert. "Banking Supervision." *Finance & Development* (March 2000): 27.

Replogle, Jill. "Hunger on the Rise in Central America." *The Lancet* 363(19) (June 2004): 2056, www.thelancet.com.

Report on the Binational Commission, International Studies Association meetings, Washington, D.C., February 20, 1999.

"Responsible Regionalism." *The Economist,* December 2, 2000.

"Revolution Ends, Change Begins." *The Economist,* October 28, 2000.

Rich, Jennifer L. "Compressed Data: Brazilians Think Basic to Bridge the Digital Divide." *New York Times,* February 12, 2001.

Richards, Michael. "Alternative Approaches and Problems in Protected Area Management and Forest Conservation in Honduras." In *Sustainable Agriculture in Central America,* ed. Jan P. de Groot and Ruerd Ruben. New York: St. Martin's, 1997.

"Rich Is Rich and Poor Is Poor." *The Economist,* October 28, 2000.

RICYT. "El Estado de la Ciencia. Principales Indicadores de Ciencia y Tecnología Iberoamericanos / InterAmericanos 2004." The Network on Science and Technology Indicators, Ibero-American and Inter-American, www.ricyt.edu.ar.

Rivoli, Pietra. *The Travels of a T-Shirt in the Global Economy.* Hoboken, N.J.: John Wiley and Sons, 2005.

Rizvi, Haider. "Biodiversity: Brazil's Lula Lashes Out At Rich Nations." *IPS Terraviva,* March 28, 2006.

Rodriguez-Clare, Andres. *Innovation and Technology Adoption in Central America.* Inter-American Development Bank Research Department, Working Paper Series 525, July 2005.

Rodriguez-Garcia, Rosalia, and Ann Goldman, eds. *The Health-Development Link.* Washington, D.C.: PAHO, 1994.

Rodriguez-Mendoz, Miguel. "The Andean Group's Integration Strategy." In *Integrating the Hemisphere, 1997: The Inter-American Dialogue,* ed. Ana Julia Jatar and Sidney Weintraub. Santafé de Bogotá, Colombia: Tercer Mundo, 1997.

Rodrik, Dani. "Growth and Poverty Reduction: What Are the Real Questions?" *Finance & Development* (August 2000), http://ksghome.harvard.edu/~drodrik/poverty.pdf.

———. "Institutions for High-Quality Growth: What They Are and How to Acquire Them." *International Monetary Fund 1999.* Available at www.imf.org/external/pubs/ft/seminar/1999/reforms/rodrik/htm.

———. *King Kong Meets Godzilla: The World Bank and the East Asian Miracle.* CEPR Discussion Paper No. 944. London: Centre for Economic Policy Research, 1994.

———. "Why Do More Open Economies Have Bigger Governments?" *Journal of Political Economy* 16(5) (1998).

Rodrik, Dani, and Arvind Subramanian. "The Primacy of Institutions (and What This Does and Does Not Mean)." *Finance and Development* (June 2003): 32.

Rohloff, Greg. "Beef Processor IBP Inc. Agrees to Buyout by Investment Bank." *Amarillo Daily News,* October 5, 2000.

Rohter, Larry. "Brazilians Uneasy Despite Help by I.M.F." *New York Times,* August 6, 2001.

———. "Bush and Brazil Chief Have Politics, If Not Trade, to Discuss." *New York Times,* March 30, 2001.

———. "Crisis Whipsaws Brazilian Workers." *New York Times,* January 16, 1999. Online edition.

———. "Ecuadorian President Imposes Sweeping Austerity Measures." *New York Times,* March 21, 1999.

————. "For Brazil's College-Bound, a Brutal Test of Mettle." *New York Times,* December 29, 2000.

————. "Loggers, Scorning the Law, Ravage the Amazon." *New York Times,* October 16, 2005.

————. "U.S. Aid to Colombia Worries Hemisphere's Defense Leaders." *New York Times,* October 18, 2000.

————. "Where Darwin Mused, Strife over Ecosystem." *New York Times,* December 27, 2000.

————. "With a Big Boost from Sugar Cane, Brazil is Satisfying Its Fuel Needs." *New York Times,* April 10, 2006.

Rohter, Larry, and Elizabeth Johnson. "Brazil Deforestation: Pioneer Loggers Suffer a Setback." *FT News Alerts,* October 7, 2005, www.ft.com.

Rojas, Eduardo. *The IDB in Low-Cost Housing the First Three Decades.* Strategic Planning and Operational Policy Department, February 1995.

Rojas, Patricia. "IDB Welcomes Creation of Brazilian Carbon Market." *IDB America,* April 2, 2006, www.iadb.org.

Rojas-Suarez, Liliana. "Dollarization in Latin America." Presented to the Hearing on Official Dollarization in Latin America for the Senate Banking Committee, July 15, 1999.

Rojas-Suarez, Liliana, and Steven R. Weisbrod. "Building Stability in Latin American Financial Markets." In *Securing Stability and Growth in Latin America,* ed. Ricardo Hausmann and Helmut Reisen. Paris: OECD Publications, 1996.

Roldán, Jorge. Interview. *IDB Extra,* June 14, 1998. Online edition.

Romero, Simon. "Where the Risk Is Riskier Yet." *New York Times,* December 16, 1999.

Rosegrant, Susan. *Banana Wars: Challenges to the European Union's Banana Regime.* Abstract. 1999.

Rosenthal, Gert. "Development Thinking and Policies: The Way Ahead." *CEPAL Review* 60 (December 1996).

————. "On Poverty and Inequality in Latin America." *Journal of Inter-American Studies and World Affairs* 38(2–3) (Summer–Fall 1996).

Ross, Jen. "Brazil's Disappearing Jungle." *Toronto Star,* August 6, 2005.

Rothkopf, David J. "Rising Above the Moment." *New Democrat* (September/October 1997).

Russell, Clifford S., and Philip T. Powell. *Choosing Environmental Policy Tools: Theoretical Cautions and Practical Considerations.* No. ENV-102. Washington, D.C.: IADB, June 1996.

Ryan, John. "The Shrinking Forest." *NACLA Report on the Americas* 25(2) (September 1991).

Saavedra, Jaime, and Omar S. Arias. "Stuck in a Rut." *Finance and Development* 42(4) (December 2005).

Sachs, Jeffery. *The End of Poverty.* New York: Penguin, 2005, 253–254.

————. *Tropical Underdevelopment.* CID Working Paper No. 57. Cambridge: Harvard University Press, December 2000.

Sachs, Jeffrey, and Alvaro Zini. "Brazilian Inflation and the Plano Real." *World Economy* 19(1) (January 1996).

Sachs, Wolfgang, ed. *The Development Dictionary: A Guide to Knowledge As Power.* London: Zed, 1992.

"Safeguarding against Crisis: The Near-Term Agenda." *Global Development Finance.* Washington, D.C.: World Bank, 2000.

Salzinger, Leslie. "Making Fantasies Real—Producing Women and Men on the Maquila Shop Floor." *NACLA Report on the Americas* 34(5) (March/April 2001).

"The Samba and the Tango." *The Economist,* February 24, 1996.

Samor, Geraldo. "Brazil's Petrobras Self-Reliant or Pliant?" *Wall Street Journal,* April 21, 2006, A7.

Sampaio Malan, Pedro, and Arminio Fraga Neto. "Brazil—Memorandum of Economic Policies." Washington, D.C.: IMF, April 20, 2000.

Samuelson, Robert J. "Dollarization—a Black Hole." *Washington Post,* May 12, 1999, A27.

Sánchez, M., R. Corona, L. F. Herrera, and O. Ochoa. "A Comparison of Privatization Experiences: Chile, Mexico, Colombia, and Argentina." In *Privatization in Latin America,* ed. M. Sánchez and R. Corona. Baltimore: Johns Hopkins University Press, 1994.

Sanchez, Ricardo, and Gordon Wilmsmeier. "Bridging Infrastructural Gaps in Central America: Prospects and Potential for Maritime Transport." ECLAC, Series CEPAL, Recursos Naturales e Infraestructura, No. 97, September 2005.

Santiso, Javier. *Latin America's Political Economy of the Possible.* Cambridge, MA: MIT Press, 2006.

———. "Political Sluggishness and Economic Speed: A Latin American Perspective." *Social Science Information* 39(2) (2000).

Savedoff, William, Antonio Giuffrida, and Roberto Iunes, *Economic and Health Effects of Occupational Hazards.* IADB, Sustainable Development Department, June 2001.

Sawers, Larry. "Nontraditional or New Traditional Exports." *Latin American Research Review* 40(3) (October 2005): 1.

Sawyer, Suzana. "Indigenous Initiatives and Petroleum Politics in the Ecuadorian Amazon." *Cultural Survival* (Spring 1996).

Schemo, Diana Jean. "The ABC's of Doing Business in Brazil." *New York Times,* July 16, 1998. Online edition.

———. "Brazil Farmers Feel Squeezed by Tobacco Companies." *New York Times,* April 6, 1998. Online edition.

———. "Brazilians Fret As Economic Threat Moves Closer." *New York Times,* September 20, 1998. Online edition.

———. "Ecuadorians Want Texaco to Clear Toxic Residue." *New York Times,* January 31, 1998.

———. "A Latin Bloc Asks U.S. and Europe to Ease Trade Barriers." *New York Times,* February 23, 1999. Online edition.

Scherr, Sara J., Andy White, and David Kaimowitz. "Making Markets Work for Forest Communities." *Forest Trends.* Washington, D.C., 2002.

Schiesel, Seth. "Brazil Sells Most of State Phone Utility." *New York Times,* July 30, 1998, D1.

Schiff, Maurice, and Alberto Valdes. "The Plundering of Agriculture in Developing Countries." 1994 draft paper, available at www.worldbank.org/html/extpb/PlunderingAgri.html.

Schmitz, Hubert, and José Cassiolato. *Hi-Tech for Industrial Development: Lessons from the Brazilian Experience in Electronics and Automation.* London: Routledge, 1992.

Schneider, Stephen, Armin Rosencranz, and John O. Niles, eds. *Climate Change Policy: A Survey.* Washington, D.C.: Island Press, 2002.

Schott, Jeffrey J. "NAFTA: An Interim Report." In *Trade: Towards Open Regionalism,* Proceedings of the 1997 World Bank Conference on Development in Latin America and the Caribbean. Washington, D.C.: World Bank 1998.

Searcey, Dionne, and David Lubnow. "Verizon Pulls Out of Latin America." *Wall Street Journal,* April 4, 2006, A18.

Sedelnik, Lisa. "CANTV: Inside the IPO." *Latin Finance* 83 (1997): 43–46.

Seers, Dudley. "What Are We Trying to Measure?" *Journal of Development Studies* (April 1972).

Sekles, Flavia. "Brazil's AIDS Policies Tightly Link Prevention and Treatment." March 2005, www.prb.org.

SELA. "Current Trends in Migrants' Remittances in Latin America and the Caribbean." Caracas, Venezuela, November 2003, sela.org.

Sen, Amartya. "The Concept of Development." In *Handbook of Development Economics,* Vol. 1. Netherlands: North-Holland, 1988.

Serant, Claire. "Sony Will Play Solectron—Sale of Two Plants May Fling Open Japan's Doors." *Electronic Buyers News,* October 23, 2000.

Shah, Fared, David Zilberman, and Ujjayant Chakravorty. "Water Rights Doctrines and Technology Adoption." In *The Economics of Rural Organization,* ed. Karla Hoff, Avishay Braverman, and Joseph Stiglitz. New York: Oxford University Press/World Bank, 1993.

Shapiro, Helen. *Engines of Growth: The State and Transnational Auto Companies in Brazil.* Cambridge: Cambridge University Press, 1994.

———. *Mexico: Escaping the Debt Crisis.* Harvard Business School Case. Boston: Harvard Business School, 1991.

———. *North American Free Trade Agreement: Free for Whom?* Harvard Business School case #5-792-059. Boston: Harvard Business School, 1993.

Shatz, Howard, "Expanding Foreign Direct Investment in the Andean Countries." CID Working Paper No. 64. Cambridge, Mass.: Center for International Development at Harvard University, March 2001.

Sheahan, John, and Enrique Iglesias. "Kinds and Causes of Inequality in Latin America." In *Beyond Trade-Offs: Market Reform and Equitable Growth in Latin America,* ed. Nancy Birdsall, Carol Graham, and Richard Sabot. Washington, D.C.: Brookings Institution Press/IADB, 1998.

Shinkai, Naoko. *Does Stolper-Samuelson Theorem Explain the Movement in Wages? The Linkage between Trade and Wages in Latin American Countries.* Working Paper #436. Washington, D.C.: IADB, November 2000.

Shore, Keane. *Harvard Economist Calls for New Approach to International Development.* IRDC Report, August 9, 2001.

Shoumatoff, Alex. *The World Is Burning.* Boston: Little, Brown, 1990.

Sillars, Les. "A Bull Market for Beef and Pork: Investment in Western Meat Processing Continues to Surge." *Alberta Report,* April 14, 1997.

Silviera, Patrícia Pelufo, André Krumel Portella, and Marcelo Zubaran Goldani. "Obesity in Latin America." *The Lancet* 366 (August 6, 2005).

Simons, Marlise. "A Talk with Gabriel García Marquez." *New York Times,* December 5, 1982, sec. 7, p. 7. Available at www.nytimes.com/books/97/06/15/reviews/marquez-talk .html and in the LEXIS-NEXIS database.

Sims, Calvin. "Peruvians Climb onto the Web." *New York Times,* May 27, 1996.

Singh, Anoop, Agneés Belaisch, Charles Collyns, Paula DeMasi, Reva Krieger, Guy Meredith, and Robert Renhack. "Stabilization and Reform in Latin America: A Macro-economicPerspective on the Experience since the Early 1990's." International Monetary Fund, Occasional Paper No. 238, February 2005.

Skidmore, Thomas E. "Brazil's Persistent Income Inequality." *Latin American Politics and Society* 46(2) (2004): 133–150.

"Skills Gap May Be Biggest Trade Barrier." *Journal of Commerce.* April 20, 1998. Online edition. Available at www.alca-cupula.org.

"Slicing the Cake: What Is the Relationship between Inequality and Economic Growth?" *The Economist,* October 19, 1996.

"The Slow Road to Reform." *The Economist,* December 2, 2000.

Smith, Geri. "Slim's New World." *Business Week* (International edition), February 2000.

Smith, James F. "Mexican Beef Growers Decry Duties on U.S. As Too Low." *Los Angeles Times,* August 4, 1999.

Sokoloff, Kenneth. "Inequality and the Evolution of Institutions of Taxation: Evidence from the Economic History of the Americas." In *Growth Institutions and Crises: Latin America from a Historical Perspective,* ed. Sebastian Edwards. Washington, D.C.: National Bureau of Economic Research, 2005.

Sola, Lourdes, Christopher Garman, and Moises S. Marques. *Central Reform and Overcoming the Moral Hazard Problem: The Case of Brazil.* Paper Presented for the XXII International Latin American Studies Association Congress, 2000.

"Some Mutual Funds Go Back Full Throttle to Emerging Markets." *Wall Street Journal,* November 12, 1996.

"Something for a Refresco." *The Economist,* October 28, 2000.

Spar, Debora. *Regarding NAFTA.* Harvard Business School Case #5-798-122. Boston: Harvard Business School, 1998.

Sprague, Courtnay. *Debt Restructuring under the Brady Plan.* Harvard Business School case #9-796-130. Boston: Harvard Business School, 1998.

"The Sputtering Spark from South America's Car Industry." *The Economist,* April 15, 1995.

Stahl, Karin. "Anti-Poverty Programs: Making Structural Adjustment More Palatable." *NACLA Report on the Americas* 29(6) (May–June 1995).

Stallings, Barbara, and Wilson Peres. *Growth, Employment, and Equity: The Impact of the Economic Reforms in Latin America and the Caribbean.* Summary. ECLAC, Spring 2000.

Stauder, Monique. "Colombian Cocaine Runs through It." *Christian Science Monitor,* June 13, 2001.

Steele, Diane. "Guatemala." In *Indigenous People and Poverty in Latin America,* ed. George Psacharopoulos and Harry Anthony Patrinos. Washington, D.C.: World Bank, 1994.

Stein, Elizabeth. *Regarding NAFTA.* Harvard Business School Case #9-797-013. Boston: Harvard Business School, 1998.

Stein, Ernesto, Ernesto Talvi, and Alejandro Grisanti. *Institutional Arrangements and Fiscal Performance: The Latin American Experience.* National Bureau of Economic Research Working Paper No. 6358. Cambridge, Mass.: National Bureau of Economic Research, 1998.

Stenfeld, Jacob. "Development and Foreign Investment: Lessons Learned from Mexican Banking." Carnegie Papers No. 47, Carnegie Endowment for International Peace, July 2004.

Stephens, Carolyn, Clive Nettleton, John Porter, Ruth Willis, and Stephanie Clark. "Indigenous People's Health—Why Are They Behind Everyone, Everywhere?" *The Lancet* 366 (July 2, 2005): 11. www.thelancet.com.

Stewart, Frances. *Adjustment and Poverty: Options and Choices.* London: Routledge, 1995.

Stiglitz, Joseph. "More Instruments and Broader Goals: Moving toward the Post-Washington Consensus." *The 1998 WIDER Annual Lecture.* The World Bank Group, Washington, D.C.: 1998.

———. "Post–Washington Consensus." *Initiative for Policy Dialogue,* Working Paper Series, Columbia University, 2005.

———. "The Role of Government in Economic Development." In *Annual World Bank Conference on Development Economics 1996.* Washington, D.C.: World Bank, 1997.

"Stopping the Rot in Public Life." *The Economist,* September 16, 2000.

Strahan, Spencer, and Adrian Wood. "Making the Financial Sector Work for the Poor." *Journal of Development Studies* 41(4) (May 2005): 657–675.

Streeten, Paul. "A Basic Needs Approach to Economic Development." In *Directions in Economic Development,* ed. Kenneth P. Jameson and Charles K. Wilber. Notre Dame, Ind.: University of Notre Dame Press, 1979.

———. "From Growth to Basic Needs." In *Latin America's Economic Development: Institutionalist and Structuralist Perspectives,* ed. James L. Dietz and James H. Street. Boulder, Colo.: Rienner, 1987.

Sturzenegger, Federico A. "Description of a Populist Experience: Argentina, 1973–1976." In *The Macroeconomics of Populism in Latin America,* ed. Rudiger Dornbusch and Sebastian Edwards. Chicago: University of Chicago Press, 1991.

Sullivan, Mark P. "Panama: Political and Economic Conditions and U.S. Relation." Congressional Research Service Report RL30981, February 15, 2006, www.opencrs.cdt.org.

"Summing Up by the Chairman of the IMF Executive Board Enhanced Initiative for Heavily Indebted Poor Countries (HIPC) and Poverty Reduction Strategy Papers (PRSP)—Progress Reports and Review of Implementation." Executive Board Meeting of September 5, 2000. Washington, D.C.: IMF, September 11, 2000.

"The Summiteers Go to School." *The Economist,* April 25, 1998, 37–38.

Sunkel, Osvaldo. *Development from Within: Toward a Neostructuralist Approach for Latin America.* Boulder, Colo.: Rienner, 1993.

Suro, Roberto. "Remittances Senders and Receivers: Tracking Transnational Channels." Joint Report of the MIF and the Pew Hispanic Center, Washington, D.C., November 24, 2003.

Swafford, David. "A Healthy Trend: Health Care Reform in Latin America." *Latin Finance* 83 (December 1996).

Swinton, Scott M., Germán Escobar, and Thomas Reardon. "Poverty and Environment in Latin America: Concepts, Evidence and Policy Implications." *World Development* 31(11) (November 2003): 1865.

Sylos Labini, Paolo. "The Classical Roots of Development Theory." In *Economic Development: Handbook of Comparative Economic Policies,* ed. Enzo Grilli and Dominick Salvatore. Westport, Conn.: Greenwood, 1994.

"A System That Needs Some Simplifying." *Financial Times,* December 14, 2000.

Székely, Miguel. *The 1990s in Latin America: Another Decade of Persistent Inequality, but with Somewhat Lower Poverty.* Working Paper No. 454. IADB, June 2001.

Székely, Miguel, Nora Lustig, Martin Cumpa, and José Antonio Mejía. *Do We Know How Much Poverty There Is?* Working Paper 437. IADB, December 2000.

Tanzi, Vito, "Fiscal Federalism and Decentralization: A Review of Some Efficiency and Macroeconomic Aspects." Paper presented at the World Bank Conference on Development Economics, World Bank, May 1995. As summarized by *The Economist,* June 3, 1995.

Tanzi, Vito, and Howell Zee. *Tax Policy for Developing Countries.* Washington, D.C.: IMF, 2001.

Tardanico, Richard, and Rafael Menjívar Larraín. "Restructuring, Employment, and Social Inequality: Comparative Urban Latin American Patterns." In *Global Restructuring, Employment, and Social Inequality in Urban Latin America,* ed. Richard Tardanico and Rafael Menjívar Larraín. Miami: University of Miami North-South Center Press, 1997.

"A Taxing Problem." *The Economist,* June 3, 1995.

Taylor, Alan. *Argentina and the World Capital Market: Saving, Investment and International Capital Mobility in the Twentieth Century.* National Bureau of Economic Research Working Paper No. 6302. Cambridge, Mass.: National Bureau of Economic Research, 1997.

———. "Foreign Capital in Latin America in the Nineteenth and Twentieth Centuries." NBER Working Paper No. W9580, March 2003.

———. "On the Costs of Inward-Looking Development: Price Distortions, Growth and Divergence in Latin America." *Journal of Economic History* 58(1) (March 1998).

Taylor, Jerry. "The Challenge of Sustainable Development." *Regulation* 17(1) (1994): 35–50.

Taylor, Lance, and Ute Piper. *Reconciling Economic Reform and Sustainable Human Development: Social Consequences of Neo-Liberalism.* UNDP Discussion Paper Series. New York: United Nations Development Programme, 1996.

"A Teacher's Lot." *The IDB,* May 1996.

Teichman, Judith. "Policy Networks and Policy Reform in Mexico: Technocrats, the World Bank and the Private Sector." Paper presented to the Congress of the Latin American Studies Association, March 16, 2000.

"Telebras Sold for US$19.lB." *Latin American Weekly Report,* August 4, 1998.

Templeman, John. "Is Europe Elbowing the U.S. Out of South America?" *BusinessWeek,* August 4, 1997, 56.

Tendler, Judith. *Good Government in the Tropics.* Baltimore: Johns Hopkins University Press, 1997.

"Tequila Freeways." *The Economist,* December 16, 1996.

Thatcher, Peter S. "The Role of the United Nations." In *The International Politics of the Environment: Actors, Interests, and Institutions,* ed. Andrew Hurrell and Benedict Kingsbury. Oxford, UK: Clarendon, 1992.

Thomas, Vinod. "Why Quality Matters." *The Economist,* October 7, 2000.

Thompson, Ginger. "At Home, Mexico Mistreats Its Farmhands." *New York Times,* May 6, 2001.

———. "Chasing Mexico's Dream into Squalor." *New York Times,* February 11, 2001.

———. "In Guatemalan Town Buried by Mud, Unyielding Hope for a Little Girl." *New York Times,* October 9, 2005.

Thomson, Adam. "US Latin American Trade Policy under Scrutiny As FTAA Fall Off Summit." *Financial Times,* November 7, 2005.

Thorp, Rosemary. "Import Substitution: A Good Idea in Principle." In *Latin America and the World Economy: Dependency and Beyond,* ed. Richard J. Salvucci. Lexington, Mass.: Heath, 1996.

———. *Progress, Poverty, and Exclusion: An Economic History of Latin America in the 20th Century.* Baltimore: Johns Hopkins University Press/IADB, 1998.

Thorpe, Andy. "Sustainable Agriculture in Latin America." In *Sustainable Agriculture in Central America,* ed. Jan P. de Groot and Ruerd Ruben. New York: St. Martin's, 1997.

Thrupp, Lori Ann. *Bittersweet Harvests for Global Supermarkets: Challenges in Latin America's Agricultural Export Boom.* Washington, D.C.: World Resources Institute, 1995.

"'Til Debt Do Us Part." *The Economist,* February 28, 1987.

Todaro, Michael P. *Economic Development.* 5th ed. White Plains, N.Y.: Longham, 1994.

Tokman, Victor E. "Jobs and Solidarity: Challenges for Post-Adjustment in Latin America." In *Economic and Social Development in the XXI Century,* Proceedings of the 1997 IADB conference, ed. Louis Emmerij. Available at www.iadb.org/exr/pub/xxi/sec4.htm.

Tokman, Viktor. *Beyond Regulation: The Informal Economy in Latin America.* Boulder, Colo.: Rienner, 1992.

———. "Policies for a Heterogeneous Informal Sector." *World Development* 17(7) (1989): 1067–1076.

Toman, Michael A. "Economics and 'Sustainability': Balancing the Trade-offs and Imperatives." *Land Economics* 70(4) (November 1994): 399–413.

Toomy, Gerry. "Combining Environmental Protection and Poverty Alleviation in Colombia." *Science from the Developing World,* August 7, 2001.

Torres, Carlos A. *Education and Social Change in Latin America.* Albert Park, Australia: James Nicolas, 1997.

Torres, Carlos Alberto, and Adriana Puiggrós. "The State and Public Education in Latin America." *Comparative Education Review* 39(1) (1995).

"Trade in the Americas." *The Economist,* April 21, 2001.

Transparency International, Global Corruption Reports 2001, www.transparency.org.

Trebat, Thomas. *Brazil's State-Owned Enterprises: A Case Study of the State As Entrepreneur.* New York: Cambridge University Press, 1983.

Tricks, Henry. "Electronic Expansion for Cemex." *Financial Times,* December 13, 2000.

Trivelli, Carolina, Javier Alvarado, Francisco Galarza. *Increasing Indebtedness, Institutional Change and Credit Contracts in Peru.* IADB, Office of the Chief Economist. Working Paper #R-378. Washington, D.C.: IADB, 1999.

"Trouble Brewing." *The Economist,* March 10, 2001.

Tullio, G., and M. Ronci. "Brazilian Inflation from 1980 to 1993: Causes Consequences and Dynamics." *Journal of Latin American Studies* 28 (October 1996): 635–666.

Tussie, Diana. *The Multilateral Development Banks,* Vol. 4, *The Inter-American Development Bank.* Ottawa: North-South Institute, 1995.

Tussie, Diana, and Cintia Quiliconi. "The Current Trade Context." HDR Publications, Background Papers, 2005. Available at hdr.undp.org/publications/.

Tussie, Diana, and María Fernanda Tuozzo. "Multilateral Development Banks and Civil Society Participation in Latin America." Presented to Facultad Latinoamericana de Ciencias Sociales for the LASA Conference, March 2000.

"21 anos da morte de Margarida Alves," http://www.mmcbrasil.com.br/noticias/21margarida.htm.

Twomey, Michael J. *Multinational Corporations and the North American Free Trade Agreement.* Westport, Conn.: Praeger, 1993.

UNESCO. *Educational Panorama 2005: Progressing Toward the Goals.* Regional Education Indicators Project, Summit of the Americas, November 2005, www.unesco.cl.

———. "Education for All, Literacy for Life 2005." *Education for all Global Monitoring Report,* www.unesco.org.

"Unfinished Business." *The Economist,* March 2, 1996.

United Nations. "AIDS Epidemic in Latin America: Fact Sheet." www.unaids.org.

———. *Human Development Report 2005.* Human Development Indicators, http://hdr.undp.org/reports/global/2005/.

———. "A Latin American and Caribbean Perspective." United Nations Development Programme, Millennium Development Goals, August 2005, 232.

———. "Millennium Development Goals: A Latin American and Caribbean Perspective." www.unesco.org, August 2005.

——— "State of the World Population 2003." www.unfpa.org.

———. Unicef Child Survival Report Card, Progress for Children, 2004, Vol. 1, www.unicef.org.

———. "United Nations Framework Convention on Climate Change." www.unfccc.org.

———. *World Economic and Social Survey 2005: Financing for Development.* www.un.org.

———. *World Investment Report 1994.* New York: United Nations, 1994.

United Nations Development Programme. *Human Development Report, 1997.* New York: Oxford University Press.

United Nations Office for Drug Control and Crime Prevention. *World Drug Report 2000.* Oxford University Press, 2000, Annex 1, www.odccp.org/pdf/world_drug_report2000/report_2001-01-22_1.pdf.

"U.S. and Mexican Labor Secretaries Sign Consultation Agreements." *PR Newswire,* May 22, 2000.

U.S. Department of State. *1996 Country Reports on Economic Policy and Trade Practices.* January 1997. Available at www.state.gov/www/issues/trade_reports/latin_america99/costarica96.html and www.state.gov/www/issues/economic/trade_reports/latin_america96/panama96.html.

U.S. Trade Representative "Mexico." Foreign Trade Barriers. 2000 National Trade Estimate Report. www.ustr.gov.

Valcarel, Juan Manuel. "Calling Someone in Argentina: Dial M for Monopoly." *Wall Street Journal,* August 16, 1996.

Valdivia, Martin. "Peru: Is Identifying the Poor the Main Problem?" In *Reaching the Poor with Health, Nutrition and Population Services,* ed. Wagstaff A. Gwatkin and A. S. Yazbeck. Washington, D.C.: World Bank, 2005.

Valente, Marcela. "Argentina: The Environmental Costs of Biofuel." *IPS Terraviva* Online, April 21, 2006.

———. "Fighting Chagas Disease, Camera in Hand." *IPS Terraviva* Online, August 30, 2005.

———. "Latin America: End to Subsidies Would Not End Rural Poverty." *IPS Terraviva* Online, December 5, 2005.

Van der Hoeven, Rolph, and Gyorgy Sziraczi. *Lesson from Privatization.* Geneva: International Labour Office, 1997.

Vandermeer, John, and Ivette Perfecto. *Breakfast of Biodiversity: The Truth about Rain Forest Destruction.* Oakland, Calif.: Institute for Food and Development Policy, 1995.

Varo, Vicente. "Argentine Stocks Rebound on Budget Cut Accord." *Financial Times,* July 17, 2001.

Veiga, Petro da Motta. "Mercosur: In Search of a New Agenda." *The Challenges of a Project in Crisis.* INTAL-ITD, July 2004, www.iadb.org.

Velzboer-Salcedo, Markjke, and Julie Novick. "Violence against Women in the Americas," *PAHO Perspectives in Health* 5(2) (2000), www.paho.org.

"Venezuela: Accession Will Not Affect Mercosur's Economy." *Latinnews Daily,* January 26, 2006.

"Venezuela: Blitz of Ranch and Industrial Plant Seizures." *Latin American Weekly Report,* September 13, 2005.

"Venezuela on Wrong Path: Seizing Assets of Resource Firms Will Scare Off Foreign Investment." *Calgary Herald* (Alberta), April 10, 2006, A14.

"Venezuela's Chaotic Land Reform," *Economist* 374(8409) (January 15, 2005): 34.

Vera-Vassallo, Alejandro C. "Foreign Investment and Competitive Development in Latin America and the Caribbean." *CEPAL Review* 60 (December 1996).

Verhovek, Sam Howe. "Pollution Problems Fester South of the Border." *New York Times,* July 4, 1998. Online edition.

Vetter, Stephen G. "The Business of Grassroots Development." *Grassroots Development* 19(2) (1995): 2–12.

Villarreal, M. Angeles. "Trade Integration in the Americas." Congressional Research Service Report RL33162, November 22, 2005. Washington D.C.: Library of Congress, www.opencrs.cdt.org.

Vives, Antonio. *Private Infrastructure: Ten Commandments for Sustainability.* The IADB, Sustainable Development Department, February 1997, www.iadb.org/SDS/doc/ifm%2D303e.pdf.

Vogel, Thomas T., Jr. "Venezuela Privatization Proves Paltry." *Wall Street Journal,* July 17, 1996.

Vosti, Stephen A., Evaldo Munoz Braz, Chantal Line Carpentier, Marcus D'Olveira, and Julie Witcover. "Rights to Forest Products, Deforestation and Smallholder Income: Evidence from the Western Brazilian Amazon." *World Development* 31(11) (November 2003): 1889–1901.

Wacziarg, Romain, and Karen Horn Welch. *Trade Liberalization and Growth: New Evidence.* National Bureau of Economic Research Working Paper 10152, December 2003.

Wade, Robert. "The Asian Crisis and the Global Economy: Causes, Consequences and Cure." *Current History,* November 1998.

Wallace, Robert Bruce. "Policies of Protection in Mexico." In *Protection and Economic*

Development in Mexico, ed. Adriaan ten Kate and Robert Bruce Wallace. Hampshire, UK: Gower, 1980.

Walsh, Sharon. "Tyson Foods to Buy Competitor Hudson; Rival Had Been Hit by Massive Beef Recall." *Washington Post,* September 5, 1997.

Warburg, Dillon Read. "The Impact of the Asian Crisis on Latin America." Fax newsletter, July 14, 1998, 2.

———. *The Latin American Adviser.* Fax newsletter, February 1998.

———. *The Latin American Adviser.* Fax newsletter, July 9, 1998.

Warts, Tom. "Protection and Private Foreign Investment." In *Protection and Economic Development in Mexico,* ed. Adriaan ten Kate and Robert Bruce Wallace. Hampshire, UK: Gower, 1980.

"Water Works in Buenos Aires." *The Economist,* February 24, 1996.

Weeks, John. "Macroeconomic Adjustment." As noted in *Economic and Social Progress in Latin America 1992 Report,* special section, "Latin America's Export of Manufactured Goods." Washington, D.C.: IADB, 1992.

———. "The Manufacturing Sector in Latin America and the New Economic Model." In *The New Economic Model in Latin America and Its Impact on Income Distribution and Poverty,* ed. Victor Bulmer-Thomas. New York: St. Martin's, 1996.

Weersma-Haworth, Teresa S. "Export Processing Free Zones as Export Strategy." In *Latin America's New Insertion in the World Economy,* ed. Ruud Buitelaar and Pitou Van Dijck. New York: St. Martin's, 1996.

Weinberg, Bill. *War on the Land: Ecology and Politics in Central America.* Atlantic Highlands, N.J.: Zed, 1991.

Weiner, Tim. "Terrific News in Mexico City: Air Is Sometimes Breathable." *New York Times,* January 5, 2001.

Weintraub, Sidney. "Ideological Generalizations about Financial Rescue Packages." *Issues in International Political Economy,* No. 15. Washington, D.C.: CSIS.

———. "In the Debate about NAFTA, Just the Facts, Please." *Wall Street Journal,* June 20, 1997, A19.

Welch, John. "The New Face of Latin America: Financial Flows, Markets, and Institutions in the 1990s." *Journal of Latin American Studies* 25 (1993): 1–24.

Weyland, Kurt. *The Politics of Market Reform in Fragile Democracies.* Princeton, N.J.: Princeton University Press, 2002.

Wheeler, David, "Racing to the Bottom? Foreign Investment and Air Pollution in Developing Countries." Washington, D.C.: World Bank, Environmental Division.

White, Allen T. "Venezuela's Organic Law: Regulating Pollution in an Industrializing Country." *Environment* 33(7) (September 1991).

Wilber, Charles K. *The Political Economy of Development and Underdevelopment.* New York: Random House, 1973.

Wilber, Charles K., and Steven Francis. "The Methodological Basis of Hirschman's Development Economics: Pattern Modeling vs. General Laws." *World Development* 14(2), special issue (February 1986): 181–191.

Williams, Frances, and Michael Mann. "Delay Threat to US and EU Banana Deal." *Financial Times,* August 1, 2000.

Williamson, John. *Dollarization Does Not Make Sense Everywhere.* Institute for International Economics, 2001. Available at www.iie.com/TESTMONY.jwdollar.htm.

———. "What Should the Bank Think about the Washington Consensus?" Institute for International Economics paper prepared as a background to the World Bank's 2000 World Development Report. July 1999, www.iie.com.

———. "What Washington Means by Policy Reform." In J. Williamson, ed., *Latin American*

Adjustment: How Much Has Happened? Washington: Institute for International Economics, 1990.

Willis, Eliza, Christopher da C. B. Garman, and Stephan Haggard. "The Politics of Decentralization in Latin America." *Latin American Research Review* 43(1) (1999).

Wills, Rick. "Mexico Beef Dispute." *New York Times,* August 3, 1999.

Winters, L. Allan. "Assessing Regional Integration." *In Trade: Towards Open Regionalism,* Proceedings of the 1997 World Bank Conference on Development in Latin America and the Caribbean. Washington, D.C.: World Bank, 1998.

Wise, Carol. "Latin America and the State-Market Debate: Beyond Stylized Facts." Paper presented to the Latin American Studies Association, March 16, 2000.

Wolfensohn, James D. *Building an Equitable World—Address to the Board of Governors.* Prague: The World Bank Group, September 26, 2000.

———. Remarks to the Board of Governors of the World Bank Group, October 1, 1996. Available at the LEXIS-NEXIS database.

Wolff, Laurence. "Educational Assessments in Latin America: Current Progress and Future Challenges." *Partnership for Educational Revitalization in the Americas.* June 1998. Online publication, available at www.preal.cl/index-i.htm.

Wolff, Laurence, Juan Carlos Navarro, and Pablo González. *Private Education and Public Policy in Latin America.* Washington, D.C.: PREAL, 2005.

Wolff, Laurence, Ernesto Schiefelbeing, and Jorge Valenzuela. *Improving the Quality of Primary Education in Latin America and the Caribbean: Toward the 21st Century.* Washington, D.C.: World Bank, 1994.

Wood, Bill, and Harry Anthony Patrinos. "Urban Bolivia." In *Indigenous People and Poverty in Latin America,* ed. George Psacharopoulus and Harry Anthony Patrinos. Washington, D.C.: World Bank, 1994.

Woodruff, David, Ian Katz, and Keith Naughton. "VW's Factory of the Future." *BusinessWeek,* October 7, 1996.

World Bank. *Beyond the Washington Consensus: Institutions Matter.* Regional Brief. Washington, D.C.: World Bank, 1998. Available at www.worldbank.org.

———. "Challenges & Opportunities for Gender Equality in Latin America and the Caribbean." www.worldbank.org, 2003.

———. *Economic Growth and Returns to Work.* Washington, D.C.: World Bank, 1995.

———. *Ecuador—Public Enterprise Reform and Privatization Technical Assistance Project.* June 1999.

———. Education Program Objectives, www.worldbank.org.

———. *Energy Efficiency and Conservation in the Developing World: The World Bank's Role.* Washington, D.C.: World Bank, 1993.

———. *Environment and Development in Latin America and the Caribbean: The Role of the World Bank.* Washington, D.C.: World Bank, 1996.

———. *Fighting Poverty in Latin America and the Caribbean.* The World Bank Group, September 2000.

———. *Global Development Finance 1997.* Washington, D.C.: World Bank, 1997.

———. *Global Development Finance 1998.* Washington, D.C.: World Bank, 1998.

———. *Global Development Finance 1999.* Washington, D.C.: World Bank, 1999.

———. *Global Economic Prospects 2005: Trade, Regionalism and Development.* World Bank Annual Report 2005. www.worldbank.org.

———. "Global Harnessing Cyclical Gains for Development." Global Development Finance 2004, World Bank, Washington, D.C.

———. "Government of Ecuador Program Information Document, Health Insurance Project, Approved." www.worldbank.org, January 19, 2006.

————. *Guatemala—Infrastructure, Privatization, Technical Assistance Loan.* April 1997.

————. *IFC: Making a Positive Difference for Sustainable Development.* Issue Brief. Washington, D.C.: The World Bank Group.

————. "Inequality in Latin America and the Caribbean: Breaking with History." Draft publication, October 2003.

————. *Labor and Economic Reforms in Latin America and the Caribbean: Regional Perspectives on World Development Report.* Washington, D.C.: World Bank, 1995.

————. *Meeting the Infrastructure Challenge in Latin America and the Caribbean.* Washington, D.C.: World Bank, 1995.

————. "Mexico—Municipal Development in Rural Areas Project." July 2002, www.worldbank.org.

————. "Mexico: Schools without Leaks." World Bank external news, August 29, 2005, www.worldbank.org.

————. *Other Financial Mechanisms: Debt-for-Nature Swaps and Social Funds.* Available at www-esd.worldbank.org/html/esd/env/publicat/edp/edp1116.htm.

————. *Privatization Principles and Practice.* IFC Lessons of Experience Series. Washington, D.C.: World Bank, 1995.

————. "Reaching the Rural Poor: A Rural Development Strategy for the Latin American and Caribbean Region." Box A4.1, Public/Private Partnerships in Research and Extension Projects, 2002.

————. *Rural Development: From Vision to Action.* Environmentally and Socially Sustainable Development Studies and Monographs Series No. 12. Washington, D.C.: World Bank, 1997.

————. *Rural Poverty Alleviation in Brazil: Toward an Integrated Strategy.* Washington, D.C.: World Bank, 2003.

————. *Ten Things You Never Knew about the World Bank.* Issue Brief. Washington, D.C.: The World Bank Group.

————. *Trade: Towards Open Regionalism,* Proceedings of the 1997 World Bank Conference on Development in Latin America and the Caribbean. Washington, D.C.: World Bank, 1998.

————. *Update on Implementation of HIPC Debt Relief Programs and Poverty Reduction Strategy Papers.* Press Conference. Washington, D.C.: The World Bank Group, April 23, 2001.

————. *World Debt Tables.* Washington, D.C. World Bank, various years. "World Bank and the IMF Agree on Debt Relief for Poor Countries."

————. *World Development Indicators, 1997.* Washington, D.C.: World Bank 1997.

————. *World Development Report 1988/9.* New York: Oxford University Press/World Bank, 1989.

————. *World Development Report 1992.* New York: Oxford University Press/World Bank, 1992.

————. *World Development Report 1994.* New York: Oxford University Press/World Bank, 1994.

————. *World Development Report 1995.* New York: Oxford University Press/World Bank, 1995.

World Bank Poverty Net. "Too Much or Too Little Water Can Spell Disaster in the World's Poorest Nations." *World Bank,* March 17, 2006, www.worldbank.org.

World Bank Staff and IMF Staff. *100 Percent Debt Cancellation? A Response from the IMF and the World Bank.* Washington, D.C.: IMF, July 2001.

World Commission on Environment and Development. *Our Common Future.* Oxford: Oxford University Press, 1987.

World Health Organization. *Integration of Health Care Delivery: Report of a WHO Study Group.* WHO Technical Report Series 861. Geneva: World Health Organization, 1996.

———. *Report on the Global HIV/AIDS Epidemic, June 1998.* Geneva: UNAIDS, 1998. Available at www.who.int/emc-hiv.

———. "Strategic Direction for Chagas Disease Research." www.who.org.

World Press Review. "Brazil's Amazon Rainforest Twice As Deforested As Estimated." October 21, 2005, newsbureau@worldbank.org.

World Resources Institute. *World Resources: A Guide to the Global Environment 1996–7.* New York: Oxford University Press, 1997.

———. *World Resources, 1994–5.* New York: Oxford University Press, 1995.

World Trade Organization. "World Merchandise Trade in 1996 by Region and Leading Trader." *International Trade,* July 30, 1997, available at www.wto/intltrad/iiworld.htm.

Worley, Heidi. "Chronic Diseases Beleaguer Developing Countries." Population Reference Bureau, January 2006.

Wrobel, Paulo. "A Free Trade Area of the Americas in 2005?" *International Affairs* 74(3) (1998).

"WTO Adopts Panel Findings against Mexican Measure on High-Fructose Corn Syrup." Press Release. Office of the United States Trade Representative. Washington, D.C.: World Trade Organization, February 28, 2000. www.iadb.org.

Yeager, Timothy. "Encomienda or Slavery? The Spanish Crown's Choice of Labor Organization in Sixteenth-Century Spanish America." *Journal of Economic History* 55(4) (December 1995).

Young, Kate. *Planning Development with Women: Making a World of Difference.* New York: St. Martin's, 1993.

Zbinden, Simon, and David Lee. "Paying for Environmental Services: An Analysis of Participation in Costa Rica's PSA Program." *World Development 33* 2 (February 2005): 255–272.

Zimbalist, Andrew. "Costa Rica." In *Struggle against Dependence: Nontraditional Export Growth in Central America and the Caribbean,* ed. Eva Paus. Boulder, Colo.: Westview, 1988.

Zoninsein, Jonas. *The Economic Case for Combating Racial and Ethnic Exclusion in Latin America and Caribbean Countries.* Research Report. Washington, D.C.: IADB, May 2001.

Zuckerman, Laurence. "In South America Car Makers See One Big Showroom." *New York Times,* April 25, 1997.

Index

Page numbers cited in *italics* refer to pages where tables, boxes, and figures appear.

About the Author

Patrice M. Franko is the Grossman Professor of Economics in the Economics Department and Professor in the International Studies Program at Colby College in Waterville, Maine, where she teaches international finance, Latin American economic policy, and microeconomics. She currently directs Colby's Oak Institute for Human Rights. At Colby she has also chaired the International Studies Program, the Economics Department, and East Asian Studies and is also an active member of the Latin America Studies Program. Nationally, she has been a Pew Faculty Fellow in International Affairs and an American Association for the Advancement of Science Fellow in International Security Affairs, and she lectures for EMIL, the executive masters program in logistics at Georgia Tech. She has served as a consultant for the Office of Inter-American Affairs in the Department of Defense, for the Center for Hemispheric Defense Studies at the National Defense University, and for the Office of International Affairs at the National Academy of Sciences. She currently serves on the boards of the Mid-Maine Global Forum, the AIDS Responsibility Project, and the Global Studies Foundation. She holds a PhD from the University of Notre Dame, and her many publications include *Toward a New Security Architecture in the Americas: The Strategic Implications of the FTAA* (2000) and *The Brazilian Defense Industry* (1992). She is currently working on a project on corporate social responsibility in Latin America. She lives on Great Pond in Rome, Maine, with her husband Sandy Maisel and their dog Nicklaus.